W9-AVM-764

English Language Learner Resource Book

Mc Graw Hill Macmillan/McGraw-Hill

Program Author
Dr. Diane August
Educational Researcher
• Principal Investigator, Developing Literacy in Second-Language Learners: Report of the National Literacy Panel on Language-Minority Children and Youth
• Member of the New Standards Literacy Project, Grades 4-5

Program Consultant
Dr. Cheryl Dressler
Literacy Consultant
English Learners

A

The McGraw·Hill Companies

Macmillan/McGraw-Hill

Published by Macmillan/McGraw-Hill, of McGraw-Hill Education, a division of The McGraw-Hill Companies, Inc., Two Penn Plaza, New York, New York 10121.

Copyright © by The McGraw-Hill Companies, Inc. All rights reserved. The contents, or parts thereof, may be reproduced in print form for non-profit educational use with Macmillan/McGraw-Hill *Treasures,* provided such reproductions bear copyright notice, but may not be reproduced in any form for any other purpose without the prior written consent of The McGraw-Hill Companies, Inc., including, but not limited to, network storage or transmission, or broadcast for distance learning.

Printed in the United States of America

4 5 6 7 8 9 10 HES 13 12 11 10

Table of Contents

How to Use This Book

Purpose and Structure

The **English Language Learner Resource Book** provides additional language and concept support for the English language learners using the *Treasures* Reading/Language Arts program.

This **ELL Resource Book** is organized by units to follow the organization of the *Treasures* program. Each unit begins with a **Unit Planner** that identifies the weekly support, which includes:

- Interactive Question-Response Guide

The Unit Planner identifies pages from the **English Language Learner Practice Book** which provides ELLs practice on the target weekly skills taught in *Treasures*.

The **ELL Resource Book** also includes an **Oral Language Proficiency Benchmark Assessment** to help you monitor children's oral language proficiency growth.

Interactive Question-Response Guide

A question-response guide is provided for each main selection and paired selection. Each lesson focuses on the weekly theme, key skills, strategies, concepts, and vocabulary. This conversational, interactive instruction creates context and provides opportunities for children to learn how information builds and connects. The interactive scripts help children use what they already know as they add new knowledge. This instruction also provides ample opportunities for children to speak and use new language learned.

Instructional Techniques and Learning Strategies

The scripted lessons are easy to navigate: each page is divided into labeled sections that correspond to the child's page. The lessons provide language and vocabulary support in a variety of ways. Instructional techniques include:

- providing a brief "set purpose" statement at the beginning of a new section
- connecting to prior lessons and literature
- presenting extra background or context

© Macmillan/McGraw-Hill

- defining vocabulary using simple language or including synonyms (circumlocution) within the flow of instruction to clarify new words
- asking the right types of questions that focus on the basic meaning of the text and build overall understanding
- using visual elements for support to clarify or elicit language
- supporting text features, such as captions, sidebars, illustrations, and charts

English Language Learner Practice Book

Use the activities in the **English Language Learner Practice Book** to provide practice opportunities for the target skill or strategy taught each week:

- Phonics
- Vocabulary
- Grammar
- Writing
- Book Talk

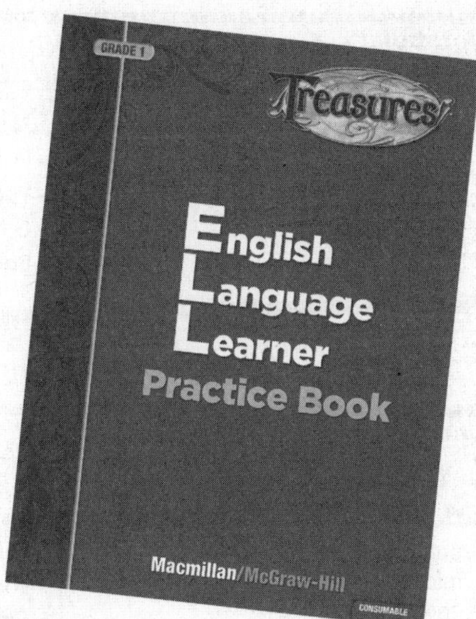

© Macmillan/McGraw-Hill

Weekly Planners

Week 1

Selections	Vocabulary		ELL Practice Book
	Oral Vocabulary Words/Cognates	Academic Language/Cognates	
Pam and Sam *Rules at School*	cheerful genuine *genuino* interest *interés* prefer *preferir* unique *único/a*	character setting story structure analyze *analizar*	• Phonics, p. 1 • Vocabulary, p. 2 • Grammar, p. 3 • Book Talk, p. 4

Week 2

Selections	Vocabulary		ELL Practice Book
	Oral Vocabulary Words/Cognates	Academic Language/Cognates	
I Can, Too! *Run! Jump! Swim!*	stretch exhausted energy *energía* express *expresar* movements *movimiento*	label word order sequence *secuencia* events *eventos*	• Phonics, p. 5 • Vocabulary, p. 6 • Grammar, p. 7 • Book Talk, p. 8

Week 3

TIME FOR KIDS®	Vocabulary		ELL Practice Book
	Oral Vocabulary Words/Cognates	Academic Language/Cognates	
How You Grew	change learn adult *adulto* imitate *imitar* practice *practicar*	statement capitalization sequence *secuencia* analyze *analizar* text *texto* structure *estructura*	• Phonics, p. 9 • Vocabulary, p. 10 • Grammar, p. 11 • Book Talk, p. 12

Week 4

Selections	Vocabulary		ELL Practice Book
	Oral Vocabulary Words/Cognates	Academic Language/Cognates	
Flip *What Pets Need*	dear needs train adorable *adorable* sensible *sensible*	beginning middle end lists *listas* exclamation *exclamación*	• Phonics, p. 13 • Vocabulary, p. 14 • Grammar, p. 15 • Book Talk, p. 16

Week 5

Selections	Vocabulary		ELL Practice Book
	Oral Vocabulary Words/Cognates	Academic Language/Cognates	
Soccer *Guess What!*	challenging charity focus admire *admirar* offer *ofrecer*	capital letters author's purpose evaluate *evaluar*	• Phonics, p. 17 • Vocabulary, p. 18 • Grammar, p. 19 • Book Talk, p. 20

© Macmillan/McGraw-Hill

Student Response Strategies

Use the following strategies to help English Language Learners move to the next proficiency level.

✔ **WAIT** Give children ample time to respond.

- Let children know that they can respond in different ways depending on their levels of proficiency, but all should be encouraged to answer questions related to the main point of the picture or text.
- Allow children to respond in their native language if they are very limited proficient. Ask a more proficient student to repeat the answer in English.

✔ **REPEAT** If the child's response is correct, the teacher can repeat what the child has said slowly and clearly for the rest of the class to hear.

✔ **REVISE for FORM** Generally the teacher will be repeating what the child has said but with corrections for grammar and pronunciation. The correction can be implicit or explicit (where teacher calls attention to the correction).

✔ **REVISE for MEANING** Teachers should also correct responses for meaning.

✔ **ELABORATE** Here, the teacher elaborates on a child's response or states the response in another way in order to more fully develop children's comprehension and oral language proficiency.

✔ **ELICIT** Finally, the teacher can also elicit a more comprehensive response from the child by prompting him or her for further information.

Newcomers

Basic and Social Language Each week you will be focusing on an important aspect of classroom communication to teach or reinforce with your newcomers. Children will expand and internalize initial English vocabulary by learning and using routine language needed for classroom communication.

Introduce Self Teach children how to introduce themselves, ask for other classmates´ names, and say Hello/Goodbye. Use the sentence frames *My name is* _____ and *What is your name?* Model dialogues, such as *Hello. My name is (name). What is your name?* Have children repeat and practice with a partner.

Basic Requests Teach children sentence frames for basic requests, such as *I need* _____, *I want* _____, and *Do you have* _____*?* Teach them how to ask for permission, such as *May I use the restroom, please?* And to respond with *thank you*. Provide daily opportunities to model and practice each request. Reinforce *please* and *thank you*.

Classroom Items Teach children the names of commonly used classroom items, such as, pencils, paper, book, chair, and desk. Reinforce each using the sentence frames *This is my* _____. *That is your* _____. and *This is a* _____. These sentence frames focus on possession. Provide daily practice, for example, *This is my book. That is your book.*

LOG ON Have children use **Newcomer Games** to expand and internalize language needed for classroom communication. **www.macmillanmh.com**

© Macmillan/McGraw-Hill

Pam and Sam

Pages 12–13

Prior to reading the selection with children, they should have listened to the selection on **StudentWorks Plus**, the interactive eBook. In addition, selection vocabulary should have been pretaught using the **Visual Vocabulary Resources**.

Access Core Content

Page 13

Title

- *Listen as I read the title of the story:* Pam and Sam. *What is the title?* (Pam and Sam)

Illustration

- *I see a rabbit. The rabbit's name is Pam. Point to the rabbit and say* Pam *with me:* Pam. *I also see a bird. The bird's name is Sam. Point to the bird and say* Sam *with me:* Sam.
- *Where is Sam the bird in this picture?* (Sam is in a nest.)
- *Pam and Sam are friends. Let's read the story to find out what Pam and Sam do together and how each friend is special.*

Page 14

Text

- *Read the page with me:* Pam and Sam play. *What do Pam and Sam do?* (Pam and Sam play.)

Illustration

- *Point to Pam the rabbit. Now point to Sam the bird. Is Sam flying out of the nest or into the nest?* (Sam is flying out of the nest.) *Pretend you are Sam. Flap your arms as if you are flying.* (Demonstrate the movement.) *What would you say if you were Sam?* ("Let's play, Pam!")

This story takes place outside in the country. That is where Pam and Sam live. There are other animals that live there, too. Can you find a butterfly in this picture? Point to the butterfly. Can you find a bee? Point to the bee.

Pages 12–13

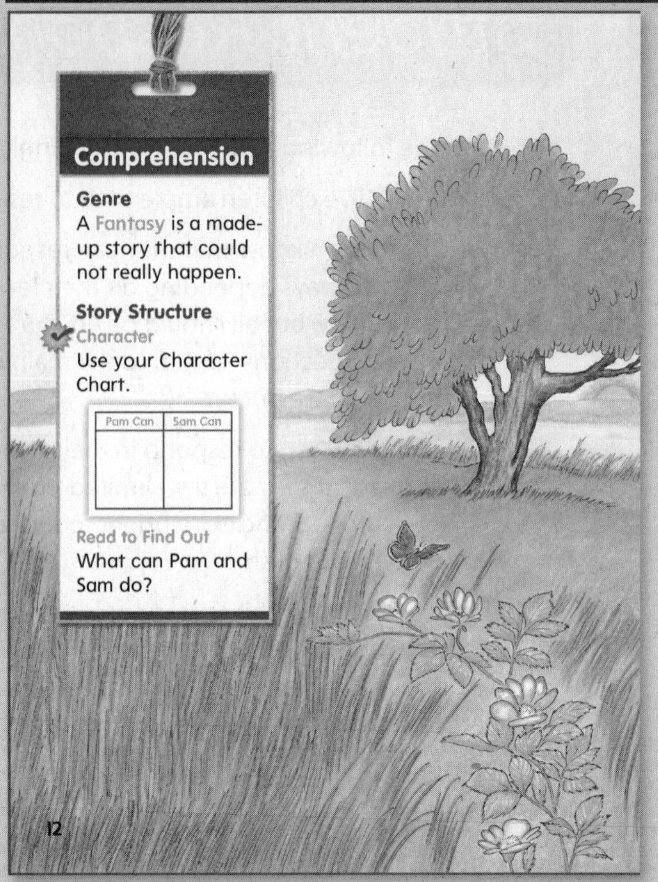

Comprehension
Genre
A Fantasy is a made-up story that could not really happen.
Story Structure
Character
Use your Character Chart.
Pam Can
Sam Can
Read to Find Out
What can Pam and Sam do?
12

Pages 14–15

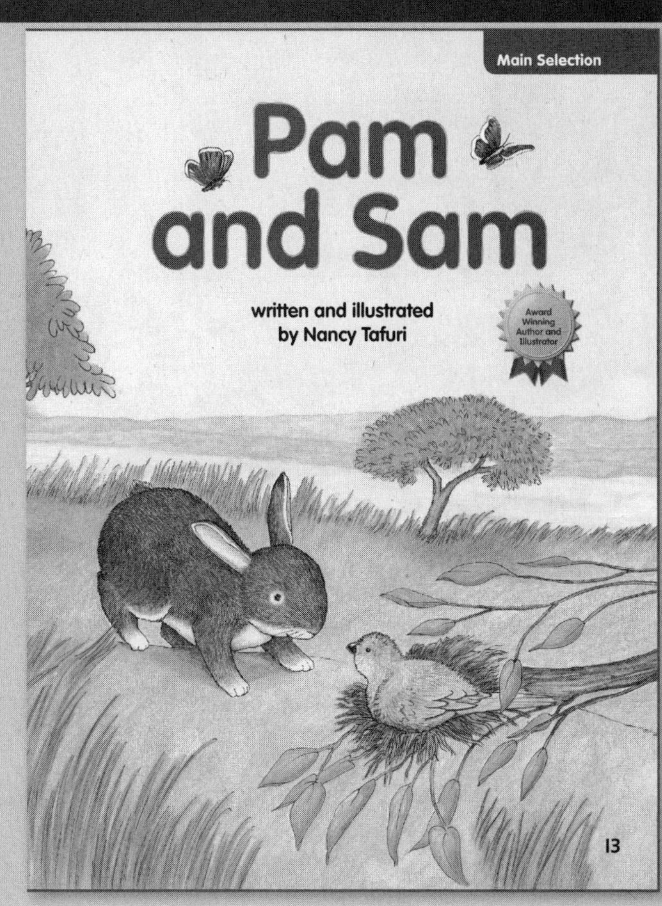

Main Selection
Pam and Sam
written and illustrated by Nancy Tafuri
Award Winning Author and Illustrator
13

Page 15

Text

- *Now let's read this page together:* Pam ran up. *Who ran up, Pam or Sam?* (Pam ran up.)

Illustration

- *Let's look at the picture. Point to Sam the bird. Now point to Pam the rabbit. Pam the rabbit ran up a hill. Put your fingers on the hill in the picture. Show me how Pam ran up the hill.* (Put your fingers on the picture and demonstrate how the rabbit would run up the hill.)
- *I see the butterfly in this picture, too. Can you find the butterfly? Point to the butterfly.*

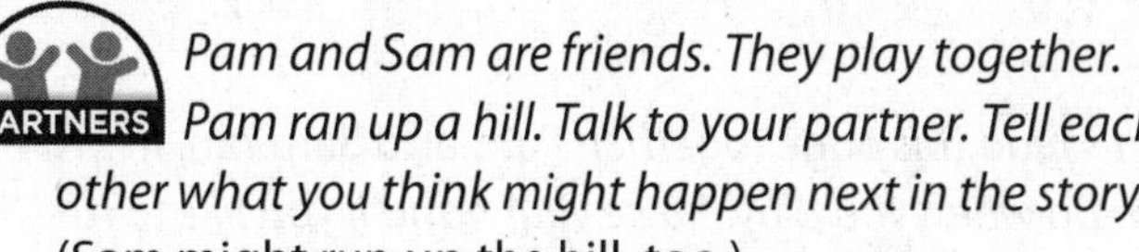

Pam and Sam are friends. They play together. Pam ran up a hill. Talk to your partner. Tell each other what you think might happen next in the story. (Sam might run up the hill, too.)

Request Assistance

Remind children of expressions they can use to request assistance from the teacher or their partners, such as *What is "ran"? Can you show me in the picture?*

Pam and Sam

Page 16

Text

- *Read this page with me:* Sam ran up. *Who ran up the hill first, Pam or Sam?* (Pam ran up the hill first.) *Then who ran up the hill?* (Then Sam ran up the hill.)

Illustration

- *Look at Sam in the picture. Put your fingers on the hill in the picture. Show me how Sam ran up.* (Demonstrate the action with your fingers.)
- *Do you see the butterfly in this picture, too? Point to the butterfly. Say the word with me:* butterfly.

Page 17

Text

- *Let's read this page together:* Pam and Sam ran. *It is fun to run when you play. Raise your hand if you like to run when you play.*

Illustration

- *Look at Pam and Sam in the picture. Point to Sam. Point to Pam. What does Pam have in her mouth?* (Pam has a flower in her mouth.)
- *What might Sam be saying to Pam as they run?* (Question is open.) *Who follows Pam and Sam as they run?* (The butterfly follows Pam and Sam.)

-

Directionality

Ask children to place their finger where you start reading (left). Ask where you finish reading on this page (right).

Pages 16–17

Sam ran up.

16

Pages 18–19

Pam can **jump**.

18

Pam and Sam ran.

17

Sam can **not** jump.

19

Page 18

Text

- *Read the page with me:* Pam can jump. *What can Pam do?* (Pam can jump.) *Rabbits like to jump! Let's all jump like a rabbit.* (Demonstrate jumping.)
- *We read another story about an animal that can jump. What other animal can jump?* (A kangaroo can jump. A frog can jump.)

Illustration

Look closely at Pam jumping. What is Pam jumping across? (Pam is jumping across the water.)

- *The butterfly is still with Pam. The butterfly must like Pam! Point to the butterfly again.*

Page 19

Text

- *Let's read this page:* Sam can not jump.

Illustration

- *Look at Sam. Sam is a bird. Sam cannot jump across the water like Pam the rabbit.*

What do you think Sam might do to get across the water? Talk to your partner about what Sam might do.

Non-verbal Cues

Remind children that they can use non-verbal cues to share information when they are not able to do so verbally. Encourage children to use pantomime or draw.

Pam and Sam

Page 20

Text

- *Let's read this page:* Sam can not go with Pam.

Illustration

- *Point to Sam. Point to Pam. Why can't Sam go with Pam?* (Pam jumped across the water. Sam can not jump.)
- *Point to the butterfly. The butterfly can fly across the water. What do you think Sam might do?* (Sam might fly across the water, too.)
- *Can you find the fish in the water? Point to the fish. The fish can't fly like a butterfly. The fish can't jump like a rabbit. The fish can swim. What can the fish do?* (The fish can swim.) *Pretend you are a fish. Show me how you swim in the water.* (Demonstrate the action.)

Page 21

Whole Page

- *Let's look at the picture and read the page:* Look at Sam! *What is Sam doing?* (Sam is flying across the water.) *Sam is flying across the water to be with Pam.*

Pages 20–21

Sam can not go with Pam.

20

Pages 22–23

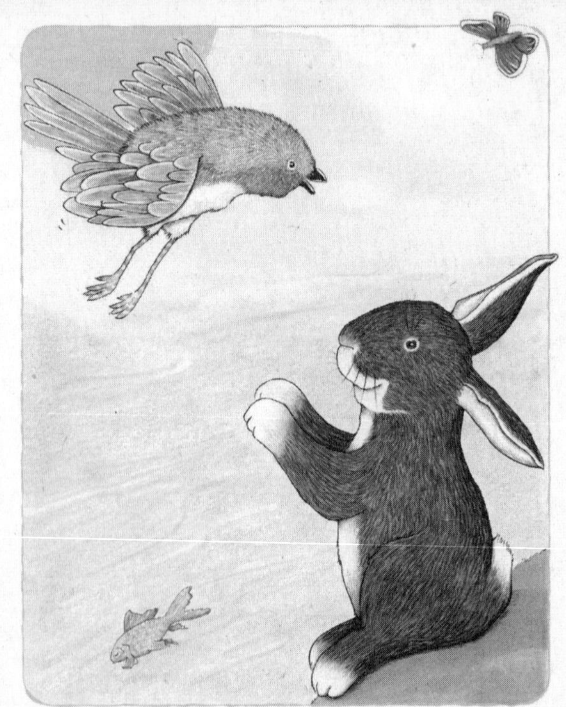

Sam can fly!

22

Look at Sam!

21

Pam and Sam can play.

23

Page 22

Text

- *Read the page with me:* Sam can fly! *He can get across the water by flying!*

Illustration

- *Now Pam and Sam are together again. Look at the picture. How do you think Pam and Sam feel: happy* (smile) *or sad* (frown)? (Pam and Sam are happy to be together again.)
- *Point to the animals in the picture and name them with me: Sam, butterfly, Pam, fish.*

Page 23

Whole Page

- *Read the end of the story with me:* Pam and Sam can play. *What might Pam and Sam do next time they play?* (Question is open.)
- *Let's say good-bye to Pam and Sam:* Good-bye, Pam! Good-bye, Sam!

What special thing can Pam do? (Pam can jump.) *What special thing can Sam do?* (Sam can fly.)

Would you rather be Pam the rabbit or Sam the bird? Tell your partner why. (Question is open.)

Rules at School

Pages 26–27

Access Core Content

Page 26

Teacher Note Pose the questions after you read the paragraph or page indicated.

Title

- (Point to title.) *Let's read the title together:* Rules at School. (Point to the word *rules*.) *This word says "rules." Say it with me:* rules. *Rules tell us what to do. Different places have different rules. Rules at school tell us what to do at school.*

Photo

- *Look at the photo. The girl is holding a sign.* (Point to sign.) *One word on the sign is* rules. *Point to it. Let's read the sign together:* Our School Rules.

Text

- *Let's read this question together:* Why do we have rules at school? *Let's read to find out.*

Page 27

Photo

- *Look at the children in the photo. Are they sitting or standing?* (standing) *Are they standing in line?* (yes) *Standing in line is a rule. Do we have that rule at our school?*

We stand in line to go to recess. At what other times do we stand in line? Tell your partner.

Text

- *Listen as I read the page.* (Read page.)
- Get along *means we work and play together with no fighting. When we have rules, do we fight or do we get along?* (We get along.) Safe *means we don't get hurt. When we have rules, do we stay safe or do we get hurt?* (We stay safe.)

Pages 26–27

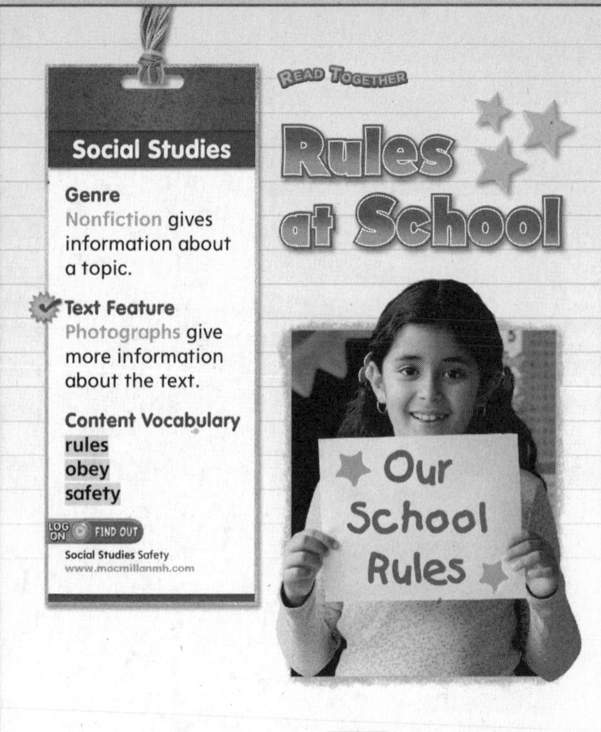

Social Studies
Genre
Nonfiction gives information about a topic.
Text Feature
Photographs give more information about the text.
Content Vocabulary
rules
obey
safety
LOG ON FIND OUT
Social Studies Safety
www.macmillanmh.com
Read Together
Rules at School
Our School Rules

Why do we have **rules** at school?

26

Pages 28–29

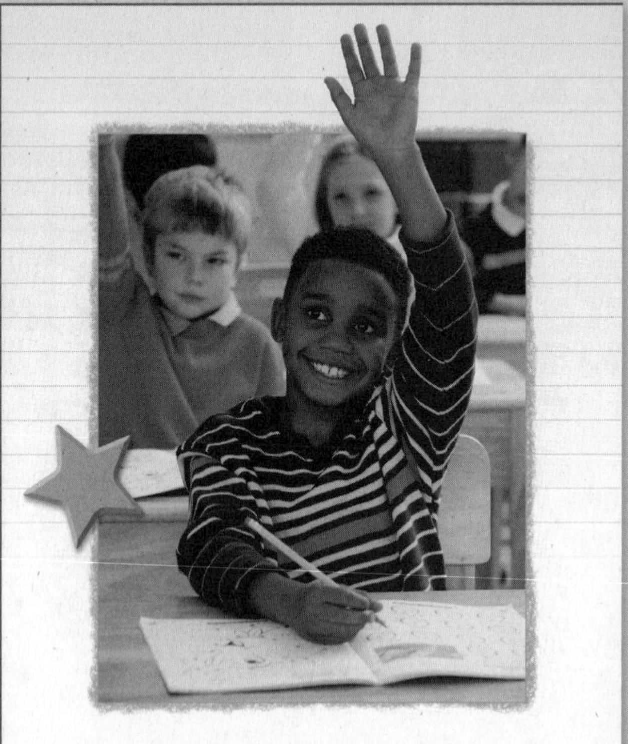

We raise our hands.

28

Rules can help us get along.
Rules can help us stay safe.

27

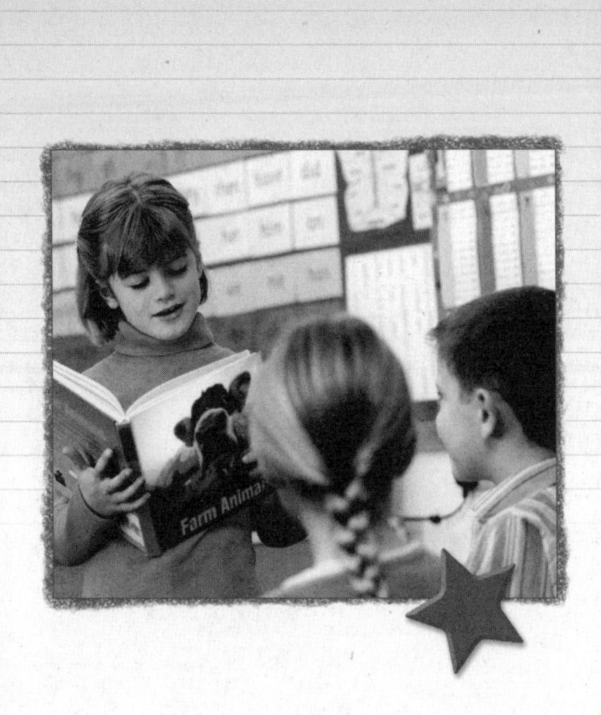

We listen quietly.

29

Page 28

Photo

- (Point to boy's raised hand.) *This boy is raising his hand. Can you raise your hand like the boy?* (Raise hand and encourage children to imitate you.)

There is another boy in the photo. Show your partner. Is he raising his hand, too? (yes) *Show your partner the girl in the photo. Is she raising her hand, too?* (yes)

Text

- *Listen as I read the page.* (Read page.) *Now let's read this page together.*
- *When do we raise our hands? Do we raise our hands to ask a question?* (yes) *When is another time we raise our hands?* (possible answer: to answer a question)

Page 29

Photo

- (Point to girl reading.) *This girl is reading.* (Point to girl listening.) *Is she reading, too?* (no) (Point to your ear.) *She's listening.* (Point to boy listening.) *Is he reading?* (no) (Point to your ear.) *He's listening. The boy and girl aren't talking. They're listening quietly.* (Put finger on lips.)

Text

- *I am going to read. Can you listen quietly while I read?* (Read page with a quiet voice.) *Now, let's read this page together:* We listen quietly.

Rules at School

Page 30

Photo

- *These two girls are crossing the street. Often, there are many cars on the street. We have to follow rules to stay safe on the street. Cars have to follow rules, too.*

Do you see a red stop sign in the photo? Show your partner. We have to stop for the red stop sign. That is a rule. Cars have to stop for the red stop sign, too. That is a safety rule.

Text

- *Listen as I read the page.* (Read page.) Obey *means "follow the rules." Say it with me:* obey. *When we see a stop sign, we obey the sign. We stop.*

Pages 30–31

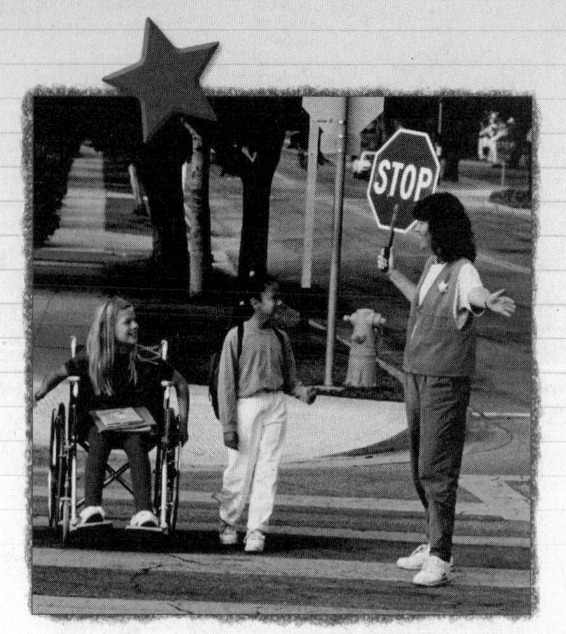

We **obey** **safety** rules.

30

We let everyone play!
What are your school rules?

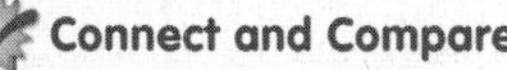

Connect and Compare

What rules might Pam and Sam follow to get along and stay safe?

31

Page 31

Photo

- *Look at the children in the photo. Are they in class or at recess?* (at recess) *Are they playing or working?* (playing) *They are having a good time. They are playing together. Everyone can play.*

What do you like to play at recess? Tell your partner. Who do you like to play with at recess? Tell your partner.

Text

- *Listen as I read the page.*
- *Let's remember some school rules.* (Raise your hand.) *I want to ask a question. What do I do?* (I raise my hand.) (Put your hand to your ear.) *Another person is talking. What do I do?* (I listen quietly.)

Tell your partner some more rules at school. Look at the book to help you remember. (possible answers: stand in line, stop for the red stop sign, let everyone play at recess)

Name ______________________________

Copy each new word on the line.
Draw a picture.

Word	Illustration
cheese	
nut	

© Macmillan/McGraw-Hill

Name ______________________________

Book Talk

Read each question and prompt. Discuss the answers with your group. Use your Leveled Reader to find details to support your answers. Then write your answers on another sheet of paper.

1. Name the characters in your book.

2. Tell what is special about one character.

3. Talk about the pictures in your book. Which picture is your favorite?

4. How do friends help one another in your book?

5. What surprised you in the story you read?

© Macmillan/McGraw-Hill

I Can, Too!

Pages 40–41

Prior to reading the selection with children, they should have listened to the selection on **StudentWorks Plus**, the interactive eBook. In addition, selection vocabulary should have been pretaught using the **Visual Vocabulary Resources**.

Access Core Content

Page 41

Title

- *Read the title of this story with me:* I Can, Too! *Do you remember the story of the two pigs? When one pig said it could jump over the puddle, the other pig said, "I can, too." We say "I can, too" when we can do something that someone else has done.*

Illustration

- *I see a boy in this picture. Point to the boy. I also see a girl. Point to the girl. The boy and the girl will have fun doing things together in this story. Let's read to find out what they do and who says "I can, too!"*

Pages 42–43

Text and Illustrations

- *Point to the girl on these pages. Let's read what the girl says:* Can you do what I can do? *The girl is putting on a hat. What can the girl do?* (The girl can put a hat on her head.)
- *Now point to the boy. Let's read what the boy says:* I can! I can do it, too. *What can the boy do, too?* (The boy can put a hat on his head, too.)
- *Are the hats the same?* (no) *No, the hats are not the same. The girl's hat is big. It has a flower and a ribbon on it. The boy's hat is small. It is a baseball cap.*

Pages 40–41

Comprehension
Genre
In a Rhyming Story, some words end with the same sound.
Story Structure
Sequence
Use your Sequence Chart.
First
Next
Last
Read to Find Out
What will the girl and boy do first, next, and last?
40

Pages 42–43

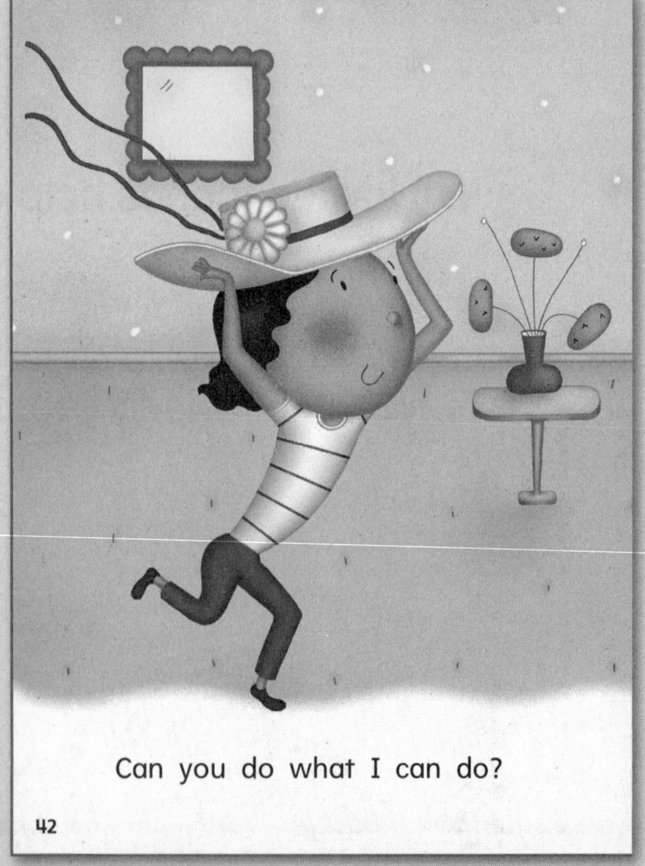
Can you do what I can do?
42

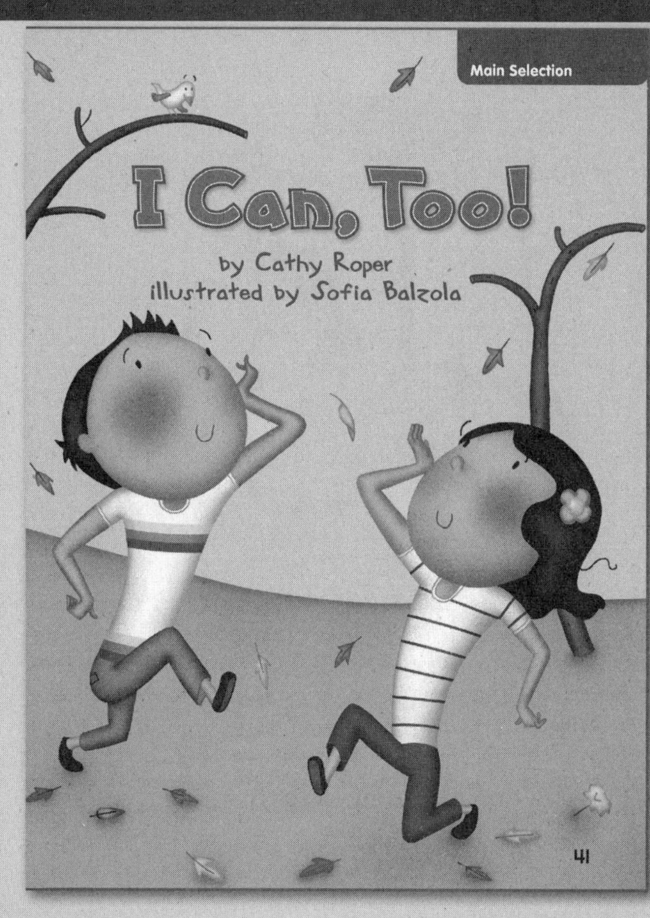
Main Selection
I Can, Too!
by Cathy Roper
illustrated by Sofia Balzola
41

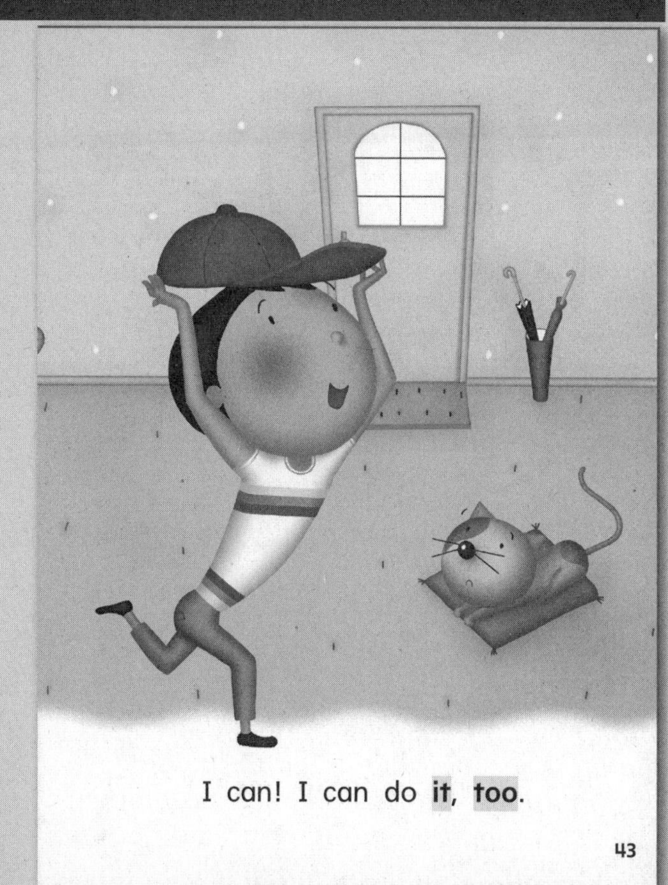
I can! I can do it, too.
43

- *Now let's read both of these pages together and listen for the words that rhyme. Remember, rhyming words are words that end with the same sound. Read the pages with me:* Can you do what I can do? I can! I can do it, too.
- *Listen as I say the last word on each page:* do, too. *Now say the words with me:* do, too. *Do the words* do *and* too *rhyme?* (Yes, the words rhyme.) *The words* do *and* too *rhyme because they end with the same sound.*
- *Let's read the pages one more time. As we read, listen for the rhyming words* do *and* too: Can you do what I can do? I can! I can do it, too.
- *What other words rhyme with* do *and* too*? Let's name some other rhyming words.* (Possible words include: *blue, boo, chew, clue, drew, flew, moo, new, Sue, stew, threw, who, you.*)

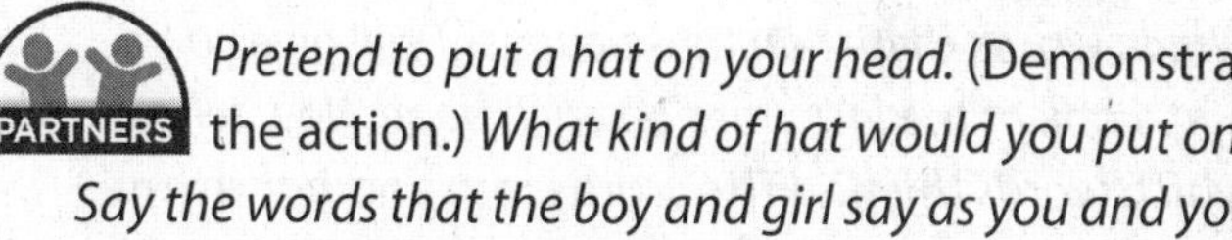
PARTNERS
Pretend to put a hat on your head. (Demonstrate the action.) *What kind of hat would you put on? Say the words that the boy and girl say as you and your partner pretend to put on hats.*

Directionality

Ask children to place their finger where you start reading (top left). Ask where you finish reading on this page (bottom right).

I Can, Too!

Pages 44–45

Text and Illustrations

- *Let's read what the girl says on these two pages:* Can you jump over a mat? Can you jump over a hat?
- *Point to the girl jumping over the mat. When the girl jumps over the mat, her hat comes off! Point to the hat coming off the girl's head.*

What does the girl do after she jumps over the mat? (The girl jumps over her hat.) *Point to the girl jumping over her hat.*

- *Pretend you are jumping over a hat. Show me how you would jump. Try to jump high!*
- *Let's read these pages together again and listen for the words that rhyme:* Can you jump over a mat? Can you jump over a hat?
- *Which words rhyme on these pages? I will give you a hint. Look at the last word on each page. Now tell me which words rhyme.* (The words *mat* and *hat* rhyme.)
- *Point to the cat in the pictures. Does the word* cat *rhyme with* mat *and* hat? (Yes, the word *cat* rhymes with *mat* and *hat*.) *The words* mat, hat, *and* cat *rhyme because they all end with the same sound.*

Monitor Oral Production

Remember to model self-corrective techniques on a regular basis as you speak to children. Pretend to mispronounce words and self-correct.

Pages 44–45

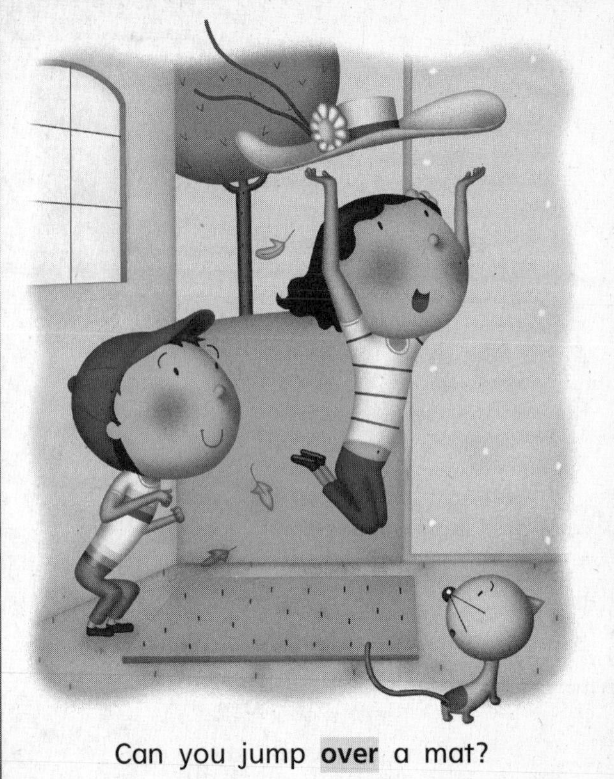

Can you jump **over** a mat?

44

Pages 46–47

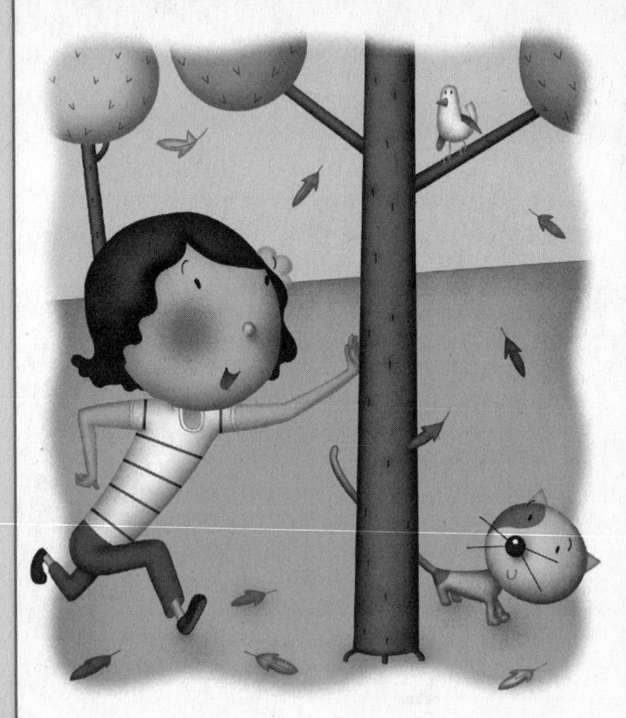

Can you tag a tree?

46

Can you jump over a hat?

45

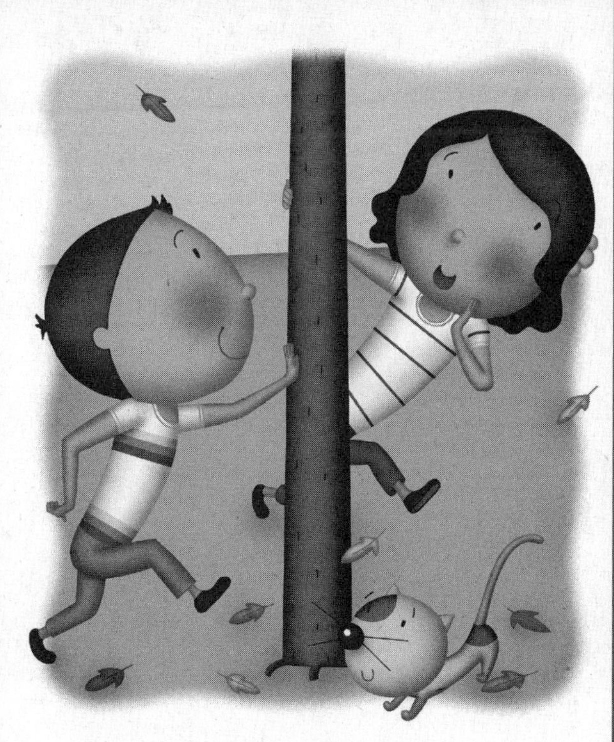

Can you tag me?

47

Pages 46–47

Text and Illustrations

- *Now let's read the girl's words on these pages:* Can you tag a tree? Can you tag me?
- *When you tag someone or something, you touch that person or thing. You can play a game with a friend by running and tagging each other. Have you played tag? Who did you play tag with?* (Questions are open.)

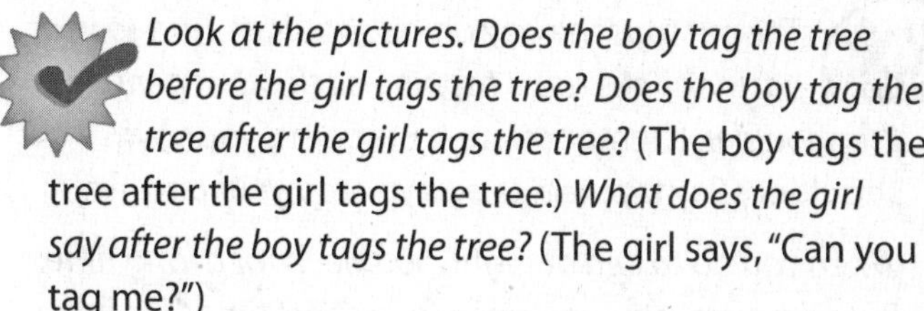

Look at the pictures. Does the boy tag the tree before the girl tags the tree? Does the boy tag the tree after the girl tags the tree? (The boy tags the tree after the girl tags the tree.) *What does the girl say after the boy tags the tree?* (The girl says, "Can you tag me?")

- *Which two words rhyme on these pages?* (The words *tree* and *me* rhyme.) *Can you name other words that rhyme with* tree *and* me? (Possible words include: *be, free, he, key, knee, see, three, we.*)

Tell your partner something that you can do. Have your partner tell you if he or she can do it, too. Take turns naming things you can do. Use words like jump, skip, run, hop, *and* walk.

I Can, Too!

Pages 48–49

Text and Illustrations

- *Read these pages aloud with me:* Can you tap, tap, tap? I can nap, nap, nap. *The girl taps the boy on the shoulder. Who says:* Can you tap, tap, tap? (The girl says, "Can you tap, tap, tap?")
- *When you tap someone, you touch them lightly. Let's tap our desks.* (Model tapping.)

The girl taps the boy on his shoulder. Turn to your partner. Take turns tapping each other gently on the shoulder. (Demonstrate by tapping your own shoulder.) *Say* tap, tap, tap *as you tap your partner.*

- *When you go to bed at night, you sleep for a long time. But when you nap, you sleep for a short time. The boy is napping in the leaves. Who says:* I can nap, nap, nap? (The boy says, "I can nap, nap, nap.") *How do you know?* (The picture shows the boy closing his eyes.)
- *What does the boy nap on?* (The boy naps on a pile of leaves.) *Who naps with the boy?* (The cat naps with the boy.)
- *Now let's read these pages again. Listen for the rhyming words as we read:* Can you tap, tap, tap? I can nap, nap, nap. *Which words rhyme on these pages?* (The words *tap, tap, tap* rhyme with *nap, nap, nap.*)

Synonyms and Circumlocution

Remind children that they can ask for synonyms to help clarify words or expressions they do not understand. Ask, *What is another word for "nap"?* (sleep)

Pages 48–49

Pages 50–51

I can nap, nap, nap.

49

51

Pages 50–51

Text and Illustrations

- *Let's find out what happens at the end of the story. First, let's read what the boy says:* Can you do what I can do? *Now let's read what the girl says:* I can! I can, too!
- *Look at the picture of the boy. I see leaves on the ground and in the air. Point to the leaves on the ground. Now point to the leaves in the air. What can the boy do?* (The boy can throw leaves into the air.)
- *Can the girl throw leaves into the air, too?* (Yes, the girl can throw leaves into the air, too.) *How do you know?* (The picture shows the girl throwing leaves into the air. The girl says, "I can! I can, too!")
- *Read the pages with me again and listen for the rhyming words:* Can you do what I can do? I can! I can, too! *Which words rhyme on these pages?* (The words *do* and *too* rhyme.)

Let's think about what the boy and girl do in the story. First, they put on hats and jump. What do they do next? (The boy and girl play tag.) *What does the boy say after the girl says she can tap, tap, tap?* (The boy says he can nap, nap, nap.) *What do the boy and girl do at the end of the story?* (They throw leaves into the air.)

Now do the things the girl and boy do in the story. You and your partner can use the pictures and the words for help.

Run! Jump! Swim!

Access Core Content

Page 54

Title

- *Listen as I read the title of the selection. Point to each word as you read it:* Run! Jump! Swim!

Text

- *Now listen while I read this page:* What helps animals move? *When animals move, they make their bodies go. Animals can move just a little, or they can move a lot. They can move quickly, or they can move slowly. Each animal has a special way of moving.*

Photo

- *Point to the animal in the photograph. This animal is a lion. Say* lion *with me:* lion. *A lion's legs help it move as it runs. Now let's read about what helps other animals move.*

Page 55

Photo

- *Point to the animal on this page. This animal is a kangaroo. Say* kangaroo *with me:* kangaroo. *Now point to the label on the photograph.* (Point to the label to demonstrate.) *Listen as I read the label:* back legs. *The label helps us find the back legs of the kangaroo. Point to the kangaroo's back legs.*

Text

- *Listen as I read about the kangaroo:* This kangaroo can jump high. Strong back legs help it jump. *What can a kangaroo do?* (A kangaroo can jump high.) *What helps a kangaroo jump?* (A kangaroo's strong back legs help it jump.)

Pages 54–55

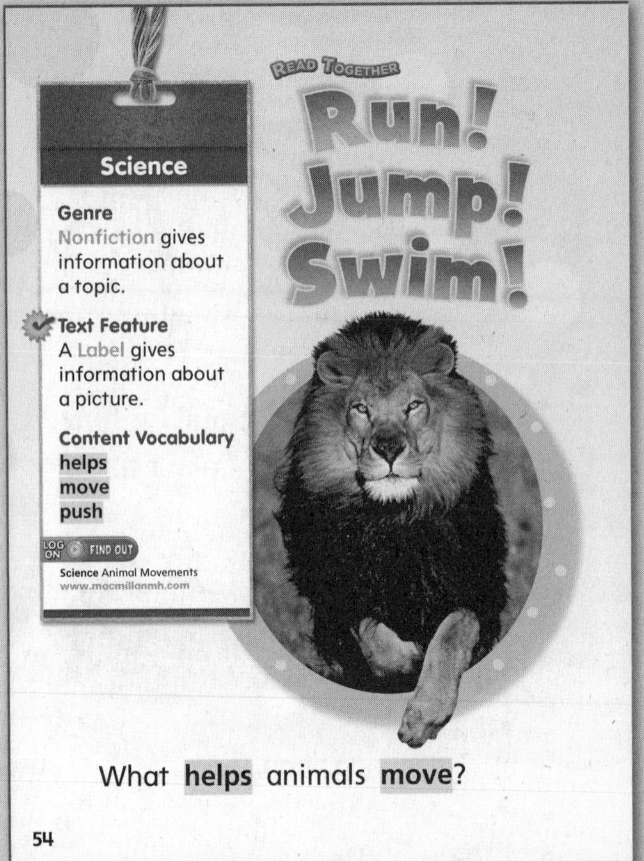

Read Together
Run! Jump! Swim!
Science
Genre
Nonfiction gives information about a topic.
Text Feature
A Label gives information about a picture.
Content Vocabulary
helps
move
push
LOG ON FIND OUT
Science Animal Movements
www.macmillanmh.com
What helps animals move?
54

Pages 56–57

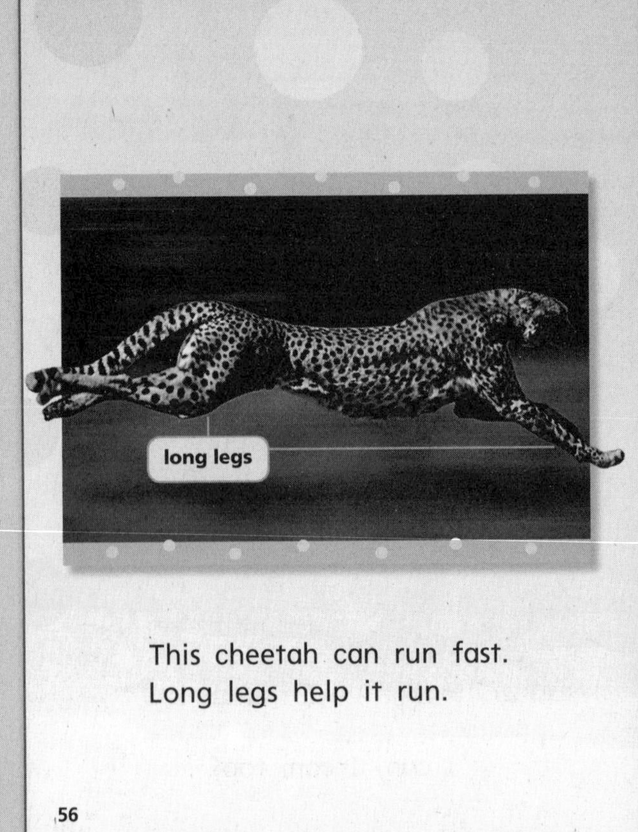

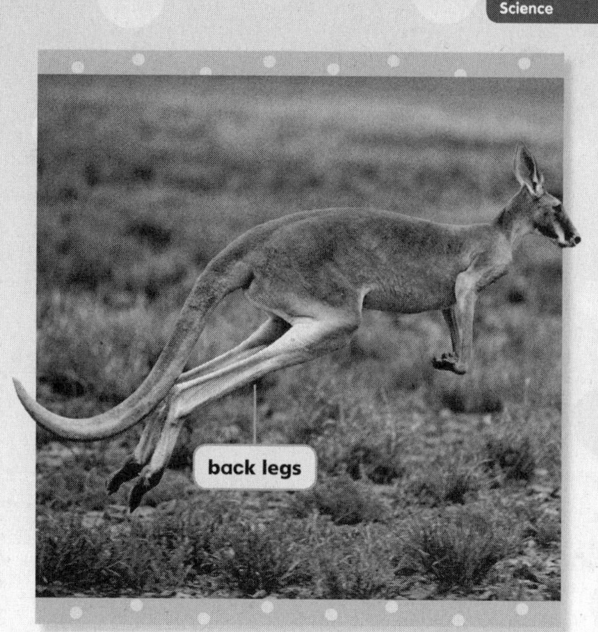

This kangaroo can jump high.
Strong back legs help it jump.

55

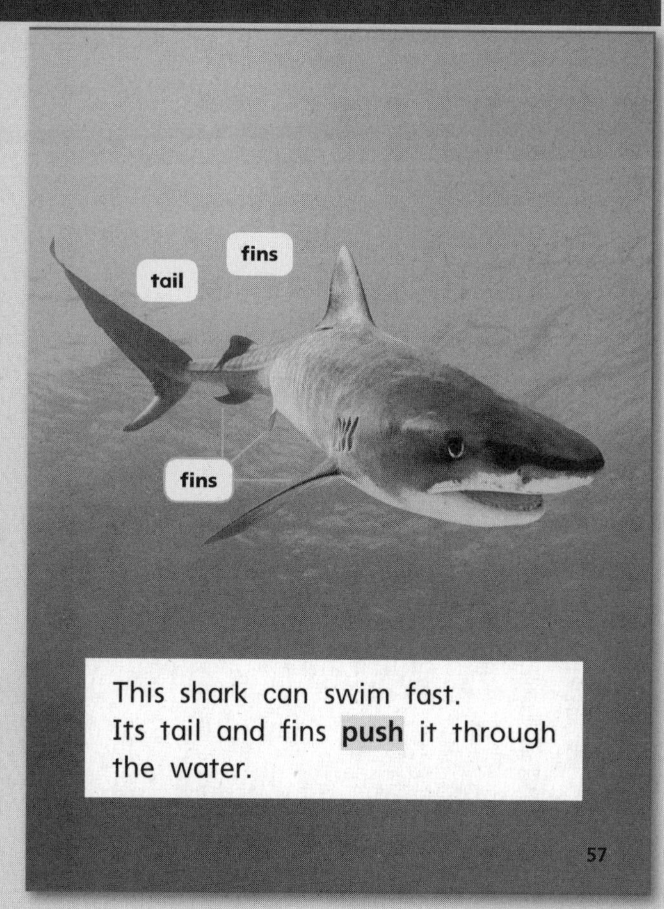

This shark can swim fast.
Its tail and fins **push** it through the water.

57

Page 56

Photo

- *This is a fast animal! The animal is called a* cheetah. *Say* cheetah *with me:* cheetah. *Listen as I read the label on the photograph:* long legs. (Point to the label.) *A cheetah has long legs. Point to the cheetah's long legs.*

Text

- *Listen as I read to find out how the cheetah moves:* This cheetah can run fast. Long legs help it run. *What helps a cheetah run?* (The cheetah's long legs help it run.)

Page 57

Photo

- *Who knows what kind of animal this is?* (shark) *Yes, this animal is a shark. As I read the labels on the photograph, point to the labels:* tail, fins, fins. (Model pointing to the labels.) *Point to the shark's tail. Now point to the shark's fins.*

Text

- *Listen as I read about the shark:* This shark can swim fast. Its tail and fins push it through the water. *What pushes a shark through the water?* (A shark's tail and fins push it through the water.)

- *Sharks have strong tails. What parts of your body are strong?* (My legs are strong. My arms are strong.)

Pretend you are a lion, a kangaroo, a cheetah, or a shark. Move like the animal. Have your partner guess which animal you are. Then guess the animal that your partner is pretending to be.

Page 58

Photo

- *This is a seal. The seal is a fast swimmer. Say* seal *with me:* seal. *Point to the labels on the photograph. Listen as I read the labels:* flipper, flippers. *What do the labels tell us about a seal?* (A seal has flippers.) *Point to the seal's flippers.*

Text

- *Now listen as I read about the seal and its flippers:* This seal is slow on land. It is fast in the water. It swims with wide flippers. *The seal's flippers are not good for walking on land. What are they good for?* (swimming fast)

Pretend that you and your partner are seals. Walk around on your flippers.

Pages 58–59

This seal is slow on land.
It is fast in the water.
It swims with wide flippers.

58

Kids can run, jump, and swim, too. What helps kids move?

Critical Thinking

Think about *I Can, Too!* How could animals join the fun?

59

Page 59

Photo

- *Look at the kids in this photograph. What are they doing?* (The kids are jumping.)

Text

- *Listen as I read about the kids:* Kids can run, jump, and swim, too. What helps kids move? *What helps you run?* (Our legs help us run.) *What helps you jump?* (Our legs and feet help us jump.) *What helps you swim?* (Our arms and legs help us swim.)
- *If you could be any of the animals in this selection for a day, which animal would you be? Why would you want to be that animal?* (Questions are open.)

Name ____________________

Copy each new word on the line.
Draw a picture.

Word	Illustration
jump	
stop	

© Macmillan/McGraw-Hill

Name ______________________________

Book Talk

Read each question and prompt. Discuss the answers with your group. Use your Leveled Reader to find details to support your answers. Then write your answers on another sheet of paper.

1. Tell about the characters in your book.

2. Describe the setting. Where does the story take place?

3. Give examples of things the characters can do.

4. What do the characters like to do?

5. What animals are named in your book?

© Macmillan/McGraw-Hill

How You Grew

Pages 66–67

Prior to reading the selection with children, they should have listened to the selection on **StudentWorks Plus**, the interactive eBook. In addition, selection vocabulary should have been pretaught using the **Visual Vocabulary Resources**.

Access Core Content

Teacher Note Pose the questions after you read the paragraph or page indicated.

Page 66

Title

- (Point to the title.) *This is the title. Listen as I read it:* How You Grew. *Once you were very little.* (Hold your hands close together to indicate *little.*) *Then you grew.* (Slowly move your hands apart.) *Now you are big.* (Hold your hands far apart to indicate *big.*) *But you are still growing.* (Move your hands a little farther apart.)

Text

- *Listen as I read the text. Getting older means you are growing and changing.*
- *Tell me about some things that you can do now that you could not do when you were little.*

Photo

- *I see a girl in this picture. Point to the girl. I see a mother, too. Point to the mother. The girl is tying her shoe. Point to the shoe.*
- (Mime tying shoes.) *Can you tie your shoes? Show me.*

Page 67

Photo

- *I see a baby in this picture. Point to the baby. You were a baby once, too. You were very little.* (Gesture *little* with your hands.)

Pages 66–67

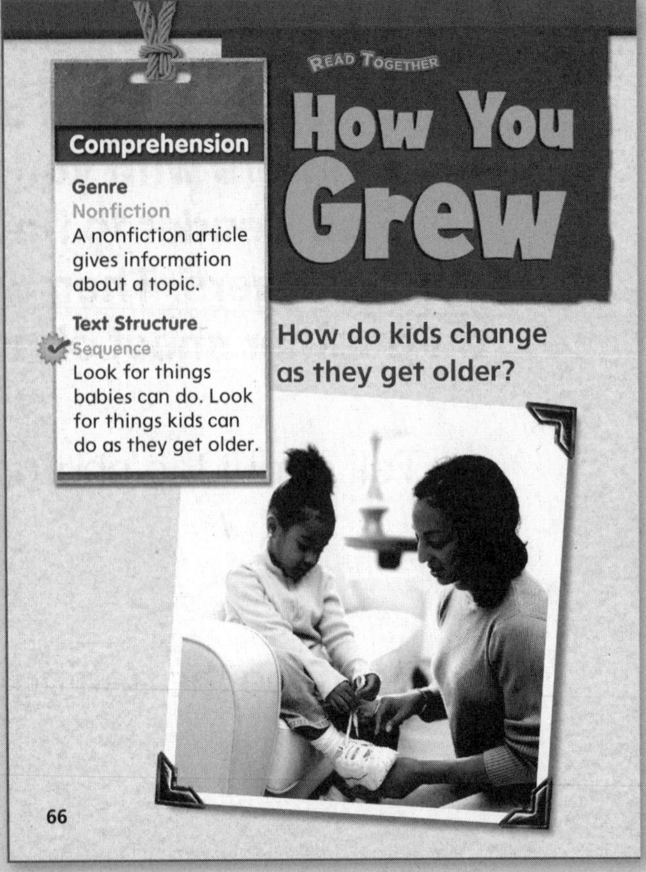

Comprehension
Genre
Nonfiction
A nonfiction article gives information about a topic.
Text Structure
Sequence
Look for things babies can do. Look for things kids can do as they get older.
Read Together
How You Grew
How do kids change as they get older?
66

Pages 68–69

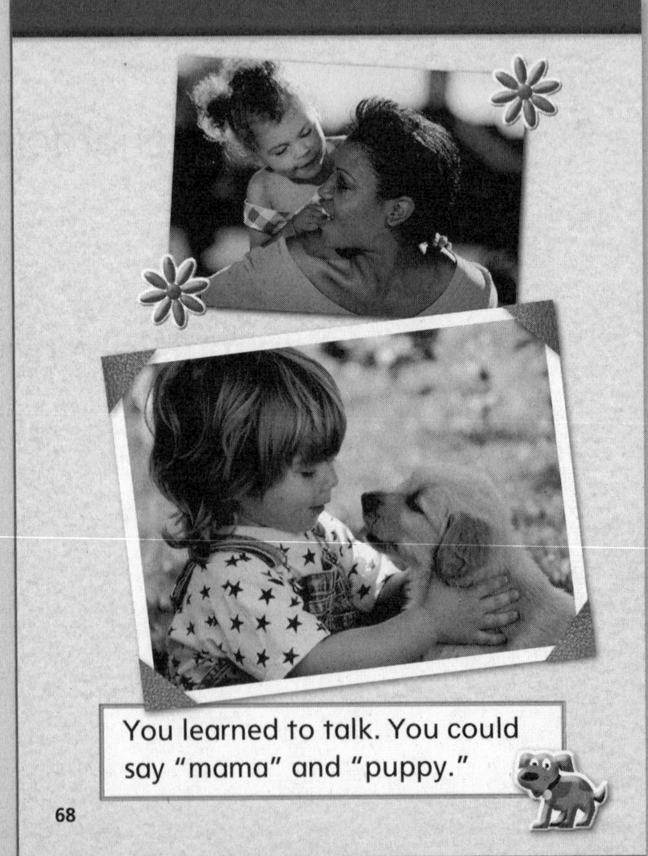

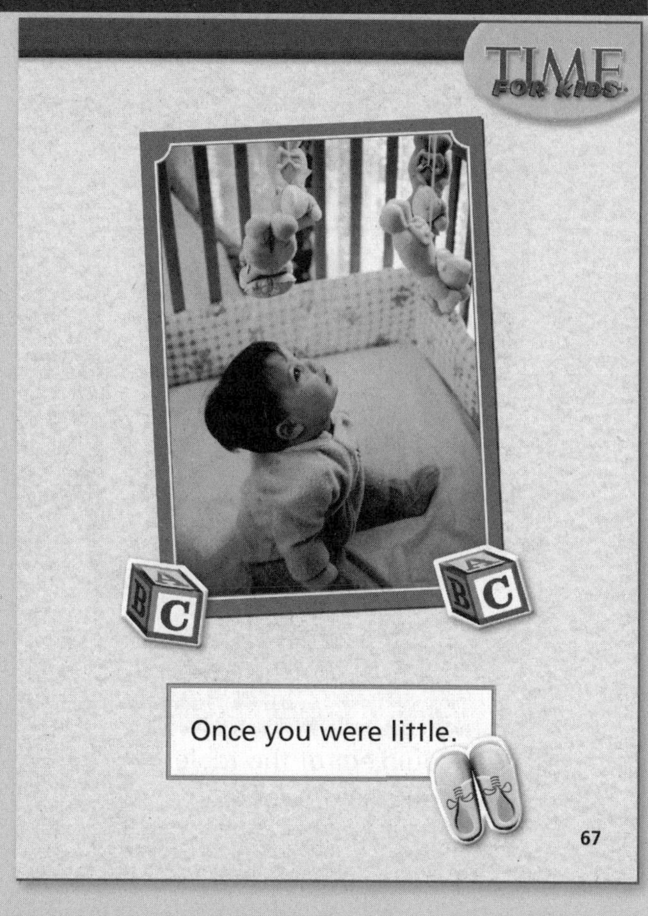

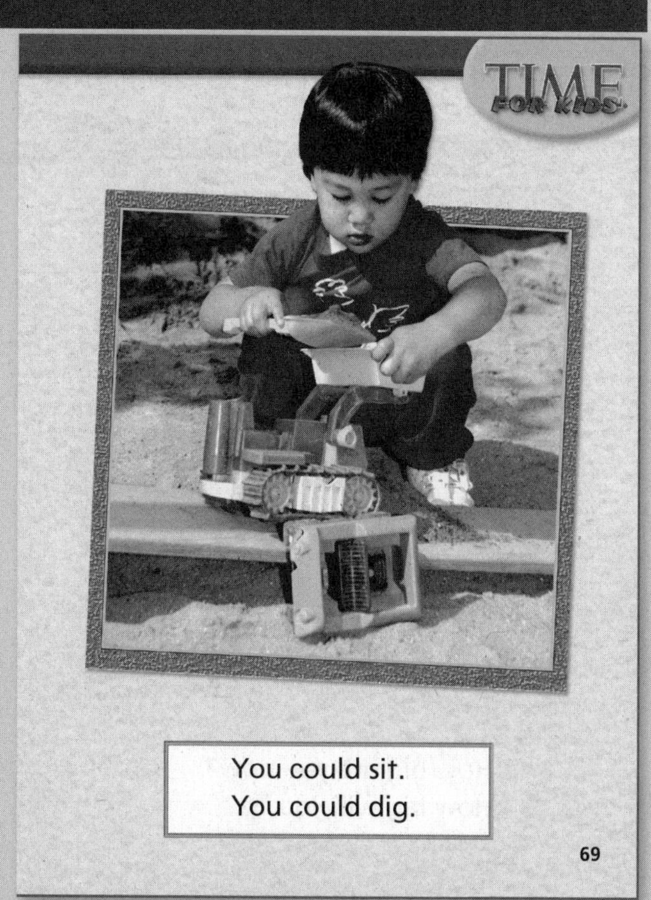

TIME FOR KIDS
You could sit.
You could dig.
69

Page 68

Text

- *Listen as I read the text:* You learned to talk. You could say "mama" and "puppy." Mama *is another word for* mother. *A puppy is a baby dog.*

Photo

Show your partner the mother in the picture. Show your partner the puppy in the picture.

Page 69

Photo

- *Look at the boy. He is playing in the sand.* (Point to the sand.) *When might you play in the sand? The little boy likes to dig.* (Point to the shovel, then mime digging.) *Do you like to dig in the sand?*

Text

- *Once you were little.* (Gesture *little* with your hands close together.) *You learned to sit.* (Demonstrate sitting.) *You learned to dig.* (Mime digging.) *You are big now.* (Gesture *big* with your hands apart.) *Can you sit now? Can you dig now?*

Seek Clarification

Some children may be confused by unfamiliar words. Encourage children to always seek clarification when they encounter a word or phrase that does not make sense to them. For example, *I don't understand this. Can you show me?*

How You Grew

Page 70

Text and Photo

- *Listen as I read the text:* You could eat at the table. You could sing a song. *I see a boy eating. Point to the boy who is eating. I see a boy singing. Point to the boy who is singing.*
- *Tell me about some foods that you like to eat. Tell me about some songs that you like to sing.*

Page 71

Text

- *When you were little, you learned to run and ride.* (Gesture *little* with your hands close together.) *You could go fast. This is what* fast *means.* (Demonstrate walking fast.) Fast *is the opposite of* slow. (Demonstrate walking slowly.)

Photo

- *I see a boy riding a bicycle. Point to the bicycle. What are some other things you can ride?* (a skateboard, a horse, a scooter)

One kid can run. One kid can ride. Show your partner how you run. Show your partner how you ride.

-

Directionality

Ask children to place their finger where you start reading (top left). Ask where you finish reading on this page (bottom right).

Pages 70–71

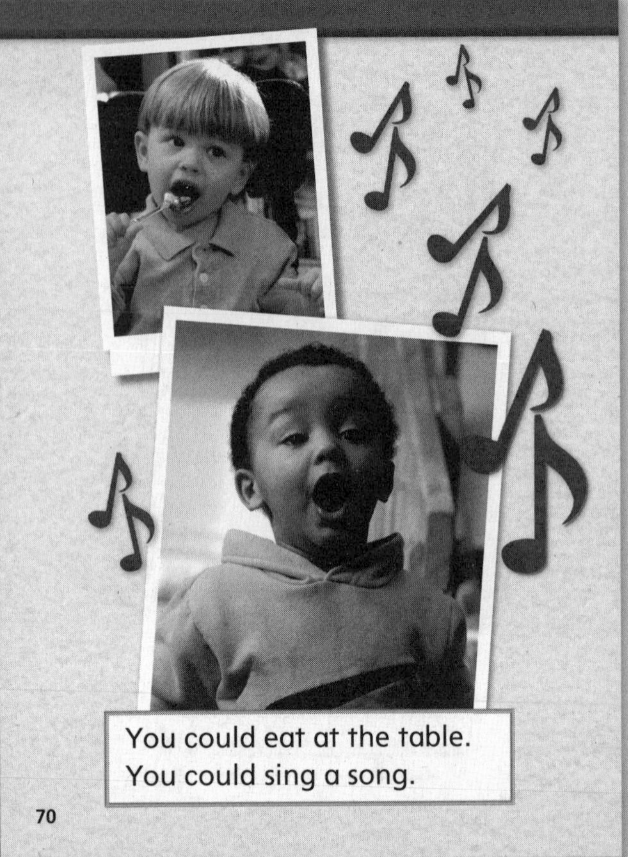

Pages 72–73

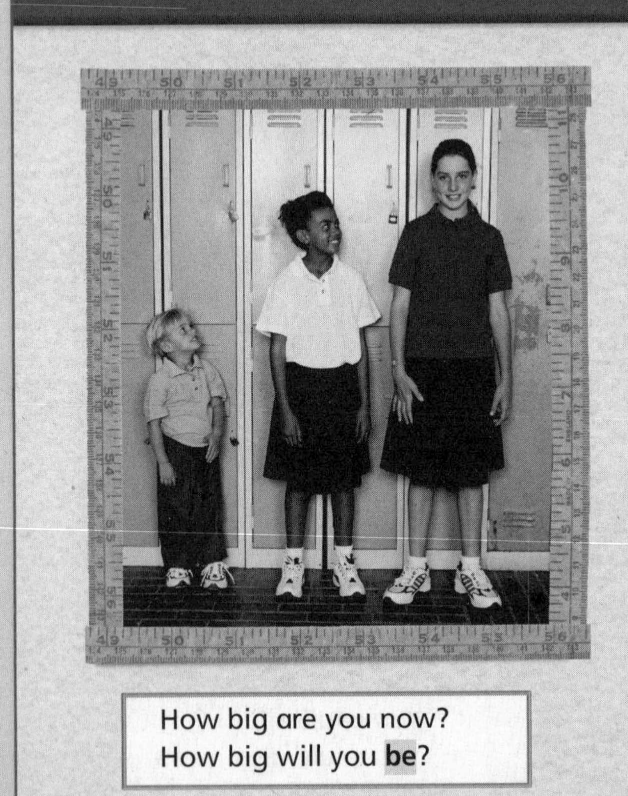

How big are you now?
How big will you be?
72

You learned to **run** and **ride**.
You could go fast.

71

 **Comprehension Check**

Tell What You Learned

Describe what kids learn to do as they get bigger.

Think and Compare

1. Name one thing kids learn to do when they are little.
2. How do children change as they get older?
3. Why can kids do harder things as they get older?
4. How are the kids in "I Am a Big Kid" different from the kids in "How You Grew"?

73

Page 72

Photo

I see a boy and two girls in this picture. The boy is smaller than the girls. Point to the boy. Look at these big girls. They are taller than the boy.

Text

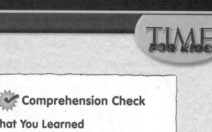

(Encourage children to do all the following gestures with you.) *First we are little.* (Hold your hands close together to indicate *little.*) *Then we grow big.* (Slowly move your hands apart to indicate growing.) *As we grow, we learn. Let's remember what we learn. We learn to talk. Show me how you talk. We learn to sit. Show me how you sit. We learn to dig. Show me how you dig. We learn to eat. Show me how you eat. We learn to run. Show me how you run. We learn to ride. Show me how you ride. Now we are big. We can do many things.*

Request Assistance

Remind children of expressions they can use to request assistance from the teacher or their partners, such as *Can you show me in the picture?*

Name ______________________

Copy each new word on the line.
Draw a picture.

Word	Illustration
milk	
apple	

© Macmillan/McGraw-Hill

Name ________________________________

Book Talk

Read each question and prompt. Discuss the answers with your group. Use your Leveled Reader to find details to support your answers. Then write your answers on another sheet of paper.

1. Tell what you learned about frogs.

2. Show classmates the different parts of a frog.

3. Describe what frog eggs look like.

4. Explain what happens to a tadpole as it grows up.

5. Give examples of things frogs can do.

© Macmillan/McGraw-Hill

Flip

Pages 84–85

Prior to reading the selection with children, they should have listened to the selection on **StudentWorks Plus,** the interactive eBook. In addition, selection vocabulary should have been pretaught using the **Visual Vocabulary Resources.**

Access Core Content

Teacher Note Pose the questions after you read the paragraph or page indicated.

Pages 84–85

Title and Illustration

- *Let's read the title of this story together:* Flip. *One of the main characters is named Flip. Do you think Flip is the animal or the girl?* (the animal, because I never knew a girl named Flip) *What kind of animal do you think Flip is?* (a dinosaur)
- *Do you think this story will tell about something that could really happen? Why or why not?* (no, because there are no dinosaurs alive today and because a girl could not ride a dinosaur)
- *The girl is smiling at Flip. He is smiling, too. Is she afraid of him or friends with him?* (She is friends with him.) *Let's smile at each other.*

Page 86

Illustration

- *The girl in the picture is holding a leash. Point to the leash and say the word:* leash. *Why does she have a leash?* (so she can hold onto Flip and walk with him; so she can keep Flip from running away)
- *A wild animal lives in the woods or water away from people. A pet lives in a house with people. Do you think Flip is a pet or a wild animal? How can you tell?* (Flip is the girl's pet. He is on a leash, like a pet dog.)

Pages 84–85

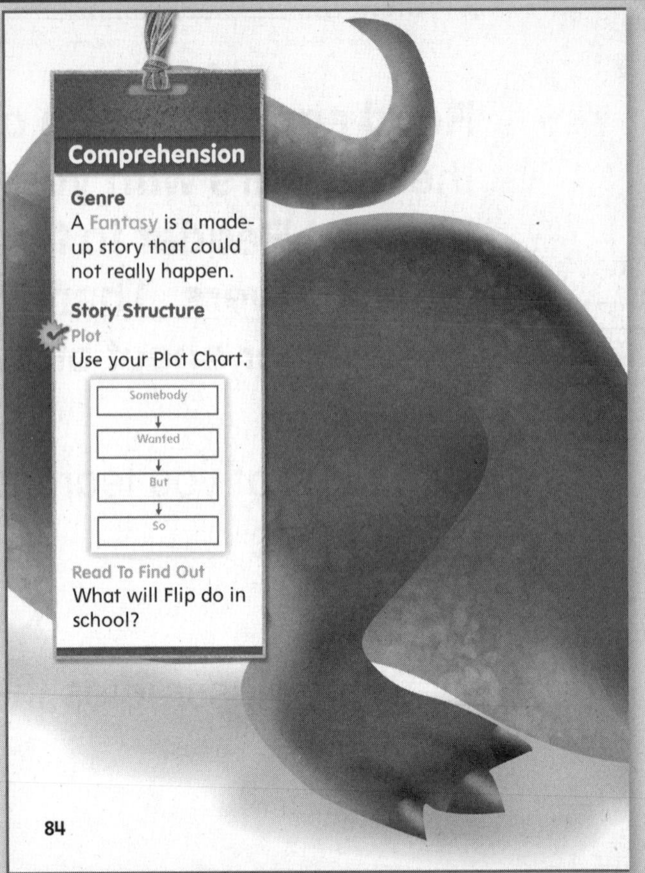

Comprehension
Genre
A Fantasy is a made-up story that could not really happen.
Story Structure
Plot
Use your Plot Chart.
Somebody
Wanted
But
So
Read To Find Out
What will Flip do in school?
84

Pages 86–87

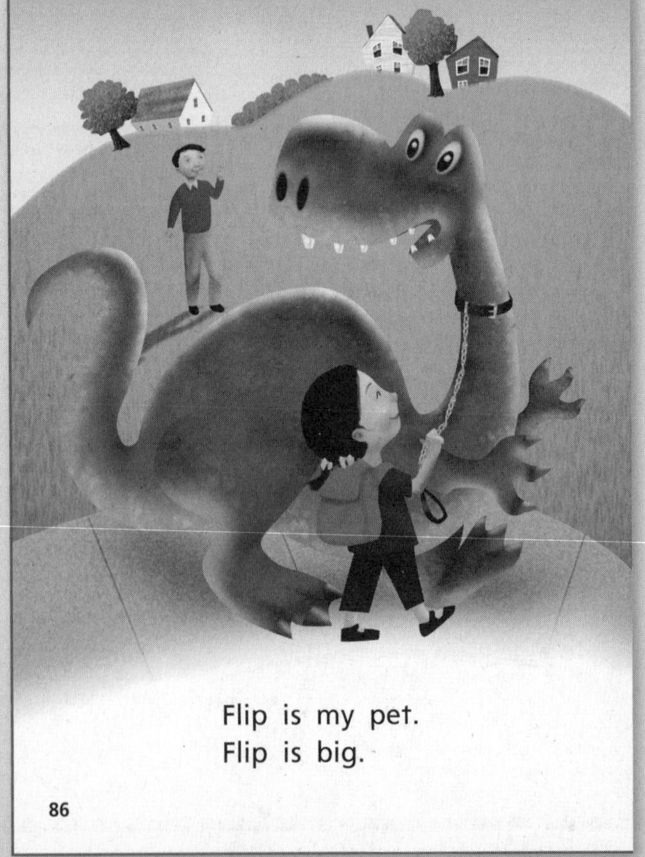

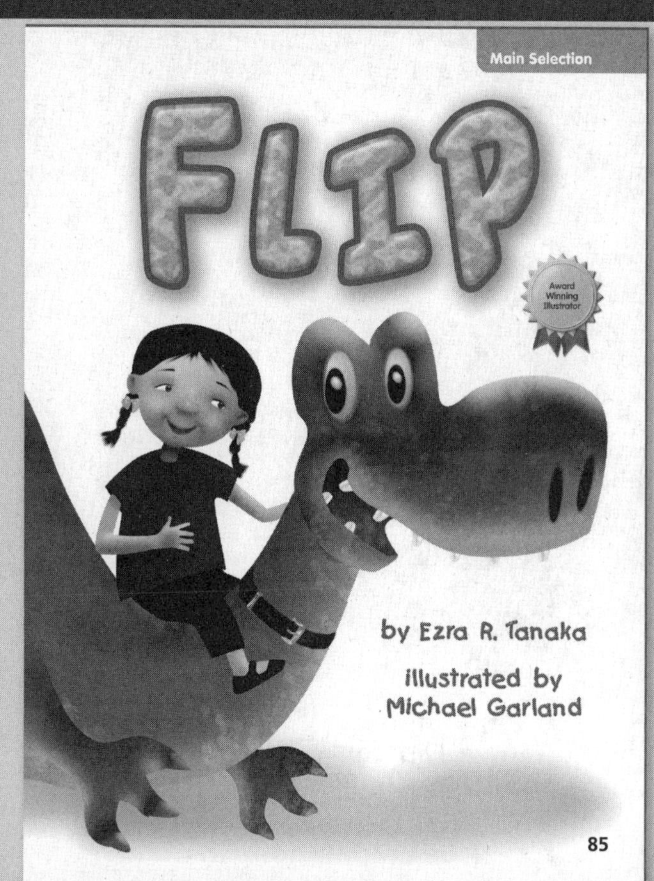

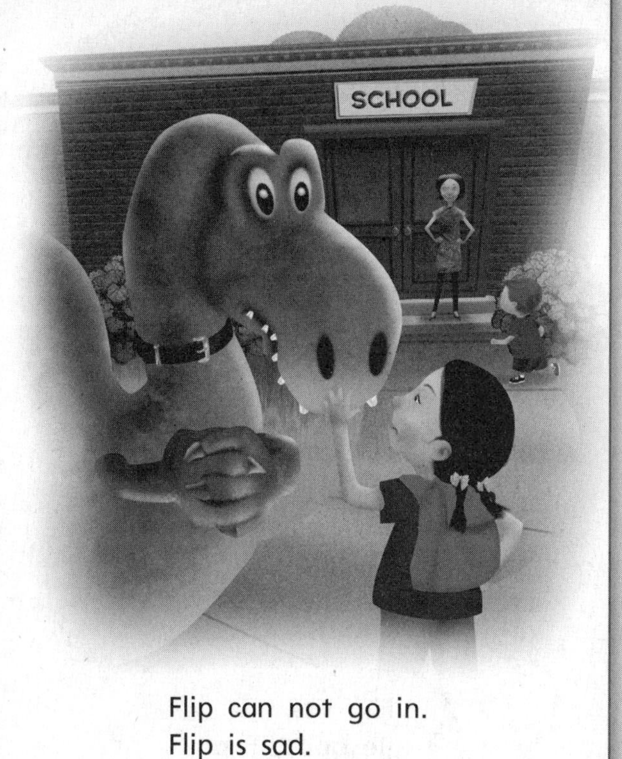

Whole Page

- *Let's read this page together:* Flip is my pet. Flip is big.
- *The story says,* Flip is my pet. *Which character do you think is talking: the man on the hill, the dinosaur, or the girl holding the leash?* (girl)
- *Could an animal as big as Flip really be a pet? Why or why not?* (no, he would be too big to take care of; He couldn't fit in someone's house.)

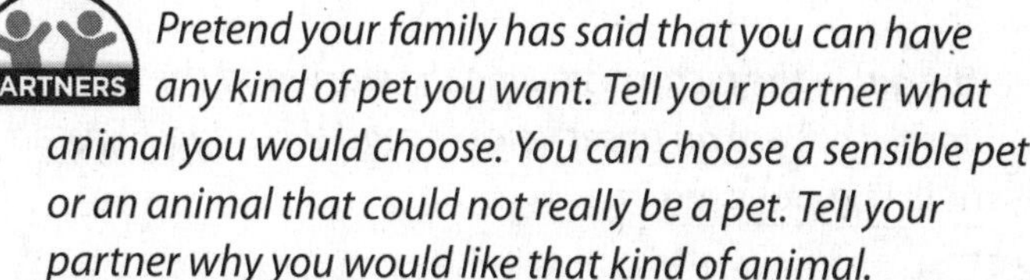

PARTNERS *Pretend your family has said that you can have any kind of pet you want. Tell your partner what animal you would choose. You can choose a sensible pet or an animal that could not really be a pet. Tell your partner why you would like that kind of animal.*

Page 87

Whole Page

- *Let's read this page together:* Flip can not go in. Flip is sad. *How does Flip feel?* (sad) *Why?* (because he can not go into school with the girl)
- *The girl in the picture looks sad. Why do you think she feels that way?* (She loves Flip and wants him with her. She also doesn't want him to feel sad.)
- *Tell what you think might happen if Flip does go into school.* (Answers will vary. Flip might knock desks over because he is so big. He would make it hard for the children to study. They would want to play with him.)

PARTNERS *What do you think I would say if Flip came into our classroom? Pretend to be me and say what I would say. Then your partner will pretend to be me.* (You cannot bring a dinosaur in here. Take it outside right now!)

Directionality

Ask children to place their finger where you start reading (top left). Ask where you finish reading on this page (bottom right).

Flip

Page 88

Whole Page

- *Flip is going into the school. Look at the girl's face in the picture. Is the girl happy or upset?* (upset) *Why is she upset?* (She is afraid that Flip will cause trouble. She is afraid that her teacher will be angry.)
- *Point to the leash. Why can't the girl pull on the leash to make Flip stop?* (He is too big. He is too strong for the girl to stop him.)
- *The girl in the picture is telling the story, and she is upset. Let's use an upset voice to read this page:* Flip can pull! Flip pulls me in.

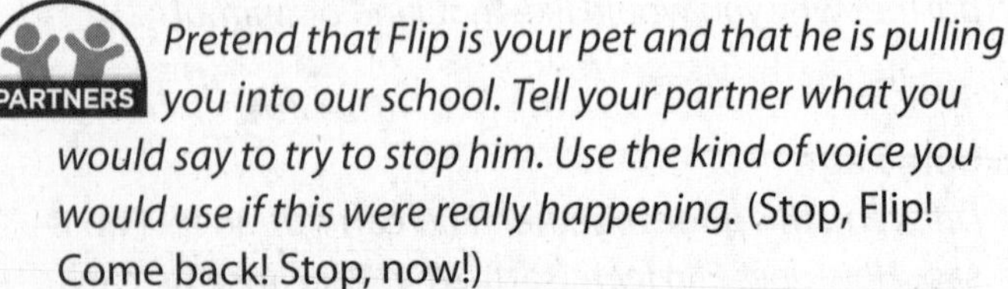
PARTNERS

Pretend that Flip is your pet and that he is pulling you into our school. Tell your partner what you would say to try to stop him. Use the kind of voice you would use if this were really happening. (Stop, Flip! Come back! Stop, now!)

Page 89

Whole Page

- *Look at the picture on this page. Do the girl's classmates know that Flip is in the school? How do you know?* (no, they are just paying attention to the teacher; They are doing their work.)
- *Pretend to be one of the children sitting at a desk. Use your face to show me what you will do when you turn around and see Flip.* (Children may gasp and open their eyes and mouths wide.)

Pages 88–89

SCHOOL
Flip can **pull**!
Flip pulls me in.
88

Pages 90–91

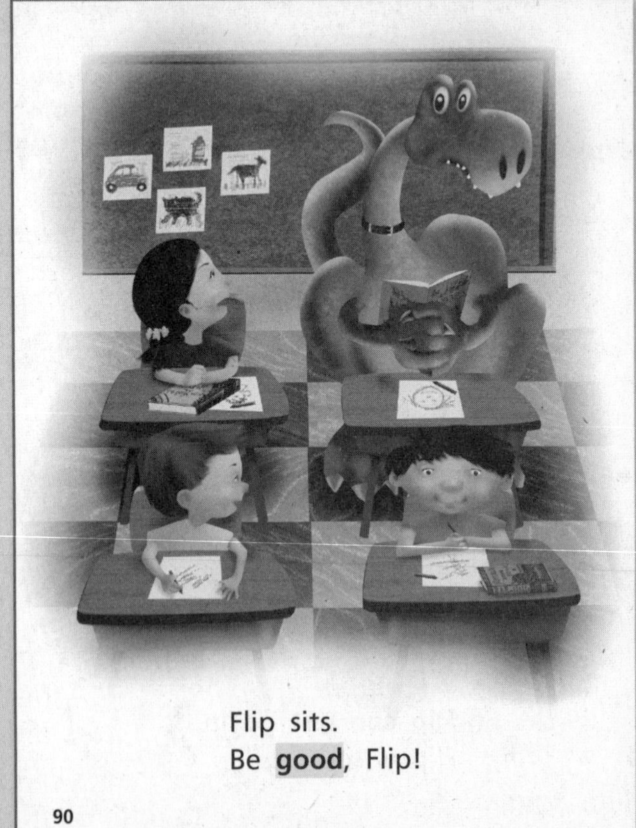
Flip sits.
Be **good**, Flip!
90

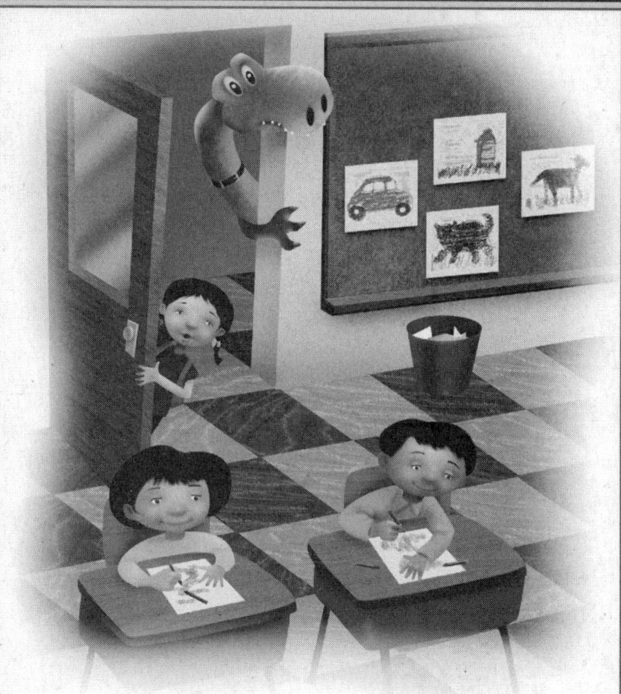

Flip and I go to class.

89

Flip likes class.

91

Pages 90–91

Text and Illustrations

- *Let's read this page together:* Flip sits. Be good, Flip! *Could Flip really sit down at a desk? Why or why not?* (Flip couldn't really sit at a desk. He would break it.)
- *What else makes this part of the story silly? Look at the picture on page 90.* (A dinosaur cannot read a book. The other children would not quietly work if Flip were in their classroom.)
- *Look at the picture on page 91. Flip and the children are painting. they are holding the brush in different ways. The children are using their _____. (hands) Flip is using his _____. (tail)*

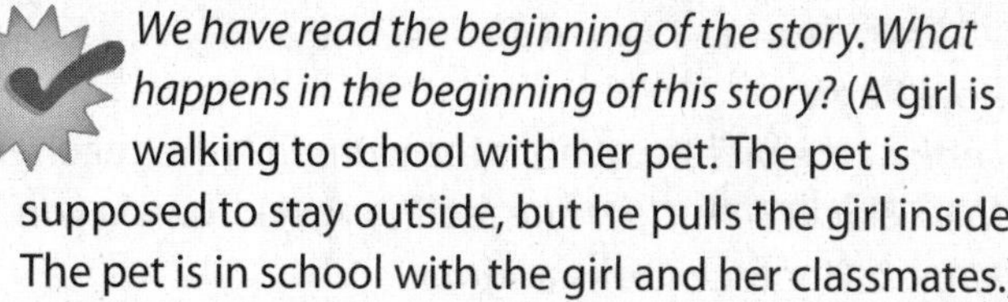

We have read the beginning of the story. What happens in the beginning of this story? (A girl is walking to school with her pet. The pet is supposed to stay outside, but he pulls the girl inside. The pet is in school with the girl and her classmates.)

Patterns in Language

Some grammatical structures, such as the ending -*s* in the present tense, pose difficulties to ELLs. Point out that there are several examples of words ending in -*s* in this selection, such as *pulls, sits, likes*. Help children find a pattern.

Flip

Page 92

Whole Page

- *Look at the picture. The children are climbing all over Flip. Do they look like they are having fun?* (yes)
- *Let's read this page together:* The kids like Flip. *Why do you think they like him?* (He is fun. He does things kids like to do.)

Talk with your partner about what it might be like to have Flip in our room. What would be good about having Flip here? (He would make us laugh. He could play with us at recess.) *What would be bad?* (He might break things. Some children might be scared of him.)

Page 93

Whole Page

- *Look at the picture. Who is the woman?* (the teacher, Miss Black) *How does she feel?* (angry) *How do you know?* (Her face looks angry.)
- *Let's read the first sentence together:* Miss Black is mad. *Now let's use an angry voice to read what she says:* Sit down, Flip!
- *Why is the teacher angry?* (The children made a mess with paints. Now they are playing with Flip instead of doing their work.)

Formal and Informal English

When children encounter a word used in a formal setting in the text, discuss other ways the character would communicate with more informal language. For example: *Miss Black / Flip*

Pages 92–93

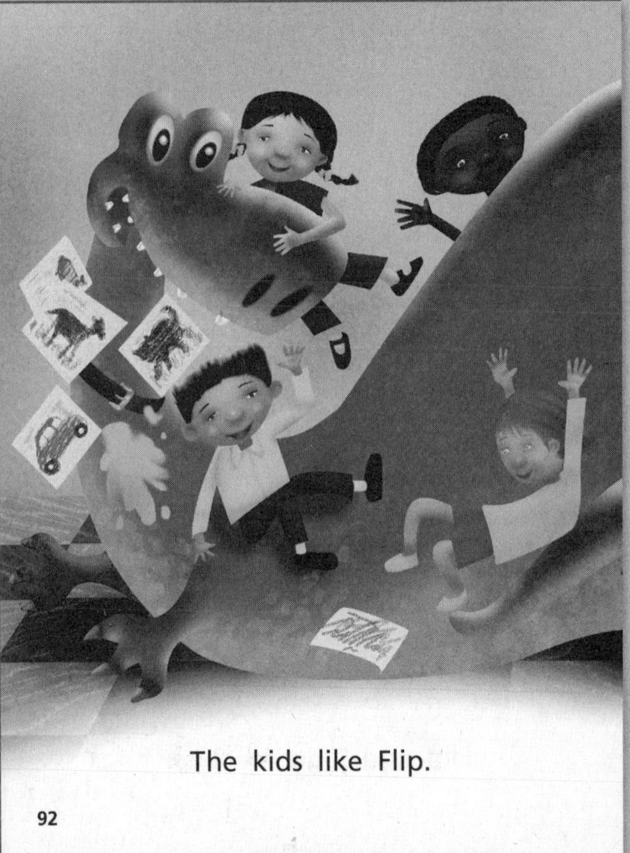

Pages 94–95

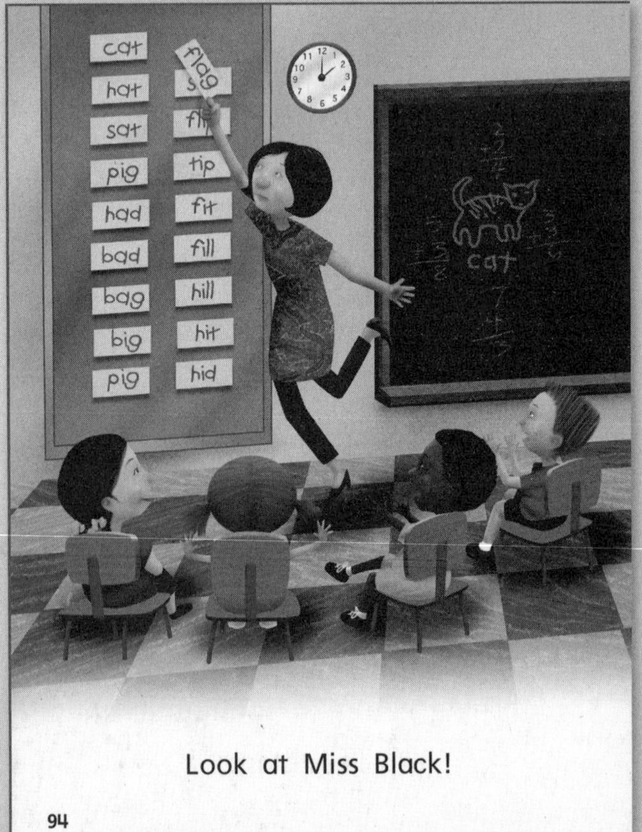

Miss Black is mad.
Sit **down**, Flip!

93

Page 94

Whole Page

- *Look at the picture. What is Miss Black trying to do?* (put up the word card) *What is the problem?* (She can't reach high enough.) *Let's stand up and pretend we are trying to hang something up high.* (Demonstrate trying to reach very high.)
- *In a real classroom, how would a teacher solve this problem?* (use a ladder, put the card at the bottom)

Page 95

Whole Page

- *Look at the picture. Flip is looking at Miss Black. He looks like he is thinking. Let's fold our hands like Flip.* (Demonstrate standing with hands folded.)
- Let's read this page together: Flip has a plan. *What do you think Flip's plan is? How might he help Miss Black?* (Answers will vary.)

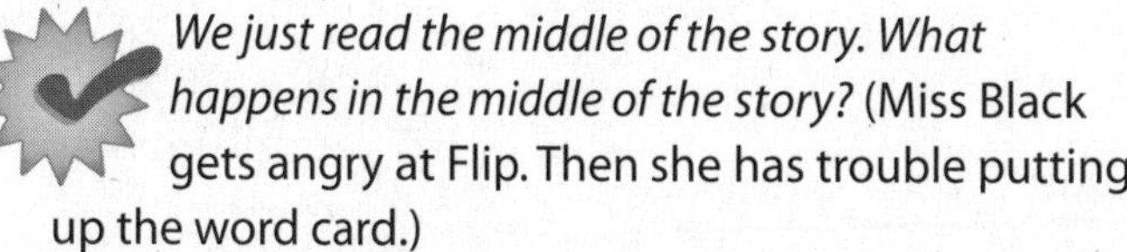

We just read the middle of the story. What happens in the middle of the story? (Miss Black gets angry at Flip. Then she has trouble putting up the word card.)

- *Who in this story is having a good day? Why?* (Flip and the children are having a good day because they are having fun in school.) *Who in this story is having a bad day? Why?* (Miss Black is having a bad day because everything is going wrong.)

Page 96

Whole Page

- *The picture shows Flip's plan. What is it?* (He lets Miss Black climb up on his neck so she can reach higher.) *Does his plan work?* (yes)
- *Say each sentence on this page after me, and do what I do:* Look at Flip! (Point up as if pointing to Flip.) The class claps. (clap)
- *Why does the class clap?* (The children want Flip to know they like his idea.)

PARTNERS *Talk with your partner about what Miss Black might say to Flip when she gets down.* (Thank you. You were a big help.) *What might Flip say?* (I'm so glad I could help you.) *Take turns pretending to be these characters and saying their lines.*

Pages 96–97

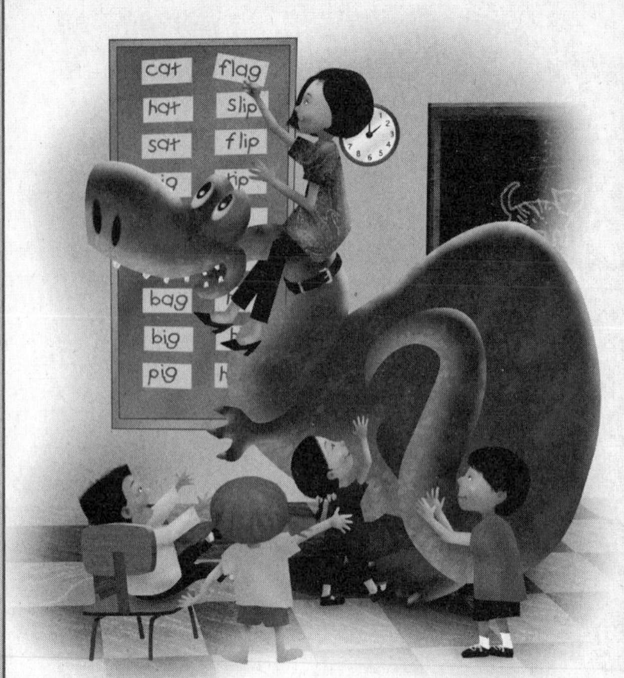

Flip did it!
The class claps.

96

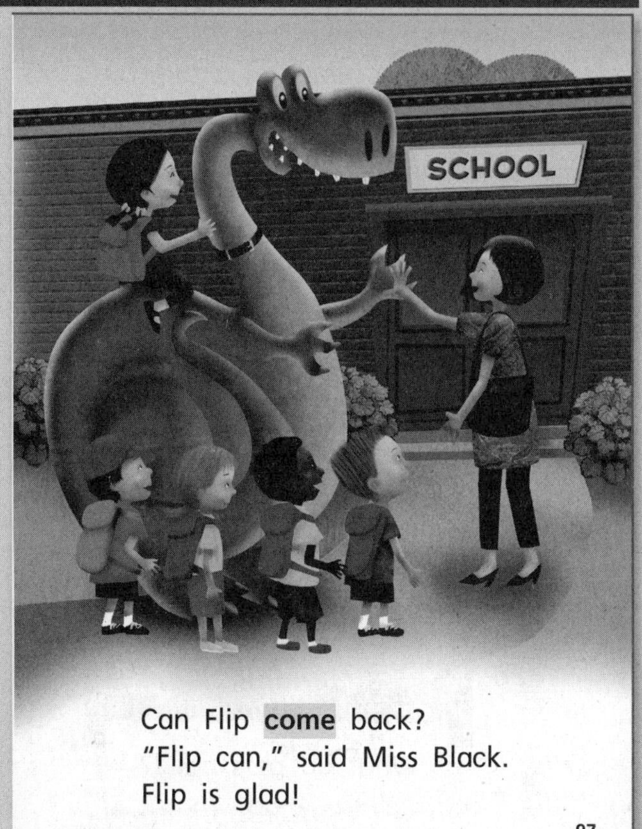

Can Flip **come** back?
"Flip can," said Miss Black.
Flip is glad!

97

Page 97

Whole Page

- *The girl says:* "Can Flip come back?" *Who do you think she means?* (She wants to know if she can bring her pet back to school.)
- *Let's read parts of this page together. You will read the question. I will read the teacher's part.* (Children:) Can Flip come back? (Teacher:) Flip can!

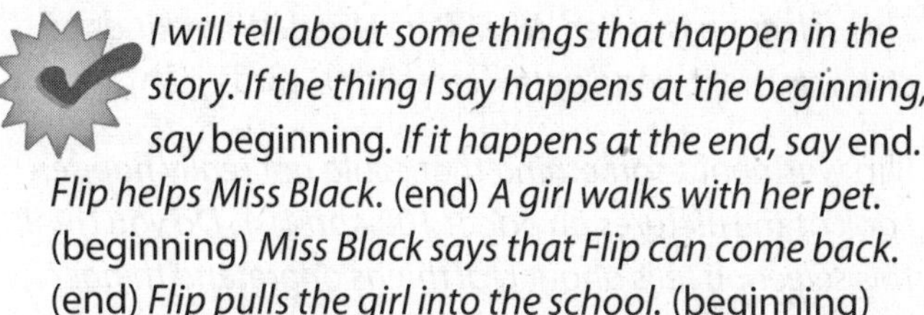

I will tell about some things that happen in the story. If the thing I say happens at the beginning, say beginning. *If it happens at the end, say* end. *Flip helps Miss Black.* (end) *A girl walks with her pet.* (beginning) *Miss Black says that Flip can come back.* (end) *Flip pulls the girl into the school.* (beginning)

- *What do you think will happen when Flip comes back to school?* (He will do artwork and read with the children. He will help Miss Black.)

What Pets Need

Access Core Content

Teacher Note Pose the questions after you read the paragraph or page indicated.

Page 100

Title and Photos

- *This selection is called* What Pets Need. *What kinds of animals make good pets?* (cats, dogs, birds, fish)
- Flip *was about something that could not really happen. Look at the pictures on pages 100 and 101. Do you think this selection tells about real things or pretend things? How can you tell?* (It tells about real things. The pictures are of real people and animals.)

Text

- *This page asks a question that the book will answer. Listen as I read the question aloud:* What do pets need?

PARTNERS

Tell your partner about a pet you have. Tell what your pet needs and how you care for it. If you don't have a pet, talk about a pet you would like to have.

Page 101

Whole Page

- *Listen as I read this page.*
- *What do all pets need?* (food) *What do some pets eat?* (plants, seeds)
- *This page shows two animals. Point to the bird. Point to the lizard. Which animal is eating a plant?* (lizard) *Which animal is eating seeds?* (bird)

Page 102

Text

- *Listen as I read to find out something else that pets need:* Some pets eat meat or fish. All pets need fresh water. *What do all pets need?* (fresh water)

Pages 100–101

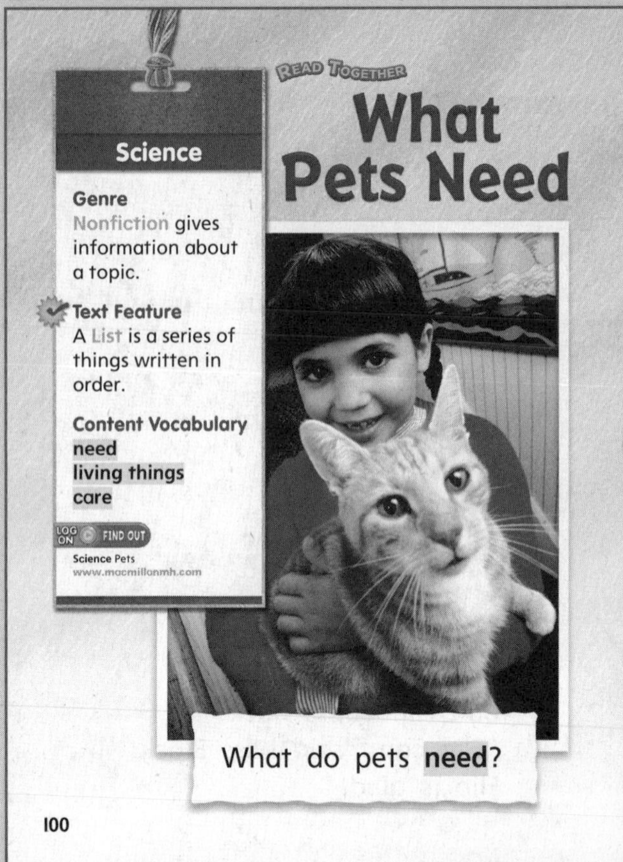
Read Together
What Pets Need
Science
Genre
Nonfiction gives information about a topic.
Text Feature
A List is a series of things written in order.
Content Vocabulary
need
living things
care
LOG ON FIND OUT
Science Pets
www.macmillanmh.com
What do pets need?
100

Pages 102–103

Some pets eat meat or fish.
All pets need fresh water.
102

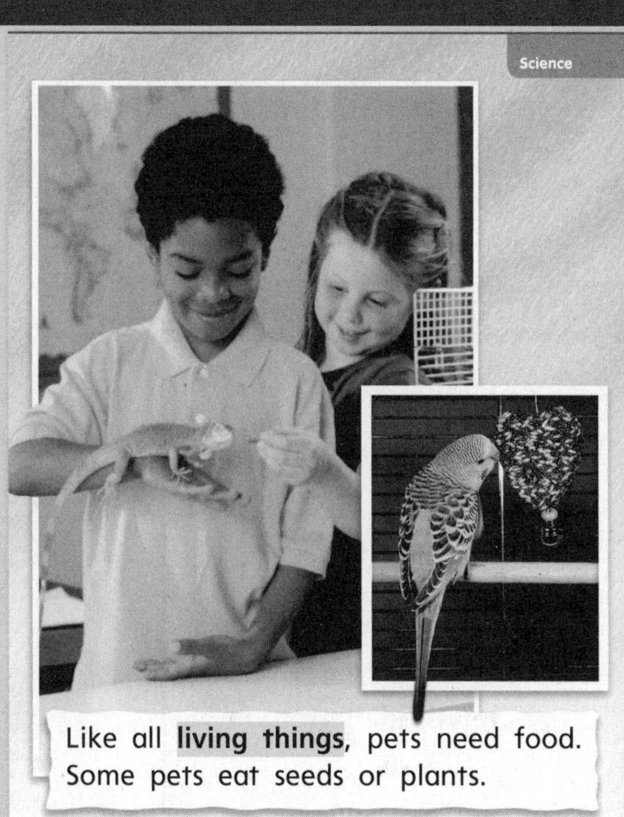
Science
Like all living things, pets need food.
Some pets eat seeds or plants.
101

Caring for My Rabbit
• Give it food.
• Give it water.
• Change the bedding.
• Brush the fur.
Pets need a safe home.
Pets need our love and care.
Connect and Compare
How would you take care of Flip?
103

Photo

- *The picture shows us a pet that eats meat. What pet is it?* (dog) *What is another kind of pet that eats meat or fish?* (cat)
- *Pets can eat other foods, too. Name some.* (fish food, vegetables, fruits)

Page 103

Text

- *Listen as I read the sentences under the picture:* Pets need a safe home. Pets need our love and care. *What is one way we show love to cats and dogs? (by* petting them)

Text Box

- *Point to the list at the top of the page. Listen as I read the title:* Caring for My Rabbit. *This list tells things to do to care for a pet rabbit.*
- *Point to the the first thing on the list. It says:* Give it food. *Point to the second thing on the list. It says:* Give it water.
- *Point to the third thing on the list. It says:* Change the bedding. *The bedding is what goes in the rabbit's cage.*
- *Now let's make our own list to show the things that all pets need.* (food, water, bed, love, care)

Name ______________________________

Copy each new word on the line.
Draw a picture.

Word	Illustration
turtle ______________________	
whale ______________________	

© Macmillan/McGraw-Hill

Name ____________________

Book Talk

Read each question and prompt. Discuss the answers with your group. Use your Leveled Reader to find details to support your answers. Then write your answers on another sheet of paper.

1. Talk about the pet in your story.

2. How does the main character take care of the pet?

3. Give examples of things a good pet can do.

4. Do you have a pet? Does a friend have a pet? Share ideas with your classmates.

5. What did you learn about pets from your story?

© Macmillan/McGraw-Hill

Soccer

Pages 112–113

Prior to reading the selection with students, they should have listened to the selection on **StudentWorks Plus**, the interactive eBook. In addition, selection vocabulary should have been pretaught using the **Visual Vocabulary Resources**.

Access Core Content

Teacher Note Pose the questions after you read the paragraph or page indicated.

Pages 112–113

Title

- (Point to the title.) *This is the title of the story. Let's read it together:* Soccer.

Photo

- *These children are playing soccer. Soccer is a game where the players kick the ball into a net. I see a soccer ball in this picture. Point to the ball.*

Look at the picture. One girl can kick. Stand away from your partner and show your partner how you can kick a ball, into the air. Two children can run. Show your partner how you run.

Page 114

Photo

- *Look at these children. They play soccer.*

Text

- *Let's read this page together. I'll read the words first, and then you say the words after me:* We play soccer.

Find the word soccer. Show and read it to your partner.

Pages 112–113

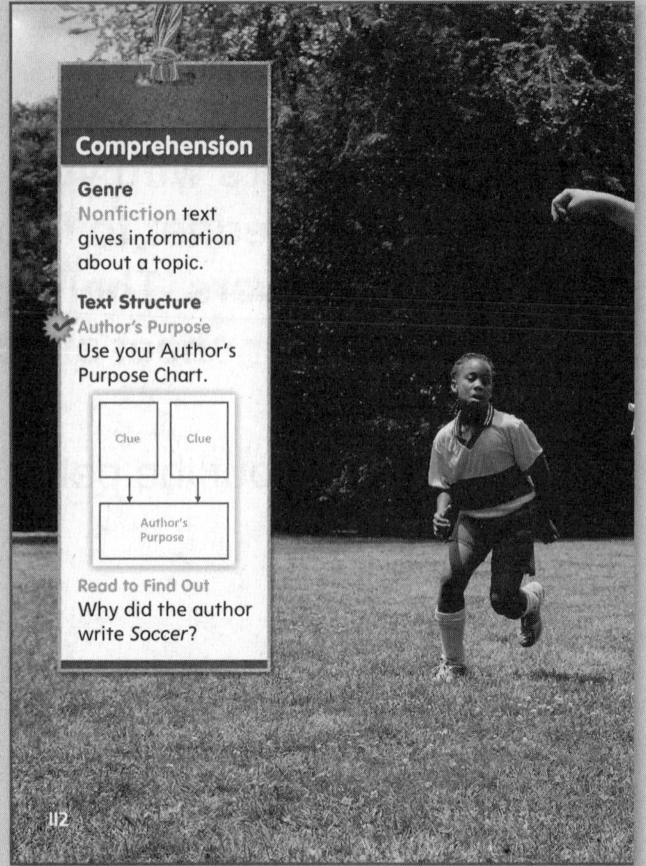

Comprehension
Genre
Nonfiction text gives information about a topic.
Text Structure
Author's Purpose
Use your Author's Purpose Chart.
Clue
Clue
Author's Purpose
Read to Find Out
Why did the author write Soccer?
112

Pages 114–115

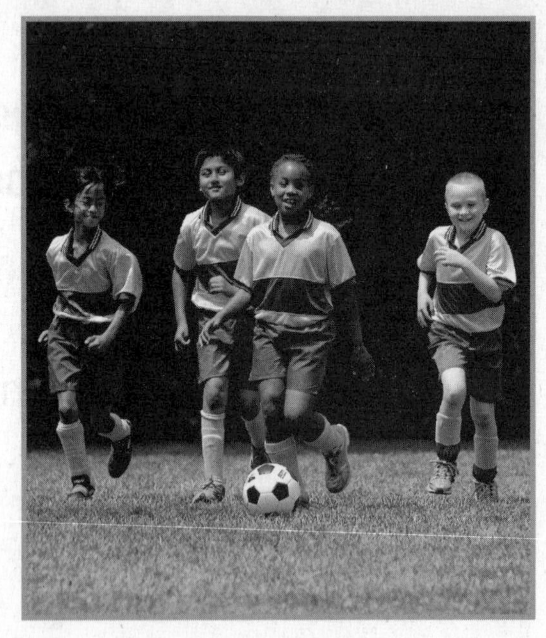

We play soccer.

114

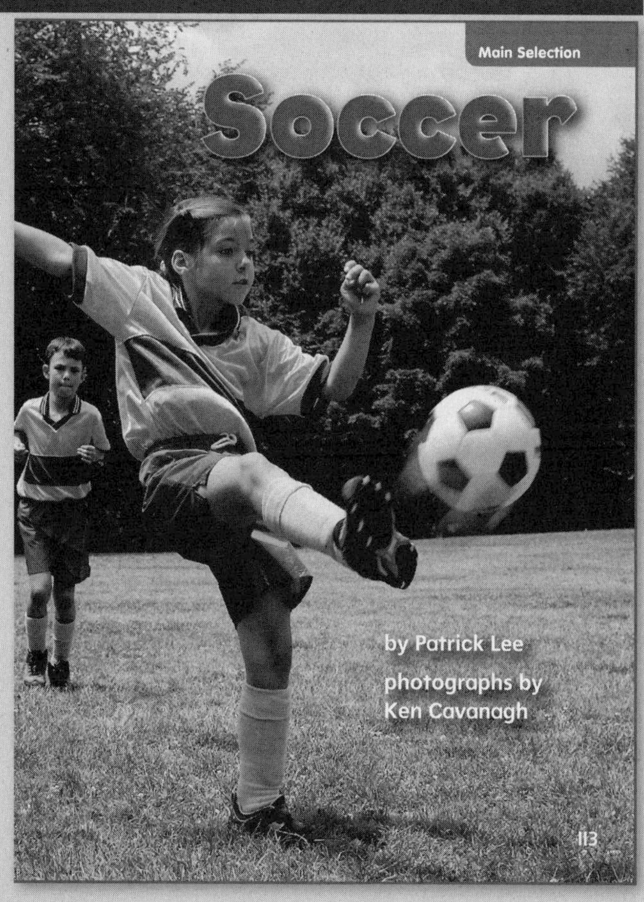

Hank will **help**.

115

Page 115

Text

- *Let's read this page together. I'll read the words first, and then you say the words after me:* Hank will help.

Photo

- *Hank can play soccer. He can help the children. He is the coach, or teacher. He is an adult. Look at the picture. Find Hank. How can Hank, the coach, help the children?* (He can teach them how to play. He can teach them the rules of the game.)

Soccer

Page 116

Photo

- *I see a girl kicking a soccer ball. Point to her. I see two children running. Point to them.*

Text, Choral Reading

- *Let's read this page together.*

Point to the word run. *Name some other games where you run. Point to the word* kick. *Name some other games where you kick.*

Page 117

Photo

- *I see a boy kicking a soccer ball. What can he do?* (He can kick.)

Page 118

Text and Photo

- *Listen as I read this page:* I am very fast. I am as fast as the wind! *Look at the boy in the picture. What is he doing?* (He is running.)
- *This boy is as fast as the wind. When the wind is blowing hard, it can be very fast. Let's pretend to be the wind.* (Blow out your breath and sway as if you're moved by a fast wind.) *The wind can be very fast!*

You need to be fast for many games. Can you think of some? Tell your partner about these games.

Directionality

Ask children to place their finger where you start reading (top left). Ask where you finish reading on this page (bottom right).

Pages 116–117

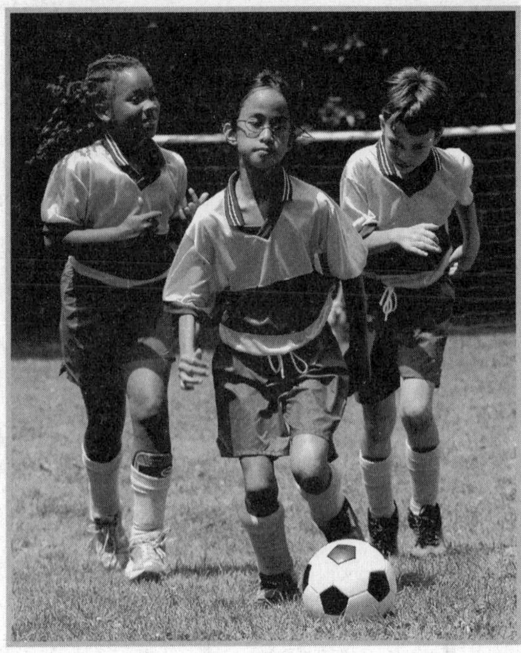

We run and kick.

116

Pages 118–119

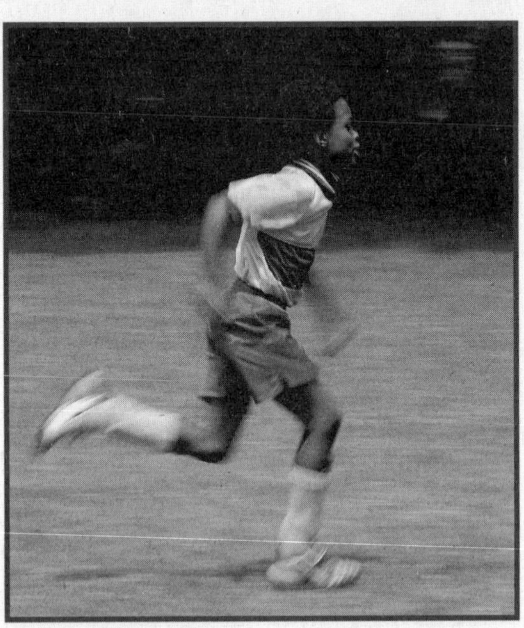

I am **very** fast.
I am as fast as the wind!

118

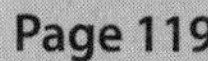

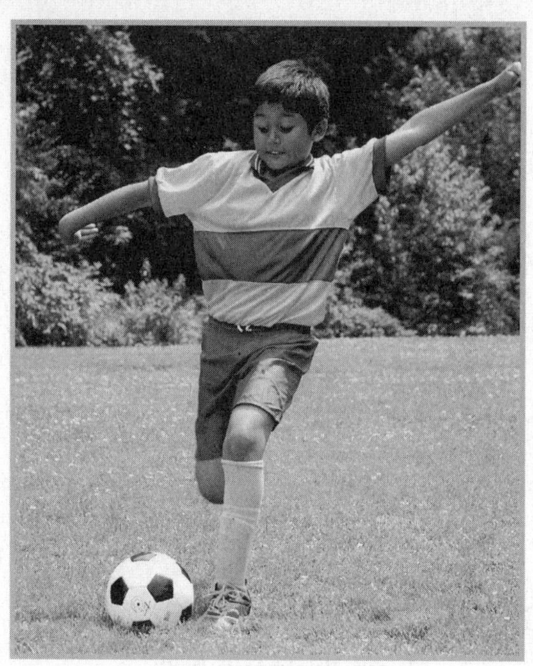

I kick and kick.

117

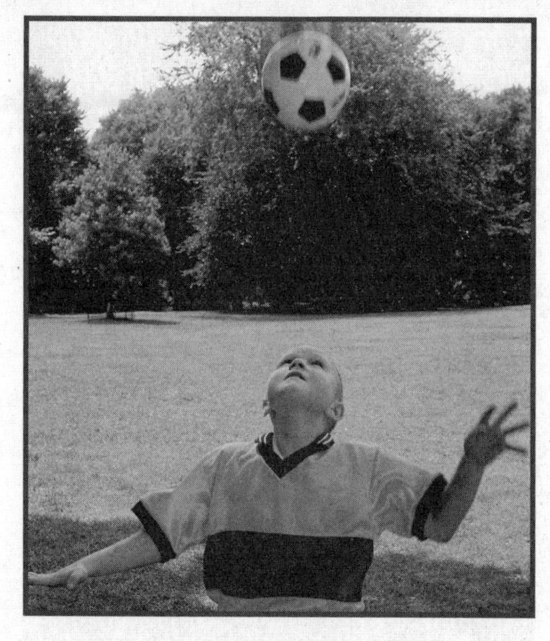

I can not use hands.

119

Page 119

Photo

- *We have two hands.* (Hold your hands up in front of you.) *Let me see your hands. Say it with me:* hands. *Look at the boy in the picture. Point to his hands.*
- *In soccer, most players cannot touch the ball with their hands. Let's think of some other body parts you could use to hit the ball.* (Point to the body parts as you say the words: *feet, head, body.*)
- *Point to the soccer ball. The ball is up in the air. Can the boy touch the ball with his hands?* (no) *No, he cannot touch the ball with his hands.*

Text, Choral Reading

- *Let's read this page together.*

Soccer

Page 120

Photo and Text

- *I see a girl and a boy in this picture. The girl's name is Jill. Point to the girl. The boy is going to kick the ball. Point to the boy.*
- *Let's read the second sentence on this page:* I will pass it to Jill. *You pass the ball when you kick it to another player. Say it with me:* pass.

PARTNERS *Pretend you are playing soccer with your partner. Show me how you would pass the ball to each other.*

Page 121

Photo

- *Sometimes we run straight, like this.* (Run straight across the room.) *Look at this boy. He can run very fast. He can run like this.* (Run in a zigzag motion.) *This is zigzag. Say it with me:* zigzag. *Can you zigzag when you run?* (Repeat zigzag motion.) *Can you run straight?* (Repeat straight motion.) *Show me.*

Text

- *Let's read the first sentence on this page:* I can zig and zag. *What can the boy do when he runs?* (He can zigzag.)

Page 122

Photo

- *I see a boy and a girl in this picture. The girl is the goalie. She makes sure the ball doesn't go into the goal. The goal is where the other team tries to put the ball to score a point. Say* goal *and* goalie *with me:* goal, goalie.

Text

- *Listen as I read this page:* I can use hands. *If you are the goalie, you can touch the ball with your hands. Let's pretend we are goalies catching the ball.*

Pages 120–121

I can kick the ball.
I will pass it to Jill.

120

Pages 122–123

I can use hands.

122

I can zig and zag.
I am very fast.

121

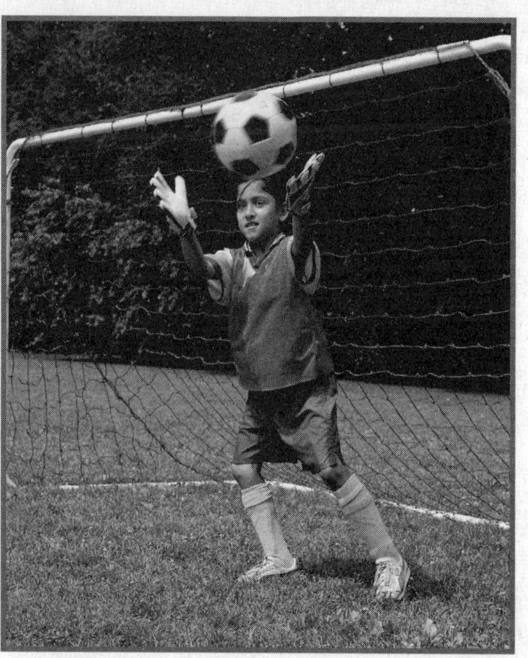

Where will the ball land?

123

Page 123

Photo

- *I see the goalie in this picture. Point to the goalie. She is ready to catch the ball.* (Mime catching a ball.)

Text

- Let's read the sentence together: Where will the ball land? *The ball is in the air. When it comes down, it will land somewhere. Where might the ball land?* (It will land in the goalie's hands.)

Seek Clarification

Some children may be confused by unfamiliar words. Encourage children to always seek clarification when they encounter a word or phrase that does not make sense to them. For example, *I don't understand "land." Can you show me?*

Soccer

Page 124

Photo

- *Look at the goalie. She can stop the ball!*
- *Let's read this page together:* I did it. I am very glad. *What did the goalie do?* (She stopped the ball from going into the net.)

Page 125

Photo

- *Do you remember Hank? He is the coach. Point to Hank. Why do you think they look happy?*

Text

- *Let's read this page together:* Now it is over. We like soccer! *The game is over. It is the end.* Over *means "the end."*
- *The children are happy because they like soccer. Do you like soccer?*

Pages 124–125

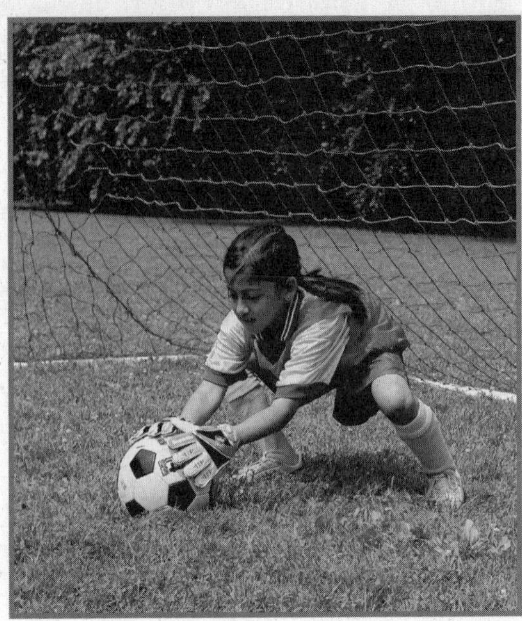

I did it.
I am very glad!

124

Now it is over.
We like soccer!

125

A man named Patrick Lee wrote this story. Let's find his name at the front of the book. (Point to the author's name.) *Patrick Lee is the author of the story. Say it with me:* author. *Why did he write it? Did he want to tell us about baseball?* (no) *Did he want to tell us about basketball?* (no) *Did he want to tell us about soccer?* (yes) *That's right, he wrote the story to tell us about soccer.*

Guess What!

Access Core Content

Teacher Note Pose the questions after you read the line indicated.

Page 128

Illustration

- I see a goal and a goalie in this picture. *Point to the goal. Point to the goalie. What is the goalie doing?* (He is ready to catch the ball.) (Point to the other children.) *What are these children doing?* (running)
- *We are going to read a poem. The poem has words that rhyme, or sound the same. Let's listen for rhyming words as we read.*

Page 129

Title

- (Point to the title.) *This is the title of the poem. Listen as I read the title:* Guess What! *The poem will tell us about something. We will have to guess what it is. Is it a soccer shoe?* (Point to a shoe in the picture.) *Is it a soccer shirt?* (Point to a shirt in the picture.) *Let's read to find out.*

Lines 1–2

- *Listen as I read the first two lines:* Black and white / Kicked with might. White *and* might *have the same sound. They rhyme.*
- *When you kick something with might, you kick it very hard. Look at the picture of the girl kicking hard.*

Lines 3–4

- *Listen as I read the next two lines:* Smooth and round / Air bound. *What two words sound the same in these lines?* (round, bound)
- *When something is air bound, it is going into the air, like an airplane. What are some other things that could be air bound?*

Pages 128–129

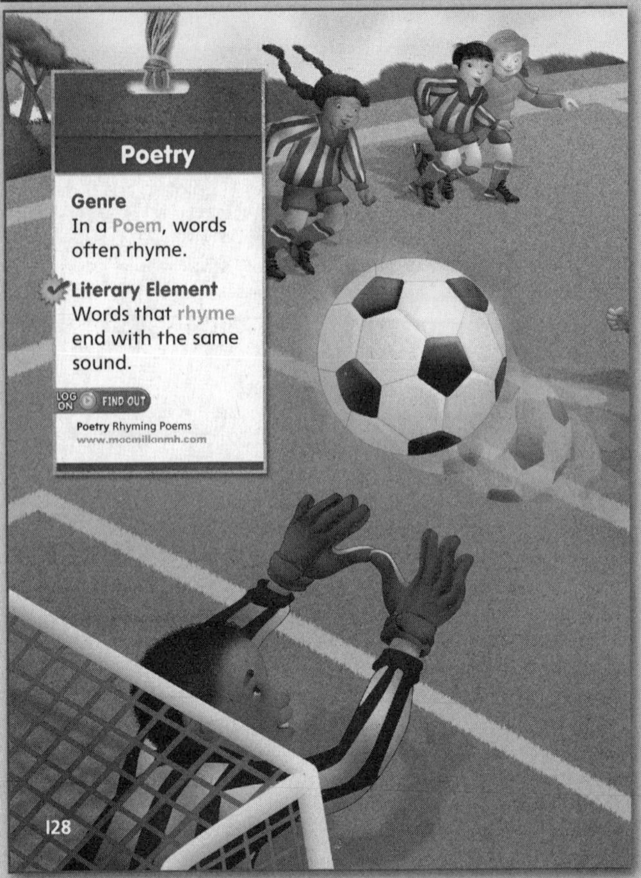
Poetry
Genre
In a Poem, words often rhyme.
Literary Element
Words that rhyme end with the same sound.
LOG ON FIND OUT
Poetry Rhyming Poems
www.macmillanmh.com
128

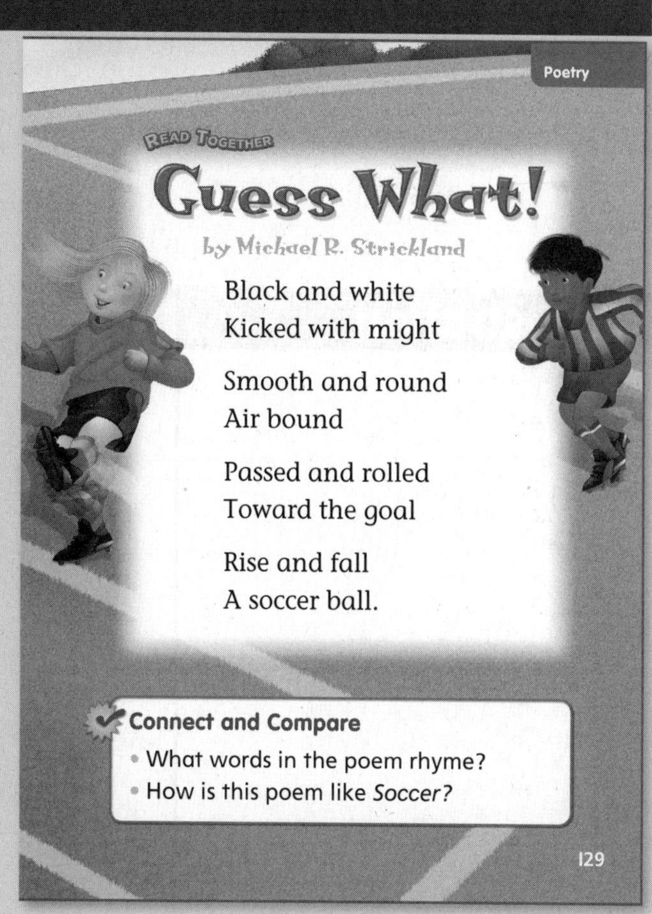

Poetry

READ TOGETHER

Guess What!

by Michael R. Strickland

Black and white
Kicked with might

Smooth and round
Air bound

Passed and rolled
Toward the goal

Rise and fall
A soccer ball.

Connect and Compare

- What words in the poem rhyme?
- How is this poem like *Soccer?*

129

Lines 5–6

- *Listen as I read the next two lines:* Passed and rolled / Toward the goal. *Tell me how we pass a ball.* (We kick it to another player.)
- *Do you think that the poem describes a soccer ball? Why?* (yes, because it describes something black and white that gets kicked and rolled)

Lines 7–8

- *Listen as I read the last two lines:* Rise and fall / A soccer ball. *What two words sound the same in these lines?* (fall, ball) *Yes,* fall *and* ball *rhyme.*
- *What was the poem about?* (a soccer ball)

Analyze Sayings and Expressions

Help children recognize that *with might* is an expression that means strongly or with lots of energy. Help them create other examples using this expression.

Name ______________________________

Copy each new word on the line.
Draw a picture.

Word	Illustration
soccer ______________________	
baseball ______________________	

© Macmillan/McGraw-Hill

Name ______________________

Read each question and prompt. Discuss the answers with your group. Use your Leveled Reader to find details to support your answers. Then write your answers on another sheet of paper.

1. Name the friends in your community who help you.

2. Describe what the crossing guard does to help you.

3. Talk about how the police officer keeps you safe.

4. Which helper in your community do you think is the most important?

5. Which helper would you like to be? Explain your answer to your group.

© Macmillan/McGraw-Hill

Weekly Planners

Week 1

Selections	Vocabulary		ELL Practice Book
	Oral Vocabulary Words/Cognates	Academic Language/Cognates	
Animal Moms and Dads *Over in the Meadow*	provide wild guide *guiar* protect *proteger* separate *separar*	main idea summarize nouns details *detalles*	• Phonics, p. 21 • Vocabulary, p. 22 • Grammar, p. 23 • Book Talk, p. 24

Week 2

Selections	Vocabulary		ELL Practice Book
	Oral Vocabulary Words/Cognates	Academic Language/Cognates	
Little Red Hen *From Wheat to Bread*	appreciate partner scrumptious cooperate *cooperar* responsibility *responsibilidad*	retell folktale plural nouns diagrams *diagramas*	• Phonics, p. 25 • Vocabulary, p. 26 • Grammar, p. 27 • Book Talk, p. 28

Week 3

TIME FOR KIDS®	Vocabulary		ELL Practice Book
	Oral Vocabulary Words/Cognates	Academic Language/Cognates	
On the Map	amazed frequently useful service *servicio* variety *variedad*	main idea detail summarize irregular plural nouns dictionary *diccionario* thesaurus *tesauro*	• Phonics, p. 29 • Vocabulary, p. 30 • Grammar, p. 31 • Book Talk, p. 32

Week 4

Selections	Vocabulary		ELL Practice Book
	Oral Vocabulary Words/Cognates	Academic Language/Cognates	
The Pigs, the Wolf, and the Mud *Homes Around the World*	collapse company *compañía* construct *construir* entire *entero/a* material *material*	proper noun plot analyze *analizar* photos *fotos*	• Phonics, p. 33 • Vocabulary, p. 34 • Grammar, p. 35 • Book Talk, p. 36

Week 5

Selections	Vocabulary		ELL Practice Book
	Oral Vocabulary Words/Cognates	Academic Language/Cognates	
Beth and the Band *Shake a Rattle!*	perform enjoy entertain *entretener* brilliant *brillante* audience *audiencia*	retell months holidays visualize *visualizar* directions *direcciones*	• Phonics, p. 37 • Vocabulary, p. 38 • Grammar, p. 39 • Book Talk, p. 40

© Macmillan/McGraw-Hill

Student Response Strategies

Use the following strategies to help English Language Learners move to the next proficiency level.

✔ **WAIT** Give children ample time to respond.

- Let children know that they can respond in different ways depending on their levels of proficiency, but all should be encouraged to answer questions related to the main point of the picture or text.
- Allow children to respond in their native language if they are very limited proficient. Ask a more proficient student to repeat the answer in English.

✔ **REPEAT** If the child's response is correct, the teacher can repeat what the child has said slowly and clearly for the rest of the class to hear.

✔ **REVISE for FORM** Generally the teacher will be repeating what the child has said but with corrections for grammar and pronunciation. The correction can be implicit or explicit (where teacher calls attention to the correction).

✔ **REVISE for MEANING** Teachers should also correct responses for meaning.

✔ **ELABORATE** Here, the teacher elaborates on a child's response or states the response in another way in order to more fully develop children's comprehension and oral language proficiency.

✔ **ELICIT** Finally, the teacher can also elicit a more comprehensive response from the child by prompting him or her for further information.

Newcomers

Basic and Social Language Each week you will be focusing on an important aspect of classroom communication to teach or reinforce with your newcomers. Children will expand and internalize initial English vocabulary by learning and using routine language needed for classroom communication.

Introduce Self Teach children how to introduce themselves, ask for other classmates' names, and say Hello/Goodbye. Use the sentence frames *My name is* ____ and *What is your name?* Model dialogues, such as *Hello. My name is (name). What is your name?* Have children repeat and practice with a partner.

Basic Requests Teach children sentence frames for basic requests, such as *I need* ____, *I want* ____, and *Do you have* ____*?* Teach them how to ask for permission, such as *May I use the restroom, please?* And to respond with *thank you.* Provide daily opportunities to model and practice each request. Reinforce *please* and *thank you.*

Classroom Items Teach children the names of commonly used classroom items, such as, pencils, paper, book, chair, and desk. Reinforce each using the sentence frames *This is my* ____*. That is your* ____*.* and *This is a* ____. These sentence frames focus on possession. Provide daily practice, for example, *This is my book. That is your book.*

LOG ON Have children use **Newcomer Games** to expand and internalize language needed for classroom communication. **www.macmillanmh.com**

© Macmillan/McGraw-Hill

Interactive Question - Response Guide

Animal Moms and Dads

Pages 12–13

Prior to reading the selection with children, they should have listened to the selection on **StudentWorks Plus**, the interactive eBook. In addition, selection vocabulary should have been pretaught using the **Visual Vocabulary Resources.**

Access Core Content

Teacher Note Pose the questions after you read the paragraph or page indicated.

Page 13

Title

- *Let's read the title of this story together:* Animal Moms and Dads. *Boys and girls have moms and dads. Animals have moms and dads, too.*

Photo

- *I see zebras in this photo. Zebras are black and white. Point to the zebras. Which zebra do you think is the baby zebra?* (the smaller one) *Another name for* mom or dad *is* parent. *Which one looks like the parent?* (the bigger zebra)
- *Human moms and dads do a lot of things for their children. What are some things human parents do for their children?* (feed them, teach them, play with them) *Animal moms and dads do a lot of things for their children, too. We will read about some of the things they do.*

Formal and Informal English

When children encounter a colloquial or informal word in the text, discuss other ways of saying the same word with more formal language. For example, *moms/mothers, dads/fathers.*

Pages 12–13

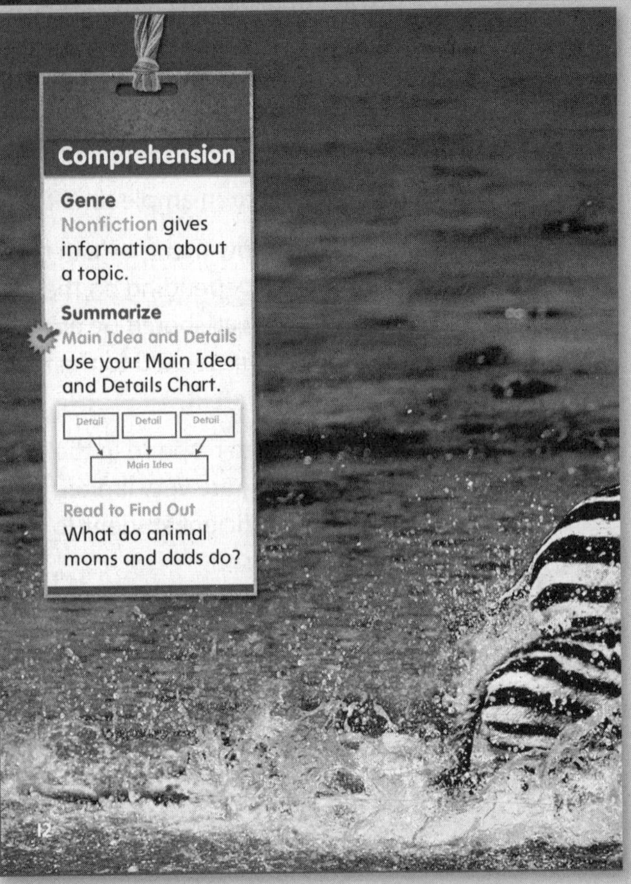

Comprehension
Genre
Nonfiction gives information about a topic.
Summarize
Main Idea and Details
Use your Main Idea and Details Chart.
Read to Find Out
What do animal moms and dads do?
12

Pages 14–15

What do animal moms do?
They do a lot.

14

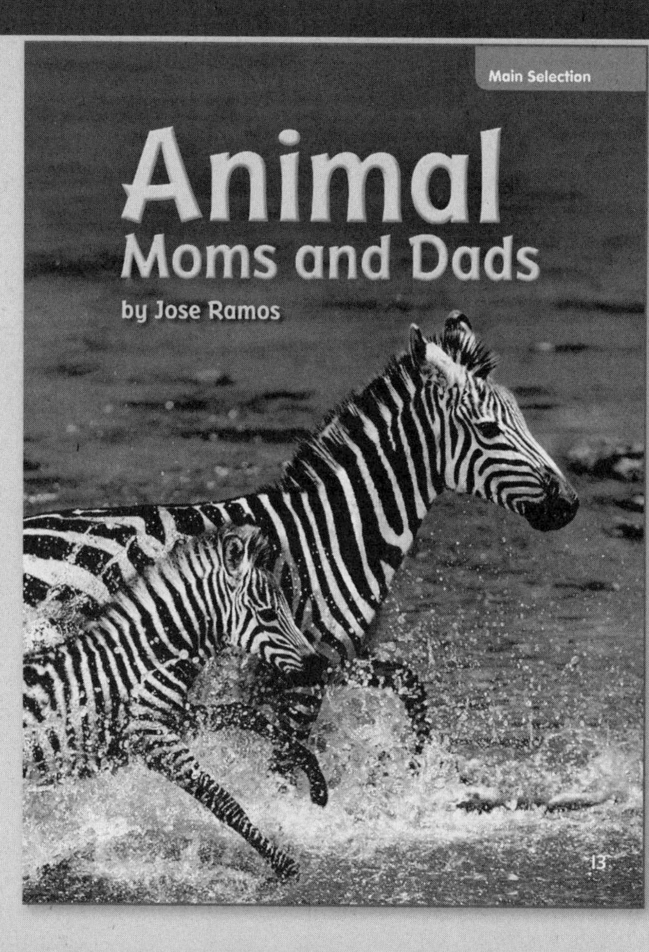

Main Selection
Animal
Moms and Dads
by Jose Ramos
13

Page 14

Photo

- I see giraffes in this picture. Giraffes have long necks. *Point to the giraffe. Point to the mom. Point to the baby.*
- *What else do you know about giraffes?* (They are yellow with brown spots. They run fast.)

Text

- *Let's read this page together:* What do animal moms do? They do a lot.
- *Who is "they" in "They do a lot." Does "they" mean animal children, animal dads, or animal moms?* (animal moms)

What do you think the mom giraffe is doing in the picture? Tell your partner. (feeding her baby, kissing her baby)

Page 15

Text

- *Let's read this page together:* What do animal dads do? They do a lot, too.

Photo

- *I see penguins in this picture. Penguins live in the South Pole. Point to the dad penguin. Point to the baby penguin.*
- *The father penguin is protecting the baby penguin. How is the dad protecting the baby?* (The father is using his body to keep the baby warm.)
-

Directionality

Ask children to place their finger where you start reading (top left). Ask where you finish reading on this page (bottom right).

Animal Moms and Dads

Page 16

Photo

- *I see chipmunks in this picture. Chipmunks have black stripes on their backs. How many baby chipmunks do you see?* (two)
- *The parts of an animal that are like our hands are called paws. The mom chipmunk has a berry in her paws. What is she going to do with it?* (feed it to her babies)

Text

- *I will read the first sentence. You echo it after me.* My mom has food. *Now I will read the second sentence and you echo it. Put your finger on the mark at the end of the second sentence. The mark tells us to read the sentence with excitement. Listen as I read the sentence with an excited voice. Use the same kind of voice when you echo the sentence.* It is good!

Page 17

Photo

- *I see two eagles on this page. Eagle babies look very different from their parents. The father eagle has a white head. Point to the father eagle.*

Text

- *The father bird has big feathers. He can fly to places where there is food. He can pick up the food in his beak. He can bring the food back to his children. Why do you think baby birds cannot get food for themselves?* (They are too little. They cannot fly yet.)

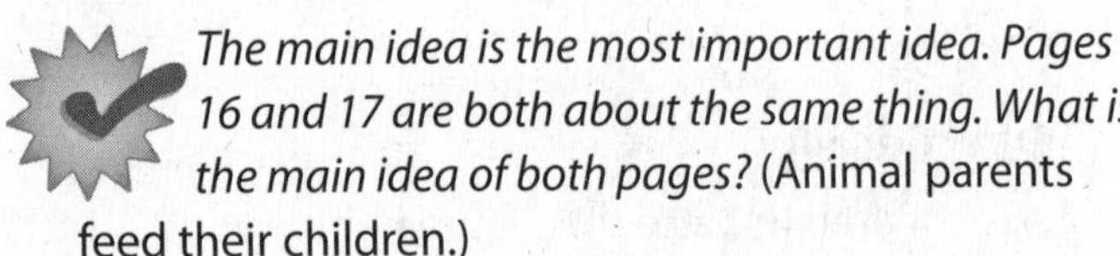

The main idea is the most important idea. Pages 16 and 17 are both about the same thing. What is the main idea of both pages? (Animal parents feed their children.)

- *How do human parents feed their children? Let's make a sequence chain to show what they do.* (Draw a series of boxes with connecting arrows.) *We will put one step in each box.* (They work to get money. They buy food with the money. They cook the food. They give it to their children.)

Pages 16–17

My mom has food.
It is very good!

16

Pages 18–19

My mom licks and licks.
I am clean.

18

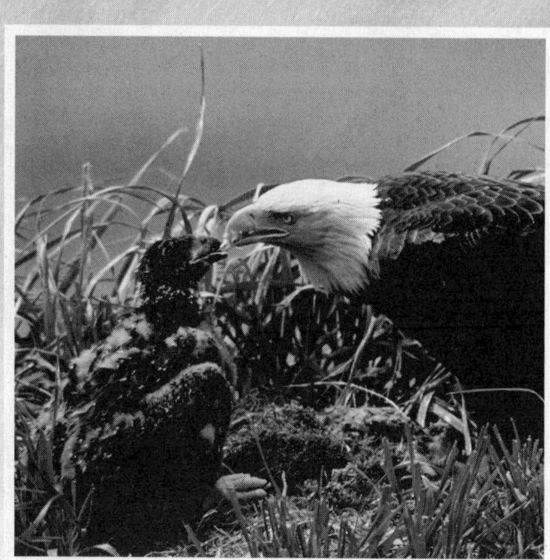

My dad got food.
Dad and I like it a lot.

17

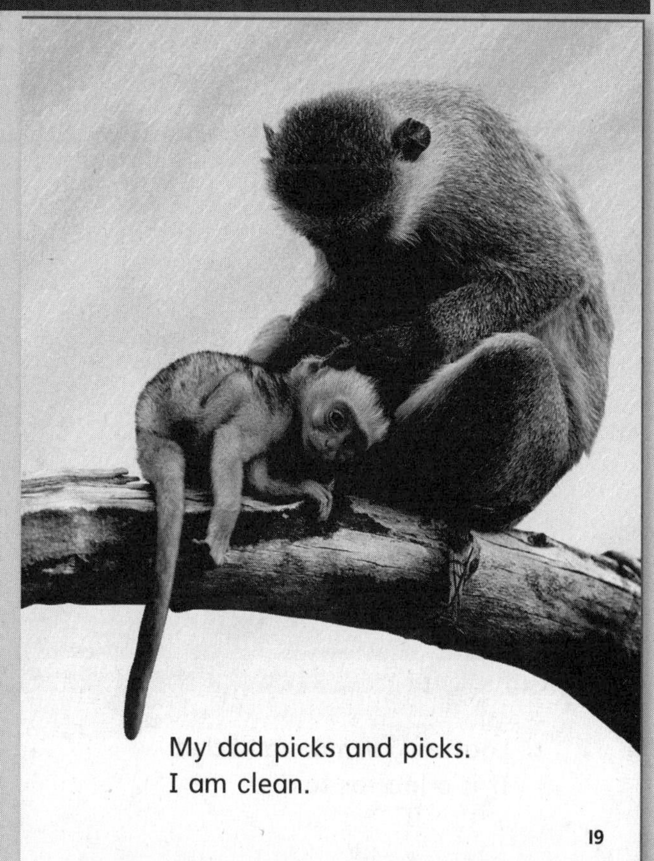

My dad picks and picks.
I am clean.

19

Page 18

Photo

- *The animals on page 18 are a kind of cat. They are leopards. Leopards have black spots. Are leopards bigger or smaller than house cats?* (They are bigger.)

Text

- *Why is the mother licking her child?* (to get the child clean)

Page 19

Photo

- *What is the animal dad doing?* (picking dirt off the baby's fur) *What kinds of things might the baby have on its fur?* (bugs, bits of leaves, mud)
- *How do human parents clean their babies?* (give them baths, wash their hands and faces, shampoo their hair)

Text

- *Let's read pages 18 and 19 together.* My mom licks and licks. I am clean. My dad picks and picks. Now I am clean.

Now let's summarize what the pages are about. We will tell the most important ideas from these pages. We will say the ideas in our own words. (Animal parents clean their children.)

Animal Moms and Dads

Page 20

Photo

I see two kangaroos on this page. Point to them. Tell your partner what you know about kangaroos. (They are big. They hop. They carry their babies in pouches.)

Text

- *Let's read this page together:* Mom and I will hop, hop, hop. I am in her sack. *Let's hop like kangaroos.*
- *The author says the baby kangaroo is in the mother's sack. Point to the sack.*
- *Why do you think the baby rides in the mother's sack?* (The baby is too little to hop on its own. When it is in the sack, the mother can protect it from getting hurt.)

What is the most important idea on this page? (Kangaroo mothers help their babies get from place to place.)

Page 21

Photo

- *I see lions on this page. A baby lion is called a cub. Where is the cub?* (on the father lion's back)
- *Tell me what you know about lions.* (They roar. They are big and strong.)

Text

- *Let's read this page together. What do you remember about the mark at the end of the second sentence?* (It means to read with an excited voice.) My dad has a very big back. I sit on top!

Fold a paper into four parts. Take turns with your partner. Draw ways that human parents help their children get from place to place. Draw one way in each box. (car, baby stroller, carrying in arms, wagon)

Pages 20–21

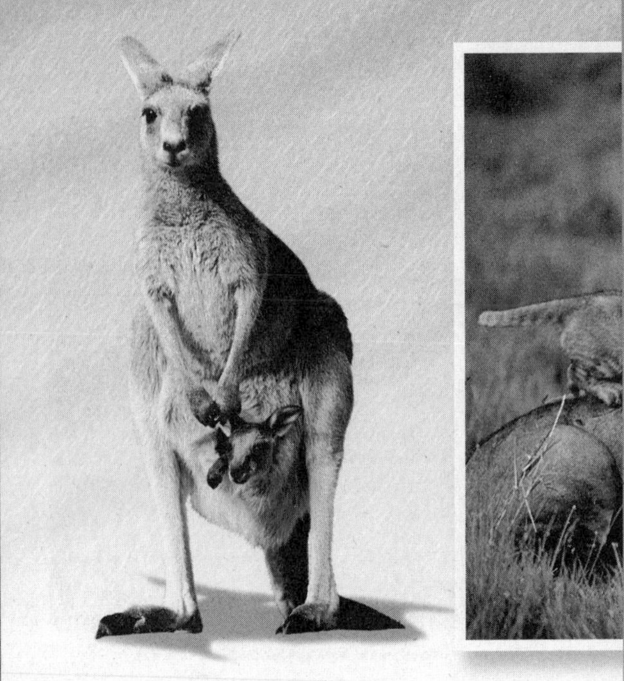

Mom and I will hop, hop, hop.
I am in **her** sack.

20

Pages 22–23

Look at **our** mom and dad.
It is a job for **two**.

22

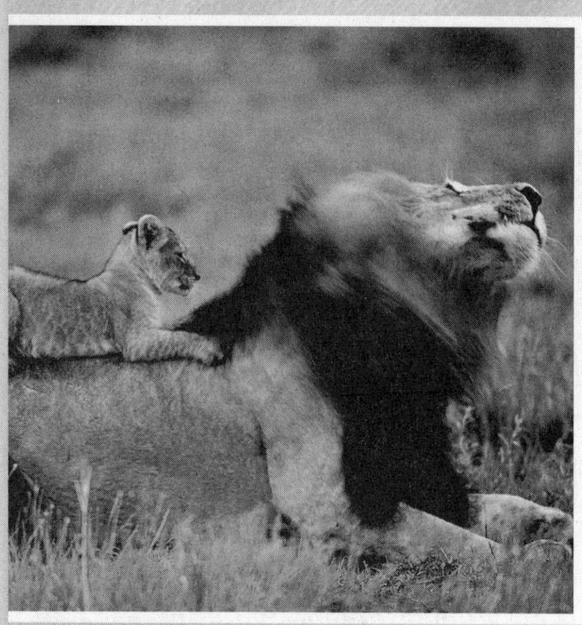

My dad has a big back.
I can sit on top!

21

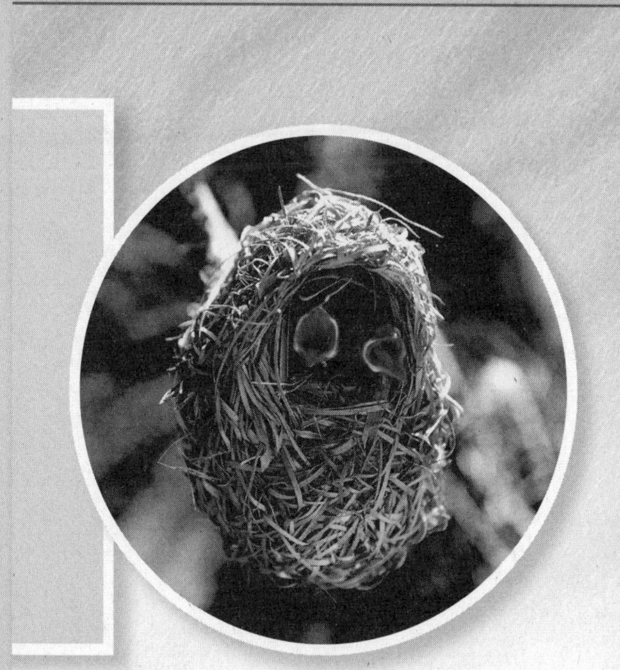

We are in it.
Good job, Mom and Dad!

23

Page 22

Photo

- *The birds are building a round nest. Put your finger on what they are building. Say* nest *with me:* nest.
- *How many birds are on this page?* (two) *Where are they?* (One is on top of the nest, and one is on the bottom.)
- *What are some things the birds are putting in their nest?* (twigs, leaves)

Page 23

Photo

- Now the nest is done. I see baby birds inside the nest. *Point to the baby birds in the nest.* (in the hole in the center) *How does the nest protect the babies?* (It keeps the sun and rain off them. It protects them from other animals.)

Draw a nest you have seen. Show where it was. Tell your partner about your picture.

What is the main idea of pages 22 and 23? (Mom and dad birds make nests for their babies.)

Analyze Sayings and Expressions

Help children recognize that *good job* is an expression used to encourage someone or recognize when they have done something well. Help them create other examples using this expression.

Animal Moms and Dads

Page 24

Photo

- *I see pandas in this picture. How many are there?* (three) *Point to the baby pandas as we count them together:* (one, two.)

Text

Let's read the question together: What can moms and dads do? *We have learned some answers to that question. Tell me what we have learned so far.* (Animal moms and dads feed their babies. They clean them. They help them get from place to place. They protect their babies.)

Page 25

Text

- *Animal moms and dads help their children in many ways. What else does this page tell us they do with their babies?* (play)
- *How do human parents play with their children?* (Sample answers: play board games, play ball, splash in a pool)
- *I will say some ways that human parents and children play and have fun. Nod your head "yes" or shake your head "no" to tell me whether animal parents and children can do each of the things: run* (yes), *jump* (yes), *toss balls* (no), *splash water* (yes), *read* (no), *tell jokes* (no), *make noises* (yes).

Whole Story

- *What are some things that both animal and human parents give to their children?* (food, a place to live, a way to get from place to place, fun)

Pages 24–25

What can moms and dads do?

24

Moms and dads can play, too!

25

I'm going to read you a sentence. Tell me if it is the main idea of the story or not. "Animal moms and dads do a lot" (yes, it is) *How do you know that is the main idea?* (Every page of the story tells about animal moms and dads doing a lot.)

The whole story is about how animal moms and dads take care of their children. The author tells us many facts about what moms and dads do. Take turns with your partner acting out a fact from the book. Then guess what your partner is acting out.

- *What are some other things animal parents do for their children that the book did not tell?* (teach them, comfort them)

Over in the Meadow

Access Core Content

Teacher Note Pose the questions after you read the paragraph or page indicated.

Page 28

Illustration

- *I see two turtles on this page. Let's point to them and count them. Tell me what you know about turtles.* (They are slow. They have hard shells. They can hide their heads and legs inside their shells.)
- *We read "Animal Moms and Dads." It told true facts about animals. It had pictures of real animals in it. Look at the picture of the turtles again. Are they real turtles? How do you know?* (No, they have smiling faces and do not look real.) *We will learn real facts about animals, but we have to remember that real animals do no talk as humans do.*
- *This is a poem. The author did not write it to tell animal facts. The author wrote the poem so readers could have fun reading it.*

Page 29

Text

- *Listen as I read the title:* Over in the Meadow. *A meadow is a grassy place or field. Look at the picture. I see flowers, grass, and the sun. Let's point to each of them as we say their names.*
- *Who lives in this meadow?* (a turtle and his mother) *Use your hands to show me what the turtle and his mother do.* (Make a digging motion.)
- *This poem is a counting rhyme. It has numbers in it. What number does this part have in it?* (one) *Show me one finger.* (Children hold up one finger.)

Pages 28–29

Poetry
Genre
In a Poem, words are often put together so that they are fun to say.
Literary Elements
Rhythm Poems are written so that the words have a certain beat when you say them aloud.
Rhyme Words that rhyme end in the same sounds.
LOG ON FIND OUT
Poetry Rhythm and Rhyme
www.macmillanmh.com
28

Pages 30–31

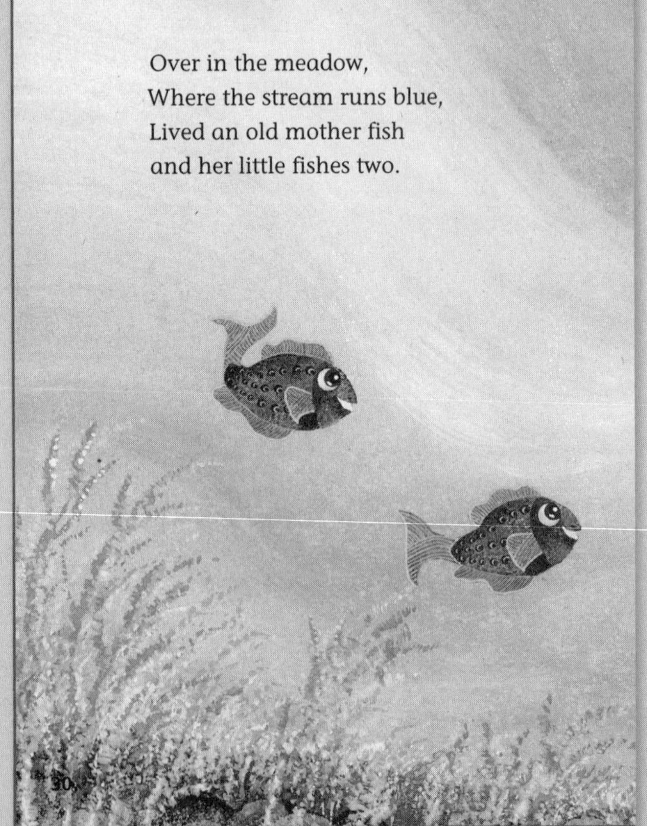

Poetry
Read Together
Over in the Meadow
An Old Counting Rhyme
Over in the meadow,
In the sand in the sun,
Lived an old mother turtle
And her little turtle one.
"Dig," said the mother.
"I dig," said the one.
So they dug all day
In the sand in the sun.
29

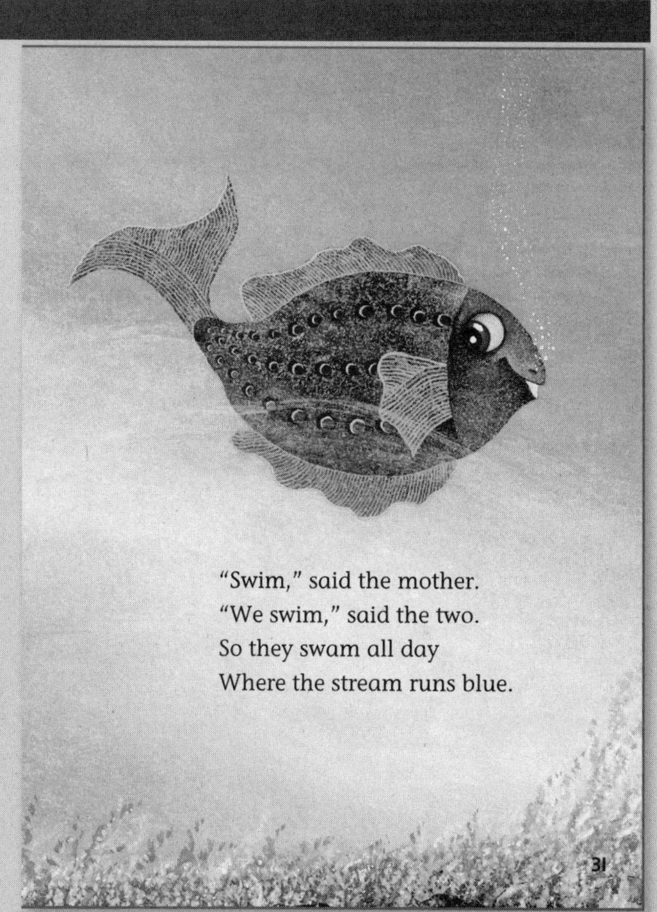

"Swim," said the mother.
"We swim," said the two.
So they swam all day
Where the stream runs blue.
31

Page 30

Text

- *Listen as I read this page:* Over in the meadow, / Where the stream runs blue, / Lived an old mother fish / and her little fishes two.
- *Does this page tell more about the turtles?* (No, it tells about fish.)

Illustration

- *How many children does this mother have? Count them with me:* one, two. *Is the fish family or the turtle family bigger? Tell me why.* (The fish family is bigger. The turtle has one baby, but the fish has two.)

Describe for your partner a real turtle or fish you have seen. How were they like the ones in the pictures? How were they different?

Page 31

Text

- *Make a fish with your hands.* (Demonstrate putting your hands together in front of you, flat and palm-to-palm.) *Show me what the mother fish told her children to do.* (Children move their hands to show a swimming motion.)

Pages 32–33

Illustration

- *I see four owls on this page. Let's point to them and count them. How many baby owls are there?* (three)
- *Tell me some things you know about owls.* (They come out at night. They hoot.)
- *Which animal family in this poem is the smallest?* (turtle family) *Which animal family in this poem is the biggest?* (owl family)

Text

- *Listen as I read the part of the poem that tells what these animals did:* "Whoo," said the mother. / "Whoo, Whoo," said the three. *What does the word* whoo *mean?* (It is the sound owls make.)

Pages 32–33

Over in the meadow,
In the wide oak tree,
Lived an old mother owl
And her little owls three.
"Whoo," said the mother.
"Whoo, Whoo," said the three.
So they whooed all night
In the wide oak tree.
32

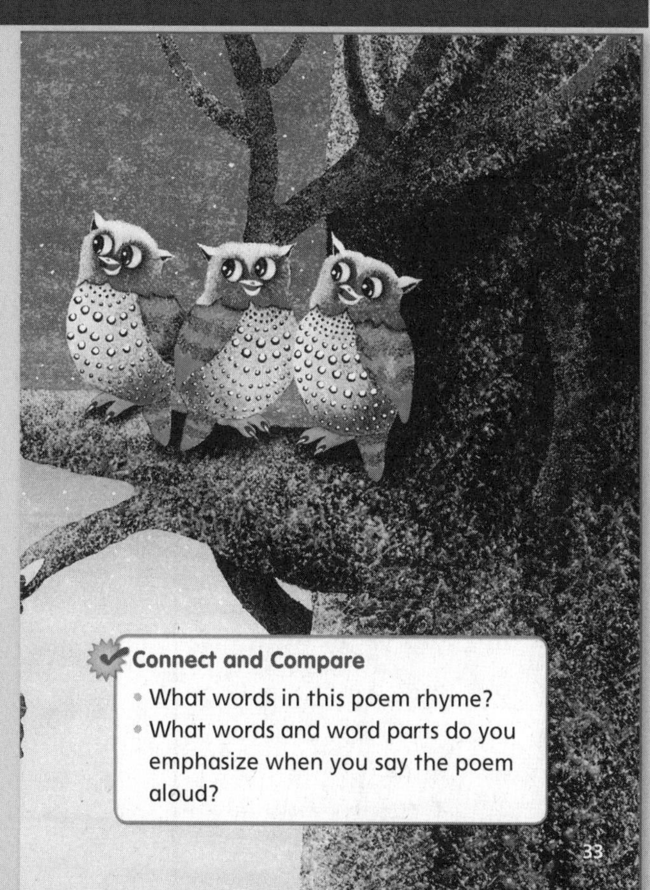

Connect and Compare
• What words in this poem rhyme?
• What words and word parts do you emphasize when you say the poem aloud?
33

Whole Poem

- *How is this poem like the story "One Frog, Two Frogs"?* (They both count animals.)
- *How is this poem like the story "Animal Moms and Dads"?* (They both tell about animal parents and children.)

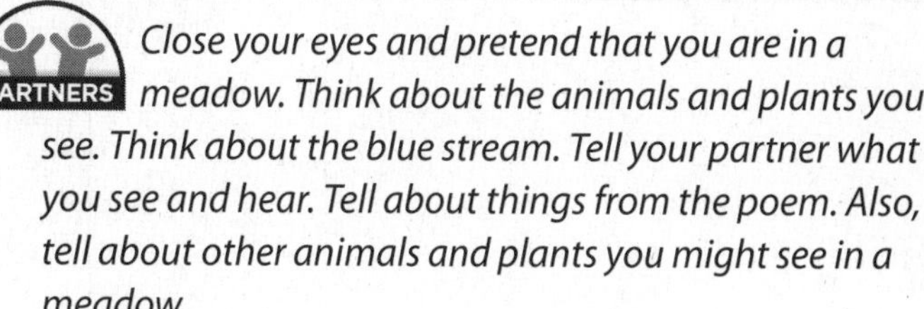

PARTNERS *Close your eyes and pretend that you are in a meadow. Think about the animals and plants you see. Think about the blue stream. Tell your partner what you see and hear. Tell about things from the poem. Also, tell about other animals and plants you might see in a meadow.*

Name ______________________________

Copy each new word on the line.
Draw a picture.

Word	Illustration
father ______________________ - - - - - - - - - - - - - - ______________________	
mother ______________________ - - - - - - - - - - - - - - ______________________	

© Macmillan/McGraw-Hill

Name ______________________________

Book Talk

Read each question and prompt. Discuss the answers with your group. Use your Leveled Reader to find details to support your answers. Then write your answers on another sheet of paper.

1. What is a baby elephant called?

2. Explain what the big elephants show the baby elephants.

3. Tell how humans and elephants eat differently.

4. How do elephants use their trunks?

5. Tell how grown-up male and female elephants live.

© Macmillan/McGraw-Hill

Little Red Hen

Pages 42–43

Prior to reading the selection with children, they should have listened to the selection on **StudentWorks Plus**, the interactive eBook. In addition, selection vocabulary should have been pretaught using the **Visual Vocabulary Resources**.

Access Core Content

Teacher Note Pose the questions after you read the page indicated.

Pages 42–43

Illustration

- *Let's read the title of this story together:* Little Red Hen. *I see Little Red Hen below the title. Point to her. Little Red Hen is the main character in this story. She is the most important character.*

Page 44

Whole page

Today we are going to read about someone else who needs help. How can people help each other? Do you think people should help each other? Why? (They can help each other do tasks. Helping is a way of being kind to others.)

Illustration

- *Wheat is a grain that grows. We plant wheat grains in the ground. We use wheat to make bread. Point to the grains of wheat that Little Red Hen is throwing. Let's say* wheat *together:* wheat.
- *What is Little Red Hen doing?* (She is planting wheat.)

Last Sentence, Echo Reading

- *I'll read the last sentence on the page. Then you repeat it:* "Who will help plant?" asked Hen. *What does Little Red Hen want?* (She wants someone to help her plant the wheat.)

What are some other things we plant? Have you ever planted anything? What did you plant? (flowers, vegetables)

Pages 42–43

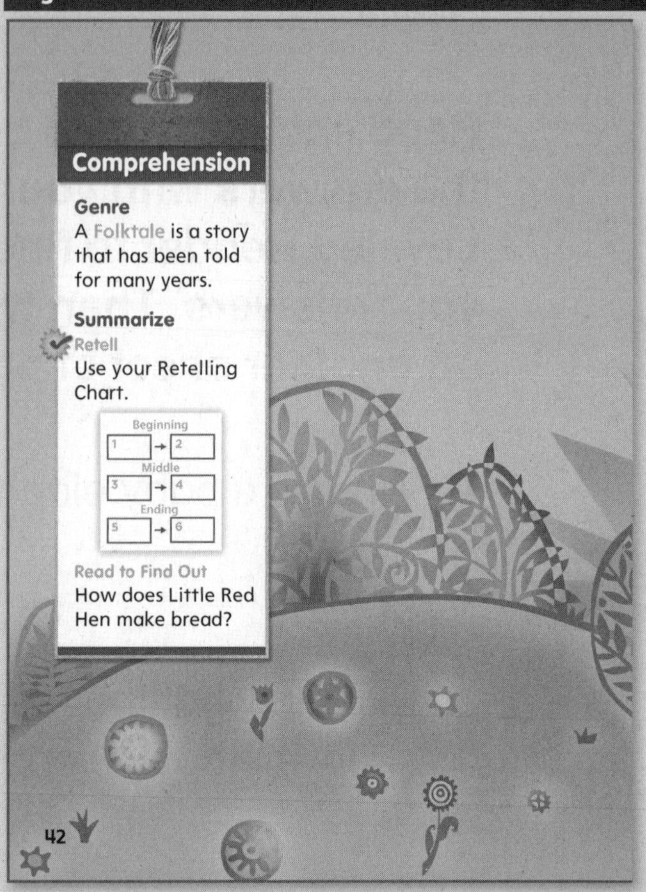

Comprehension
Genre
A Folktale is a story that has been told for many years.
Summarize
Retell
Use your Retelling Chart.
Beginning
1 → 2
Middle
3 → 4
Ending
5 → 6
Read to Find Out
How does Little Red Hen make bread?
42

Pages 44–45

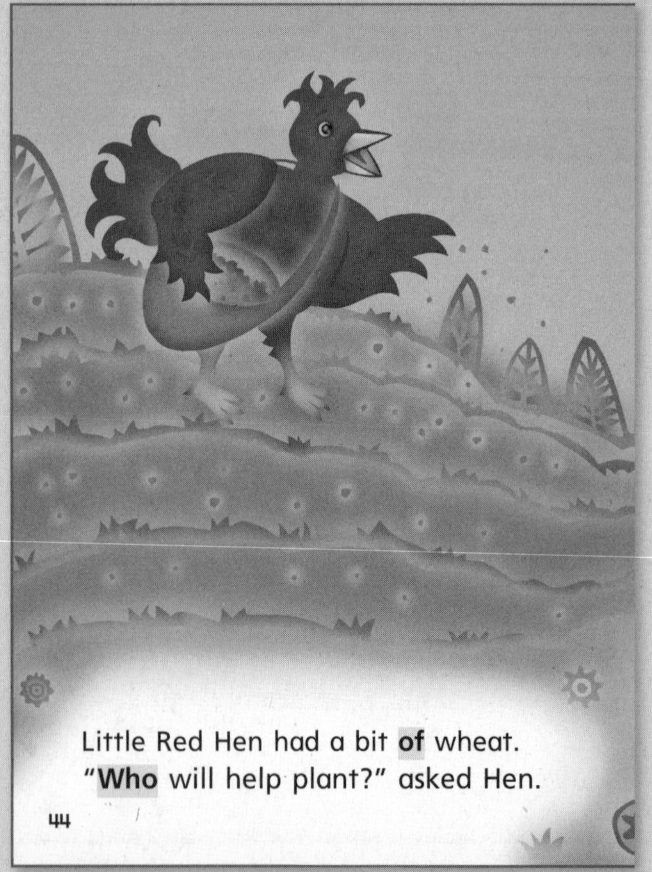

Little Red Hen had a bit of wheat.
"Who will help plant?" asked Hen.
44

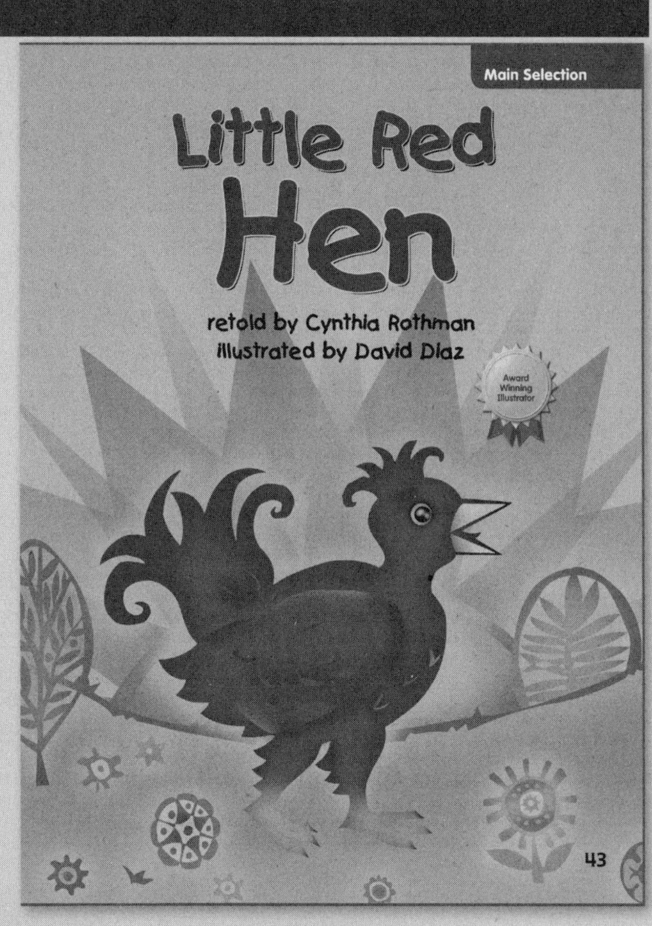
Main Selection
Little Red Hen
retold by Cynthia Rothman
illustrated by David Diaz
43

"Not I," said Dog.
"Not I," said Pig.
"Not I," said Cat.
45

- *Let's pretend that we are planting wheat like Little Red Hen.* Demonstrate taking seeds from a pouch and spreading them as shown in the illustration.

Page 45

Whole Page, Choral Reading

- *Let's read this page together. Try to sound the way Dog, Pig, and Cat might sound.*
  "Not I," said Dog.
  "Not I," said Pig.
  "Not I," said Cat.
- *Let's role-play what has happened so far. Read the words the characters have said. Use movements or gestures to show how the characters might act. For example, shake your head while saying "Not I."* (Demonstrate shaking your head.)

Tell me what has happened so far in this story. (Little Red Hen wants help planting wheat, but no one will help her.)

- **Directionality**

  Ask children to place their finger where you start reading (top left). Ask where you finish reading on this page (bottom right).

Little Red Hen

Page 46

Illustration

- *Point to Little Red Hen. She is holding a pail to carry water. Point to the pail.*
- *Point to the well. A well is a big hole in the ground. Inside the well is water. We get our water from a water faucet. Little Red Hen will get water from the well.*
- *Let's pretend we are getting water from the well.* (Demonstrate putting the pail down the well, cranking it down and up, then carrying the pail of water. As you demonstrate, describe each action.) *First I will put the pail in the well. Then I will lower the pail and get a bit of water. Now I will get the pail up. Now I will carry my pail of water.*

Page 47

Whole Page, Choral Reading

Let's read this page together.

"Not I," said Dog.
"Not I," said Pig.
"Not I," said Cat.

- *Did some of Little Red Hen's friends help?* (no) *That's right. All of them said no.*

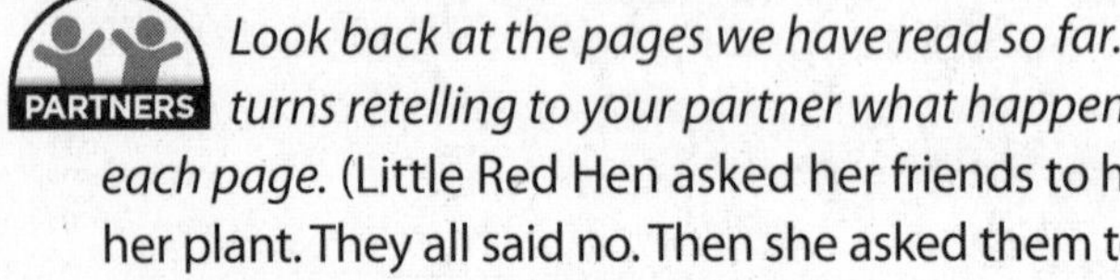

Look back at the pages we have read so far. Take turns retelling to your partner what happened on each page. (Little Red Hen asked her friends to help her plant. They all said no. Then she asked them to help her get some water. They all said no.)

- *What might happen next? Let's read on to find out.*

Pages 46–47

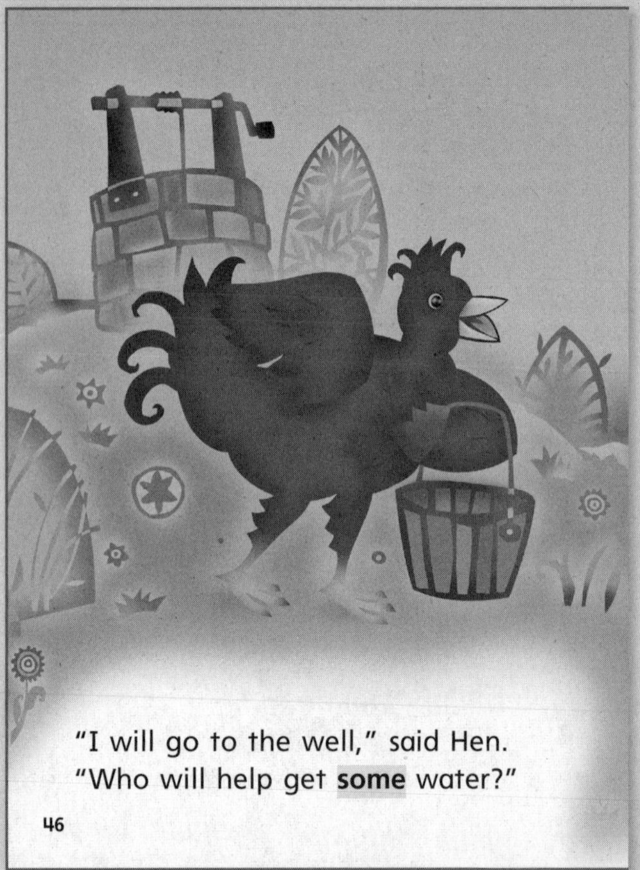

"I will go to the well," said Hen.
"Who will help get **some** water?"
46

Pages 48–49

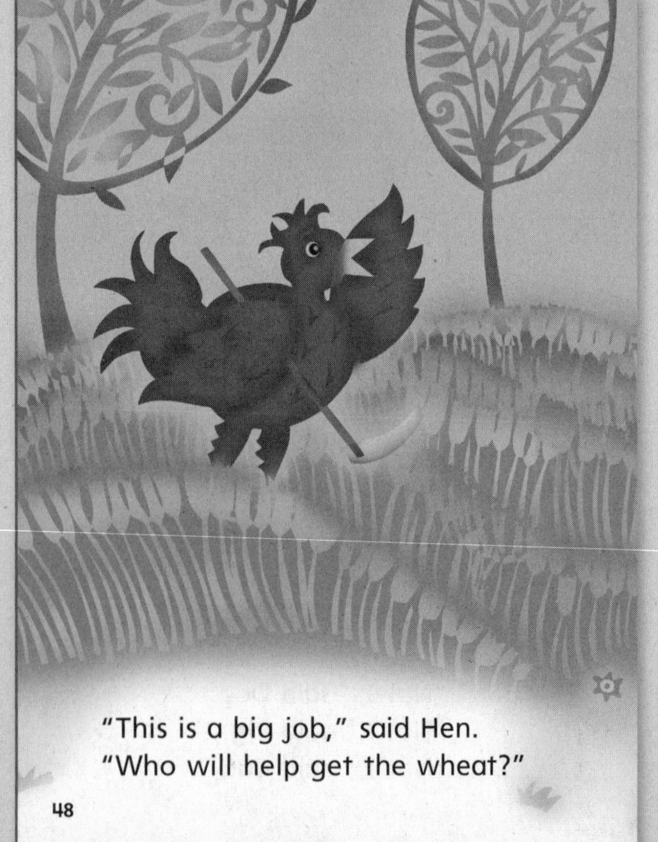

"This is a big job," said Hen.
"Who will help get the wheat?"
48

"Not I," said Cat.
"Not I," said Dog.
"Not I," said Pig.
47

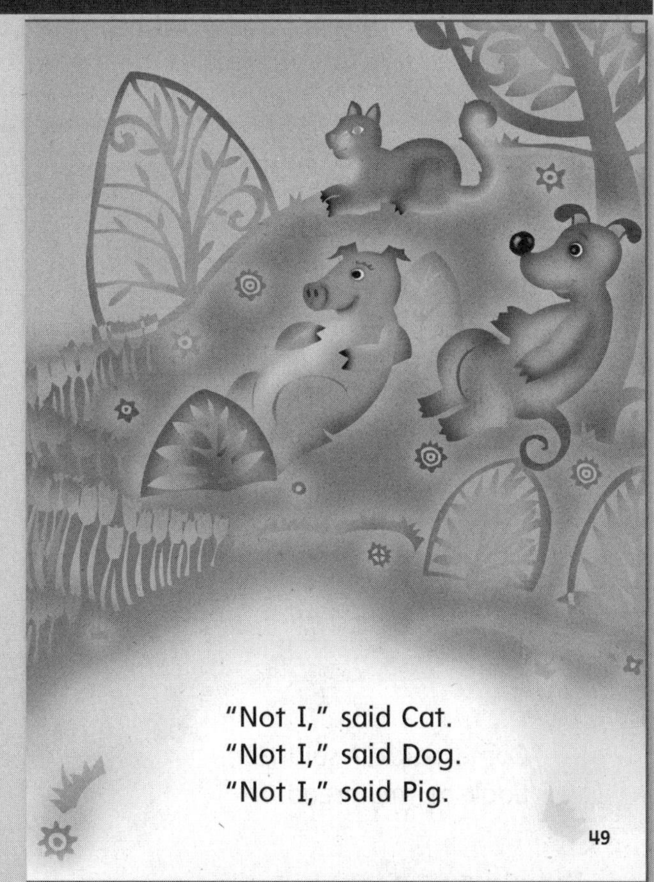

Page 48

Whole Page

- *Look at this picture. I see wheat growing from the ground. Point to the wheat. What has happened to the wheat?* (It grew.) *How can you tell?* (It is tall now.)
- *After the wheat grows, it needs to be cut and gathered. Little Red Hen thinks this is a big job. Let's say her words together:* This is a big job.
- *What does the word* job *mean?* (work, something you have to do)
- *Look at the tool Little Red Hen is holding. It is called a sickle. We use a sickle to cut down the wheat. Point to the tool and say its name:* sickle.
- *Let's pretend we are cutting down the wheat with a sickle.* (Demonstrate how to use a sickle to cut the wheat.)

Page 49

Whole Page

- *Have all of Little Red Hen's friends helped so far?* (no) *Have some of her friends helped so far?* (no) *Have most of her friends helped so far?* (no) *That's right, none of her friends have helped so far.*
- *Let's role-play what has happened on these pages. Read the words the characters say. Use gestures or movements to show how your character might act. Remember to sound like your character might sound when saying the words.*

Little Red Hen

Page 50

Illustration

- *Little Red Hen is holding a spoon. Point to the spoon. What is she doing with the spoon?* (She is mixing.) *Yes, she is mixing something in a bowl.*
- *Let's pretend we are mixing something in a bowl.* (Demonstrate stirring the mixture with a spoon.)

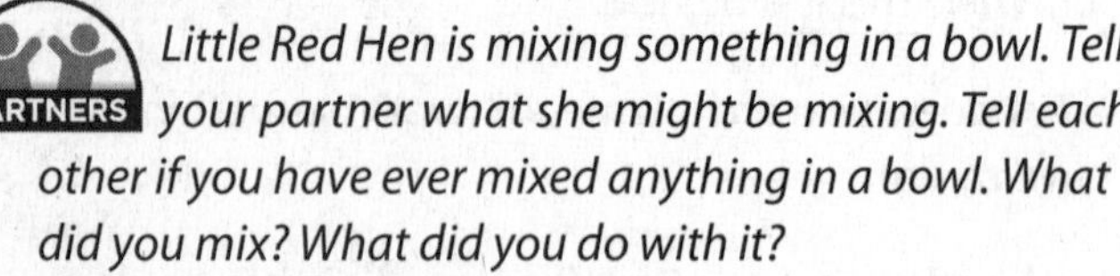

PARTNERS *Little Red Hen is mixing something in a bowl. Tell your partner what she might be mixing. Tell each other if you have ever mixed anything in a bowl. What did you mix? What did you do with it?*

- *I think Little Red Hen is mixing dough. You make dough with flour and water. Maybe she made the dough with flour she made from the wheat. Let's see if my guess is right by reading on.*

Page 51

Whole Page, Choral Reading

- *Let's read this page together. Point to each animal as you say the words that each one says. Remember to sound the way Cat, Dog, and Pig might sound when they say these words.*
- *Did some of Little Red Hens friends help?* (no) *That's right. All of them said no.*

Tell me again what happened on these pages. (Little Red Hen asked her friends to help her mix. They all said no.)

Synonyms and Circumlocution

Remind children that they can ask for synonyms to help clarify words or expressions they do not understand. Ask, *What is another way of saying "quick"?* (fast).

Pages 50–51

"I will mix and mix," said Hen.
"Who will help mix?"
50

Pages 52–53

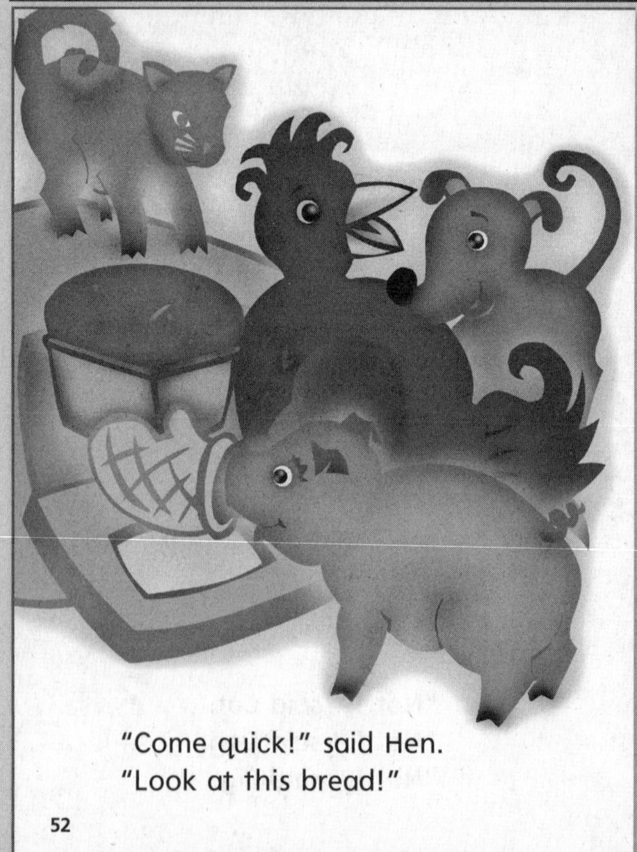

"Come quick!" said Hen.
"Look at this bread!"
52

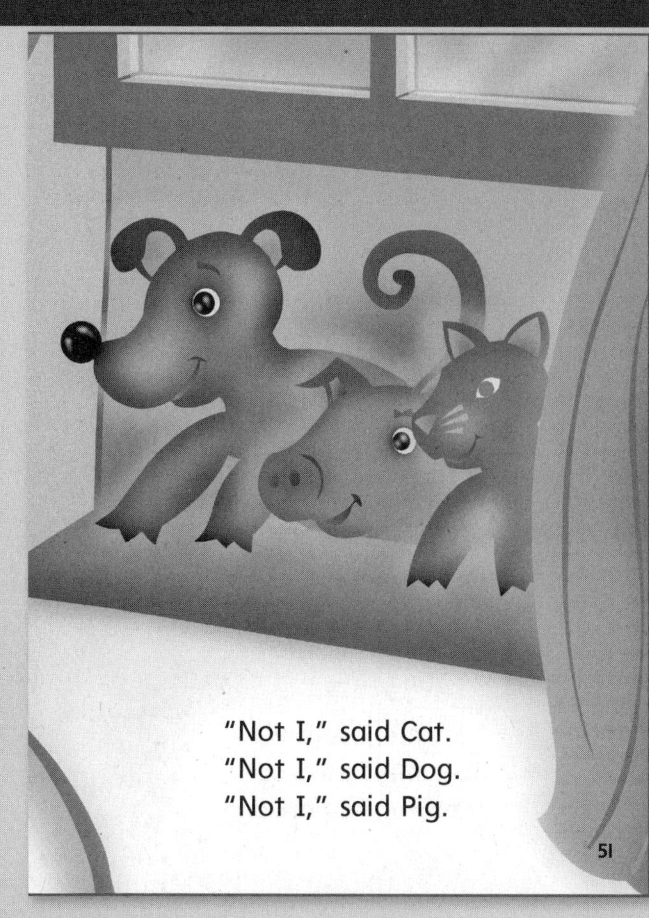

"Not I," said Cat.
"Not I," said Dog.
"Not I," said Pig.
51

Page 52

Illustration

- *Look at this picture. All of Little Red Hen's friends are there. Point to each friend and say the name:* Cat, Dog, Pig.

Text

- *Let's look at the words Little Red Hen says. Look at the exclamation marks. They show that Little Red Hen sounds excited. Let's take turns reading her words aloud. Remember to sound excited:* Come quick! Look at this bread!

- *This part of the story shows what Little Red Hen was mixing in the bowl. Do you think she was mixing dough?* (Yes, she was mixing flour and water to make dough.) *Dough is used to make bread. It is put into a bread pan and then cooked in an oven. Point to the bread. Say the word:* bread.

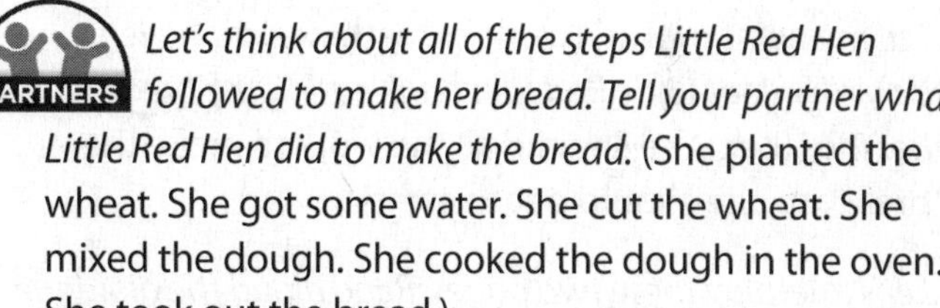

Let's think about all of the steps Little Red Hen followed to make her bread. Tell your partner what Little Red Hen did to make the bread. (She planted the wheat. She got some water. She cut the wheat. She mixed the dough. She cooked the dough in the oven. She took out the bread.)

Page 53

Illustration

- *Little Red Hen is cutting the bread. Point to the slice of bread she just cut. She used a knife to cut the bread. Point to the knife.*

Text, Choral Reading

- *Let's pretend we are Little Red Hen. Let's say her words together. Remember to make your voice go up at the end of the question:* "This is the best bread. Who will help me eat some?"

- *Do you think her friends might help Little Red Hen eat some bread?*

Page 54

Whole Page, Choral Reading

- *Let's read this page together.*
- *What do Pig, Cat, and Dog want to do?* (They want to help Little Red Hen eat the bread.)
- *Do you think Little Red Hen will let them help eat the bread? Why or why not?* (no, because they didn't help Little Red Hen make the bread) *Let's read the next page to find out.*

Page 55

Whole Page

- *Did Little Red Hen let them help eat the bread?* (no)

Last Sentence

- *Let's read the last sentence together.* "This is a job for me!" *Tell me what a job is.* (work, something you have to do) *Why does Little Red Hen think eating the bread is her job?* (because she did all the work to make the bread, so she should get to eat it)
- *Let's role-play these two pages. Read aloud the dialogue and use actions to show what the characters might do.* (Demonstrate raising your hands and jumping up and down as you say "Let me!" Wave your finger and shake your head as you say "No! No!")

Pages 54–55

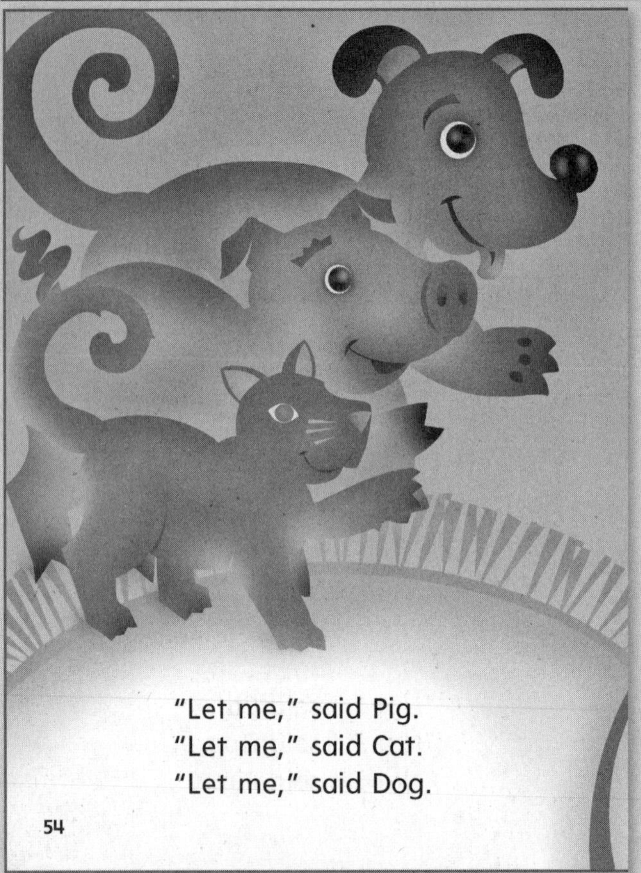

"Let me," said Pig.
"Let me," said Cat.
"Let me," said Dog.
54

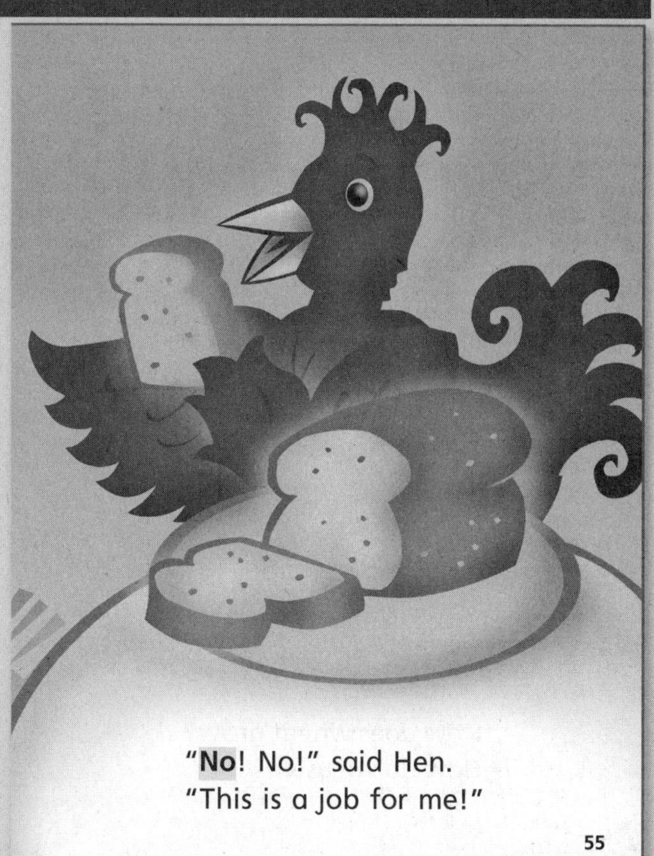

"**No**! No!" said Hen.
"This is a job for me!"

55

Let's retell this story together. I'll say part of a sentence, then you repeat that part and finish the sentence by retelling the story.

Little Red Hen asked her friends to help her plant ______. (wheat) *They all said* ______. (no) *Then, Little Red Hen asked her friends to help get* ______. (water) *They all said* ______. (no) *Next, Little Red Hen asked her friends to help cut* ______. (wheat) *They all said* ______. (no) *Next, Little Red Hen asked her friends to help* ______. (mix the dough) *They all said* ______. (no) *At the end, Little Red Hen baked* ______. (bread) *Her friends wanted to help her* ______. (eat the bread) *But Little Red Hen said* ______. (no)

Monitor Oral Production

Remember to model self-corrective techniques on a regular basis as you speak to children. Pretend to mispronounce words and self-correct.

Interactive Question - Response Guide

From Wheat to Bread

Access Core Content

Teacher Note Pose the questions after you read the paragraph or page indicated.

Page 58

Photo

- *Look at the picture on pages 58–59. Is shows a field of wheat. What will this article be about?* (wheat)

Title

- *Let's read the title together:* From Wheat to Bread.

Talk to your partner about what you learned about wheat in the story Little Red Hen. *How did Little Red Hen grow wheat?* (She planted it. She watered it.) *What did she use it for?* (to make bread)

Page 59

Photo

- *Farmers grow food for themselves and other people. Point to the farmer in this picture.*
- *Look at the picture labeled* Seeds. *What kind of seeds are they?* (wheat)
- *Wheat is planted in a field. Point to the field the farmer is in. What do you see?* (dirt, small green plants) *Point to the field on page 58. What do you see?* (wheat that has grown)

Whole Page, Choral Reading

- *Let's read this page together.*
- *Wheat starts out as a little seed. It grows and grows into tall plants. Let's find out how the wheat grows from a seed to a tall plant.*

Pages 58–59

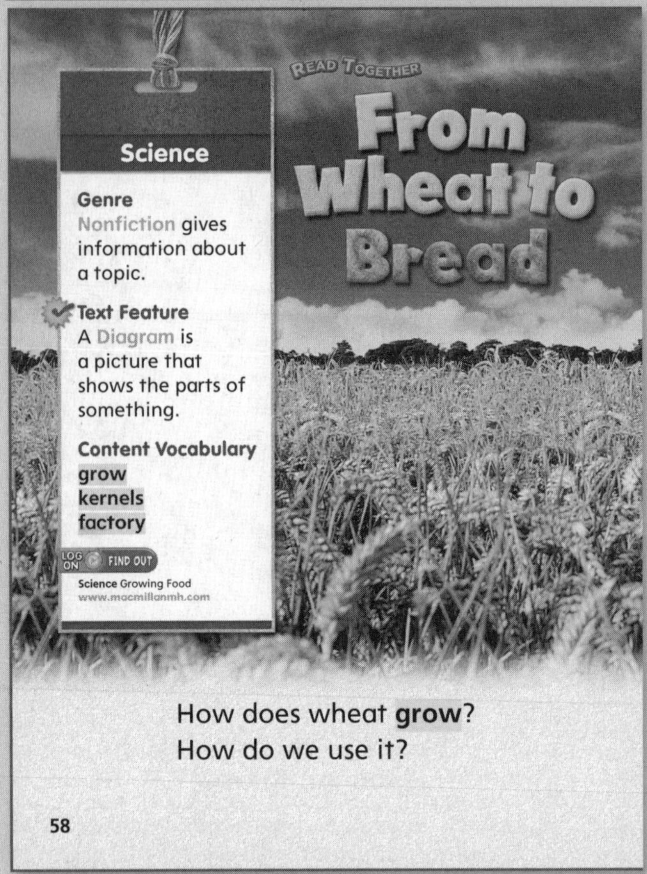

Pages 60–61

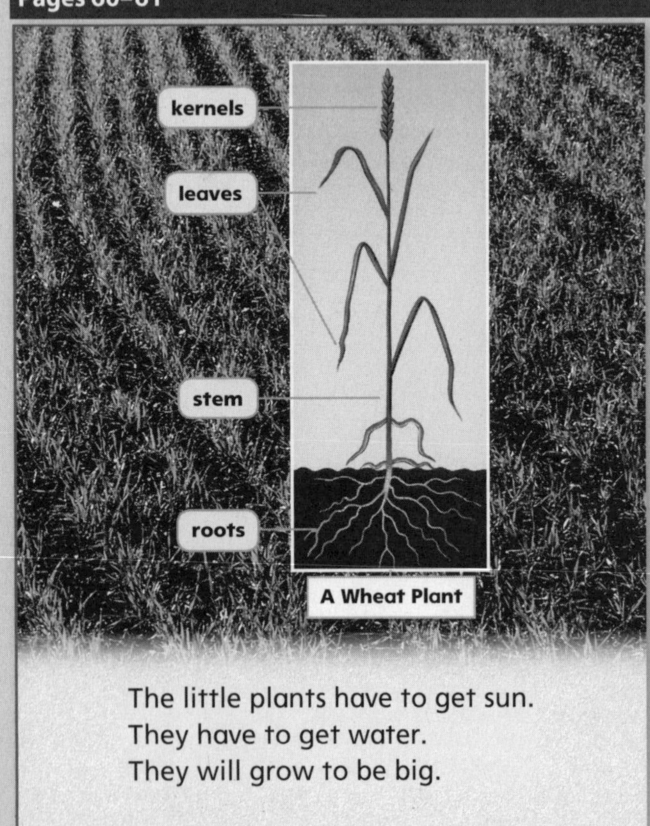

kernels
leaves
stem
roots
A Wheat Plant
The little plants have to get sun.
They have to get water.
They will grow to be big.
60

Science
Seeds
Wheat starts as a little seed.
Farmers plant the seeds.
59

Page 60

Caption

- *The caption at the bottom tells us what this picture is. It is a wheat plant. Point to the wheat plant in the picture. Say it with me:* A Wheat Plant.
- *The labels on the side tell about the parts of a wheat plant. Say each part with me. Point to each part as you say it with me:* kernels, leaves, stem, roots.

Whole Page, Choral Reading

- *Let's read this page together.*

Retell what you just read in your own words. What do wheat plants need to grow? (sun and water)

Page 61

Whole Page

- *Let's read the first sentence together:* Now the wheat is tan. *Tan is a color like light brown. Point to something in the room that is tan.*
- *Let's read the next sentence together.* The farmer picks off the kernels. *I see a picture of the kernels at the bottom of the page. Point to the kernels. Say it with me:* kernels.
- *Let's read the last sentence together:* The kernels are good to eat. *Let's pretend we are eating the kernels.*

Photo

- *Now look at the picture of the machine in the middle of the page. It is called a thresher. Point to the thresher. The thresher removes, or picks off, the kernels from the wheat stem. Which sentence on this page tells what the farmer does to the kernels?* (The farmer picks off the kernels.)

From Wheat to Bread

Page 62

Whole Page, Choral Reading

- *Let's read this page together.*

Photo

- *Look at the picture. Point to the man working. Where is he working?* (in a factory)

Look at the picture with a partner. Take turns telling what you see in the picture. Point to each part of the picture you are telling about. (machine, bags, worker, flour, cup)

- *Look at the pictures at the bottom of the page. What do you see? Point to each picture you name. Why do you think there are pictures of bread and cookies?* (Those are things you can make with flour from wheat.)

Page 63

Photo

- *Look at the picture. What kind of work, or job, do you think the woman does?* (She makes bread.)

Whole Page

- *Let's read this page together.*
- *We read that wheat is used in good things to eat. I will say the name of a food. Say "yes" if you think we can use wheat to make it. Say "no" if you do not think we can use wheat to make it:*

  bread (yes)
  cookies (yes)
  cheese (no)
  cake (yes)
  milk (no)

Pages 62–63

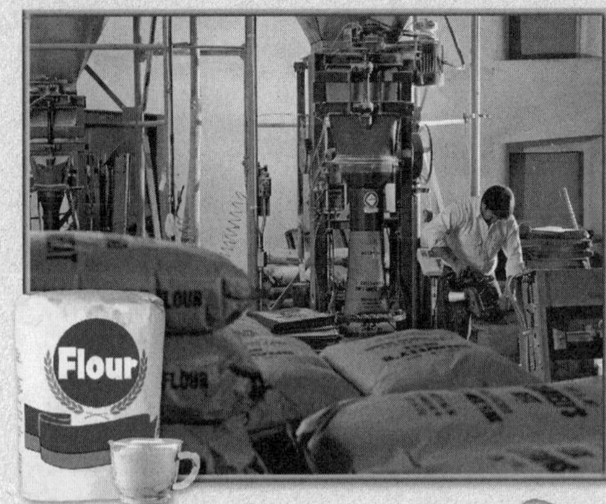

The kernels go to a **factory**.
Here they are crushed.
The little bits of wheat are flour.

62

We use flour to make bread.
We use it in good things to eat.
That is what we do with wheat!

Connect and Compare

- Who helps Little Red Hen make bread?
- How is bread made in "From Wheat to Bread"?
- What does the diagram tell you about wheat?

63

From Wheat to Bread

- *Let's retell this story together. I'll say part of a sentence, and then you repeat that part and finish the sentence by retelling the story. You can look back at the story for help.*

Wheat starts out as a little _______. (seed)
Farmers plant the _______. (seeds)
The plants need _______. (sun and water)
The plants will _______. (grow big)
The farmers pick off the _______. (kernels)
The kernels go to a _______. (factory)
The kernels are crushed into _______. (flour)
We use flour to make _______. (bread)

Name ______________________________

Copy each new word on the line.
Draw a picture.

Word	Illustration
cookie ________	
cake ________	

© Macmillan/McGraw-Hill

Name ______________________________

Book Talk

Read each question and prompt. Discuss the answers with your group. Use your Leveled Reader to find details to support your answers. Then write your answers on another sheet of paper.

1. Tell what you learned about trees.

2. Give examples of the different ways that animals use trees.

3. Give examples of things that can come from trees.

4. Explain the many ways that trees help us.

5. Describe your favorite tree to your classmates and tell why you like it.

© Macmillan/McGraw-Hill

Interactive Question - Response Guide

On the Map

Pages 70–71

Prior to reading the selection with children, they should have listened to the selection on **StudentWorks Plus,** the interactive eBook. In addition, selection vocabulary should have been pretaught using the **Visual Vocabulary Resources.**

Access Core Content

Teacher Note Pose the questions after you read the paragraph or page indicated.

Pages 70–71

Title and Map

- *Read the title of this selection with me:* On the Map.
- Maps show where places are. You can use a map to figure out how to get to a new place. Look at the map on page 71. *Does a map have words and drawings on it?* (yes) *Does a map tell a story?* (no)
- *Let's read the first page together:* Greg and Stef live in a big town. They go out a lot. *Is our school in a big or little town?* (Children's answer will be appropriate to the school community.)
- *This page says that the children go out a lot. This means that the children go to a lot of places. Where are some places children can go to in a town?* (school, friends' houses, playground, stores)
- *Look at the map on page 71 again. What other ideas does it give you about where Greg and Stef might go?* (library, playground)
-

Directionality

Ask children to place their finger where you start reading (top left). Ask where you finish reading on this page (bottom right).

Pages 70–71

Comprehension

Genre
Nonfiction
A nonfiction article gives information about a topic.

Summarize
Main Idea and Details
Look for details that show what the town is like.

On the Map

Greg and Stef **live** in a big town.

They go **out** a lot.

70

Pages 72–73

Greg and Stef go here a lot.
It is red. It has bricks.
It has **many** steps.
What is it?

72

Here is the town on a map.

71

Can you spot it on the map?

73

Page 72

Illustration

- *This page tells about a large building where the children go almost every day. It is next to the park. Point to a part of the building that is red. Point to the steps.*
- *What kind of building do you think this is? How do you know?* (It is a school. School is a place where children go almost every day. The picture shows a building where many classrooms could fit.)

Talk to your partner about Greg and Stef's school. How is their school like our school? How is it different? (Answers will vary.)

Text

- *Let's read this page together.*
- *This place has many steps.* Many *means "a lot." Here is one pencil.* (Hold up one pencil.) *Here are* many *pencils.* (Hold up several pencils.)

Page 73

Text

- *The author asks:* Can you spot it on the map? *What is another way to say* Can you spot it?("Can you see it?" or "Can you find it?") *What does the author mean by* it? (the school)

Map

- *Find Greg and Stef's school on the map. Point to it. What kinds of buildings are in front of the school and beside the school?* (houses) *Where is the library? Point to it.*
- *The spaces between the buildings on this map are streets. Pretend that your finger is Greg or Stef. Pretend that you are going to the library after school. Show me how you would walk.*

Synonyms and Circumlocution

Remind children that they can ask for synonyms to help clarify words or expressions they do not understand. Ask, *What is another way of saying "spot"?* (find, see)

On the Map

Page 74

Text

- *Let's read this page together.*
- *We will answer the question on this page. I will give you some choices. Pick the best answer, and tell me why it is best. Is this place the school, the library, or the park?* (the park, because that is where there are trees and swings)

Page 75

Whole Page

- *Point to the park on the map on page 75. Tell me how you know it is the park.* (Children should point to the part of the map that has swings and sand. Page 74 said that the place has swings and sand.)
- *Find the pond or lake. How can you tell?* (Children should point to the upper-left part of the map. The wavy lines mean water. There is a boat on the water.)
- *The author tells us about the swings and sand. Find some other things that are in the park.* (a slide, a seesaw)
- *If the children want to take a snack to the park, where could they go to buy one? Show me on the map. Why is that a good place to go for a snack?* (They could go to the market. Markets sell food.)

Tell your partner what you like to do in parks or on playgrounds. (Answers will vary.)

> **Non-verbal Cues**
> Remind children that they can use non-verbal cues to share information when they are not able to do so verbally. Encourage children to use visuals.

Pages 74–75

Greg and Stef like this
place a lot!
It has swings and sand.
What is it?
74

Pages 76–77

Greg and Stef go here
to get stamps.
What is it?
Can you spot it on the map?
MARKET
CITY HALL
CAFE
76

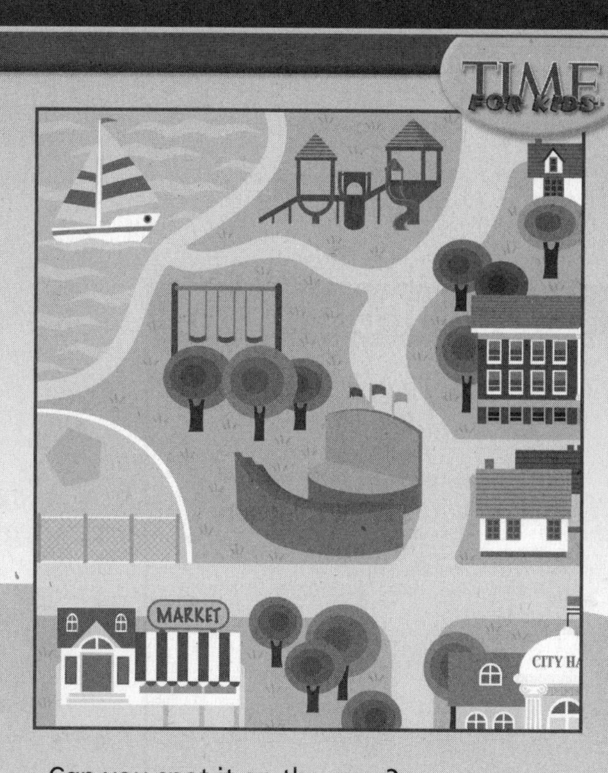

Can you spot it on the map?

75

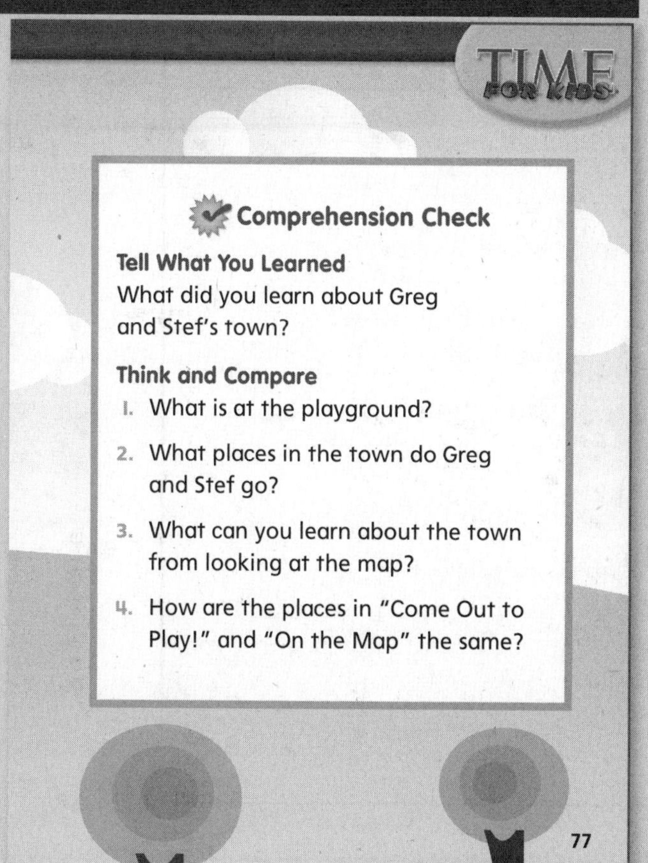

TIME FOR KIDS
Comprehension Check
Tell What You Learned
What did you learn about Greg and Stef's town?
Think and Compare
1. What is at the playground?
2. What places in the town do Greg and Stef go?
3. What can you learn about the town from looking at the map?
4. How are the places in "Come Out to Play!" and "On the Map" the same?
77

Page 76

Text

- *Let's read this page together.*
- *What is the name of the place where people go to buy stamps and mail packages?* (post office)

Map

- *Point to the post office on the map.* (Children should point to the post offfice.) *Is the post office closer to the Café or to City Hall?* (City Hall)
- *Point to the post office again. What is sitting outside the post office on the left side?* (mailbox) *Let's pretend to mail something in the mailbox.* (Demonstrate opening the small door on the box, dropping in a make-believe letter, and closing the door.)

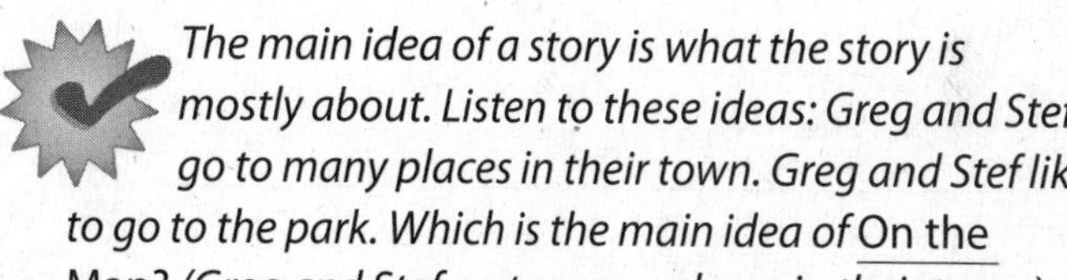

The main idea of a story is what the story is mostly about. Listen to these ideas: Greg and Stef go to many places in their town. Greg and Stef like to go to the park. Which is the main idea of On the Map? *(Greg and Stef go to many places in their town.)*

Name ________________________________

Copy each new word on the line.
Draw a picture.

Word	Illustration
park ______________________	
school ______________________	

© Macmillan/McGraw-Hill

Name ______________________________

Book Talk

Read each question and prompt. Discuss the answers with your group. Use your Leveled Reader to find details to support your answers. Then write your answers on another sheet of paper.

1. Explain how maps help people.

2. Describe a fun thing to do in San Francisco.

3. Tell about a fun thing to do in Monterey.

4. Describe what you can see at an aquarium.

5. Describe what a map of your city would show.

© Macmillan/McGraw-Hill

The Pigs, the Wolf, and the Mud

Pages 88–89

Prior to reading the selection with children, they should have listened to the selection on **StudentWorks Plus,** the interactive eBook. In addition, selection vocabulary should have been pretaught using the **Visual Vocabulary Resources.**

Access Core Content

Teacher Note Pose the questions after you read the paragraph or page indicated.

Pages 88–89

Title and Illustration

- *This story is called* The Pigs, the Wolf, and the Mud. *What other story do you know about pigs and a wolf.* (The Three Little Pigs) *This story is a different version of that story.*
- *Point to the mud and the wolf in the picture. Now point to the pigs. How can you tell that this is not a true story?* (Real pigs do not eat at a table and wear clothes.)
- *Even though this is a made-up story that couldn't happen, real pigs are often muddy. They roll in mud because it cools them down on hot days.*
- *The pigs in this story like mud, too. Look at the picture. Point to the mud on the pigs' clothes and on their bodies. Do you think they mind being messy?* (no) *There is mud everywhere!*

Pages 88–89

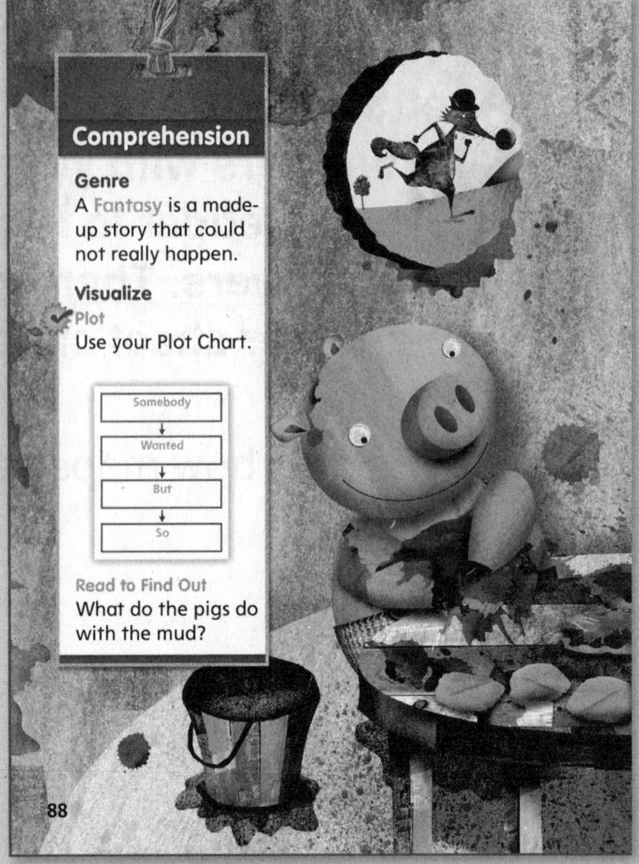

Comprehension
Genre
A Fantasy is a made-up story that could not really happen.
Visualize
Plot
Use your Plot Chart.
Somebody
Wanted
But
So
Read to Find Out
What do the pigs do with the mud?
88

Pages 90–91

Three little pigs lived in a mud hut.
90

"It is a mess," said Pig **One**.
"But pigs like a mess," said Pig Two.
"Mud is fun!" said Pig Three.

91

Page 90

Whole Page

- *Point to the three little pigs in the picture. Where are they?* (in the hut) *What are they doing?* (looking out the windows)
- *The story says they lived in a mud hut. The hut is their home. What is another word for* hut? (*house*)
- *Point to the parts of the house that are made out of mud. These are the walls. Say* walls. *Now point to the roof, which is the top of the house. Say* roof. *What do you think the pigs used to make the roof?* (straw, hay, twigs, branches)

Page 91

Whole Page

- *Let's read this page together.* (Divide the group into three subgroups.) *Children in group one will read what Pig One says with me:* "It is a mess," said Pig One.
- *Children in group two will read what Pig Two says with me:* "But pigs like a mess," said Pig Two.
- *Children in group three will read what Pig Three says with me:* "Mud is fun!" said Pig Three.
- *Our classroom is not a mess. If we walked into this room with mud on our feet, we would make a mess on the floor.*
- *Let's pretend to throw papers around the room.* (demonstrate) *That would be another way to make a mess.*

Pig Three said that mud is fun. Tell your partner whether you think mud is fun. Also tell why you think the way you do. (Responses are open.)

- **Directionality**

  Ask children to place their finger where you start reading (top left). Ask where you finish reading on this page (bottom right).

The Pigs, the Wolf, and the Mud

Page 92

Whole Page

- *Pig One says:* "Get this!" *What does the word* this *mean in the sentence?* (mud) "Get this!" *means "Catch the mud!"*
- *Let's read the page aloud and act it out. We'll pretend to throw a handful of mud when we tell what Pig One did. We'll also pretend to be Pig Two and catch the mud.*
- *Read the first two lines with me, and do what I do:* "Get this!" yelled Pig One. She tossed mud to Pig Two. (Pretend to toss a handful of mud.)
- *Let's pretend to catch the handful of mud.* (Demonstrate catching the mud.)
- *Now let's read the last sentence:* "Mud is fun!" yelled Pig Three.

Page 93

Whole Page

- *Look at the picture. Who is ringing the doorbell?* (a wolf)
- Let's read what the wolf says: "Little pigs, little pigs, let me in."
- *Wolves in made-up stories are often bad. Why do you think the wolf may be coming to the pigs' hut?* (Answers will vary.)

Tell your partner what you think the pigs will do. Tell why you think so. (They will try to keep the wolf out so they will be safe.)

Pages 92–93

"Get this!" yelled Pig One.
She tossed mud to Pig Two.
"Mud is fun!" yelled Pig Three.

92

Pages 94–95

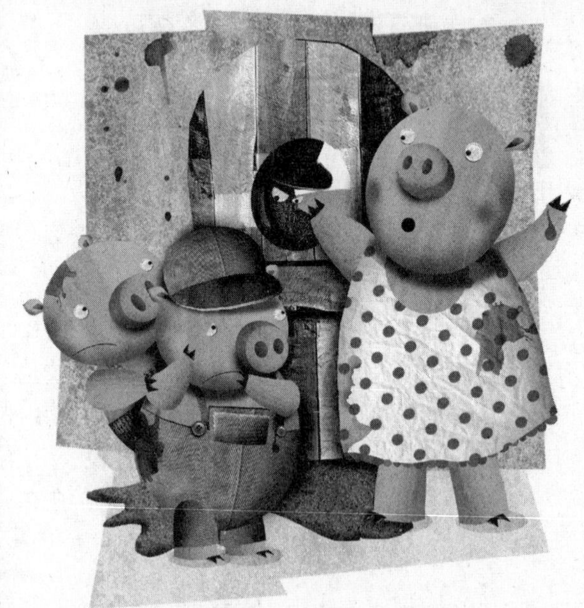

"It is the Big Bad Wolf!" said Pig One.
"We can not let you in," yelled the pigs. "You will eat us up."

94

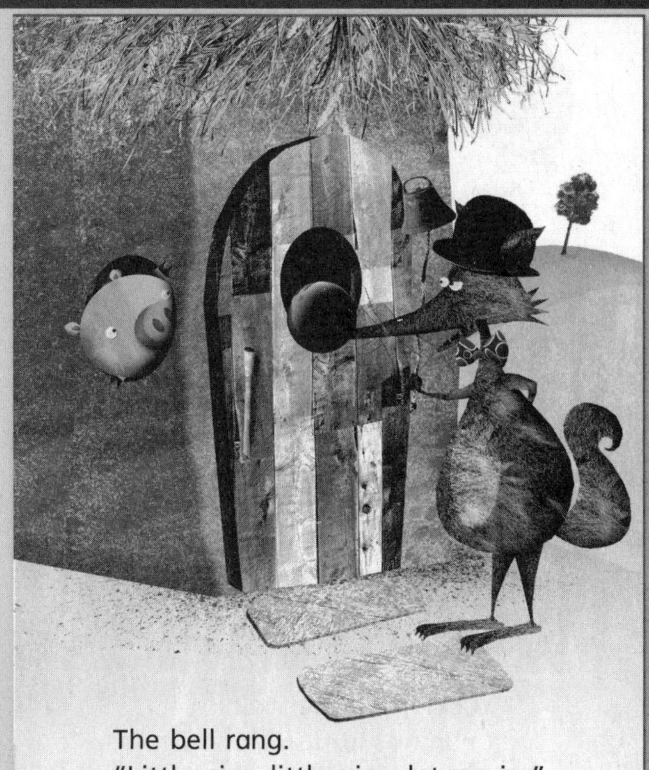

"**Then** I must huff and puff,"
said the wolf.
He huffed and huffed.
He puffed and puffed.
95

Page 94

Whole Page

- *Look at the faces of the pigs in the picture. How do you think they feel?* (scared) *Let's look scared.*
- *Let's make our faces look scared like the pigs. Let's use a scared voice to read what Pig One says:* "It is the Big Bad Wolf!" said Pig One.
- *Now let's use a scared voice to read what the other pigs say:* "We can not let you in," yelled the pigs. "You will eat us up."

Characters in a story usually have a problem. What problem do the pigs have? (The wolf wants to come in. They're afraid he will eat them. They have to try to keep him out.)

Page 95

Whole Page

- *The wolf is huffing and puffing. Huffing and puffing is blowing really hard. Let me show you how huffing and puffing looks and sounds.* (Demonstrate huffing and puffing.) *Let's all huff and puff together.*
- *The wolf starts huffing and puffing when the pigs say he can't come in? Why do you think he is huffing and puffing?* (He wants to blow down the hut so he can get to the pigs.)

The Pigs, the Wolf, and the Mud

Page 96

Whole Page

- *Mud is wet and squishy. What happens when the sun shines on mud for a long time?* (It gets dry and dusty.) *What do the clouds all over this page show?* (They show the dust from the pigs' messy house.)
- *What would happen if you tried to huff and puff in a dusty place?* (All the dust would blow around.) *What is happening in the picture. (It's getting dustier and dustier.)*
- *The wolf does not like the dust. Let's read what the wolf says together:* "Yuck!" said the wolf. "I can not huff in this dust. I can not puff in this dust."

Page 97

Illustration

- *The wolf just rang the bell for the second time. Look at the picture. Do you think the pigs are more scared or less scared than they were before? Why?* (They are probably more scared because the wolf is not giving up and going away.)

Text

- *How do you think the wolf feels now? Why?* (The wolf is probably angry and frustrated because the pigs won't let him in, and he can't huff and puff down the door.)
- *Let's read the wolf's part in an angry voice:* "Little pigs, let me in!" he yelled.
- *Now let's read what the pigs say in a scared voice:* "We will not let you in!" the pigs yelled back.

Analyze Sayings and Expressions

Help children recognize that *Yuck!* is an expression used when you think something is disgusting or unpleasant. Find other examples while reading the selection.

Pages 96–97

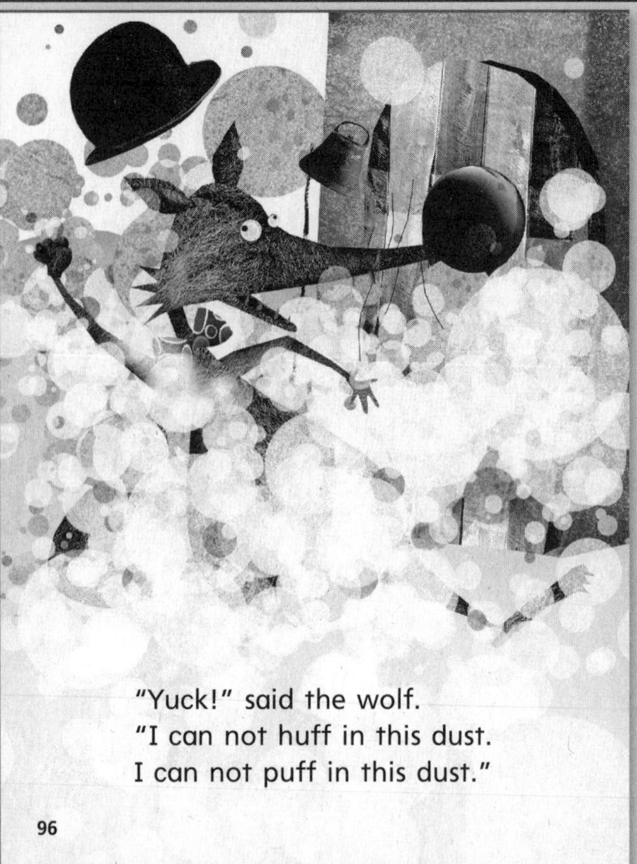

Pages 98–99

"Then I must kick," said the wolf.
He kicked and kicked.
98

The wolf rang the bell again.
"Little pigs, let me in!" he yelled.
"We will not let you in!" the pigs yelled back.

97

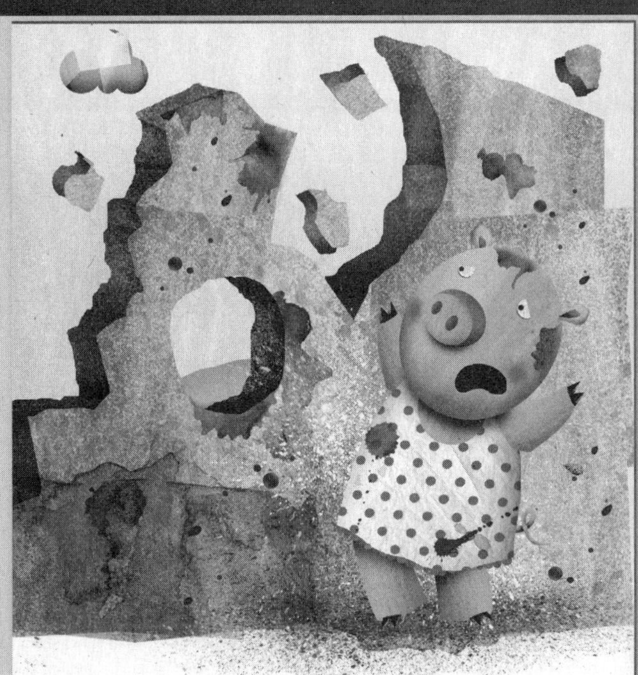

The hut fell in!
"Yuck!" said the wolf.
"Just look at this mud."

99

Page 98

Whole Page

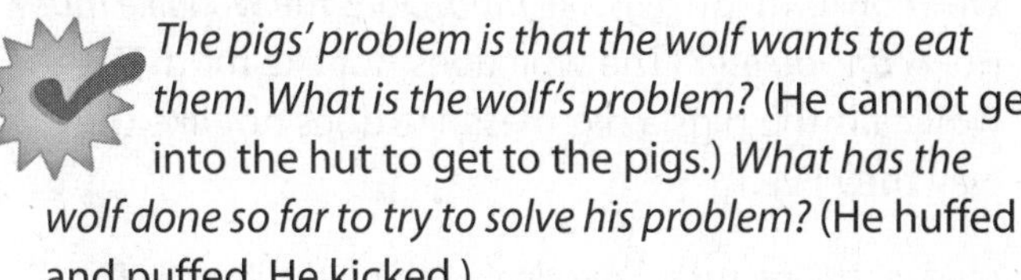

The pigs' problem is that the wolf wants to eat them. What is the wolf's problem? (He cannot get into the hut to get to the pigs.) *What has the wolf done so far to try to solve his problem?* (He huffed and puffed. He kicked.)

- *Look at the picture. Now the wolf is kicking. Why do you think he is doing that?* (to kick open the door, to knock down the walls)

Page 99

Whole Page

- *Look at the picture. The walls are breaking, and there is no more roof. What made the hut fall in?* (The wolf kicked it apart.)
- *The wolf says:* "Yuck!" *When do people say* yuck? (when something is horrible or disgusting) *Let's read what the wolf says in a disgusted voice:* "Yuck!" said the wolf. "Just look at this mud."

Bugs, mud, and snakes are things that make some people say "Yuck!" Do any of these things make you say "Yuck"? Do you feel that way about any foods? Talk with your partner and see if you feel the same way. (Responses are open.)

Patterns in Language

Some grammatical structures, such as past tense "ed," pose difficulties to ELLs. Point out that there are several examples of words ending in *-ed* in this selection, such as *yelled* and *kicked*. Help children find a pattern.

The Pigs, the Wolf, and the Mud

Page 100

Whole Page

- *We know that the pigs like mud. Does the wolf like mud? How can you tell?* (The wolf does not like mud. The wolf calls the pigs a big mess. He does not like the way they live.)
- *Look at the picture. How do you think the pigs feel? What makes you think so?* (They seem happy. They are smiling at the wolf.)
- *The wolf calls the pigs a big mess. He does not mean it in a nice way, but the pigs like what he says. What do they say?* ("Yes! Pigs like a big mess!")
- *The pigs don't seem afraid at all. Why do you think they aren't afraid?* (Maybe they think the wolf will leave them alone because he is disgusted with them.)

Page 101

Whole Page

- *The wolf yells: "I do not!" What did the pigs say to him before he said that?* ("Pigs like a big mess!") *So what does the wolf mean when he says, "I do not"?* (He does not like a big mess.)
- *Look at the picture. What is all over the wolf?* (mud) *The wolf says: "Good-bye, pigs." What do you think he is going to do now?* (He will go take a bath.)

PARTNERS *Talk with your partner. Do you think the wolf will come back to eat the pigs? Why or why not?* (No, because he doesn't like their mess, and he probably doesn't like to eat muddy things.)

Pages 100–101

"You pigs are a big mess!"
"Yes!" yelled the pigs.
"Pigs like a big mess!"

100

Pages 102–103

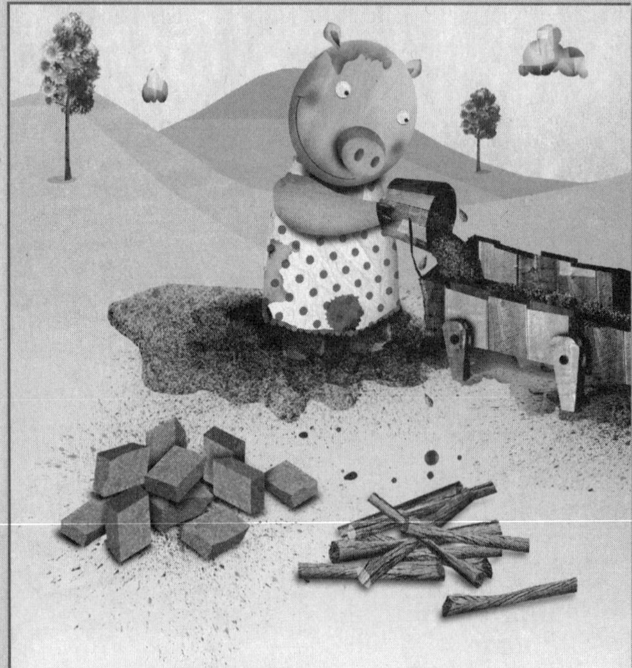

"Let's **make** a hut," said Pig One.
"We **could** use bricks," said Pig Two.
"We could use sticks," said Pig Three.

102

"I do not!" yelled the Wolf.
"I must get this mud off.
Good-bye, pigs."

101

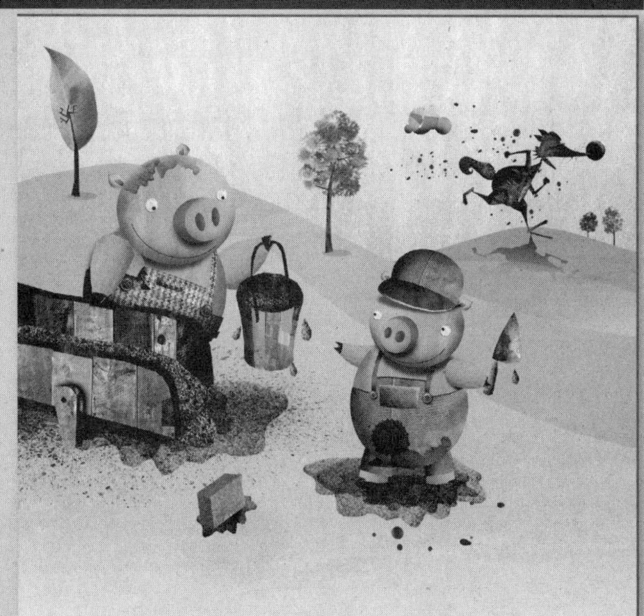

"Let's use mud," said Pig One.
"Mud is best!" said Pig Two.
"Mud is fun!" said Pig Three.
"Yuck!" said the wolf.

103

Pages 102–103

Text and Illustrations

- *Now the pigs need to build another house. Let's read their ideas for building it on page 102:* "Let's make a hut," said Pig One. "We could use bricks," said Pig Two. "We could use sticks," said Pig Three."
- *In the story* The Three Little Pigs, *one pig builds his house with sticks. The wolf is able to blow it in. But the wolf is not able to blow in the house that is made from bricks.*
- *Let's read page 103 together to see what the pigs decide to do.*
- *Why do the pigs choose mud?* (They love it.)
- *Look at the picture. The pigs are using mud. Are they being neat or messy?* (messy) *What does the wolf say as he is running off?* ("Yuck!")

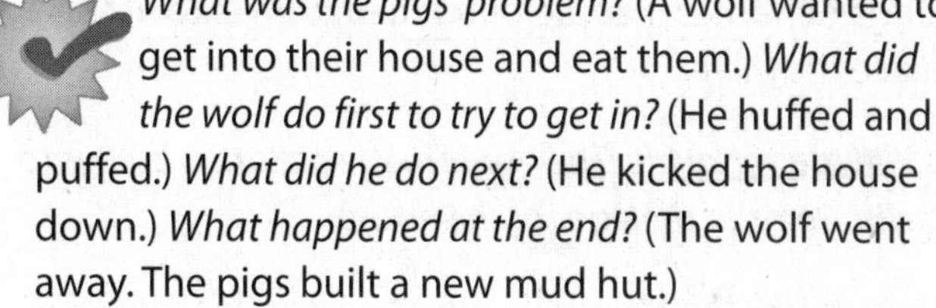

What was the pigs' problem? (A wolf wanted to get into their house and eat them.) *What did the wolf do first to try to get in?* (He huffed and puffed.) *What did he do next?* (He kicked the house down.) *What happened at the end?* (The wolf went away. The pigs built a new mud hut.)

Interactive Question - Response Guide

Homes Around the World

Access Core Content

Teacher Note Pose the questions after you read the paragraph or page indicated.

Page 106

Title and Photos

- *The title of this selection is* Homes Around the World. *Look at the pictures. Do you think this selection is about pretend homes or real homes? Why?* (real, because the pictures show homes that people could live in)
- *In the story* The Pigs, the Wolf, and the Mud, *the pigs' home was made of mud. What are real houses made of?* (bricks, wood, stone)

Text

- *Listen as I read the first paragraph:* There are many kinds of homes. People build their homes to fit the place they live.
- *A cliff is a rocky hill. The home in the picture is built into a cliff. Point to the door of the house.*
- *Now think about the walls. What do you think they are made of?* (rocks) *Why do you think so?* (The house is built into a rocky cliff.)
- *We find cliffs where there is high, rocky land. Is the home most likely in a flat place or a place with mountains and hills?* (a place with mountains and hills)

Page 107

Whole Page

- *Look at the picture. This is a stilt.* (Point to one of the stilts.) *Which one of these words could we use instead of* stilt: pole, wall, *or* line? (pole)
- *Listen as I read this page to find out about houses that are built on stilts. The stilts hold the houses up above the water.*

Pages 106–107

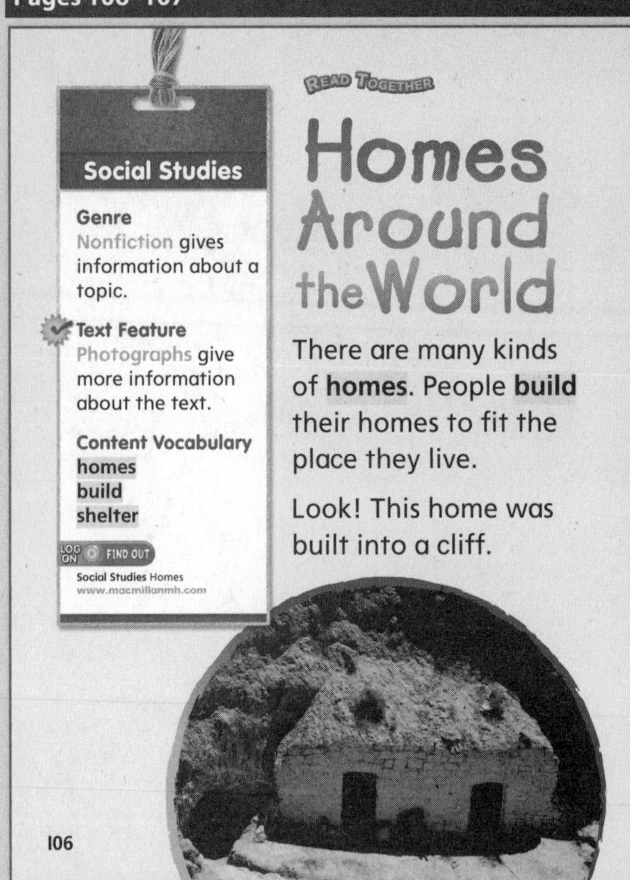

Social Studies
Genre
Nonfiction gives information about a topic.
Text Feature
Photographs give more information about the text.
Content Vocabulary
homes
build
shelter
LOG ON FIND OUT
Social Studies Homes
www.macmillanmh.com
READ TOGETHER
Homes Around the World
There are many kinds of **homes**. People **build** their homes to fit the place they live.
Look! This home was built into a cliff.
106

Pages 108–109

This is a good home for a hot place. There is a lot of clay in this place. People use it to build homes. Clay keeps the home cool inside.
108

This is a good home for a wet place. There is a lot of water here. The stilts help keep this home dry.

107

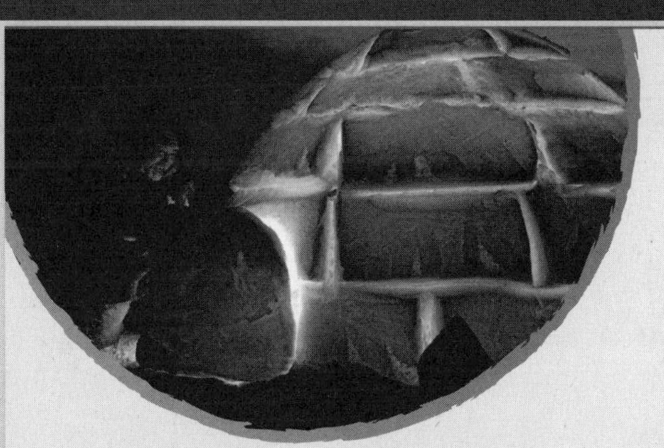

There is a lot of ice in this place. People can use it to build. This is an igloo. Igloos are good **shelter** from the cold.

What is your home like?

Connect and Compare
How are the igloo and the clay hut the same? How are they different? Use the photographs.

109

Work with your partner to draw a picture of a house on the water that is not on stilts. Then draw a picture of what would happen to the house when the water came up high.

Page 108

Whole Page

- *Listen as I read this page about houses made of clay.*
- *How do families keep cool in these houses?* (The clay keeps the house cool.) *How do we keep cool in our houses?* (We use air conditioners or fans.)
- *Look at the ground. Is it the same color as the house or different?* (the same) *The clay for the house comes from the land around it. Remember:* There is a lot of clay in this place.

Page 109

Whole Page

- *Listen as I read this page about houses called igloos.*
- *What do people use to build igloos?* (ice) *Where do you think they find it.* (all around them)
- The selection says: Igloos are good shelter from the cold. *That means igloos can protect people from the cold. An igloo keeps out the wind and keeps the heat inside.*
- *Look at the igloo in the picture. Point to a block of ice.*

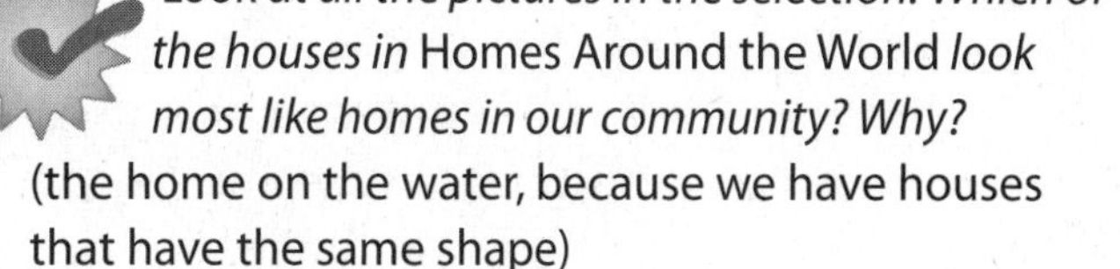

Look at all the pictures in the selection. Which of the houses in Homes Around the World *look most like homes in our community? Why?* (the home on the water, because we have houses that have the same shape)

Name ______________________________

Copy each new word on the line.
Draw a picture.

Word	Illustration
mess ______________	
trash ______________	

© Macmillan/McGraw-Hill

Name ______________________________

Book Talk

Read each question and prompt. Discuss the answers with your group. Use your Leveled Reader to find details to support your answers. Then write your answers on another sheet of paper.

1. Describe the characters in your book.

2. Explain what problem the family has.

3. Tell what happens when characters in your book go out of their home.

4. Describe a lesson learned by a character in your book.

5. Share something you learned from your book.

© Macmillan/McGraw-Hill

Beth and the Band

Pages 118–119

Prior to reading the selection with students, they should have listened to the selection on **StudentWorks Plus**, the interactive eBook. In addition, selection vocabulary should have been pretaught using the **Visual Vocabulary Resources**.

Access Core Content

Teacher Note Pose the questions after you read the paragraph or page indicated.

Pages 118–119

Title and Illustrations

- *The title of the story is* Beth and the Band. *Let's read the title of this story together.*
- *Beth is the girl on page 119. Point to Beth.*
- *Now say the word* band. *A band is a group of people who play music together.*
- *Look at the man who is wearing a red suit and hat. He is the leader of the band. He is called the bandleader. Point to him.*
- *Point to the things the the children are holding. They will use them to make music. These are their instruments. Say it with me:* instruments. *What will they use their instruments for?* (to make music in the band)
- *The children are going to play music in a band. Look at the musical notes.* (Point to the notes.) *These stand for the sounds they will make. Let's read to find out how they meet the bandleader.*

Pages 118–119

Comprehension
Genre
Fiction is a story with made-up characters and events.
Visualize
Retell
Use your Retelling Chart.
Beginning
Middle
Ending
Read to Find Out
What does Beth do with the band?
118

Pages 120–121

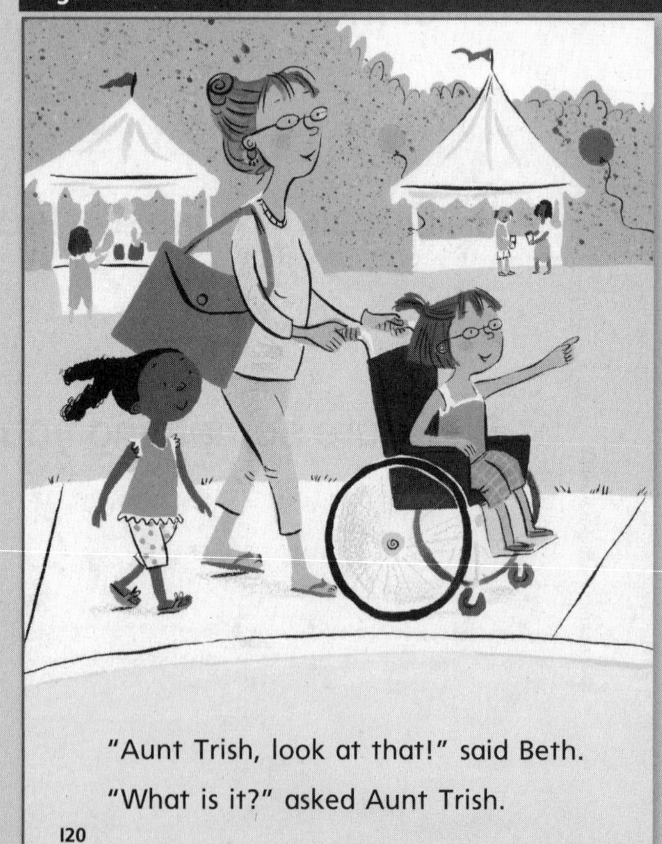

KIDS' BAND
"It is a band for kids," said Ann.
121

Pages 120–121

Illustrations

- *Beth is taking a walk with her Aunt Trish. Point to Beth. Point to Aunt Trish. Beth's friend Ann is also in the picture. Point to Ann. What are they doing?* (They're taking a walk.)
- *Let's look at the picture on page 121 to see what Beth is pointing to. Look at the bandleader. He is on a bandstand. A bandstand is an outdoor stage where bands play. Point to it.*
- *The sign on the bandstand says* Kids' Band. *Read it with me:* Kids' Band.

Text

- *Listen as I read:* "Aunt Trish, look at that" said Beth. *Does Beth sound excited or bored?* (excited)
- *Look at the exclamation point.* (Point to the exclamation point in the first line.) *It tells us that Beth is excited when she speaks. Let's read what Beth says together.*
- *Let's read what Aunt Trish says together:* "What is it?" asked Aunt Trish.
- *Now let's read what Ann says:* "It is a band for kids." *How does she know that?* (She sees the sign: *Kids' Band.*)

Formal and Informal English

When children encounter a colloquial or informal word in the text, discuss other ways of saying the same word with more formal language. For example, *kids/children.*

Beth and the Band

Page 122

Whole Page

- *Follow along as I read this page.* "We want to play in the band!" said Beth, Bud, Ann, and Will. *Who wants to play in the band?* (Beth, Bud, Ann, and Will)
- *Look at the picture. How can you tell that everyone is excited?* (Beth and Bud are moving their hands. Ann is looking at Aunt Trish.) *Copy the children's hand movements.*
- *Now let's read the page together with excitement.*

Page 123

Whole Page

- *Look at the picture. Shep is the bandleader. The bandleader helps everyone play music together. Shep tells players when to start and when to ____.* (stop) *He also tells players when to play softly and when to play ____.* (loudly)
- *Now let's read the page together.*
- *Shep tells the children to make instruments. A drum is an instrument. Let's name some other instruments.* (horn, piano, guitar)
- *Let's act out making music with the instruments we named.* (Name each instrument, and lead students in pretending to make music with it.)

Let's retell what has happened in the story so far. (Aunt Trish, Beth, Bud, Ann, and Will see a sign for a kids' band. The children want to play in the band. The leader tells them to make instruments.)

- **Directionality**
  Ask children to place their finger where you start reading (top left). Ask where you finish reading on this page (bottom right).

Pages 122–123

"We **want** to play in the band!" said Beth, Bud, Ann, and Will.

122

Pages 124–125

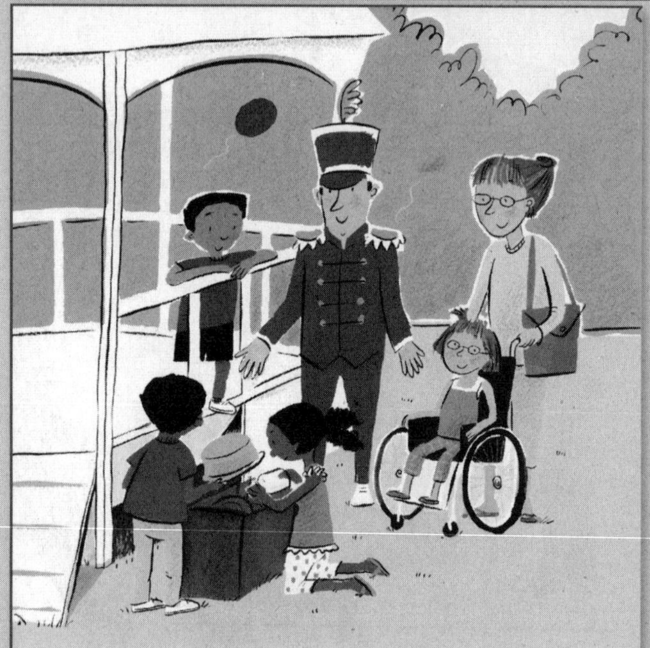

"Make instruments?" asked the kids.

"Yes. Use the things in the box. It is **under** the bandstand," said Shep.

124

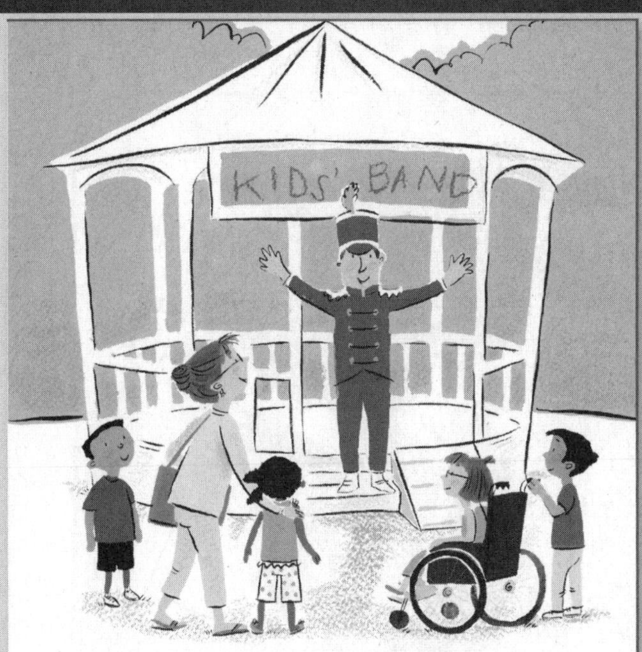

"Can the kids all play?" asked Aunt Trish.

"Yes!" said a man in a red hat. "I am Shep. Make some instruments, kids."

123

"I can hit this tub!" said Bud. "It sounds just like a drum." Rap! Tap! Tap!

125

Page 124

Whole Page

- *Listen to what the children say when Shep tells them to make instruments:* "Make instruments?" *Do the children seem surprised, or did they expect him to say that?* (They seem surprised.)
- *Let's sound surprised as we read the children's question together:* "Make instruments?" asked the kids.
- *Look at the picture. Point to the boy in red who is standing on the bandstand, or the stage where bands play. Now point to the box. Is the box under the bandstand or on top of it?* (under)

Shep tells the children to use the things in the box to make instruments. The boy is pulling out a tub. How can you make music with a tub? (You can bang on it.) *What other things might be in the box?* (Question is open.)

Page 125

Whole Page

- *Bud is playing a drum. Let's say it together:* drum. *What did he use to make the drum?* (tub, string, sticks) *Where did he get the things for the drum?* (from the box)
- *Let's read together the sound that Bud's drum makes:* Rap! Tap! Tap! *Let's pretend we are banging a drum as we say the sound.* (Demonstrate banging a pretend drum as you say the sound.)

Non-verbal Cues

Remind children that they can use non-verbal cues to share information when they are not able to do so verbally. Encourage children to use pantomime and sounds.

Pages 126–127

Illustrations

- *Ann's instrument is a jug. Point to it. What sound does Ann make with the jug?* (hum, hum, hum)
- *Will takes two lids out of the box. Let's pretend to hold the lids like Will does and bang them together.* (Demonstrate banging the lids together.) *What sound does Will's instrument make?* (crish, crush, crash)

Text

Which child's instrument is probably the loudest? (Will's) *Why?* (Banging metal lids together is loud.)

- *Let's read together what Ann and Will say. First, the girls in the group will read with me about what Ann made:* "I can play this jug!" said Ann. Hum! Hum! Hum!
- *Now the boys will read with me about what Will made:* "I can play the lids!" said Will. Crish! Crush! Crash!

Pages 126–127

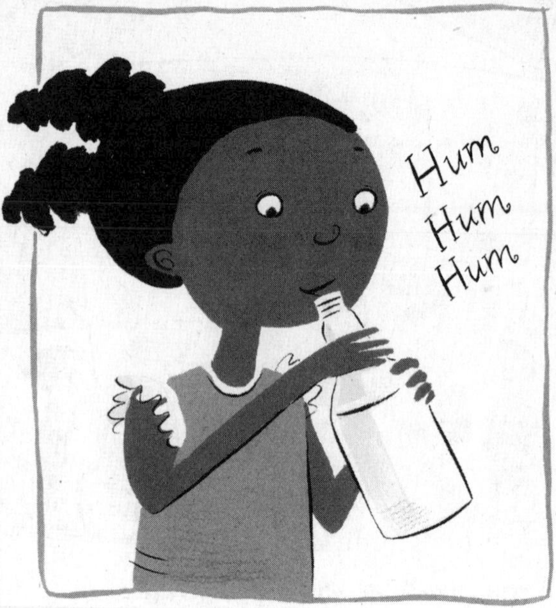

"I can play this jug!" said Ann.
Hum! Hum! Hum!

126

Pages 128–129

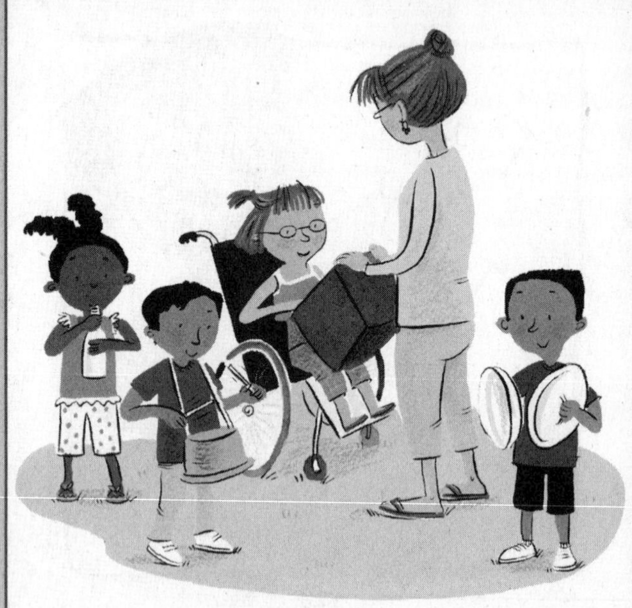

"What do you want to make, Beth?" asked Aunt Trish.

"I just want to sing," said Beth.

128

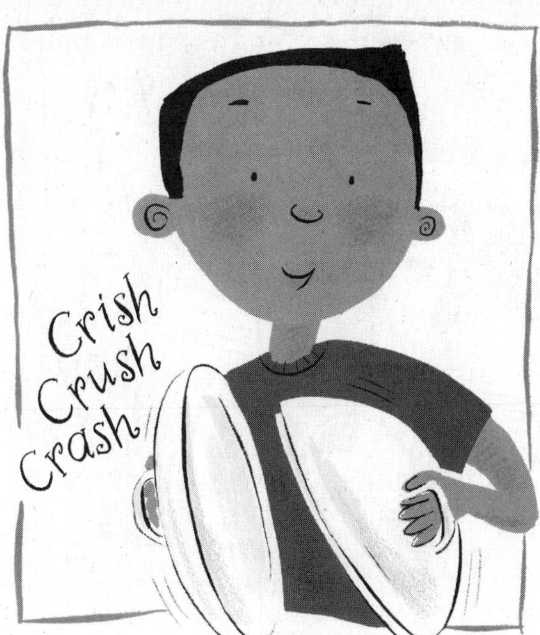

"I can play the lids!" said Will.
Crish! Crush! Crash!

127

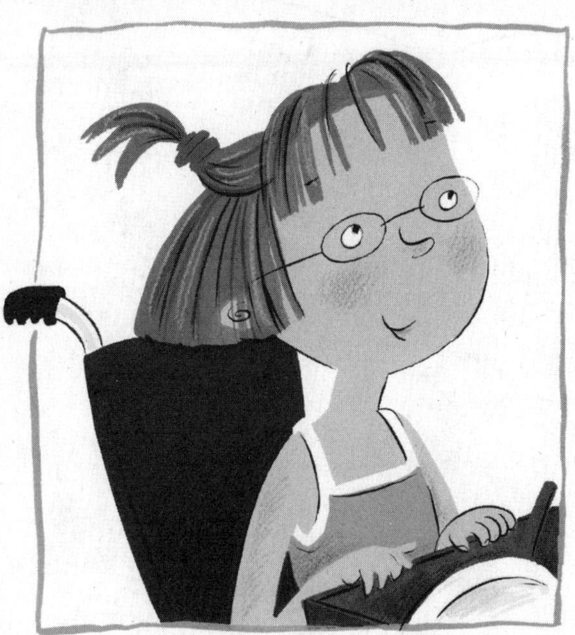

"Can I sing in the **show**?" she asked. "That will be fun for me."

129

- *Let's pretend we are Bud, Ann, and Will. We will make the sounds their instruments make. We will do it together so we sound like a band.* (Divide the group into three parts, and assign each to make the sound of the tub, jug, or lids.)
- *I will be the bandleader. I will raise my hands to start the music. I will put my hands down to stop it.* (Have the three groups simultaneously say their sounds: *Rap! Tap! Tap! Hum! Hum! Hum! Crish! Crush! Crash!*)

Pages 128–129

Text and Illustrations

- *Let's read what Beth says together. What does Beth want to do in the band?* (sing) *Will she need anything from the box? Why or why not?* (No, she will use her voice to make music.)

Some of the children want to play musical instruments in the show. Beth wants to sing. Pretend we are going to have a show. Tell your partner what you would like to do in the show. Tell why.

Beth and the Band

Page 130

Text and Illustration

- *Let's read what the kids say. Do they want Beth to sing?* (yes) *Why do you think they want her to sing?* (They want her to do what she thinks is fun. They already have enough instruments.)
- *Look at the picture. What is Will holding?* (one of the lids) *Does he look like he is inviting Beth to sing with the band or telling her not to?* (inviting her)
- *Let's read the rest of the page together:* "Come on," said Will. "Sing with us!"

Page 131

Text and Illustration

- *The children and Shep are excited about the show. Let's read this page with excited voices:* "Beth and the band will put on a show," said Shep. "Yes!" yelled the kids.
- *Point to the people in front of the bandstand. They are the audience. Say* audience. *Point to the person in the audience that you have seen before.* (Aunt Trish)

Talk with your partner. Who do you think the other people might be? (family and friends of the other children, people who are walking by and are curious)

Pages 130–131

"That will be fun for us, too," said the kids.

"Come on," said Will. "Sing with us!"

130

Pages 132–133

"Let's all play **together**," said Shep. "One, two, three! Play with me!"

132

"Beth and the band will **put** on a show," said Shep.

"Yes!" yelled the kids.

131

"Jam! Jim! Jam!
Sing with the band!
This fun kids' band
is the best in the land!"
133

Page 132

- *Let's read what Shep said together:* "One, two, three! Play with me!" *Which two words rhyme?* (*three* and *me*)
- *What do you think happened next?* (The children started playing.)

Page 133

- *Let's read together what Beth sings:* Jam! Jim! Jam! Sing with the band! This fun kids' band is the best in the land! *Which two words in the song rhyme?* (*band* and *land*)
- *Do you think the band enjoyed playing together? Will they want to play together again? Why or why not?* (Yes, they are having fun playing. They are smiling. They will want to do it again.)

Let's retell the story together. (Aunt Trish, Beth, Bud, Ann, and Will were taking a walk. They saw a bandleader who wanted to start a kids' band. Ann, Will, and Bud made instruments and played them. Beth sang. Everyone had a good time.)

Shake a Rattle!

Access Core Content

Teacher Note Pose the questions after you read the paragraph or page indicated.

Page 136

Title and Text

- *The title of this selection is* Shake a Rattle! *What is the title?* (*Shake a Rattle!*)
- *A rattle can be a baby's toy. It can also be something to make music. Look at the pictures in this selection. Which kind of rattle do you think we will learn about?* (something to make music)
- *Listen as I read the page to see if we are right:* What instruments do you see here? Shaking rattles is a fun way to make music. *Remember that instruments are things that make music.*

Photo

The people who made these rattles got ideas from nature. Look at the shapes of the rattles. Look at the way they are painted. What kinds of things from nature do you see? (mountains, a bug, the shell of a turtle)

Page 137

Whole Page

- *Listen as I read this page to find out what rattles are like:* Rattles can be big or little. *Can rattles be big?* (yes) *Can they be little?* (yes)
- *Now listen to find out what can make the sound inside a rattle:* Some have sand in them. Some have beans. *What can make the sound?* (sand, beans) *When you shake a rattle, these things hit the sides and make noise.*
- *The boy in the picture is wearing special clothing for a holiday or other event. What is he doing with the rattles?* (shaking them, making music) *Let's pretend we are shaking the rattles, too.*

Pages 136–137

Social Studies
Genre
Nonfiction can tell how to do or make something.
Text Feature
Directions are the steps to follow to make something.
Content Vocabulary
instruments
rattles
music
LOG ON FIND OUT
Social Studies
Instruments Around the World
www.macmillanmh.com
READ TOGETHER
Shake a Rattle!
What **instruments** do you see here? Shaking **rattles** is a fun way to make **music**.
136

Pages 138–139

Do you want to make a rattle? Here's how!
How to Make a Rattle
What You Need
plastic bottle
dried beans
stickers
What to Do
1 Put beans into the bottle.
2 Put fun stickers on.
3 Shake it and have fun!
138

Social Studies

Rattles can be big or little. They can be made of many things. Some have sand in them. Some have beans.

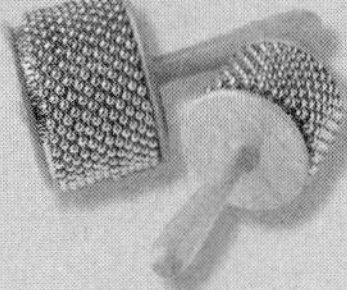

137

Can you play the rattle loud? Can you play it soft? Can you make up a song?

Connect and Compare

How is a rattle like the instruments the kids made in *Beth and the Band*?

139

Page 138

Whole Page

- *Now listen as I read the sentences at the top of the page:* Do you want to make a rattle? Here's how!
- *Put your finger on the part of the page that shows the things we need.* (Demonstrate.) *We will point to each thing, and I will say the word. Then you will say it after me.*
- *Now let's point to the part of the page that says* What to Do. (Demonstrate.) *These are the steps for making a rattle. Why do you think there are numbers?* (to help us do the steps in order)
- *Point to Step 1, and listen as I read:* Put beans into the bottle. *Pretend you are holding a bottle. Pretend to put beans in it.*
- *Now point to Step 2, and listen as I read:* Put fun stickers on. *What are the stickers for? Do they make the music sound better or make the instrument look pretty?* (look pretty)
- *Now point to Step 3.* Shake it and have fun! *Shake a pretend rattle.*
- *Look at pictures of the rattles. Why did the author put them there?* (to help us know what to do)

Page 139

Whole Page

- *Now listen as I read the page, and copy my movements:* Can you play the rattle loud? (Shake the pretend rattle hard.) Can you play it soft? (Shake it easy.) Can you make up a song?
- *Let's shake our pretend rattles as though we are playing a song.*
- *Let's retell this selection in our own words.* (Rattles make music. They can be big or small. They can have different things inside. They're easy to make. They can make a loud or soft sound.)

Name ______________________

Vocabulary

Copy each new word on the line.
Draw a picture.

Word	Illustration
band	
drum	

© Macmillan/McGraw-Hill

Name____________________________________

Book Talk

Read each question and prompt. Discuss the answers with your group. Use your Leveled Reader to find details to support your answers. Then write your answers on another sheet of paper.

1. Explain what the friends in your book want to do together.

2. Describe what they do to get ready.

3. Share your ideas about something fun people in your neighborhood might do together.

4. Tell about a problem someone in your book has.

5. Explain how the problem is solved.

© Macmillan/McGraw-Hill

Weekly Planners

Week 1

Selections	Vocabulary		ELL Practice Book
	Oral Vocabulary Words/Cognates	Academic Language/Cognates	
On My Way to School *Signs We See*	amuse delighted mood humorous *humorístico* ridiculous *ridículo*	retell signs visualize *visualizar* verbs *verbos* symbols *símbolos*	• Phonics, p. 41 • Vocabulary, p. 42 • Grammar, p. 43 • Book Talk, p. 44

Week 2

Selections	Vocabulary		ELL Practice Book
	Oral Vocabulary Words/Cognates	Academic Language/Cognates	
Smile, Mike! *Healthy Eating*	relief support connection *conexión* possessions *posesiones* typical *típico*	present tense chart predictions *predicciones* analyze *analizar*	• Phonics, p. 45 • Vocabulary, p. 46 • Grammar, p. 47 • Book Talk, p. 48

Week 3

TIME FOR KIDS®	Vocabulary		ELL Practice Book
	Oral Vocabulary Words/Cognates	Academic Language/Cognates	
Masks! Masks! Masks!	talented astonishing complicated *complicado* original *original* continue *continuar*	main idea detail *detalle* past tense periodical newspaper	• Phonics, p. 49 • Vocabulary, p. 50 • Grammar, p. 51 • Book Talk, p. 52

Week 4

Selections	Vocabulary		ELL Practice Book
	Oral Vocabulary Words/Cognates	Academic Language/Cognates	
Rose Robot Cleans Up *A Bottle Takes a Trip*	inspire *inspirar* resourceful structure *estructura* create *crear* hobby	draw conclusions reread silent letters present-tense verbs	• Phonics, p. 53 • Vocabulary, p. 54 • Grammar, p. 55 • Book Talk, p. 56

Week 5

Selections	Vocabulary		ELL Practice Book
	Oral Vocabulary Words/Cognates	Academic Language/Cognates	
Kids Have Fun! *Kids' Poems from Around the World*	language skill culture *cultura* custom *costumbre* similar *similar*	compare *comparar* contrast *contrastar* blends contractions	• Phonics, p. 57 • Vocabulary, p. 58 • Grammar, p. 59 • Book Talk, p. 60

© Macmillan/McGraw-Hill

Student Response Strategies

Use the following strategies to help English Language Learners move to the next proficiency level.

✔ **WAIT** Give children ample time to respond.

- Let children know that they can respond in different ways depending on their levels of proficiency, but all should be encouraged to answer questions related to the main point of the picture or text.
- Allow children to respond in their native language if they are very limited proficient. Ask a more proficient student to repeat the answer in English.

✔ **REPEAT** If the child's response is correct, the teacher can repeat what the child has said slowly and clearly for the rest of the class to hear.

✔ **REVISE for FORM** Generally the teacher will be repeating what the child has said but with corrections for grammar and pronunciation. The correction can be implicit or explicit (where teacher calls attention to the correction).

✔ **REVISE for MEANING** Teachers should also correct responses for meaning.

✔ **ELABORATE** Here, the teacher elaborates on a child's response or states the response in another way in order to more fully develop children's comprehension and oral language proficiency.

✔ **ELICIT** Finally, the teacher can also elicit a more comprehensive response from the child by prompting him or her for further information.

Newcomers

Basic and Social Language Each week you will be focusing on an important aspect of classroom communication to teach or reinforce with your newcomers. Children will expand and internalize initial English vocabulary by learning and using routine language needed for classroom communication.

Introduce Self Teach children how to introduce themselves, ask for other classmates' names, and say Hello/Goodbye. Use the sentence frames *My name is* ____ and *What is your name?* Model dialogues, such as *Hello. My name is (name). What is your name?* Have children repeat and practice with a partner.

Basic Requests Teach children sentence frames for basic requests, such as *I need* ____, *I want* ____, and *Do you have* ____*?* Teach them how to ask for permission, such as *May I use the restroom, please?* And to respond with *thank you*. Provide daily opportunities to model and practice each request. Reinforce *please* and *thank you*.

Classroom Items Teach children the names of commonly used classroom items, such as, pencils, paper, book, chair, and desk. Reinforce each using the sentence frames *This is my* ____. *That is your* ____. and *This is a* ____. These sentence frames focus on possession. Provide daily practice, for example, *This is my book. That is your book.*

LOG ON Have children use **Newcomer Games** to expand and internalize language needed for classroom communication. **www.macmillanmh.com**

© Macmillan/McGraw-Hill

Interactive Question - Response Guide

On My Way to School

Pages 12–13

Prior to reading the selection with children, they should have listened to the selection on **StudentWorks Plus**, the interactive eBook. In addition, selection vocabulary should have been pretaught using the **Visual Vocabulary Resources**.

Access Core Content

Teacher Note Pose the questions after you read the paragraph or page indicated.

Pages 12–13

Title and Illustrations

- *The title of this story is* On My Way to School. *What's the title? (On My Way to School)*
- *We all come to school each day. Some of us walk to school, and some of us get here in other ways. Some of us come by bus. Say the words on the sign on the front of the bus after me:* SCHOOL BUS. (Point to the sign.)
- *Look at the sign on the side of the bus. The word on this sign is* STOP. *What does this word tell people in cars to do when they see the bus?* (It tells them to stop.)
- *A boy and a pig are behind the door of the bus. Point to them. Have you ever seen a pig on a school bus?* (no) *Is the driver a person or an ape?* (ape)
- *This is a very special school bus! It has animals and people on it. Point to the duck on the bus. What animals are jumping from the tree and hopping in front of the bus?* (frogs) *Do you think they are going to school, too?* (Question is open.)
- *Do pigs, ducks, and frogs really ride on a bus or go to school?* (no) *Many of the things that happen in this story could not happen in real life.*
- *Does a school bus take one child to school, or many children?* (many children)

Pages 12–13

Comprehension
Genre
In a Rhyming Story, some words end with the same sounds.
Story Structure
Retell
Use your Retelling Chart.
Beginning
Middle
Ending
Read to Find Out
What happens to the boy on his way to school?
12

Pages 14–15

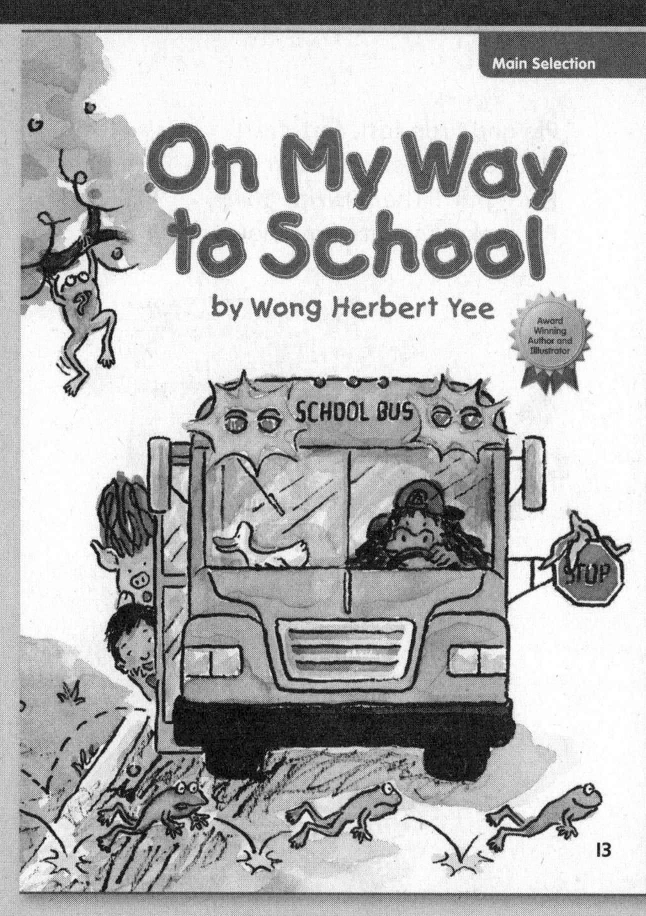

It's not just a pig.
It's a pig in a wig!
We run for the bus,
just the two of us.

15

Page 14

Whole Page

- *What kind of animal do you see in this picture?* (pig) *Point to the pig. Point to the boy.*
- *The pig is holding a ball. Do you think pigs can really play ball?* (no)
- *Let's read this page together:* On my way to school today, a pig asks me to come and play.
- *Who is* me *in* a pig asks me? *Is it the pig or the boy?* (the boy)

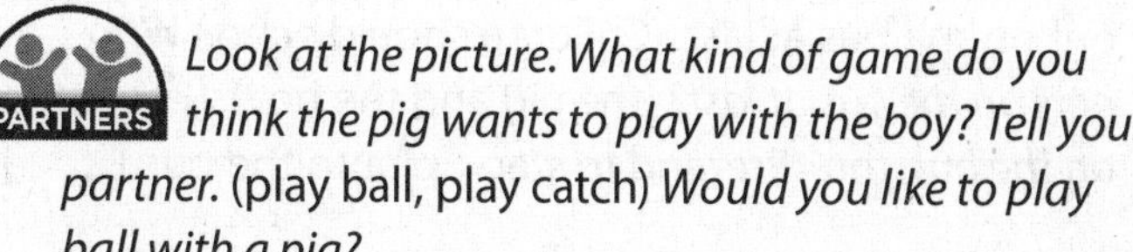

PARTNERS *Look at the picture. What kind of game do you think the pig wants to play with the boy? Tell your partner.* (play ball, play catch) *Would you like to play ball with a pig?*

Page 15

Whole Page

- *Let's read this page together:* It's not just a pig. It's a pig in a wig! We run for the bus, just the two of us.
- *Who is running for the bus in this picture?* (the boy and the pig) *Where do you think they want to go?* (to school)
- *Point to the bus. What kind of bus is this?* (a school bus) *Do you see the front of the bus or the back of the bus?* (the back)
- *The pig is wearing a wig. Point to the wig. A wig is made to look like hair. Some people wear wigs on their heads. Do you think a pig would really wear a wig?* (no)

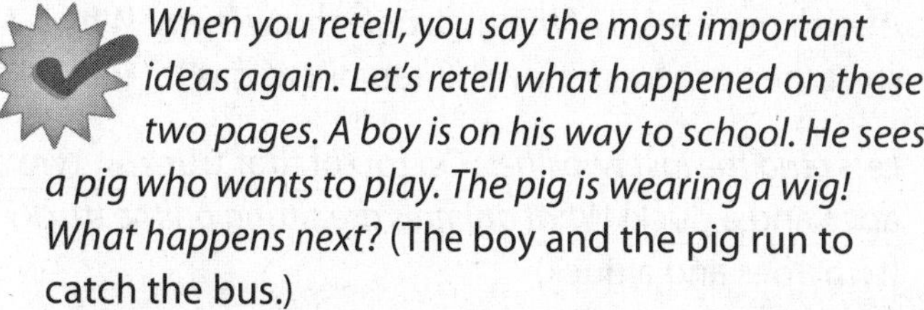

When you retell, you say the most important ideas again. Let's retell what happened on these two pages. A boy is on his way to school. He sees a pig who wants to play. The pig is wearing a wig! What happens next? (The boy and the pig run to catch the bus.)

- **Directionality**

  Ask children to place their finger where you start reading (top left). Ask where you finish reading on this page (bottom right).

On My Way to School

Page 16

Whole Page

- *Look at the picture of the top bus. Who do you see?* (a pig, a boy, and a girl) *What are they doing?* (running to catch the bus)
- *Point to the exclamation point at the end of the first sentence. It tells us to read the sentence with excitement. Now you echo it after me:* Pig and I run fast, fast, fast! (Children should echo.) *Now let's run for the bus, too.* (Demonstrate running in place quickly.)
- *Now I will read the second sentence, and you echo it.* We get on the bus at last. (Children should echo.) *Who gets on the bus at last?* (the pig and the boy) *Let's get on the bus, too.* (Pretend to step up onto the bus.)
- *Let's read the last three sentences together. Remember to use your excited voice when a sentence ends with an exclamation point.*
- *When you run fast, you huff and puff. Let's run again and huff and puff.* (Run in place and breathe loudly.) *Point to the bus at the bottom of the page. The bus goes away fast. It zips away!*
- *The boy says,* Pig makes me late for school today! *Does the boy get to school on time?* (No, he is late.) *Who makes him late for school?* (the pig)

Page 17

Whole Page

- *Let's read the first two lines together:* On my way to school, we pass a trash truck that ran out of gas.
- *A trash truck is full of things people throw away. Why can't the trash truck move?* (It ran out of gas.)
- *Lets read the last two lines:* On top of that truck sit two apes and a duck! *What animals are sitting on the truck?* (two apes and a duck)

Is it normal to see two apes and a duck sitting on a trash truck? Tell your partner why or why not.

Pages 16–17

Pig and I run fast, fast, fast!
We get on the bus at last.
Huff, puff! The bus zips **away**.
Pig makes me late for school today!

16

Pages 18–19

Apes and a duck hop in the bus.
They sit down with the rest of us.

18

On my way to school, we pass
a trash truck that ran out of gas.
On top of that truck,
sit two apes and a duck!

17

Slip, flip! The bus zips away.
Apes make me late for school today!

19

Page 18

Whole Page

- *Let's read this page together:* Apes and a duck hop in the bus. They sit down with the rest of us.
- *Who gets on the bus on this page?* (apes and a duck) *Look at the picture. What is the second ape carrying?* (bananas)

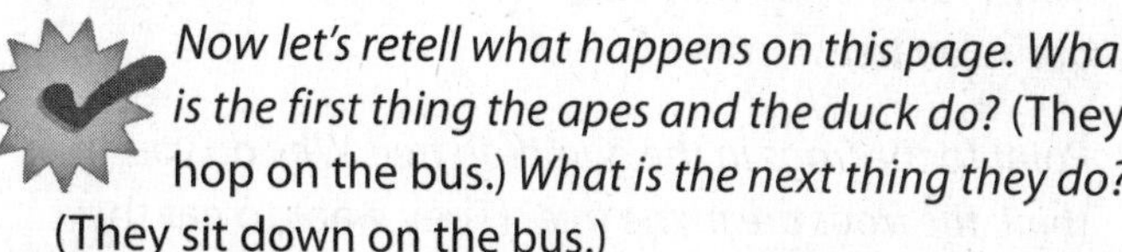

Now let's retell what happens on this page. What is the first thing the apes and the duck do? (They hop on the bus.) *What is the next thing they do?* (They sit down on the bus.)

Page 19

Whole Page

- *What does the bus do?* (It zips away.)
- *Point to the dog in the picture. Does the dog get on the bus?* (no) *Does the dog stand still, or does it slip and flip?* (The dog slips and flips.)
- *Let's read page 19 together.* Slip, flip! The bus zips away. Apes make me late for school today!
- *Does the boy get to school on time?* (No, he is late.) *What animals are making him late for school?* (a pig, a duck, apes)

Synonyms and Circumlocution

Remind children that they can ask for synonyms to help clarify words or expressions they do not understand. Ask, *What is another way of saying "zips away"?* (leaves quickly)

On My Way to School

Page 20

Whole Page

- *What kind of animals do you see on this page?* (frogs)
- *Let's read this page together:* On my way to school, I see frogs up in a gumdrop tree.
- *Gumdrops are a kind of candy. Gumdrops taste like fruit. Fruit grows on trees. Do you think gumdrop candy grows on trees?* (no)
- *Point to the frogs in the gumdrop tree. Why do you think the frogs are in the tree?* (They want to eat the gumdrops.)
- *Are frogs in gumdrop trees a normal thing to see on the way to school?* (no)

Page 21

Whole Page

- *What do you see falling from the tree?* (gumdrops)
- *The frogs in the tree are holding scissors. Why are they cutting the gumdrops?* (to make them fall)
- *The frogs on the ground are holding mops. What are they mopping up?* (gumdrops)
- *Let's read this page together in an excited voice:* Plip, plop! The gumdrops drop. Two frogs cut. Two frogs mop.
- Plip, plop *is a sound. What is making the sound* plip, plop? (the falling gumdrops)

Now let's retell what happens on these two pages. (The boy is still on the bus. He sees frogs in a gumdrop tree. The frogs cut down the gumdrops and mop them up.)

Pages 20–21

On my way to school, I see frogs up in a gumdrop tree.

20

Pages 22–23

Frogs hop in the bus.
They sit down with the rest of us.
Hip! Hop! The bus zips away.
Frogs make me late for school today!

22

Plip, plop! The gumdrops drop.
Two frogs cut. Two frogs mop.

21

Here we go, just one last stop.
Frogs hop in the lake. Plip, plop!

23

Page 22

Whole Page

- *Two frogs are carrying something. Put your finger on what they are carrying. What do you think is in the bags?* (gumdrops)
- *Let's read the page together.*
- *The bus stops to pick up the frogs. Will the boy get to school on time?* (No, he is late.) *What animals are making him late for school?* (a pig, two apes, a duck, and some frogs)

Page 23

Whole Page

- *Let's read this page together:* Here we go, just one last stop. Frogs hop in the lake. Plip, plop!
- *What does the bus do on this page?* (It stops.) *What do the frogs do then?* (They hop in the lake.)

PARTNERS *Point to the frogs in the water. Do you think the frogs are having fun? Tell your partner how you know.* (Yes, they are hopping and splashing.)

Page 24

Whole Page

- *What kind of animals do you see on this page?* (two apes and a duck) *Point to the duck. Point to the apes.*
- *Let's read this page:* Duck is off to get some gas. Apes fish and nap in the grass.

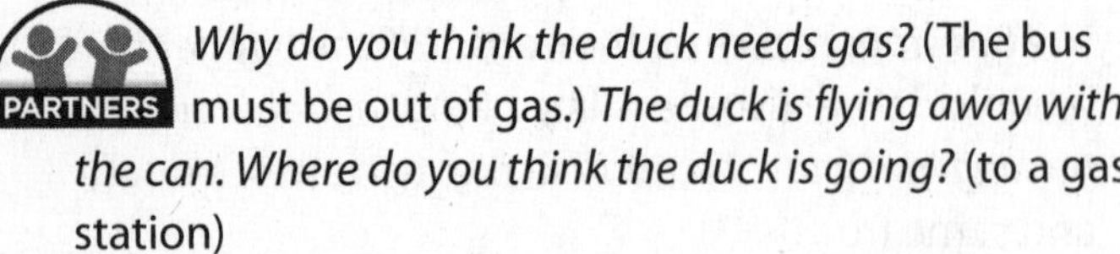

Why do you think the duck needs gas? (The bus must be out of gas.) *The duck is flying away with the can. Where do you think the duck is going?* (to a gas station)

- *Point to the apes. What are the apes doing?* (One ape is fishing. One ape is taking a nap.)

Page 25

Whole Page

- *Let's read page 25:* Tick, tock! The bus zips away. It looks like I am late today!
- *The bus is finally going again! Do you think the boy is going to get to school on time? Or is he going to be late?* (He'll probably be late.)
- *The words* tick *and* tock *sound like noises made by a clock. The author probably uses the clock sound to remind us that the boy is late. Let's say it together:* tick, tock, tick, tock.
- *Point to the banana. Who do you think tossed it out of the bus?* (one of the apes)

Pages 24–25

Duck is off to get some gas.
Apes fish and nap in the grass.

24

Pages 26–27

Now the bus drops me off at school.
I see a crocodile slink out of a pool!

26

Tick, tock! The bus zips away.
It looks like I am late today!

25

I think it slid under the gate.
And that, Miss Blake, is **why** I am late!

27

Page 26

Whole Page

- *Let's read this page together:* Now the bus drops me off at school. I see a crocodile slink out of a pool!

  The boy finally gets to school. But what does he see then? (a crocodile) *Point to the crocodile. The crocodile slinks out of the pool. Let's pretend we are crocodiles that slink.* (Demonstrate slinking.)

Page 27

Whole Page

- *Let's read the first sentence together:* I think it slid under the gate. *Who does the word* it *tell about? Who slid under the gate?* (the crocodile)
- *The boy tells Miss Blake why he is late. Who is Miss Blake?* (the boy's teacher)

Let's go back to the beginning and use the pictures to help us retell the story. (Help children retell the story spread-by-spread.)

Seek Clarification

Some children may be confused by complex syntax. Encourage children to always seek clarification when they encounter a sentence that does not make sense to them. For example, *I don't understand this sentence.*

Signs We See

Access Core Content

Teacher Note Pose the questions after you read the paragraph or page indicated.

Page 30

Photo

- *Look at the photos on this page. There are many signs.* (Point to signs.) *The title of this article is "Signs We See." Say it with me:* Signs We See.
- *Signs give us information. They tell us things we need to know. You have seen this red sign before.* (Point to the stop sign.) *Let's read it together:* stop. *This sign can tell people to stop walking. It can tell people driving cars to stop, too.*
- (Point to picture on "Crossing Ahead" sign.) *Is this a picture or words?* (a picture) *It's a picture, or a symbol. Say it with me:* symbol. *It shows us something we need to know, but not with words.*
- (Point to the words "Crossing Ahead" sign.) *Here are the words. They say* Crossing Ahead. *This sign tells people to drive carefully because children are crossing the street.*

Text

- *Let's read this page together.* (Read one sentence at a time and have children repeat.) *Now read this page after me.*

Page 31

Photo

- *Do you see a stop sign in the picture? Show your partner. Are these children going to school or to a playground? How do you know?* (They are going to school because they are carrying book bags.)

Text

- *Listen as I read this page.* (Read page.) *Does Zack take a bus to school, or does he walk to school?* (He walks to school.) *Raise your hand if you walk to school. How do signs help Zack?* (They help him get to school safely.)

(Point to the word *signs* in the second sentence.) *This word is* signs. *Read it with me:* signs. *Help your partner find the word* signs *two more times on this page.*

Pages 30–31

Read Together
Social Studies
Genre
Nonfiction gives information about a topic.
Text Feature
A Sign uses words or pictures to give information.
Content Vocabulary
signs
symbol
map
LOG ON FIND OUT
Social Studies Signs and Symbols
www.macmillanmh.com
Signs We See
STOP
What helps you get to school?
Signs, symbols, and maps help kids get to school.
STOP
SCHOOL XING
CROSSING AHEAD
30

Pages 32–33

Jake rides the bus to school. The bus driver sees signs on the way. Some signs have words on them. The signs help the bus driver get to school safely.

SCHOOL BUS

32

Social Studies

Zack walks to school. He sees signs on the way. Some signs have symbols on them. The signs help Zack get to school safely.

31

Pam's mother drives her to a new school today. She looks at a map. The map shows where the school is.

Signs, symbols, and maps help us get to where we want to go safely and easily.

Connect and Compare

- What signs and symbols do you see in this piece? What do they tell you?
- What signs and symbols might the bus pass in *On My Way to School*?

33

Page 32

Photo

- *Look at the large photo. Show your partner the children getting on the school bus.* (Point to boy at the front of the line.) *This boy's name is Jack. He takes the bus to school. Raise your hand if you come to school on a bus.*
- *Who drives a school bus?* (a bus driver) *Let's all point to a bus driver on this page.* (Point to the humorous elephant bus driver.)
- *Look at the photo of the sign. Show your partner the sign. This sign has a word. It says "Yield." It tells the bus driver to let other buses and cars go first.*

Text

- *Listen as I read this page.* (Read page.) *How do signs help the bus driver?* (Signs help the bus driver get to school safely.)

Page 33

Photo

- *Look at the large photo. Show your partner the girl and her mother. The girl's name is Pam. Are Pam and her mother walking or in a car?* (They are in a car.) *Raise your hand if you come to school in a car.*
- *Look at the small photo.* (Point to map in inset.) *This is a map. Say it with me:* map. *A map shows streets and roads. It can help you find places you need to get to.*

Paragraph 1

- *Listen as I read this paragraph.* (Read paragraph.) *Are Pam and her mother going home or to school?* (to school) *Why are they looking at a map?* (They need to find Pam's new school.)

Paragraph 2

- *Let's read this paragraph together.*

I see many signs on the way to school. What signs do you see on the way to school? Tell your partner about a sign you see.

Name ______________________

Vocabulary

Copy each new word on the line.
Draw a picture.

Word	Illustration
bus ______	
bicycle ______	

© Macmillan/McGraw-Hill

Name ____

Read each question and prompt. Discuss the answers with your group. Use your Leveled Reader to find details to support your answers. Then write your answers on another sheet of paper.

1. Tell about the characters in your book.

2. Tell three things that happen in the story. Tell what happens first, next, and last.

3. Talk about how friends help each other in the story.

4. Is there a big surprise for one character? Describe it for your classmates.

5. Show your favorite illustration to the group. Why do you like it?

© Macmillan/McGraw-Hill

Smile, Mike!

Pages 42–43

Prior to reading the selection with children, they should have listened to the selection on **StudentWorks Plus**, the interactive eBook. In addition, selection vocabulary should have been pretaught using the **Visual Vocabulary Resources**.

Access Core Content

Teacher Note Pose the questions after you read the paragraph or page indicated.

Pages 42–43

Title and Illustrations

- *Look at the pictures on pages 42 and 43. I see people in a family.* (Point to family members as you name them.) *Point to the grandmother. Point to the grandfather.*
- *Now point to the children. How many children do you see?* (two) *Point to the brother. That's the boy. Now point to the sister. That's the girl. Who is holding a cat, the brother or the sister?* (brother)
- *I also see a mother and father with a baby. Mike is the baby. Point to Mike. Is Mike smiling in the picture?* (yes) *Is he happy or sad?* (He is happy.)

Point to the dog. Tell your partner who is holding the dog. Is it Mike's mother or his father? (The father is holding the dog.)

- *Let's read the title of this story together:* Smile, Mike!
- Smile, Mike! *is a play. A play is usually read out loud. Each person who helps to read a play pretends to be one of the characters.*

Pages 42–43

Pages 44–45

 **Mike:** Waaaah!

 **Mom:** Here we are, little Mike.

 **Dad:** Did you **call** us?
Do you want to eat?
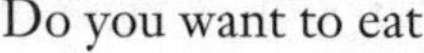

 **Mom:** No, he just had a fine snack.

45

Page 44

Whole Page

- *The top of this page says* Meet the Characters. *The page shows the names and faces of the characters in the play.*
- *Mike is a character in the play.* (Point to Mike.) *Say his name after me:* Mike. (Point to the other characters in turn, and have children repeat each name.)
- *You probably already know that* Mom *and* Dad *are names children use for their mother and father.* Gram *is another name for a grandmother, and* Pops *is another name for a grandfather.*

Page 45

Whole Page

PARTNERS *Look at the picture. Mike in his crib. Tell your partner what Mike is doing.* (crying, yelling) *Who else do you see in the picture?* (the mother and father)

- *Look at the first line. The picture and the first word in the line let you know who is speaking. The first word is* Mike. *Who says this first line?* (Mike)
- *The other word on this line tells what Mike says. He is making a loud crying sound. I don't think he's happy! Say the sound after me:* Waaaah!
- *What are some things that make babies cry?* (They cry if they are tired. They cry if they are hungry.) *Why do you think Mike is crying?* (Question is open.)
- *Who is the next character? Look at the picture and the word.* (Mom) *Let's read Mom's words together:* Here we are, little Mike.
- *Who speaks next?* (Dad) *Let's read Dad's words together:* Did you call us? Do you want to eat? *Who is* you *in* Did you call us? (Mike)
- *Mom answers Dad's question. I'll read her answer, and you repeat it after me:* No, he just had a fine snack. (Children should echo.) *Do you think Mike is hungry?* (no) *How do you know?* (He had a snack. He just ate something.)

Smile, Mike!

Page 46

Whole Page

- *Juan is holding a cat.* (Point to the cat in the picture.) *Does Mike look happy to see the cat?* (no) *How do you know?* (He is still crying. He is not happy.)
- *That's right. Mike is not happy, even when he sees the cat.* (Point to the picture and the word *Mike* in the first line.) *This tells us that what Mike says. Let's read the word together:* Waaaah!
- *Point to Ana's picture and name in the second line. Mike's sister Ana says the next words. Let's read Ana's words together:* Why is Mike so sad? *Do we know why Mike is sad?* (no)
- Point to Juan's picture and name in the third line. *Let's say this name together:* Juan. *Who is talking now?* (Juan) *Say his words after me:* Let's make him happy. Do you want this cat, Mike? (Children should echo.)
- *Mike answers Juan's question. Now he uses words, not a crying sound. Repeat Mike's words after me:* No! No! No cat! (Children should echo.)

Page 47

Whole Page

- *People are singing in this picture. Who is singing?* (Mom, Dad, Ana, Juan) *Why do you think they are singing to Mike?* (They want to make him happy.)
- *This is Ana's picture and her name. Ana talks and sings. Let's read her words together:* Let's sing. *Listen as I sing her song:* A-B-C-D-E-F-G-H-I- *What song is she singing?* (the alphabet song) *Let's sing the letters together.*

✔ *Think about the last letter that Ana sang.* What was it? (*I*) *What letter do you think Dad will start with?* (*J*) *Let's sing Dad's part of the song together:* J-K-L-M-N-O-P-.

- *Now Juan will sing the last part of the song. What letter do you think he will start with?* (Q) *Let's sing Juan's part of the song together.*
- *Does Mike want to hear his family sing? How do you know?* (No, he does not want them to sing. He says No! No! No sing!)

Pages 46–47

 **Mike:** Waaaah!

 **Ana:** Why is Mike **so** sad?

 **Juan:** Let's make him happy.
Do you want this cat, Mike?

 **Mike:** No! No! No cat!

46

Pages 48–49

 **Gram:** Why is our little Mike so sad?

 **Mike:** Waaaah!

 **Pops:** **How** can we make him smile?

Gram: Let's clap hands!

48

 **Ana:** Let's sing. 

 **Dad:** J - K - L - M - N - O - P -

 **Juan:** Q - R - S - T - U - V - W - X - Y - Z.

 **Mike:** No! No! No sing!

47

 **Pops:** Clap with us, Mike.

 **Mike:** Waaah!

 **Gram:** Clap hands with us.

 **Mike:** No! No! No clap!

49

Page 48

Whole Page

- *Gram is clapping her hands. Point to Gram in the picture.*
- *Let's think about what we've read already. Why do you think Gram is clapping her hands?* (to make Mike happy)
- *Gram and Pops talk to Mike on this page. Let's read the whole page together. Make sure you look at each picture and read each name so you know who is speaking.*

Page 49

Whole Page

- *Who is clapping their hands in the picture?* (Mom, Dad, and Pops) *What do you think they are trying to do?* (make Mike stop crying)
- *Pops talks first on this page. Let's read his words together:* Clap with us, Mike. *What does Pops want Mike to do? Why?* (He wants Mike to clap his hands. He wants Mike to be happy.)
- *Let's read the rest of this page together.*
- *Does Mike want to clap with his family? How do you know?* (No, he does not want to clap with them. He says No! No! No clap!)

PARTNERS *What has the family done so far to make Mike stop crying?* (brought the cat, sang a song, clapped) *What else might they do to make Mike happy?* (They might tickle him, bring a toy, or pick him up.)

- **Directionality**
  Ask children to place their finger where you start reading (top left). Ask where you finish reading on this page (bottom right).

Smile, Mike!

Page 50

Whole Page

- *I see a duck.* (Point to the duck as you name it.) *Who is holding the duck, Mom or Ana?* (Ana)
- *Why do you think Ana shows Mike the duck?* (She wants to make him happy.)
- *Let's read what Ana says:* This funny duck will make Mike smile. *Does it?* (No, he cries.)
- *Let's read what Mom says to Mike:* Do not be sad, Mike. Quack with us. *A duck makes a quacking sound. Let's do what Mom says.* (Demonstrate quacking.)
- *Does the duck make Mike happy?* (no) *How do you know?* (Mike says, No! No! No quack!)

Page 51

Whole Page

- *I see bubbles.* (Point to the bubbles as you name them.) *Who is blowing bubbles?* (Dad)

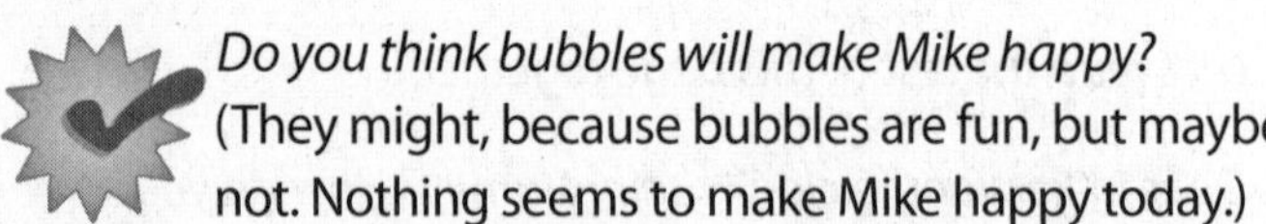

Do you think bubbles will make Mike happy? (They might, because bubbles are fun, but maybe not. Nothing seems to make Mike happy today.)

- *Let's read this page together. Remember to use an excited voice when you read a sentence that ends in an exclamation mark.*

Pages 50–51

 **Ana:** This **funny** duck will make Mike smile.

 **Mike:** Waaah!

 **Mom:** Do not be sad, Mike. Quack with us. Quack! Quack!

Mike: No! No! No quack!

50

Pages 52–53

 **Ana:** Mike, look at my funny duck.

 **Mike:** Waaah!

 **Juan:** And look at my little cat.

52

 **Dad:** Look, Mike! I can make bubbles!

 **Mike:** Waaah!

 **Gram:** And I can get a bubble.

 **Mike:** No! No! No bubbles!

51

 **Gram:** Look at me, Mike.

 **Mike:** Waaah!

 **Dad:** Look! **There** are **more** bubbles!

53

Pages 52–53

Whole Page

- *These pictures show ways the family has tried to make Mike stop crying. What is each person doing?* (Juan is showing Mike the cat. Ana is showing him the duck. Dad is blowing bubbles, and Gram is trying to catch them.)
- *The whole family is trying to make Mike happy. Let's read the lines together.*
- *The family is doing a lot to make Mike happy. Do you think it's working? Why or why not?* (It's not working. Mike keeps crying.)

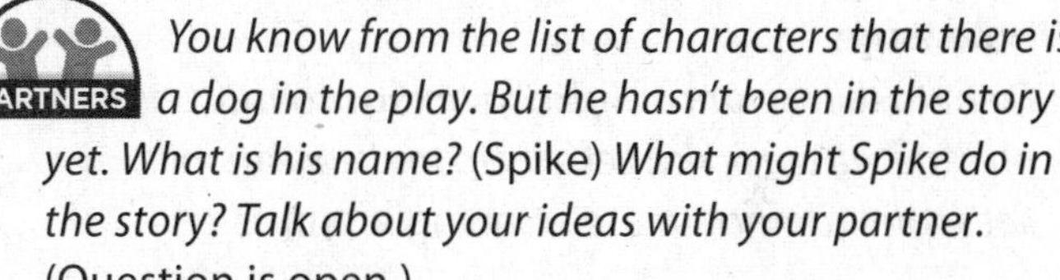

PARTNERS *You know from the list of characters that there is a dog in the play. But he hasn't been in the story yet. What is his name?* (Spike) *What might Spike do in the story? Talk about your ideas with your partner.* (Question is open.)

Non-verbal Cues

Remind children that they can use non-verbal cues to share information when they are not able to do so verbally. Encourage children to use pantomime or draw.

Smile, Mike!

Page 54

Whole Page

- *Point to Spike. Why did do you think he came to see Mike?* (He heard him crying. He wants to make him smile.)
- *Let's read the page together.*

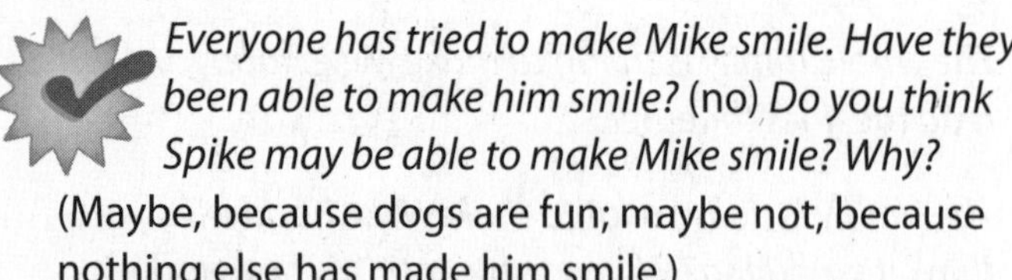

Everyone has tried to make Mike smile. Have they been able to make him smile? (no) *Do you think Spike may be able to make Mike smile? Why?* (Maybe, because dogs are fun; maybe not, because nothing else has made him smile.)

Page 55

Whole Page

- *Point to the picture of Spike spinning around. Let's pretend we are Spike. Let's try to make Mike smile. Let's spin!* (Demonstrate spinning around.)
- *Now listen as I read this page. Who says Spike is funny?* (Ana)
- *Gram says that Mike has a big smile. Look at the picture. Is she right?* (yes)
- *Who made Mike smile?* (Spike) *Which words let you know?* (Spike made Mike smile.)

Request Assistance

Remind children of expressions they can use to request assistance from the teacher or their partners, such as *Can you show me in the picture? Can you repeat it, please?*

Pages 54–55

Pops: Look, Mike! There is Spike.

Mike: Waaah!

Juan: Did you come to see Mike, Spike?

Ana: Spike wants to make Mike smile.

54

Pages 56–57

Juan: Good dog! This is for you, Spike.

Dad: Show us how you can jump.

Mike: Jump, Spike! Jump!

Spike: Ruff! Ruff!

56

 **Gram:** Look at Spike spin.

 **Ana:** Spike is funny!

 **Gram:** Look! Mike has a big smile.

 **Pops:** Spike made Mike smile.

55

 **Dad:** At last, Mike is happy.

 **Mom:** Now it is time for bed.

 **Ana:** Mike will get some rest now.

Gram: And so will we!

57

Pages 56–57

Whole Page

- *I see a dog treat.* (Point to the dog treat in the picture on page 56.) *It has a shape like a bone. Dogs love to eat dog treats.*
- *Who do you think will get the treat?* (Spike) *Does Spike look happy to get a treat?* (yes) *Listen as I read page 56.*
- *Mike and Dad want Spike to jump for the bone. What does Spike say as he jumps?* (Ruff! Ruff!) *He is excited.*
- *Now let's read pages 56 and 57 like a play. Each of you will read a part, and I'll help you.* (Assign parts and have children read. Depending on the number of children in the group, you may have to read a part yourself or repeat the activity to give everyone a chance to read.)

Look at the picture on page 57. What is MIke doing? (sleeping) *What is Spike doing?* (sleeping) *Look at Mike's family. They are leaving the room. What do you think they will do next?* (go to sleep)

Healthy Eating

Access Core Content

Teacher Note Pose the questions after you read the paragraph or page indicated.

Page 60

Title and Photo

- *Listen as I read the title:* Healthy Eating. *Say the first word with me:* healthy. *When you are healthy, you feel good and your body is strong.*
- *Point to the boy in the picture. This boy will tell us about his family and the foods they eat. Let's read the rest of the page together.*

Text

- *Healthful foods make people healthy. Say the word with me:* healthful. *Do healthful foods make people sick or healthy?* (They make people healthy.)
- *What do healthful foods give the family?* (energy) *How do you know?* (The article says, Healthful foods give us energy to walk, work, and have fun.)
- *When you have energy, you can do a lot of things. If you have energy, you are not tired. Let's walk as if we are really tired.* (Demonstrate walking slowly, as if exhausted.) *Now let's walk as if we have a lot of energy.* (Demonstrate walking briskly, with energy.)

Page 61

Diagram

- *Let's look at the diagram together.* (Point to the word Grains in the diagram.) *Say this word with me:* grains. (Point to the grains in the picture.) *These are some foods made with grains. What foods do you see here?* (bread, cereal, rice) (Repeat the procedure with each food group shown on the page.)

Text

- *Now listen as I read this page.*
- *Muscles make us strong. We use them to move our arms and legs. What do meat and fish help muscles do?* (grow)

Pages 60–61

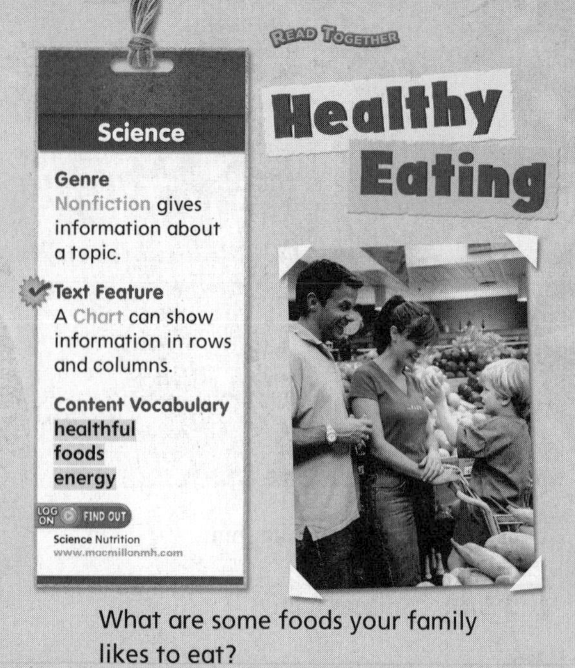

Science
Genre
Nonfiction gives information about a topic.
Text Feature
A Chart can show information in rows and columns.
Content Vocabulary
healthful
foods
energy
LOG ON FIND OUT
Science Nutrition
www.macmillanmh.com
READ TOGETHER
Healthy Eating

What are some foods your family likes to eat?

My family likes to eat **healthful foods**. Healthful foods give us **energy** to walk, work, and have fun.

60

Pages 62–63

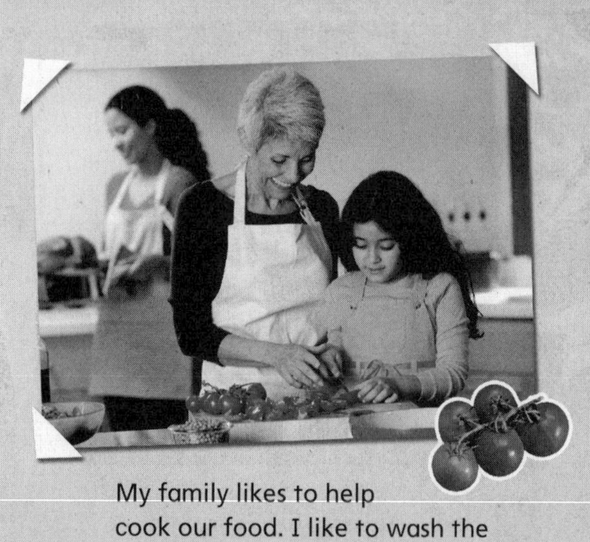

My family likes to help cook our food. I like to wash the vegetables. Grandmother chops them. Then I put them in a big bowl. We made a salad!

62

Science

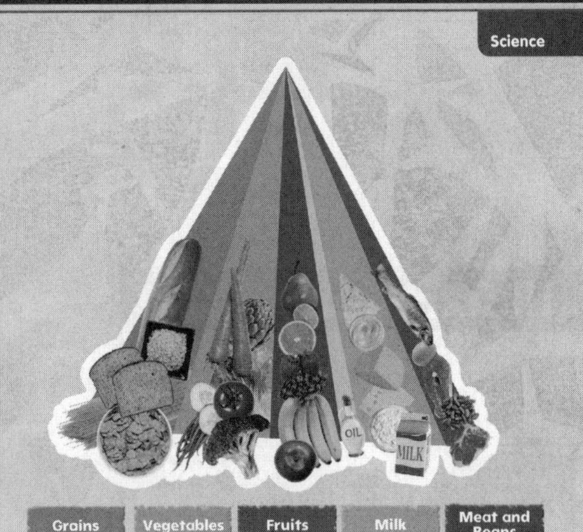

Grains | Vegetables | Fruits | Milk | Meat and Beans

Mom and Dad buy foods that are good for our family to eat. They pick healthful foods like milk, bread, meat, fish, fruits, and vegetables. Grains give us energy. Meat and fish help our muscles grow.

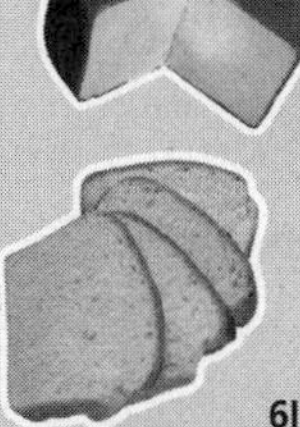

61

My family made fish, carrots, and rice. They are all healthful foods. They taste good, too!

What healthful foods does your family like to eat?

Connect and Compare

- What does the chart tell you about food?
- What other foods can you think of for each category?

63

Page 62

Photo

- *Point to the family in the picture. Are they cooking or eating?* (cooking) *What do you think they are making?* (Question is open, though the text will identify the food as salad.)

Text

- *Let's read the first sentence:* My family likes to help cook our food. *Let's read the rest of the page. As we read, we will stop and do the action that each sentence tells about.* (Chorally read one sentence at a time. Stop after each sentence and demonstrate the action of washing vegetables, chopping vegetables, and putting them in a big bowl.)
- *What healthful food did the girl and her grandmother make?* (salad) *What words tell you?* (We made a salad!)

Page 63

Photo

- *Point to the family in the picture. Are they cooking or eating?* (eating) *What makes you think so?* (They are sitting at the table. Some of the food is on the plates.)

Text

- *Listen as I read the first sentence:* My family made fish, carrots, and rice. *What healthful foods did we read about on this page?* (fish, carrots, and rice)
- *Now listen as I read the rest of the page.*

Talk with your partner. Do you think healthful foods taste good? Tell your partner what healthful foods your family likes to eat.

Vocabulary

Name ______________________________

Copy each new word on the line.
Draw a picture.

Word	Illustration
clap	
cry	

© Macmillan/McGraw-Hill

Name ____________________

Book Talk

Read each question and prompt. Discuss the answers with your group. Use your Leveled Reader to find details to support your answers. Then write your answers on another sheet of paper.

1. Tell about the family in your book.

2. What is different about an older child and a younger child in your book? What is the same?

3. Describe a problem one child has.

4. How is the problem solved?

5. Which character seemed a lot like you? Share your ideas.

© Macmillan/McGraw-Hill

Masks! Masks! Masks!

Pages 70–71

Prior to reading the selection with children, they should have listened to the selection on **StudentWorks Plus,** the interactive eBook. In addition, selection vocabulary should have been pretaught using the **Visual Vocabulary Resources.**

Access Core Content

Teacher Note Pose the questions after you read the paragraph or page indicated.

Page 70

Title and Photos

- The *title of the article is* Masks! Masks! Masks! *Let's point to the two masks on this page.* (Point to them.) *Now say the word* masks *with me:* masks.

Text

- *A mask hides your face so that no one can see it.* (Cover your face with your hands.) *Say the word* hide *with me:* hide.
- *You can put on a mask.* (Mime putting on mask.) *You can put on a jacket.* (Mime putting on a jacket.) *Say the words* put on *with me:* put on. *Let's pretend to put on mittens. Let's pretend to put on a hat. Now let's pretend to put on a mask.*
- *A mask can make you look different. You can also act different in a mask. What sound might you make if you had on a cat mask?* (purr, meow)

Page 71

Whole Page

- *Point to the mask in the picture. The person in the picture is also wearing a costume, or special clothing. Say the word* costume *with me:* costume.
- *A tale is another word for story. Find the word* tales *on the page, and point to it. Then say it with me:* tales. *What other tales, or stories have we read?* (Responses will vary.)

Pages 70–71

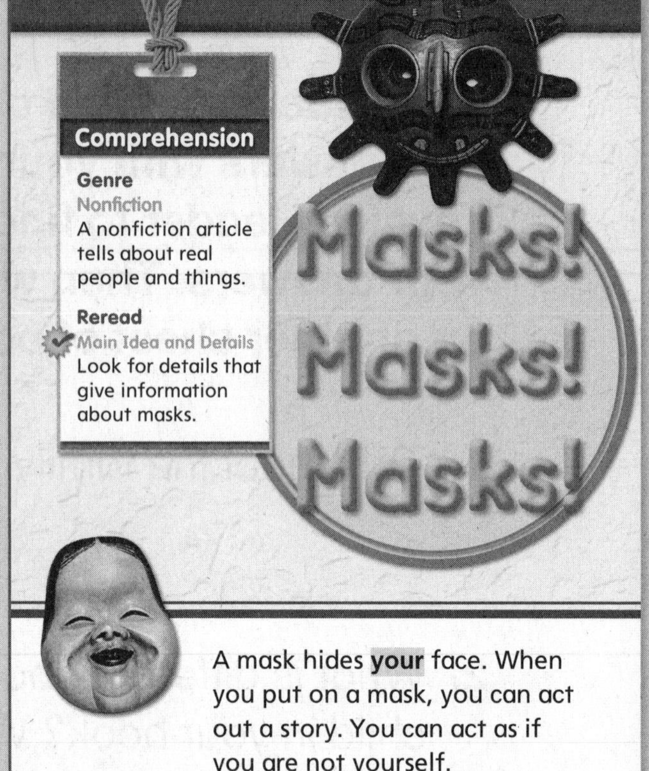

Pages 72–73

This mask is **from** Africa. What shapes can you see on the mask? Which animal is on top?
72

People make masks in **every** land.
Masks help them tell tales.
And masks help them have fun.

71

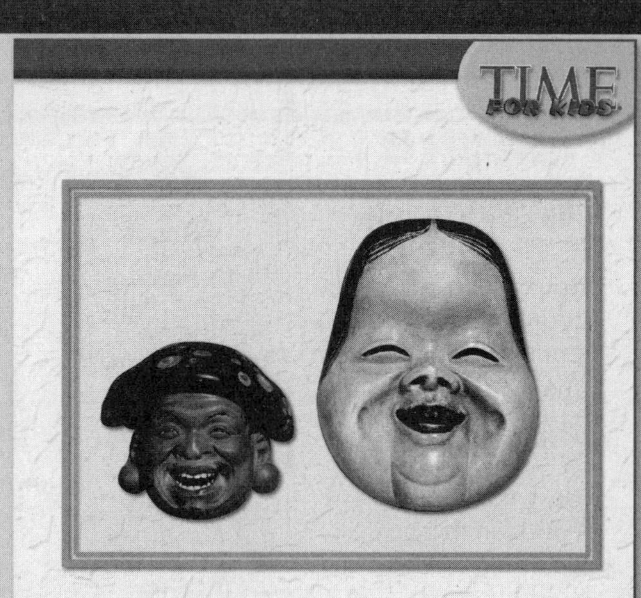

The masks on this page are from Japan. People use them when they act in plays. What tales could they tell with such masks?

73

- *Let's read the page together:* People make masks in every land. Masks help them tell tales. And masks help them have fun. *What do people use masks for?* (to tell tales, to have fun)

Page 72

Whole Page

- *Let's read this page together.*
- *Point to the mask in this picture. Where is it from?* (Africa) *Africa is a very big land across the ocean. It is made up of many countries.*
- *Let's name some of the shapes on the mask.* (Help students name shapes as you point to them: oval, circle, rectangle, triangle.) *You can also see a bird.*

Page 73

Whole Page

- *These masks are from Japan. Point to them. Japan is a country. It is made up of many islands. Islands are land with water on all sides.* (Draw a group of islands on the board.)
- *Let's read the second sentence about the masks together:* People use them when they act in plays. *A play is a story that is acted out. You can watch it! Where do actors usually stand and move when they are in a play?* (on a stage)
- *When people act, they pretend to be another person or even an animal. How does the mask help them?* (The mask helps them look like someone else. It also helps them feel like someone else.)
- *The actors might tell scary tales with these masks.* (Make a scared face.) *What other kinds of tales might they tell?* (happy, sad)

Make up a story about one of these masks with your partner. Then share it with the group.

Directionality

Ask children to place their finger where you start reading (top left). Ask where you finish reading on this page (bottom right).

Masks! Masks! Masks!

Page 74

Whole Page

- *Look at the mask in the picture. It is a bird. Let's point to the beak.* (Point to it.)
- *Let's think about what the mask is mostly made of. Is it made out of paper?* (Point to a piece of paper.) (no) *Is it made out of cloth?* (Point to a piece of cloth.) (no) *Is it made out of wood?* (Point to something wooden.) (yes) *How did the artist make the eye and all the colorful shapes?* (with paint)
- *It takes a lot of skill to make this mask. You have to learn how to do it. Then you have to practice a lot to do it well. What skills do we practice in class every day?* (reading, writing, spelling)

Page 75

Whole Page

- *Look at this mask from a country called Peru. What does the mask look like?* (the sun) *Point to the snakes.*
- *A snake is long and has no legs. Let's hiss like a snake and use our hands to show how snakes move.* (demonstrate)
- *Let's read this page together.*

Page 76

Illustration and Paragraph 1

- *Let's read the first sentence together:* You can make a mask, too! *What do you think we will learn from this page?* (how to make a mask)
- *Now let's read the rest of the paragraph together:* First, get a plate. Cut holes into it. Check that you can see. *Should we use a real plate or a paper plate? Why?* (paper, so we can cut into it) *When you check something, you make sure of it.*
- *Look at the first picture. The girl folded the plate in half like this.* (Demonstrate folding a piece of paper.) *She is cutting two holes in the plate. Say it with me:* holes. *Why does she need holes?* (to see; for eyes)

Pages 74–75

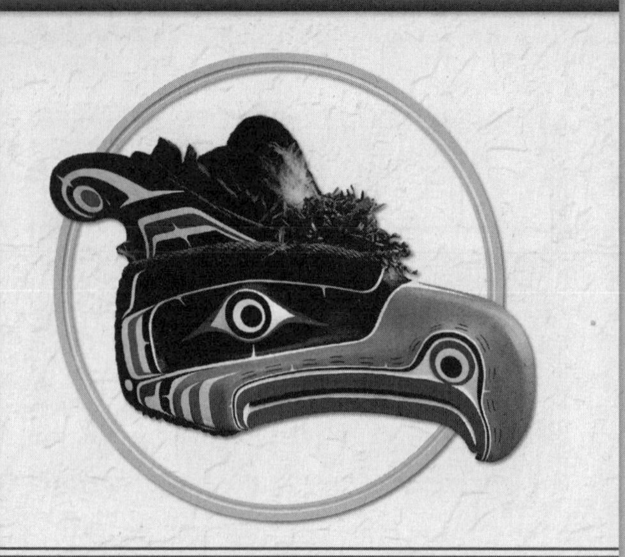

Look at this bird. How do you think this mask was made? What is it made from?

It takes much skill to make such a mask.

74

Page 76

Make a Mask

You can make a mask, too! First, get a plate. Cut holes **into** it. Check that you can see.

Next, color the mask. Paste fun things on it. **Soon** you will have a mask!

Last, tape a band on the back of the mask. Put the mask on. Who are you?

76

This mask is from Peru. It is shaped like the sun. Look at it. Can you see snakes?

75

Illustration and Paragraph 2

- *Let's read the second step together:* Next, color the mask. Paste fun things on it. Soon you will have a mask!
- *Look at the picture. The girl is coloring in her mask. What is she using to color it in?* (paint and a paintbrush)

Illustration and Paragraph 3

- *Let's read the last step together:* Last, tape a band on the back of the mask. Put the mask on. Who are you?

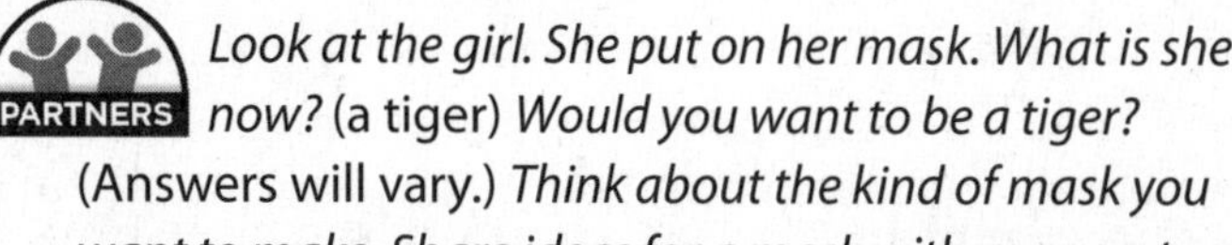

PARTNERS *Look at the girl. She put on her mask. What is she now?* (a tiger) *Would you want to be a tiger?* (Answers will vary.) *Think about the kind of mask you want to make. Share ideas for a mask with your partner.*

- *When you put on a mask, you use a band.* (Mime putting on a mask that has a band on the back.) *A band holds the mask on your head so it doesn't fall off.*

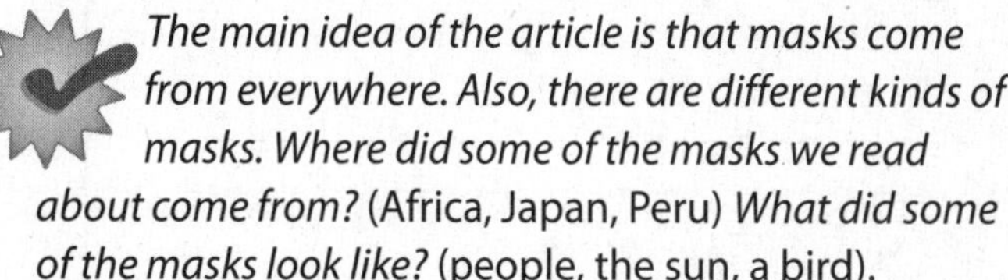

The main idea of the article is that masks come from everywhere. Also, there are different kinds of masks. Where did some of the masks we read about come from? (Africa, Japan, Peru) *What did some of the masks look like?* (people, the sun, a bird).

Monitor Oral Production

Remember to model self-corrective techniques on a regular basis as you speak to children. Pretend to mispronounce words and self-correct.

Name ______________________________

Copy each new word on the line.
Draw a picture.

Word	Illustration
tear	
shake	

© Macmillan/McGraw-Hill

Name ____________________

Book Talk

Read each question and prompt. Discuss the answers with your group. Use your Leveled Reader to find details to support your answers. Then write your answers on another sheet of paper.

1. What are some of the ways that art can be made?

2. Tell what fire does to glass so it can be made into art.

3. Explain how creating art with ice is the same as creating art with rock.

4. Describe what happens to clay when you put it into an oven.

5. Tell your group how you would like to make art.

© Macmillan/McGraw-Hill

Interactive Question - Response Guide

Rose Robot Cleans Up

Pages 88–89

Prior to reading the selection with children, they should have listened to the selection on **StudentWorks Plus**, the Interactive eBook. In addition, selection vocabulary should have been pretaught using the **Visual Vocabulary Resources**.

Access Core Content

Teacher Note Pose the questions after you read the paragraph or page indicated.

Pages 88–89

Illustration and Title

- *Let's look at the picture. I see two robots. Point to the robot boy. Now point to the robot girl.*
- *A robot is a machine that can look like a person. It can do some of the things that people do. This is a make-believe story about some robots.*
- *Look at the floor in the picture.* (Point to it.) *There are so many things there. I see a tambourine for making music. I see a key. I see nails and other things for building.* (Point to the things as you name them.) *What are some things that you see?* (boots, drum, wagon or cart)
- *There is so much stuff in this room! Do you think the room is neat or messy?* (messy)
- *Let's read the title of the story together:* Rose Robot Cleans Up. *This story is about a robot named Rose. Rose is a girl's name. Let's point to Rose Robot.*
- Clean up *means "to make something clean or neat." What do you see that is messy?* (the room) *What do you think Rose Robot is going to clean up?* (the mess in the room)?
-

Directionality

Ask children to place their finger where you start reading (top left). Ask where you finish reading on this page (bottom right).

Pages 88–89

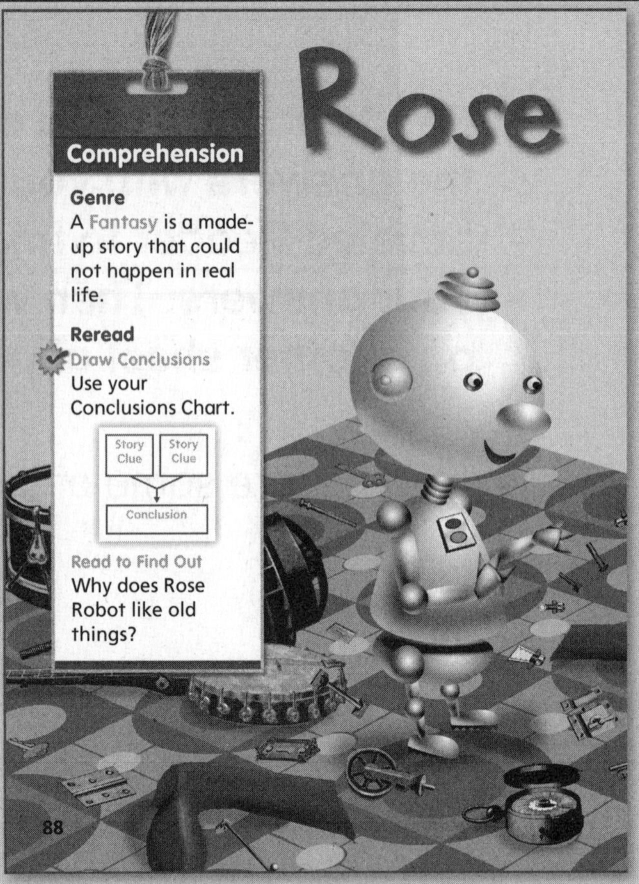

Rose
Comprehension
Genre
A Fantasy is a made-up story that could not happen in real life.
Reread
Draw Conclusions
Use your Conclusions Chart.
Story Clue
Story Clue
Conclusion
Read to Find Out
Why does Rose Robot like old things?
88

Pages 90–91

Rose Robot liked to **find old** things. Her little brother, Rob, liked to help.

"Rose, what will we do with this old junk?" asked Rob.

"We will use it," said Rose.

90

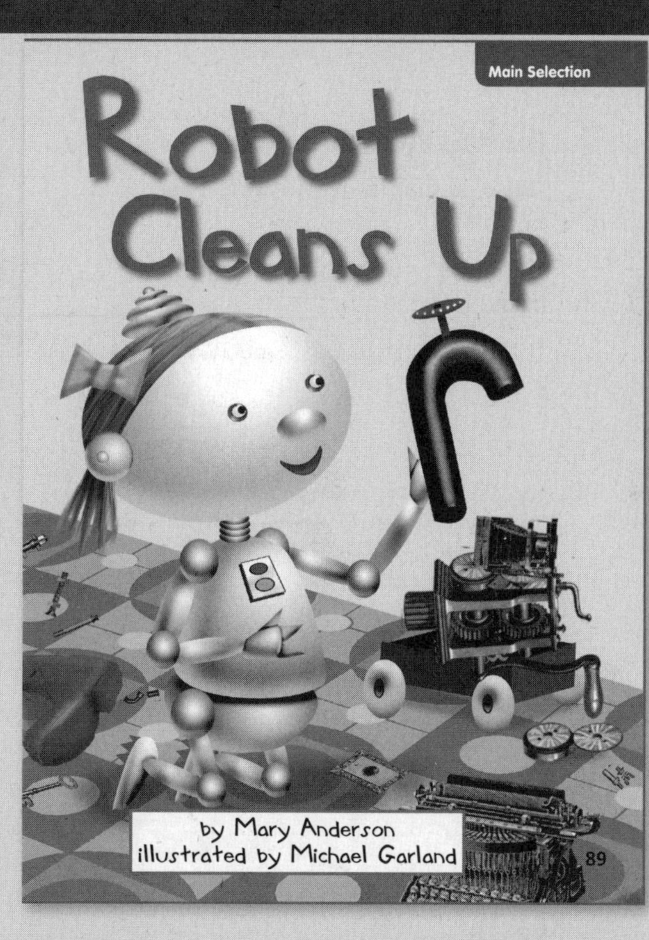

They passed Luke and his dad.

"This stuff broke," said Luke. "We are bringing it to the dump."

"But it is such good stuff!" said Rose. "I can use it."

Luke gave his old stuff to Rose.

91

Page 90

Illustration

- *Look at the picture. Rose is pulling a wagon. Say it with me:* wagon. *The wagon is full of old things.*

Text

- *Let's read the first sentence together:* Rose Robot liked to find old things. *Point to the word* find. *We look for something that is lost until we find it. We also find things that we weren't looking for. Say it with me:* find.
- *Now point to the word* old. *Something that is old is not new. Say it with me:* old.
- *Rose likes to find old things. Her little brother Rob likes to help her. Where do you think they are taking the old things?* (Question is open.)
- *Rob calls Rose's old things* junk. *Point to the word* junk. Junk *is stuff that nobody wants, like trash. Rob wants to know what they are going to do with all the junk.*
- *Let's read the last sentence on this page together:* "We will use it," said Rose. *Does Rose think that old things are junk?* (no) *Why does she want to keep everything and not throw it away?* (She wants to use it.) *I wonder how she will use all these things.*

Page 91

Whole Page

- *I see two more robots on this page. They are Luke and his dad. Point to Luke. Point to Luke's dad. Look at all the stuff on the grass! Why do you think Rose is talking to Luke and his dad.* (She probably wants the stuff.)
- *Let's read what Luke says together:* "This stuff broke," said Luke. "We are bringing it to the dump." *Luke and his dad have a lot of things that broke. The things don't work anymore.*
- *Luke and his dad want to take their broken things to the dump. The dump is a place people take trash. Does your family have to bring trash to the dump, or do trucks from the city or town pick it up?* (Answers will vary.)
- *Luke and his dad think this stuff is junk because it is broken. What does Rose think?* (She thinks it's good stuff. She can use it.)

Rose Robot Cleans Up

Page 92

Illustration

- *Look at the picture. I see Rose talking to two grown-up robots. Who do you think they are?* (Rose's parents) *What is behind Rose?* (her wagon full of old stuff) *Rose and her parents are talking about all the stuff.*

Text

- *Let's read the sentence that tells what Rose's mom said:* "Rose, is that more old stuff?" asked her mom.
- *Now let's read the sentence that tells what her dad said:* "What will you do with that junk?" asked her dad.
- *Rose called everything "good stuff" when she was talking to Luke. What does her mother call it?* (more old stuff) *What does her father call it?* (junk)

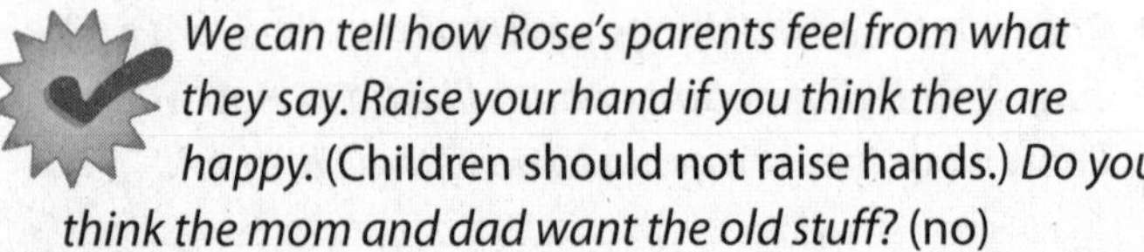

We can tell how Rose's parents feel from what they say. Raise your hand if you think they are happy. (Children should not raise hands.) *Do you think the mom and dad want the old stuff?* (no)

Page 93

Whole Page

- *Let's look at the picture together. Point to Rose. Rose is very busy doing something. Does Rose look happy or sad?* (happy)
- *Let's read this page together.*
- *Rose wants Rob to help her make a new toy. Point to the word* new. *Rose is using something old to make something new!*
- *Rose is putting a spring on a boot.* (Point to the spring and boot.) *Say* spring *with me:* spring. *Say* boot *with me:* boot. *Rose wants the boot and the spring to stick together. She is using glue to make them stick.*
- *Rose is making a new toy for Rob to jump in. Look at Rob. How do you think he feels?* (Question is open.)

Pages 92–93

Rose and Rob went home.

"Rose, is that more old stuff?" asked her mom.

"What will you do with that junk?" asked her dad.

"I am going to use it," said Rose.

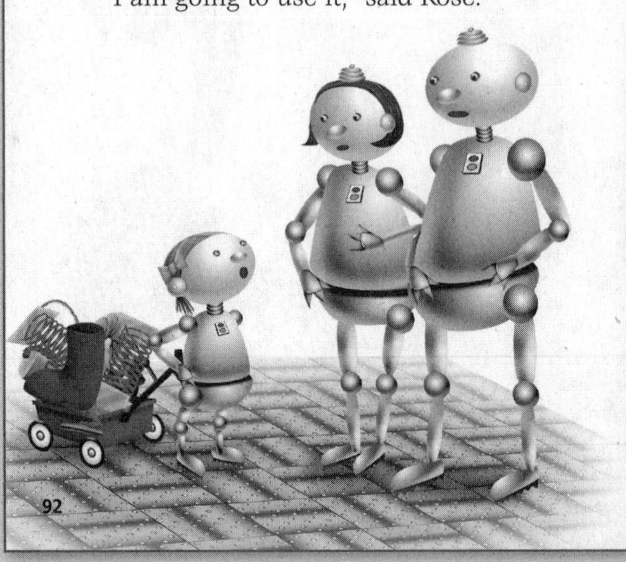

92

Pages 94–95

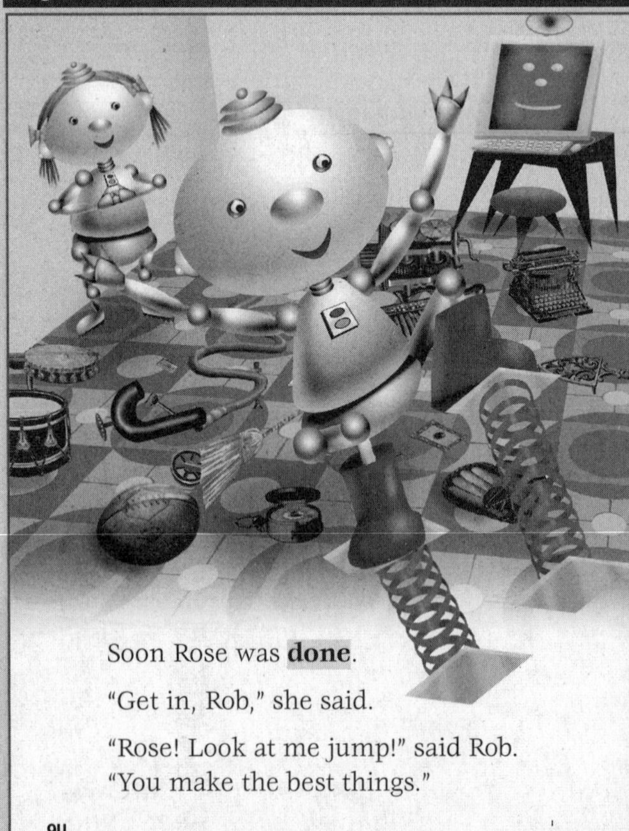

Soon Rose was **done**.

"Get in, Rob," she said.

"Rose! Look at me jump!" said Rob. "You make the best things."

94

Rose went to her room.

"Come and help me, Rob," she said. "I will make a **new** toy for you to jump in."

93

"What is that thumping?" asked Mom.

"What is going on up there?" asked Dad.

"Let's go find out," they said.

Page 94

Whole Page

- *Let's read the first sentence together:* Soon Rose was done. *Point to the word done. Done means "to be finished." So Rose was finished with what she was making.*
- *Look at the picture. What did Rose make?* (jumping boots for Rob) *Let's read the rest of the page together:* "Get in, Rob," she said. "Rose! Look at me jump!" said Rob. "You make the best things."

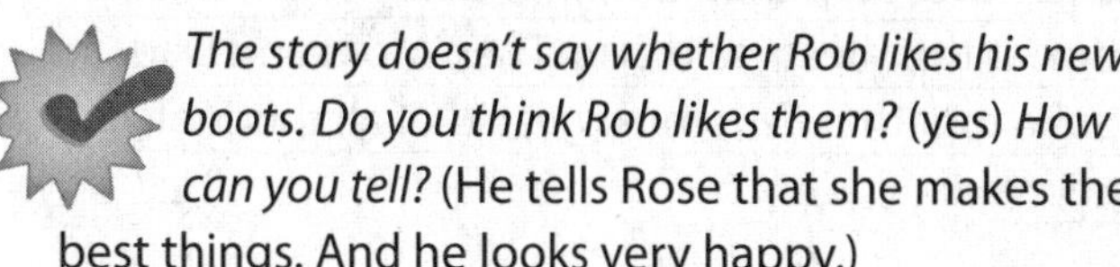

The story doesn't say whether Rob likes his new boots. Do you think Rob likes them? (yes) *How can you tell?* (He tells Rose that she makes the best things. And he looks very happy.)

- *Let's pretend to wear jumping boots like Rob's. Let's pull on the boots. There are springs on the bottom to help us jump. Now let's jump high!*

Page 95

Whole Page

- *Look at the picture on page 95. Mom is knitting, or making something out of yarn. Dad is reading a newspaper. Do people usually like to read in noisy places or quiet places?* (quiet places)
- *Mom and Dad are looking up. What makes them look up?* (They hear a noise.)
- *Let's read the first sentence together:* "What is that thumping?" asked Mom. *Mom hears a loud noise that sounds like this.* (Pound on the desk with your fist.)

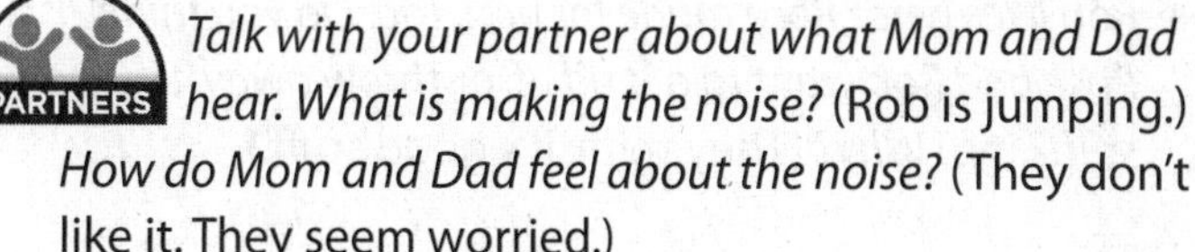

Talk with your partner about what Mom and Dad hear. What is making the noise? (Rob is jumping.) *How do Mom and Dad feel about the noise?* (They don't like it. They seem worried.)

> **Non-verbal Cues**
>
> Remind children that they can use non-verbal cues to share information when they are not able to do so verbally. Encourage children to use pantomime and sounds.

Rose Robot Cleans Up

Page 96

Illustration

- *Look at Rob. What is he doing?* (jumping) *Look at Rose's room. Is it neat or messy?* (messy)
- *Look at Mom and Dad. They see Rob jump. They see a mess in Rose's room. Do Mom and Dad like what they see?* (no) *How do you know?* (They look angry.)

Text

- *Let's read together what Mom and Dad say to Rob and Rose:* "Rob! Stop that jumping!" said Mom." "Rose! Look at this mess," said Dad. Then Mom and Dad spoke together. "We must get rid of all this junk," they said.
- *Mom and Dad are not very happy about this mess! They want to get rid of Rose's stuff. That means they want to take it out of the house.*

Page 97

Illustration

- *Let's look at what Rose made. This is a lampshade.* (Point to it.) *These are flashlights.* (Point to them.) *Point to the bottles Rob is holding. It looks like Rose has made some other new things from old stuff.*

Text

- *Rose made a special light to help her read. She made an instrument for Rob to play music on. Let's pretend we're holding the instrument and blowing the bottles to make music.* (demonstrate) *How do you think Rose feels about what she made?* (proud, happy, good)
- *Rob likes what Rose made for him, too. Do you think Rose and Rob want to get rid of, or throw away, the old stuff?* (no) *Why?* (They think it's good stuff.)

Pages 96–97

"Rob! Stop that jumping!" said Mom.

"Rose! Look at this mess," said Dad.

Then Mom and Dad spoke together. "We must get rid of all this junk," they said.

96

Pages 98–99

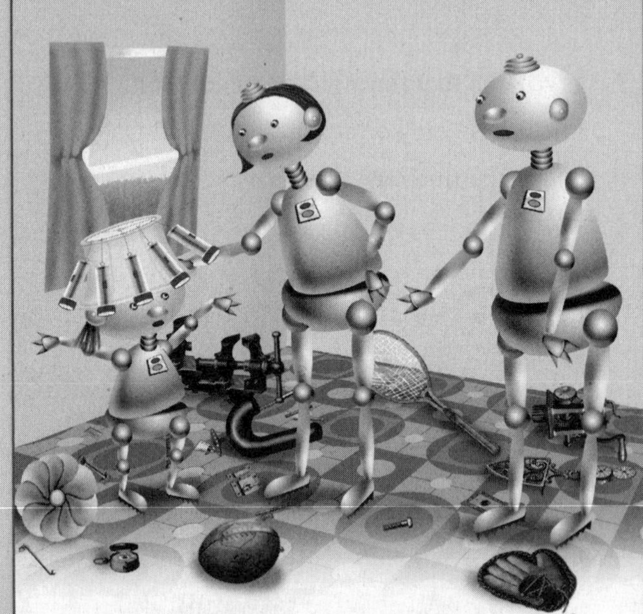

"Very cute," said Mom. "But this mess has to go!"

"Tomorrow we will bring the things you can't use to the dump," said Dad.

98

"But this is such good stuff!" said Rose. "Look! I made this for reading in bed."

"And she made this for me to play a tune on!" said Rob.

97

After Mom and Dad left, Rose looked at her stuff.

"Rob, I have a plan," said Rose. "I can have a clean room and still keep my stuff."

"Can I help?" asked Rob.

99

Page 98

Illustration

- *Look at Mom and Dad. How do you think they feel about the mess in Rose's room?* (not happy)

Text

- *Mom says that the mess has to go. Does she want a mess in the house?* (no)
- *Dad wants to take Rose's things to the dump. Why won't Rose like that idea?* (She thinks it's all good stuff.)

Page 99

Whole Page

- *Look at the picture. Rose is touching a vacuum cleaner.* (Point to the vacuum cleaner.) *Now say it with me:* vacuum cleaner. *A vacuum cleaner is a machine that we use to clean a rug. It sucks things up like this.* (Make a sucking noise.) Let's make the vacuum cleaner noise together.

Rose has a plan! She knows a way to clean her room and keep her stuff. What do you think her plan is? Talk with your partner. (Answers will vary.)

Rose Robot Cleans Up

Page 100

Whole Page

- *Look at the picture. I see the vacuum cleaner again. It must be part of the plan.*
- *Let's read the first two sentences together:* Rose and Rob went to work. "We can use so much of this stuff," said Rose. *Work is what someone does.*

Let's try to figure out what kind of work it was. We know it has something to do with the vacuum and the stuff in the room. How did Rose use old stuff before? (to make new things) *What do you think the work is?* (to make something out of the vacuum cleaner and other stuff)

Page 101

Whole Page

- *Look at what Rose and Rob painted on the vacuum cleaner. What do you see?* (eyes, nose, mouth; a face)
- *Let's read what Rose said:* "This is my best thing yet." *Now let's read what Rob said:* "I'll get Mom and Dad." *Do you think that Mom and Dad like what Rose and Rob made? Give a thumbs up for* yes *and a thumbs down for* no. (Responses may vary.)

Monitor Oral Production

Remember to model self-corrective techniques on a regular basis as you speak to children. Pretend to mispronounce words and self-correct.

Pages 100–101

Rose and Rob went to **work**.

"We can use so much of this stuff," said Rose.

"I hope Mom and Dad like this!" said Rob.

100

Pages 102–103

"Mom and Dad!" said Rob. "Look at what we made."

"What is it?" they asked.

"You'll see," said Rose. "I just have to pull this knob."

102

Rose and Rob worked and worked.
At last, they were done. Rose smiled.
"This is my best thing yet," she said.
"I'll get Mom and Dad," said Rob.

101

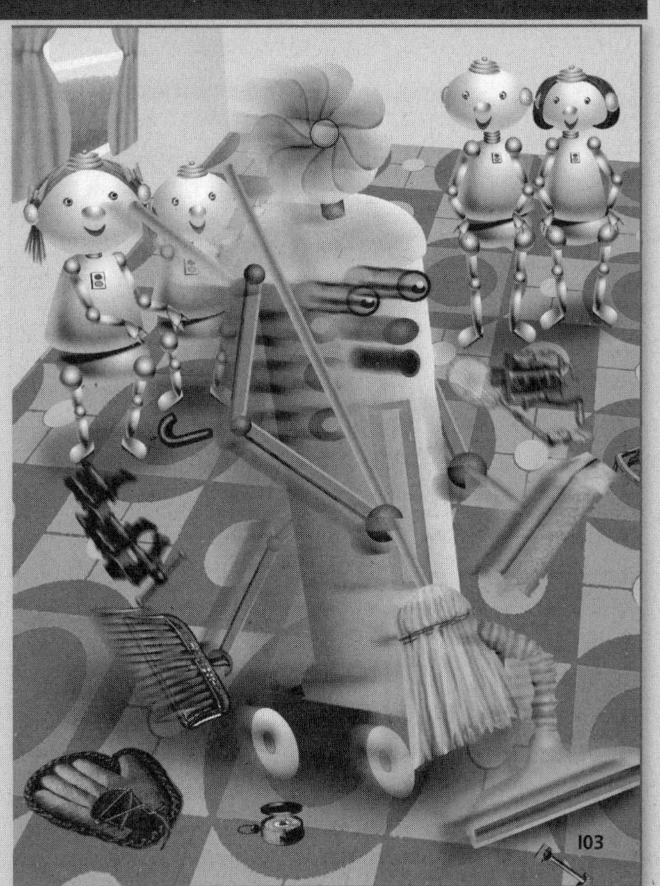

103

Page 102

Illustration

- *Let's look at the picture. Rose and Rob used a lot of old things to make something new.*
- *Rose and Rob made a robot. What do you think it can do?* (clean)

Text

- *Rose and Rob want to show the robot to Mom and Dad. Rose will show them how the robot works. Let's read the last sentence together:* I just have to pull this knob. *A knob can make a radio go on or off.* (demonstrate) *A knob can also make something louder or softer, such as the sound on a radio.*

Page 103

Whole Page

- *Let's look at the picture of the robot now. What happened when Rose pulled the switch?* (The robot started moving fast.)
- *The robot's body is moving. So are the brooms, fan, and dustpan. What is the robot doing?* (cleaning up the mess.)
- *Look at Rose and Rob. How do they feel?* (happy) *How do Mom and Dad feel?* (happy)

Let's take turns pretending to work like Rose's robot. You are the robot. Ask your partner to pull the switch. Show us how Rose's robot works. Trade places with your partner.

Rose Robot Cleans Up

Pages 104–105

Whole Page

- *Look at the picture. Is the room clean or dirty?* (clean) *Where are Rose's things?* (in the toy box)
- *Let's read Mom and Dad's words together in grown-up voices.* "Your room is so clean," said Mom. And you used so much old stuff," said Dad.

Page 105

Whole Page

- *Did Rose and Rob use all the old stuff?* (no) *There are a few things left. Do Mom and Dad still want to take what's left to the dump?* (no)
- *Let's read the last two sentences together:* "But Rose can make something new with it" said Mom and Dad. "I can!" said Rose.

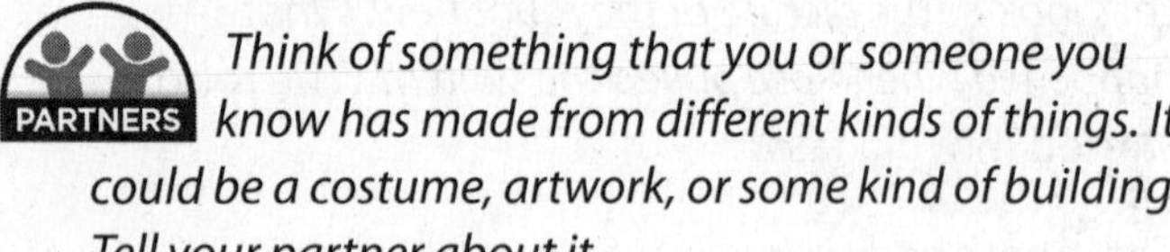

Think of something that you or someone you know has made from different kinds of things. It could be a costume, artwork, or some kind of building. Tell your partner about it.

Pages 104–105

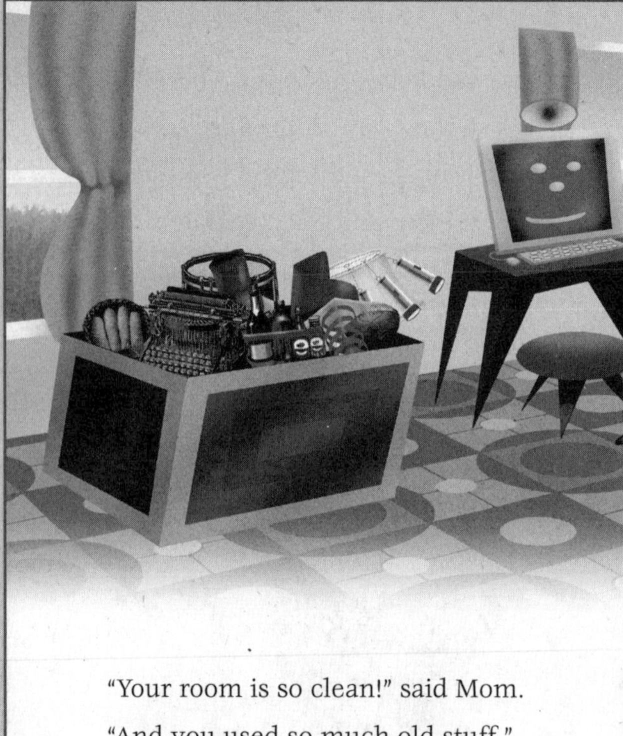

"Your room is so clean!" said Mom.

"And you used so much old stuff," said Dad.

104

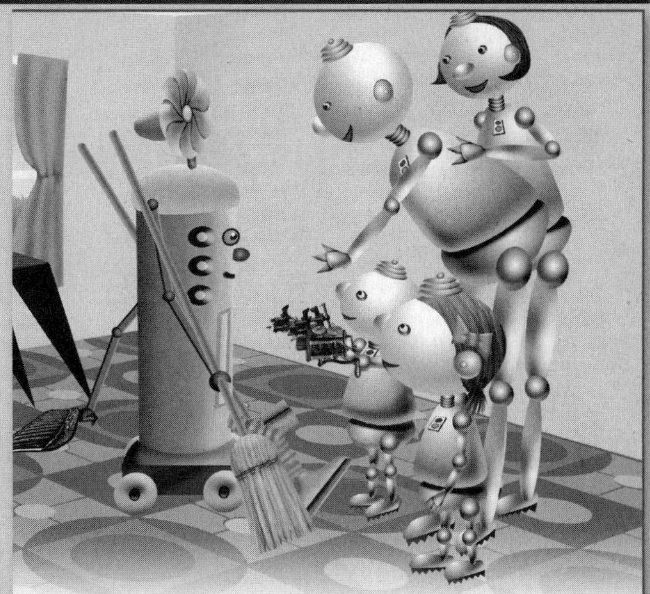

"Look!" said Rob. "This is the stuff we didn't use. You can bring it to the dump."

"But Rose can make something new with it," said Mom and Dad.

"I can!" said Rose.

105

- *At the end of the story, Mom and Dad change their minds about Rose's stuff. How do they feel about Rose's stuff at first?* (They think it is junk.) *How do they feel about Rose's stuff at the end of the story?* (They think that Rose can make something new with it.)

The story doesn't tell us why Mom and Dad change their minds. We have to use the information in the story to figure it out. Why do you think Mom and Dad change their minds about Rose's stuff? (They see what Rose can make out of it. They also see how Rose got the mess cleaned up.)

A Bottle Takes a Trip

Pages 108–109

Access Core Content

Teacher Note Pose the questions after you read the paragraph or page indicated.

Page 108

Illustrations

- *Look at the picture. I see a boy drinking from a water bottle. Point to him. I see cans and bottles in a special box called a recycling bin. Point to the bin.*
- Recycle *means "to use again." Say it with me:* recycle. *This is the recycle symbol.* (Point to the symbol on the bin.) *Look at the arrows. They show that something old can be turned into something new, over and over again.*

PARTNERS

Think about Rose Robot. How did she recycle things? Tell your partner. (She used old things to make new things.)

Text

- *Listen as I read the page aloud. Let's pretend to put a water bottle in a recycle bin.* (Demonstrate drinking out of a water bottle and then placing it in a bin.) *Now let's find out where it goes next!*

Page 109

Text and Illustration

- *Look at the pictures. Let's point to the house. Let's point to the recycling bin. Let's point to the truck.*
- *At the bottom of the page, I see a big slide.* (Point to it.) *I see bottles going down it. The slide is at a recycling center. Say it with me:* recycling center. *Old things are made into new things at a recycling center.*
- *Now listen as I read the page.*
- *A truck picks up the bottles we put in a recycling bin. Where does the truck take the bottles?* (It takes them to the recycling center)
- *At the recycling center, the bottles go down a big* ______. (slide) .

Pages 108–109

Social Studies
Genre
Nonfiction gives information about a topic.
Text Feature
A Floor Plan is a drawing that shows where things are in a room.
Content Vocabulary
recycling
sort
plastic
LOG ON FIND OUT
Social Studies Recycling
www.macmillanmh.com
READ TOGETHER
A Bottle Takes a Trip
Ahh! You just drank some water. Now you toss the bottle in a blue bin for recycling. What will happen to that bottle?
WE RECYCLE
108

Pages 110–111

Now people **sort** the cans, bottles, and paper.

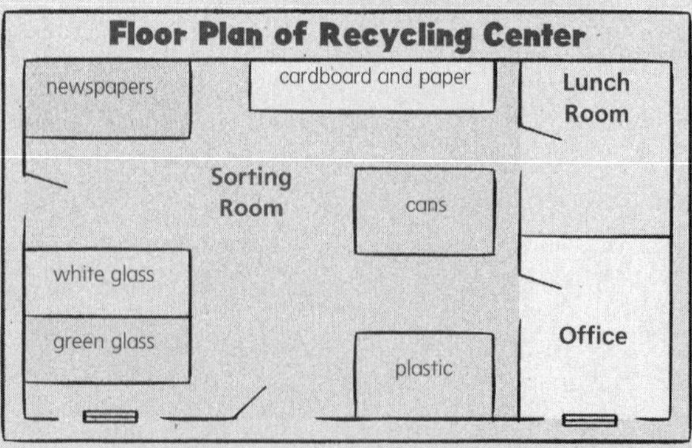
Floor Plan of Recycling Center
newspapers
cardboard and paper
Lunch Room
Sorting Room
cans
white glass
green glass
plastic
Office

Look at this floor plan of a recycling center. What kinds of things do you see being recycled?

110

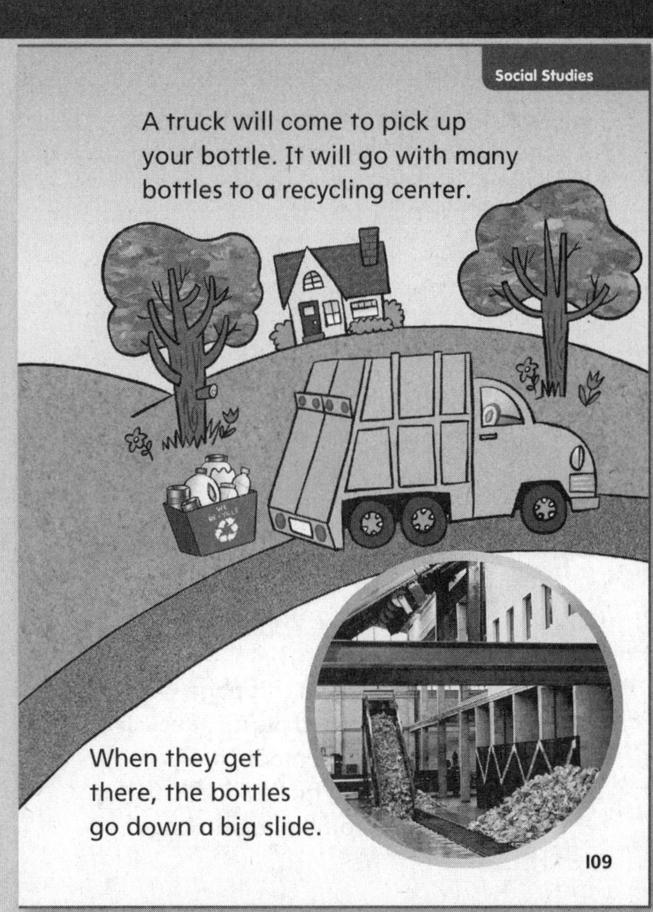

Social Studies
A truck will come to pick up your bottle. It will go with many bottles to a recycling center.
When they get there, the bottles go down a big slide.
109

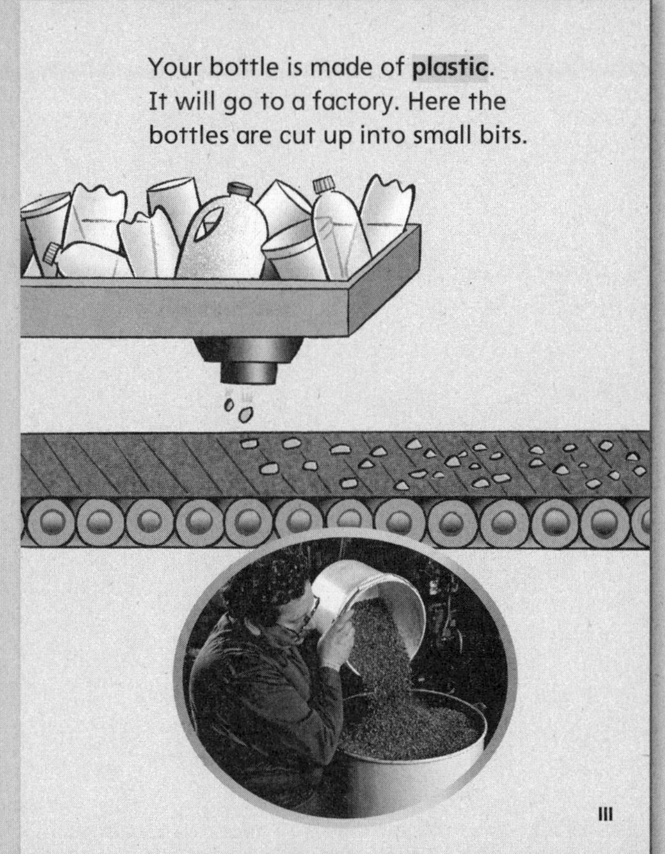

Your bottle is made of **plastic**. It will go to a factory. Here the bottles are cut up into small bits.
111

Page 110

Whole Page

- *Listen as I read the sentence at the top of the page.*
- *Now look at the workers in the picture. They are sorting the cans, bottles, and paper. When we sort things, we put them in groups. The workers will put the cans together in a group. They'll put the bottles together in a group. What will be in the third group?* (paper)
- *The drawing at the bottom of the page shows the floor plan of a recycling center. Does a floor plan look like a painting or a map?* (a map) *We'll point to the places on the floor plan as I describe them.*
- *Let's point to the office. That's where people work at desks.*
- *Let's point to the lunchroom. What do you think the workers do there?* (eat lunch). *Now let's point to the sorting room. That's where the workers sort things. What three groups of things did we just read about?* (cans, papers, bottles)
- *The workers do even more sorting. They sort the glass into white glass and green glass.* (Point to each kind as you say it.) *They sort the papers into newspapers, cardboard, and regular paper.* (Point to each kind as you say it.)
- *The workers also put cans here and plastic there.* (Point to each as you say it.)

Page 111

Whole Page

- *Listen as I read the page aloud.*
- *Water bottles are made of plastic. Say it with me:* plastic. *What other things are made of plastic?* (Responses will vary.)
- *Look at the picture. The plastic bottles are cut up into small bits, or little pieces.Point to the small bits falling out of the machine. Now point to the small bits on the moving belt. Let's find out where they go next!*

A Bottle Takes a Trip

Page 112

Whole Page

- *Listen as I read the top paragraph aloud.*
- *When plastic gets hot, it gets soft and melts. The melted plastic is used to make new things. Look at the picture with me. Point to the bits dropping into the pan. Now point to melted plastic inside the pan.*
- *The picture shows a man making green plastic rulers. They are made from recycled plastic.*
- *Listen as I read the bottom paragraph.*
- *What other kinds of things are made from recycled plastic?* (yarn, socks, sweaters)

Pages 112–113

Next the plastic bits are melted until they are soft. The soft plastic can be used to make many new things.

The green rulers on this page were made from recycled plastic. Recycled plastic can also be made into yarn. It can be used to make socks and sweaters and to fill sleeping bags.

112

All of the things this girl has were made out of recycled plastic. One of them could have come from your bottle!

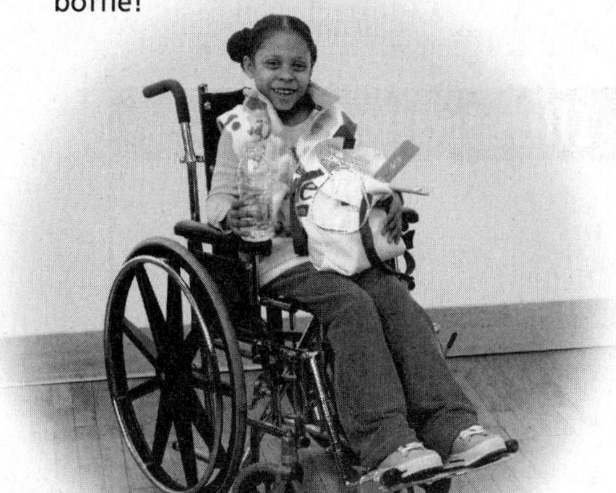

Connect and Compare

- How is what Rose Robot does like the recycling in "A Bottle Takes a Trip"?
- What recycled things does the girl in the picture have?

113

Page 113

Whole Page

- *Listen as I read this page aloud.*

PARTNERS *Look at the picture with your partner. Find things that were made from recycled plastic. Name some of them.* (bottle, bag, ruler)

Name ______________________________

Copy each new word on the line.
Draw a picture.

Word	Illustration
shoe ______________	
coat ______________	

© Macmillan/McGraw-Hill

Name ____

Read each question and prompt. Discuss the answers with your group. Use your Leveled Reader to find details to support your answers. Then write your answers on another sheet of paper.

1. Tell about the characters in your book.

2. Explain what painting the main character is looking at.

3. What happens when the character falls asleep?

4. Can a person really become part of a painting? Share your ideas.

5. Did you ever have a dream like this? Tell the group about it.

© Macmillan/McGraw-Hill

Kids Have Fun!

Pages 122–123

Prior to reading the selection with children, they should have listened to the selection on **StudentWorks Plus,** the interactive eBook. In addition, selection vocabulary should have been pretaught using the **Visual Vocabulary Resources.**

Access Core Content

Teacher Note Pose the questions after you read the paragraph or page indicated.

Page 123–124

Title

- *We read* It's Fun to Help. *That selection said that kids have fun helping others. How did they help?* (washing dishes, making bread, shoveling snow)
- *In this selection, we will read about some other ways kids have fun. We will read how kids play. What do you do when you play with your friends?* (Answers will vary.)
- *Point to the punctuation mark at the end of the title. It is called an exclamation mark. It tells you to read the title with an excited, happy voice.*
- *Now let's read the title with an excited, happy voice:* Kids Have Fun! *Why do you think the author used an exclamation point?* (because people are excited and happy when they do something fun)

Photo and Illustrations

- *Look at the boy in the picture? He is holding a pinwheel He has fun watching it twirl in the wind. What other kinds of fun things are moved by the wind?* (kites, wind chimes, sailboats)
- *Now look at the next page. What things do you see that you can use to have fun?* (scissors, crayons, snowflakes) *What kinds of things can you do with them?* (cut out shapes with scissors, draw with crayons, cut out snowflakes, catch real snowflakes with your tongue)

Pages 122–123

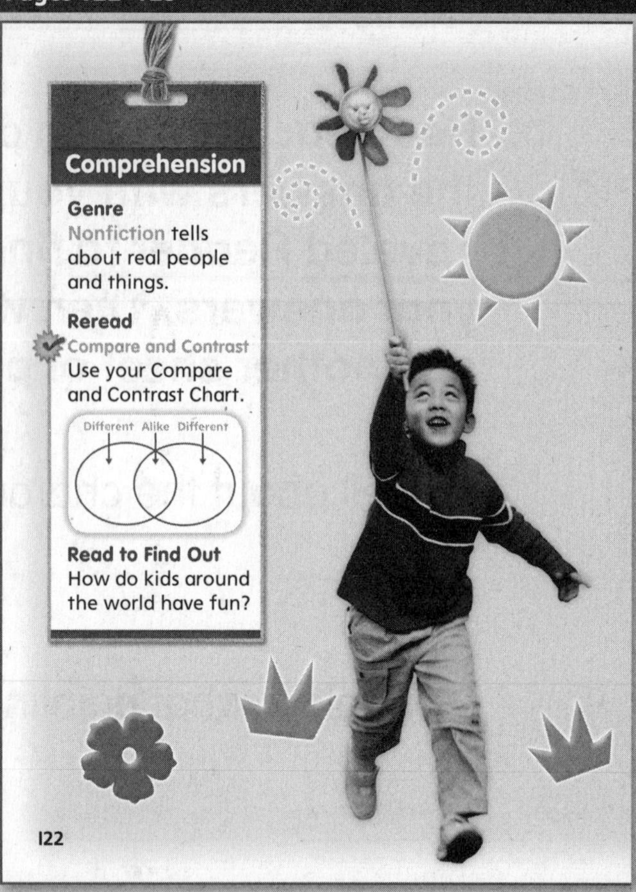

Comprehension
Genre
Nonfiction tells about real people and things.
Reread
Compare and Contrast
Use your Compare and Contrast Chart.
Different Alike Different
Read to Find Out
How do kids around the world have fun?
122

Pages 124–125

Kids have fun in every land.
They have fun doing many things.

It's fun to play games.
Kids in this icy land like to jump rope.

124

This **boy** plays a game with a flat bat.
Will he strike the ball?
Do you play **any** games with a bat?
125

Page 124

Whole Page

- *The two sentences at the top of the page tell the main idea. They tell what the whole selection is about. Let's read them together:* Kids have fun in every land. They have fun doing many things.
- *Point to the word* land *at the end of the first sentence.* The *word* land *is another way to say* place *or* country. *What land do you come from?* (Answers will vary.)
- *Look at the picture. Point to the snow on the mountain. Point to the snow-covered ground. It looks hard and icy. Do you think this is a cold place or a hot place?* (a cold place) *How can you tell?* (from the ice and snow; from the children's clothes)
- *When you run or jump, do you get hot or cold?* (hot) *What are the children doing? (jumping rope) Do you think that jumping rope helps the children stay warm?* (yes)

 *Think of something fun to do outside in cold weather, and pretend to do it. Have your partner try to tell what you are doing.* (If children are not familiar with cold weather, share some activities.)

Page 125

Whole Page

- Strike *is another word for* hit. *The boy in the picture is holding a bat. Point to it. Pretend you are holding a bat. Show me how you would strike the ball.*
- *Look at the man behind the boy. The man is holding out his hands like this.* (Demonstrate holding out hands to catch something.) *Why do you think the man is standing behind the boy?* (He will catch the ball if the boy misses it.)
- *The boy is playing a game called cricket. Say* cricket. *People play cricket with a flat bat and a ball. What is another game that we play with a bat and a ball?* (baseball)
- *Let's read this page together.*

Kids Have Fun!

Page 126

Whole Page

- *The girl in the picture is playing with a toy called a hoop. Say* hoop. *A hoop is a big ring. The girl has to swing her hips to make the hoop spin, or go around. What do you think will happen when the girl stops moving?* (The hoop will fall down to the ground.)
- *Let's pretend we have hoops. Show me how you would move as you played with your hoop.*

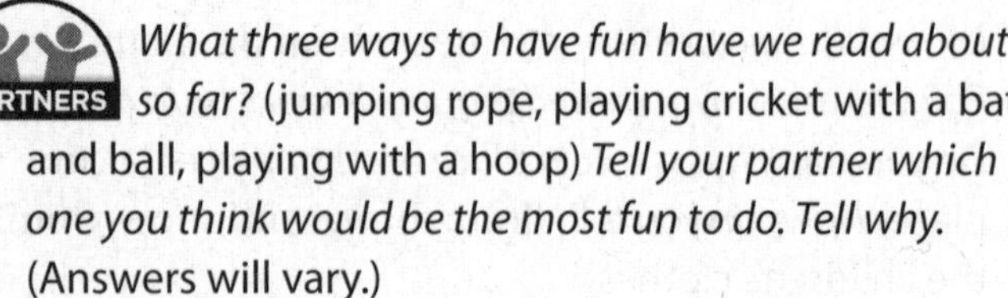

PARTNERS *What three ways to have fun have we read about so far?* (jumping rope, playing cricket with a bat and ball, playing with a hoop) *Tell your partner which one you think would be the most fun to do. Tell why.* (Answers will vary.)

Page 127

Whole Page

- *Let's read this page together.*
- *We read about other children who jumped over ropes. Where did they live? (in a cold, icy land) Two children held the rope for their game. One child held the rope at each end. This boy is holding the rope by himself. He also does other tricks with his rope.*

Look at the toys on pages 126 and 127. How is their shape the same? (They are both rings.) *Now let's think about how the toys are different. The hoop is hard and does not bend. A rope is soft. Can you bend it?* (yes) *Let's pretend to make different shapes with a rope.* (demonstrate)

Request Assistance

Remind children of expressions they can use to request assistance from the teacher or their partners, such as *Can you show me in the picture? Can you do it?*

Pages 126–127

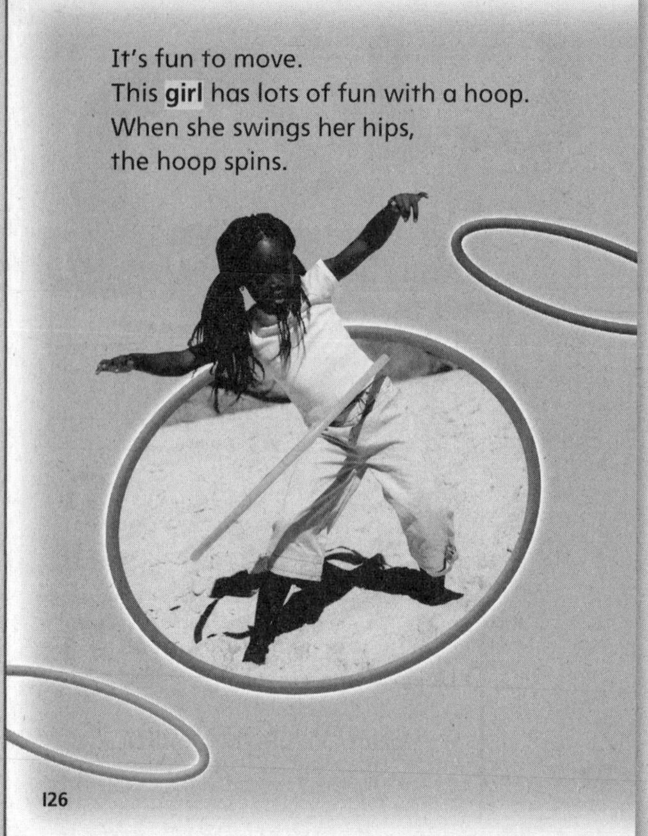

It's fun to move.
This **girl** has lots of fun with a hoop.
When she swings her hips,
the hoop spins.

126

Pages 128–129

It is fun to make things!
This boy cuts up scraps.
Snip, snip!
What shape did he make?

128

This boy **does** tricks with a rope.
He can make a ring with it.
Then he jumps into it and out again.

127

This girl makes things from leaves.
She cuts them in strips.
She will use them to make a box.

129

Page 128

Whole Page

- *Let's read the first two lines together:* It's fun to make things! This boy cuts up scraps.
- *Now say the next two lines after me, and copy what I do:* Snip, snip! (Make a scissor shape with the index and middle finger of one hand, and pretend to cut twice.) What shape did he make? (Trace a circle in the air with the index finger of one hand.)
- *What are some fun things you like to do with paper and scissors?* (make snowflakes, make paper chains)

Think about the fun activities we have read about so far. Think about where kids do these things. How is the activity on page 128 different from the others? (People usually make things with paper and scissors indoors. The other activities are for outside.)

Page 129

Whole Page

- *Look at the girl in the picture. She is making things out of leaves. She cut the leaves in strips first. Strips are long, thin shapes. Do you think the leaves were big or little?* (big) *Why do you think so?* (because the strips are very long)
- The girl is making a box from the leaves. *An adult probably taught her because it must be hard to make a box from leaves. What is something fun to do that someone taught you?* (Answers will vary.)
- *The girl is working on the box outside. Do you think she lives in a warm or cold place?* (warm)
- *Which of these things could the girl put in her box— a rock, pretty stones, or water? Why?* (She could put pretty stones in the box because they are small and light. A rock would be too big and heavy. Water would run out.)

Kids Have Fun!

Page 130

Whole Page

- *The boy in the picture is wearing a lion costume. Point to the furry part around the boy's head. It is called a mane. Say it with me:* mane. *Male lions have manes.*
- *Let's read this page together:* It's fun to make things up. This boy acts like a lion. He shakes his mane. But then he smiles.
- *Let's pretend we are lions and shake our manes like the boy does.* (Lead children in pretending to be lions.) *What else can we do to act like lions?* (roar, stretch out our claws) *Let's act like lions again and do all the things we said.*
- *Why does the boy smile?* (He is having fun pretending to be a lion.)

PARTNERS

Tell your partner what kind of costume you would like to wear. Tell your partner how you could make that kind of costume. (Responses are open.)

Page 131

Whole Page

- *Let's read this page together.*
- *Look at the picture of the ship. It looks like a sailboat. The kids made it from sticks, cloth, and a box. Which part of the ship is the sail?* (the cloth) *Which part is the boat?* (the box)
- *The part of the ship that the sail hangs on is called the mast. The mast on this ship is made of sticks.* (Point to the mast.) *Say it with me:* mast.

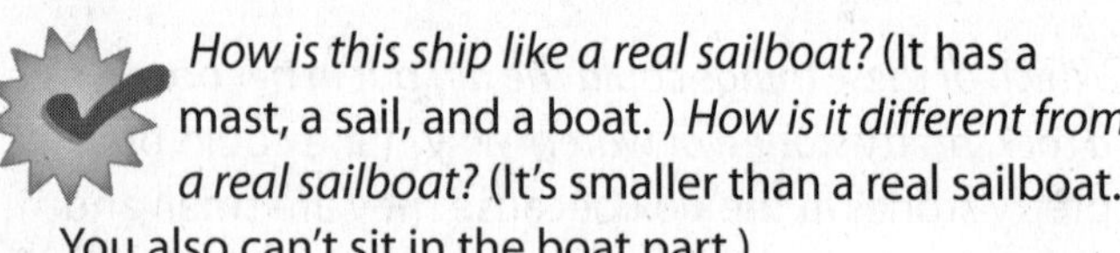

How is this ship like a real sailboat? (It has a mast, a sail, and a boat.) *How is it different from a real sailboat?* (It's smaller than a real sailboat. You also can't sit in the boat part.)

Pages 130–131

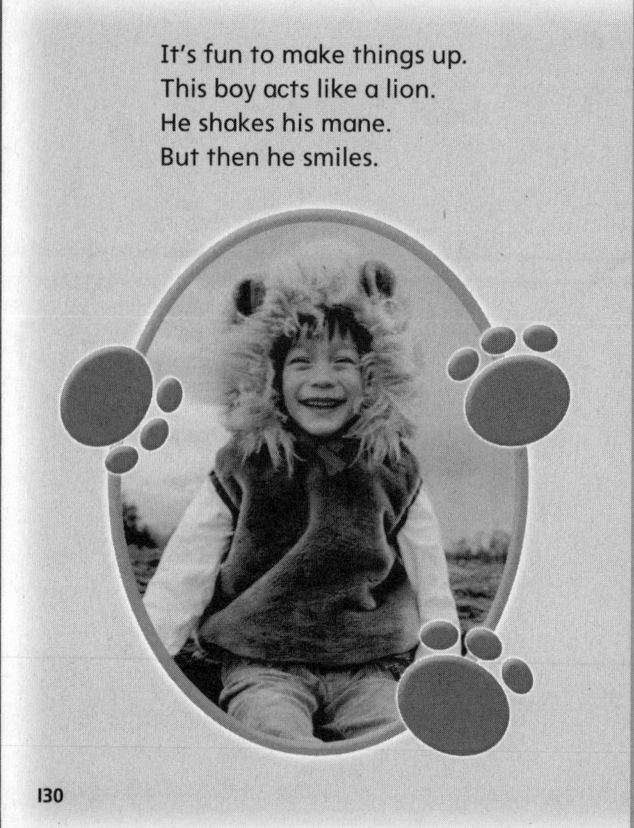
It's fun to make things up.
This boy acts like a lion.
He shakes his mane.
But then he smiles.
130

Pages 132–133

It's fun to see new things.
This boy finds new things under **water**.
Look at what he picked up!

132

These kids like to make up games.
They made a ship.
They used sticks, cloth, and a box.

131

What does this boy see?
It is wide.
How wide can he stretch?

133

Page 132

Illustration

- *The boy wears a mask to see underwater. The mask looks like eyeglasses. Point to the mask. The mask keeps the water out. Do you think the mask needs to be tight or loose to keep out the water?* (tight)
- *The boy uses a snorkel to breathe underwater. The tube that sticks out of the water is the snorkel.* (Point to it.) *Say* it *with me:* snorkel. *The snorkel lets the boy breathe in air while he is under the water.*

Text

- *Let's read this page together.*
- *The boy picked up a fish that looks like a star. What is its name?* (starfish)
- *Do you think it would be fun to go underwater with a mask and snorkel? Why or why not?* (Answers will vary.)

Page 133

Whole Page

- *Let's read this page together.*
- *The boy sees a bridge. Say it with me:* bridge. *Can the boy stretch as wide as the bridge?* (no)

Perhaps the boy is pretending to be a bridge. What other ways could you pretend to be a bridge? (Responses will vary.) *Pretend to be another thing or an animal, and have your partner try to figure out what it is.*

Kids Have Fun!

Page 134

Whole Page

- *This girl's mom is helping her learn to do something. How do people help others learn?* (They tell them what to do. They show them how to do it.)
- *The mother makes the rug out of string. Say* string *with me and point to it. She uses a special tool to weave the rug. The tool is a special frame called a loom. Say* loom *with me and point to it.*
- *Let's read the page together.*

Now tell your partner about something new you have learned to do this year. Who helped you learn? (Responses will vary.)

Page 135

Whole Page

- *This boy and his father are sitting outside. Do you think the weather is cold or hot?* (hot) *What makes you think so?* They are wearing shorts and no shoes.)
- *The boy and his father are making pots. They shape the clay into pots. Then what do they do to the pots?* (paint them)
- *We read about a mother teaching her daughter to make a string rug. We read about a father teaching his son to make pots. What are some other things parents teach their children to do?* (Answers will vary.)

Pages 134–135

It's fun to learn new things.
This girl's mom shows her
how to make a rug from string.

134

Pages 136–137

Holidays are fun!
This boy is all dressed up.
He has a mask.
He acts strong.

136

This boy's dad shows him how to make pots.
They have fun doing it together.

135

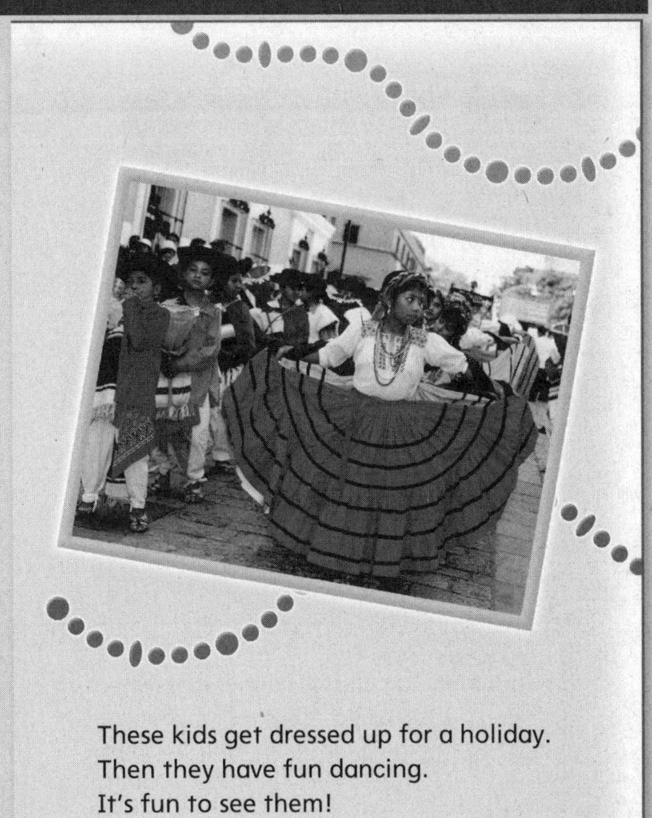

These kids get dressed up for a holiday.
Then they have fun dancing.
It's fun to see them!

137

Page 136

Whole Page

- *Let's read this page together:* Holidays are fun! This boy is all dressed up. He has a mask. He acts strong. *How is the boy acting strong?* (He is holding up the mask high over his head.)
- *The boy is all dressed up in black. He is also wearing a special belt around his waist. Point to it.*

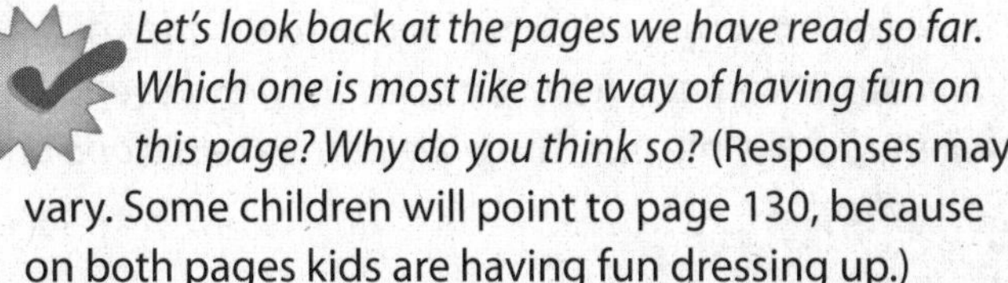

Let's look back at the pages we have read so far. Which one is most like the way of having fun on this page? Why do you think so? (Responses may vary. Some children will point to page 130, because on both pages kids are having fun dressing up.)

Page 137

Whole Page

- *Let's read this page together. Why might it be fun to celebrate this holiday?* (You could get dressed up. You could see bright colors. You could hear music. You could dance.)

Tell your partner about your favorite holiday. What makes it fun? (Answers will vary.)

Request Assistance

Remind children that they can ask for synonyms to help clarify words or expressions they do not understand. Ask, *What is another way of saying "holiday"?* (celebration)

Kids Have Fun!

Page 138

Whole Page

- *These kids are playing a game called wheelbarrow. Say it with me:* wheelbarrow.
- *A real wheelbarrow is a big cart. People use it to move things in a garden. What kinds of things might people put in a wheelbarrow when they are planting? (dirt, plants, seeds)*
- *A wheelbarrow has one wheel in the front and two handles in the back. A person holds the handles and lifts up the back of the tray. The wheelbarrow rolls along on the wheel.*
- *Which boy is acting like a wheelbarrow, the one standing or the one on the ground?* (the one on the ground) *Which parts of the boy are like the handles?* (his legs) *Which parts are like the wheel?* (his arms)

PARTNERS *Talk with your partner about things you like to do outdoors with friends. Then talk about things you like to do indoors with friends.* (Responses will vary.)

Pages 138–139

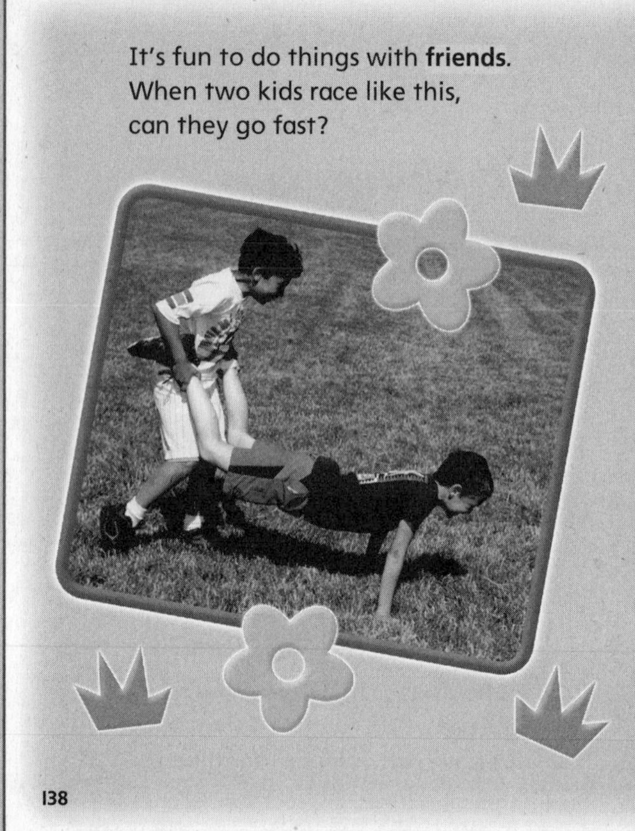

It's fun to do things with **friends**.
When two kids race like this,
can they go fast?
138

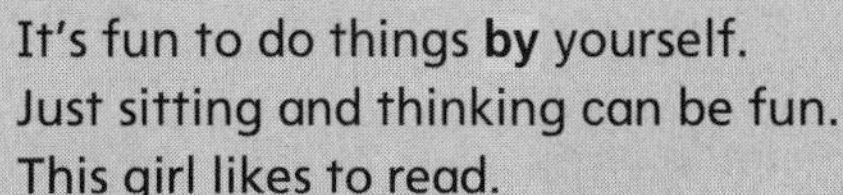
It's fun to do things **by** yourself.
Just sitting and thinking can be fun.
This girl likes to read.

Lots of things are fun.
How do you have fun?

139

Page 139

Whole Page

- *This girl thinks reading is a fun thing to do by herself. She likes to read when she is alone. What do you like to do by yourself?* (Responses will vary.)
- *Let's read together the sentences at the bottom of the page:* Lots of things are fun. How do you have fun? *Let's make a list of our favorite things to do on the board.*

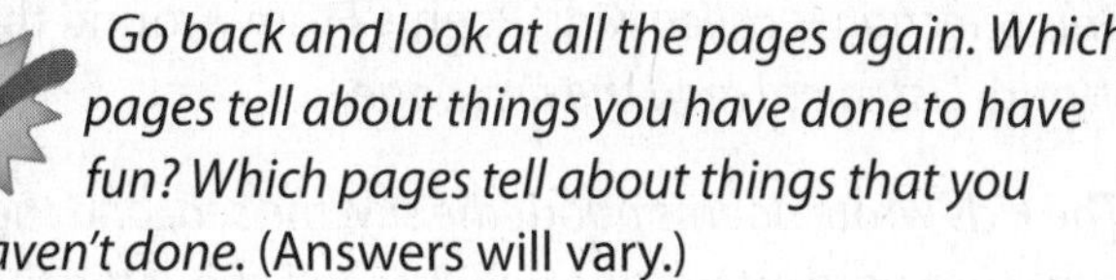
Go back and look at all the pages again. Which pages tell about things you have done to have fun? Which pages tell about things that you haven't done. (Answers will vary.)

Kids' Poems From Around the World

Access Core Content

Teacher Note Pose the questions after you read the paragraph or page indicated.

Page 142

Whole Page

- *This selection is called* Kids' Poems From Around the World. *Listen as I read the first page.*
- *The kids wrote poems about the sky, the sea, and the sun. They used interesting words to tell about the things in their poems. Look at the picture, and point to the sky. Point to the sea. Point to the sun.*

Page 143

Whole Page

- *The title of the first poem is* The Sky Is Busy. *When we say that a place is busy, what do we mean?* (Lots of things are happening there.)
- *Listen as I read the first three lines to find out one thing that is happening in the sky:* The lighthouse / On that island / Is shining.
- *A lighthouse is a building near the water. It has a bright light shining from the top of it. Point to the lighthouse. Point to its light. A lighthouse helps people in boats. How does it help?* (It shows them where they are.)
- *Listen as I read the next two lines:* Helicopters in the sky / Are shining. *Helicopters are in the sky, too. Point to a helicopter in the picture. How is it like a plane?* (It flies.)
- *Listen as I read the last lines:* Boats are glittering, too. / And with a bang / Someone is shooting / off fireworks. Glittering *is another word for* shining. *Say it with me:* glittering. *What glitters, gold or wood?* (gold)
- *Let's point to the sky in the picture. It takes up a lot of the page. What things make the sky busy in the poem? (light from the lighthouse, helicopters, fireworks)*
- *Now listen as I read the poem again.*

Pages 142–143

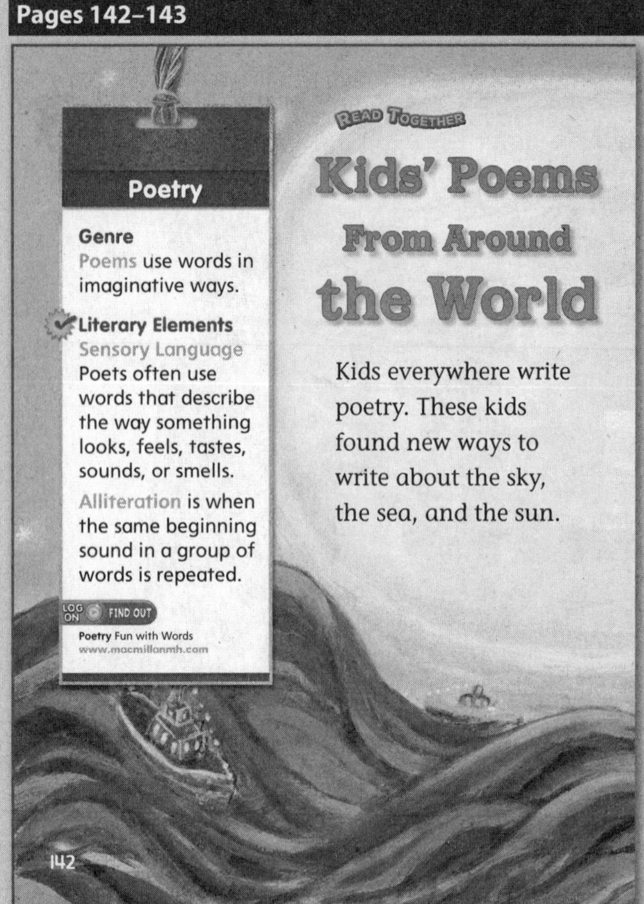

Poetry
Genre
Poems use words in imaginative ways.
Literary Elements
Sensory Language
Poets often use words that describe the way something looks, feels, tastes, sounds, or smells.
Alliteration is when the same beginning sound in a group of words is repeated.
LOG ON FIND OUT
Poetry Fun with Words
www.macmillanmh.com
Read Together
Kids' Poems From Around the World
Kids everywhere write poetry. These kids found new ways to write about the sky, the sea, and the sun.
142

Pages 144–145

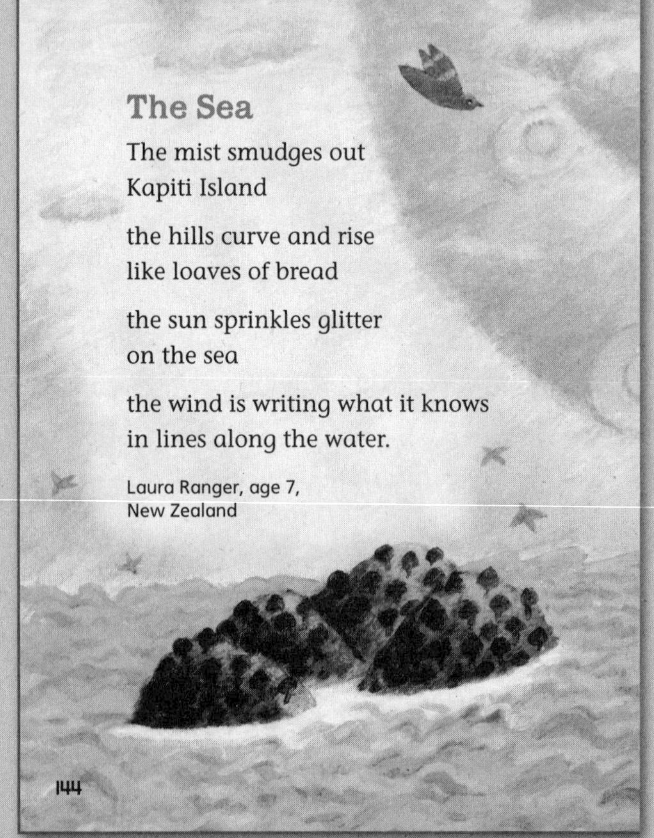

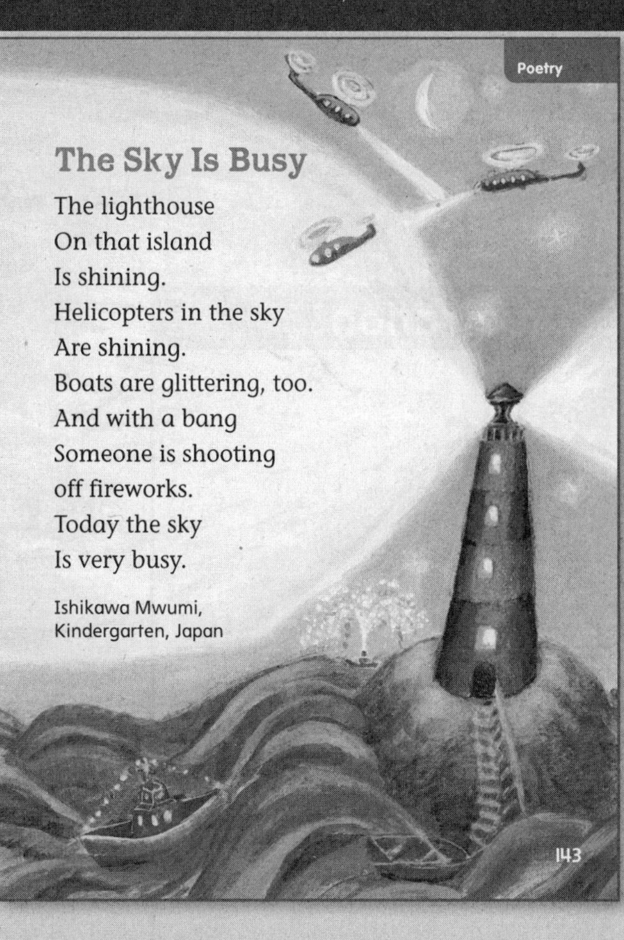

Poetry
The Sky Is Busy
The lighthouse
On that island
Is shining.
Helicopters in the sky
Are shining.
Boats are glittering, too.
And with a bang
Someone is shooting
off fireworks.
Today the sky
Is very busy.
Ishikawa Mwumi,
Kindergarten, Japan
143

Sun Rise
Sun, sun, sun
Rise up from the clouds
Spread your rays
Flowers will be happy
Birds will sing
And I shall be happy
and sing, too.
Camille Pabalan,
age 6, Canada
Connect and Compare
• What words describe the way something looks and sounds?
• What lines in "The Sea" have words that begin with the same sounds?
145

Page 144

Whole Page

- *This poem is called* The Sea. *What is another word for sea?* (ocean) *This poem tells about an island. An island is a piece of land with water all around it. Point to the island in the picture.*
- *I'm going to write the word* island *on the board and then smudge it out.* (Write it and smudge it with your finger.) *Can you read it now?* (no)
- *Now listen as I read the first two lines of the poem:* The mist smudges out / Kapiti Island. *Mist is like fog. The poet says that the mist smudges the island. Does the mist make the island easy to see or hard to see?* (hard to see) *Say the word* smudge *with me*: smudge.
- *Listen as I read the next two lines:* the hills curve and rise / like loaves of bread. *What does the poet say the islands look like?* (loaves of bread) *What else do the islands in the picture look like?* (turtle shells, upside-down bowls)
- *Now listen as I read the last four lines:* the sun sprinkles glitter / on the sea / the wind is writing what it knows / in lines along the water.
- *The poet says that the wind writes lines along the water. What kinds of lines do we see in the sea?* (lines of waves)

Page 145

Whole Page

- *This poem is called* Sun Rise. Rise *means "get up." Does sunrise take place in the morning or at night?* (in the morning) *Listen as I read the poem.*
- *Now I'm going to read it again. This time, I want you to be the sun. Start in a crouching position.* (demonstrate) *When I read the words* Rise up, *stand. When I read the words* Spread your rays, *open your arms wide.*

Make your own picture to go with the poem. Have your partner make one, too. Then share your pictures and point out the things in the poem.

Name ______________________________

Copy each new word on the line.
Draw a picture.

Word	Illustration
jump rope	
balloon	

© Macmillan/McGraw-Hill

Name ________________________________

Book Talk

Read each question and prompt. Discuss the answers with your group. Use your Leveled Reader to find details to support your answers. Then write your answers on another sheet of paper.

1. Tell why holidays are fun.

2. Describe which holiday from the book you would like to experience.

3. Tell your classmates which holiday is your favorite.

4. Give examples of foods you eat on that day.

5. Explain why you think holidays are important.

© Macmillan/McGraw-Hill

GRADE 1, UNIT 4 • Interactive Reading

Weekly Planners

Week 1

Selections	Vocabulary		ELL Practice Book
	Key Selection/Oral Vocabulary Words/Cognates	**Academic Language/Cognates**	
Drakes Tail *Busy as a Bee*	borrow encourage rely relationship *relación* suggest *sugerir* trip friendship	captions was were question predictions *predicciones* generate *generar*	• Phonics, p. 61 • Vocabulary, p. 62 • Grammar, p. 63 • Book Talk, p. 64

Week 2

Selections	Vocabulary		ELL Practice Book
	Key Selection/Oral Vocabulary Words/Cognates	**Academic Language/Cognates**	
Gram and Me *Chinese New Year*	concerned share trust concentrate *concentrarse* splendid *espléndido* fortunate *afortunado* member *miembro*	character setting has have	• Phonics, p. 65 • Vocabulary, p. 66 • Grammar, p. 67 • Book Talk, p. 68

Week 3

TIME FOR KIDS	Vocabulary		ELL Practice Book
	Oral Vocabulary Words/Cognates	**Academic Language/Cognates**	
César Chávez	ripe agree attempt difficult *difícil* accomplish argue	reread go monitor *monitorear* comprehension *comprensión* retell do	• Phonics, p. 69 • Vocabulary, p. 70 • Grammar, p. 71 • Book Talk, p. 72

Week 4

Selections	Vocabulary		ELL Practice Book
	Key Selection/Oral Vocabulary Words/Cognates	**Academic Language/Cognates**	
The Kite (from *Days with Frog and Toad*) *The Wright Brothers*	perhaps approach assist meadow view determined	chart see saw problem *problema* solution *solución*	• Phonics, p. 73 • Vocabulary, p. 74 • Grammar, p. 75 • Book Talk, p. 76

Week 5

Selections	Vocabulary		ELL Practice Book
	Key Selection/Oral Vocabulary Words/ Cognates	**Academic Language/Cognates**	
Animal Teams *Where?*	danger behavior soar group *grupo* vivid *vívido* beautiful plead	retell contraction nonfiction repetition text structure *texto*	• Phonics, p. 77 • Vocabulary, p. 78 • Grammar, p. 79 • Book Talk, p. 80

© Macmillan/McGraw-Hill

Student Response Strategies

Use the following strategies to help English Language Learners move to the next proficiency level.

✔ **WAIT** Give children ample time to respond.

- Let children know that they can respond in different ways depending on their levels of proficiency, but all should be encouraged to answer questions related to the main point of the picture or text.
- Allow children to respond in their native language if they are very limited proficient. Ask a more proficient student to repeat the answer in English.

✔ **REPEAT** If the child's response is correct, the teacher can repeat what the child has said slowly and clearly for the rest of the class to hear.

✔ **REVISE for FORM** Generally the teacher will be repeating what the child has said but with corrections for grammar and pronunciation. The correction can be implicit or explicit (where teacher calls attention to the correction).

✔ **REVISE for MEANING** Teachers should also correct responses for meaning.

✔ **ELABORATE** Here, the teacher elaborates on a child's response or states the response in another way in order to more fully develop children's comprehension and oral language proficiency.

✔ **ELICIT** Finally, the teacher can also elicit a more comprehensive response from the child by prompting him or her for further information.

Newcomers

Basic and Social Language Each week you will be focusing on an important aspect of classroom communication to teach or reinforce with your newcomers. Children will expand and internalize initial English vocabulary by learning and using routine language needed for classroom communication.

Introduce Self Teach children how to introduce themselves, ask for other classmates′ names, and say Hello/Goodbye. Use the sentence frames *My name is* _____ and *What is your name?* Model dialogues, such as *Hello. My name is (name). What is your name?* Have children repeat and practice with a partner.

Basic Requests Teach children sentence frames for basic requests, such as *I need* _____, *I want* _____, and *Do you have* _____? Teach them how to ask for permission, such as *May I use the restroom, please?* And to respond with *thank you*. Provide daily opportunities to model and practice each request. Reinforce *please* and *thank you*.

Classroom Items Teach children the names of commonly used classroom items, such as, pencils, paper, book, chair, and desk. Reinforce each using the sentence frames *This is my* _____. *That is your* _____. and *This is a* _____. These sentence frames focus on possession. Provide daily practice, for example, *This is my book. That is your book.*

LOG ON Have children use **Newcomer Games** to expand and internalize language needed for classroom communication. **www.macmillanmh.com**

© Macmillan/McGraw-Hill

Drakes Tail

Pages 10–11

Prior to reading the selection with children, they should have listened to the selection on **StudentWorks Plus**, the interactive eBook. In addition, selection vocabulary should have been pretaught using the **Visual Vocabulary Resources**.

Access Core Content

Teacher Note Pose the questions after you read the paragraph or page indicated.

Pages 10–11

Title and Illustrations

- *Let's read the title together:* Drakes Tail.
- *This big house on a hill is called a palace.* (Point to the picture of the palace.) *A king lives in this palace.*
- *Point to the duck in the picture. This duck's name is Drakes Tail, just like the title of the story. A drake is a boy duck.*

Page 12

Illustration

- *Look at the picture. The man is wearing a robe and a crown.* (Point to the robe and crown as you say them.) *This man lives in the palace. Who is he?* (the king)
- *Now point to the bag of money. Is the duck giving the money to the king or taking money from him?* (giving money to the king)

Text

- Once upon a time *is a way to begin a story. Say it with me:* once upon a time. *The first sentence tells us that this is a story about a duck. What is the duck's name?* (Drakes Tail)
- **Directionality**

  Ask children to place their finger where you start reading (top left). Ask where you finish reading on this page (bottom right).

Pages 10–11

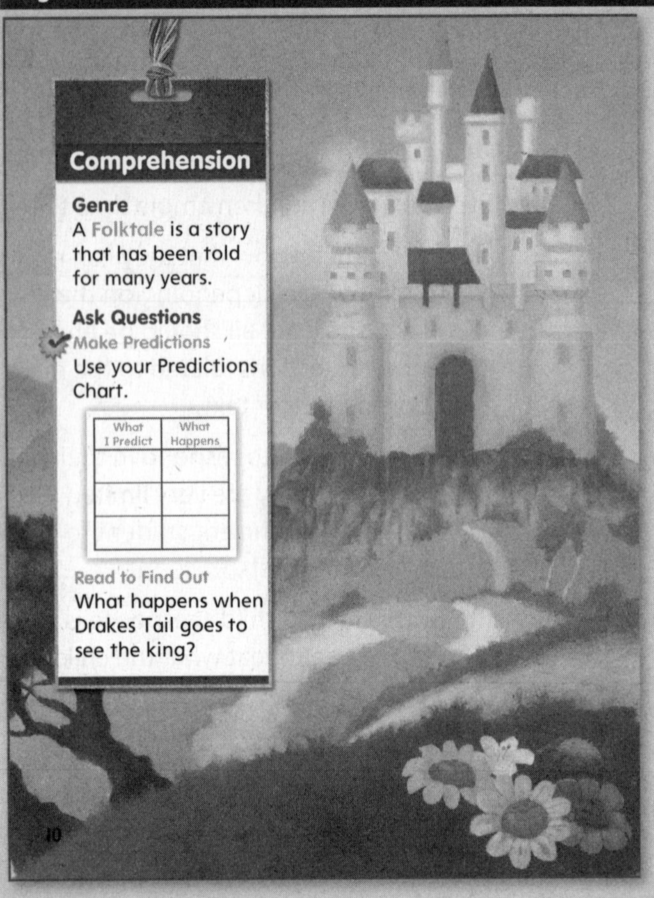

Comprehension
Genre
A Folktale is a story that has been told for many years.
Ask Questions
Make Predictions
Use your Predictions Chart.
What I Predict
What Happens
Read to Find Out
What happens when Drakes Tail goes to see the king?
10

Pages 12–13

Once upon a time, there was a duck named Drakes Tail.

Drakes Tail was a duck with brains. He saved all of his money. One day, the king asked to **borrow** some. Drakes Tail said yes.

12

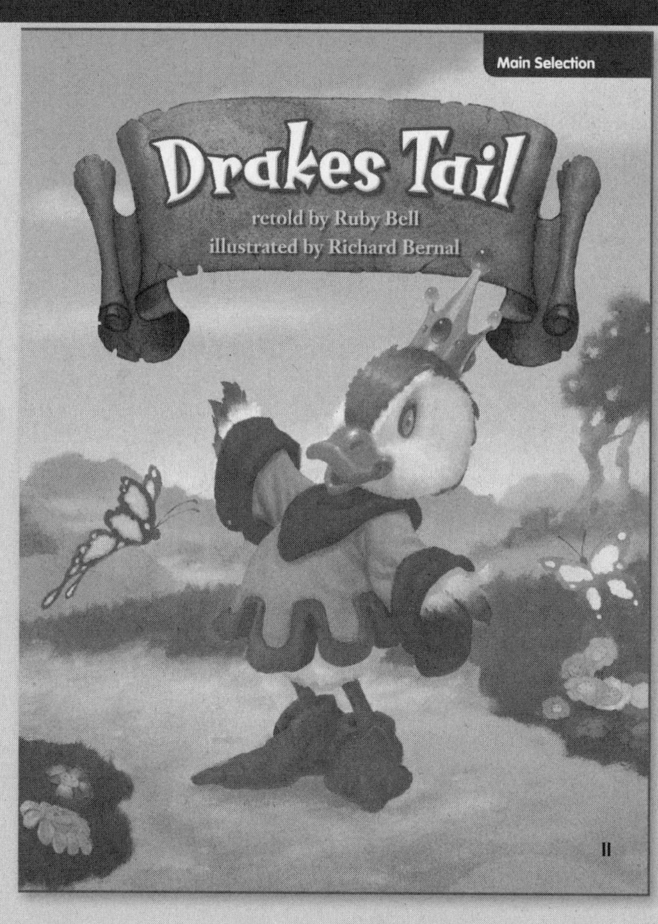

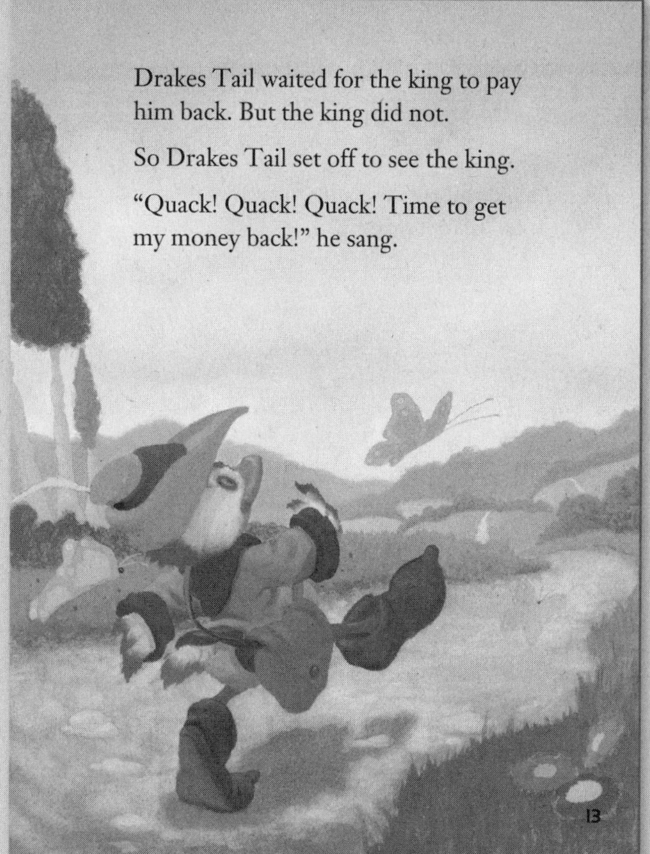

Drakes Tail waited for the king to pay him back. But the king did not.

So Drakes Tail set off to see the king.

"Quack! Quack! Quack! Time to get my money back!" he sang.

13

- Let's read the next sentence together: Drakes Tail was a duck with brains. (Tap your head.) *Drakes Tail was very smart.*
- *When you save your money, you keep it and don't spend it. Does Drakes Tail keep his money or spend it?* (He keeps it.)
- *The king wants to borrow the money. When you borrow something, you take it now and give it back later. Does Drakes Tail give the king the money?* (yes)

Page 13

Whole Page

- *The king borrowed the money. Did he give the money back later the way he was supposed to?* (no)
- *Drakes Tail sets off, or goes, to see the king. Why is he going there?* (to get his money back)
- *Drakes Tail sings a song as he walks. Let's read what he sang together:* "Quack! Quack! Quack! Time to get my money back!" *Which words rhyme, or end the same way? (quack* and *back)*
- *Look at the way Drakes Tail is walking.* (Demonstrate walking with determination.) *Do you think he is going to try very hard to get his money back?* (yes) Let's *walk like Drakes Tail and sing his song.*

Analyze Sayings and Expressions

Help children recognize that *once upon a time* is an expression used to start a story. Help them create other examples using this expression with stories they know.

Page 14

Whole Page

- *Point to the fox in the picture. Foxes often hunt, or try to catch, ducks in stories and in real life. But in this story, Fox and Drakes Tail are friends.*
- *Drakes Tail tells Fox where he is going. Let's read what Fox says together:* "Take me! I can help!"

Talk with your partner. Do you think that Drakes Tail should take Fox with him? (Question is open.)

Page 15

Whole Page

- *Fox wants to go with Drakes Tail. Let's read what Drakes Tail says together:* "OK," said Drakes Tail. "But the trip is long. You may get tired. Make yourself little and hop into my bag. I will carry you."
- *Drakes Tail thinks that Fox might get tired on such a long trip. He wants to carry Fox.* (Mime carrying something.) *Look at the picture of Fox on page 14. Do you think that Drakes Tail can carry such a big fox?* (no)
- *Drakes Tail wants Fox to fit into the bag. What does he tell fox to do?* (make himself little)
- *Stand up so I can see how big you are. Do you think you can make yourself little enough to fit into the bag?* (Use your hands to show how short a child would have to be.) (no) *But this is a make-believe story, so Fox can make himself little.*
- *Look at Fox.* (Point to the picture on page 15.) *Is he big or little now?* (little) *He is hopping into the bag. Let's hop.* (demonstrate) *Fox can hop much higher. He can hop from the ground into the bag.*

Page 16

Illustration

- *Look at this water.* (Point to the pond.) *It's called a pond. Say it with me:* pond. *This is a funny pond. It has a face. Does a pond really have a face?* (no) *But this pond is a friend of Drakes Tail.*

Pages 14–15

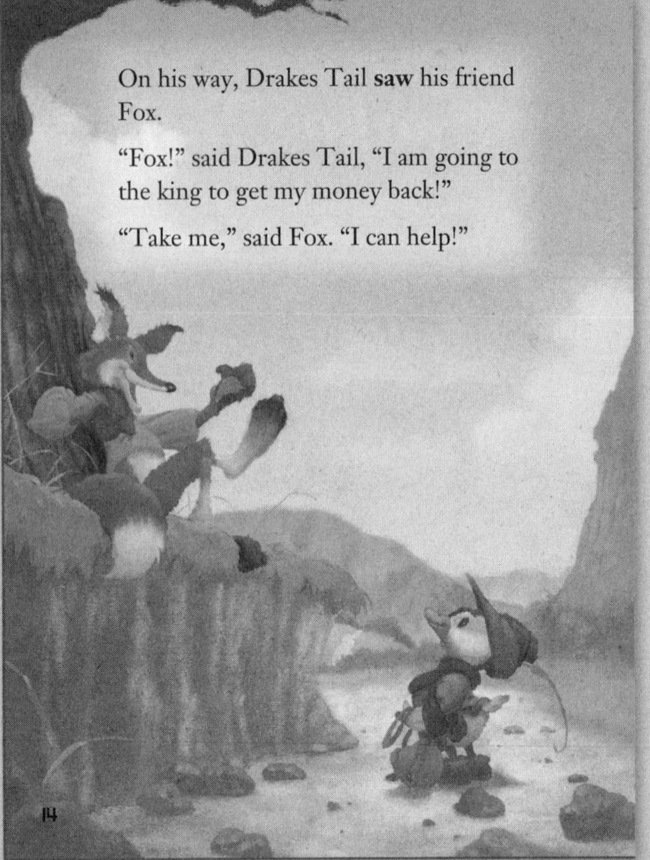

On his way, Drakes Tail **saw** his friend Fox.
"Fox!" said Drakes Tail, "I am going to the king to get my money back!"
"Take me," said Fox. "I can help!"
14

Pages 16–17

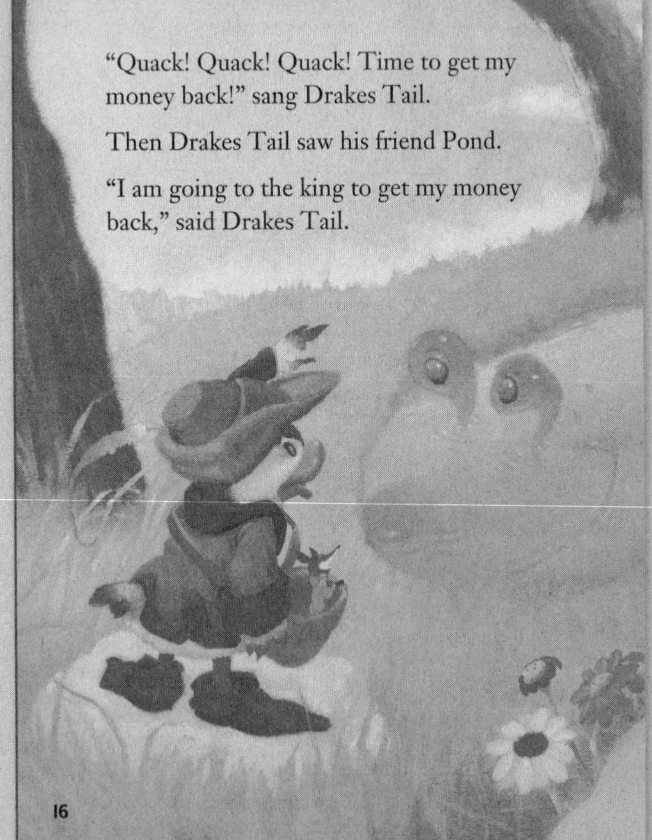

"Quack! Quack! Quack! Time to get my money back!" sang Drakes Tail.
Then Drakes Tail saw his friend Pond.
"I am going to the king to get my money back," said Drakes Tail.
16

"I will," said Drakes Tail. "But it is a long **trip**. You may get tired. Make yourself little and hop in my bag. I will **carry** you."

Fox did as Drakes Tail said.

15

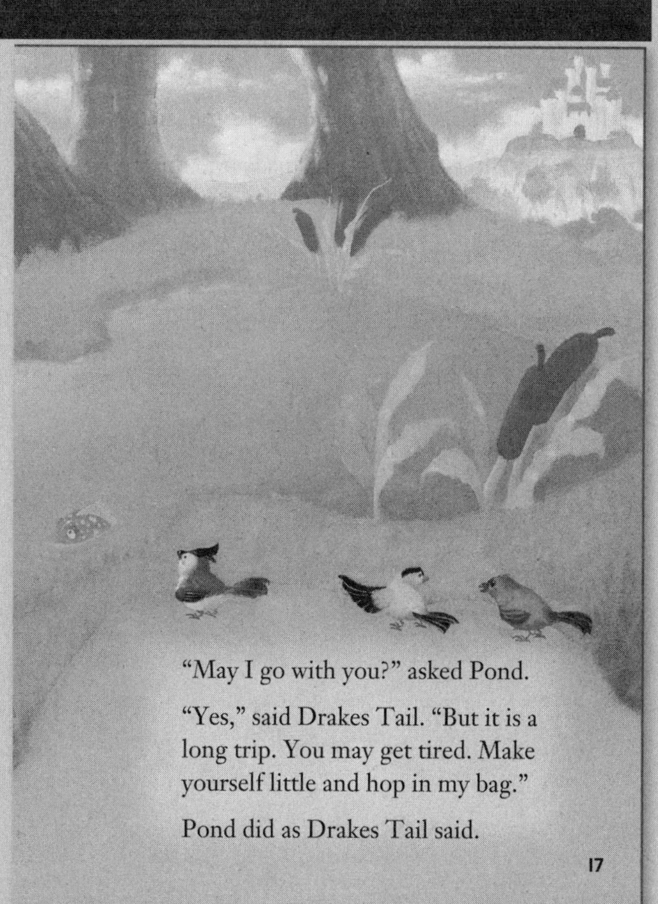

"May I go with you?" asked Pond.

"Yes," said Drakes Tail. "But it is a long trip. You may get tired. Make yourself little and hop in my bag."

Pond did as Drakes Tail said.

17

Text

- *Let's read the first sentence together:* "Quack! Quack! Quack! Time to get my money back!" sang Drakes Tail.
- *Drakes Tail sees his friend, Pond. What does Drakes Tail tell Pond?* (that he is going to see the king to get his money back)

Page 17

Whole Page

- *Pond wants to go with Drakes Tail to see the king! Does Drakes Tail say* yes *or* no? (yes)
- *Drakes Tail says:* "Make yourself little and hop into my bag." *Let's use our hands to show how Pond made himself little.* (Demonstrate holding hands apart and then moving them closer together.)
- *Now let's pretend to hold the bag with one hand.* (Demonstrate holding out one hand to stand for the bag) *Let's make Pond hop into the bag with our other hand.* (Demonstrate moving the other hand to represent Pond hopping into the bag.)

Formal and Informal English

When children encounter a formal expression, discuss other ways the character would communicate with more informal language. For example: *May I go with you?/Can I go with you?*

Page 18

Illustration

- *This is a hive.* (Point to the hive.) *Say it with me:* hive. *Bees live inside a hive.* (Move your finger around and make a buzzing sound.) *Look at these bees.* (Point to the bees.) *This hive has a face. Does a hive really have a face?* (no) *This hive is a friend of Drakes Tail.*

Text

- *What does Drakes Tail say while he walks? Let's read it together:* "Quack! Quack! Quack! Time to get my money back!"
- *Drakes Tail spots, or sees, Hive. He tells Hive about his trip to see the king.*

Let's stop here and remember the story. Drakes Tail is going to see the king. First, he sees Fox. Fox wants to go, too. Then he sees Pond. Does Pond want to go, too? (yes) *Now Drakes Tail sees Hive. What do you think will happen?* (He will want to go, too.)

Page 19

Whole Page

- *Look at the hive in the picture. Is it big or little now?* (little) *Where is it going?* (into the bag) *Point to the fox. Point to the pond.*
- *Let's read this page together:* Hive wished to come, too. So Hive got little and hopped into Drakes Tail's bag.
- *Let's use our hands again to show how Hive got little.* (Demonstrate holding hands apart and then moving them closer together.)
- *Now let's pretend to hold the bag with one hand again.* (Demonstrate holding out one hand to stand for the bag.) *Let's make Hive hop into the bag with the other hand.* (Demonstrate moving the other hand into the bag.) *Who are in the bag now?* (Fox, Pond, Hive)

Pages 18–19

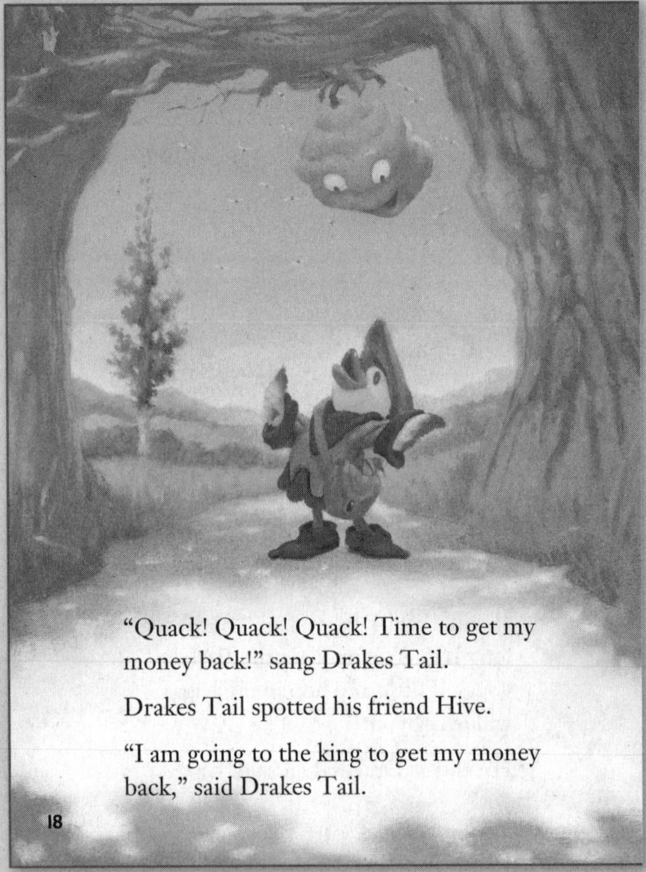
"Quack! Quack! Quack! Time to get my money back!" sang Drakes Tail.
Drakes Tail spotted his friend Hive.
"I am going to the king to get my money back," said Drakes Tail.
18

Pages 20–21

Drakes Tail **walked across** the land.

After **eight** days, he made it to the king's palace.

"Quack! Quack! Quack! Can I have my money back?" Drakes Tail asked the king.

20

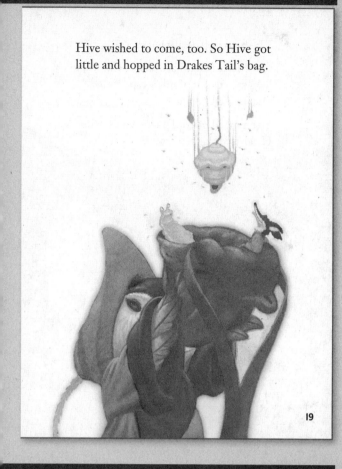

Hive wished to come, too. So Hive got little and hopped in Drakes Tail's bag.

19

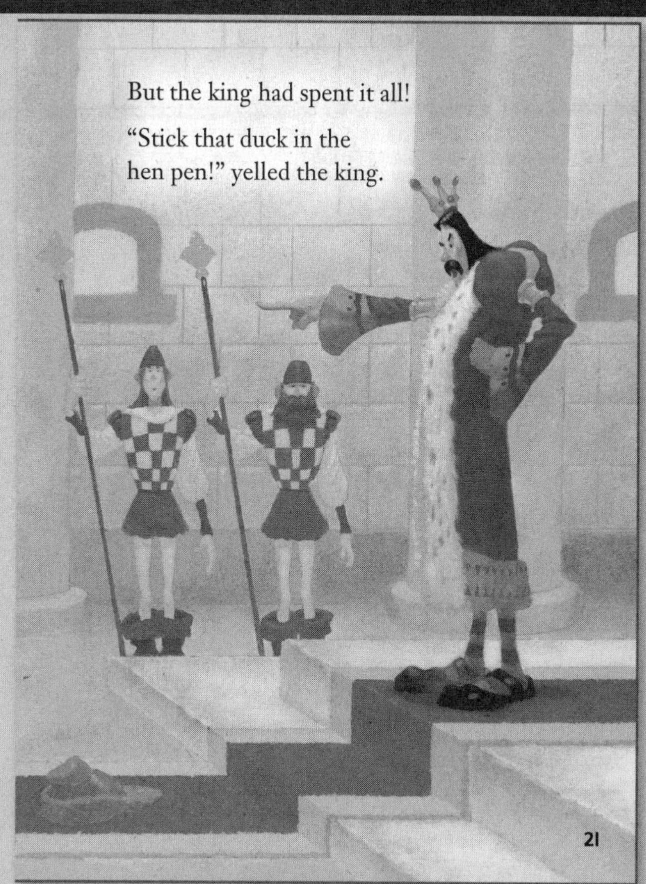

But the king had spent it all!

"Stick that duck in the hen pen!" yelled the king.

21

Pages 20–21

Text

- *Let's read the first two paragraphs together:* Drakes Tail walked and walked across the land. After eight days, he made it to the king's palace. *Is eight days a long time to walk or a short time to walk?* (a long time)
- *Let's read what Drakes Tail says when he sees the king:* "Quack! Quack! Quack! Can I have my money back?"
- *But the king doesn't have any money. Why doesn't he?* (He spent it.) *Let's read what the king says together:* "Stick that duck in the hen pen!"
- *A pen can be something that you write with. It can also be a place where animals live. Which kind of pen is a hen pen?* (a place where animals live)

Illustration

- *Look at the king in the picture. He is pointing to his men. What does he want them to do?* (take Drakes Tail to the hen pen)
- *The king looks mad. Do you think Drakes Tail looks mad or scared?* (scared) *Let's look mad like the king.* (Make a mad face.) *Now let's look scared like Drakes Tail.* (Make a scared face.)

Let's talk about what might happen next. Drakes Tail will be in the hen pen. He is scared, but he has three friends in his bag. Who are they? (Fox, Pond, Hive) *Is a fox scared of hens?* (no) *A fox likes to eat hens. Do you think Fox might help Drakes Tail?* (yes)

Page 22

Whole Page

- *Point to the hens in the picture. How many are there?* (three) *Now look at this hen's beak.* (Point to a beak.) *A beak is very hard and sharp.*
- *The hens peck at Drakes Tail with their beaks.* (*They peck him like this.* ("Peck" your hand with a finger.) *Do you think that feels good or hurts?* (hurts)
- *Drakes Tail says he is* in bad shape." In bad shape *means "in trouble." Then he says:* "Come and help me get out of this scrape!" *He means "Come and help me with this problem!"*
- *Let's read Drakes Tail's words together:* "Fox! Fox! I'm in bad shape. Come and help me get out of this scrape!" *What words rhyme, or sound the same at the end?* (*shape* and *scrape*) *Drakes Tail always sings his words.*
- *Fox hops out of the bag like this.* (Use one hand to represent the bag and the other to represent Fox hopping out of it.) *Now use your hands to make Fox hop out of the bag.* (Demonstrate the action again.)
- *Look at the picture. Is Fox big or small now?* (big) *Do the hens play with Fox or run away?* (They run away.)

Page 23

Whole Page

- *Look at the picture. Where is Drakes Tail now?* (in the palace, talking to the king)
- *What does Drakes Tail say to the king? Let's read it together:* Quack! Quack! Quack! Can I have my money back?
- *The king wants to eat the duck! He wants to cook him in a pot. Will it be hot or cold in the pot?* (hot)

Think about the things the king does in this story. Do you think he is a good king? Why or why not? Share your ideas with your partner.(Response is open.)

Pages 22–23

The hens pecked at Drakes Tail!

"Fox! Fox! I am in bad shape. Come and help me get out of this scrape!" sang Drakes Tail.

Fox hopped out of Drakes Tail's bag. He chased the hens away.

22

Pages 24–25

"Pond! Pond! I am in a bad spot. Put out the fire that is so hot!" sang Drakes Tail.

Pond gushed out of the bag and put out the fire. Drakes Tail ran.

24

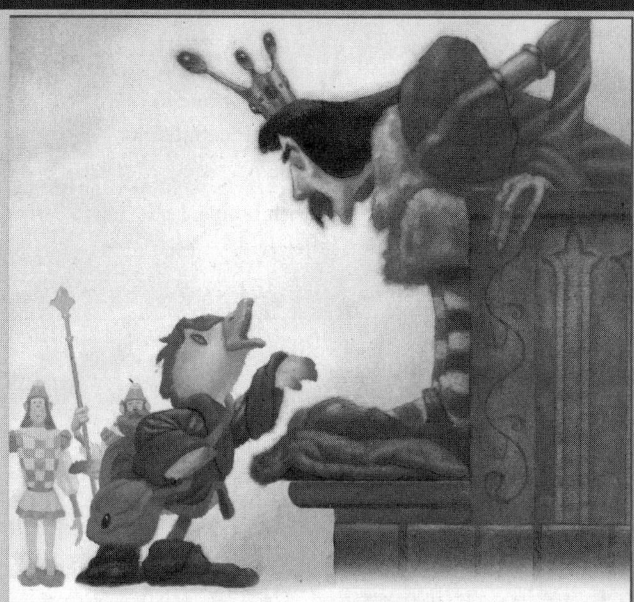

Drakes Tail went back to the king. "Quack! Quack! Quack! Can I have my money back?"

"That duck shall make a fine snack!" said the king. "Put him in a pot!"

23

"Catch that duck!" yelled the king.

Drakes Tail sang, "Hive! Hive! Help me please! It is time to send the bees!"

Hive sent its bees to sting the king and his men. They ran and ran.

25

Page 24

Illustration

- *Point to the fire under the pot. That fire is hot!*

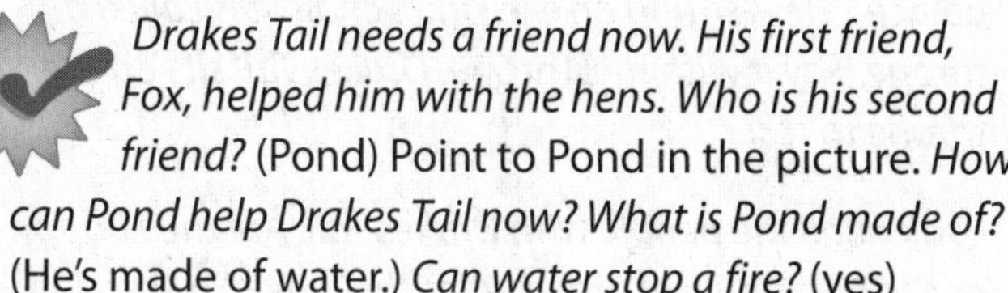

Drakes Tail needs a friend now. His first friend, Fox, helped him with the hens. Who is his second friend? (Pond) Point to Pond in the picture. *How can Pond help Drakes Tail now? What is Pond made of?* (He's made of water.) *Can water stop a fire?* (yes)

Text

- *Drakes Tail says:* "I'm in a bad spot." *He means that he is in trouble. He asks Pond for help. He wants Pond to put out, or stop, the hot fire.*
- *Let's read Drakes Tail's words together:* "Pond! Pond! I'm in a bad spot. Put out the fire that is so hot!" *What words rhyme, or sound the same at the end?* (*spot* and *hot*)
- *Pond is big again, and a lot of water gushes out of the bag, or pours out really fast. Pond puts out the fire. Drakes Tail runs away!*

Page 25

Whole Page

- *The king want his men to catch Drakes Tail. Is Drakes Tail in trouble again?* (yes) *Drakes Tail asks Hive for help. Let's read Drakes Tail's words together:* "Hive! Hive! Help me please! It is time to send out the bees."
- *Hive sends his bees to sting, like this.* ("Sting" your hand with a finger and say, "Ouch!") *Look at the picture. What are the king and his men doing?* (running from the bees)

Page 26

Whole Page

- *Look at Drakes Tail. Where is he?* (He's at the king's palace.) *He is sitting on the king's chair. It is called a throne. Say it with me:* throne. *Drakes Tail sits on the throne to rest.*
- *Look at all the people with Drakes Tail. Are they happy or sad?* (happy) *Let's read what they say:* "Drakes Tail is a duck with brains. Let's make him our king!"

Page 27

Paragraph 1

- *Let's read Drakes Tail's words together:* "I will be the king today, if you say my friends can stay!" *(What words rhyme, or sound the same at the end?* (today and *stay*)

Talk with your partner about Drakes Tail. What kind of king do you think he will be? Will he be a better king than the last one? (Questions are open.)

Pages 26–27

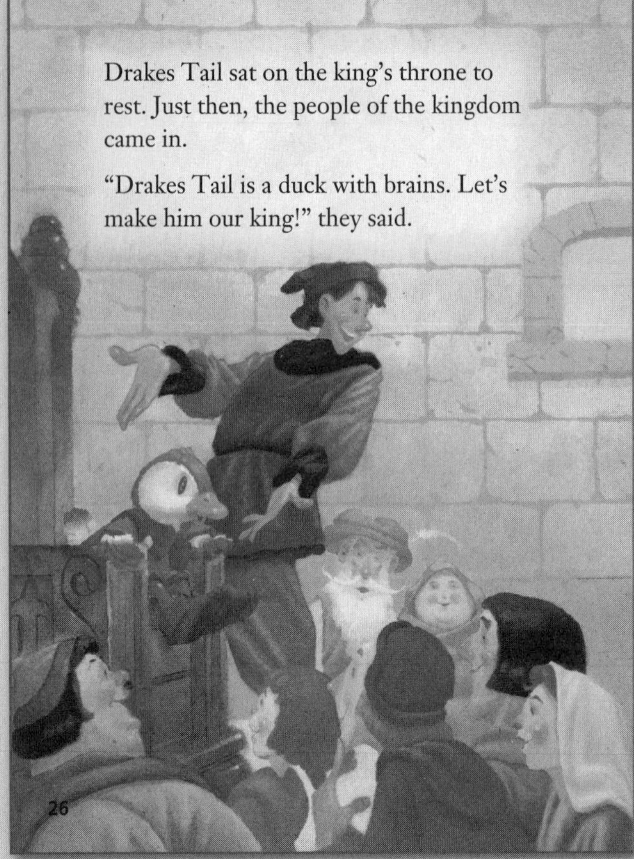

Drakes Tail sat on the king's throne to rest. Just then, the people of the kingdom came in.
"Drakes Tail is a duck with brains. Let's make him our king!" they said.
26

Drakes Tail sang, "I will be the king today, if you say my friends can stay!"

From that day on, Drakes Tail ruled the kingdom. He had Fox, Pond, and Hive at his side.

27

Illustration and Paragraph 2

- *Look at the picture. Drake's Tail is king now. What does he have on his head?* (a crown) *A crown shows who the ruler is. Who is with Drake's Tail?* (Fox, Pond, Hive) *Did the people let these friends stay?* (yes)
- Let's read the last paragraph together: From that day on, Drakes Tail ruled the kingdom. He had Fox, Pond, and Hive at his side.
- *The story stays that Drakes Tail ruled the kingdom. That means that he made all the rules and laws. Drakes Tail was king, and he always had his friends with him!*

Busy as a Bee

Access Core Content

Teacher Note Pose the questions after you read the paragraph or page indicated.

Page 30

Title and Photo

- *Listen as I read the title:* Busy as a Bee. *When you are busy, you do many things. Let's read to find out about the many things that bees do.*
- *Look at the picture. It shows a hive where bees live. Point to the hive. Do you see many bees or a few bees?* (many)
- *A caption gives us information, or tells us new things. Listen as I read the caption:* Bees can make a hive in a tree. *Where can bees make a hive?* (in a tree)

Text

- *Bees make this sound:* buzz, buzz, buzz. *Say it with me:* buzz, buzz, buzz. *Now listen as I read the page.*
- *The bees live in the hive. How do they help the hive?* (by doing jobs)

Page 31

Photo and Caption

- *Look at the bees in the big picture. They are worker bees. They are making honey. Honey is sweet, like sugar. People like to eat honey. Say it with me:* honey.
- *Listen as I read the caption for the small picture:* Worker bees make wax cups called honeycombs. *We use wax to make candles and crayons. Bees use wax to make cups. Let's point to a wax cup in the small picture.* (Point to one of the wax cups in the picture.)
- *The worker bees put honey in the wax cups. What do we call the wax cups?* (honeycombs)

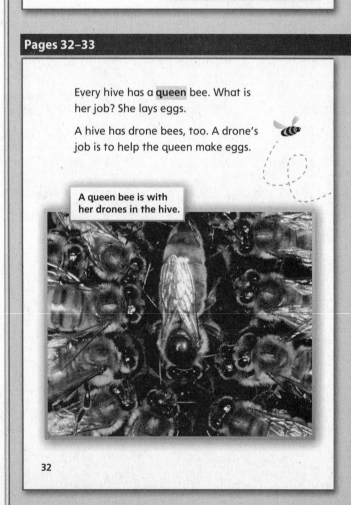

Pages 30–31

Science

Genre
Nonfiction gives information about a topic.

Text Feature
A Caption gives information about a photograph or picture.

Content Vocabulary
worker
honey
queen

LOG ON FIND OUT
Science Animals at Work
www.macmillanmh.com

Busy As a Bee

Buzz, buzz, buzz! Bees are at home in a hive. They are so busy! All of them have jobs that help the hive.

Bees can make a hive in a tree.

30

Pages 32–33

Every hive has a **queen** bee. What is her job? She lays eggs.

A hive has drone bees, too. A drone's job is to help the queen make eggs.

A queen bee is with her drones in the hive.

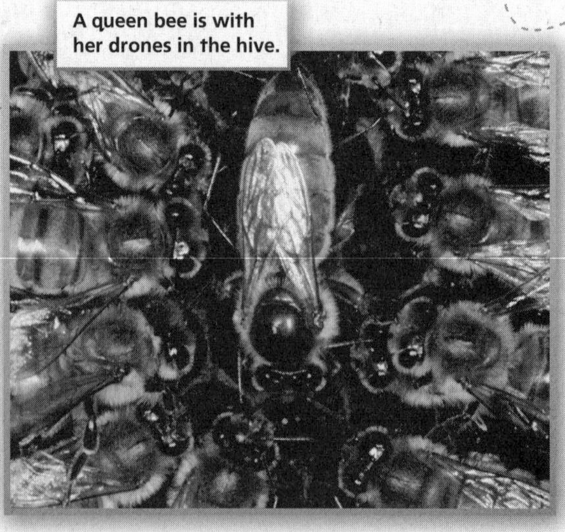

32

Science

Worker bees make wax cups called honeycombs.

Lots of worker bees live in a hive. They make honey. They help the hive stay clean. They fan the hive with their wings when it gets hot.

31

The queen lays eggs inside wax cups.

New bees hatch from these eggs. Worker bees feed them.

As time passes, a hive can get quite big. Buzz, buzz, buzz! A big hive is a busy place!

Connect and Compare

- How do the captions help you understand the pictures?
- What can you learn from the pictures? Point to the eggs in the photograph on this page.

33

Text

- *Listen as I read the page aloud.*
- *Some bees are worker bees. Worker bees have three kinds of work, or jobs.* (Hold up three fingers and count off as you explain each job.) *They make honey. They clean the hive. They fan the hive when it's hot.*
- *Lets fan our faces.* (Demonstrate fanning your face.) *Does that make you feel cooler or hotter?* (cooler) *When the hive is hot, the worker bees fan with their wings.*

Pretend that you and your partner are worker bees. Your arms are your wings. It's hot in the hive. Make buzzing sounds, and talk to each other about how hot it is. Then fan your wings to cool the hive off.

Page 32

Photo and Caption

- *Listen as I read the caption for the picture:* A queen bee and her drones in the hive. *The big bee is called the queen bee. Point to her. The smaller bees are called drones. Point to them.*

Text

- *Listen as I read the page aloud.*
- *The queen bee has a job. She lays ______.* (eggs) *Birds lay eggs, and bees lay eggs. Do you think bees' eggs are big or very small?* (very small) *Drones have a job, too. They help the queen bee make eggs.*
- *We have learned about three kinds of bees. What are they?* (worker bees, the queen bee, drones)

Page 33

Photo and Caption

- *Look at this wax.* (Point to it.) *The queen bee lays her eggs here. Listen as I read the caption aloud:* The queen lays eggs inside wax cups.

Text

- *Listen as I read the page aloud.*
- *The new bees hatch, or come out of the eggs. What do the worker bees give them?* (food)
- *A hive can get big. Do lots of bees live there, or just a few?* (lots of bees) *They are busy doing their jobs. What sounds do the bees make?* (buzz, buzz, buzz)

Name ___________________________

Use the word chart to study this week's vocabulary words. Write a sentence using each word in your writer's notebook.

Word	Context Sentence	Illustration
trip ______________	We are on a trip to see Aunt Sally.	Where would you like to take a trip?
borrow ______________	I can borrow books from the library.	Library

© Macmillan/McGraw-Hill

Name________________________________

Read each question and prompt. Discuss the answers with your group. Use your Leveled Reader to find details to support your answers. Then write your answers on another sheet of paper.

1. Tell about the characters in your book. Are they pals?

2. Talk about a mistake one character makes.

3. Retell the main events of the story.

4. Have you heard another story that is a little bit like this one? Tell your classmates about it.

5. Show your favorite illustration to the group. Why do you like it?

© Macmillan/McGraw-Hill

Gram and Me

Pages 40–41

Prior to reading the selection with children, they should have listened to the selection on **StudentWorks Plus,** the interactive eBook. In addition, selection vocabulary should have been pretaught using the **Visual Vocabulary Resources.**

Access Core Content

Teacher Note Pose the questions after you read the text indicated.

Pages 40–41

Title and Illustration

- *Read the title of this story with me:* Gram and Me. *The name Gram is short for Grandma or Grandmother. Your grandmother is the mother of your father or mother.*
- *Look at the picture and point to the boy. Now point to Gram. Who will be telling the story?* (The boy will be telling the story.) *We know this because the title of the story is* Gram and Me. *The* me *in the title is the boy.*
- *Now point to the cat in the chair. We don't know yet if it belongs to the boy or his grandmother.*

How do you think the boy feels about Gram?(The boy likes Gram a lot.) *How do you know?* (He is smiling. He looks very happy to be with Gram.)

- *Let's read to find out more about the boy, his grandmother, and the cat.*

Page 42

Text

- *Let's read the first page of this story together.*
- *The boy likes Gram a lot. Why does he like her so much? (because she is a lot of fun)*

Pages 40–41

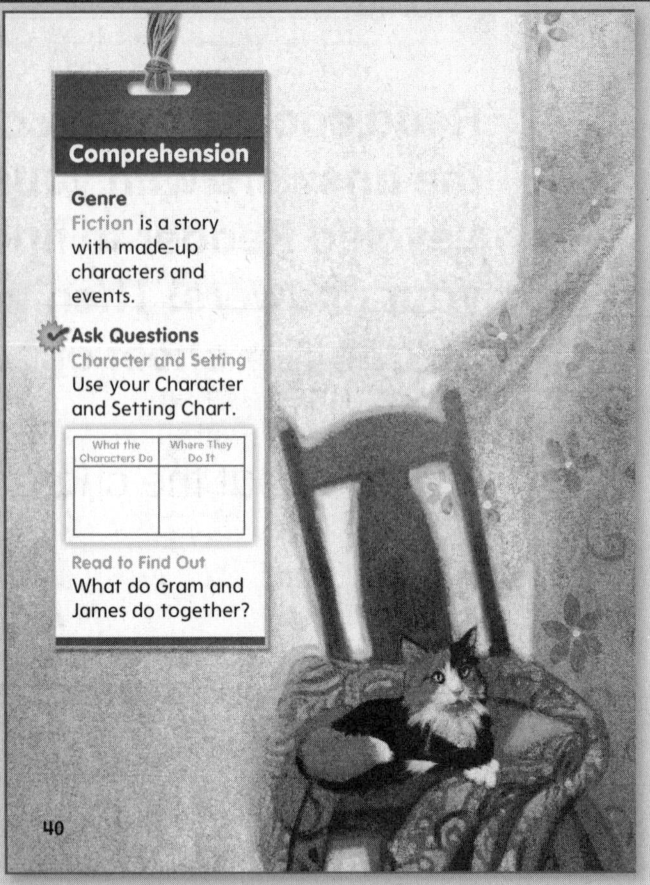

Pages 42–43

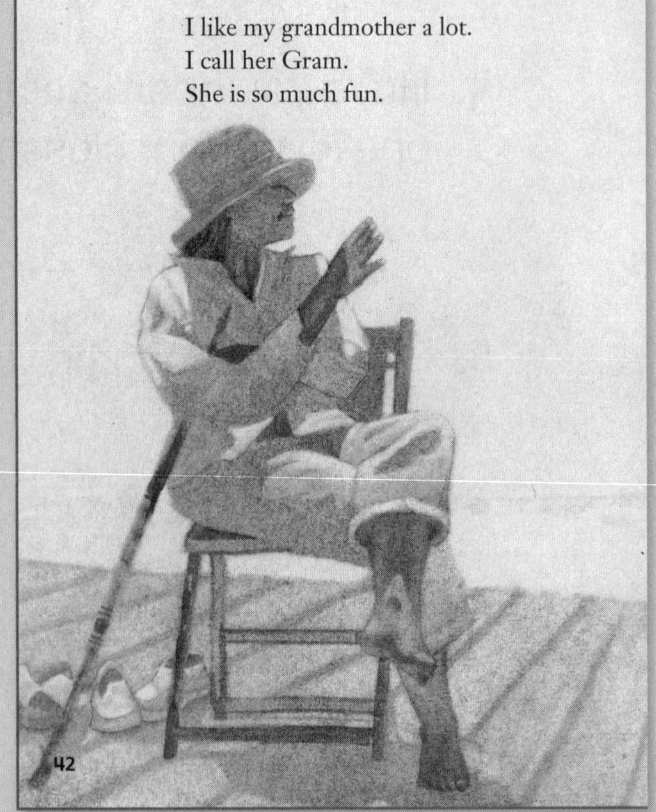

I like my grandmother a lot.
I call her Gram.
She is so much fun.
42

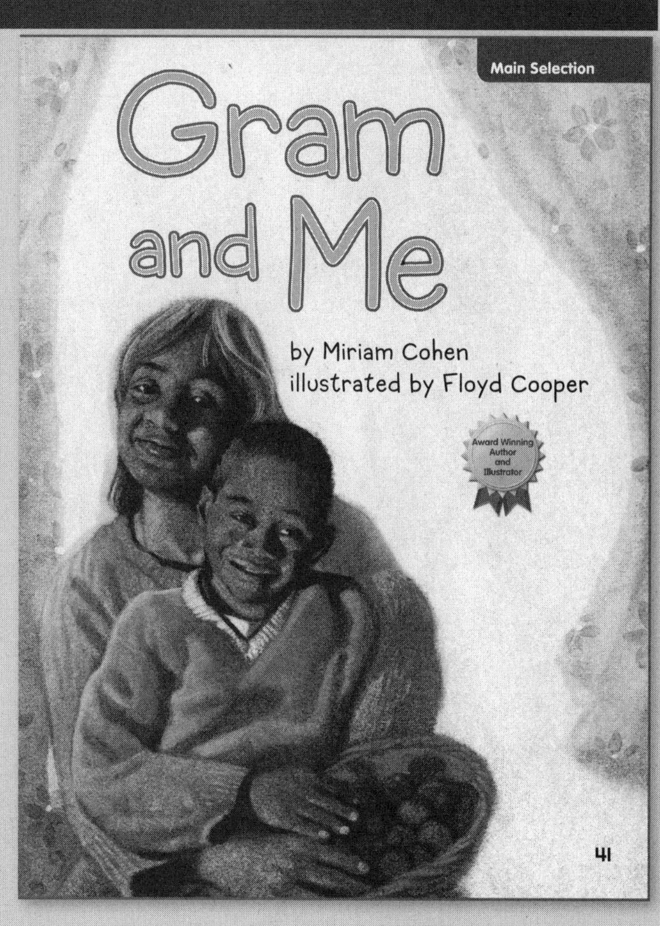

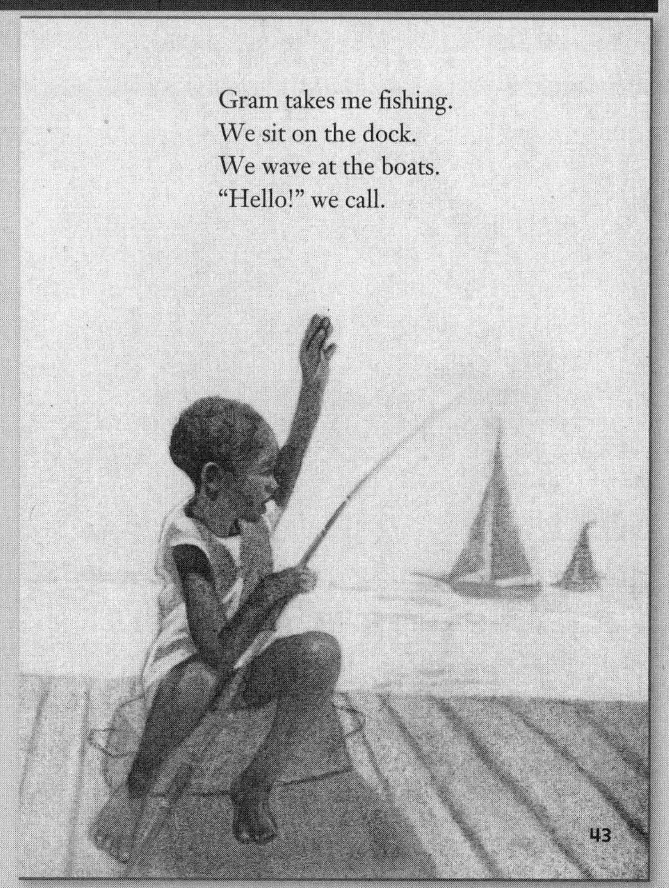

Gram takes me fishing.
We sit on the dock.
We wave at the boats.
"Hello!" we call.
43

There are lots of different names for grandmothers and grandfathers. Imagine that you are a grandmother or grandfather. What would you like your grandchildren to call you? Tell your partner.

Page 43

Whole Page

- *A dock stretches out into the water.* (Point to the dock in the picture.) *It is made of wood, and you can sit on it or walk on it. You can also fish from a dock, or you can bring a boat up to a dock. Say it with me:* dock.
- *Let's read this page together.*
- *What is one thing that the boy and Gram do together?* (The boy and Gram fish.) *Where do they fish?* (They fish on the dock.)
- *Let's pretend that we are on the dock with Gram and the boy. Let's wave at the boats and call* hello *just like the boy and Gram do:* Hello! (Demonstrate waving.)
- **Directionality**

  Ask children to place their finger where you start reading (top left). Ask where you finish reading on this page (bottom right).

Gram and Me

Page 44

Whole Page

- *Let's take a look at the picture before we read this page. What is the boy doing?* (The boy is riding a bike.) *What is Gram doing?* (Gram is helping the boy.)
- *Point to the word* wheels *on this page. What other words on the page give you clues about the meaning of the word* wheels? (The words *ride, bike,* and *two* give clues about the meaning of *wheels.*) *Point to the wheels in the picture.*
- *The boy's name is James. Let's read aloud what Gram says when James rides his bike. Say the words like Gram would say them:* "You can do it, James!"
- *Now let's read what James says. Say the words like James would say them:* "Look at me go!"

Page 45

Text

- *What kind of a pet does Gram have?* (Gram has a cat.) *What is the pet's name?* (The cat's name is Bean.)
- *Let's read aloud what Gram says to James:* "Scratch him under the chin." *This is a chin.* (Point to your chin.) *Show me where your chin is.*

Illustration

- *Look at James scratching Bean under the chin. Now pretend you are James. Show me how you would scratch Bean.* (Demonstrate scratching beneath your own chin.)

Page 46

Text

- *Chess is a board game. When you play chess, you try to capture, or take, your partner's game pieces. Chess can be hard to play. It takes a lot of thought to play chess well.*

Pages 44–45

Gram helps me ride my bike.
It has two wheels.
"You can do it, James!" she **says**.
"I can ride!" I say.

44

Pages 46–47

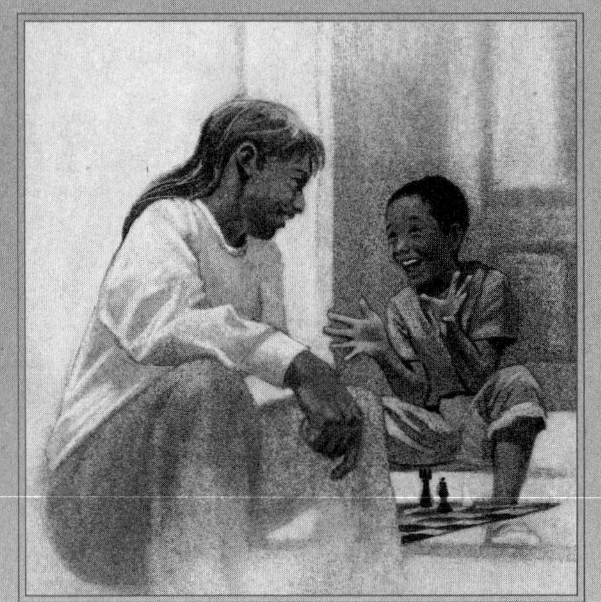

Gram and I play chess.
She helps me when we play.
"**Concentrate**, James," she says.
"I win, Gram!" I say.

46

Gram has a cat named Bean.
Bean feels soft when I pet him.
"Scratch him under his chin," she says.
"Bean likes it!" I say.

Gram has a lot of **pretty** flowers.
She lets me **give** them a drink.
"Flowers need a good drink," she says.
"Look! They drank it up," I say.

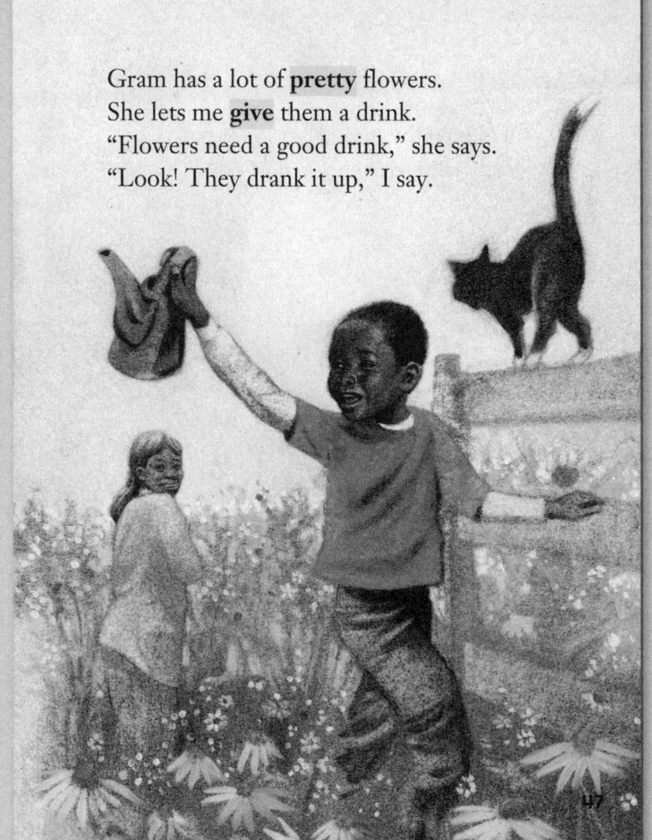

- *Gram tells James to concentrate when they play chess. When you concentrate on something, you pay close attention to it and think carefully about it. Why do you have to concentrate when playing chess?* (Chess can be hard to play. It takes a lot of thought.)
- *Who wins the chess game?* (James wins the chess game.) *How do you know?* (James says, "I win, Gram!")

Illustration

- *Point to the chessboard. You can see two of the chess pieces on it. Players move the pieces around the board. Let's pretend to move chess pieces around a board.*

Page 47

Text

- *Let's point to the word* pretty *on this page.* Pretty *means "nice to look at," or "beautiful." Now let's read the whole sentence:* Gram has a lot of pretty flowers.
- *James gives the flowers a drink. What do you think he gives the flowers to drink?* (water) *Plants need water to grow.*
- *What does James say when he gives the flowers a drink? Read his words with me:* "Look! They drank it all up."

Illustration

Where are James and Gram in this part of the story? (James and Gram are outside in Gram's garden.) *Look at their faces. How do you think they feel about being together in the garden?* (They feel happy. They are having fun.)

- *Point to the watering can that James is holding in his hand. Now pretend you are James. Show me how you would give the flowers a drink of water with the watering can.* (Demonstrate the action.)

PARTNERS *Think about all the things that James does with his grandmother. Would you rather fish, ride a bike, play chess, or help water flowers in a garden? Tell your partner which thing you would rather do and why.* (Responses are open.)

Page 48

Text

- *Why does Gram lift up James?* (Gram lifts up James so he can pick plums from the tree.)
- *Let's read what James says when Gram lifts him up. Read the words as if you were James:* "I got a ripe one!"
- *Things that are ripe are ready to eat. Plums are sweet and juicy when they are ripe. What other fruits are good to eat when they are ripe?* (Question is open.)

Illustration

- *Look at James and Gram in the picture. Gram has a basket for the plums they pick.* (Point to the basket.) *Pretend you are James. Show me how you would pick plums from the tree and put them into a basket.* (Demonstrate the action.)

Page 49

Illustration

- *Let's look at the picture before we read this page. What are James and Gram doing?* (cooking) *How do you know?* (There is a pot in the picture. Gram is putting something into the pot.)
- *Gram is holding onto the pot with a towel. Point to the towel. Do you think she needs the towel because the pot is hot or because it is cold?* (because it is hot)

Text

- *Gram and James are cooking. Gram is teaching James how to make plum jam. Jam is a spread, like jelly, that is made from fruit. You can put jam on toast or bread. What else can you put jam on?* (crackers, muffins, biscuits)
- *Let's read aloud what James says:* "Yum! This jam will taste good!"

Pages 48–49

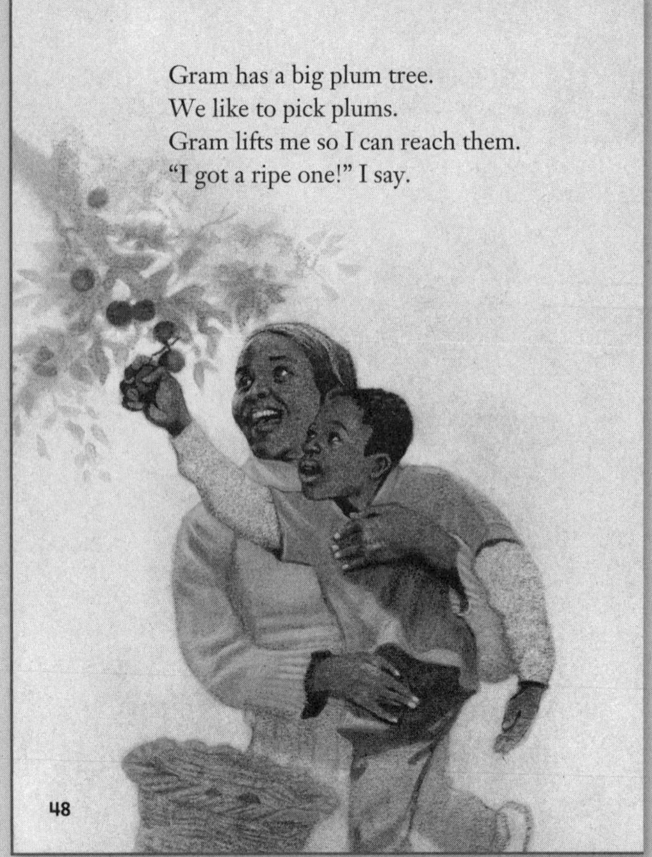

Gram has a big plum tree.
We like to pick plums.
Gram lifts me so I can reach them.
"I got a ripe one!" I say.
48

Pages 50–51

"Gram, did you cook when you **were** little?" I ask.
"I helped my mom," says Gram. "We made jam just like you and I do."

50

Gram teaches me how to make plum jam.
She adds salt to the pot.
"Just a bit," she says.
"Yum! This jam will taste good!" I say.

49

"Did you go to school?" I ask.
"Yes, I went to a little school," says Gram.
"My school is big," I say.
"Yes, it is," says Gram.

51

Page 50

Text

- *James is a good helper. Gram was a good helper when she was little, too. How do we know this from the story?* (Gram helped her mom make jam, just like James helps Gram make jam now.)
- *You can often learn something when you help grown-ups. What did Gram learn by helping her mother?* (how to make plum jam) *What is James learning now?* (the same thing)

Talk with your partner about a time when you helped a grown-up do something. Tell what you did and any things you learned.

Page 51

Text

- *Let's read this page together.*
- *Tell me one way that Gram's school was different from James's school.*(Gram's school was little. James's school is very big.)

Illustration

Where are James and Gram in this part of the story? (They are in Gram's kitchen.) *How do you know?* (There is a stove in the picture. Gram is making jam. James is sitting at a kitchen table.)

Formal and Informal English

When children encounter a colloquial or informal word in the text, discuss other ways of saying the same word with more formal language. For example, *Yum!/It's delicious!*

Gram and Me

Page 52

Illustration

- *James and Gram are eating the plum jam that Gram made. Are they eating it on bread or on a muffin?* (bread) *Do they look happy or sad?* (happy) *What kind of jam do you like to eat on bread?* (Question is open.)

Text

- *James is telling Gram about school. What is he learning at school?* (James is learning to read and write.)

How was Gram like James when she was his age? (Gram learned to read and write when she was the same age as James.)

- *James asks Gram a question at the bottom of the page. Let's read it together:* "Gram, can you read me a story?"

Page 53

Whole Page

- *Gram is going to read a story about cats and dogs to James. Does James like cats and dogs?* (Yes, he likes them a lot.)
- *Look at Bean in the picture. He looks like he wants to hear the story, too! Point to Bean. Now point to the book that Gram will read to James.*
- *Let's read ths page together.*

Page 54

Text

- *James likes Gram's story a lot. What does he want to do now?* (He wants to read more.)
- *Gram asks James if he can read a story to her. Let's read aloud what James says:* "I think I can."

What kinds of stories are fun to read aloud to other people? Tell your partner what kinds of stories you like to read aloud. (Responses are open.)

Pages 52–53

"I am learning to read and **write** at school," I say.
"That is good," says Gram. "I learned to read and write when I was just your age."
"Gram, can you read me a story?"

52

Pages 54–55

I like Gram's story a lot.
"Let's read more," I say.
"Can you read a story to me?" asks Gram.
"I think I can."

54

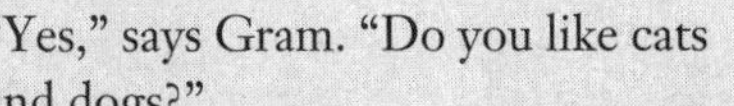

"Yes," says Gram. "Do you like cats and dogs?"
"I like them a lot!" I say.
"This is a story **about** cats and dogs."

"I will read you this story," I say.
"Is it about cats and dogs?" Gram asks.
"No, it is a story about pigs."
"Pigs are good, too," says Gram.

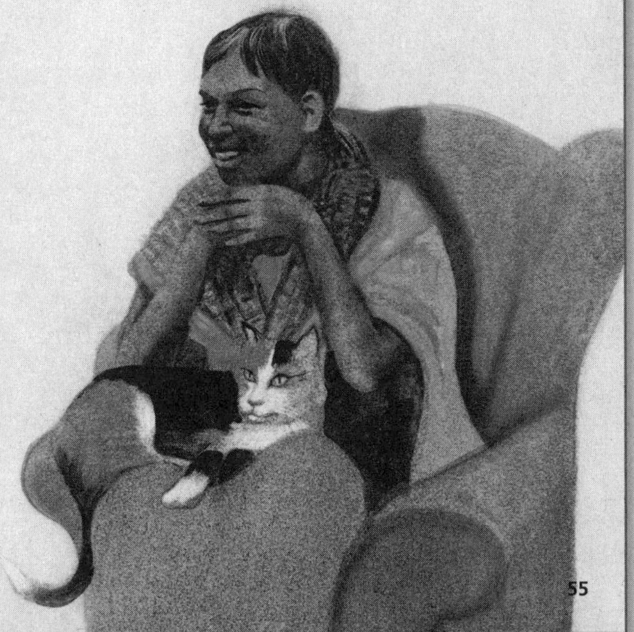

Page 55

Text

- Let's read this page together.
- James says that he will read a story about pigs. *Does Gram like that idea?* (yes) *How do you know?* (She says, "Pigs are good, too.")

We know that James and Gram like to fish and play chess. They like to make jam together. Now what else do we learn about them? (James and Gram like to read.)

Illustration

- *Look at Gram. She is listening to James read the story. Do you think Gram likes the story?* (yes) *Why do you think that?* (Gram is looking at James as he reads. Gram is smiling.)

Gram and Me

Page 56

Text

- *James reads a story about three little pigs. What story do we know about three little pigs? Let's retell the story.* (Possible version: Three little pigs build houses. A wolf blows down the house made of straw and the house made of sticks. The wolf can't blow down the house of the third pig, because it is made of bricks.)

Illustration

- *Look at James as he reads the story. He looks like he is reading in a loud, strong voice. Let's read aloud the first sentence on this page as James might read it:* "This is a story about three little pigs."
- *Then James says,* I read on and on. *He means that he keeps on reading. When do you think he stops?* (at the end of the story)

Page 57

Illustration

- *James has finished reading the book in this picture. We can tell because he is closing the book. Do you think that Gram and James enjoyed the book? Why or why not?* (yes, because they are smiling.)

PARTNERS

Imagine that you are James. What would you do with Gram next? Tell your partner what you and Gram could do. (Responses are open.)

Pages 56–57

"This is a story about three little
pigs," I say.
I read on and on.
56

At the end, Gram claps and claps.
"What a **splendid** story," she says.
"Gram, you are so much fun," I say.
"So are you," says my Gram.

57

Text

- *Let's read the end of the story together.*
- *After James reads, Gram claps and claps. I can clap.* (Demonstrate clapping.) *Show me how you clap.*
- *Something that is splendid is very, very nice. A splendid story is one that you enjoy hearing a lot. What are the names of some splendid stories that you have heard?* (Question is open.)

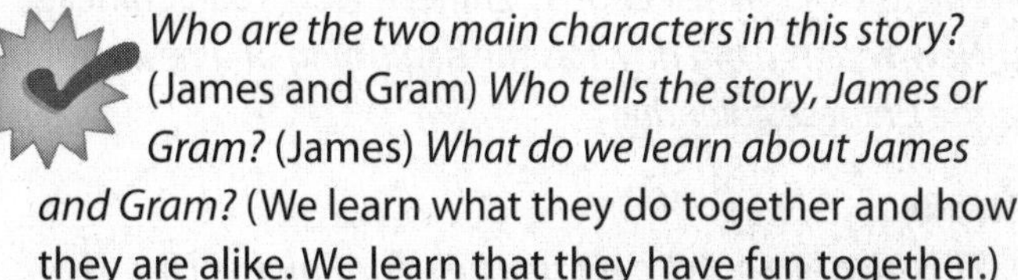

Who are the two main characters in this story? (James and Gram) *Who tells the story, James or Gram?* (James) *What do we learn about James and Gram?* (We learn what they do together and how they are alike. We learn that they have fun together.)

Seek Clarification

Some children may be confused by complex syntax. Encourage children to always seek clarification when they encounter a sentence that does not make sense to them. For example, *I don't understand "so are you."*

Chinese New Year

Access Core Content

Teacher Note Pose the questions after you read the text indicated.

Page 60

Title

- *The title of this selection is* Chinese New Year. *Chinese New Year is a big day. It is the beginning of a new year in the Chinese calendar.*

Photo

- *This picture shows a parade held for Chinese New Year. A parade is when people dance, march, and perform along a street to celebrate something, or show they are happy about it.*
- *People often wear uniforms or costumes during a parade. They often sing or play music. Let's pretend we are marching in a parade.* (Lead them in a march.)
- *The animal with teeth is a dragon. Point to the dragon. The dragon is an exciting part of a Chinese New Year parade.*

Text

- *When you celebrate a day, you do special things to enjoy that day. Listen as I read:* Chinese New Year is a lot of fun. Let's see how kids celebrate it.

Page 61

Whole Page

- *Point to the girl in the picture. Her name is Ming Lee.*
- *Listen as I read the lines at the bottom of the page:* To get set, Ming Lee makes a list. She has a lot to do! To get set *means "to get ready." What does Ming Lee do to get set for Chinese New Year?* (She makes a list.)
- *Ming's list is at the top of the page. It is called* Things to Do. *Point to Ming Lee's list.*
- *There is a number in front of each thing on Ming's list. Point to the number as I read it:* 1. Make things to eat. 2. Make a costume. 3. Get a flag. 4. Get gifts. *What is the last thing on Ming's list?* (Get gifts.)

Pages 60–61

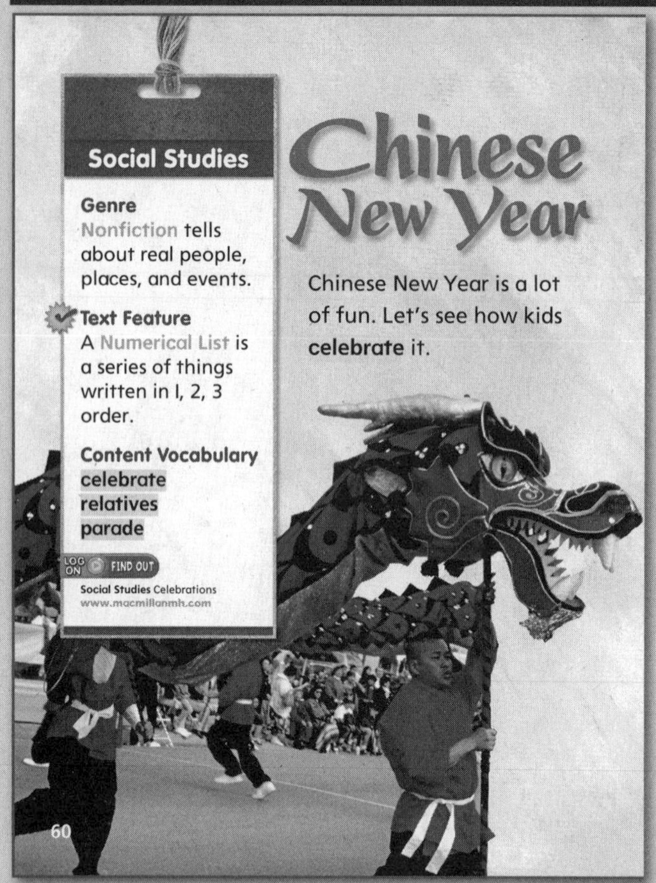

Social Studies
Genre
Nonfiction tells about real people, places, and events.
Text Feature
A Numerical List is a series of things written in 1, 2, 3 order.
Content Vocabulary
celebrate
relatives
parade
LOG ON FIND OUT
Social Studies Celebrations
www.macmillanmh.com
Chinese New Year
Chinese New Year is a lot of fun. Let's see how kids celebrate it.
60

Pages 62–63

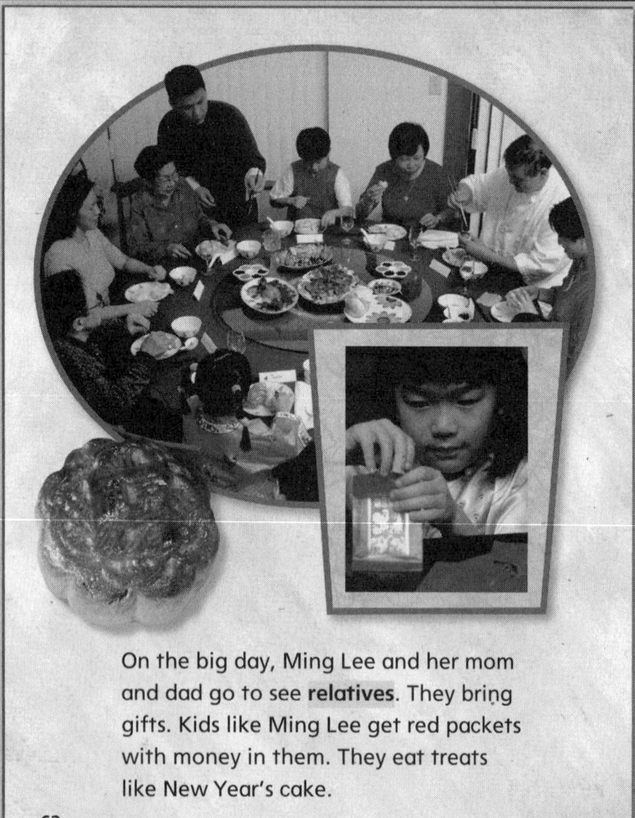

On the big day, Ming Lee and her mom and dad go to see relatives. They bring gifts. Kids like Ming Lee get red packets with money in them. They eat treats like New Year's cake.
62

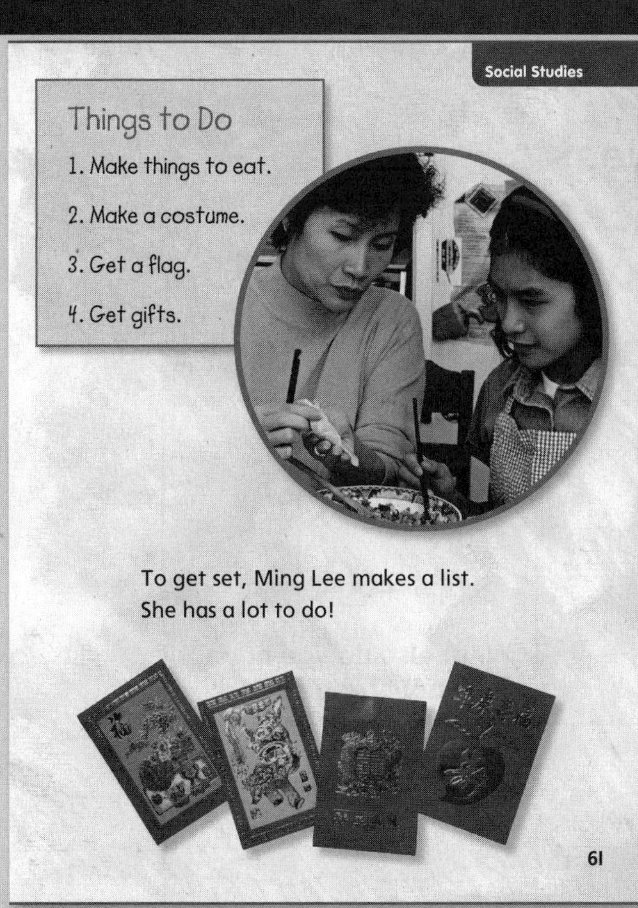
Social Studies
Things to Do
1. Make things to eat.
2. Make a costume.
3. Get a flag.
4. Get gifts.

To get set, Ming Lee makes a list. She has a lot to do!

61

The day ends in a big **parade**. People dress up. They wave big flags. It is such a fun way to start the year!

Connect and Compare
- How do you celebrate the new year?
- How might James and Gram from *Gram and Me* celebrate the new year?

63

- *The second thing on the list is* Get costumes. *A costume is a set of clothes you wear on a special day. When have you worn or seen a costume?* (Question is open.)

Page 62

Whole Page

- *Listen as I read this page to find out what happens on the big day. What do you think the big, or special, day is?* (Chinese New Year)
- *Relatives are people in your family. Your parents are your relatives. So are grandparents, aunts, uncles, and cousins. Ming Lee and her family see relatives on Chinese New Year. What do Ming Lee and her parents bring to their relatives?* (gifts)
- *Children get red packets on Chinese New Year. The girl in the small picture is opening her red packet.* (Point to it.) *What will she find in it—a toy or money?* (money)
- *The big picture shows Ming Lee's relatives enjoying a meal on Chinese New Year. Look at all the good food they are enjoying! What is one good thing they will eat?* (New Year's cake)

Page 63

Whole Page

- *Now listen as I read the last page.*
- *The special day comes to an end. What is the last thing that people do?* (They go to a parade.)
- *Point to the people waving the big flags. Now point to the children waving the small flags. What are the children wearing?* (costumes) *The costumes are just like the clothes that people once wore in China.*

PARTNERS
What part of Chinese New Year do you think you would enjoy the most? Tell your partner what you would enjoy most, and why. (Responses are open.)

Name ______________________________

Use the word chart to study this week's vocabulary words. Write a sentence using each word in your writer's notebook.

Word	Context Sentence	Illustration
concentrate ______________	If you concentrate, you will not fall.	What else do you have to concentrate on?
splendid ______________	The colors in a sunset are splendid.	

© Macmillan/McGraw-Hill

Name ____________________

Book Talk

Read each question and prompt. Discuss the answers with your group. Use your Leveled Reader to find details to support your answers. Then write your answers on another sheet of paper.

1. Tell about the child and the grownup in your book. What are they doing? What are they talking about?

2. Tell where the story takes place.

3. Tell which things the child and the grownup both like to do.

4. Give examples of some things the child and the grownup do differently.

5. Have you had a conversation like this with a grownup? What did you learn?

© Macmillan/McGraw-Hill

César Chávez

Pages 70–71

Prior to reading the selection with children, they should have listened to the selection on **StudentWorks Plus**, the interactive eBook. In addition, selection vocabulary should have been pretaught using the **Visual Vocabulary Resources**.

Access Core Content

Teacher Note Pose the questions after you read the paragraph or page indicated.

Page 70

Title and Photo

- *The title of this selection is* César Chávez. César Chávez *is the name of the person in the picture on this page. Let's say his name together:* César Chávez.

Text

- *César Chávez helped people who picked crops. Crops are plants that people grow for food. Raise your hand when I name a kind of crop:* apples, baseballs, carrots, pencils. (Children should raise hands when you say *carrots* and *apples.*)
- *When you pick crops, you take them from where they are growing. Some crops grow in the ground. Others grow on trees. Let's pretend to pick peaches from a tree.* (Mime the action and have children imitate you.)
- *Let's read together what César Chávez did:* César Chávez was a great man. In his life, he helped a lot of people. He helped people who picked crops the most.
- **Directionality**
  Ask children to place their finger where you start reading (top left). Ask where you finish reading on this page (bottom right).

Pages 70–71

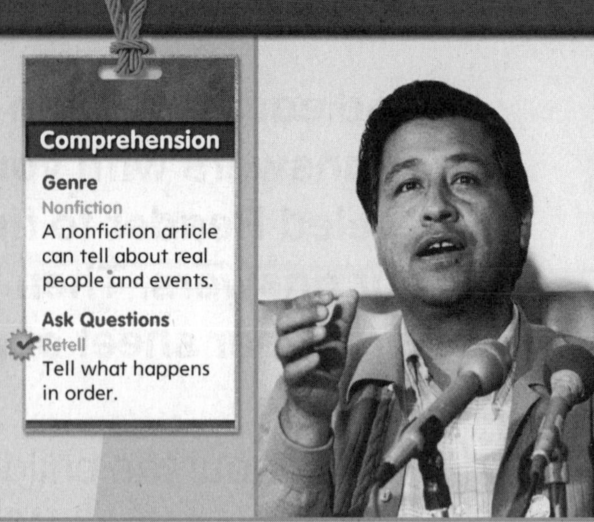

Comprehension
Genre
Nonfiction
A nonfiction article can tell about real people and events.
Ask Questions
Retell
Tell what happens in order.

César Chávez

César Chávez was a great man. In his life he helped a lot of people. He helped people who picked crops the most.

70

Pages 72–73

For a long time, these crop pickers had a **difficult** life. They picked crops in the hot sun all day. The farmers did not pay them much.

Farmers grow crops, such as grapes and peaches.

When the crops are **ripe**, they need to be picked. Then crop pickers come to pick the crops.

71

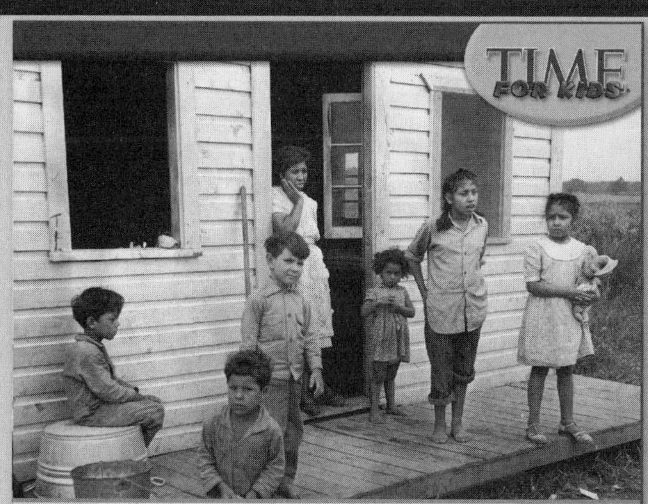

When there were no crops left, the pickers had to **move**.

They had many homes each year. But the homes were not good. The crop pickers lived in shacks.

73

Page 71

Text

- *How do farmers grow crops?* (They plant seeds. They water the plants. They pull out weeds.) *Why do you think farmers grow crops?* (to grow food to eat; to get money to buy things they need)
- *Crops need to be picked when they are ripe, or ready to eat. Is a ripe peach hard or soft?* (soft) *If crops aren't picked when they are ripe, they will rot, or turn bad.*

Page 72

Text, Choral Reading

- *This page tells us that crop pickers had a difficult, or hard, life. They worked in the hot sun. What else made their life so hard?* (They were not paid well.)
- *Let's read this page together.*

Photo

- *Look at the crop pickers. What are they wearing on their heads?* (hats) *The hats keep the hot sun off their heads.*

Page 73

Paragraph 1

- *Families who were pickers worked hard. They picked all the crops from a farmer's fields. When there were no more crops, what did they have to do?* (move to another place) *Did pickers have to move many times each year?* (yes)

How do you think the children felt when they had to move many times? Share your thoughts with your partner. (They probably felt sad to leave their friends. They might have felt scared.)

Paragraph 2 and Photo

- *Look at the shack in the picture. A shack is a very small building. It is not built very well. Dust and wind can get inside. Do you think that a shack is a nice place to live?* (no)

César Chávez

Page 74

Paragraph 1

- *Let's read the first sentence together:* César Chávez did not like this. *César Chávez did not like the way the pickers had to live. What did he think would happen if people worked together?* (Things could change.)

Paragraph 2

- *César Chávez told crop pickers not to pick _______.* (grapes) *He told people not to buy _______.* (grapes)
- *He hoped the farmers would pay attention. He hoped the farmers would try to make the pickers lives better.*

Page 75

Paragraph 1

- *The pickers didn't pick the grapes. The grapes just stayed in the fields. They began to rot, or turn bad. What happened to the grapes?* (They began to rot.)
- *The farmers couldn't sell the grapes. They could not make money. Would this make them unhappy?* (yes)

Paragraph 2 and Photo

- *Look at the picture. The crop pickers are marching with César Chávez. He is carrying a big sign. Point to it.*
- *When people march, they walk together. Sometimes people march because they are unhappy about something and want to change things. The people carry signs that tell why they are unhappy..*
- *The crop pickers were unhappy. They carried signs and spoke to the farmers. What did the crop pickers ask for?* (more pay, better homes)

Patterns in Language

Some grammatical structures, such as past tense "ed," pose difficulties to ELLs. Point out that there are several examples of words ending in *-ed* in this selection, such as *worked, marched, asked, helped.* Help children find a pattern.

Pages 74–75

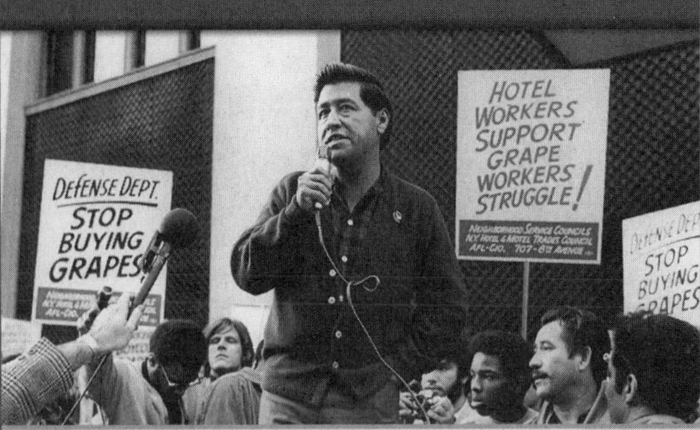

César Chávez did not like this. He wanted the crop pickers to have a **better** life. He felt that if people worked together, things could **change**.

Grapes were one of the biggest crops. César Chávez told the crop pickers not to pick grapes. He told people not to buy grapes.

74

Pages 76–77

César Chávez stands with grape pickers.

It took a long time, but the farmers did make changes.

Today crop pickers have a better life. They get more pay. They live in better homes. They thank César Chávez, who helped them work together.

76

The grapes began to rot.
The farmers did not like this.

The crop pickers marched with César Chávez. They spoke to the farmers. They asked for more pay. They asked for better homes.

75

 **Comprehension Check**

Tell What You Learned
What did you learn about César Chávez?

Think and Compare

1. Who did César Chávez help the most? Retell
2. What was it like for the crop pickers before César Chávez helped them? How did their lives change? Retell
3. Why do you think César Chávez told people not to buy grapes? Draw Conclusions
4. What might César Chávez have said to the peach pickers in "Picking Peaches"? Reading Across Texts

77

PARTNERS *We will pretend that we are pickers in one of César Chávez's marches. First, make signs with your partner. Make one sign that says:* More pay! *Make another that says:* Good houses!

- *Now let's hold our signs and march around the room.*

Page 76

Photo and Caption

- *Let's read the caption together:* César Chávez stands with grape pickers.
- *Look at the picture of César Chávez. Is he happy?* (yes) *Do you think the marches helped?* (yes)
- *Let's read the first paragraph together:* It took a long time, but the farmers did make changes.
- *Pretend that you are a picker in the time of César Chávez. What would you want to say to him?* (Thank you for helping us. You made our lives much better.)

Let's tell what we learned about the pickers' problems. (They worked hard in the heat. They did not get much pay. They lived in shacks.) *Now let's tell what César Chávez did to help.* (He marched with the pickers. He made farmers listen.)

- *Let's read aloud about pickers today:* Today, crop pickers have a better life. They get more pay. They live in better homes. They thank César Chávez who helped them work together.

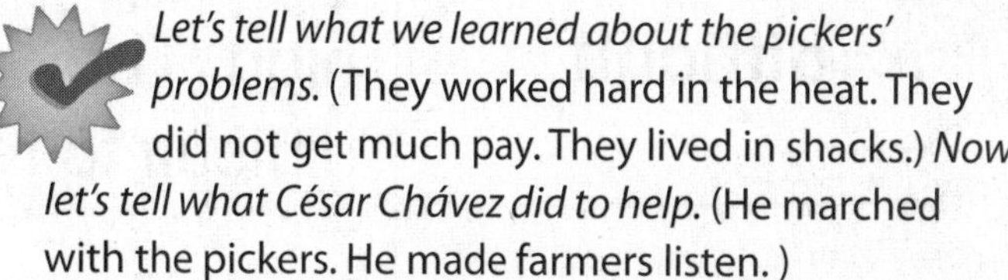

Monitor Oral Production

Remember to model self-corrective techniques on a regular basis as you speak to children. Pretend to mispronounce words and self-correct.

Name ______________________

Use the word chart to study this week's vocabulary words. Write a sentence using each word in your writer's notebook.

Word	Context Sentence	Illustration
ripe ______________	A yellow banana is ripe and good to eat.	
difficult ______________	The apples are high. They are difficult to reach.	**Name a word that means the opposite of difficult.**

© Macmillan/McGraw-Hill

Name ______________________

Book Talk

Read each question and prompt. Discuss the answers with your group. Use your Leveled Reader to find details to support your answers. Then write your answers on another sheet of paper.

1. Tell what you learned about teams.

2. Describe the kinds of teams you read about.

3. Describe the people who are in the teams you read about.

4. Give examples of things teams can do.

5. Tell what kinds of teams you are a part of.

© Macmillan/McGraw-Hill

The Kite

Pages 86–87

Prior to reading the selection with children, they should have listened to the selection on **StudentWorks Plus**, the interactive eBook. In addition, selection vocabulary should have been pretaught using the **Visual Vocabulary Resources**.

Access Core Content

Teacher Note Pose the questions after you read the text indicated.

Pages 86–87

Title and Illustration

- *Let's read the title of this story together:* The Kite. *This story comes from a book titled* Days with Frog and Toad. (Point to the title of the book on page 87.)
- *The characters in this book are named Frog and Toad. Look at Frog and Toad in the picture. They have a kite.*
- *Frog is holding the kite.* (Point to Frog.) *Toad is holding a ball of string for the kite.* (Point to Toad.) *What is Frog holding?* (a kite) *What is Toad holding?* (a ball of string)
- *Now look at the birds in the picture. The birds are robins. Say the word* robins *with me:* robins. *The robins look like they are laughing at Frog and Toad. I wonder why the robins are laughing at Frog and Toad with their kite.*
- *Let's read the story to find out what happens when Frog and Toad fly the kite.*

Page 88

Text

- *A meadow is a grassy field. The wind can be strong in a meadow because a meadow does not have a lot of trees to block the wind. Why do Frog and Toad go to the meadow?* (to fly a kite)

Think of a time that you flew a kite or saw someone else fly a kite. Tell your partner what you did or saw. (Response is open.)

Pages 86–87

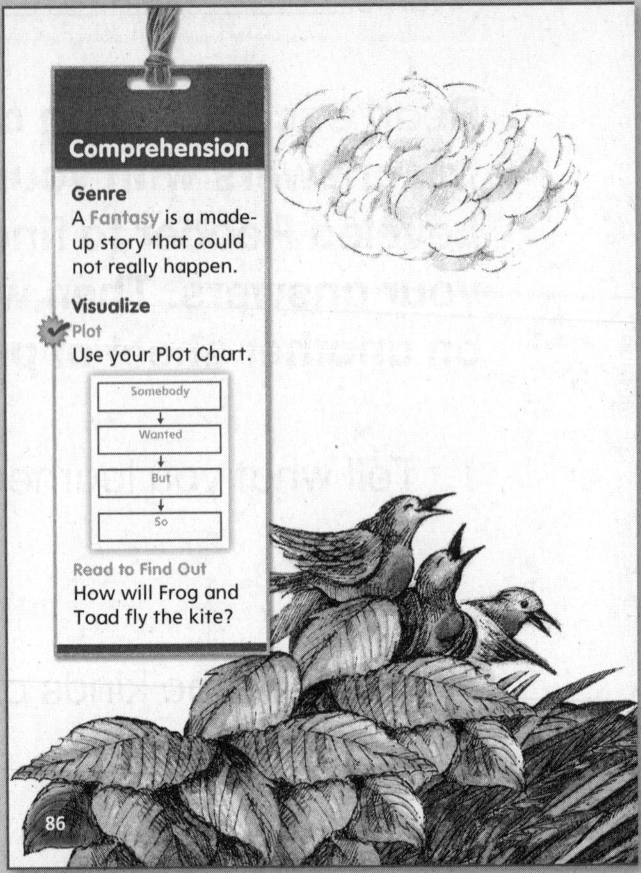

Comprehension
Genre
A Fantasy is a made-up story that could not really happen.
Visualize
Plot
Use your Plot Chart.
Somebody
Wanted
But
So
Read to Find Out
How will Frog and Toad fly the kite?
86

Pages 88–89

Frog and Toad went out
to fly a kite.
They went to
a large **meadow**
where the wind was strong.
"Our kite will fly up and up,"
said Frog.
"It will fly all the way up
to the top of the sky."

88

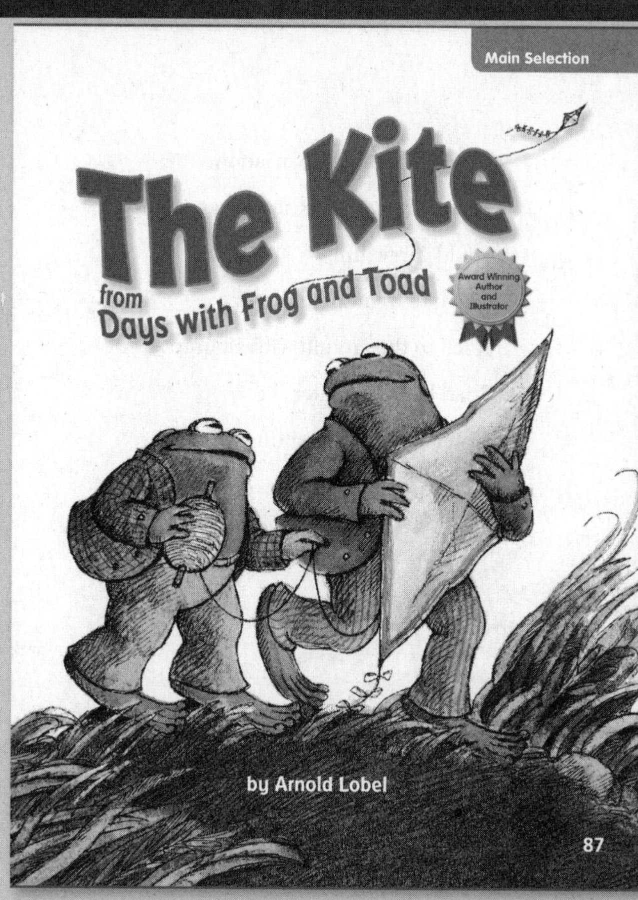

"Toad," said Frog,

"I will hold the **ball** of string.

You hold the kite and run."

89

- *Let's read what Frog says to Toad at the beginning of the story. Look for the words in quotation marks.* (Point to quotation marks in the text.) *The words in quotation marks are the words that Frog says aloud.*
- *Now read the words with me:* "Our kite will fly up and up. It will fly all the way up to the top of the sky."
- *The sky does not really have a top, but we often say that something very high is at the top of the sky. Which of these would you say flies at the top of the sky—a plane or a butterfly?* (a plane)

Page 89

Illustration

- *Look at Frog and Toad in this picture. Frog and Toad are in the meadow. Frog is pointing up to the sky. Let's all point up to the sky like Frog is doing.* (Demonstrate pointing up.)

Text

- *Frog and Toad want to fly the kite in the sky. What will Frog do to get the kite into the sky?* (Frog will hold the ball of string.) *What will Toad do to get the kite into the sky?* (Toad will hold the kite and run.)
- **Directionality**

  Ask children to place their finger where you start reading (top left). Ask where you finish reading on this page (bottom right).

The Kite

Page 90

Text

Close your eyes and imagine Toad running across the meadow. His short legs are moving fast. His kite starts to go up into the air. Then what happens to the kite? (The kite falls to the ground with a bump.)

Frog and Toad want to fly their kite, but they have a problem. What is their problem? (The kite won't stay up in the air.)

- *What does Toad hear when the kite falls to the ground?* (laughter) *Who is laughing?* (the three robins)

Illustration

- *Point to the robins laughing in the picture. Let's count them: one, two, three.* (Point to the robins as you count.) *Now let's try to sound like laughing robins:* Hee, hee! Cheep, cheep! Ha, ha! Peep, peep!

Page 91

Text

- *Let's read aloud what the robins say to Toad:* "That kite will not fly. You may as well give up." *When you give up, you stop trying.*
- *Toad runs back to Frog. Does Toad believe what the robins tell him?* (yes) *How do you know?* (Toad tells Frog the same thing that the robins say. He tells Frog that the kite will not fly. He tells Frog that he gives up.)

Illustration

- *Look at Toad talking to Frog in the picture. Pretend that you are Toad. Tell Frog that you give up. Say:* I give up.

Page 92

Text

- *When you make a second try, you try again after trying one time.*

Pages 90–91

Toad ran across the meadow.
He ran as fast as his short legs
could carry him.
The kite went up in the air.
It fell to the ground with a bump.
Toad heard laughter.
Three robins were sitting in a bush.

90

Pages 92–93

"We must make a second try,"
said Frog.
"Wave the kite over your **head**.
Perhaps that will make it fly."

Toad ran back across the meadow.
He waved the kite over his head.

92

"That kite will not fly,"
said the robins.
"You may as well give up."

Toad ran back to Frog.
"Frog," said Toad,
"this kite will not fly.
I give up."

91

The kite went up in the air
and then fell down with a thud.
"What a joke!" said the robins.
"That kite will **never**
get off the ground."

93

- *Look at Frog's words after he tells Toad that they must make a second try.* (Point to the words.) *Let's read Frog's words together:* "Wave the kite over your head. Perhaps that will make it fly." *The word* perhaps *means "maybe."*

Illustration

- *Point to Toad in the picture. What is Toad doing as he runs back across the meadow?* (Toad is waving the kite over his head.)
- *Now let's pretend to be Toad and wave the kite over our heads.* (Demonstrate the action.)

Page 93

Text

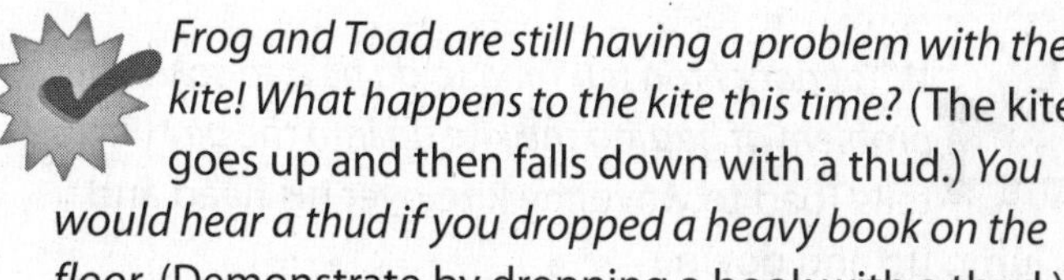

Frog and Toad are still having a problem with the kite! What happens to the kite this time? (The kite goes up and then falls down with a thud.) *You would hear a thud if you dropped a heavy book on the floor.* (Demonstrate by dropping a book with a thud.)

- *Those silly robins are still watching Toad as he tries to fly the kite. Let's read their words aloud:* "What a joke! That kite will never get off the ground."

Illustration

- *Take a look at Toad in the picture. What would you say to the robins if you were Toad?* (Question is open.)

Think about what Frog and Toad have done so far to try to get the kite to fly. Do you think they should give up trying to fly the kite? Tell your partner why or why not. (Response is open.)

Non-verbal Cues

Remind children that they can use non-verbal cues to share information when they are not able to do so verbally. Encourage children to use gestures and facial expressions.

The Kite

Page 94

Illustration

- *Look at Toad in the picture. What is he doing?* (Toad is taking the kite back to Frog.) *Toad looks like he has worked hard to try to get the kite into the air!*

Text

- *Let's read aloud what Toad says when he takes the kite back to Frog:* "This kite is a joke. It will never get off the ground." *Who else said this about the kite?* (The robins did.)
- *Frog tells Toad that they will have to make a third try. Hold up your fingers as we count the tries: first try, second try, third try.* (Hold up a corresponding number of fingers.)

What does Frog tell Toad to do next to solve the problem of getting the kite up into the air? (Frog tells Toad to wave the kite over his head and jump up and down.)

- *Let's act out what Frog wants Toad to do.* (Pantomime holding and waving a kite over your head as you jump up and down.)

Page 95

Text

- *Toad waves the kite over his head. What else does he do?* (He jumps up and down.) *What happens this time?* (The kite goes up in the air. Then it crashes down into the grass.)
- *Let's read what the robins say to Toad:* "That kite is junk. Throw it away and go home."

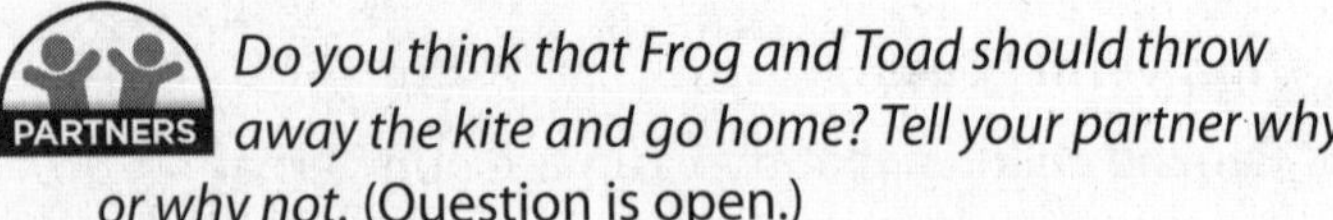

Do you think that Frog and Toad should throw away the kite and go home? Tell your partner why or why not. (Question is open.)

Pages 94–95

Toad ran back to Frog.
"This kite is a joke," he said.
"It will never get off the ground."
"We have to make
a third try," said Frog.
"Wave the kite over your head
and jump up and down.
Perhaps that will make it fly."

94

Pages 96–97

Toad ran back to Frog.
"This kite is junk," he said.
"I think we **should**
throw it away and go home."
"Toad," said Frog,
"we need one more try.
Wave the kite over your head.
Jump up and down
and **shout** UP KITE UP."
Toad ran across the meadow.
He waved the kite over his head.
He jumped up and down.
He shouted, "UP KITE UP!"

96

Toad ran across
the meadow again.
He waved the kite
over his head.
He jumped up and down.
The kite went up in the air
and crashed down into the grass.
"That kite is junk,"
said the robins.
"Throw it away and go home."

95

The kite flew into the air.
It climbed higher and higher.

97

Page 96

Text

- *When Toad goes back to Frog, he says the same thing that the robins say. He tells Frog that the kite is junk. He says they should throw it away and go home. Does Frog think that he and Toad should give up?* (No. Frog says they need one more try.)
- *Let's count down to the seventh line on this page. Then let's read aloud what Frog tells Toad to do next:* "Wave the kite over your head. Jump up and down and shout UP KITE UP."
- *How did we say the words* UP KITE UP? (in a loud voice) *Yes, we said the words in a loud voice. We used a loud voice because the words are printed in capital letters. We said the words like Frog wants Toad to say them.*
- *Now let's pretend to wave the kite over our heads, jump up and down, and shout UP KITE UP.* (Pantomime the actions as you say the words.)

Toad does what Frog tells him to do. Do you think this will solve the problem of getting the kite into the air? Why or why not? (Question is open.)

Page 97

Whole Page

- *Let's read about the kite together:* The kite flew into the air. It climbed higher and higher.
- *Point to the kite in the picture. The kite is flying high in the air!*

Pretend that you and your partner are two of the robins in the picture. What would you say to each other about the kite? (Question is open.)

The Kite

Page 98

Text

Frog and Toad wanted to get the kite into the sky. Did a running try work? (no) *Did a running and waving try work?* (no) *Did a running, waving, and jumping try work?* (no) *What finally worked?* (Toad made a running, waving, jumping, and shouting try.)

- *We can learn a lesson from Frog and Toad in this story. Say the lesson after me:* Don't give up. Try again and again until your problem is solved.

Page 99

Text

- *Let's read the first three lines together.* The robins flew out of the bush. But they could not fly as high as the kite. *What did the robins do when the kite flew into the air?* (They flew out of the bush.) *Could they fly as high as the kite?* (no)
- *Do you think the robins were surprised that they couldn't fly as high as the kite? Why or why not?* (The robins were probably surprised. They didn't think the kite would get off the ground. They told Toad to give up.)

Seek Clarification

Some children may be confused by complex syntax. Encourage children to always seek clarification when they encounter a sentence that does not make sense to them. For example, *What does "a running and waving try" mean?*

Pages 98–99

"We did it!" cried Toad.

"Yes," said Frog.

"If a running try
did not work,
and a running and waving try
did not work,
and a running, waving,
and jumping try
did not work,
I knew that
a running, waving, jumping,
and shouting try
just had to work."

98

The robins flew out of the bush.
But they could not fly
as high as the kite.
Frog and Toad sat
and watched their kite.
It seemed to be flying
way up at the top of the sky.

99

- *Let's read the last two sentences together:* Frog and Toad sat and watched their kite. It seemed to be flying way up at the top of the sky.
- *Point to the word* watched. *The word* watched *means "looked at." What letters are added to the base word* watch *to make the word* watched? (the letters *-ed*) *What other word ends with* -ed *on this page?* (seemed)

Illustration

PARTNERS *Look at Frog and Toad flying their kite. Pretend that you and your partner are Frog and Toad. What would you say to each other as you watched your kite fly way up at the top of the sky? Act out the end of the story together.* (Response is open.)

Interactive Question - Response Guide

The Wright Brothers

Access Core Content

Teacher Note Pose the questions after you read the text indicated.

Page 102

Title and Photo

- *The title of this selection is* The Wright Brothers. *Point to the Wright Brothers in the picture.*

Text

- *Listen as I read the page.*
- *The Wright brothers were named Wilbur and Orville. People shortened the Wright brothers' names. The Wright brothers were called Will and Orv for short. Say* Will *and* Orv *with me:* Will, Orv.
- *The Wright brothers lived in America over 100 years ago. Let's read to find out what important things Wilbur and Orville Wright did together.*

Page 103

Whole Page

- *Listen as I read the page.*
- *Will and Orv had a bike shop. What else did we learn about them?* (Will and Orv liked to fix things. They also liked to ride things.)
- *Point to the picture of the Wright brothers' bike shop. Bikes are sold in a bike shop. Sometimes bikes are fixed at a bike shop, too.*

Page 104

Text

- *Listen as I read the page.* The first sentence says: Will and Orv had wheels. *What kind of wheels did they have?* (bike wheels)

Pages 102–103

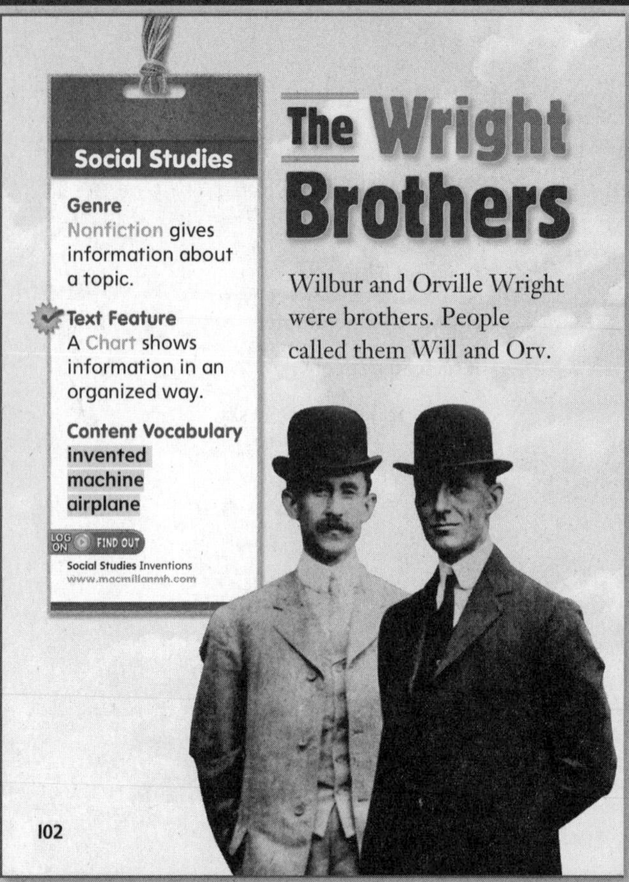

Social Studies
Genre
Nonfiction gives information about a topic.
Text Feature
A Chart shows information in an organized way.
Content Vocabulary
invented
machine
airplane
LOG ON FIND OUT
Social Studies Inventions
www.macmillanmh.com
The Wright Brothers
Wilbur and Orville Wright were brothers. People called them Will and Orv.
102

Pages 104–105

Will and Orv had wheels. But they wanted wings. They wanted to fly.

In those days long ago, there were no planes. So Will and Orv got to work. First they made a glider. A glider is like a kite that a person can ride on.

104

Social Studies

Will and Orv both liked fixing things. They liked to ride things, too.

Will and Orv liked bikes a lot. They had a bike shop.

103

Will and Orv liked the glider. But they wanted it to do more. They saw birds use their wings and tails to help them go up and down and turn.

Will and Orv got to work. They **invented** a **machine**. It was the first **airplane**. The plane had propellers and an engine. These helped the plane move like a bird.

105

- *Will and Orv wanted wings. That means that they wanted to fly like a bird. What did they make because they wanted to fly?* (a glider)
- *A glider is like a big kite. It does not have an engine to make it move. Like a kite, a glider moves with the air around it. Let's pretend we are gliders.* (Demonstrate holding your arms out and gliding around the room.)

Photo

Point to the glider in the photograph. Now point to the people waving to the glider. Would you rather be riding in the glider or waving to the person in the glider? Tell your partner what you would rather do and why. (Response is open.)

Page 105

Text

- *Listen as I read the first paragraph.*
- *What did Will and Orv want the glider to do?* (Will and Orv wanted the glider to be able to go up and down and turn.)
- *Now listen as I read the second paragraph.*
- *When you invent something, you are the first to make something. What did Will and Orv invent?* (Will and Orv invented a machine. The machine was the first airplane.)

Photo

- *The airplane that Will and Orv invented looks very different from the airplanes we have today. Let's point to the wings of the airplane in the photograph.* (Point to the wings.) *Now let's point to the propellers.* (Point to the propellers.)
- *Let's point to the pilot, or the person flying the airplane.* (Point to the pilot.) *The pilot is lying down. Today pilots sit down to fly airplanes.*

The Wright Brothers

Page 106

Text

- *Listen as I read the page aloud.*
- *Will and Orv tried out their plane on a cold day in 1903. Did the plane go up?* (yes) *How long did the plane stay up in the air?* (12 seconds)
- *Let's see just how long 12 seconds is. I will clap at the beginning of 12 seconds. Then I will clap again when 12 seconds have passed.* (Time 12 seconds in this manner.) *Twelve seconds isn't long at all!*
- *The flight, or the time that the plane stayed in the air, was very short. What did the flight show?* (The flight showed that the plane worked.)

Photo

- *Look at the plane in the picture. We know that the plane didn't fly for long. The plane also didn't fly very high!*

Page 107

Text

- *Listen as I read the first two sentences aloud.*
- *What are ways that we get to places today?* (on land, by water, and in the sky)
- *Listen as I read the last sentence aloud.*
- *What can we do thanks to Wilbur and Orville Wright?* (We can fly.)

Today thanks to the Wright Brothers we can go places in the sky. Would you rather go places on land, by water, or in the sky? Tell your partner what way you like best and why. (Response is open.)

Pages 106–107

On a cold day in 1903, Will and Orv tried the plane. It went up! It stayed up for 12 seconds. That is not a lot, but it showed that the plane worked!

106

This is how we can get places today. We can go on land, by water, and high up in the sky.

Thanks to Wilbur and Orville Wright, we can fly!

How We Get Places

Land	Sea	Air
car	sailboat	plane
train	ship	helicopter

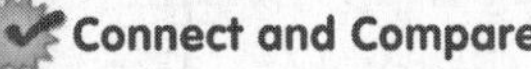

Connect and Compare

- How did the Wright brothers act like a team?
- How can we travel by land? What is shown on the chart? How else can we travel by land?

107

Chart

- *Look at the chart on this page. The name of this chart is* How We Get Places. (Point to the title.) *The chart has three columns. Let's point to the column heads as I read them:* Land, Sea, Air. (Point to the heads.)
- *Now listen as I read the label below each picture on the chart:* car, train, sailboat, ship, airplane, helicopter. (Point to each label as you read it aloud.)
- *Look at the chart again. What can we ride on land to get places?* (a car or a train) *What can we ride on the sea to get places?* (a sailboat or a ship) *What can we ride in the air to get places?* (an airplane or a helicopter)

Name ______________________

Use the word chart to study this week's vocabulary words. Write a sentence using each word in your writer's notebook.

Word	Context Sentence	Illustration
perhaps ______	It is cloudy, so perhaps it will rain.	
meadow ______	The cows graze in the meadow.	How is a meadow different from a forest?

© Macmillan/McGraw-Hill

Name ____

Book Talk

Read each question and prompt. Discuss the answers with your group. Use your Leveled Reader to find details to support your answers. Then write your answers on another sheet of paper.

1. Tell what you learned about frogs.

2. Show classmates the different parts of a frog.

3. Describe what frog eggs look like.

4. Explain what happens to a tadpole as it grows up.

5. Give examples of things frogs can do.

© Macmillan/McGraw-Hill

Animal Teams

Pages 114–115

Prior to reading the selection with children, they should have listened to the selection on **StudentWorks Plus**, the interactive eBook. In addition, selection vocabulary should have been pretaught using the **Visual Vocabulary Resources**.

Access Core Content

Teacher Note Pose the questions after you read the paragraph or page indicated.

Pages 114–115

Title and Illustration

- *This selection is called* Animal Teams. (Point to the title.) *Teams work together or help each other. What are some kinds of teams that you know?* (sports teams, partners for school activities)
- *Look at the picture. Point to the big fish. Point to the small fish. Sometimes big and small animals make a team.*

Pages 116–117

Illustrations

- *This is a giraffe.* (Point to the giraffe on page 116.) *Say it with me:* giraffe. What is the little animal called? (a bird) *Do you think the bird is afraid of the giraffe?* (no) *How can you tell?* (The bird is on the neck of the giraffe. It is not flying away.)
- *This is a fish.* (Point to the fish on page 117.) *Say it with me:* fish. *This is a shrimp.* (Point to the shrimp.) *Say it with me:* shrimp. *Do you think the fish and shrimp are afraid of each other?* (no) *How can you tell?* (They are not trying to get away from each other. They are not hurting each other.)
-

Directionality

Ask children to place their finger where you start reading (top left). Ask where you finish reading on this page (bottom right).

Pages 114–115

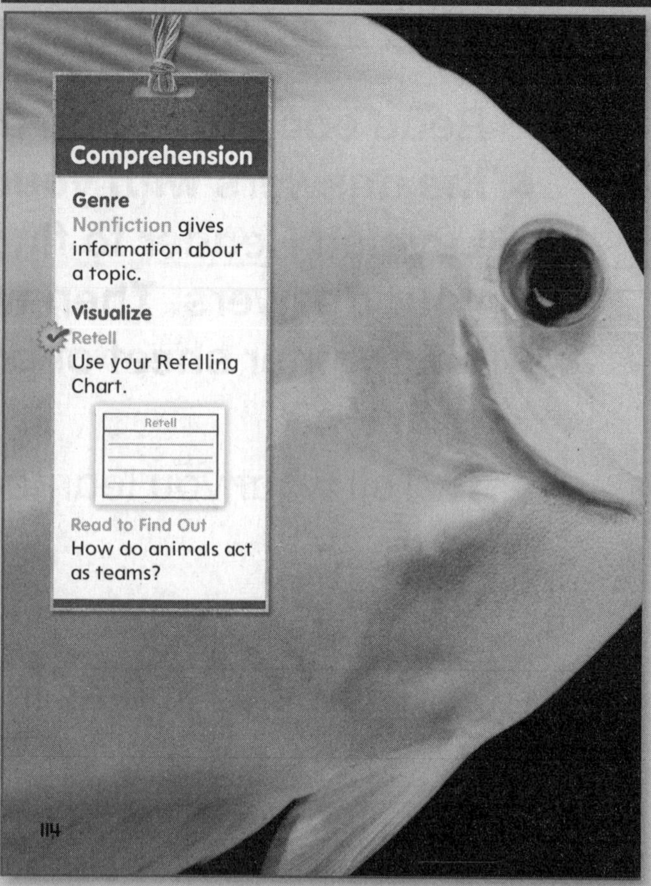

Comprehension
Genre
Nonfiction gives information about a topic.
Visualize
Retell
Use your Retelling Chart.
Retell
Read to Find Out
How do animals act as teams?
114

Pages 116–117

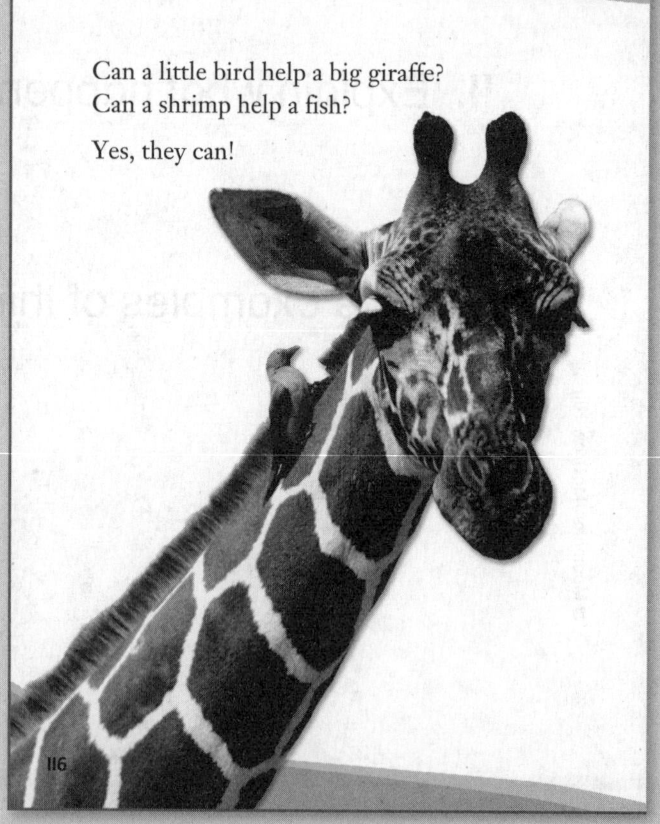

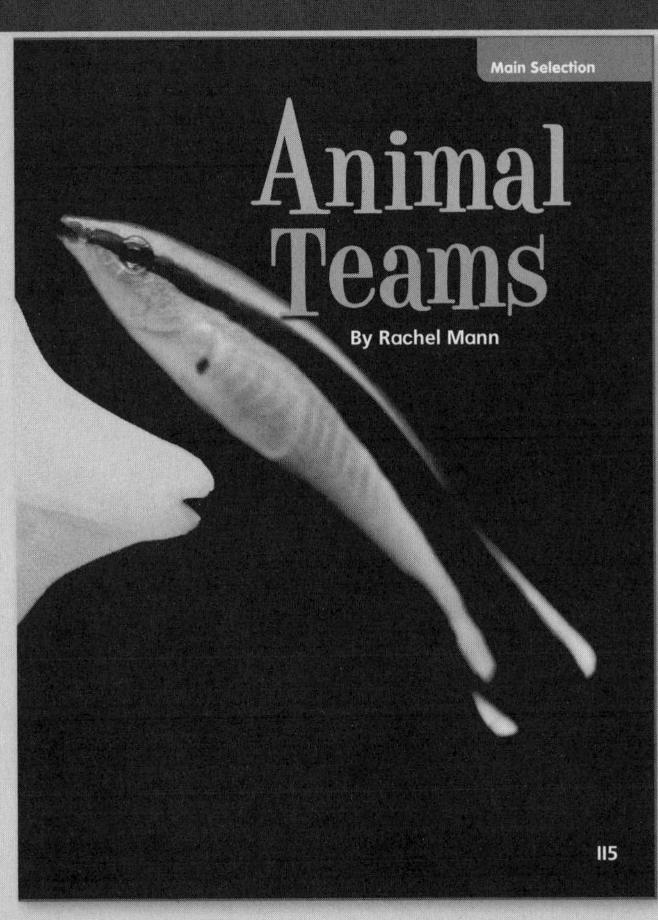

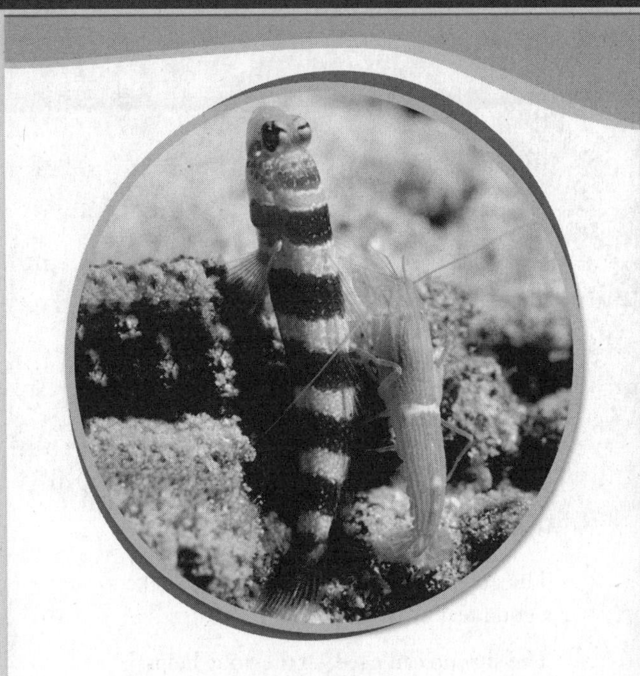

These might seem like funny friends. But many kinds of animals work together in teams. These animals help each **other** in lots of ways. Let's find out how.

117

Text

- *Let's read page 116 together:* Can a little bird help a big giraffe. Can a shrimp help a fish? Yes, they can!

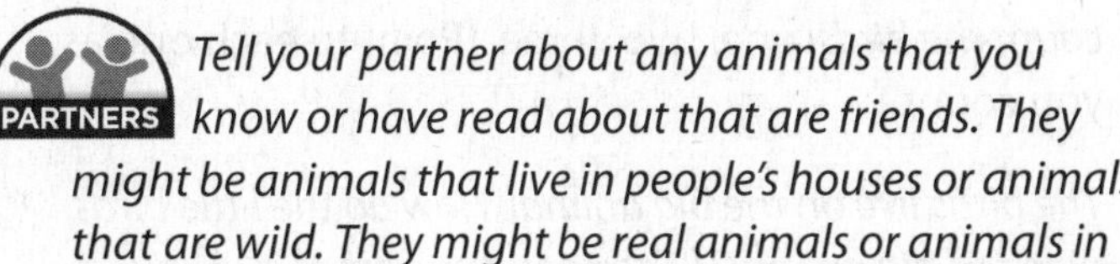

Tell your partner about any animals that you know or have read about that are friends. They might be animals that live in people's houses or animals that are wild. They might be real animals or animals in made-up stories.

- *Let's read page 117 together to find out what this book is all about:* These might seem like funny friends. But many kinds of animals work together in teams. These animals help each other in lots of ways. Let's find out how.

Synonyms and Circumlocution

Remind children that they can use circumlocution, or paraphrasing, to help clarify words or expressions they do not understand. Ask, *What is another way of saying "might seem like"?* (perhaps they look like)

Animal Teams

Page 118

Whole Page

- *Look at the picture. Little birds are on a big animal. Let's count the birds:* one, two, three. (Point to each one as you count.)
- *The birds live on the big animal. How do the little birds help the big animal?* (They eat bugs off of it.) *Why would this be good for the big animal?* (The bugs could bother or bite the big animal.)
- *Birds eat bugs off the skin of the animals. Let's point to the skin on our hands. Say it with me:* skin. *Skin is under the animal's soft fur. Point to the fur.*

Page 119

Whole Page

- Let's read the first two sentences together: The big animals help the little birds, too. The birds are safe on top of these big pals. *Are the birds high up or close to the ground?* (high up)
- *The birds are safe on top of their big pals, or friends. Why are the birds safe there?* (Animals on the ground cannot reach so high up.)

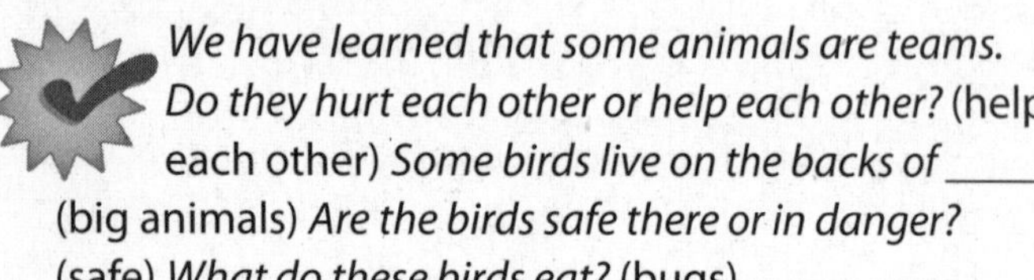

We have learned that some animals are teams. Do they hurt each other or help each other? (help each other) *Some birds live on the backs of ____.* (big animals) *Are the birds safe there or in danger?* (safe) *What do these birds eat?* (bugs)

Pages 118–119

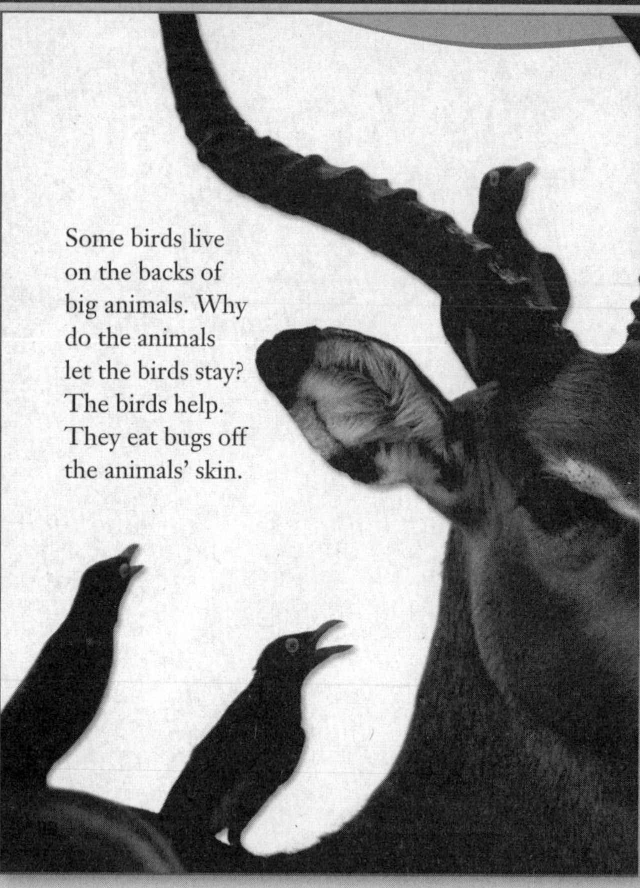

Some birds live on the backs of big animals. Why do the animals let the birds stay? The birds help. They eat bugs off the animals' skin.

Pages 120–121

The goby fish and the blind shrimp make a good team.

The shrimp can't see, so the goby helps. The goby looks out for **danger**, and the shrimp stays close. When the goby flicks its tail, it means that it is time to hide.

120

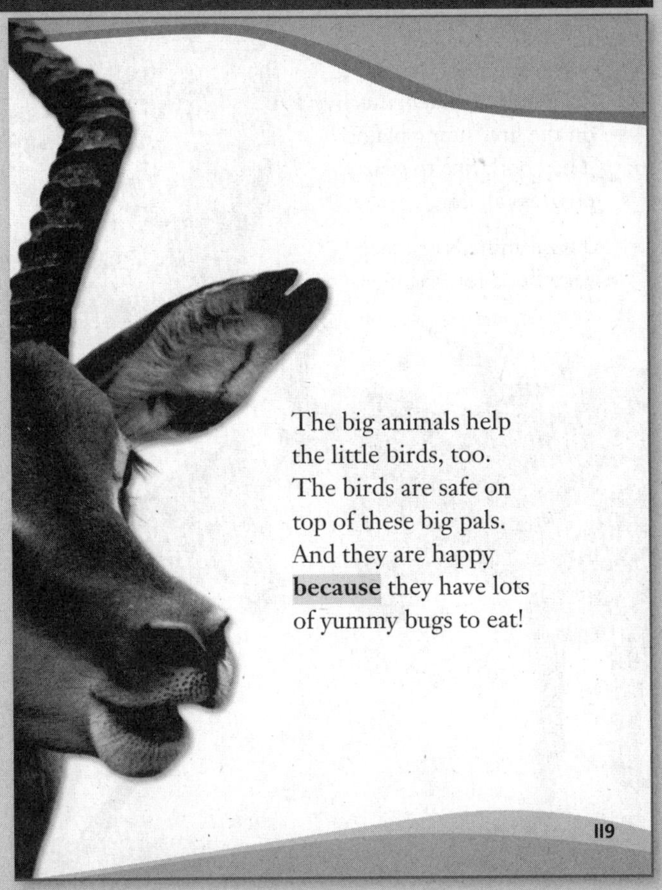

The big animals help the little birds, too. The birds are safe on top of these big pals. And they are happy **because** they have lots of yummy bugs to eat!
119

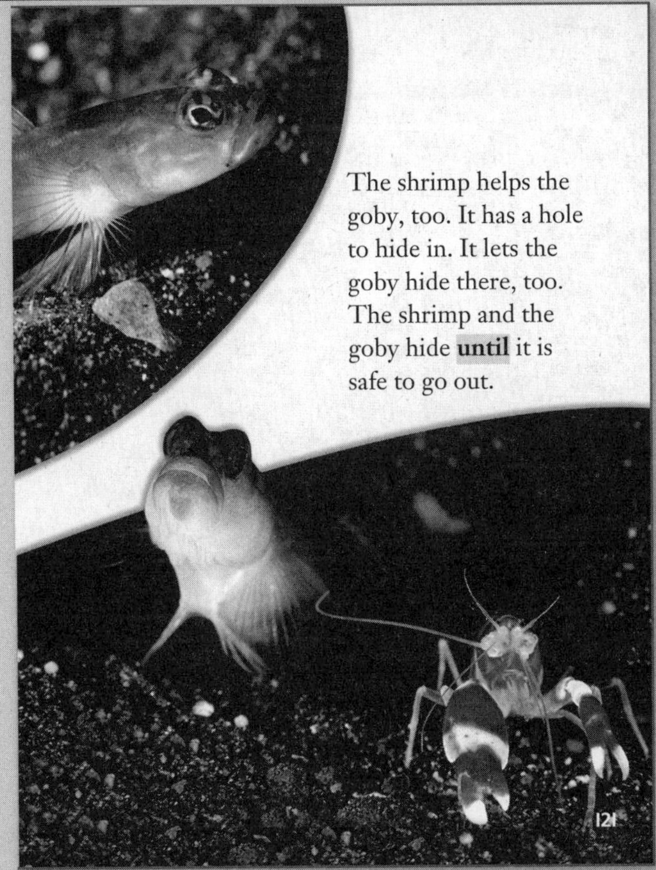

Page 120

Whole Page

- *Look at the picture of another animal team. Point to the fish. Now point to the shrimp. The shrimp is blind, or not able to see. Who do you think helps the shrimp to see?* (the fish)
- Let's read the first sentence: The goby fish and the blind shrimp make a good team. The shrimp can't see, so the goby helps. *Can the goby fish see? How do you know?* (yes, because it looks out for danger)
- *Flick means "move quickly." Let's flick our wrist.* (Demonstrate flicking your wrist.) *When does the goby fish flick its tail?* (when there is danger) *Why does it do it?* (to let the shrimp know)
- *The shrimp stays close to the goby. That way, the shrimp can tell when the goby flicks its tail. When the goby flicks its tail, it is time to hide. Let's hide our faces with our hands.* (demonstrate)

Page 121

Whole Page

- *Let's read the first three sentences together:* The shrimp helps the goby, too. It has a hole to hide in. It lets the goby hide there, too. *How does the shrimp help the goby?* (It lets the goby hide with it.)
- *What might a fish and shrimp need to hide from?* (Answers will vary but might include a bigger fish or a fishing net.)

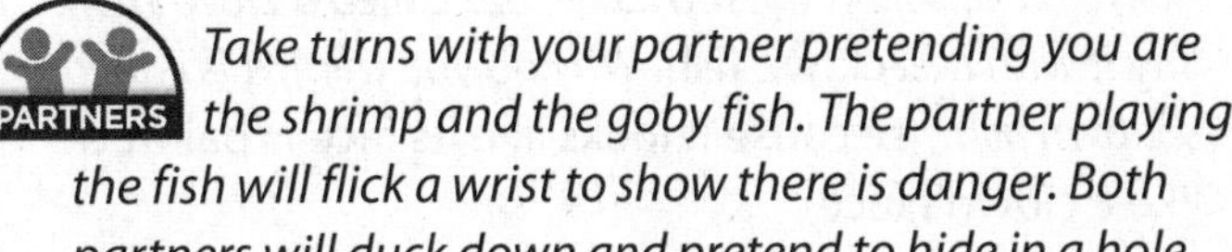

Take turns with your partner pretending you are the shrimp and the goby fish. The partner playing the fish will flick a wrist to show there is danger. Both partners will duck down and pretend to hide in a hole.

Animal Teams

Page 122

Whole Page

- *Zebras have stripes, or lines, on their bodies.* (Point to the zebra at the bottom of the page.) *Say* zebra *with me:* zebra.
- *This animal is called a wildebeest. It has horns.* (Point to the wildebeest at the bottom of the page.) *Say it with me:* wildebeest.
- *Let's read the first two sentences together:* Zebras and wildebeests live on the hot, sunny plains. They both graze on grass all day. *That means they nibble on, or eat grass all day.*
- *A plain is flat. It is not hilly. Is the plain where zebras and wildebeests live hot or cold?* (hot) *Is it rainy or sunny?* (sunny)

Page 123

Whole Page

- *Zebras and wildebeests are a team. They help each other find food. How else do they help each other?* (They help each other stay safe.)
- *Look at the top picture. The zebras and wildebeests are running. They have kicked up some dust. Why might they be running?* (They might be running away from a lion or other dangerous animal.)

Page 124

Whole Page

- *Point to the fish in the red circle. It is called a clown fish. Say it with me:* clown fish. *Why do you think it is called a clown fish?* (because it looks like its face is painted like a clown's face)
- *The animal that helps the clown fish is a sea anemone. Say it with me:* sea anemone. *A sea anemone looks like a plant, but it is an animal. Point to the sea anemone in the picture.*

Formal and Informal English

When children encounter a colloquial or informal word in the text, discuss other ways of saying the same word with more formal language. For example, *pals/friends, yummy/delicious, tasty.*

Pages 122–123

Pages 124–125

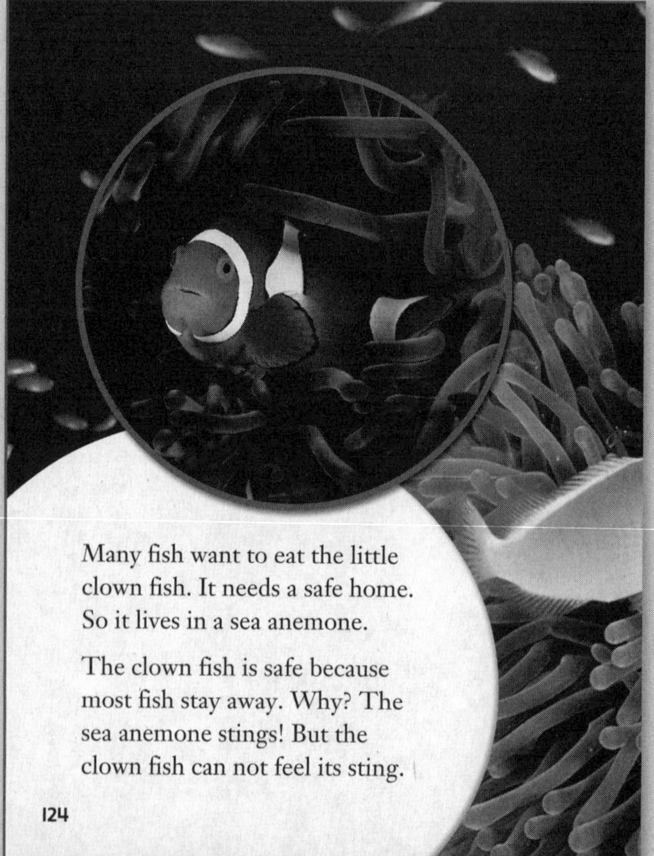

Many fish want to eat the little clown fish. It needs a safe home. So it lives in a sea anemone.
The clown fish is safe because most fish stay away. Why? The sea anemone stings! But the clown fish can not feel its sting.
124

Many fish want to eat the little clown fish. It needs a safe home. So it lives in a sea anemone.
The clown fish is safe because most fish stay away. Why? The sea anemone stings! But the clown fish can not feel its sting.
124

The clown fish helps its buddy, too. It swims in and out, in and out. It chases away big fish that might hurt its pal.
125

- *A sea anemone looks beautiful, but it can sting like a bee. Does it hurt or feel good when something stings you?* (It hurts.)
- *The clownfish lives in a sea anemone because it needs a safe home. Why do most fish stay away from the sea anemone?* (because it stings)
- *The clown fish doesn't worry about the sting. Why doesn't it?* (because it cannot feel the sting)

Page 125

Whole Page

- *Let's read this page together.* The clown fish helps its buddy, too. It swims in and out, in and out. It chases away big fish that might hurt its pal.
- *Which animal is swimming in and out?* (the clown fish) *Why is it doing that?* (to chase away the big fish)
- *Let's pretend we are clown fish. Let's hold our palms together and move them like we are swimming.* (demonstrate) *We are swimming away from a big fish. It's getting closer. Ah! There's the sea anemone. Swim into it! Zap! The big fish got stung, but we are safe!*

PARTNERS
The clown fish and the sea anemone are pals, or good friends. They help each other. Tell your partner about a time when a friend helped you or you helped a friend.

Animal Teams

Pages 126–127

Whole Page

- *Caterpillars and ants help each other. Look at the picture at the top of page 127. This is a caterpillar.* (Point to the caterpillar.) *Say it with me:* caterpillar. *Now point to the ants.*
- *Let's read the first sentence:* A caterpillar needs to be safe so that it can grow. *Look at the picture at the bottom of the page. The ants are carrying a caterpillar. Where will they take it?* (to a safe place)
- *Let's read the first sentence on page 127 together:* The caterpillar has a sweet liquid on its skin. *A liquid is something wet that you can lick or drink. The liquid is sweet. Do you think the ants like it?* (yes)

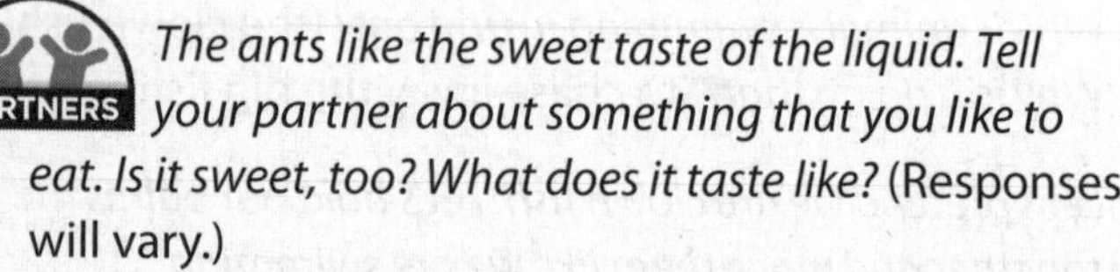

The ants like the sweet taste of the liquid. Tell your partner about something that you like to eat. Is it sweet, too? What does it taste like? (Responses will vary.)

- *The ants carry the caterpillar to somewhere safe. Let's read the last sentence together:* Soon the caterpillar will be a beautiful blue butterfly. *Point to the butterfly. Say it with me:* butterfly.
- *Let's pretend to be beautiful butterflies and fly around the room.* (Demonstrate by spreading your arms and gliding around the room.)

Formal and Informal English

When children encounter a colloquial or informal word in the text, discuss other ways of saying the same word with more formal language. For example, *buddy/friend.*

Pages 126–127

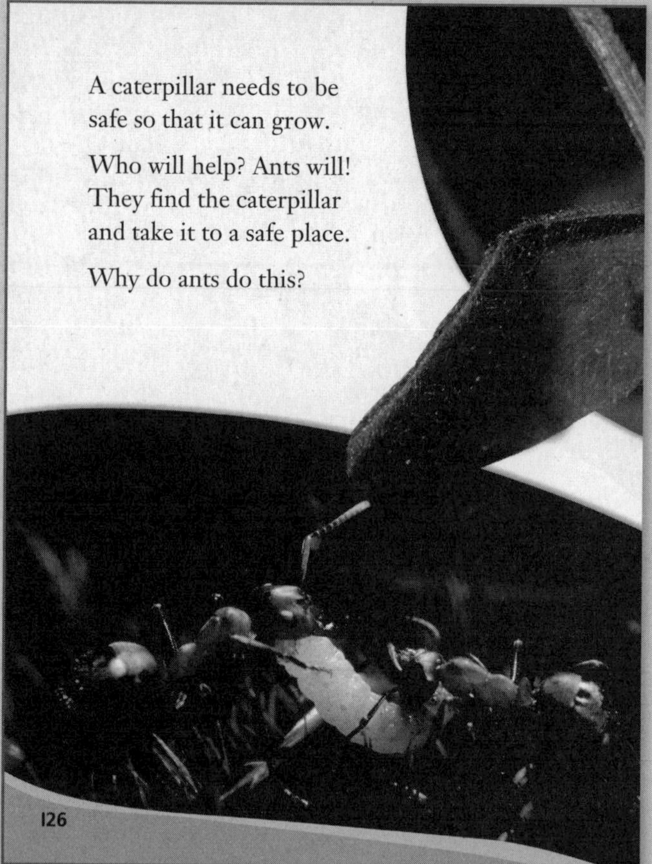

A caterpillar needs to be safe so that it can grow.
Who will help? Ants will! They find the caterpillar and take it to a safe place.
Why do ants do this?
126

Pages 128–129

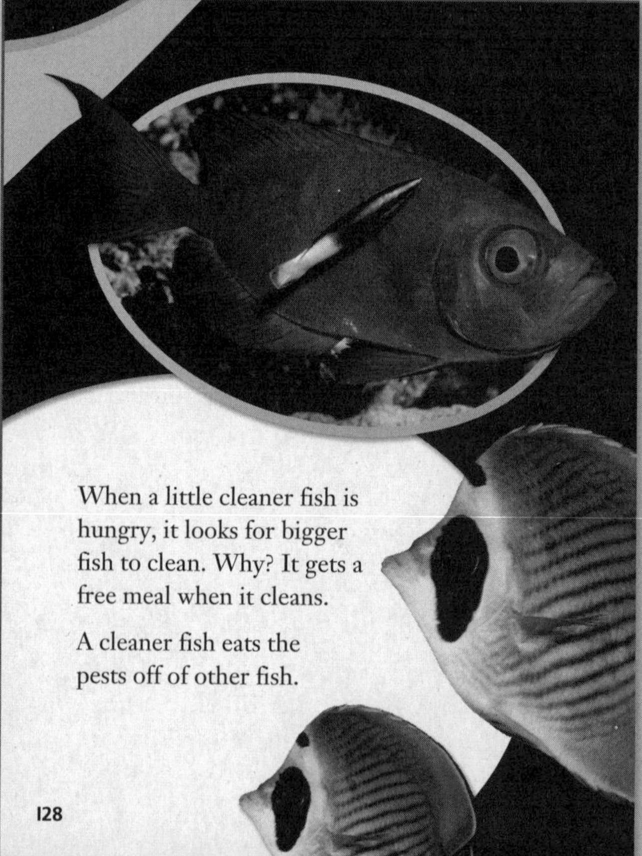

When a little cleaner fish is hungry, it looks for bigger fish to clean. Why? It gets a free meal when it cleans.
A cleaner fish eats the pests off of other fish.
128

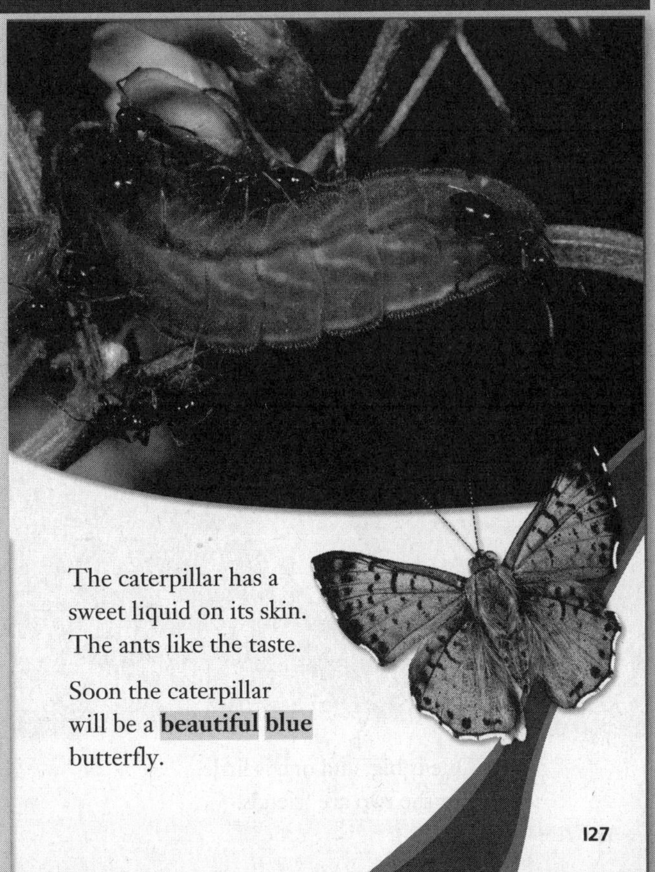

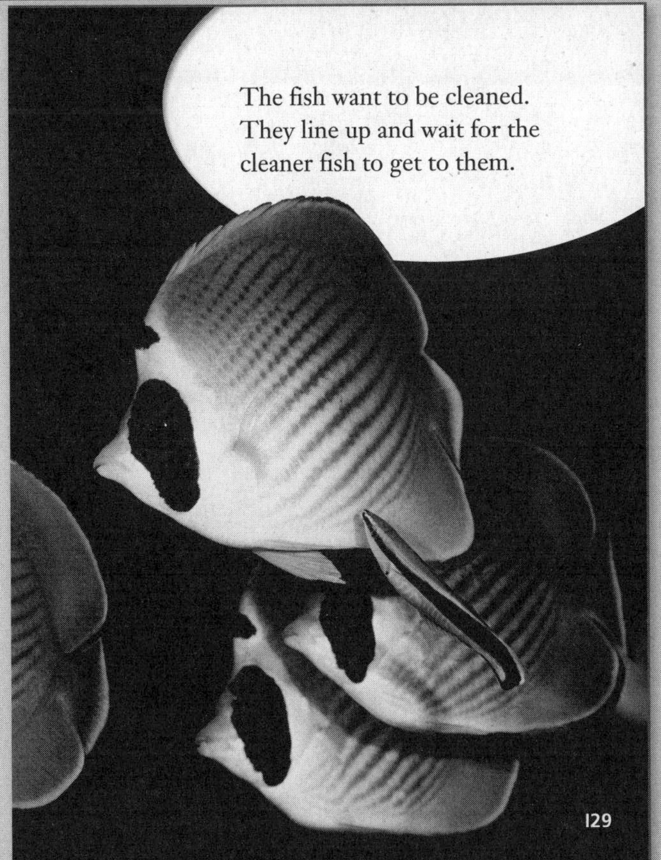

The fish want to be cleaned. They line up and wait for the cleaner fish to get to them.
129

Page 128

Whole Page

- *Point to the very small fish on top of a bigger fish. The small fish is called a cleaner fish. It is called that because it cleans other fish.*
- *Let's pretend we are cleaning our desks with a rag.* (Demonstrate cleaning with a rag.) *What part of our body helps us clean?* (our hands) *Does the little fish in the picture have hands?* (no)
- *Let's read the second paragraph together to find out how the cleaner fish cleans:* A cleaner fish eats the pests off of other fish.)
- *Pests are small animals that bother bigger animals. When does the cleaner fish eat the pests?* (when the cleaner fish is hungry)

Page 129

Whole Page

- *Point to the cleaner fish on this page. Now look at the other fish. What are they waiting for?* (They are waiting to be cleaned.)

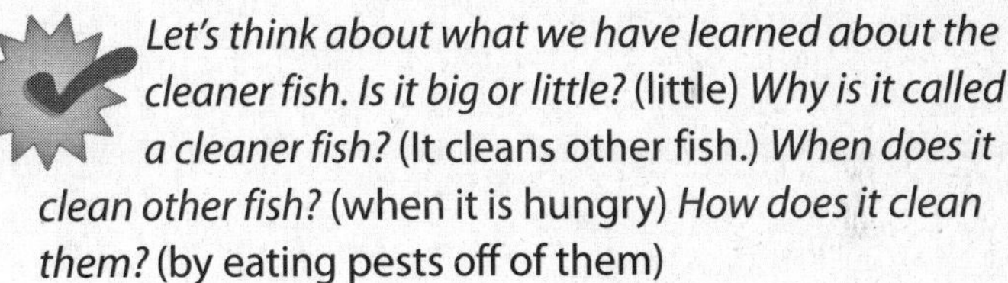

Let's think about what we have learned about the cleaner fish. Is it big or little? (little) *Why is it called a cleaner fish?* (It cleans other fish.) *When does it clean other fish?* (when it is hungry) *How does it clean them?* (by eating pests off of them)

Animal Teams

Page 130

Whole Page

- *Let's read this page together:* One is big, and one is little. But the two are friends.
- *The big animal is a rhinoceros. Point to it, and say it with me:* rhinoceros. *Think about the birds we have read about in this selection. How do they help out the big animals?* (They eat small bugs off of them.)

Think about a friend you have who is older or younger than you are. Tell your partner about your friendship.

Pages 130–131

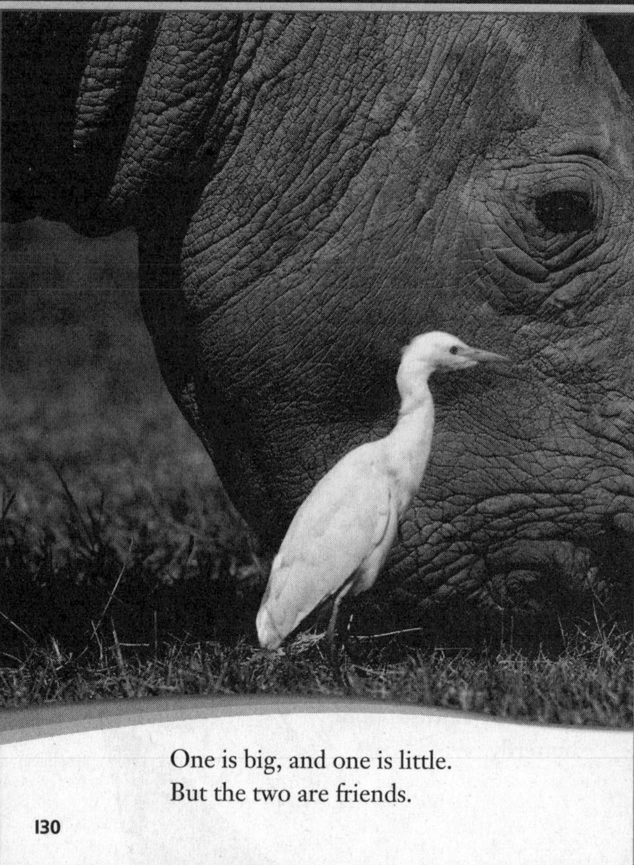

One is big, and one is little.
But the two are friends.

130

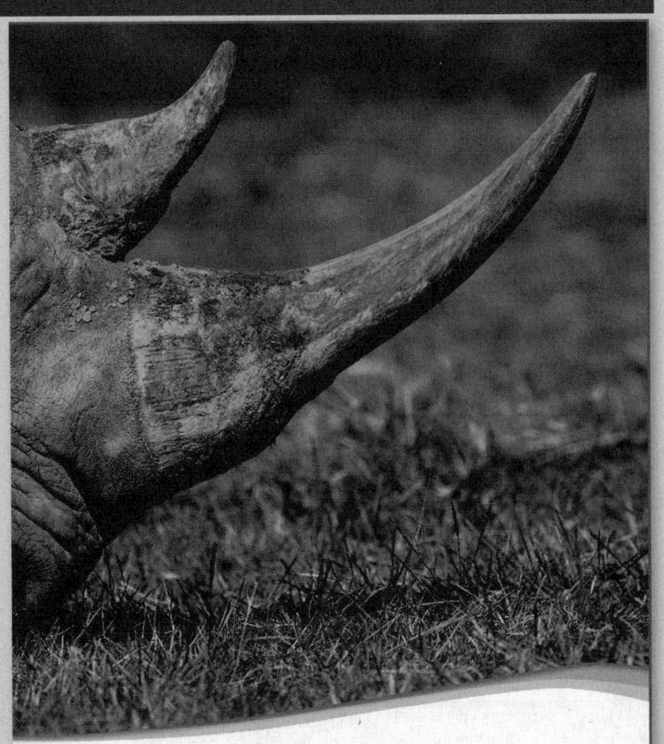

When animals team up, they do what is best for both of them.

131

Page 131

Whole Page

- *Let's read this page together:* When animals team up, they do what is best for each other.

Let's think about some teams in the selection. Birds help big animals by eating pests. How does that help the birds? (They get food.) *What fish is friends with a sea anemone?* (the clown fish) *What are some other animal friends?* (Answers will vary.)

Where?

Access Core Content

Teacher Note Pose the questions after you read the paragraph or page indicated.

Page 134

Whole Page

- *Look at the picture. The girl is sitting on a little hill. Let's point to the things around her as I say them:* grass, flowers, butterfly, trees, houses. (Point to each one as you say it.)
- *The girl is looking up. She sees clouds. Point to them. She also sees birds. Point to them.*

Tell your partner about a time when you were outdoors looking at something in nature. What did you see? What did you hear? (Responses will vary.)

Page 135

- *The title of the poem is* Where? *Listen as I read the first four lines aloud:* I look up into the sky / and see the birds / like black arrows / flying high.
- *The poet says that the birds look like black arrows.* (Draw an arrow on the board.) *When people shoot arrows with a bow, the arrows also fly. What else do you think the birds look like?* (Response is open.)

Pages 134–135

Poetry
Genre
Poetry helps readers look at things they see every day in new ways.
Literary Elements
Repetition is the way words in a poem are used more than once.
Rhythm Poems are written so that the words have a certain beat, or rhythm, when you say them aloud.
LOG ON FIND OUT
Poetry Animal Poems
www.macmillanmh.com
134

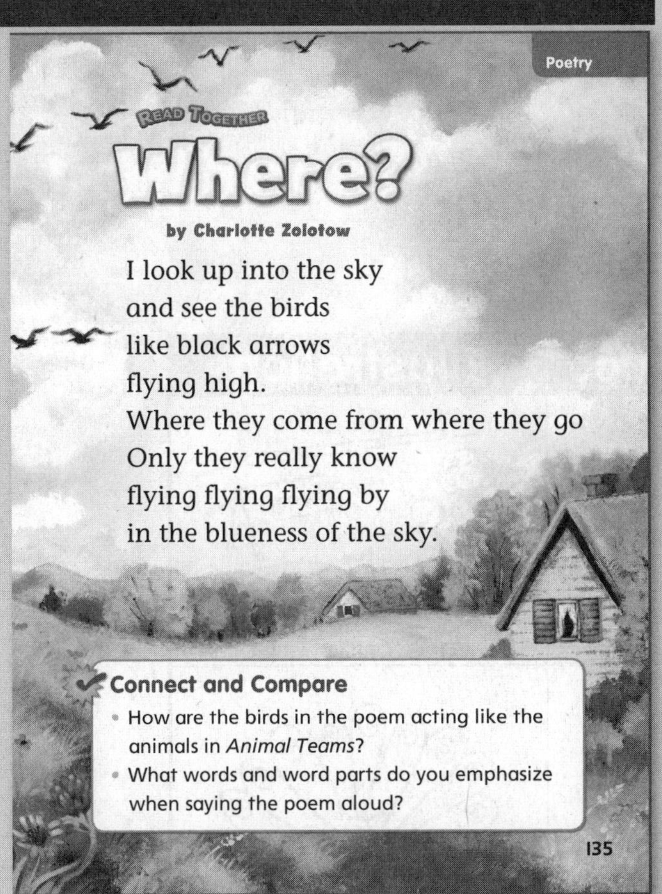

Poetry
Read Together
Where?
by Charlotte Zolotow
I look up into the sky
and see the birds
like black arrows
flying high.
Where they come from where they go
Only they really know
flying flying flying by
in the blueness of the sky.
Connect and Compare
How are the birds in the poem acting like the animals in Animal Teams?
What words and word parts do you emphasize when saying the poem aloud?
135

- *Listen as I read the next two lines:* Where they come from where they go / Only they really know. *What do the birds know?* (where they come from and where they are going) *Does anyone else know?* (no)
- *Now listen as I read the last two lines:* flying flying flying by / in the blueness of the sky. *What word did you hear three times?* (flying) *The poet wants us to keep picturing birds flying across the sky.*
- *So many birds are flying together. Birds fly as a team when they go on long trips.*
- *Listen as I read the whole poem.*

Name ______________________________

Use the word chart to study this week's vocabulary words. Write a sentence using each word in your writer's notebook.

Word	Context Sentence	Illustration
danger ______________	Look out for danger.	Danger
beautiful ______________	A peacock has beautiful feathers.	**What is a word that means the opposite of beautiful?**

© Macmillan/McGraw-Hill

Name ______________________________

Book Talk

Read each question and prompt. Discuss the answers with your group. Use your Leveled Reader to find details to support your answers. Then write your answers on another sheet of paper.

1. Name the body parts that help a penguin swim.

2. Do all penguins look the same? Describe how they might look.

3. Explain how penguins get their food and what they eat.

4. How do penguins create nests for their eggs?

5. Explain how penguins take care of their chicks.

© Macmillan/McGraw-Hill

GRADE 1, UNIT 5 • Interactive Reading
Weekly Planners

Week 1

Selections	Vocabulary: Key Selection/Oral Vocabulary Words/ Cognates	Vocabulary: Academic Language/Cognates	ELL Practice Book
Kitten's First Full Moon *Ellen Ochoa in Space*	lucky scatter discover *descubrir* mysterious *misterioso* dusk pale	captions cause *causa* effect *efecto* adjectives *adjetivos*	• Phonics, p. 81 • Vocabulary, p. 82 • Grammar, p. 83 • Book Talk, p. 84

Week 2

Selections	Vocabulary: Key Selection/Oral Vocabulary Words/ Cognates	Vocabulary: Academic Language/Cognates	ELL Practice Book
Meet Ben Franklin *A Close Look*	improve curious *curioso* idea *idea* career *carrera* fascinating *fascinante* investigate *investigar*	inference summarize adjective *adjetivo* compare *comparar* biography *biografía*	• Phonics, p. 85 • Vocabulary, p. 86 • Grammar, p. 87 • Book Talk, p. 88

Week 3

TIME FOR KIDS®	Vocabulary: Key Selection/Oral Vocabulary Words/ Cognates	Vocabulary: Academic Language/Cognates	ELL Practice Book
Stormy Weather	extreme forecast commotion *conmoción* conditions *condiciones* tranquil *tranquilo* predict breeze	monitor comprehension synonym *sinónimo* antonym *antónimo* compare *comparar* contrast *contrastar*	• Phonics, p. 89 • Vocabulary, p. 90 • Grammar, p. 91 • Book Talk, p. 92

Week 4

Selections	Vocabulary: Key Selection/Oral Vocabulary Words/ Cognates	Vocabulary: Academic Language/Cognates	ELL Practice Book
Happy Fall! (from Pinwheel Days) *Seasons*	wondered blaze outline observe *observar* season increase scorch	visualize *visualizar* sequence *secuencia* color *color* diagram *diagrama*	• Phonics, p. 93 • Vocabulary, p. 94 • Grammar, p. 95 • Book Talk, p. 96

Week 5

Selections	Vocabulary: Key Selection/Oral Vocabulary Words/ Cognates	Vocabulary: Academic Language/Cognates	ELL Practice Book
A Tiger Cub Grows Up *Gray Goose*	cub slender remain mature *maduro* process *proceso* wild newborn	summarize number compare *comparar* contrast *contrastar*	• Phonics, p. 97 • Vocabulary, p. 98 • Grammar, p. 99 • Book Talk, p. 100

© Macmillan/McGraw-Hill

Student Response Strategies

Use the following strategies to help English Language Learners move to the next proficiency level.

✔ **WAIT** Give children ample time to respond.

- Let children know that they can respond in different ways depending on their levels of proficiency, but all should be encouraged to answer questions related to the main point of the picture or text.
- Allow children to respond in their native language if they are very limited proficient. Ask a more proficient student to repeat the answer in English.

✔ **REPEAT** If the child's response is correct, the teacher can repeat what the child has said slowly and clearly for the rest of the class to hear.

✔ **REVISE for FORM** Generally the teacher will be repeating what the child has said but with corrections for grammar and pronunciation. The correction can be implicit or explicit (where teacher calls attention to the correction).

✔ **REVISE for MEANING** Teachers should also correct responses for meaning.

✔ **ELABORATE** Here, the teacher elaborates on a child's response or states the response in another way in order to more fully develop children's comprehension and oral language proficiency.

✔ **ELICIT** Finally, the teacher can also elicit a more comprehensive response from the child by prompting him or her for further information.

Newcomers

Basic and Social Language Each week you will be focusing on an important aspect of classroom communication to teach or reinforce with your newcomers. Children will expand and internalize initial English vocabulary by learning and using routine language needed for classroom communication.

Introduce Self Teach children how to introduce themselves, ask for other classmates' names, and say Hello/Goodbye. Use the sentence frames *My name is* ____ and *What is your name?* Model dialogues, such as *Hello. My name is (name). What is your name?* Have children repeat and practice with a partner.

Basic Requests Teach children sentence frames for basic requests, such as *I need* ____, *I want* ____, and *Do you have* ____? Teach them how to ask for permission, such as *May I use the restroom, please?* And to respond with *thank you.* Provide daily opportunities to model and practice each request. Reinforce *please* and *thank you.*

Classroom Items Teach children the names of commonly used classroom items, such as, pencils, paper, book, chair, and desk. Reinforce each using the sentence frames *This is my* ____. *That is your* ____. and *This is a* ____. These sentence frames focus on possession. Provide daily practice, for example, *This is my book. That is your book.*

LOG ON Have children use **Newcomer Games** to expand and internalize language needed for classroom communication. **www.macmillanmh.com**

© Macmillan/McGraw-Hill

Interactive Question - Response Guide

Kitten's First Full Moon

Pages 10–11

Prior to reading the selection with children, they should have listened to the selection on **StudentWorks Plus**, the interactive eBook. In addition, selection vocabulary should have been pretaught using the **Visual Vocabulary Resources**.

Access Core Content

Teacher Note Pose the questions after you read the paragraph or page indicated.

Pages 10–11

Title and Illustration

- *Let's read the title of the story together:* Kitten's First Full Moon.
- *A kitten is a baby cat. Point to the kitten in the picture. There is a big moon behind the kitten.* (Point to the moon.) *Do we see the moon in the day or at night?* (at night) *We see the moon in the sky at night.* (Point up.)
- *Sometimes the moon is big and round like this one.* (Trace the circumference of the moon with your finger.) *But the moon can also have other shapes.*
- *Sometimes the moon looks like this.* (Draw a half moon on the board.) *Other times, the moon looks like this.* (Draw a crescent moon.)
- *When the moon is big and round, we call it a* full moon. (Point to the circle on the board.) *Say it with me:* full moon. *In this story, Kitten sees the full moon for the first time.*
- *The full moon is round. A bowl is round, too. We eat cereal from a bowl. We eat soup from a bowl. A kitten can eat or drink from a bowl, too. What might a kitten drink from a bowl?* (water, milk)

Pages 10–11

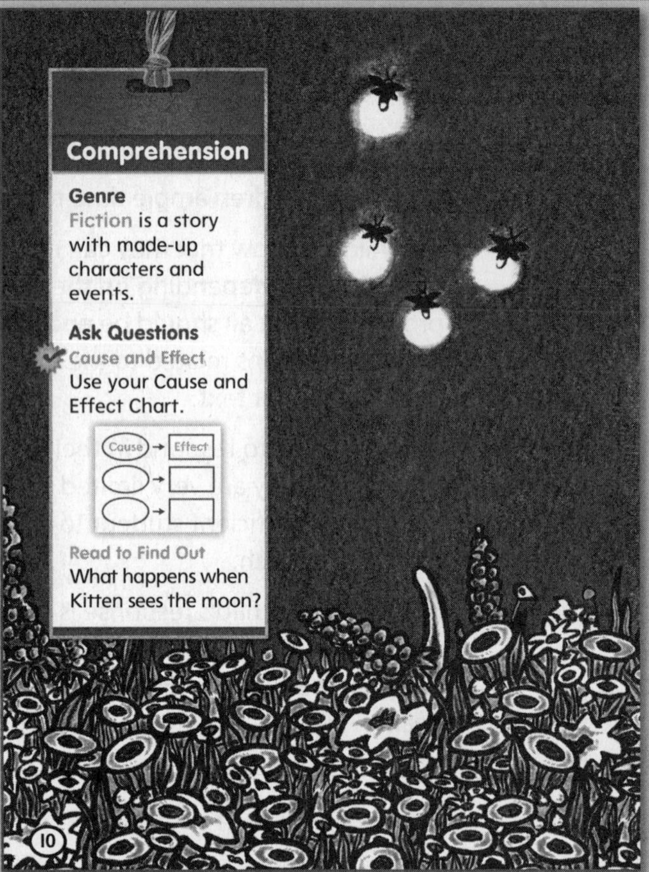

Comprehension
Genre
Fiction is a story with made-up characters and events.
Ask Questions
Cause and Effect
Use your Cause and Effect Chart.
Cause
Effect
Read to Find Out
What happens when Kitten sees the moon?
10

Pages 12–13

It was Kitten's first full moon.
When she saw it, she thought,
There's a little bowl of milk in the sky.
And she wanted it.

12

Pages 12 and 13

Text

- *Kitten sees the full moon. It is her first time. What does the moon look like to kitten?* (a bowl of milk)

Kitten likes milk. What do you like to eat or drink? Tell your partner three things that you like.

Illustration

- *Look at the moon. Is it round like a bowl?* (yes) *What color is it?* (white) *What color is milk?* (white) *The moon and milk are the same color. The moon looks like a bowl of milk to Kitten.*
- *Point to Kitten. Now point to the three bugs.* (Hold up three fingers.) *These bugs make little lights at night.*
-

Directionality

Ask children to place their finger where you start reading (top left). Ask where you finish reading on this page (bottom right).

Kitten's First Full Moon

Page 14

Illustration

- *Look at Kitten's eyes. Are they open or closed?* (closed) *I see her tongue.* (Point to Kitten's tongue.) *Say it with me:* tongue. *Kitten is trying to lick something with her tongue.* (Mime licking your hand.) *Say it with me:* lick.

Text

- *We just read that Kitten sees her first full moon. What does she think it is?* (a bowl of milk)
- *Let's read this page together:* So she closed her eyes and stretched her neck and opened her mouth and licked. (Pause very briefly after each line to pantomime the actions.)
- *Kitten is trying to lick the moon. She thinks it is a bowl of* ______. (milk)

Read this page to your partner. Have your partner pretend to be Kitten and do all the actions. Then switch roles.

Page 15

Illustration

- *Point to Kitten's tongue. What does Kitten have on her tongue?* (a bug) *Is Kitten happy?* (no)

Non-verbal Cues

Remind children that they can use non-verbal cues to share information when they are not able to do so verbally. Encourage children to use pantomime and sounds.

Pages 14–15

So she closed her eyes
and stretched her neck
and opened her mouth and licked.

14

Pages 16–17

Still, there was the little bowl

16

But Kitten only ended up with a bug on her tongue. Poor Kitten!

15

of milk, just waiting.

17

Text

- *Kitten thinks she will get milk, but ends up with a bug. That means that in the end, after all her trying, she gets a bug. Poor Kitten! Say it with me:* Poor Kitten!
- *Sometimes one thing causes another thing, or makes it happen. What happens is called the effect.*

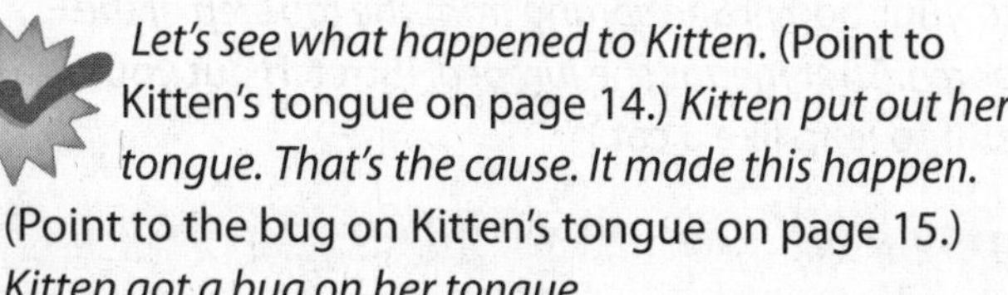

Let's see what happened to Kitten. (Point to Kitten's tongue on page 14.) *Kitten put out her tongue. That's the cause. It made this happen.* (Point to the bug on Kitten's tongue on page 15.) *Kitten got a bug on her tongue.*

Pages 16–17

Illustration

- *Point to Kitten. What is she looking at?* (the moon) *Does Kitten know it's the moon?* (no) *When Kitten looks at the moon, she sees a bowl of milk!*

Text

- *Let's read these pages together:* Still, there was the little bowl of milk, just waiting. *Kitten thinks the bowl is waiting for her to lick it!*

Page 18

Illustration

- *Look at Kitten. It looks like she wants to jump. Where does she want to jump?* (to the moon)

Text

- *Kitten pulled herself together.* (Gather your arms close to your body.) *She sprang from the top step of the porch. That means she jumped.* (Stretch out your arms as if to leap like a cat.)

Page 19

Illustration

- *Look at poor Kitten. What happened to her?* (She fell.) *These are the steps.* (Point to the steps and run your finger down them.) *Kitten fell down the steps.*

Text

- *Kitten tumbles, which means she falls. All these things happen as she falls: She bumps her nose.* (Point to your nose.) *Ouch! She bangs her ear.* (Point to your ear.) *Ouch! She pinches her tail.* (Point to Kitten's tail.) *Ouch! Poor Kitten! Read it with me:* Poor Kitten!

Pages 18–19

So she pulled herself together
and wiggled her bottom
and sprang from the top step of the porch.

18

Pages 20–21

Still, there was the little bowl

20

But Kitten only tumbled—
bumping her nose and banging her ear
and pinching her tail.
Poor Kitten!

19

of milk, just waiting.

21

Remember, cause and effect means that one thing makes another thing happen. Kitten tries to jump. That's the cause. Then what happens? Kitten tries to jump, and she ______ (falls). *The effect is that she falls.*

Pages 20–21

Illustration

- *Point to Kitten. What is she looking at?* (the moon) *Does Kitten know it's the moon?* (no) *When Kitten looks at the moon, she still sees a bowl of milk!*

Text

- *Let's read these pages together:* Still, there was the little bowl of milk, just waiting.

Pages 22–23

Illustration

- *Look at Kitten. She's running down the sidewalk.* (Run your finger along the sidewalk.) *Say it with me:* sidewalk. *Is there a sidewalk outside your house?* (Answers will vary.)
- *Look at Kitten. She's in a garden.* (Point to the garden.) *Say it with me:* garden. *A garden is a place with plants and flowers. Kitten is running through the garden.*
- *Look at the field.* (Point to the field.) *Say it with me:* field. *The field is full of grass. Kitten is running past the field.*
- *Look at the pond.* (Point to the pond.) *Say it with me:* pond. *The pond has water. Kitten is running by the pond.*
- *Kitten chases the moon past all these things. That means she runs after the moon.*
- *Look at the moon in all the pictures. Does Kitten ever get any closer to it?* (no) *The distance between her and the moon is always the same.*

Pages 22–23

So she chased it—
down the sidewalk,
through the garden,
past the field,
and by the pond.
But Kitten never seemed to get closer.
Poor Kitten!

22

Pages 24–25

Still, there was the little bowl

24

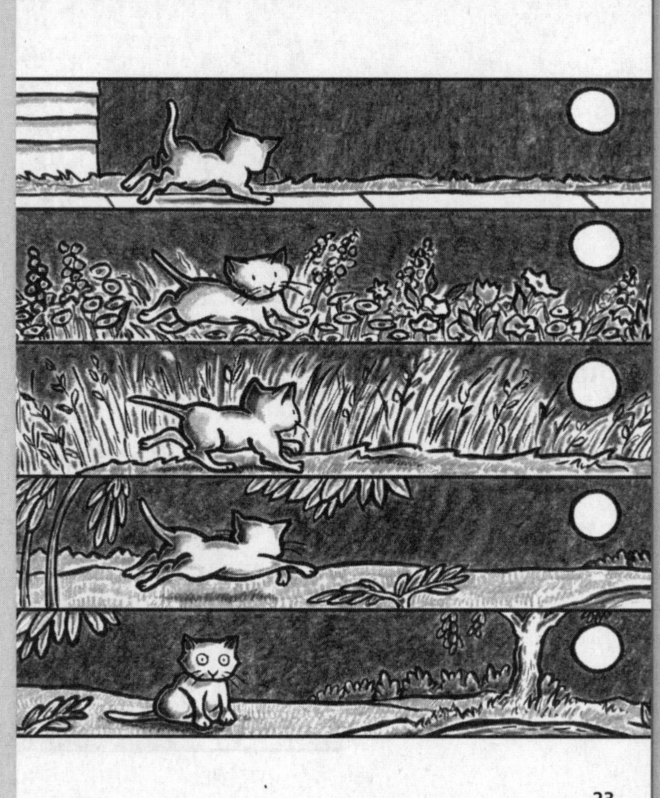

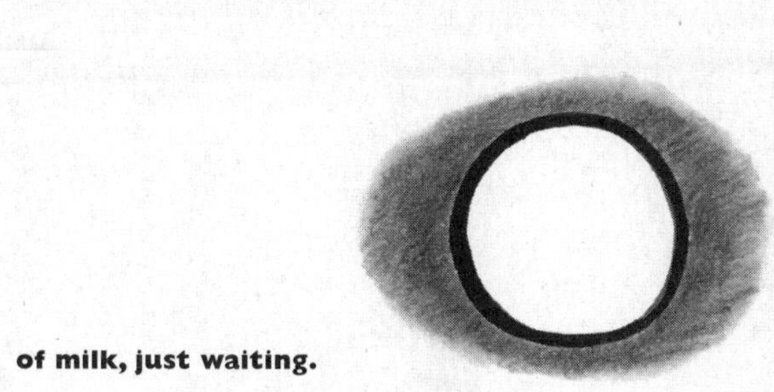

of milk, just waiting.

25

Talk with your partner about times you have seen the moon. Where were you? What did the moon look like? Did you ever watch the moon while you were walking? Did you ever watch it from a car or bus? (Questions are open.)

Text, Choral Reading

- *Let's read the first part of the page together:* So she chased it—down the sidewalk, through the garden, past the field, and by the pond.

Pages 24–25

Illustration

- *Point to Kitten. What is she looking at?* (the moon) *When Kitten looks at the moon, what does she see?* (a bowl of milk)

Text

- *Let's read these pages together:* Still, there was the little bowl of milk, just waiting.

Kitten's First Full Moon

Page 26

Illustration

- *Kitten is going up the tree. She's climbing it.* (Run your finger up tree.) *Say it with me:* climbing. *Why is Kitten climbing the tree?* (to get to the moon)

Text

- *Kitten runs to a very tall tree.* (Hold your hand up high.) *She climbs and climbs and climbs.* (Mime climbing.) *She climbs to the very top.* (Hold your hand up high.)

Page 27

Illustration

- *Look at Kitten. She's at the top of the tree. Does she look happy or scared?* (scared)

Text

- *Kitten still cannot reach the bowl of milk.* (Hold your hand up and mime reaching for the moon.) *It is just too far away. Is it really a bowl of milk?* (no)
- *Kitten feels scared. Why do you think she is afraid?* (She is very high. Maybe she has never climbed so high before.)

PARTNERS *Talk with your partner. What kinds of things do you climb at the playground? Do you ever feel scared when you are high up?* (Responses will vary.)

Pages 26–27

So she ran
to the tallest tree
she could find,
and she climbed
and climbed
and climbed
to the very top.

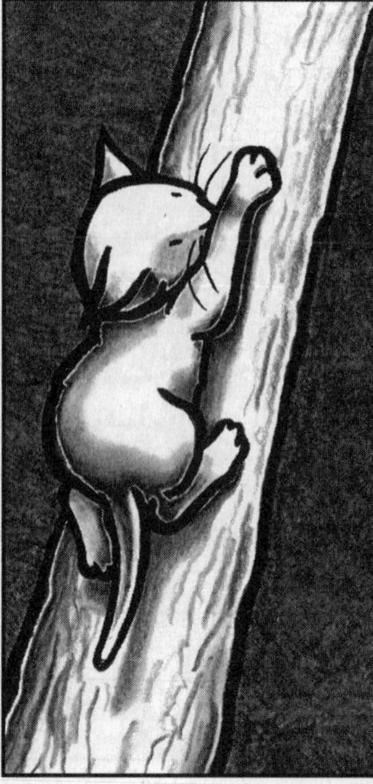

26

Pages 28–29

Then, in the pond, Kitten saw
another bowl of milk.
And it was bigger.
What a night!

28

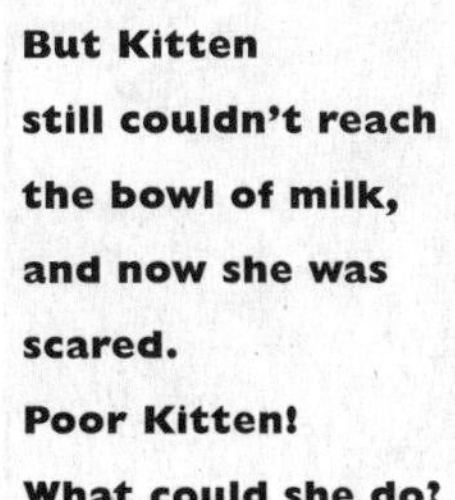

But Kitten
still couldn't reach
the bowl of milk,
and now she was
scared.
Poor Kitten!
What could she do?

27

29

Pages 28–29

Illustration

- *Look at the pond.* (Point to the pond.) *Kitten sees something in the pond. It's the light from the moon. Kitten doesn't know that's what it is. What does she think she sees?* (a bowl of milk)

Text

- *Let's read this page together:* Then, in the pond, Kitten saw another bowl of milk. And it was bigger. What a night! *How does Kitten feel now?* (happy, excited)
- *Kitten thinks she sees another bowl of milk, a different one. How many bowls of milk does she think she sees?* (two) *She is really seeing the reflection of the moon in the water. The pond is acting like a mirror.*

Kitten is looking at the pond. She wants that bowl of milk! What do you think Kitten is going to do? (Question is open.) *Tell your partner.*

Analyze Sayings and Expressions

Help children recognize that *What a night!* is an expression that means it has been a busy and eventful night. Help them create other examples using this expression.

Page 30

Illustration

- *Look at Kitten. Is she going up the tree or down the tree?* (down) *Is she going fast or slow?* (fast) *Why is she going so fast?* (She wants the bowl of milk.)

Text

- *Kitten races, or runs, down the tree. She races through the grass.* (Point to the grass.) *Where do you think she is going?* (to the pond)

Page 31

Illustration

- *Look at Kitten.* (Point to the picture on the left.) *She's right next to the pond. She's at the edge of the pond. Say it with me:* edge.
- *Look at the next picture. What is Kitten doing now?* (She's jumping into the pond.)

Text

- *Kitten runs to the edge of the pond.* (Run your finger along the edge of the pond.)
- *She leaps, or jumps, into the pond. She leaps with all her might. That means she jumps with all her strength.*
- *The pond is water. Do cats like water?* (no)

Pages 30–31

So she raced down the tree and raced through the grass

30

Pages 32–33

**Poor Kitten!
She was wet and sad and tired and hungry.**

32

and raced to the edge of the pond.

She leaped with all her might—

31

33

Pages 32–33

Illustration

- *Look at Kitten in the pond. Is she wet or dry?* (wet) *Is she happy or sad?* (sad)

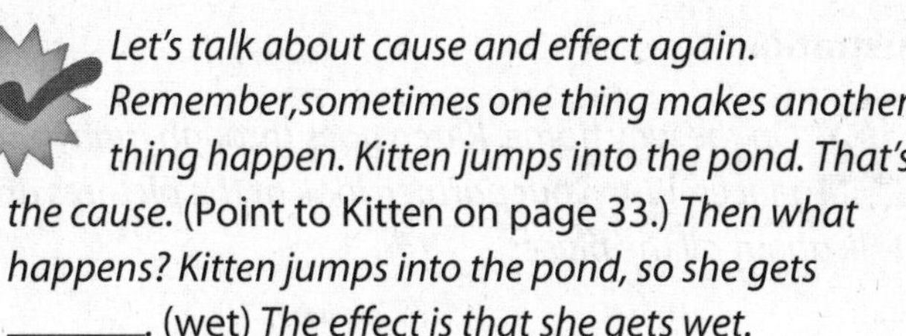

Let's talk about cause and effect again. Remember,sometimes one thing makes another thing happen. Kitten jumps into the pond. That's the cause. (Point to Kitten on page 33.) *Then what happens? Kitten jumps into the pond, so she gets ______.* (wet) *The effect is that she gets wet.*

Text

- *Let's read this page together:* Poor Kitten! She was wet and sad and tired and hungry. *Kitten is wet from the pond. She is tired from all the running and climbing and jumping. How else does she feel?* (sad and hungry)

Pages 34–35

Text

- *Kitten isn't happy, so she goes home. Let's read this page together:* So she went back home—

Illustration

On the way home, Kitten goes through many places. With your partner, look at the pictures and talk about all the places.

Pages 34–35

So she went back home—

34

Pages 36–37

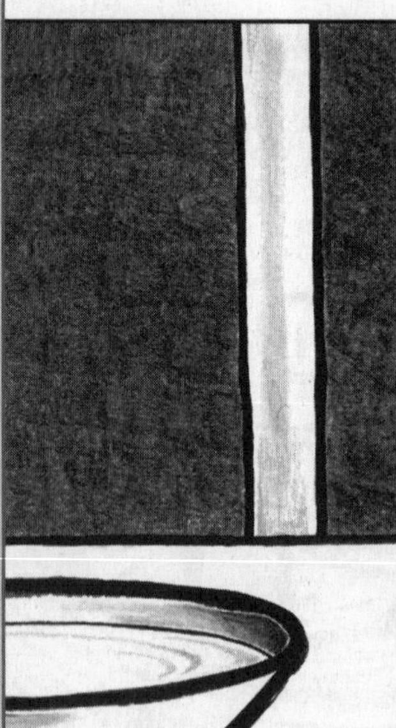

and there was a great big

36

35

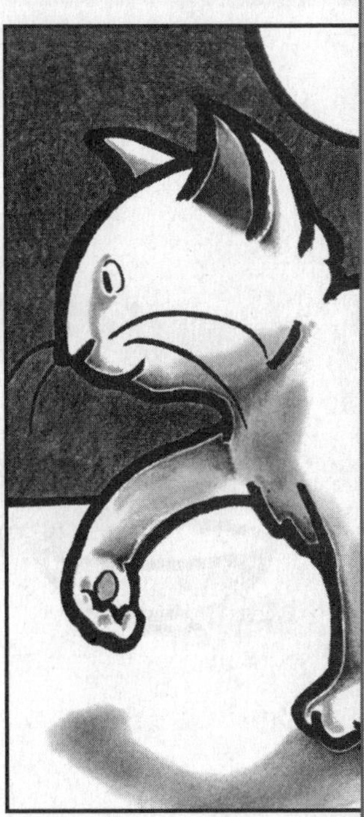

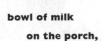

bowl of milk
on the porch,

37

Pages 36–37

Illustration

- *Look at the picture. What is it?* (Point to the bowl of milk.) *Is it the moon?* (No, it's a bowl of milk.)

Text

- *There was a bowl of milk on the porch. The milk was in front of the house, at the top of the steps.*
- *Let's read these pages together:* <u>and there was a great big bowl of milk on the porch.</u>

Kitten sees the bowl of milk. What is she going to do? Tell your partner what you think.

Kitten's First Full Moon

Pages 38–39

Text

- *The bowl of milk was waiting for Kitten! Who do you think left the milk for Kitten?* (her owners)

Illustration

- *Look at Kitten drinking the milk. Do you see her tongue? Show your partner. Is Kitten hungry now?* (no) *Is Kitten sad now?* (no)

Pages 40–41

Illustration

- *Look at Kitten. What is she doing?* (She's sleeping.) *Is she happy or sad?* (She's happy.)
- *Look at the moon.* (Trace the circumference of the moon with your finger.) *It's round and white.* (Point to the bowl.) *Look at the bowl of milk.* (Trace the circumference of the bowl with your finger.) *It's round and white.*

Text

- *Let's read this page together:* <u>Lucky Kitten!</u> *To be lucky means that things are going well for you. Do you think Kitten is lucky after all?* (yes)

Pages 38–39

just waiting for her.

38

Pages 40–41

40

39

Lucky Kitten!

41

Let's talk about cause and effect at the end of the story. Kitten finally has a bowl of milk. (Point to Kitten on page 39.) *That's the cause. How does Kitten feel when she finally gets some milk?* (happy, lucky) *The effect is that Kitten is happy!*

Ellen Ochoa in Space

Access Core Content

Teacher Note Pose the questions after you read the paragraph or page indicated.

Page 44

Title

- *Listen as I read the title:* Ellen Ochoa in Space.

Photo

- *This woman's name is Ellen Ochoa.* (Point to her.) *Look behind her.* (Point to the darkness and stars in the background.) *It's very dark. Point to the stars. The stars are in space. Say it with me:* space.

Text

- *Ellen Ochoa has a job. She is an astronaut. Say it with me:* astronaut. *She takes trips into space.*
- *Listen as I read this page:* Ellen Ochoa is an astronaut. She has been on many trips into space.

Page 45

Photo

- *Point to Ellen Ochoa in the picture. She is in space in this picture. She is very, very high up in the sky.* (Reach your arm high and point up.) *Are we high up in space?* (no) *We are down here on Earth. Ellen is looking out the window. Point to it. Ellen can see Earth far, far away.*

Text

- *Earth is the planet where we live. Ellen travels from Earth into space. She goes in a spacecraft. What does Ellen see when she looks down from space?* (Earth)
- *Ellen likes being in space. What does she like to see at night from the spacecraft?* (the moon and stars)

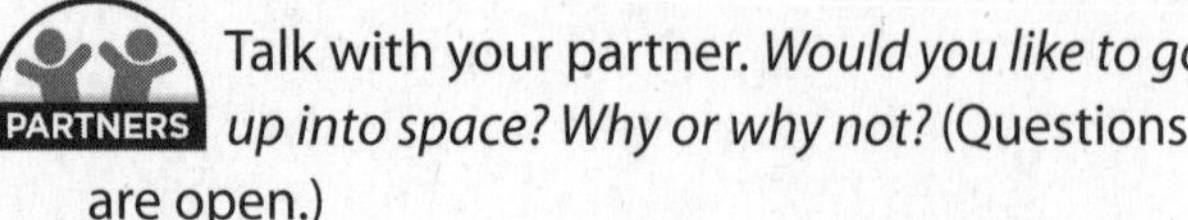

PARTNERS Talk with your partner. *Would you like to go up into space? Why or why not?* (Questions are open.)

Pages 44–45

Ellen Ochoa IN SPACE

Science

Genre
A Biography gives information about a real person.

Text Feature
A Caption gives information about a picture.

Content Vocabulary
astronaut
planet
weightless

LOG ON FIND OUT
Science Exploring Space
www.macmillanmh.com

Ellen Ochoa is an **astronaut.** She has made many trips into space. Ellen lives in Houston, Texas. She works at the Johnson Space Center there.

44

Pages 46–47

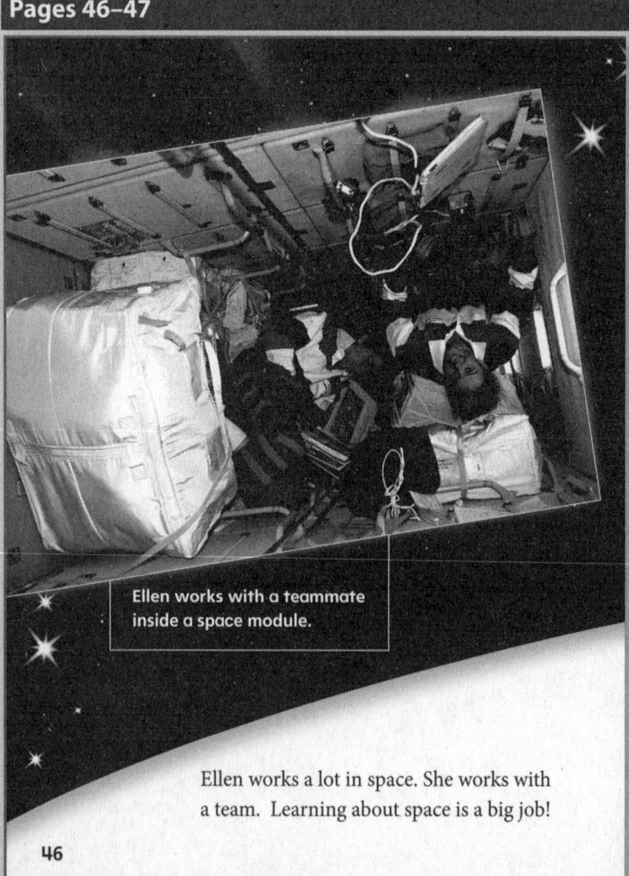

Ellen works with a teammate inside a space module.

Ellen works a lot in space. She works with a team. Learning about space is a big job!

46

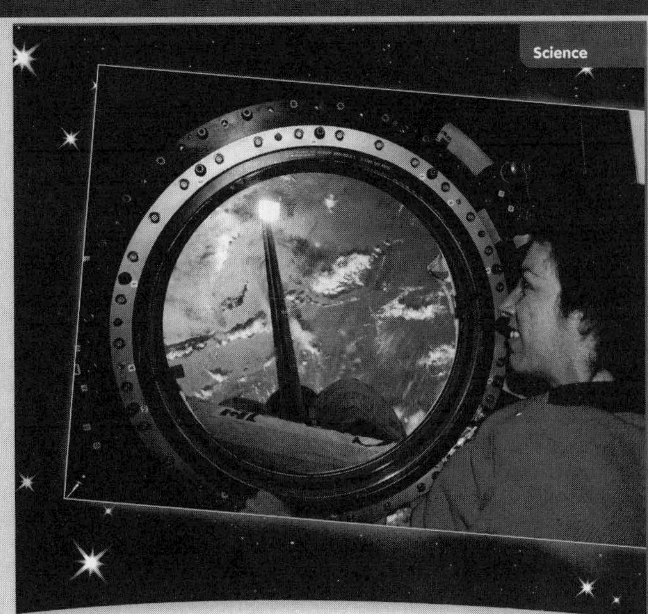

Ellen thinks space trips are exciting. She likes seeing Earth from space. She sees our **planet** as the spacecraft rises through the sky. And she sees the moon and stars at night. What a thrilling sight that is!

45

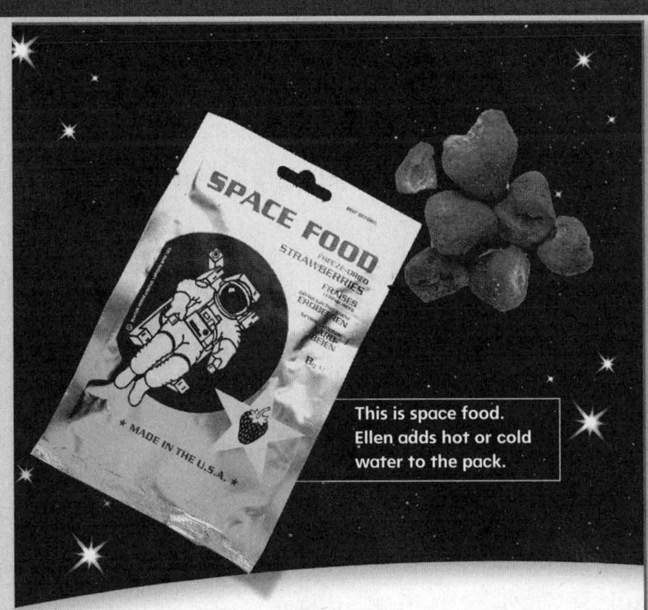

This is space food. Ellen adds hot or cold water to the pack.

In space, everything is **weightless**. Everything floats!

So how can astronauts eat? Ellen has a tray that sticks to her lap. Dried food and drinks in packs stick to the tray. She eats tortillas, as well. It is easy to stuff them with good things.

47

Page 46

Photo and Caption

- *This is where Ellen works in space.* (Point to space module.) *It's called a space module. Say it with me:* space module. *Ellen works in the space module with another astronaut.*

Text

- *Ellen works in space. Does she work a lot or a little?* (a lot) *She works with a team, or a group. They learn about space.*

Page 47

Photo and Caption

- *Look at the strawberries.* (Point to them.) *These strawberries are in space. Do they look like wet or dry?* (dry)
- *The strawberries were inside this pack of space food.* (Point to it.) *Space food is dry. What does Ellen have to add before she eats the food?* (water)

Paragraph 1

- *In space, things don't have weight. They are not heavy. They are weightless. Say it with me:* weightless. *Weightless things float. They don't stay down. Things go up and down and everywhere.* (Move hands around to demonstrate things floating everywhere.)
- *Astronauts float in space. People also can float in water. Raise your hand if you know how to float. Have you ever floated in a pool, on a lake, or in the ocean?* (Answers will vary.) *If you did, you know what it feels like to be weightless.*

Paragraph 2

- *Astronauts don't want their food to float. They want it to stay down. Ellen has a special tray on her lap. This is my lap.* (Sit down and put hands on your lap.)
- *Ellen's tray sticks to her lap. It stays down. It doesn't float. The packs of space food stick to the tray. They don't float. Ellen can eat tortillas in space! What would you like to eat in space?* (Answers will vary.)

Ellen Ochoa in Space

Page 48

Photo

- *Look at the picture. What is the astronaut doing?* (He is sleeping.) *Is he sleeping in a bed?* (no) *He is sleeping in a bag.*
- *The astronaut doesn't want to float when he sleeps. He wants to stay down. Look at these straps.* (Point to the straps.) *Say it with me:* straps. *The straps hold the sleeping bag.* (Grab one wrist to demonstrate *hold.*) *The astronaut doesn't float.*

Caption

- *Ellen sleeps in a sleeping bag, just like the astronaut in the picture. Her sleeping bag has straps, too. She doesn't fall out.*

Text

- *The sleeping bags stick to the wall of the spacecraft.* (Hold the palm of one hand tightly against the wall to demonstrate *stick.*) *The astronaut gets in the sleeping bag. The straps hold the bag.*
- *Do astronauts float when they are asleep?* (no) *What holds the sleeping bag?* (the straps)

We use straps to hold many things. Look with your partner for things that have straps in our room.

Analyze Sayings and Expressions

Help children recognize that *sleep tight* is an expression used to wish someone a good night sleep. Help them create other examples using this expression.

Pages 48–49

Ellen uses a sleeping bag like this one. With straps like these, you can't fall out.

How can astronauts sleep if everything floats? They use sleeping bags that stick to the side of the spacecraft. They just float into the bag and strap themselves in. Then it is time to curl up and sleep tight!

48

Ellen Ochoa is dressed for space.

Ellen worked hard to be an astronaut. She went to college. She learned a lot of math and science. Then she went to school to learn about space flight. She had to pass a lot of tests. At last she became an astronaut. Ellen thinks that she has a fantastic job! Do you think so, too?

Connect and Compare

- What do you think Kitten in *Kitten's First Full Moon* might do in a space module?
- What do the captions tell you about the pictures?

49

Page 49

Photo

- *Listen as I read the caption aloud:* Ellen Ochoa is dressed for space.
- *Look at Ellen. She is wearing a spacesuit. Point to it. She is also wearing a helmet.* (Point to it.) *The helmet helps her breathe in space. Can she see through it?* (yes)

Text

- *Ellen worked hard to be an astronaut. She went to college. She learned some things that we learn. What were they?* (math and science)
- *She also went to a special school for astronauts.*
- *We learned some different things about Ellen's job in space. Let's remember:*

  Does Ellen think her job is fun or not fun? (fun)
  Does Ellen work alone or with a team? (with a team)
  Is space food wet or dry? (dry)
  In space, does Ellen sleep in a bed or bag? (bag)

Name ______________________

Use the word chart to study this week's vocabulary words. Write a sentence using each word in your writer's notebook.

Word	Context Sentence	Illustration
leaped ______________	The squirrel leaped from one branch to the next.	When might someone leap?
lucky ______________	Sam was the lucky winner.	Sam

© Macmillan/McGraw-Hill

Name ____________________

Book Talk

Read each question and prompt. Discuss the answers with your group. Use your Leveled Reader to find details to support your answers. Then write your answers on another sheet of paper.

1. Explain what makes the moon shine.

2. Tell what we see as the moon circles Earth.

3. Why did Native Americans call the June full moon the Strawberry Moon?

4. Why did astronauts travel to the moon?

5. What did the first astronauts do on the moon?

© Macmillan/McGraw-Hill

Meet Ben Franklin

Pages 56–57

Prior to reading the selection with children, they should have listened to the selection on **StudentWorks Plus**, the interactive eBook. In addition, selection vocabulary should have been pretaught using the **Visual Vocabulary Resources**.

Access Core Content

Teacher Note Pose the questions after you read the paragraph or page indicated.

Pages 56–57

Title

- *Benjamin Franklin was a great American. We remember him for the special things he did.*

Illustration

- *Look at the picture. It shows the time when Benjamin Franklin lived. Do boys today wear the same kinds of shoes and clothes?* (no) *Benjamin Franklin lived a long time ago.*

- *This picture shows Benjamin Franklin as a boy. What is young Ben doing?* (flying a kite) *The string with ribbons hanging from the kite is called a tail. Some kites need a tail to fly correctly. Point to the kite. Point to the kite's tail.*

Pages 56–57

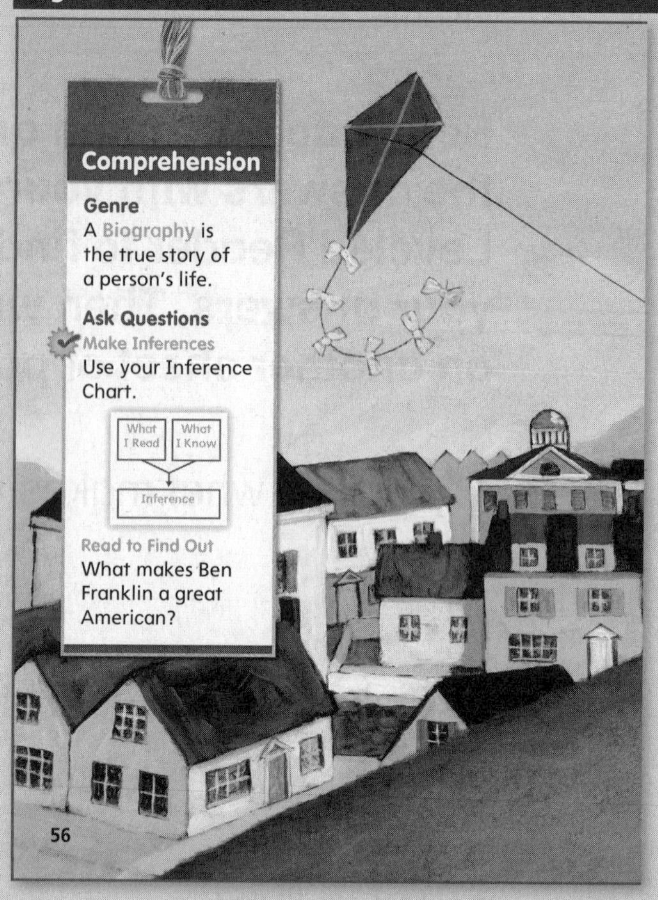

Comprehension
Genre
A Biography is the true story of a person's life.
Ask Questions
Make Inferences
Use your Inference Chart.
What I Read
What I Know
Inference
Read to Find Out
What makes Ben Franklin a great American?
56

Pages 58–59

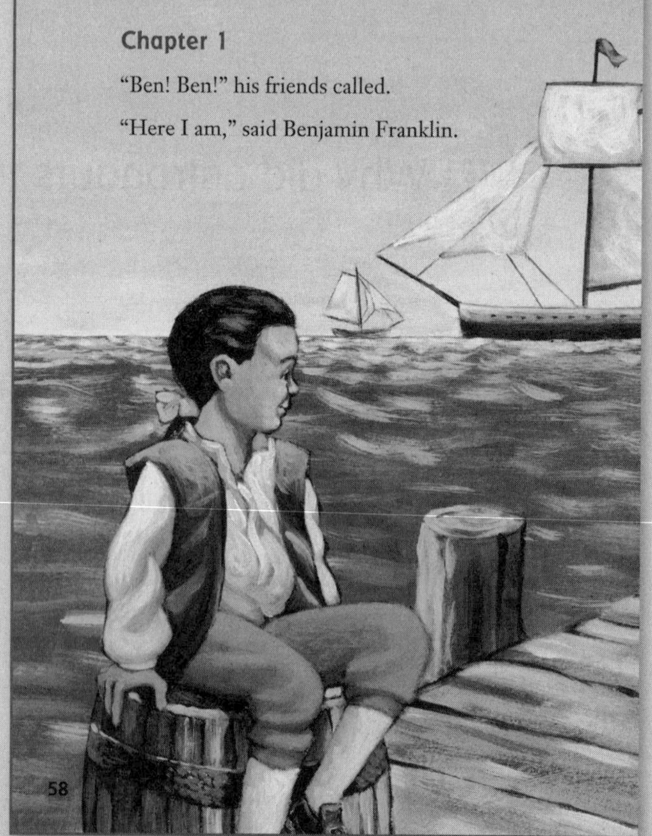

Chapter 1
"Ben! Ben!" his friends called.
"Here I am," said Benjamin Franklin.
58

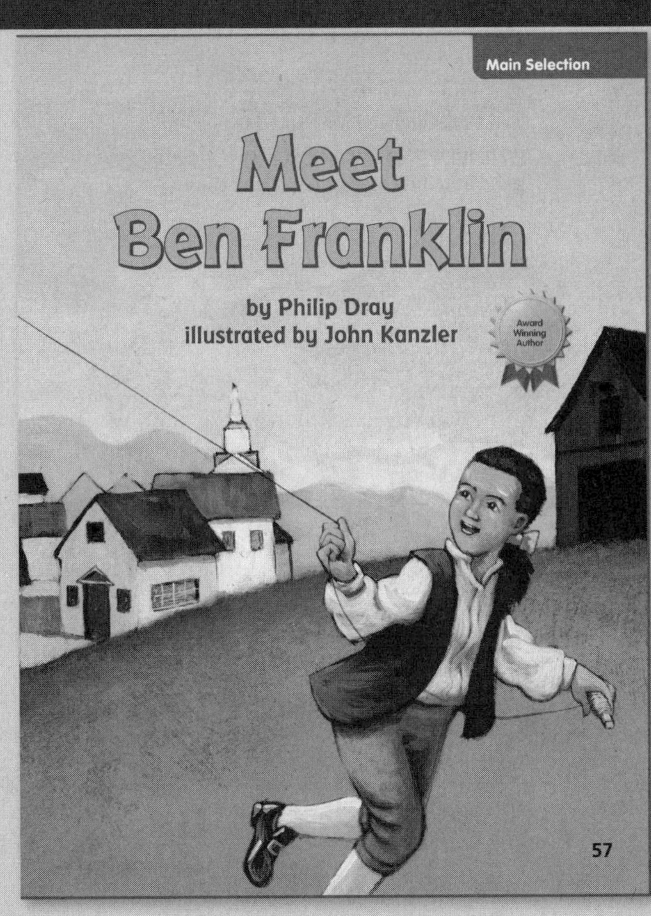

Ben was sitting on the docks. He was looking at the big ships. He liked the way the wind filled the sails.
59

Pages 58–59

Text and Illustration

- *This book has sections called chapters. Chapter 1 tells about Ben as a young boy.*
- *Look at the big ships in the picture. What makes them go?* (the wind) *The wind fills the sails, or blows into the sails.* (Blow against a piece of paper to demonstrate filling the sails.) *The wind pushes the ship forward.*
- *Look at Ben. He is watching the big ships from the docks.* (Point to the docks.) *People build docks out of wood. Docks jut out from the shore onto the water.*
- *Ben's friends are looking for Ben. Point to them. Where do they find Ben?* (on the docks)

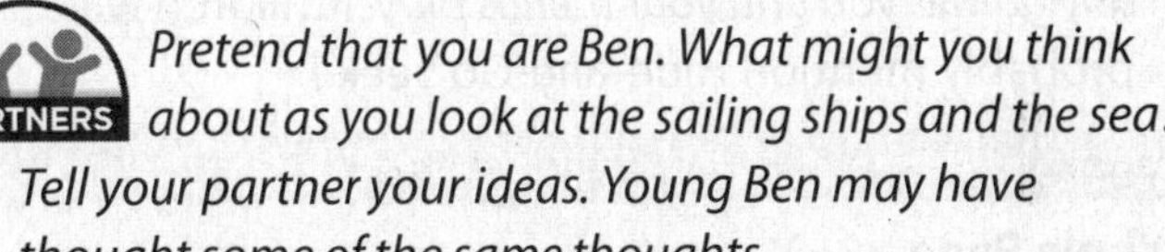

Pretend that you are Ben. What might you think about as you look at the sailing ships and the sea? Tell your partner your ideas. Young Ben may have thought some of the same thoughts.

-

Directionality

Ask children to place their finger where you start reading (top left). Ask where you finish reading on this page (bottom right).

Meet Ben Franklin

Page 60

Text

- *Let's read together to find out what Ben liked to do as a boy:* Ben Franklin lived long ago. He liked to do many things. He liked to read. He was good at telling jokes and playing games.
- *Ben liked to do many things. Which of those things do you like to do? Why do you like those things?* (Questions are open.)

Illustration

PARTNERS *Talk with your partner about what type of game Ben and his friends may be playing. Talk about whether the game you see in the picture reminds you of any games you and your friends play.* (Children will probably mention Hide-and-Go Seek.)

Page 61

Whole Page

- *Let's read the first paragraph together to find out more about young Ben:* Ben was a curious boy. He was smart, too. He liked to dream. And he liked to make things.
- *Young Ben was curious. That means that he wondered about things. Ben also liked to dream. We dream when we sleep. We also dream when we think of ideas we would like to make come true. Which kind of dream does the author mean?* (thinking of ideas)
- *We learned a fact about Ben on page 60 that tells one reason he was smart. Look back to find one thing that made him smart.* (He liked to read.)

Pages 60–61

Pages 62–63

The next time Ben went swimming, he had his kite with him.
"What will you do with that?" his friends asked.
"You will see," said Ben.
62

Ben was a **curious** boy. He was smart, too. He liked to dream. And he liked to make things.

One day, Ben made a red kite.

"This kite will be like the sails on the big ships," Ben said.

61

Ben ran with the kite. The wind lifted it. He jumped in the water. He started to go fast. The kite was pulling him!

"Look at Ben go!" said his friends.

"How did Ben think of that?" they asked.

63

Look at the picture of the kite Ben made. Draw a picture of a kite you have flown or seen. Share and talk about your picture with your partner.

- *Ben says that his kite will be like the sails on the ships. How is a kite like a sail?* (They both need wind to work.)

Page 62

Whole Page

- *Ben goes for a swim with his friends. Point to them in the picture. What does Ben have with him?* (his kite)'
- *We know that Ben is curious. He wonders about many things and wants to learn about them. What do his friends do to show that they are curious, too?* (They want to know what he will do with the kite.)

Page 63

Text, Choral Reading

- *Let's read this page together. We will use a telling voice when we read facts about what Ben does. We will use an excited voice when surprising things happen. We will use a questioning voice when someone is curious.*
- *Ben uses the kite to pull himself across the water. Do you think he got the idea from reading a book or from watching the big ships on the water?* (from watching the big ships on the water)

Patterns in Language

Some grammatical structures, such as past tense "ed," pose difficulties to ELLs. Point out that there are several examples of words ending in *-ed* in this selection, such as *lived, liked, asked, lifted, jumped.* Help children find a pattern.

Let's summarize what we learned about Ben as a young boy. (He liked to have fun. He was also smart and curious. He liked to think of new ideas. He figured out how to use a kite to take a ride across the water.)

Page 64

Whole Page

- *Chapter 2 tells about Ben as an adult.*
- *Ben has made a new kind of stove to heat houses. It is smaller than the fireplaces. Does it give lots of heat or a little bit of heat?* (lots of heat)
- *Point to the stove in the picture. Why do you think the woman is sitting close to it?* (to stay warm)

Page 65

Paragraph 1, Choral Reading

- *Let's read the first paragraph together:* Ben made a new kind of glasses. They helped people to see up close and far away.
- *Raise your hand if you wear glasses to see things that are up close, like books. Raise your hand if you wear glasses to see things that are far away.* (Allow children to respond.)

Illustration

- *Point to the person who is using glasses to see things that are close. Point to the person who is using glasses to see things that are faraway.*

Do you think that Ben was the kind of person who liked to help others? (yes) *What clues in the story helped you figure out that?* (He made things that helped other people.)

Pages 64–65

Chapter 2

Time went by. Ben **grew** up. He still liked to dream. He still liked to make things.

He made a new kind of stove. This stove was little, but it gave off lots of heat.

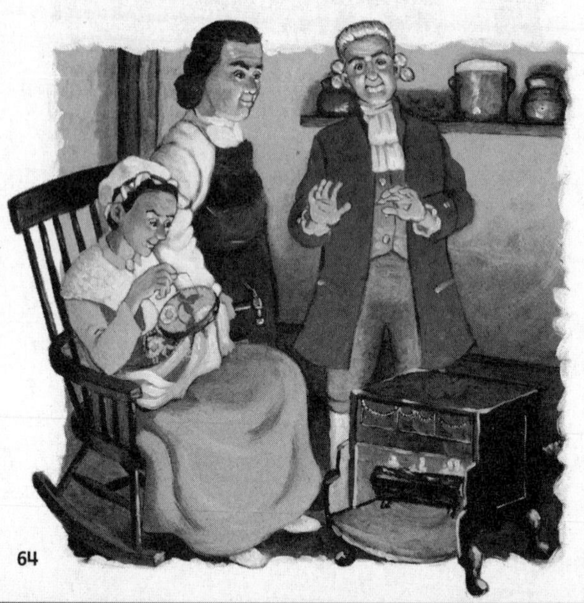

64

Pages 66–67

When Ben lived, people did not know much about electricity.

Ben was curious about it. He **knew** it could make sparks. He sometimes saw the sparks when he put his key into a lock.

66

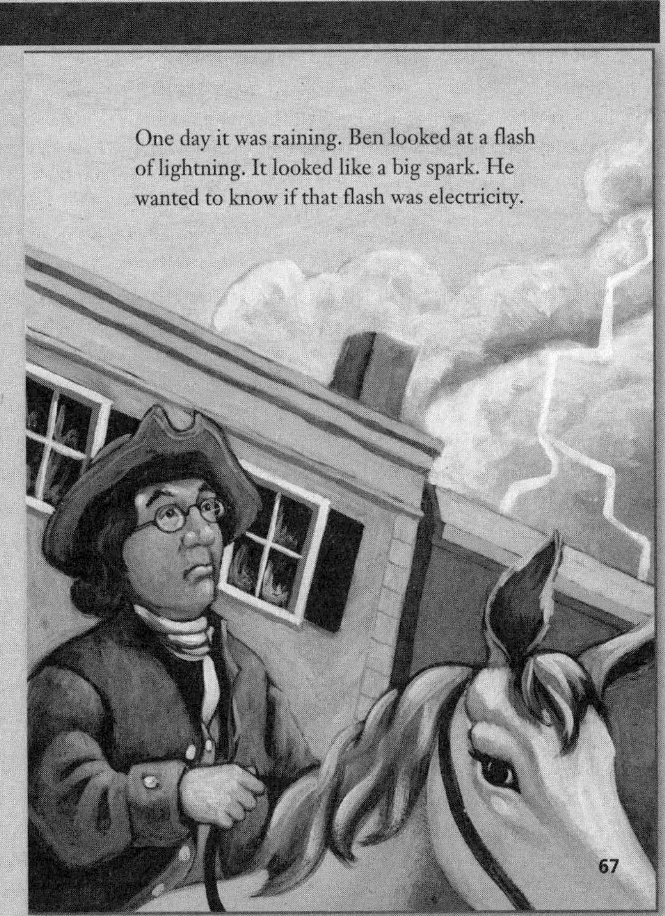

One day it was raining. Ben looked at a flash of lightning. It looked like a big spark. He wanted to know if that flash was electricity.
67

Pages 66–67

Whole Page

- *Ben was curious about electricity. Did people in his time know much about it?* (no)
- *Ben knew that electricity could make sparks. He sometimes saw sparks when he put his key in the lock.*
- *Look at the picture. Ben is putting his key into a lock. Point to the key. Point to the lock. Point to the sparks, or tiny flashes of light or fire.*

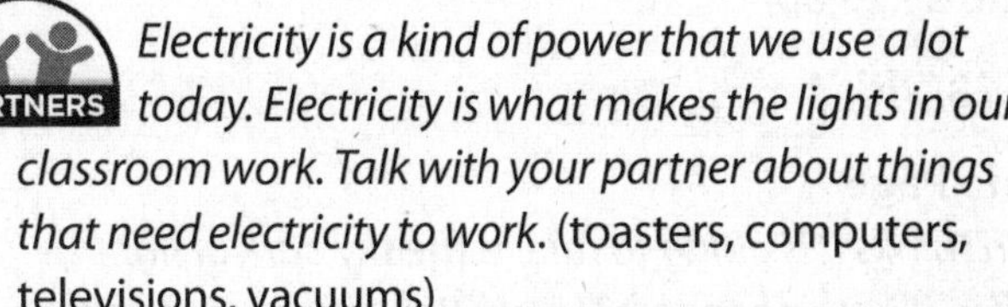

Electricity is a kind of power that we use a lot today. Electricity is what makes the lights in our classroom work. Talk with your partner about things that need electricity to work. (toasters, computers, televisions, vacuums)

Page 67

Whole Page

- *The author says that the lightning looks like a big spark, or flash of light. Point to the lightning in the picture. What do you think it looks like?* (Responses will vary.)
- *Draw a picture of lightning that you have seen.*

Meet Ben Franklin

Page 68

Whole Page

- *Chapter 3 tells what Ben does with his idea about lightning and electricity.*
- *Let's read to see what question Ben wants to answer:* "How can I find out if lightning is electricity?" Ben asked. "I can not go up in the sky."
- *Ben cannot go up in the sky. Look at the picture on page 69 to see what other idea Ben has. What is his idea?* (to send a kite up)

Page 69

Whole Page

- *Ben thinks it is going to rain. Is the sky dark or light when it is going to rain?* (dark) *Ben needs rain to check out his idea. That is when lightning happens.*
- *Ben has a kite and an iron key. Iron is a strong metal. It is used to make many things, like tools. Point to the key in the picture.*

Page 70

Whole Page

- *Lightning shakes, and Ben feels the kite string shake. He sees sparks of electricity jump off the key. Remember, sparks are small flashes of light. When sparks jump, they shoot off in different directions. Point to the sparks in the picture.*
- *Look at the picture of Ben and the boy. Does the boy look sad or surprised?* (surprised) *The boy didn't expect lightning to hit the key. Do you think that Ben did?* (yes)
- *Let's read the last sentence together:* "This shows that lightning is electricity!" said Ben.

Imagine that you and your partner are watching Ben do the experiment. Tell each other what you would say. (Responses will vary.)

Pages 68–69

Chapter 3
"How can I find out if lightning is electricity?" Ben asked. "I can not go up in the sky."
Ben had an **idea.** A kite had helped him long ago. A kite could help him again.
"I can not get up there," he said. "But a kite can."
68

Pages 70–71

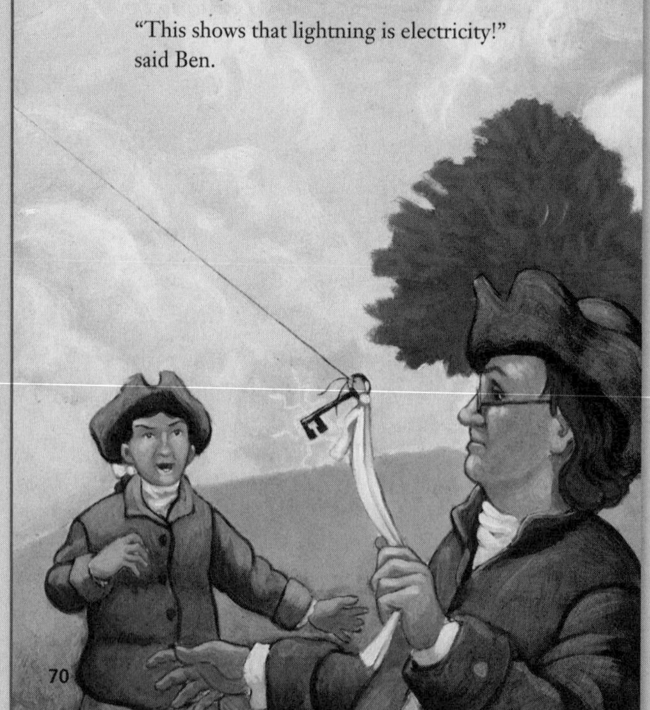

The next time it looked like rain, Ben went out. The sky was dark. Ben had a kite and an iron key. He sent the kite up.

69

Ben had an idea. He knew that if lightning struck a **house**, it could catch on fire. He put an iron rod on top of his house.

"Lightning will strike the iron rod, but not my house," Ben said. "The rod will keep my house safe."

71

Let's summarize how Ben discovers that lightning is electricity. He sees that it is going to ______. (rain) *During the storm, he sends up a ______.* (kite) *He puts an iron key on the ______.* (string) *Lightning hits, and Ben sees ______.* (sparks) *He now knows that lightning is ______.* (electricity)

Page 71

Whole Page

- *If lightning strikes, or hits a house, the house can catch on fire. That means that the house can burn.*
- *Ben has an idea. He puts an iron rod, or pole, on top of his house. Point to the iron rod in the picture.*
- *Let's read what Ben says together:* Lightning will strike the iron rod, but not my house," Ben said. "The rod will keep my house safe."

Monitor Oral Production

Remember to model self-corrective techniques on a regular basis as you speak to children. Pretend to mispronounce words and self-correct.

Page 72

Text

- *Ben's friends decide to put the iron rod on their houses, too. Do you think that Ben's idea worked?* (yes) *His friends want their houses to be safe, too.*
- *Today, we call what Ben made a lightning rod.*

Illustration

- *Point to the lightning rods in the picture. How many lightning rods do you see?* (seven)

Let's summarize some of the ways Ben helped people. He made a heating stove to help people keep_______. (warm) *He made glasses to help them _______.* (see) *Then he learned about electricity. He made lightning _______.* (rods)

Pages 72–73

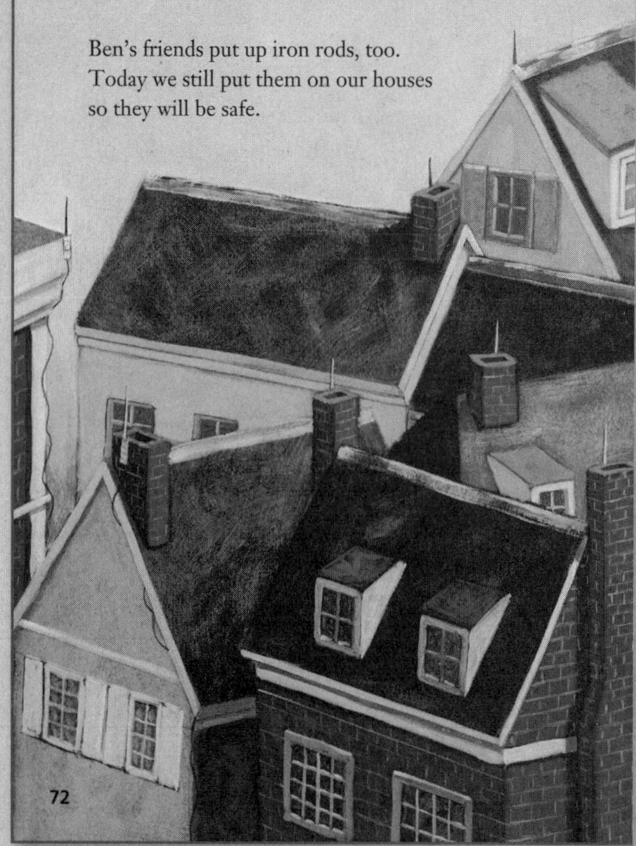

Ben's friends put up iron rods, too.
Today we still put them on our houses
so they will be safe.
72

Ben was glad that the lightning rods helped people. In his life, Ben Franklin **would** do many more things to help people. He had more things to dream about and more things to make.
73

Page 73

Whole Page

- *On page 61, it says that when Ben was a boy he liked to dream and he liked to make things. As an adult, he still liked to dream and make things. What does this tell you about the kind of person Ben was?* (He was curious and smart.)

Think about people you know. Who is curious and smart like Ben? What makes you think so. Tell your partner about the person.

A Close Look

Access Core Content

Teacher Note Pose the questions after you read the paragraph or page indicated.

Page 76

Whole Page

- *Something that is tiny is very, very small.* (Use your fingers to demonstrate tiny.) *A microscope is a machine that people look through to see things that are very tiny. Microscopes make tiny things look big.* (Use your fingers to show the difference between tiny and big.)
- *A scientist is a person who studies things in nature and in the universe to learn more about them. Scientists use tools like microscopes to learn about things. Point to the scientist on this page. Point to the microscope.*
- *Why might a scientist want to make things look bigger?* (to see how the thing is put together, to see what its parts are, to see how it works)

Scientists are curious. They ask questions. They use science ideas to try to answer their questions. Talk with your partner about whether you think Ben Franklin was a scientist.

Page 77

Whole Page

- *Listen as I read the first paragraph aloud.*
- *The first paragraph ends with a question. Let's use the pictures to figure out the answer. Point to the glass container with a metal lid. It is a salt shaker. What do you think is in it.* (salt)
- *Look at the red line. It starts on page 76 and connects all the pictures. Point to the large circle. It shows how something looks under a microscope. What does it show?* (salt)
- *Now listen as I read the last paragraph.*

Pages 76–77

Science
Genre
Nonfiction gives information about a topic.
Text Feature
Bold Print points out important words.
Content Vocabulary
scientists
microscope
photograph
LOG ON FIND OUT
Science Scientists at Work
www.macmillanmh.com
A Close Look
How do **scientists** see tiny things up close? They look through a **microscope**. That makes tiny things look big.
76

Pages 78–79

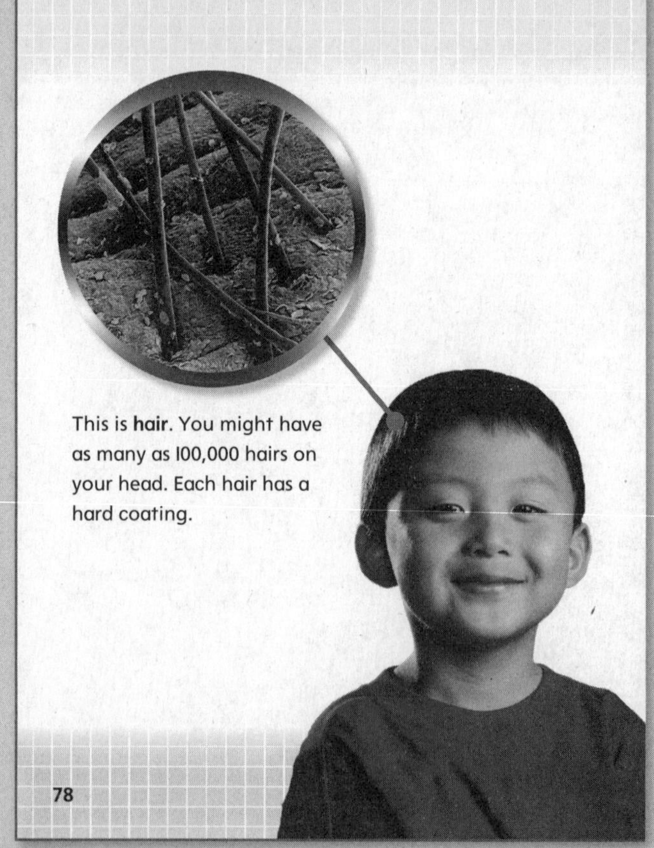

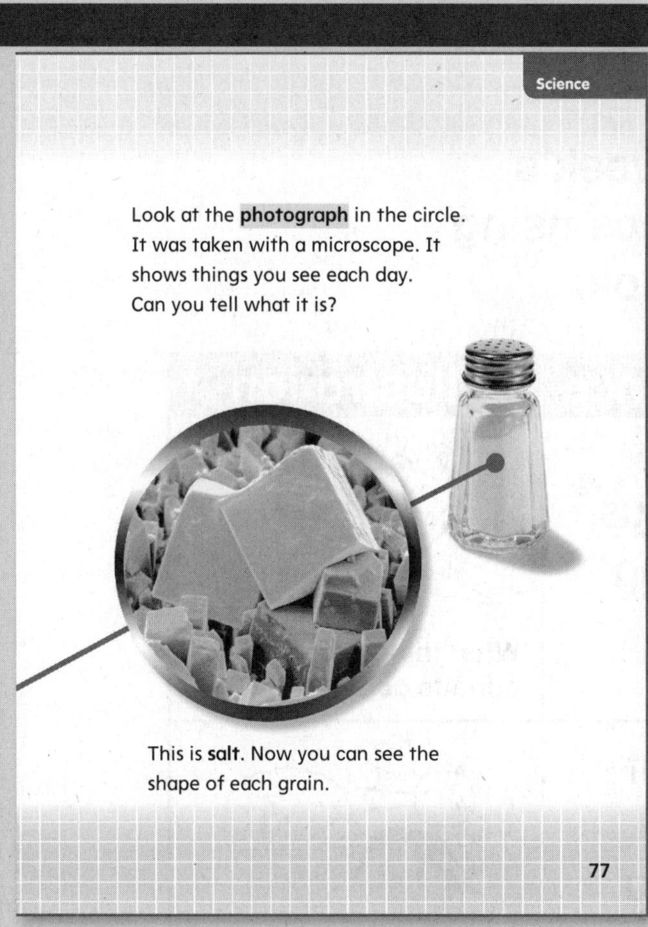

Science
Look at the photograph in the circle. It was taken with a microscope. It shows things you see each day. Can you tell what it is?
This is salt. Now you can see the shape of each grain.
77

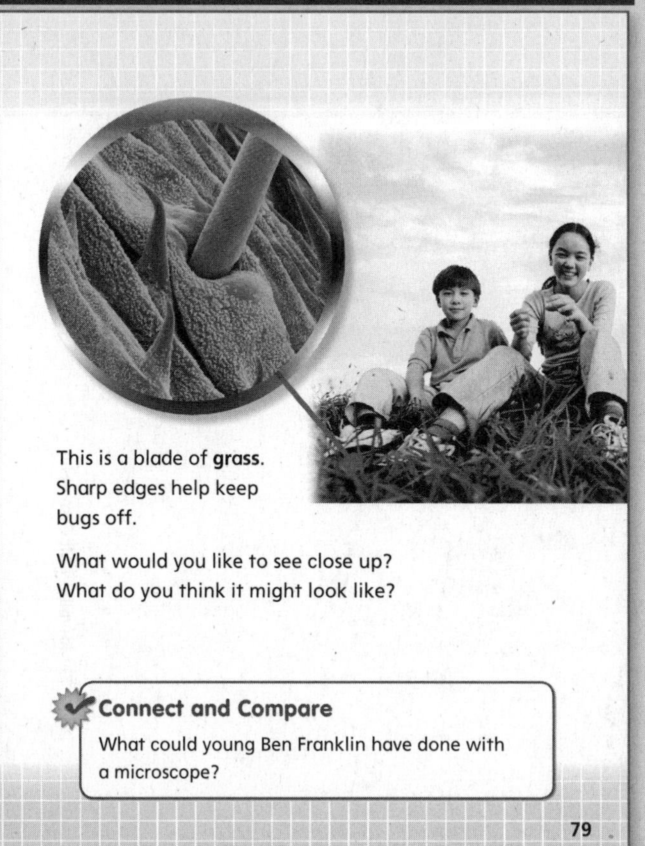

Page 78

Whole Page

- *Listen as I read this page aloud:* This is hair. You might have as many as 100,000 hairs on your head. Each hair has a hard coating.
- *A coating is a layer of something that covers another object. For example, a piece of candy may have a coating of hard sugar surrounding a chocolate center. A piece of hair has a hard coating, just like that candy does. The coating protects what is inside.*
- *We might have as many as 100,000 hairs growing out of our heads. That's a lot of hairs! Do you think you could count how many hairs are on your head? Why or why not?* (No. There are too many to count.)

Page 79

Whole Page

- *This page tells us about a blade of grass. A blade is something that is flat with a thin edge. Grass grows in blades.*
- *Grass has sharp edges. Point to a sharp edge on a piece of grass in the microscope picture.* The *sharp edges keep bugs off. Do you think the sharp edges would hurt the bugs if they land on them?* (yes)

Answer these questions from the selection with your partner: What else would you like to see close up? What do you think it would look like? (Responses will vary.)

Name ______________________________

Use the word chart to study this week's vocabulary words. Write a sentence using each word in your writer's notebook.

Word	Context Sentence	Illustration
curious ______________	My dog is curious about everything around him.	**What things are you curious about?**
idea ______________	Dan had a great idea about how to stay cool on a hot day.	

© Macmillan/McGraw-Hill

Name ____________________________________

Book Talk

Read each question and prompt. Discuss the answers with your group. Use your Leveled Reader to find details to support your answers. Then write your answers on another sheet of paper.

1. Tell why Sylvia became curious about the sea.

2. What did Sylvia want to learn about?

3. Explain how Sylvia was able to dive.

4. Describe what a sea lab is.

5. What did Sylvia put on the sea floor?

© Macmillan/McGraw-Hill

Stormy Weather

Pages 86–87

Prior to reading the selection with children, they should have listened to the selection on **StudentWorks Plus**, the interactive eBook. In addition, selection vocabulary should have been pretaught using the **Visual Vocabulary Resources**.

Access Core Content

Teacher Note Pose the questions after you read the paragraph or page indicated.

Page 86

Title and Text

- *Read the title of this selection with me:* Stormy Weather. *Let's read the question under the title:* How many sorts of storms do you know about?
- *Think about storms you have seen. Have you seen any big rainstorms? Was the rain pouring down. Have you seen any snowstorms? Was there a lot of deep snow after the storm?* (Questions are open.) We're going to read about different kinds of storms.

Page 87

Text, Choral Reading

- *Let's read this page together:* On some days, the sky is gray. That could mean a storm is on the way. *When a storm is on the way, we mean that a storm is coming.*
- *Sometimes the sky is blue. Is it usually sunny or rainy when the sky is blue?* (sunny)

Photo

- *Look at the picture. I see a cloud in the sky. Point to it. When a storm is coming, the sky is full of clouds, or cloudy. Say* cloudy *with me:* cloudy.
- *What is the boy in the picture doing?* (flying a kite) *We need wind to fly a kite. Wind is something else that happens in storms.*

Pages 86–87

Comprehension

Genre
Nonfiction
A nonfiction article gives information about a topic.

Ask Questions
Compare and Contrast
Look for ways that storms are alike and ways they are different.

Stormy Weather

How many sorts of storms do you know about?

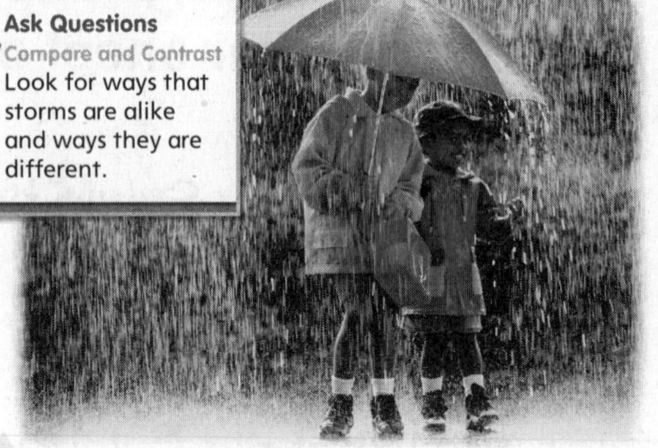

There are all sorts of storms. Which storms do you see where you live?

86

Pages 88–89

A gray sky can mean a thunderstorm. You will see **great** flashes of lightning. Next comes a loud **sound**. That is a thunderstorm. It's time to go inside!

Lightning can make a tree catch fire.

88

TIME FOR KIDS
Thunderstorms may have strong winds. The winds can blow branches off trees. Balls of ice may fall from the sky. This is hail. It can hail when it is warm or cold.
89

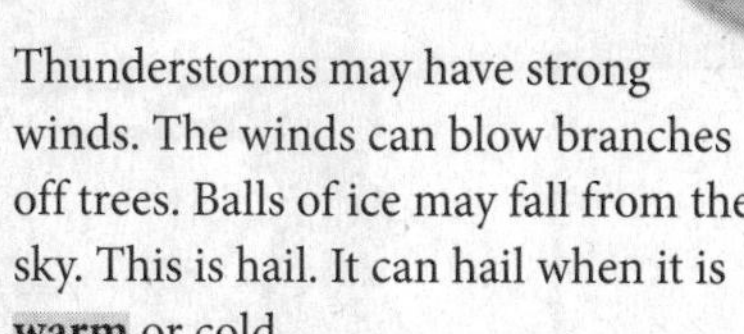

Page 88

Text

- *I'll read this page to you. When I tell about lightning, use your finger to draw an imaginary zigzag line of lightning in the air.* (demonstrate) *When I read about thunder say, "Boom!" loudly.*
- *Remember to do your part as I read:* A gray sky can mean rainstorms. You may see great flashes of lightning. (Lead students in making a zigzag line.) Next comes a loud sound. That is thunder. (Lead children in saying, "Boom!") Time to go inside!

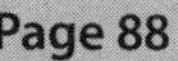

Lightning and thunder usually go together, but they are different. Lightning is something we see. Say it with me: lightning. *Thunder is something we hear.* Say it with me: thunder. *Which do we see?* (lightning) *Which do we hear?* (thunder)

- *The author says:* Time to go inside! *You could get hit by lightning if you stay outside. What are you supposed to do when there is thunder and lightning?* (go inside)

Photo

- *Look at the picture. I see lightning hitting a tree. Point to it.*
- *Listen as I read the caption, and echo it after me:* Lightning can make a tree catch fire.

Page 89

Whole Page

- *Sentence 1 talks about thunderstorms.* Thunderstorm *is another word for* rainstorm.
- *This paragraph also talks about hail. Hail is a ball of ice. Some hail is small, like this.* (Use your fingers to show tiny hail.) *Some hail is bigger than a tennis ball. Point to the tennis ball in the little picture.*
- *Let's think about all the things that can happen during a thunderstorm, or rainstorm. Would the sky be blue or gray?* (gray) *Would there be clouds and wind?* (yes) *There might also be thunder, lightning, and hail.*

With your partner, draw a thunderstorm. Take turns adding parts to the drawing.

Stormy Weather

Page 90

Whole Page, Choral Reading

- *Let's read this page together:* Some storms come when it is very cold. It can snow so much that you can't see. Strong winds can blow snow into big piles. This is a blizzard.
- *A pile of snow looks like a small hill of snow. Point to the pile of snow in the picture. Strong winds blew the snow into big piles. What made the piles of snow?* (strong winds)
- *Look at the picture. What color is the sky?* (blue) *Is it still snowing?* (no) *Is the storm over?* (yes)
- *People use snow plows to move snow from driveways and roads. I see a person with a snow plow. Point to the snow plow. People also use shovels to move snow.*

Thunderstorms and blizzards are alike in some ways. The sky gets gray and cloudy. It is windy. But different things fall from the sky. Which falls from the sky in a thunderstorm—rain or snow? (rain) *Which falls from the sky in a blizzard—rain or snow?* (snow)

Page 91

Whole Page

- *Look at the smaller picture. The buildings have fallen down. They are smashed and broken. Point to them.*
- *Let's read the caption together to find out what happened:* A tornado can destroy buildings. *This page tells about the kind of storm called a tornado.*
- *Let's get an idea of how the winds of a tornado spin. Hold your arm like this.* (Bend your arm at the elbow so that your hand and lower arm stick straight up.)
- *Now move your hand and lower arm around very fast in circles.* (demonstrate)*This is something like the way the wind of a tornado spins. Look at the spinning tornado in the picture.*

Request Assistance

Remind children of expressions they can use to request assistance from the teacher or their partners, such as *Can you repeat it, please? Can you show me?*

Pages 90–91

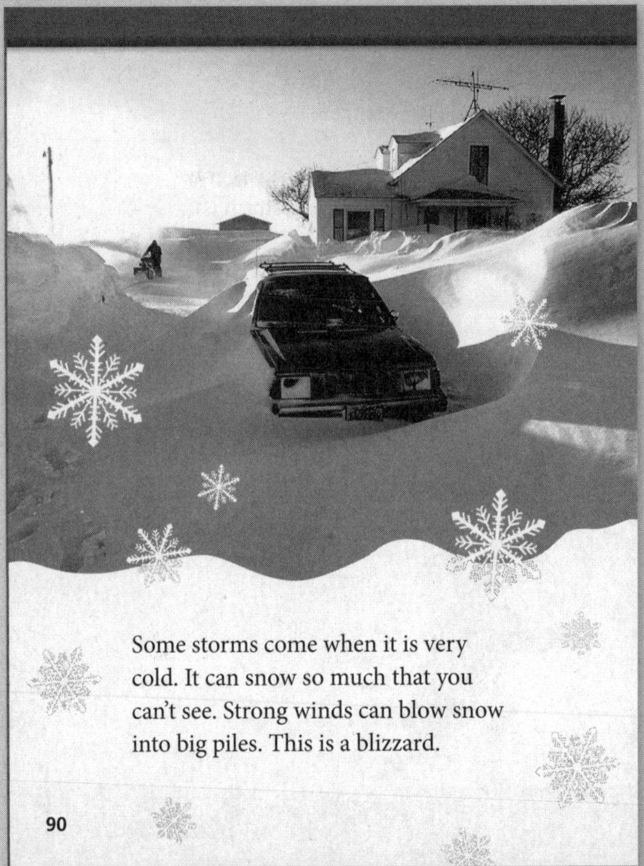

Some storms come when it is very cold. It can snow so much that you can't see. Strong winds can blow snow into big piles. This is a blizzard.

90

Pages 92–93

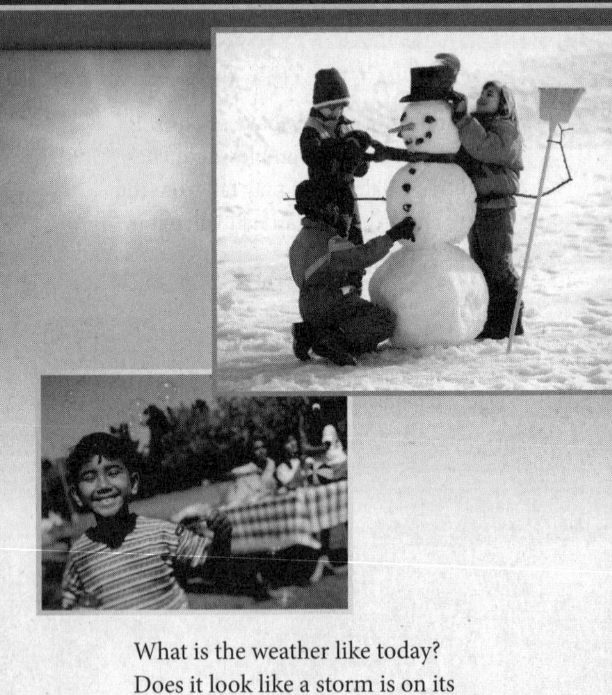

What is the weather like today? Does it look like a storm is on its way? Or is it a great day for playing outside?

92

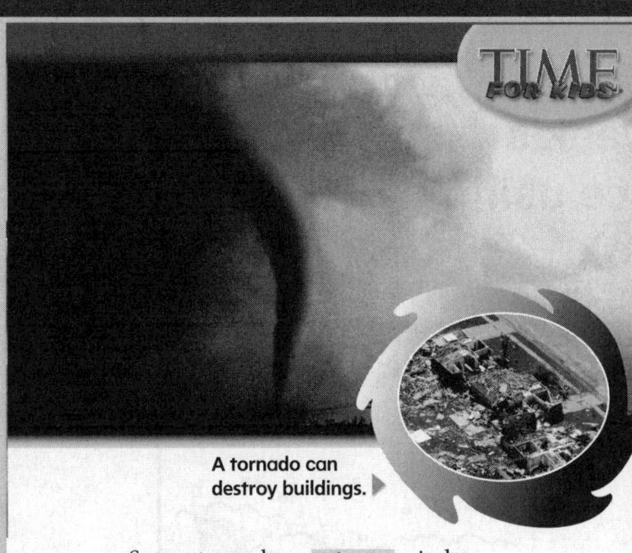

A tornado can destroy buildings.

Some storms have **extreme** winds. Tornadoes are made of fast winds that spin and spin. The winds can pick up trucks and homes.

Scientists have ways to **predict** when tornadoes will come. Then people can get out of **their** way.

91

 **Comprehension Check**

Tell What You Learned
What did you learn about storms?

Think and Compare

1. What is hail? Details
2. What can happen during a thunderstorm? Retell
3. How are a thunderstorm and a blizzard the same? How are they different? Compare and Contrast
4. How are the storms in "Stormy Weather" and "Warm and Cold Days" alike? Read Across Texts

93

- *To* predict *means to "make a guess about what will happen." Let's read the last paragraph together:* Scientists have ways to predict when tornadoes will come. Then people can get out of their way.
- *One safe place to go in a tornado is a basement. But it is important to stay away from any windows.*

Page 92

Whole Page

- *Look at the picture of the children playing in the snow. They are making a snowman. Say it with me:* snowman. *Is it a cold day or a hot day?* (cold day)
- *We can tell that it is cold because the children are wearing clothes for cold weather. Also, the snowman is not melting, or turning to water.*
- *Look at the boy blowing bubbbles. Point to him. The boy's family is having a picnic. Point to them. Look at the sky. Is it gray or blue?* (blue) *Is a storm coming?* (no)
- *Look at the boy's clothes. Is the day warm or cold?* (warm) *It is a warm, sunny day.*

Predict the weather for today with your partner. Will the day be warm or cold? Will it be sunny? Will there be a storm? Look at the sky for clues. What color is it? Are there clouds? Look at the trees. Are they blowing in the wind? (Questions are open.)

Seek Clarification

Some children may be confused by unfamiliar words. Encourage children to always seek clarification when they encounter a word or phrase that does not make sense to them. For example, *I don't understand this word.*

Name ____________________

Use the word chart to study this week's vocabulary words. Write a sentence using each word in your writer's notebook.

Word	Context Sentence	Illustration
extreme	It snowed a lot. The snow was extreme.	
predict	Will the sun shine tomorrow? I predict it will.	What kinds of things can you predict?

© Macmillan/McGraw-Hill

Name ____________________________________

Book Talk

Read each question and prompt. Discuss the answers with your group. Use your Leveled Reader to find details to support your answers. Then write your answers on another sheet of paper.

1. Retell what the weather was like on each day of the week.

2. Explain why it is safe to go swimming on one day but not on another.

3. Show classmates what days people needed to use umbrellas.

4. Tell what you learned about the weather.

© Macmillan/McGraw-Hill

Happy Fall!

Pages 102–103

Prior to reading the selection with children, they should have listened to the selection on **StudentWorks Plus**, the interactive eBook. In addition, selection vocabulary should have been pretaught using the **Visual Vocabulary Resources**.

Access Core Content

Teacher Note Pose the questions after you read the paragraph or page indicated.

Page 102

Illustration

- *Look at the picture with me. I see leaves falling down. Say leaves with me:* leaves. (Use hand to demonstrate leaves floating to the ground.) *I see leaves on the ground.* (Point to the ground.)
- *In the fall, leaves fall to the ground. We move the leaves into big piles. We use a tool called a rake.* (Draw a rake on the board.) *We can jump and play in the fall leaves.* (Demonstrate jumping.)
- *Let's pretend to rake the leaves. Pretend to hold a rake in your hands. Let's rake the fall leaves into a big pile.* (demonstrate) *Now let's pretend to put down the rake and jump into the pile of leaves.*

Page 103

Title and Illustration

- *The title of this story is* Happy Fall! *Let's read the title together:* Happy Fall!
- *This story is about Pinwheel, the donkey, and his friend, Squirrel. Point to Pinwheel the donkey. Point to Squirrel.*
- *Look at the picture. What do you see in the air?* (leaves) *What are they doing?* (falling) *They are falling from the trees. That's why there are so many leaves on the ground. Look at all the different colors!*

Pages 102–103

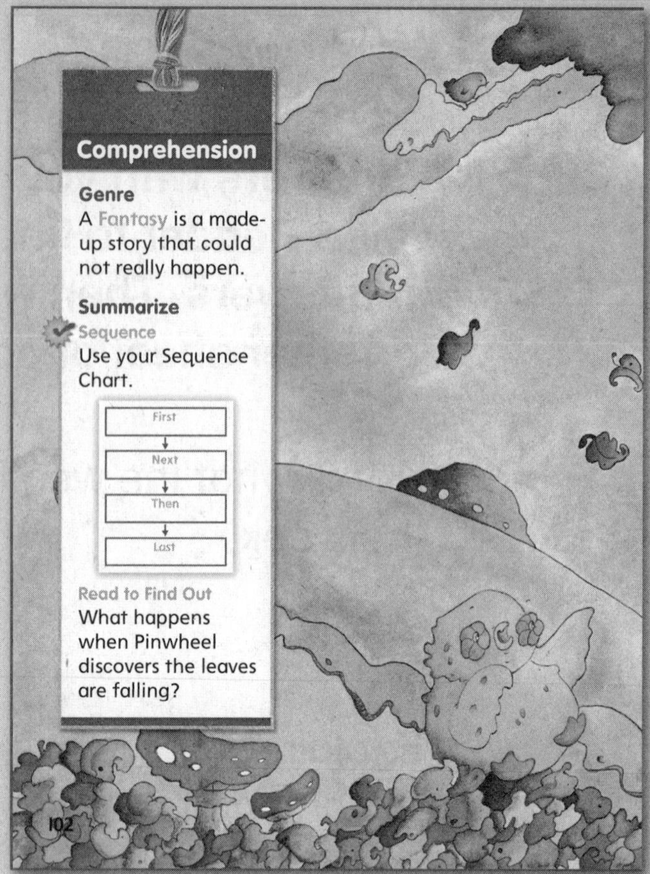

Comprehension
Genre
A Fantasy is a made-up story that could not really happen.
Summarize
Sequence
Use your Sequence Chart.
First
Next
Then
Last
Read to Find Out
What happens when Pinwheel discovers the leaves are falling?
102

Pages 104–105

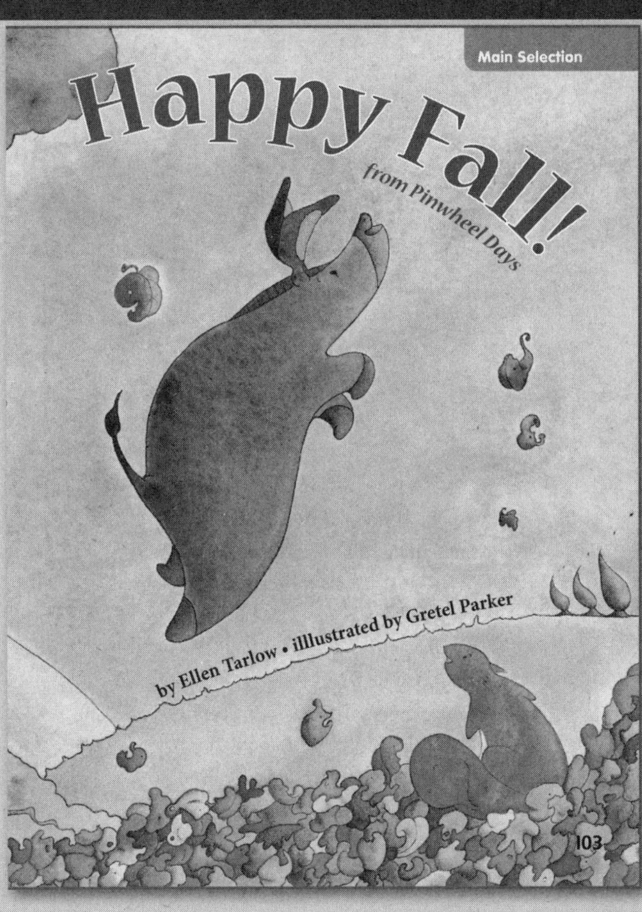

Main Selection
Happy Fall!
from Pinwheel Days
by Ellen Tarlow • illustrated by Gretel Parker
103

Pinwheel was waiting for Squirrel.
"I like Squirrel and Squirrel likes me,"
he sang.
"Pinwheel! Be quiet!" came a voice.
"I am trying to sleep."
It was Owl.
"I am sorry, Owl," said Pinwheel.
Pinwheel felt an itch.
He rubbed **against** the tree.
"Pinwheel!" shouted Owl.
"Stop bumping the tree!
My bed is shaking."
"I am sorry, Owl," said Pinwheel.

105

Page 104

Illustration

- *Let's look at the picture together. Pinwheel is waiting for someone. He is looking up at a tree. Who do you think Pinwheel is waiting for?* (Question is open.)
- *Point to the other animal in the picture. It's a bird called an owl.*

Page 105

Text

- *Pinwheel is singing while he waits. Let's read his song together:* "I like Squirrel and Squirrel likes me." *Does Owl want Pinwheel to sing or to be quiet?* (to be quiet) *Owl wants to sleep! Owls sleep during the day.*

Role-play this part of the story with your partner. One of you can be Pinwheel singing his song. The other can be the owl who wants to sleep. Then switch roles.

- *Then Pinwheel feels an itch in his back. When something itches, we scratch it.* (Demonstrate scratching your arm.) *Pinwheel rubs his back against the tree, which means that he rubs his back on the tree trunk.*
- *Owl's bed is shaking.* (Demonstrate making a desk or table shake.) *Owl tells Pinwheel to stop bumping the tree. Where is owl's bed?* (in the tree)
- *Let's read Pinwheel's words together:* "I'm sorry, Owl," said Pinwheel.

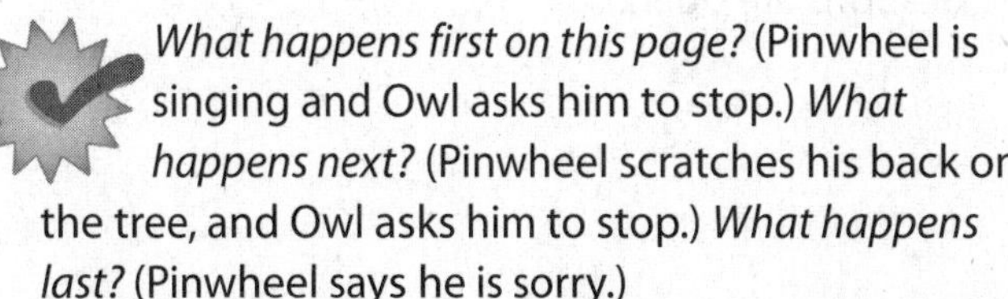

What happens first on this page? (Pinwheel is singing and Owl asks him to stop.) *What happens next?* (Pinwheel scratches his back on the tree, and Owl asks him to stop.) *What happens last?* (Pinwheel says he is sorry.)

- **Directionality**
  Ask children to place their finger where you start reading (top left). Ask where you finish reading on this page (bottom right).

Page 106

Illustration

- *Look at the picture. Pinwheel is standing very still. What do you see on Pinwheel's head?* (a leaf)

Text

- *Pinwheel feels something touching his head. "What is that?" he wonders.* (Make an expression as if you are wondering about something.) *Do we know what's on his head?* (yes)
- *Pinwheel shakes his head. What happens to the leaf when he does that?* (The leaf falls.)
- *Then the wind blows. What happens when the wind blows?* (The leaves fall.)
- *Pinwheel sees all the leaves falling down and thinks he broke the tree! Did he?* (no) *What time of year is it in the story?* (fall) *Do leaves fall at this time of year?* (yes)

Page 107

Whole Page

- *Look at the picture. I see Pinwheel's friend, Squirrel, in the tree. Point to Squirrel.*
- *Squirrel is talking to Pinwheel. Pinwheel seems very worried. Why is he so upset?* (He thinks he broke the tree. He thinks Owl will be angry with him.)

Talk with your partner. Do you think that Owl will be angry about the tree? Why or why not? (Questions are open.)

Pages 106–107

Pinwheel stood as still as he could.
Something soft touched his head.
"What is that?" he **wondered**.
He shook his head.
A red leaf fell.
The wind blew.
More leaves fell.
"1, 2, 3, 4, 5," Pinwheel counted.
"Oh, no!" he said. "I broke the tree."

106

Pages 108–109

"Are you **sure** it's broken?"
asked Squirrel.
The wind blew.
More leaves fell.
"6, 7, 8, 9, 10," Pinwheel counted.
"See?" he said. "Broken."
"Very broken," said Squirrel.
They looked up.
More leaves fell.
"Go back!" they shouted.

108

"Hello, Pinwheel," said Squirrel.
"Squirrel, I broke the tree!
Owl is going to be so mad at me!"
cried Pinwheel.

107

But the leaves kept on falling.

Red leaves.

Orange leaves.

Yellow leaves.

There were too many to count.

109

Page 108

Illustration

- *Look at the picture with me. What are Pinwheel and Squirrel watching?* (More leaves are falling.) *Pinwheel looks worried.*

Text

- *Look at the word* sure in Sentence 1. *Pinwheel is sure that the tree is broken. The wind blows and more leaves fall. Pinwheel is certain that he broke the tree.*
- *Let's count five falling leaves:* 1, 2, 3, 4, 5. *Now let's blow like the wind. Let's count more falling leaves:* 6, 7, 8, 9, 10.

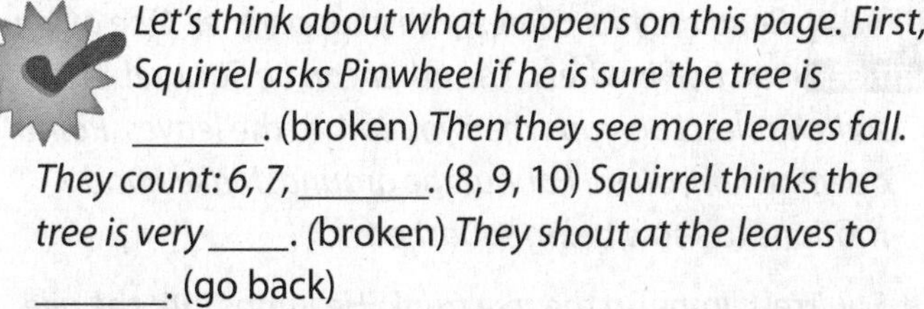

Let's think about what happens on this page. First, Squirrel asks Pinwheel if he is sure the tree is _______. (broken) *Then they see more leaves fall. They count: 6, 7,* _______. (8, 9, 10) *Squirrel thinks the tree is very* _____. (broken) *They shout at the leaves to* _____. (go back)

Page 109

Illustration and Text

- *Look at the falling leaves. Let's point to the color words and read them together:* red, orange, yellow.
- *Let's read this page together:* But the leaves kept on falling. Red leaves. Orange leaves. Yellow leaves. There were too many to count.

Non-verbal Cues

Remind children that they can use non-verbal cues to share information when they are not able to do so verbally. Encourage children to use pantomime and sounds.

Pages 110–111

Illustration

- *Look at all the leaves on the ground! What colors do you see?* (red, yellow, orange)
- *I see Squirrel. Point to him. What is he doing?* (playing in the leaves) *Look at his face. Do you think that Squirrel is happy or sad?* (happy)

Text

- *Pinwheel and Squirrel talk to the leaves. They tell the leaves they won't like it on the ground because they will get stepped on and squashed.* (Use your hands to demonstrate squashing something between them.)

PARTNERS *Read the first 6 lines with your partner. One of you can be Pinwheel. The other can be Squirrel. Then switch roles. Look up when you talk to the leaves. Point down when you talk about the ground. Make hand motions to show being squashed.*

- *Squirrel climbs up the tree trunk. He jumps into the pile of leaves. He wants to show the leaves how they'll get stepped on and squashed if they fall on the ground. He laughs and tells Pinwheel to jump in.*
- *Let's pretend to climb up the tree trunk.* (demonstrate) *Then we'll pretend to jump into a pile of leaves.* (Demonstrate jumping in place.) *Then let's laugh and say, "Jump in!"*

Pages 110–111

"You won't like it down here,"
Pinwheel told the leaves.
"You will only get stepped on,"
said Squirrel.
"And squashed," added Pinwheel.
"Very squashed," said Squirrel.
"Let's show them," said Pinwheel.
"Good thinking," said Squirrel.
He climbed up the tree trunk.
"Look out **below**!" he shouted.
He jumped into a pile of leaves.
"See?" Pinwheel told the leaves.
"Squashed!"

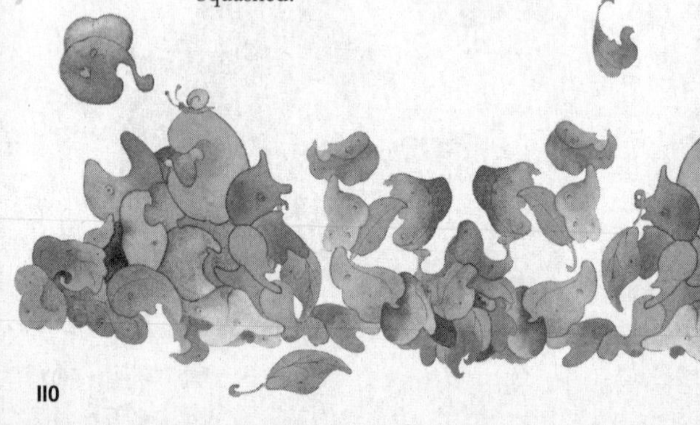

110

Pages 112–113

Squirrel popped out of the leaves.
He jumped back in.

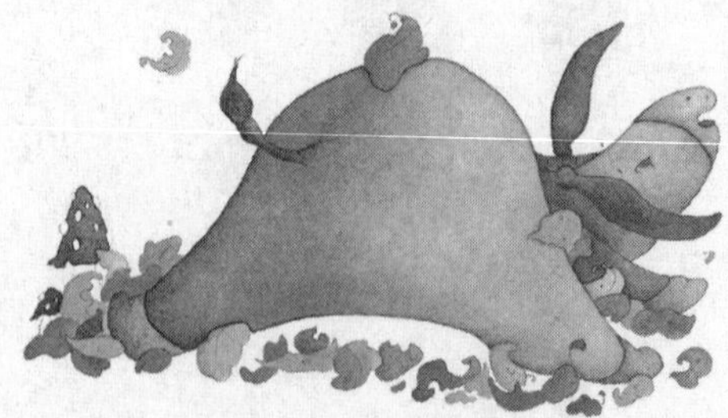

Then Pinwheel jumped in.
"Catch me!" called Squirrel.

112

Then he heard laughing.
"Pinwheel," laughed Squirrel.
"Jump in!"

111

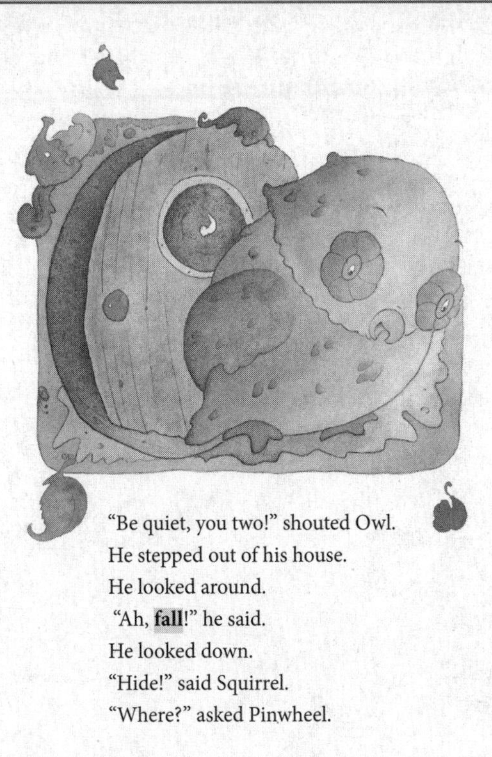

"Be quiet, you two!" shouted Owl.
He stepped out of his house.
He looked around.
"Ah, **fall**!" he said.
He looked down.
"Hide!" said Squirrel.
"Where?" asked Pinwheel.

113

Page 112

Illustrations and Text

- *Let's look at the pictures together. What is squirrel doing?* (playing in the leaves)
- *Let's read the sentences under the pictures together*: Squirrel popped out of the leaves. He jumped back in. Then Pinwheel jumped in. "Catch me!" called Squirrel.
- *Is Squirrel still playing alone, or his he playing a game?* (He is playing a game.) *Who is playing with him?* (Pinwheel) *It looks like they're having a lot of fun!*

Page 113

Illustration

- *Look at the picture. Owl has come out of his house. Look at Owl's face. Does he look happy?* (no) *Remember, Owl is trying to sleep. What do you think Owl might say to Squirrel and Pinwheel?* (Question is open.)

Text

- Let's read what Owl says together: "Be quiet, you two!" shouted Owl. *Who is Owl shouting at?* (Pinwheel and Squirrel)
- *Owl looks around and says,* "Ah, fall!" *How does Owl know that it is the time of year called fall?* (He sees the falling leaves.)
- *Squirrel and Pinwheel want to hide from Owl. Why are they afraid?* (because they think Pinwheel broke Owl's tree) *Where do you think Owl and Pinwheel might hide?* (Question is open.)

Patterns in Language

Some grammatical structures, such as past tense "ed," pose difficulties to ELLs. Point out that there are several examples of words ending in *-ed* in this selection, such as *popped, called, stepped, looked, asked.* Help children find a pattern.

Happy Fall!

Page 114

Illustration

- *Look at the picture. What is Owl doing?* (Owl is jumping in the leaves.)

Text, Choral Reading

- *Owl calls:* "Look out below!" *Let's read the rest of the page together.*
- *Squirrel wants to run away, but it is too* _______. (late)
- *Owl says something to Squirrel and Pinwheel that surprises them. What does he say?* ("Happy fall!") *Does Owl seem angry, or does he look like he's having fun?* (He looks like he's having fun.)
- *Squirrel and Pinwheel seem confused, or puzzled. What do they say?* ("Fall?") *Let's say,* Fall? *together and look really puzzled.* (Demonstrate a puzzled expression)

Pages 114–115

"Look out below!" called Owl.
He jumped into the leaves.
"Run!" said Squirrel.
But it was too late.
"Hello," said Owl. "Happy fall!"
"Fall?" asked Pinwheel.
"Fall?" asked Squirrel.

114

"It's my favorite **season**," said Owl.
Pinwheel looked at the colorful leaves.
"Happy fall!" he shouted as loudly as he could.
Then he jumped in to find Squirrel.

115

Page 115

Whole Page

- *Let's read together what Owl says to Pinwheel and Squirrel:* "It's my favorite season," said Owl.
- So *Owl isn't angry about the leaves falling. He doesn't think Pinwheel broke his house. He knows that the leaves are falling because it's fall. Leaves fall in the season we call fall! Let's name the seasons together:* winter, spring, summer, fall.

PARTNERS *What is your favorite season? Tell your partner and explain why you like that time of year.*

- *Pinwheel shouts,* "Happy fall!" *Let's shout it together! Then Pinwheel jumps in to find Squirrel. Look at the picture. Point to Squirrel's tail. Then point to his head!*

Let's tell what happens after the leaf falls on Pinwheel's head. Pinwheel sees other leaves. He thinks the tree is _______. (broken) *He and Squirrel tell the leaves to _______.* (go back up) *Then they play in the _______.* (leaves) *Their sounds wake up _______.* (Owl) *At first, he is _______.*(angry) *Then he joins them.*

Seasons

Access Core Content

Teacher Note Pose the questions after you read the paragraph or page indicated.

Page 118

Title and Text

- *Let's read the title together:* Seasons. *We read a story about an owl who loves the fall. Fall is Owl's favorite season. Now we are going to read about all four seasons.*
- *Listen as I read this page aloud. Then let's read the names of the seasons together. I'll point to each word as we say it:* spring, summer, fall, winter.

Page 119

Photo

- *Look at the big picture. The woman and child are planting flowers. Everything is green and growing. What season is this?* (spring)
- *Listen as I read the caption for the small picture:* <u>In spring, leaves on trees start to come out.</u>

Text

- *In spring, the sun and rain help plants to grow. The leaves on trees come out. Animal babies are born.*
- *Now I'm going to list things that people like to do in the spring. Raise your hand when you hear something that you like to do:* fly a kite, ride a bike, play soccer, play baseball, plant flowers, take a walk, go to the playground. (Responses will vary.)
- *Now raise your hand if spring is your favorite season.*

Pages 118–119

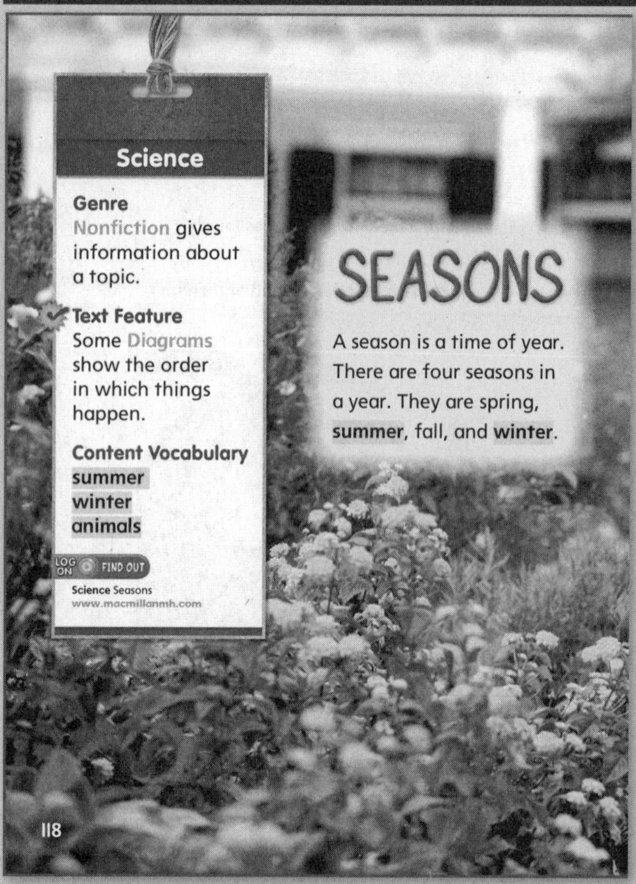

Pages 120–121

Summer comes after spring. Summer has the most daylight. That means more time to play outside! The weather gets hot in a lot of places. Plants grow big in summer. Animals eat and grow big, too.
In summer the leaves on trees get bigger.
120

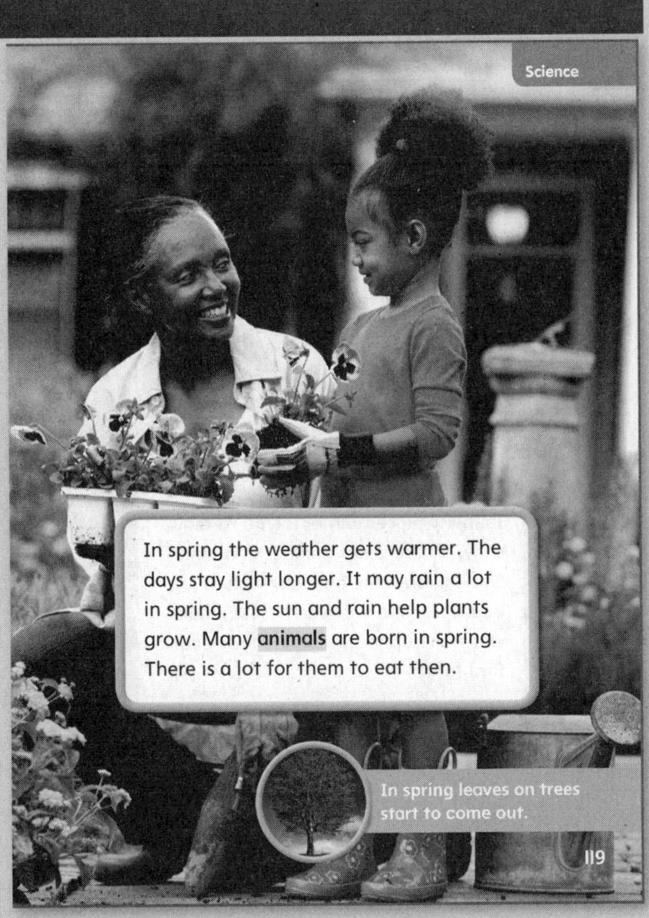

Science

In spring the weather gets warmer. The days stay light longer. It may rain a lot in spring. The sun and rain help plants grow. Many **animals** are born in spring. There is a lot for them to eat then.

In spring leaves on trees start to come out.

119

Fall follows summer. There is less daylight in fall. The weather starts to get colder. Plants stop growing. Some animals save food for when it will get much colder. Other animals go where they will find more food.

In fall leaves may turn red, yellow, and orange.

121

Page 120

Photo

- *Look at the big picture. The children are playing in water. Are they wearing bathing suits or snowsuits?* (bathing suits) *It must be hot outside. What season is this?* (summer)
- *Look at the small picture. Are the leaves bigger or smaller than they were in the spring?* (bigger)

Text

- *Summer is the season right after spring. The sun stays out longer in summer. Is there more or less time to play outside?* (more time) *The weather is hot in summer. Plants and animals grow big in summer.*
- *Now I'm going to list some things that people like to do in the summer. Raise your hand when you hear something that you like to do:* swim, go fishing, go camping, go to the park, go to a fair, go to a parade, go to the seashore.
- *Raise your hand if summer is your favorite season.*

Page 121

Photo

- *Look at the picture with me. Children are getting off a school bus. Point to them. The children are wearing long-sleeved shirts and pants. Do you think it is very hot or a little cool?* (a little cool)
- Look at the trees in the picture. *Are the leaves all green, or are they many colors?* (many colors) *What season is it?* (fall)

Text

- *Fall is the season after summer. Fall is the time to go back to school. The weather starts to get cooler, so we wear clothes to keep us warm. Plants stop growing. Animals look for food to save. Are they saving it for summer or for winter?* (winter)
- *Now I'm going to list some things that people like to do in the fall. Raise your hand when you hear something that you like to do:* play soccer, pick apples, pick pumpkins, hike in the woods, rake leaves, jump in leaves.
- *Raise your hand if fall is your favorite season.*

Seasons

Page 122

Photo

- *Look at the picture. What is the girl doing?* (playing in the snow) *She is wearing a coat because it is cold outside. What season is this?* (winter)

Text

- *Winter is the season after fall. In many places, the weather is cold in winter. Some animals sleep during the winter. People stay inside much of the time in winter.*
- *Now I'm going to list some things that people like to do in the winter. Raise your hand when you hear something that you like to do:* ice skate, ski, play in the snow, read books, play board games.
- *Raise your hand if winter is your favorite season.*
- *The seasons always happen in the same order. What season is it right now? Starting with* (current season), *let's name all the seasons in order.*

Pages 122–123

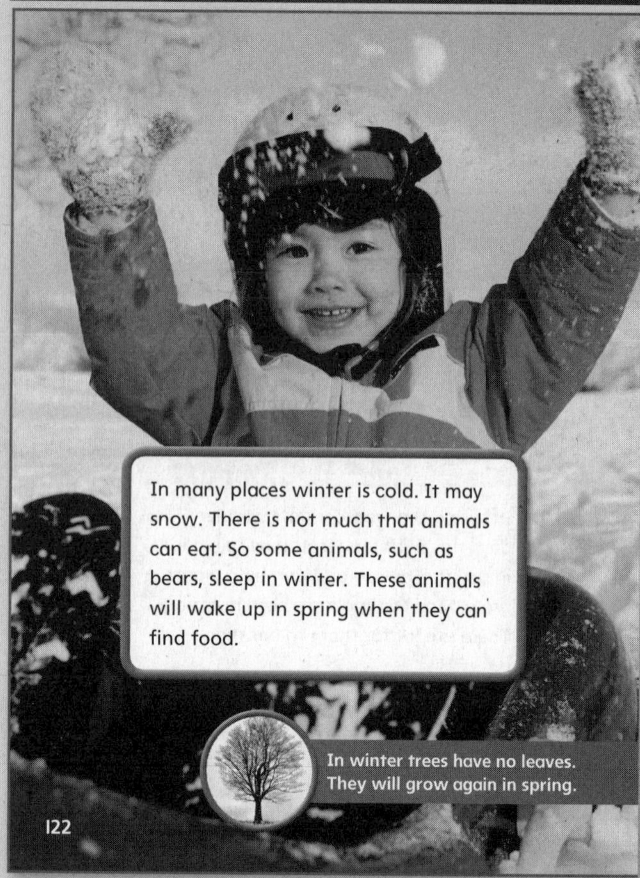

In many places winter is cold. It may snow. There is not much that animals can eat. So some animals, such as bears, sleep in winter. These animals will wake up in spring when they can find food.
In winter trees have no leaves. They will grow again in spring.
122

Look at these trees. How do they change over a year? In which season do trees have the most leaves? The fewest?

Connect and Compare

- How do the pictures show the way seasons change over a year?
- What does the diagram tell you about seasons?

123

Page 123

Diagram

- *This diagram shows what happens to trees in each of the four seasons.*
- *Put your finger on the fall tree. What color are the leaves?* (yellow and orange)
- *Follow the arrow to the next season. What season follows fall?* (winter) *Are there leaves on the trees?* (no)
- *Look at the next picture. Do you see leaves on the tree now?* (yes) *New leaves start to come out on the trees in spring.*
- *Which season follows spring?* (summer) *Are the leaves bigger in the summer than in the spring?* (yes)

Draw a picture of your favorite season. Share it with your partner.

Name ____________________

Use the word chart to study this week's vocabulary words. Write a sentence using each word in your writer's notebook.

Word	Context Sentence	Illustration
wondered ____________	Pam wondered if it would snow today.	Snow?
season ____________	Sara likes all four seasons.	**Which is your favorite season?**

© Macmillan/McGraw-Hill

Name ____________________

Read each question and prompt. Discuss the answers with your group. Use your Leveled Reader to find details to support your answers. Then write your answers on another sheet of paper.

1. Describe what a strawberry looks like.

2. What is the best season for picking strawberries?

3. Explain how strawberries grow.

4. Why should you put nets or little fences around strawberry plants?

5. Tell your group how you like to eat strawberries.

© Macmillan/McGraw-Hill

Interactive Question - Response Guide

A Tiger Cub Grows Up

Pages 130–131

Prior to reading the selection with children, they should have listened to the selection on **StudentWorks Plus**, the interactive eBook. In addition, selection vocabulary should have been pretaught using the **Visual Vocabulary Resources**.

Access Core Content

Teacher Note Pose the questions after you read the paragraph or page indicated.

Pages 130–131

Title and Photo

- *Let's read the title together:* A Tiger Cub Grows Up. *Tiger babies are called cubs. Tell me another animal that has cubs.* (bear, lion)
- *Look at the tiger cub. It's little now, but it will grow up. It will get big like its mother and father.*

Page 132

Heading and Photo

- *Let's read the section heading together:* In the Nursery. *A nursery is a place for babies. This nursery is for tiger cubs.*
- *The tiger cub is drinking from a bottle, just like a baby. What is it drinking?* (milk)

Text

- *This tiger cub's name is Tara. Say it with me:* Tara.
- *Tara lives in a special park. Other wild animals live there, too. A tiger is a wild animal. Is a pet dog a wild animal?* (no) *Is a pet cat a wild animal?* (no) *Pet dogs and cats live with people. They aren't wild animals.*
- *Tara lives with people, but most tigers and other wild animals usually don't live with people.*

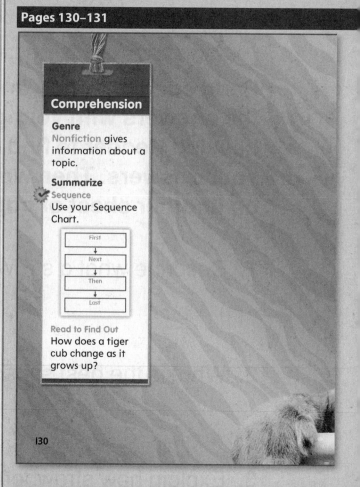

Pages 130–131

Comprehension

Genre
Nonfiction gives information about a topic.

Summarize
Sequence
Use your Sequence Chart.

First → Next → Then → Last

Read to Find Out
How does a tiger cub change as it grows up?

130

Pages 132–133

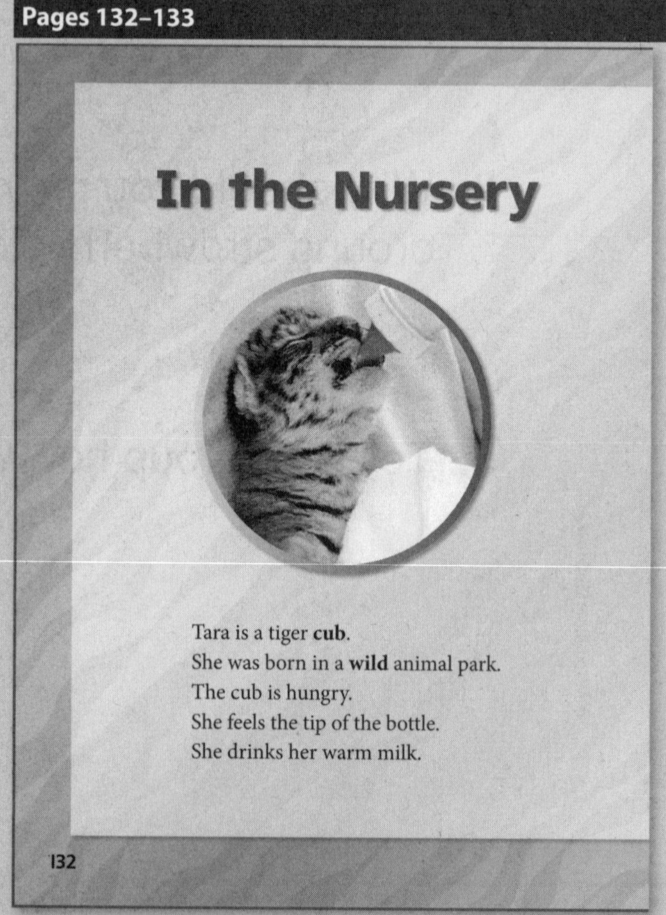

In the Nursery

Tara is a tiger **cub**.
She was born in a **wild** animal park.
The cub is hungry.
She feels the tip of the bottle.
She drinks her warm milk.

132

PARTNERS *A tiger is a wild animal. What other wild animals do you know? Tell your partner.* (Responses will vary.)

- *Tara drinks milk from a bottle. The tip of the bottle is in her mouth.* (Point to the bottle tip in the picture.) *Tara drinks warm milk. Do you like warm milk or cold milk?* (Responses will vary.)
- *Tara is hungry. Sy it with me:* hungry. *She will drink until she is full.*
- *Let's read the last three lines on the page together:* The cub is hungry. She feels the tip of the bottle. She drinks her warm milk.

Page 133

Photo

- *Look at Tara. She's a very little baby. Point to Tara's eyes. Are they open or closed?* (closed) *When tiger cubs are born, their eyes are closed. They stay closed for a number of days.*
-

Directionality

Ask children to place their finger where you start reading (top left). Ask where you finish reading on this page (bottom right).

A Tiger Cub Grows Up

Page 134

Whole Page

- *Look at Tara, and point to her eyes. Are they open or closed?* (open)
- *Let's read this page together:* When Tara is 9 days old, her eyes open. *How old is Tara when her eyes open?* (nine days old)

Page 135

Whole Page

- *Look at Tara. What is she doing?* (taking a bath)
- *Grown-up tigers like to swim. They like the water. But little Tara does not like her bath. Do you like to take a bath?* (Responses will vary.)

Let's compare grown-up tigers to little tigers like Tara. Grown-up tigers like the water. Does little Tara like the water? (no) *So they are different in one way. Grown-up tigers like the water, but tiger cubs do not.*

Pages 134–135

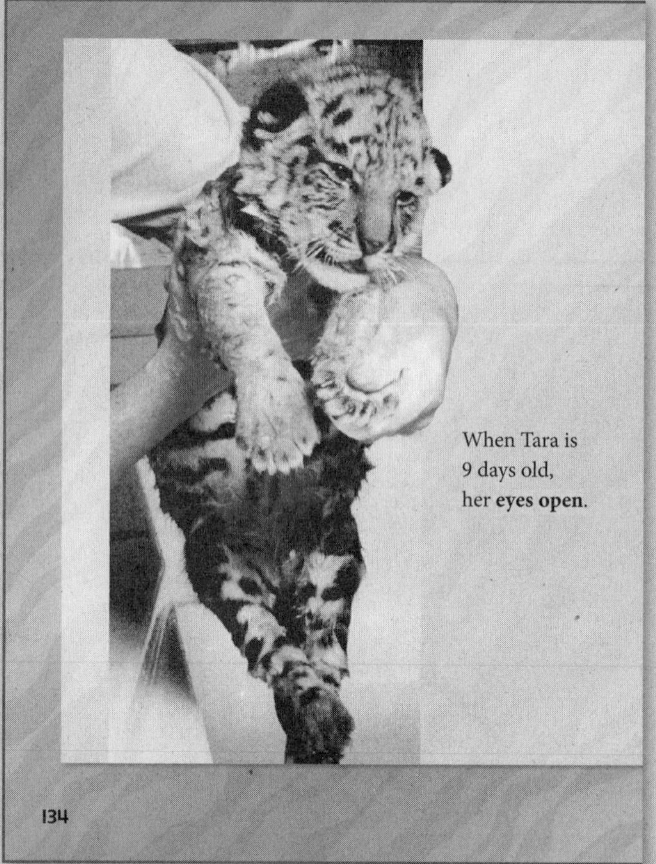

When Tara is
9 days old,
her **eyes open**.

134

Pages 136–137

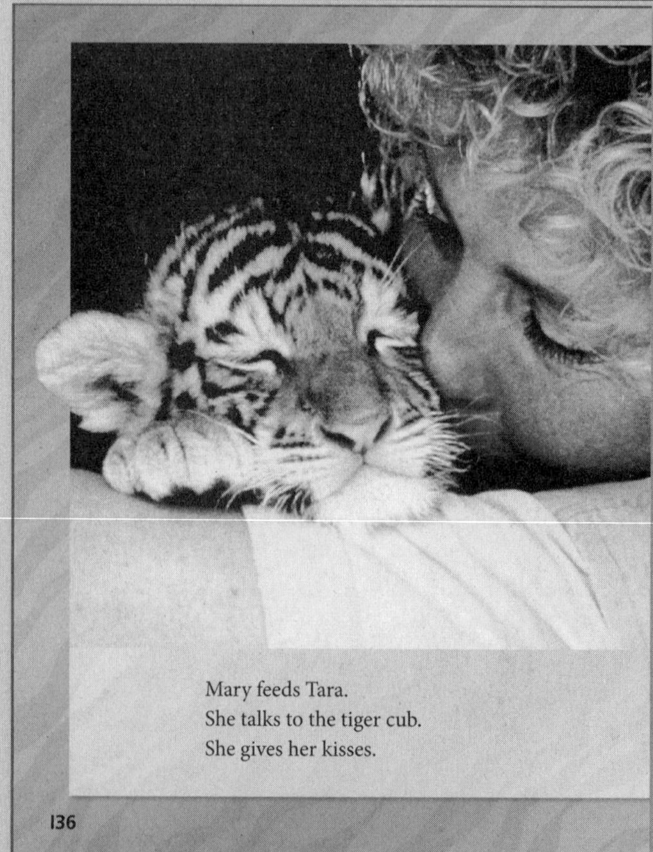

Mary feeds Tara.
She talks to the tiger cub.
She gives her kisses.

136

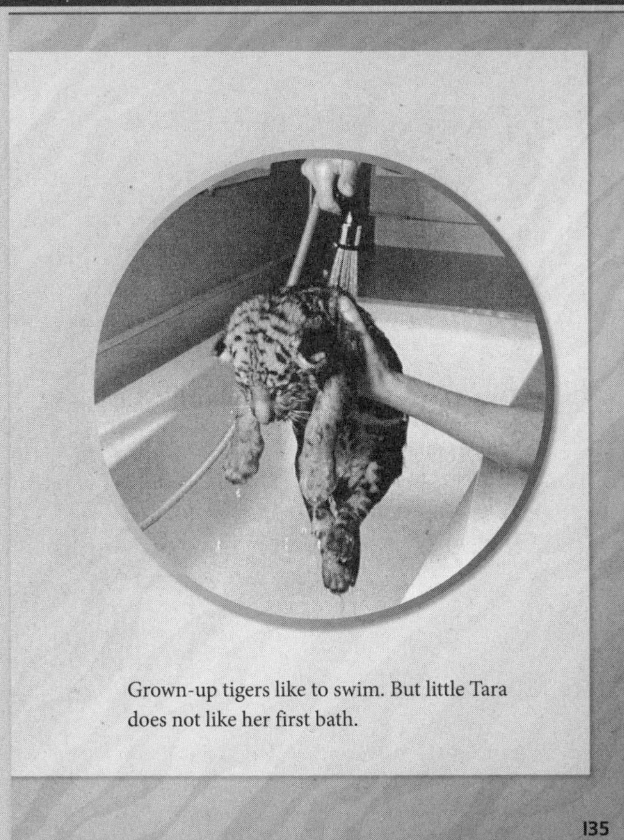

Grown-up tigers like to swim. But little Tara does not like her first bath.

135

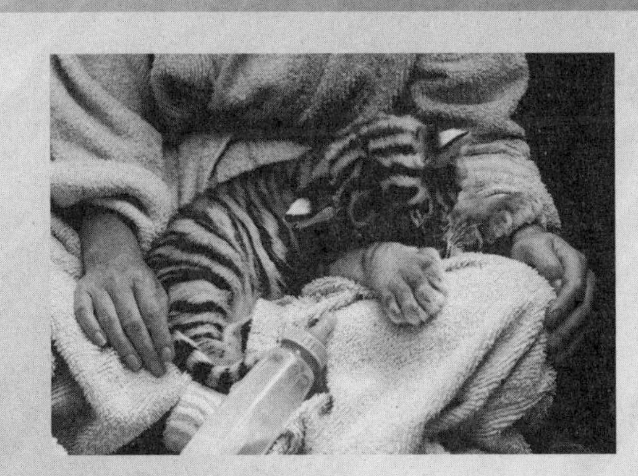

At night, Mary takes the cub home with her.
Tara drinks her milk.
She falls asleep.

Then Tara wakes up.
She is hungry!
She wants more milk.

137

Page 136

Photo

- *This is Mary.* (Point to the woman in the photo.) *She takes care of Tara. She loves Tara.*

Text

- *Mary feeds Tara—she gives her food. She talks to Tara. She kisses Tara.*

Mary talks to Tara. What would you say to Tara? Tell your partner. (Responses will vary.)

Page 137

Photos

- *Look at Tara in the top picture. Point to her bottle of milk. There is only a little bit of milk in the bottle now. It's almost empty. Did Tara drink a lot of milk?* (yes)
- *Look at the bottom picture. Tara isn't sleeping now. She is awake. What do you think she wants now?* (Question is open.)

Text

- *Mary takes Tara to her house at night. Tara drinks milk.* (Point to the milk bottle.) *Then she sleeps.* (Point to Tara sleeping.)
- *Let's read the last three lines together:* Then Tara wakes up. She is hungry! She wants more milk. *Cubs must be hungry a lot. They are growing!*

A Tiger Cub Grows Up

Page 138

Photo

- *Point to the picture of Tara drinking milk again!*

Text

- *Tara drinks some more milk. Now her belly is full.* (Pat your stomach.) *She isn't hungry now.*
- *Tara goes to sleep again. She grunts as she sleeps.* (Make a soft grunting sound.) *She squeals, too.* (Make a soft squealing sound.)
- *Let's grunt and squeal like Tara, but very, very quietly. Remember, she is sleeping.* (Make soft grunting and squealing sounds and encourage children to imitate you.)

Page 139

Photo

- *Look at Tara's teeth. Point to them. Say it with me:* teeth. *Let's read to find out what she can eat with those teeth.*

Text

- *Now Tara is three weeks old. Her teeth are growing. What can Tara eat with her teeth?* (meat)
- *Tara has pointed teeth.* (Point to her pointed teeth in the photo.) *Her teeth have little points at the end.*
- *Tara can tear meat with those teeth. I can tear this paper with my fingers.* (Tear paper into a few pieces.) *Tara uses her teeth to tear the meat into small pieces.*

Formal and Informal English

When children encounter a colloquial or informal word in the text, discuss other ways of saying the same word with more formal language. For example, *belly/stomach.*

Pages 138–139

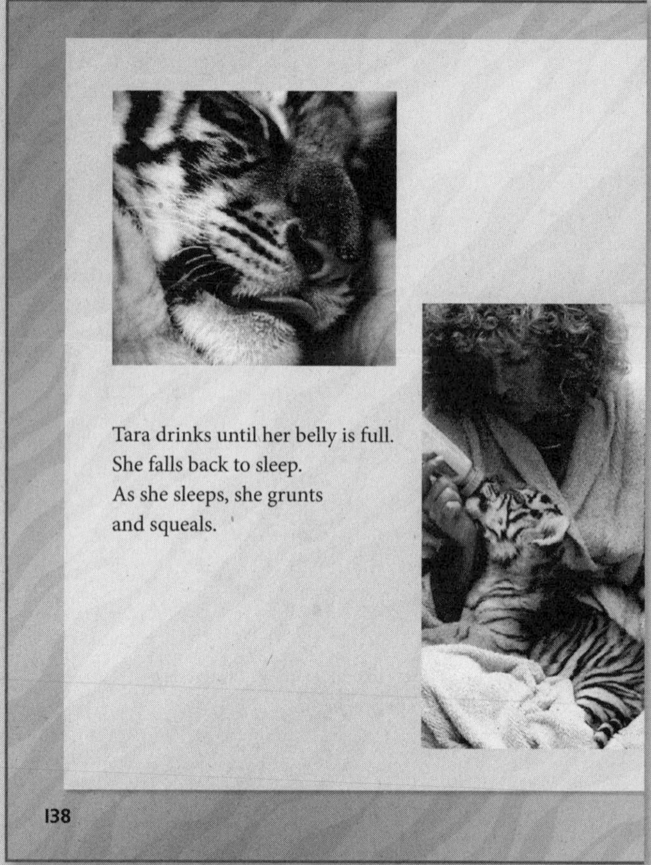

Pages 140–141

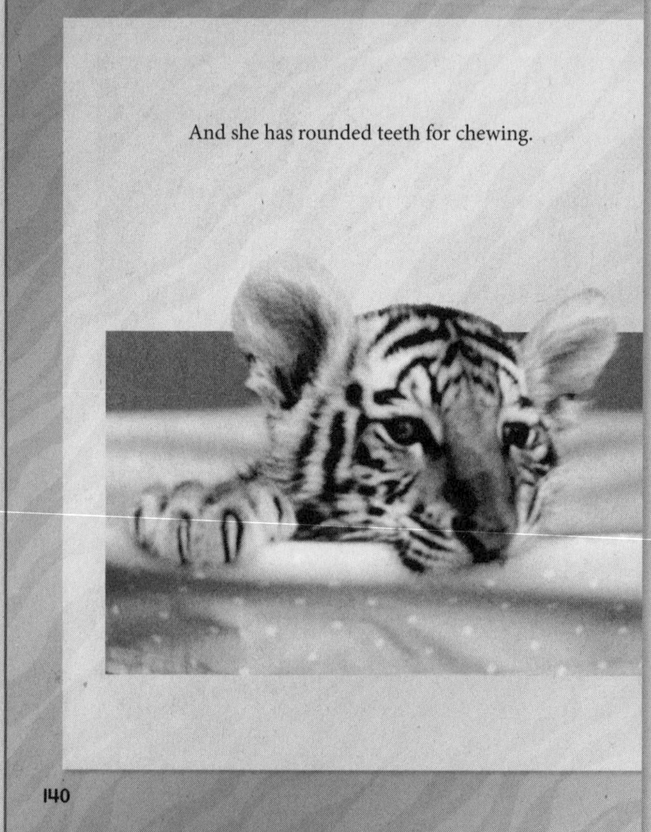

And she has rounded teeth for chewing.
140

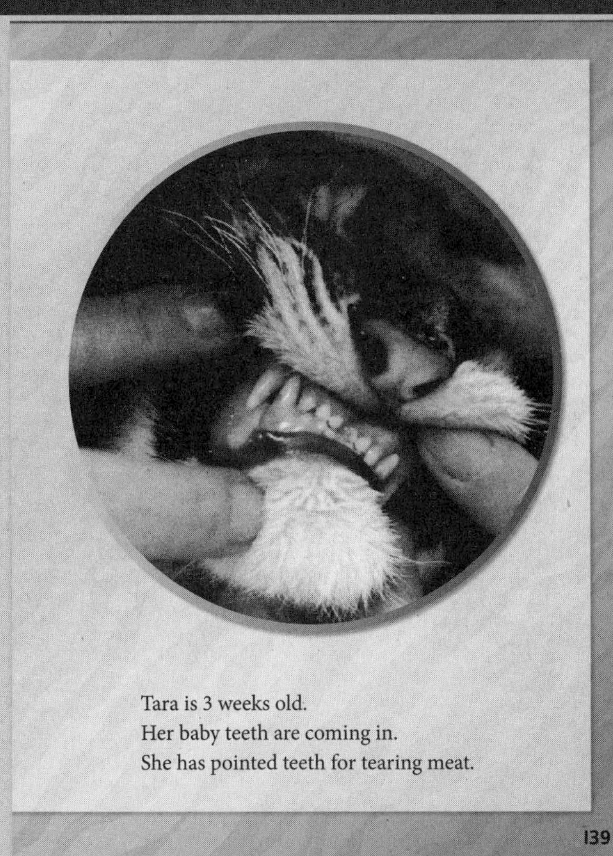
Tara is 3 weeks old.
Her baby teeth are coming in.
She has pointed teeth for tearing meat.

139

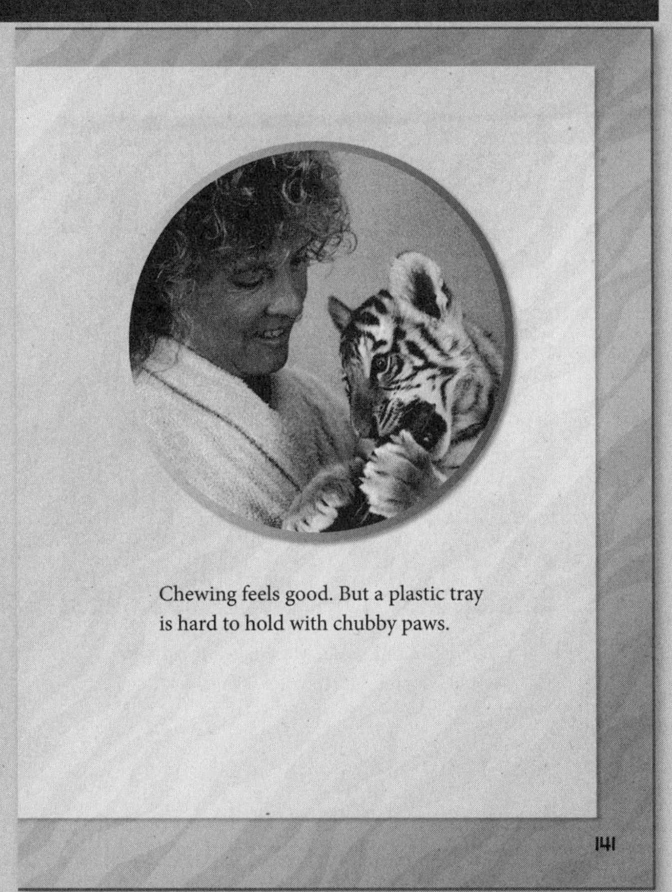
Chewing feels good. But a plastic tray
is hard to hold with chubby paws.

141

Page 140

Text

- *Tara also has rounded teeth. She can chew with those teeth. Say and do it with me:* chew. (Mime chewing and encourage children to imitate you.)

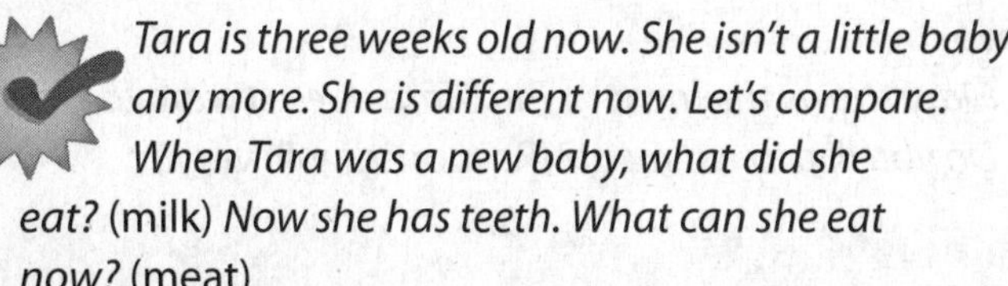

Tara is three weeks old now. She isn't a little baby any more. She is different now. Let's compare. When Tara was a new baby, what did she eat? (milk) *Now she has teeth. What can she eat now?* (meat)

Page 141

Photo

- *Look at Tara chew.* (Point to the tray in the photo.) *She is chewing a plastic tray.*
- *Look at Tara's feet.* (Point to Tara's feet.) *We call tiger's feet paws. Say it with me:* paws. *Tara is little, but her paws are big.*

Text, Choral Reading

- *Tara likes to chew. Her paws are chubby.* Chubby *is another word for* fat. *It isn't easy to hold the tray with her fat paws!*
- *Let's read this page together:* Chewing feels good. But a plastic tray is hard to hold with chubby paws.

A Tiger Cub Grows Up

Page 142

Photo

- Look at the picture. *Mary has a piece of meat in her hand. Point to it. Does she look like she wants to try it?* (no)

Text

- *Mary shows the meat to Tara. Tara doesn't want to eat it. Do you like to eat meat?* (Responses will vary.)

Page 143

Photo

- *Look at Tara bite Mary.* (Mime biting your arm.) *Say it with me:* bite. *Do you think Tara bites Mary hard or softly?* (softly)

Text, Choral Reading

- *When Tara plays, she learns. She learns to move. She learns to bite.*
- *Let's read this page together:* Playtime is time to learn. Can Tara crawl over Mary's legs? How hard will Mary let her bite?

Page 144

Photo

- *Tara is visiting the doctor. Point to her. The doctor is looking in Tara's ear.*
- *Look at Tara. Do you think she likes visiting the doctor?* (no) *Mary is holding Tara very tight. Can Tara get away?* (no)

Pages 142–143

Each day, Mary shows the cub a piece of meat. Tara does not want to try it. Not yet!

142

Pages 144–145

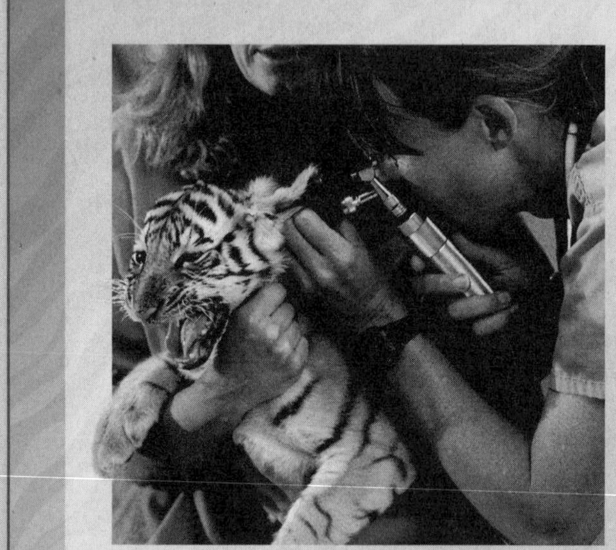

Tara is 3 months old. Mary takes Tara to the animal doctor. It is time for a checkup.

144

Playtime is a time to **learn**.
Can Tara crawl over Mary's legs?
How hard will Mary let her bite?

143

The bright lights are scary. The tiger cub roars.

145

Text

- *Tara is three months old now. Mary takes Tara to the animal doctor for a checkup. Say it with me:* checkup. *The doctor will check Tara. She will see if Tara is healthy.*

Page 145

Photo

- *Tara is standing under some big lights. Point to the lights. Those big lights make a lot of light. They are bright. Say it with me:* bright.
- *Look at Tara. Do you think she feels happy or scared?* (scared)

Text

- *Tara is scared of the bright lights. She roars.* (Make roaring sound.) *Say it with me:* roar.
- *Let's read this page together and roar at the end:* The bright lights are scary. The tiger cub roars. H-O-W-R-R.
- *Tara roars because she is scared. What do you do when you are scared?* (cry, hide, ask for help)

 *Tigers, like Tara, roar. Talk with your partner about some other animals that roar. Then think of sounds that other animals make.* (Responses will vary.)

Patterns in Language

Some grammatical structures, such as the ending –*s* in the present tense, pose difficulties to ELLs. Point out that there are several examples of words ending in -*s* in this selection, such as *takes* and *roars*. Help children find a pattern.

A Tiger Cub Grows Up

Page 146

Heading and Text

- *Let's read the section heading together:* Tara Goes Outdoors. Outdoors *means "outside."*
- *Tara is healthy. She's big now. She can go outside. Do you think Tara will like it outside?* (yes)

Page 147

Photo

- *Look at Tara run. She is so long now that she doesn't fit in the picture.*
- *There's grass in the picture. Show your partner the grass.*

Text

- *What does Tara see outside? She looks up and sees the* _______. (sky) *She runs on the* _______. (grass)
- *The grass and sky are strange to Tara. Say it with me:* strange. *This is Tara's first time to see grass and sky. They are new for her.*
- *Tara smells new smells, too.* (Point to your nose and sniff.) *She follows her nose. That means that when she smells something, she tries to find it.*

Think about how small Tara was at 9 days old, when she first opened her eyes. Look how big she is now! What could she do when she was 9 days old? (sleep and drink milk) *What can she do now?* (run, go outside, follow her nose, chew, play, take baths)

Pages 146–147

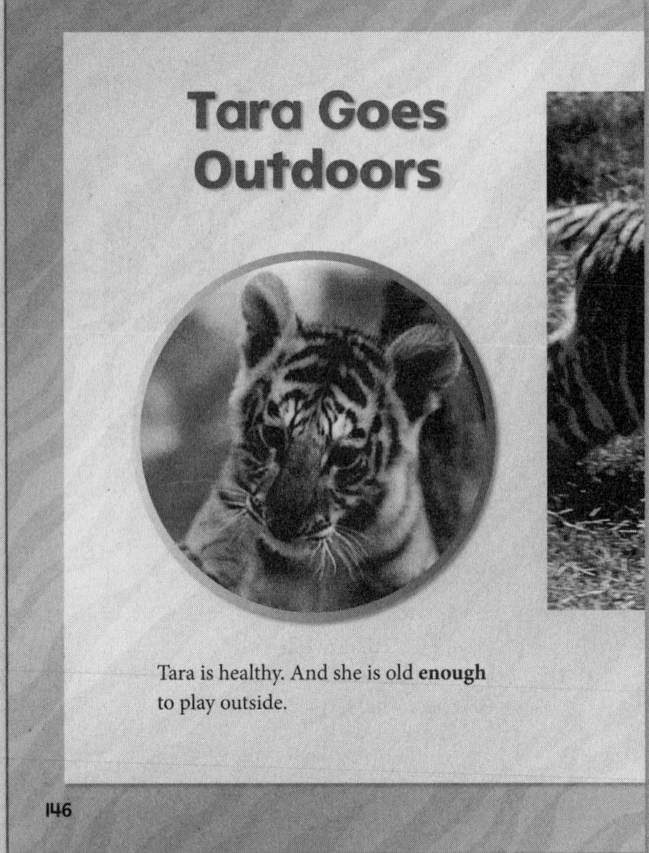

Tara Goes Outdoors
Tara is healthy. And she is old **enough** to play outside.
146

Pages 148–149

Lynn takes care of Tara now.
Lynn hugs Tara. She plays with Tara.
She shows her falling leaves.

148

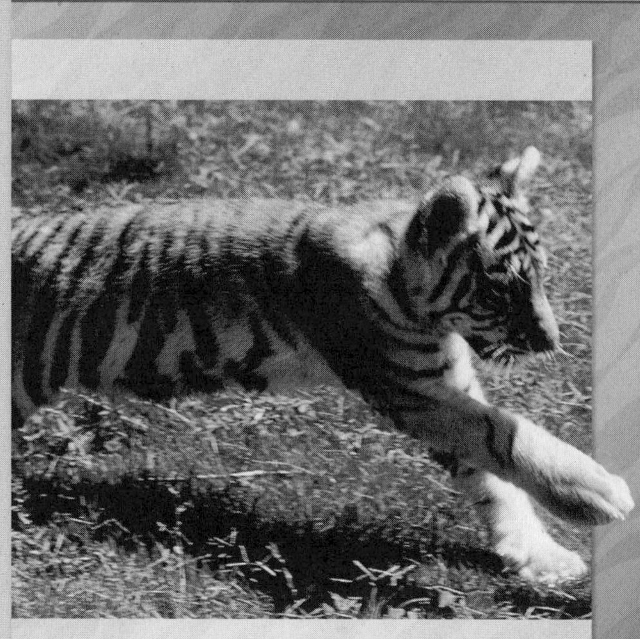

Grass and sky seem strange to Tara.
The **air** is filled with new smells.
The tiger cub follows her nose.
She runs across the grass.

147

Lynn plays with Tara every day.
She teaches Tara what she can do.
She teaches Tara what she cannot do.

149

Page 148

Photo

- *This is Lynn.* (Point to Lynn.) *Now that Tara is too big for the nursery, Lynn takes care of her. Lynn hugs Tara.*

Text

- *Tell me some things that Lynn does with Tara.* (Lynn plays with Tara. Lynn hugs Tara. Lynn takes care of Tara. Lynn shows Tara leaves.)

Page 149

Photo

- *Look at Tara on the tree. Tigers can get stuck in trees. Lynn is teaching Tara not to climb a tree.*

Think about some animals that can climb trees. Tell your partner. (Responses will vary.)

Text

- *Lynn plays with Tara and teaches her. Let's read this page together:* Lynn plays with Tara every day. She teaches Tara what she can do. She teaches Tara what she cannot do.

A Tiger Cub Grows Up

Page 150

Text

- *Tara doesn't say* hello *when she greets Lynn. She makes a chuffing sound, like this.* (Make a sound similar the sound of the word. Tigers make this sound by expelling air through the nostril.) *Lynn does the same. She greets Tara with a chuffing sound*

When people greet, they say hello. *When tigers greet, the make a chuffing sound. Greet your partner like a person. Then greet your partner like a tiger.*

Page 151

Photos

- *Look at the top picture. Tara is climbing over Lynn.*
- *Look at Lynn.* (Point to Lynn in the bottom photo.) *Is she happy or mad?* (happy) *Lynn and Tara are playing.*

Text

- *Tara climbs on Lynn and follows Lynn. Tara creeps, or moves very slowly and close to the ground. Then she pounces. That means she jumps on Lynn. Say it with me:* pounces.
- *Let's read this page together:* Climbing over Lynn is fun. Following Lynn is fun. Tara creeps along the ground. Then she pounces!

Pages 150–151

Tara greets Lynn with a friendly chuffing sound. Lynn returns the greeting.

150

Pages 152–153

Tara Joins the Grown-up Tigers

Tara is 9 months old. She is big and strong. She can join the park's grown-up tigers. Tara likes her new home. She can run across the grass. She can climb on logs. She can nap under leafy trees.

152

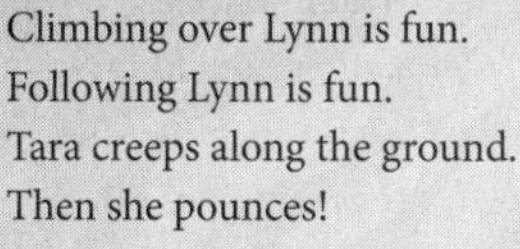

Climbing over Lynn is fun.
Following Lynn is fun.
Tara creeps along the ground.
Then she pounces!

151

Tara watches the big tigers swim.
She walks around the pond. It is hot.
So Tara jumps in. Tara is 1 year old.
The tiger cub has grown up.

S- P- L- A- S- H

153

Page 152

Heading and Photo

- *Let's read the section heading together:* Tara Joins the Grown-up Tigers.
- *Look at these big tigers. Maybe one of these tigers is Tara. Tara isn't a little cub any more.*
- *A log is a tree trunk that has fallen or been cut. Point to the log in the picture. The tiger is climbing on the log.*

Text

- *Now Tara is nine months old. She lives in the park with the grown-up tigers. She runs in the grass and naps under trees. She climbs on logs.*

Page 153

Photo

- *Look at Tara. She is jumping into the water. Do you think she likes the water now?* (yes)

Text

- *Tara watches the big tigers. They swim in the water. It is hot. Tara jumps in the water, too.*
- *Tara is one year old. She's a grown-up tiger now. She's big. She makes a big sound when she jumps in the water*—splash! *Read it with me:* Splash! (Point to the letters spelling out *splash*.)

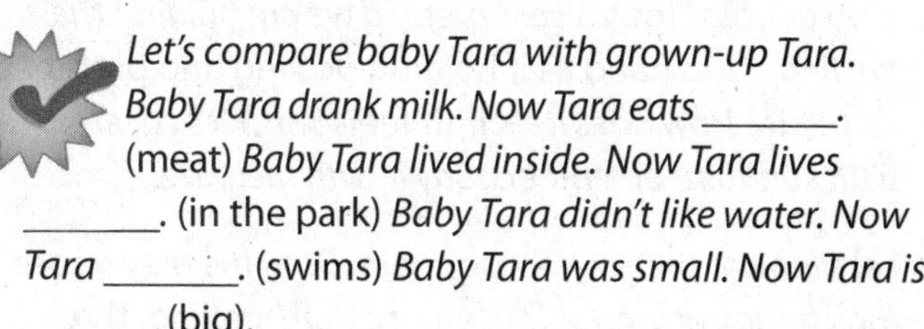

Let's compare baby Tara with grown-up Tara. Baby Tara drank milk. Now Tara eats _______. (meat) *Baby Tara lived inside. Now Tara lives* _______. (in the park) *Baby Tara didn't like water. Now Tara* _______. (swims) *Baby Tara was small. Now Tara is* _______ (big).

Gray Goose

Access Core Content

Teacher Note Pose the questions after you read the lines indicated.

Pages 156–157

Title

- *Poems have words that sound nice together. One way to make words sound nice together is to use alliteration. That means using words that begin with the same sound. Say it with me:* alliteration. *The title of the poem has alliteration. Let's read it together:* Gray Goose. Gray *and* goose *begin with the same sound.* (Say the hard *g* sound and encourage children to repeat.)

Illustration

- *Look at the illustration on page 157. A goose has a long neck. It changes color as it grows. Point to the gray goose in the picture.*
- *Now point to the gray goose's feet. They're webbed feet. Say it with me:* webbed feet. *Webbed feet are good for swimming.*
- *Show your partner the baby goose. A baby goose is called a gosling. Say it with me:* gosling. *Is the gosling gray or gold?* (gold) *Let's pretend we are holding the gosling.* (Cup hand as if holding gosling and pretend to pet it.) *How does it feel?* (It feels soft.) *It's covered with soft fuzz, or feathers. Say it with me:* fuzz.
- *Let's look at the grey goose again. Does the grey goose look happy or worried?* (Demonstrate smiling, then frowning.) (worried)

Lines 1–4

- *Listen while I read the first four lines.* (Read lines 1–4.)
- *How do we know the gray goose is a mother goose? Say the first line with me:* Gray mama goose. *The word* mama *means "mother."*

(Twirl finger around to represent dizziness.) *The goose is dizzy because she's running around looking for her gosling, her baby. She's also making a sound. What sound does she make?* (honk, honk) *Is this an example of alliteration?* (yes) *Say it with me:* honk, honk. (Say the *h* sound and encourage children to repeat.)

Pages 156–157

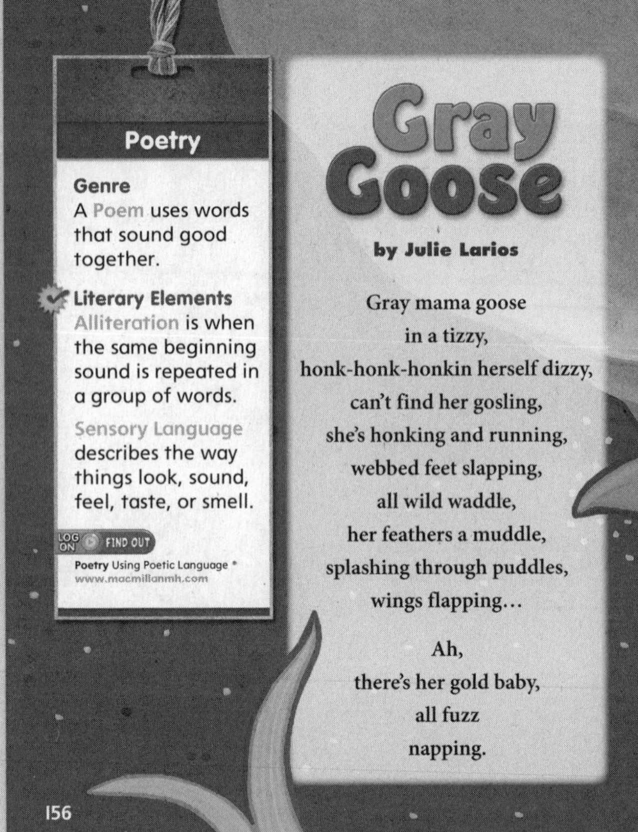

Poetry

Genre
A Poem uses words that sound good together.

Literary Elements
Alliteration is when the same beginning sound is repeated in a group of words.

Sensory Language describes the way things look, sound, feel, taste, or smell.

LOG ON FIND OUT
Poetry Using Poetic Language • www.macmillanmh.com

Gray Goose

by Julie Larios

Gray mama goose
in a tizzy,
honk-honk-honkin herself dizzy,
can't find her gosling,
she's honking and running,
webbed feet slapping,
all wild waddle,
her feathers a muddle,
splashing through puddles,
wings flapping…

Ah,
there's her gold baby,
all fuzz
napping.

156

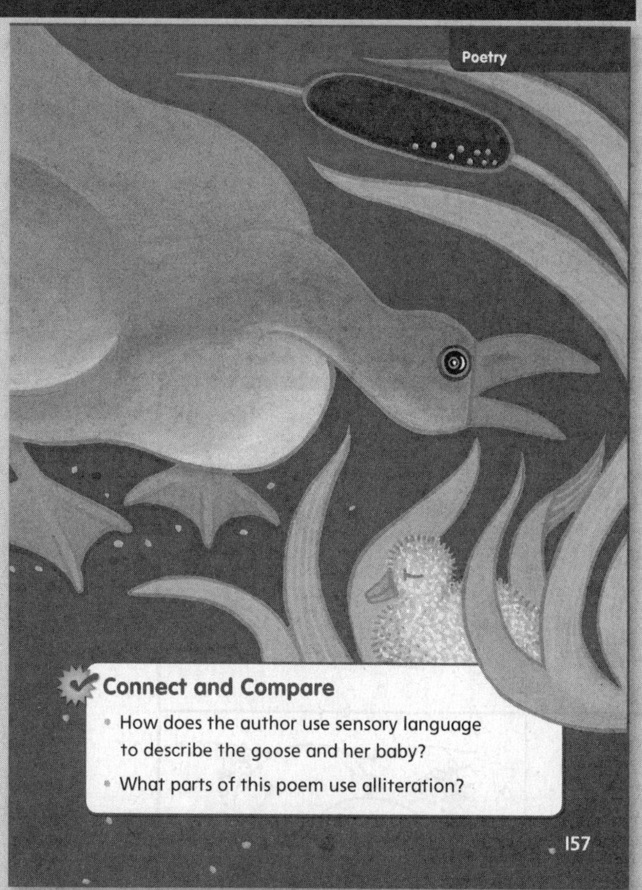

Poetry
Connect and Compare
How does the author use sensory language to describe the goose and her baby?
What parts of this poem use alliteration?
157

Lines 5–7

- *Now listen while I read lines five through seven.* (Read lines 5–7.) *The goose's webbed feet are slapping, like this.* (Slap one hand against the other.) *She is doing a wild waddle.* (Demonstrate waddling.) *Say these words with me:* wild waddle. *This is another example of alliteration.* Wild *and* waddle *begin with the same sound.* (Say the *w* sound and encourage children to repeat.)
- *Now let's read these three lines together and do the motions:* she's honking and running, webbed feet slapping, all wild waddle.

Lines 8–10

- *The gray goose is splashing through puddles.* (Demonstrate.) *Let's all pretend to splash through puddles.* (Lead children in splashing and stomping motion.)
- *The goose is flapping her wings, like this.* (Demonstrate by flapping arms.) *Let's all flap our wings.* (Lead children in flapping arms.) *What sound do you think the goose's flapping wings make?* (Answers will vary.)

Lines 11–14

- *The mama goose has found her gosling. It's napping, or sleeping. Point to the napping gosling in the picture. Now let's all pretend to nap.* (Demonstrate.)

Talk to your partner. Is the goose worried or happy now? Why? (She's happy. She's happy because she found her baby.)

The goose in this poem makes a lot of sounds. Let's remember them. Let's honk like the goose. (Lead children in honking.) *Let's make a slapping sound, like the goose's webbed feet.* (Lead children in making slapping sound.) *Let's make a flapping sound, like the goose's wings.* (Lead children in flapping arms and making flapping sound.)

- *That's a noisy goose! What about the gosling in the picture. What sound do you think it's making?* (possible answers: peep peep; snoring sound; no sound)

Choral Response

- *Let's read the title and the poem together.* (Read poem line by line expressively, using motions. Pause to allow children to repeat.)

Name ______________________________

Use the word chart to study this week's vocabulary words. Write a sentence using each word in your writer's notebook.

Word	Context Sentence	Illustration
cub ____________	The mother bear carries her cub on her back.	
wild ____________	Bears live in the wild, not in houses.	**Describe something you might see in the wild.**

© Macmillan/McGraw-Hill

Name ______________________________

Read each question and prompt. Discuss the answers with your group. Use your Leveled Reader to find details to support your answers. Then write your answers on another sheet of paper.

1. Tell what you learned about living things.

2. Describe what living things need to survive.

3. Give examples of living things and nonliving things from the book.

4. Explain what living things can do that nonliving things cannot.

5. What are the two types of living things that are talked about in the book?

© Macmillan/McGraw-Hill

GRADE 1, UNIT 6 • Interactive Reading
Weekly Planners

Week 1

Selections	Vocabulary		ELL Practice Book
	Key Selection/Oral Vocabulary Words/ Cognates	Academic Language/Cognates	
Olivia *National Parks*	anxious supposed *supuesto* firm *firme* adventurous *aventurero* inquisitive *inquisitivo* insignificant *insignificante* route *ruta*	visualize *visualizar* fantasy *fantasía* reality *realidad* subject *sujeto* captions	• Phonics, p. 101 • Vocabulary, p. 102 • Grammar, p. 103 • Book Talk, p. 104

Week 2

Selections	Vocabulary		ELL Practice Book
	Key Selection/Oral Vocabulary Words/ Cognates	Academic Language/Cognates	
Whistle for Willie *Seeing-Eye Dogs*	errand suddenly dare humble predicament permit *permitir* solution *solución*	ask questions make inferences *inferencias* predicate *predicado*	• Phonics, p. 105 • Vocabulary, p. 106 • Grammar, p. 107 • Book Talk, p. 108

Week 3

TIME FOR KIDS®	Vocabulary		ELL Practice Book
	Key Selection/Oral Vocabulary Words/ Cognates	Academic Language/Cognates	
Cool Jobs	ordinary duty equipment thorough interesting *interesante* profession *profesión* satisfaction *satisfacción*	reread categorize pronoun classify *clasificar*	• Phonics, p. 109 • Vocabulary, p. 110 • Grammar, p. 111 • Book Talk, p. 112

Week 4

Selections	Vocabulary		ELL Practice Book
	Key Selection/Oral Vocabulary Words/ Cognates	Academic Language/Cognates	
Dot and Jabber and the Big Bug Mystery *The World of Insects*	clues feature swift habit understand dull invisible *invisible*	monitor comprehension heads prediction *predicción*	• Phonics, p. 113 • Vocabulary, p. 114 • Grammar, p. 115 • Book Talk, p. 116

Week 5

Selections	Vocabulary		ELL Practice Book
	Key Selection/Oral Vocabulary Words/ Cognates	Academic Language/Cognates	
Super Oscar *Dancing Paper*	daydream cancel nutritious plentiful stubborn fantastic *fantástico*	analyze story structure character setting plot rhyming pattern	• Phonics, p. 117 • Vocabulary, p. 118 • Grammar, p. 119 • Book Talk, p. 120

© Macmillan/McGraw-Hill

Student Response Strategies

Use the following strategies to help English Language Learners move to the next proficiency level.

✔ **WAIT** Give children ample time to respond.

- Let children know that they can respond in different ways depending on their levels of proficiency, but all should be encouraged to answer questions related to the main point of the picture or text.
- Allow children to respond in their native language if they are very limited proficient. Ask a more proficient student to repeat the answer in English.

✔ **REPEAT** If the child's response is correct, the teacher can repeat what the child has said slowly and clearly for the rest of the class to hear.

✔ **REVISE for FORM** Generally the teacher will be repeating what the child has said but with corrections for grammar and pronunciation. The correction can be implicit or explicit (where teacher calls attention to the correction).

✔ **REVISE for MEANING** Teachers should also correct responses for meaning.

✔ **ELABORATE** Here, the teacher elaborates on a child's response or states the response in another way in order to more fully develop children's comprehension and oral language proficiency.

✔ **ELICIT** Finally, the teacher can also elicit a more comprehensive response from the child by prompting him or her for further information.

Newcomers

Basic and Social Language Each week you will be focusing on an important aspect of classroom communication to teach or reinforce with your newcomers. Children will expand and internalize initial English vocabulary by learning and using routine language needed for classroom communication.

Introduce Self Teach children how to introduce themselves, ask for other classmates′ names, and say Hello/Goodbye. Use the sentence frames *My name is* _____ and *What is your name?* Model dialogues, such as *Hello. My name is (name). What is your name?* Have children repeat and practice with a partner.

Basic Requests Teach children sentence frames for basic requests, such as *I need* _____, *I want* _____, and *Do you have* _____*?* Teach them how to ask for permission, such as *May I use the restroom, please?* And to respond with *thank you.* Provide daily opportunities to model and practice each request. Reinforce *please* and *thank you.*

Classroom Items Teach children the names of commonly used classroom items, such as, pencils, paper, book, chair, and desk. Reinforce each using the sentence frames *This is my* _____. *That is your* _____. and *This is a* _____. These sentence frames focus on possession. Provide daily practice, for example, *This is my book. That is your book.*

LOG ON Have children use **Newcomer Games** to expand and internalize language needed for classroom communication. **www.macmillanmh.com**

© Macmillan/McGraw-Hill

Olivia

Pages 10–11

Prior to reading the selection with children, they should have listened to the selection on **StudentWorks Plus**, the interactive eBook. In addition, selection vocabulary should have been pretaught using the **Visual Vocabulary Resources**.

Access Core Content

Teacher Note Pose the questions after you read the paragraph or page indicated.

Pages 10–11

Title and Illustration

- Olivia *is the title of this book. Olivia is also the name of the main character. Say the name with me:* Olivia.

Look at Olivia. What kind of animal is she? (a pig) *Is she a real pig or a made-up pig?* (She is a made-up pig.) *How do you know?* (Real pigs don't wear clothes.)

Page 12

Whole Page

- *Let's read the first page together to find out something about Olivia:* This is Olivia. She is good at lots of things.
- *Look at the picture to see one thing that Olivia is good at. Let's read the title of the book she is holding:* 40 Very Loud Songs. *What is one thing that Olivia can do well?* (sing) *Why is her mouth open so wide in the picture?* (to show that she is singing loudly)
- *Olivia likes to sing loud songs. This is* loud. (Model a loud sound.) *The opposite of* loud *is* soft. *This is* soft. (Model a soft sound.)
- *Let's sing a song that we all know.* (Choose a song for students to sing.) *We'll pretend to be Olivia and sing it loudly.*

Pages 10–11

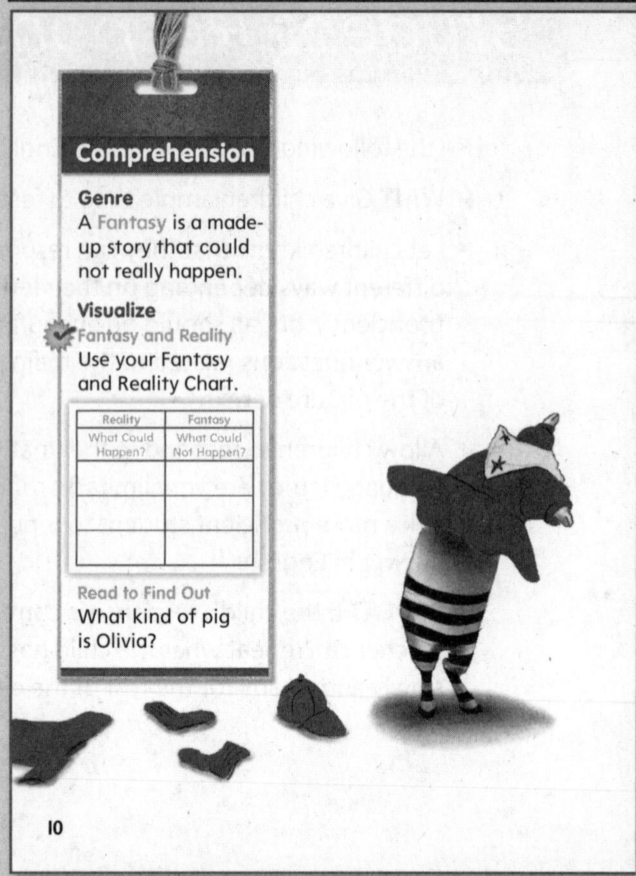

Comprehension
Genre
A Fantasy is a made-up story that could not really happen.
Visualize
Fantasy and Reality
Use your Fantasy and Reality Chart.
Reality
What Could Happen?
Fantasy
What Could Not Happen?
Read to Find Out
What kind of pig is Olivia?
10

Pages 12–13

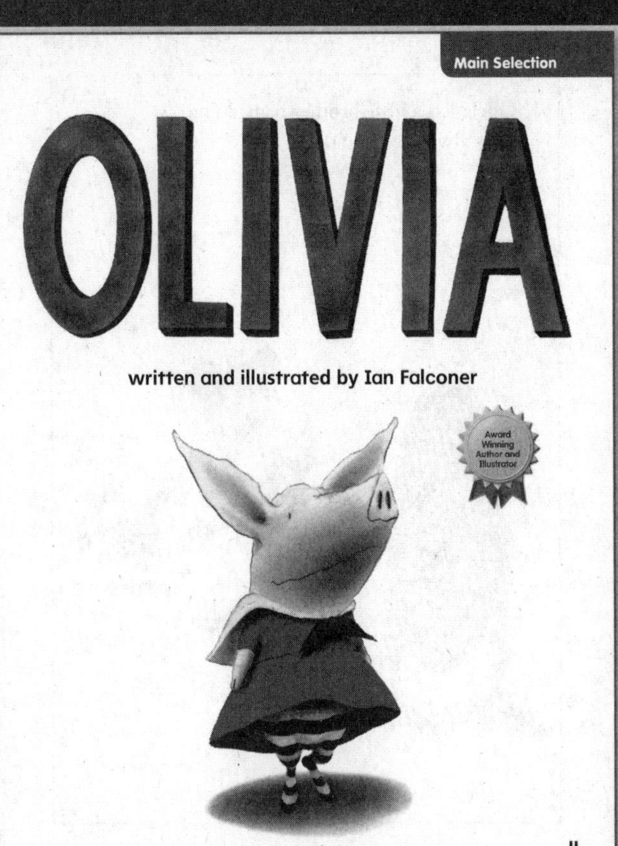

Main Selection
OLIVIA
written and illustrated by Ian Falconer
Award Winning Author and Illustrator
11

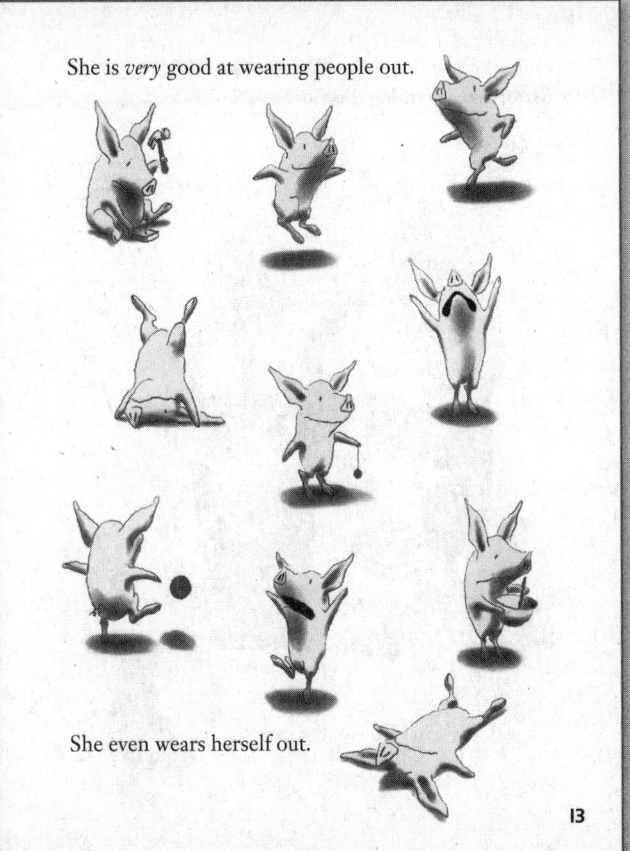

She is *very* good at wearing people out.
She even wears herself out.
13

- *When you are good at something, that means you "do it well." Here are some things I am good at.* (Name some things you do well.)

Tell your partner some things you are good at. Then listen to your partner tell you things he or she is good at.

Page 13

Whole Page

- *Olivia wears people out. She makes people tired. Long walks in hilly places wear me out. What are some things that wear you out?* (raking leaves, running all the way home)

- *We see lots of pictures of Olivia on this page. Look at each picture carefully. Name some of the things Olivia is doing in the pictures.* (making something, playing with a yoyo, jumping, standing on her head, cooking) *Point to the picture that shows Olivia being worn out.*

- *Why does Olivia wear herself out?* (She is always doing something.) *Why might she wear others out?* (They try to keep up with her.)

Synonyms and Circumlocution

Remind children that they can use circumlocution, or paraphrasing, to help clarify words or expressions they do not understand. Ask, *What is another way of saying "wearing people out"?* (making people tired)

Page 14

Whole Page

- *Olivia has a brother. We see him on this page. Let's read together about her brother:* <u>Olivia has a little brother named Ian. He's always copying.</u>
- *Look at the picture. Point to Olivia. Point to Ian. The author says that Ian is always copying Olivia. That means Ian is always doing the same things that Olivia does. What is Ian doing to copy Olivia?* (standing like she does, wearing lipstick)
- *How do you feel when somebody copies everything you do?* (I think it is funny. It makes me mad.)

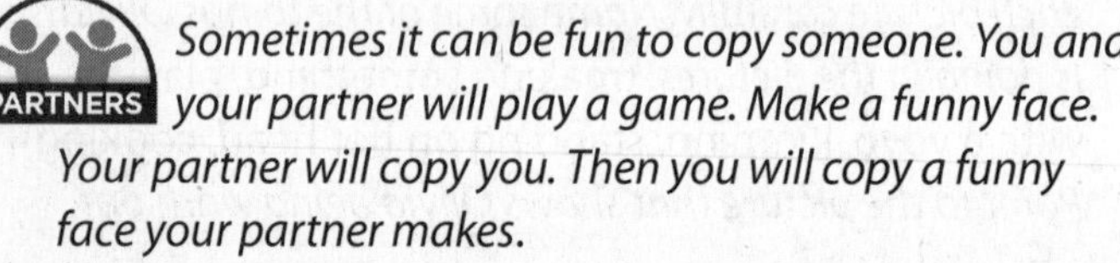

PARTNERS *Sometimes it can be fun to copy someone. You and your partner will play a game. Make a funny face. Your partner will copy you. Then you will copy a funny face your partner makes.*

Page 15

Whole Page

- *Look at the picture. Find Olivia and point to her. Why is she wearing a scary bag mask?* (She wants to scare Ian away so he won't copy her anymore.)
- *What are some other ways Olivia might get Ian to leave her alone?* (give him something else to do, tell Mom or Dad, go to her room and close the door)
-

Directionality

Ask children to place their finger where you start reading (top left). Ask where you finish reading on this page (bottom right).

Pages 14–15

Pages 16–17

Olivia lives with her **mother**, her **father**,
her brother, her dog, Perry,
and Edwin, the cat.
16

Sometimes Ian just won't leave her alone, so Olivia has to be **firm**.

15

In the morning, after she gets up, and moves the cat,

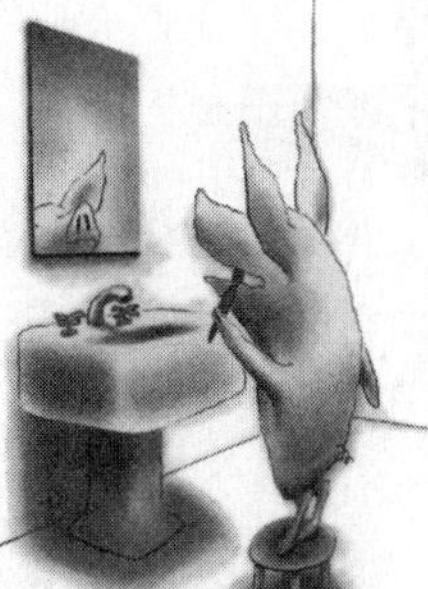

and brushes her teeth, and combs her ears,

and moves the cat,

17

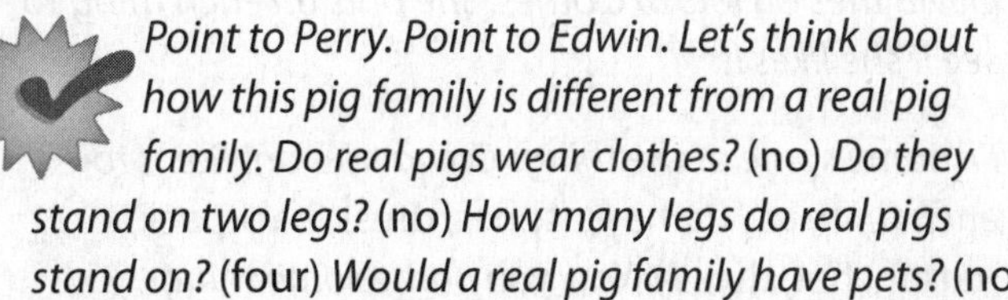

Page 16

Whole Page

Point to Perry. Point to Edwin. Let's think about how this pig family is different from a real pig family. Do real pigs wear clothes? (no) *Do they stand on two legs?* (no) *How many legs do real pigs stand on?* (four) *Would a real pig family have pets?* (no)

Page 17

Whole Page

- *A real pig sleeps in a field or in a barn. Close your eyes and imagine where Olivia might sleep.* (pause) *Now, open your eyes. Tell me what kind of bedroom you pictured in your mind for Olivia.*
- *Olivia brushes her teeth in the morning. Do you do the same thing?* (yes) *She also combs her ears. Point to them. What do you comb?* (my hair)
- *Olivia keeps moving the cat. Why do you think she does that?* (Question is open.)

Pages 18–19

Text and Illustrations

- *Olivia tries on lots of clothes. She puts on each thing to see if she likes it.*
- *I'll name some of the things Olivia tries on. Point to each thing as I name it.* (shoes, dress, backpack, mitten, hat, dress.) *Now you name some things, and I'll point to them.*

You and your partner will take turns. Pretend to try on different kinds of clothes. See if your partner can guess what you are pretending to put on.

Page 20

Whole Page

- *Olivia likes to go to the beach, a place where there is sand and water. Does she like to go when it is sunny or when it is cloudy?* (when it is sunny)

Look at the top picture. What is Olivia holding? (a beach ball) *Do real pigs usually go to the beach?* (no) *If a real pig did go to the beach, do you think it would play* ball? (no) *What might it do?* (play in the mud)

- To be prepared *means "to be ready for what will happen." Look at the bottom picture.* (Point to it.) *What is Olivia prepared to do?* (swim) *She is wearing a bathing suit and flippers on her feet. Point to the flippers and say the word with me:* flippers.

Pages 18–19

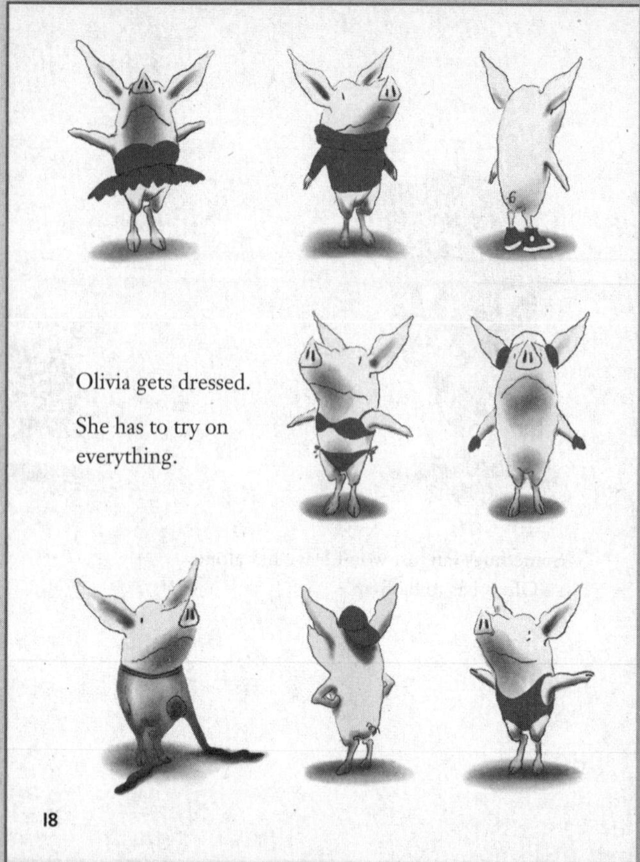

Olivia gets dressed.
She has to try on everything.
18

Pages 20–21

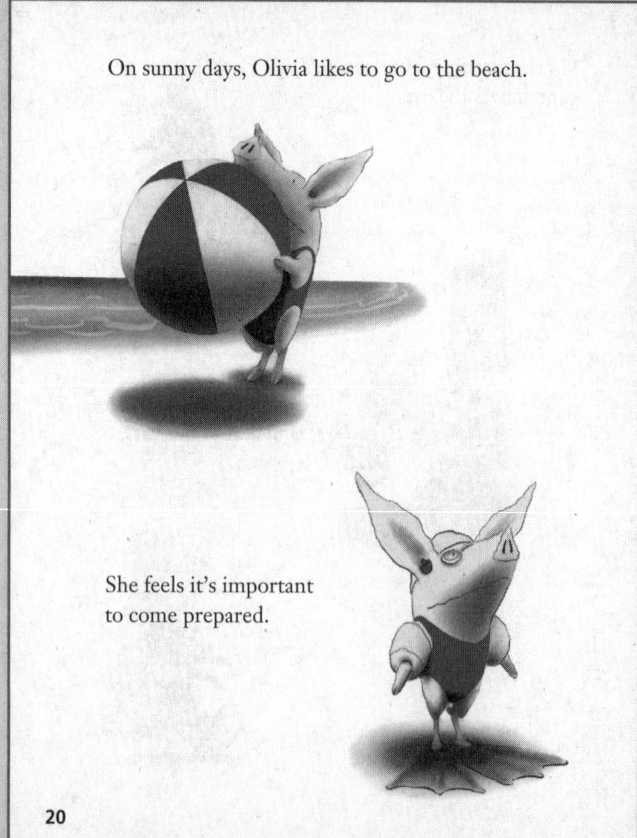

On sunny days, Olivia likes to go to the beach.
She feels it's important to come prepared.
20

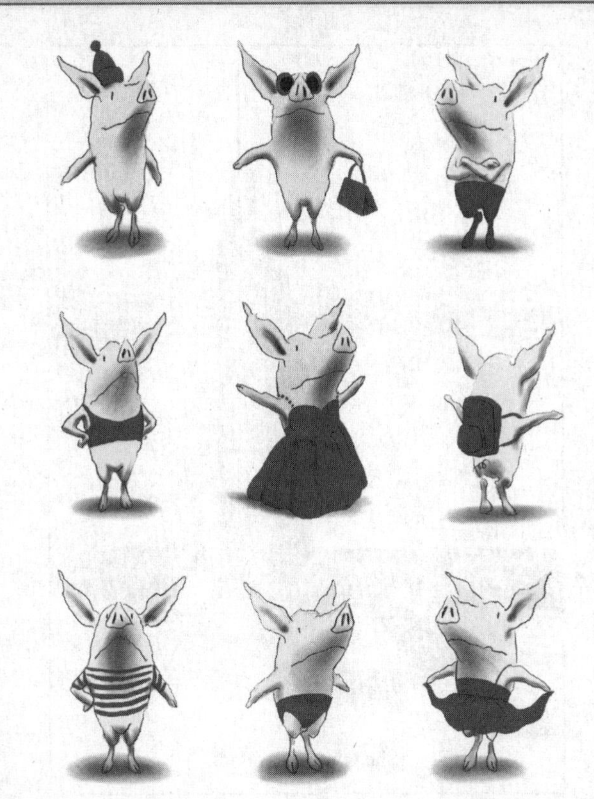

19

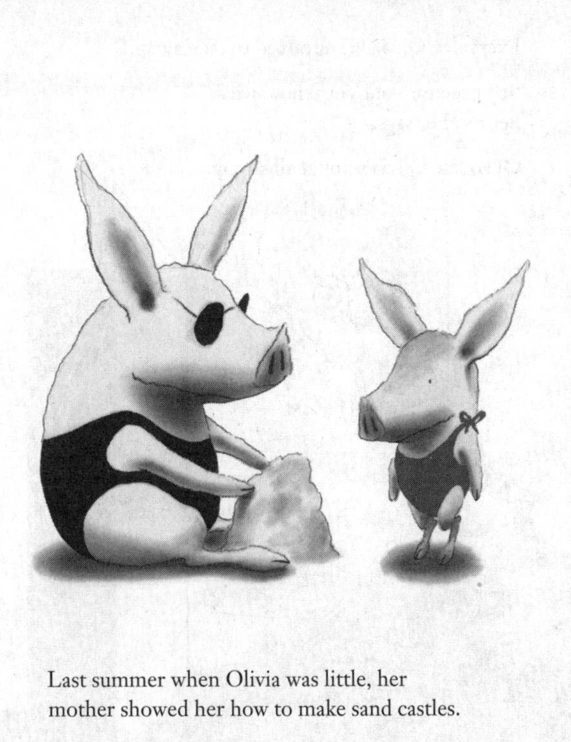

Last summer when Olivia was little, her mother showed her how to make sand castles.

21

Page 21

Whole Page

- *A castle is a special house for a king and queen. A sand castle is made from sand. People often make sand castles at the beach. They build towers and walls out of sand.*
- *Pretend you are Olivia's mother. What might you tell Olivia about how to build a sand castle?* (First, you have to scoop together a pile of sand. Then you have to make it into the shape of a castle.)
- *We read that Olivia is good at many things. Do you think that she will make a good sand castle?* (yes)

Monitor Oral Production

Remember to model self-corrective techniques on a regular basis as you speak to children. Pretend to mispronounce words and self-correct.

Page 22

Whole Page

- *Look at that sandcastle! Let's read what the author says about it:* She got pretty good. *What is another way to say that Olivia got pretty good at building sand castles?* (She was a really good builder. She did it very well.)
- *This castle would be hard to make out of sand. It is also much taller than sand castles you usually see. What are some words we could use to tell about the sand castle?* (huge, pointed)

Could Olivia, a pig, really build a sand castle like this? Why or why not? (No, because sand would fall down. A pig could not reach high enough to pile up the sand. Pigs can't really build sand castles.)

Page 23

Top of the Page

- *Let's read together what else Olivia likes to do at the beach:* Sometimes Olivia likes to bask in the sun.
- *Look at the picture at the top of the page. What is Olivia doing?* (She is lying in the sun.) *Does it look like she is enjoying herself?* (Yes, she is smiling.) To bask *means "to lie and soak up the sun."*

Middle and Bottom of the Page

- *Olivia's mother thinks Olivia has had enough. What has she had enough of?* (sun) *How does Olivia's mom know that Olivia has had enough sun?* (Olivia's skin is red.)
- *Pretend that you are Olivia. Show me how your sunburn makes you feel.* (Children might touch their skin and say, "Ow!" They may say," I feel hot and sore.")

Pages 22–23

Pages 24–25

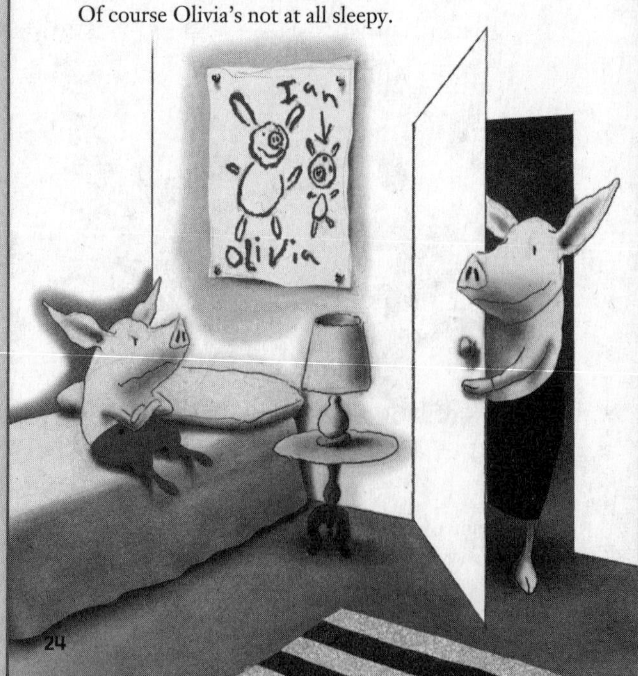

Every day Olivia is **supposed** to take a nap.
"It's time for your you-know-what," her mother says.
Of course Olivia's not at all sleepy.
Ian
Olivia
24

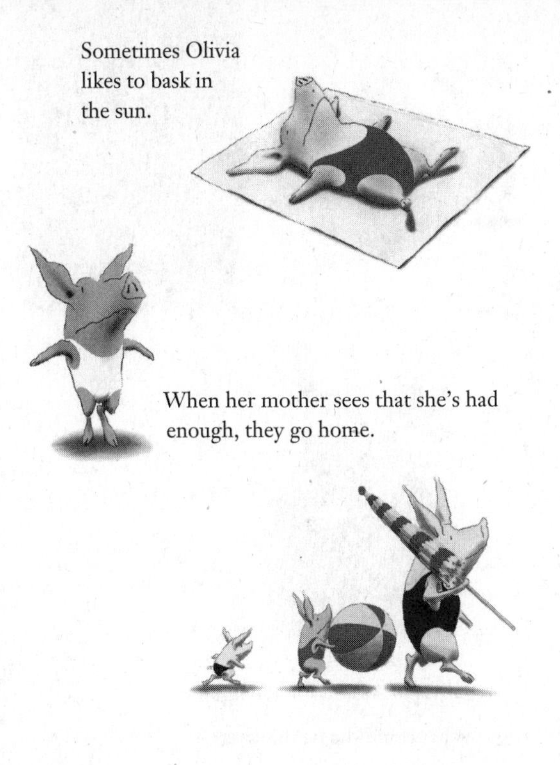

Sometimes Olivia likes to bask in the sun.
When her mother sees that she's had enough, they go home.
23

On rainy days, Olivia likes to go to the museum.
She heads straight for her favorite picture.
25

Page 24

Text

- *Olivia is supposed to, or has to, take a nap every day. Why is it a good idea for Olivia to take naps? Look back on page 13 for a clue.* (She does so many things that she wears herself out.)
- *Let's read what Olivia's mother says:* "It's time for your you-know-what," her mother says. *What does she mean by* your you-know-what? (your nap)

Illustration

- *Look at Olivia. Is she happy or mad?* (mad) *Why?* (She does not want to take a nap.)

Talk with your partner about some things little children do to try to get out of naps. (Responses will vary.)

Page 25

Text and Illustration

- *A museum is a building where people go to see important artwork or important things from the past.*
- *Does Olivia go to museums on sunny days or rainy days?* (rainy days) *Why might a museum be a good place for a rainy day?* (It is indoors.)

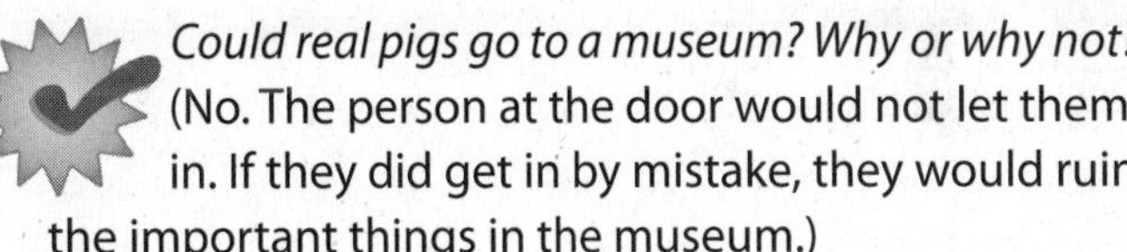
Could real pigs go to a museum? Why or why not? (No. The person at the door would not let them in. If they did get in by mistake, they would ruin the important things in the museum.)

- *Look at Olivia's favorite picture. Girls are dancing in it. Why might Olivia like this picture?* (Maybe she likes it because it has girls in it. Maybe she likes to dance.)

Page 26

Whole Page

- *Let's read this page together:* Olivia looks at it for a long time. What could she be thinking? *What do you think Olivia is thinking? Look at the picture for a clue.* (She is imagining herself in the painting. She is imagining that she is a dancer.)

PARTNERS

Talk with your partner about a painting that you like. It could be one that you have seen somewhere or one that you have made.

Page 27

Whole Page

- *Olivia doesn't get the painting we see on this page. That means that Olivia doesn't understand the painting.*
- *Let's read together what Olivia says about the painting:* "I could do that in about five minutes," she says to her mother. *She means she could make a picture like that in five minutes. She doesn't think the painting is very good.*

Pages 26–27

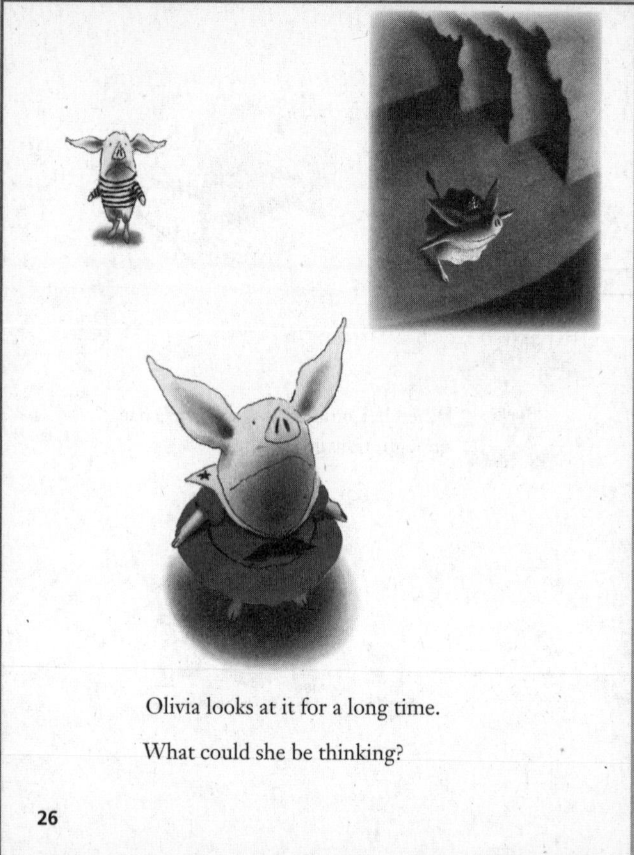
Olivia looks at it for a long time.
What could she be thinking?
26

Pages 28–29

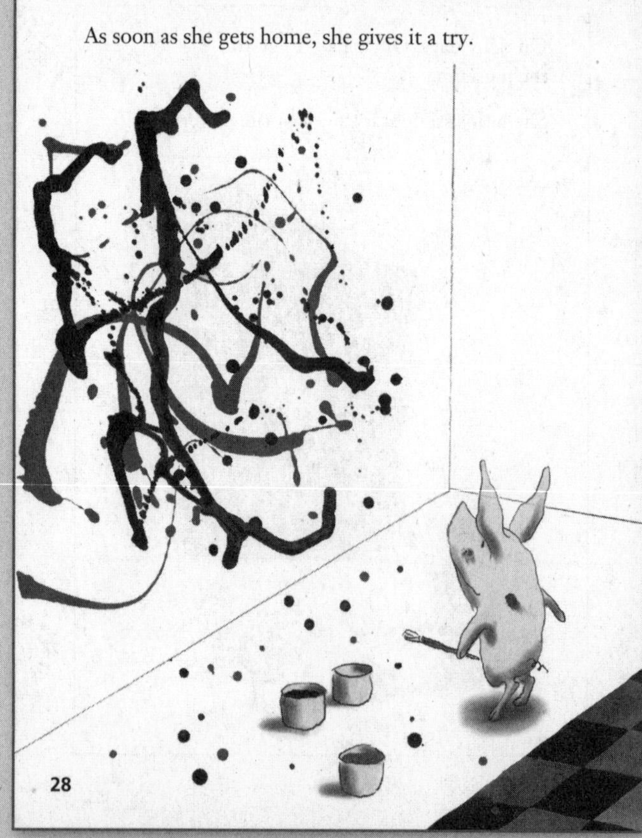
As soon as she gets home, she gives it a try.
28

But there is one painting Olivia just doesn't get.

"I could do that in about five minutes," she says to her mother.

27

29

Page 28

Whole Page

- *It says on this page that Olivia* gives it a try. *That means that Olivia tries to make a painting like the one she saw in the museum. What did she do? Where did she do it?* (She made a scribble painting on the wall.)

Page 29

Illustration

- *Look at the mother's face on this page. Is she happy or angry?* (She is angry that Olivia painted on the wall.)

One of you will pretend to be Olivia. The other will pretend to be Olivia's mother. What do you think Olivia and her mother would say to each other? Make up the words.

Page 30

Whole Page

- *Let's read the words together:* Time out. *That means that Olivia has to stop what she is doing. She has to sit and think about what she has done. Who told Olivia to do this?* (her mother)
- *Olivia is sitting on the chair. Does she look happy or sad?* (sad) *Why might she feel this way?* (Olivia probably feels sorry that she painted on the wall. She is probably not happy that she has to sit there. She would like to get up and play.)

Page 31

Top of Page

- *Look at the marks across the middle of the page and on the bathtub.* (Point to them.) *What are these marks?* (They are paint.)
- *Why is it important for Olivia to take a bath before she does anything else?* (So she won't get paint on anything else in the house.)

Bottom of Page

- *Most parents read one or two books to their children before bed. Olivia says she wants her mother to read five books. Do you think Olivia wants to stay up later?* (yes) She is not sleepy.

Talk with your partner about other things children do to try to stay up later. (Responses will vary.)

Pages 30–31

Pages 32–33

"No, Olivia, just one."

"How about **four**?"

"Two."

"Three."

"Oh, all right, three.
But that's *it*!"

32

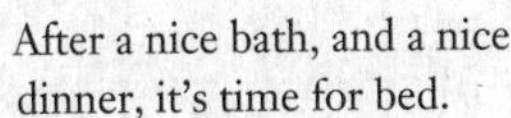

After a nice bath, and a nice dinner, it's time for bed.

But of course Olivia's not at all sleepy.

"Only five books tonight, Mommy," she says.

31

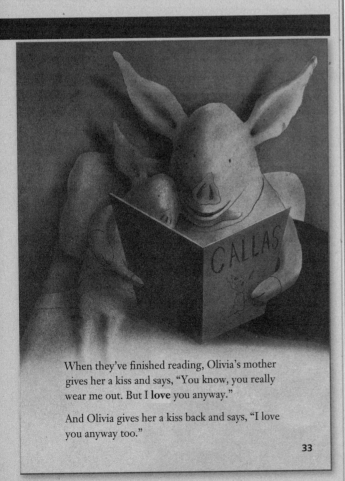

When they've finished reading, Olivia's mother gives her a kiss and says, "You know, you really wear me out. But I **love** you anyway."

And Olivia gives her a kiss back and says, "I love you anyway too."

33

Page 32

Text

- *On this page, Olivia and her mother talk about how many books to read. It is hard to tell who is talking because the author does not say:* Olivia said *or* her mother said.
- *We will do something to help us understand. Half of our group will read what the mother says. Half will read what Olivia says.* (Designate groups.)
- *I will point to the group that will read.* (Point to the Mother group.) "No, Olivia, just one." (Point to the Olivia group.) "How about four?" (Point to the mother group.) "Two." (Point to the Olivia group.) "Three." (Point to the mother group.) "Oh, all right, three. But that's *it*!"
- *Olivia's mother says* "But that's *it*!" *She means that she will read only three books, and no more.*

Page 33

Text

- *How does Olivia wear her mother out?* (She wears her mother out because she is always busy. Also, she gets into trouble sometimes.)

Tell some things that happened in the story that could not happen in real life. (Pigs wear clothes, build sand castles, paint, and read.)

- *Let's read this page aloud together.*

National Parks

Pages 36–37

Access Core Content

Page 36

Teacher Note Pose the questions after you read the paragraph or page indicated.

Title

- *Let's read the title together:* National Parks. *We are going to read about some special parks called "national parks."* National *means they belong to everyone in the country. Say it with me:* national.

Photo

- (Point to photo.) *Look at the photo. This is the Grand Canyon. A canyon is a deep valley. Say it with me:* canyon. (Point to river.) *At the bottom is a river.*

Text

- *The Grand Canyon is made of many kinds of rocks. Let's point to the different colors of the rocks.* (Demonstrate pointing to various layers of rock.)
- *How deep is the Grand Canyon?* (about one mile deep) *Put your finger on the river at the bottom of the canyon. Now move it to the top of the canyon. That is one mile.*

Page 37

Photo

- Look at this photo. This is a national park, too. It has a deep canyon with a river at the bottom.

PARTNERS
Show your partner the river. Show your partner the boat. Would it be fun or scary to be in that boat?

Paragraph 1

- *Tell me the name of this national park.* (Big Bend National Park) *Let's say the name of the river in this park:* Rio Grande.
- *The river runs along the park's border. Say it with me:* border. Border *means "edge."* (Point to a classroom wall.) *The walls are the borders of our classroom.*
- *The river bends, like this.* (Demonstrate bending.) *Let's pretend to be the river. Our river will bend along the border of our classroom.* (Lead children in a line that "bends" as it reaches and turns a corner.)

Pages 36–37

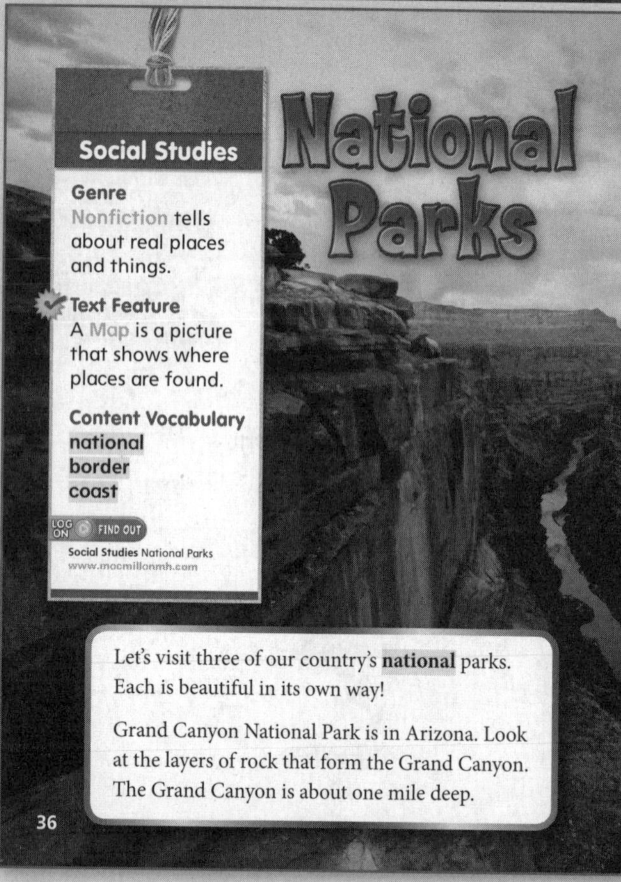
National Parks
Social Studies
Genre
Nonfiction tells about real places and things.
Text Feature
A Map is a picture that shows where places are found.
Content Vocabulary
national
border
coast
LOG ON FIND OUT
Social Studies National Parks
www.macmillanmh.com

Let's visit three of our country's **national** parks. Each is beautiful in its own way!

Grand Canyon National Park is in Arizona. Look at the layers of rock that form the Grand Canyon. The Grand Canyon is about one mile deep.

36

Pages 38–39

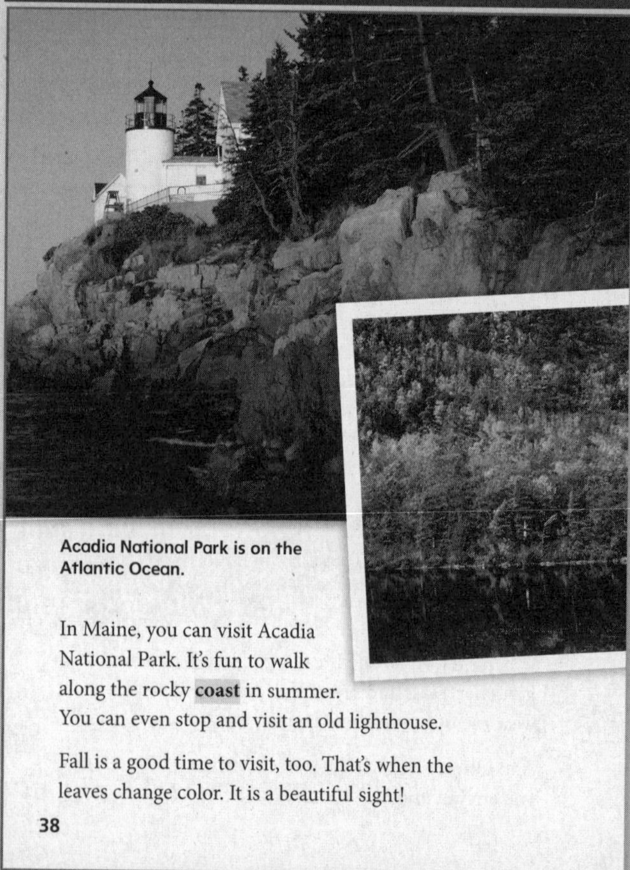

Acadia National Park is on the Atlantic Ocean.

In Maine, you can visit Acadia National Park. It's fun to walk along the rocky **coast** in summer. You can even stop and visit an old lighthouse.

Fall is a good time to visit, too. That's when the leaves change color. It is a beautiful sight!

38

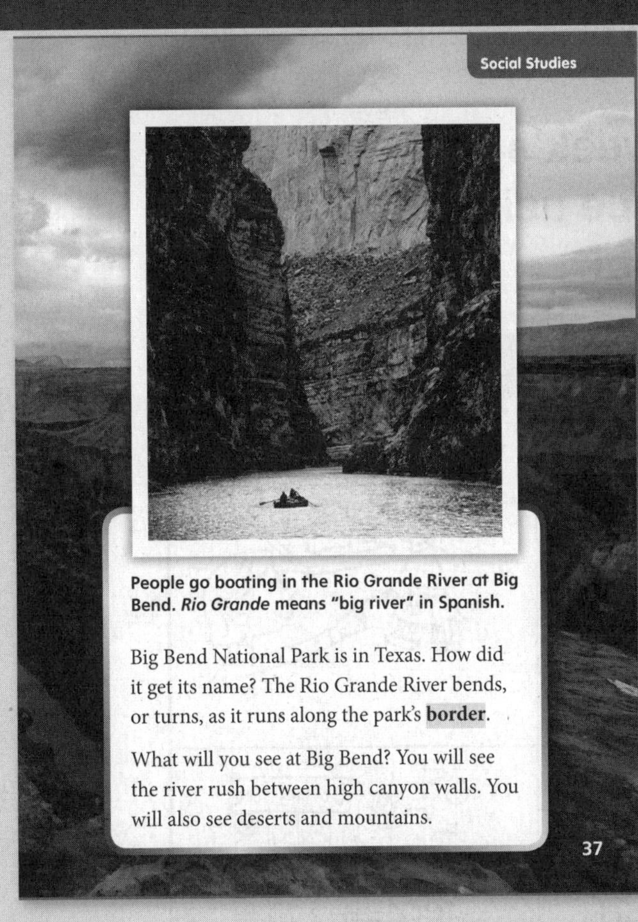

Social Studies

People go boating in the Rio Grande River at Big Bend. *Rio Grande* means "big river" in Spanish.

Big Bend National Park is in Texas. How did it get its name? The Rio Grande River bends, or turns, as it runs along the park's **border**.

What will you see at Big Bend? You will see the river rush between high canyon walls. You will also see deserts and mountains.

37

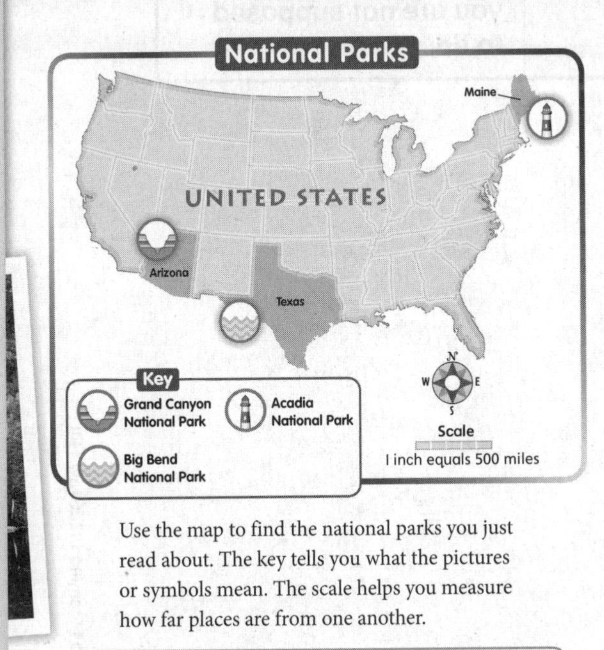

Use the map to find the national parks you just read about. The key tells you what the pictures or symbols mean. The scale helps you measure how far places are from one another.

Connect and Compare

- How does the key help you understand the map?
- What do the symbols on the key show?

39

Paragraph 2

- *Deserts are dry places. Mountains are high places. At Big Bend National Park, we can see deserts and mountains. What else can we see?* (a river)
- *Look at the photo of the river again. Listen as I read the words in the caption. Then we will say the words together.* (Read the caption once. Then read it slowly in phrases, pausing for children to repeat.)

Page 38

Photo

- (Point to the top photo.) *Look at this photo. There is water in the photo, but it is not a river. It is an ocean.* (Read photo caption aloud.)
- *Point to the house in the photo. This is a special kind of house called a lighthouse. Let's say it together:* lighthouse. *It has a big light to show boats where to go.*

Text

- *This is the coast.* (Run finger along coast in top photo.) *The coast is where the ocean meets the land. Say it with me:* coast. *There are rocks all along the coast in Maine.*
- (Point to small photo.) *This is the park in the fall. What happens to the leaves in the fall?* (They change color.)

Pretend you are at Acadia National Park. What would you like to do in the park? Tell your partner.

Page 39

Text

- *This is a map of the United States. Let's read the title together:* National Parks in the United States.
- *We read about three national parks. Let's find them on the map.* (Point to each state as you name it.)
- *Grand Canyon National Park is in the state of Arizona. Say it with me:* Arizona. *Point to Arizona on the map.*
- *Big Bend National Park is in the state of Texas. Where is Texas? Let's all point to Texas on the map and say:* Texas.
- *Point to the state of Maine on the map. Acadia National Park is in Maine. Remember, it is on the coast. Let's say the name of this state together:* Maine.

Name____

Use the word chart to study this week's vocabulary words. Write a sentence using each word in your writer's notebook.

Word	Context Sentence	Illustration
firm	Mom is <u>firm</u> about my bedtime.	
supposed	We are not <u>supposed</u> to feed the monkeys.	Do not feed **Name something that you are not supposed to do.**

© Macmillan/McGraw-Hill

Name ___________________________________

Read each question and prompt. Discuss the answers with your group. Use your Leveled Reader to find details to support your answers. Then write your answers on another sheet of paper.

1. Tell about the characters in the book you read. Are they friends?

2. The friends decide to be in a show. Give some details about the show.

3. Tell about something surprising that happens in the story.

4. What did you like best about this story? Share your ideas with the group.

5. Describe a show you have been in with your friends or family.

© Macmillan/McGraw-Hill

Whistle for Willie

Pages 46–47

Prior to reading the selection with children, they should have listened to the selection on **StudentWorks Plus**, the interactive eBook. In addition, selection vocabulary should have been pretaught using the **Visual Vocabulary Resources**.

Access Core Content

Teacher Note Pose the questions after you read the paragraph or page indicated.

Pages 46–47

Title and Illustration

- *Let's read the title together:* Whistle for Willie. *When you whistle, you make this sound.* (Demonstrate whistling.) *Say the word* whistle *with me:* whistle.

Practice whistling with your partner. If you do not know how to whistle, and your partner does, try to learn from your partner. If you know how to whistle and your partner does not, try to teach your partner.

- *I see a boy in the picture. Point to him. The boy's name is Peter. What is Peter doing?* (whistling)
- *I also see a dog in the picture. Point to him. The dog's name is Willie. Willie is Peter's dog. What does Willie have in his mouth—a ball or a piece of paper? (a piece of paper) We'll find out why later in the story.*
- *I see a tall brick wall.* (Point to it.) *It is the outside of a large building. Do you usually see tall brick buildings in the city or in the country?* (in the city) *Where do you think this story takes place?* (in the city)

Pages 46–47

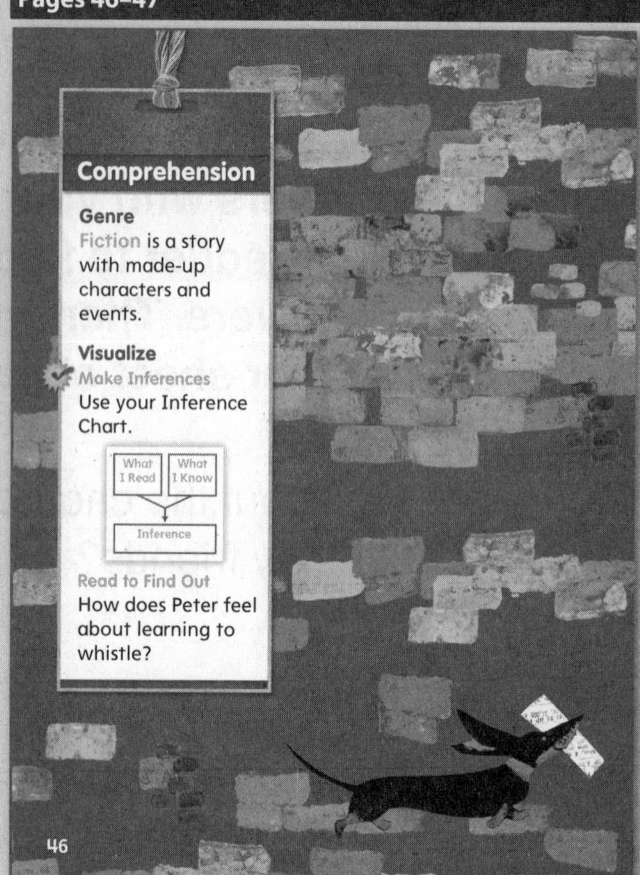

Comprehension
Genre
Fiction is a story with made-up characters and events.
Visualize
Make Inferences
Use your Inference Chart.
What I Read
What I Know
Inference
Read to Find Out
How does Peter feel about learning to whistle?
46

Pages 48–49

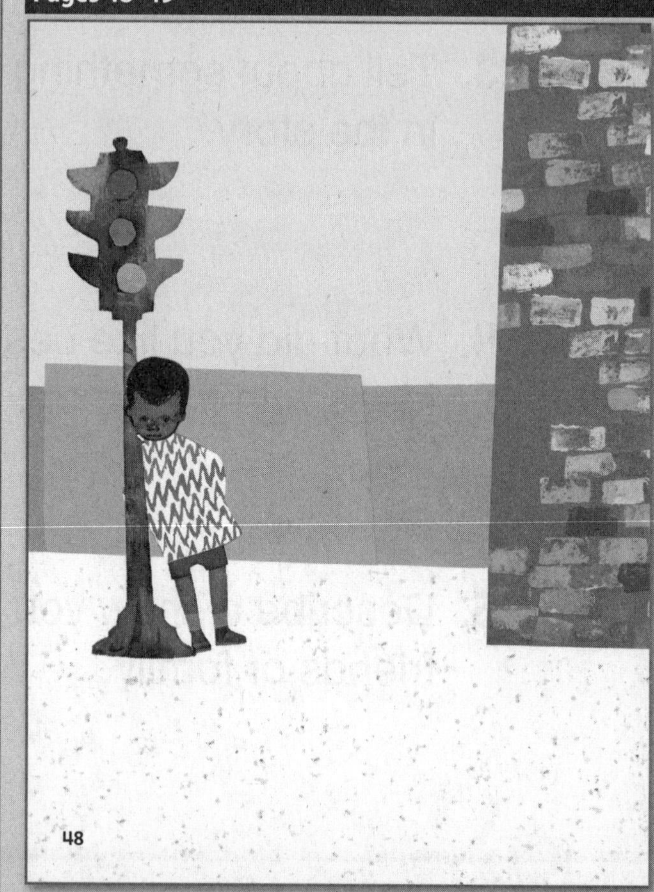

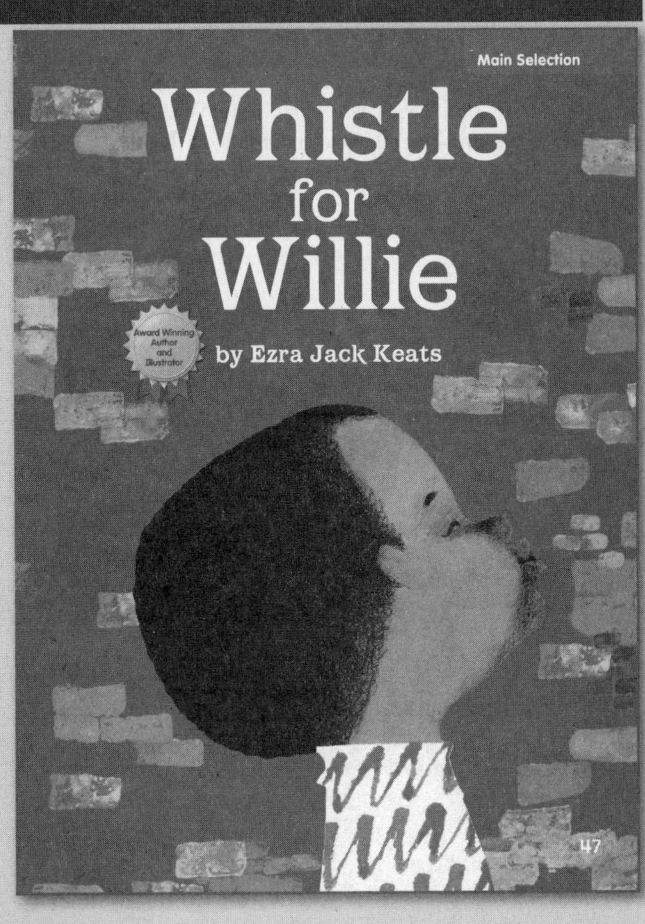

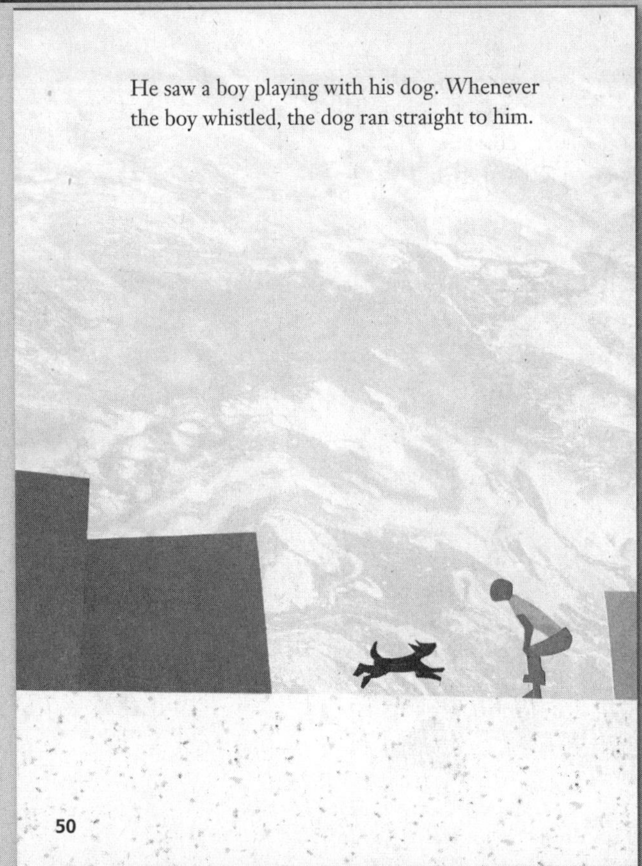

He saw a boy playing with his dog. Whenever the boy whistled, the dog ran straight to him.
50

Pages 48–49

Whole Page

- *Peter is leaning against a traffic light.* (Point to it.) *Does he look like he has somewhere to go, or is he just standing there?* (He is just standing there.) *Let's stand up and lean against our desks.* (demonstrate)
- *Look at Peter's face in this picture. Do you think he feels sad or happy?* (sad) *What are some things that could make a child feel this way?* (Question is open.)
- *This page tells why Peter is sad. Let's read it together:* Oh, how Peter wished he could whistle!

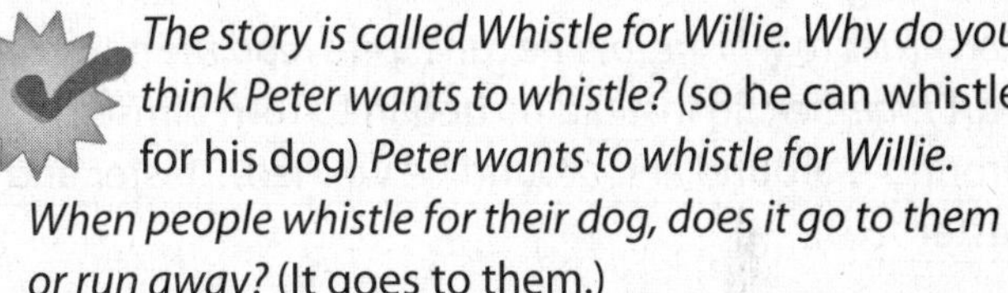
The story is called Whistle for Willie. Why do you think Peter wants to whistle? (so he can whistle for his dog) *Peter wants to whistle for Willie. When people whistle for their dog, does it go to them or run away?* (It goes to them.)

Seek Clarification

Some children may be confused by complex syntax. Encourage children to always seek clarification when they encounter a sentence that does not make sense to them. For example, *I don't understand "how Peter wished he could whistle."*

Page 50

Whole Page

- *Look at the picture. Is the dog running away from the boy or running to him?* (running to him)
- *Peter sees a boy playing with his dog. Can the other boy whistle?* (yes) *What happens when the other boy whistles?* (The dog runs to him.)
- *The dog runs straight to the boy. That means that the dog goes to the boy right away.*

Page 51

Whole Page

- *Peter tries to whistle, but he can't. Let's read the next part together:* So instead he began to turn himself around—around and around he whirled...faster and faster....
- *The author tells us that Peter turned himself around and around. Then the author uses another word that means almost the same thing as* turned around and around. *What is the word?* (whirled)
- *Look at the picture. Show me what Peter does with his arms when he whirls.* (Children should hold out their arms.)
- *The author doesn't tell us why Peter starts to whirl around. We have to figure it out for ourselves. Let's think about what we know. Does Peter want to whistle?* (yes) *Can he do it when he tries?* (no)

How do you feel when you can't do something you really want to do? (upset, frustrated) *Is Peter good at whirling?* (yes) *Do you think he likes it?* (yes) *Why do you think he starts whirling?* (to make himself feel better; because it is fun for him)

-

Directionality

Ask children to place their finger where you start reading (top left). Ask where you finish reading on this page (bottom right).

Pages 50–51

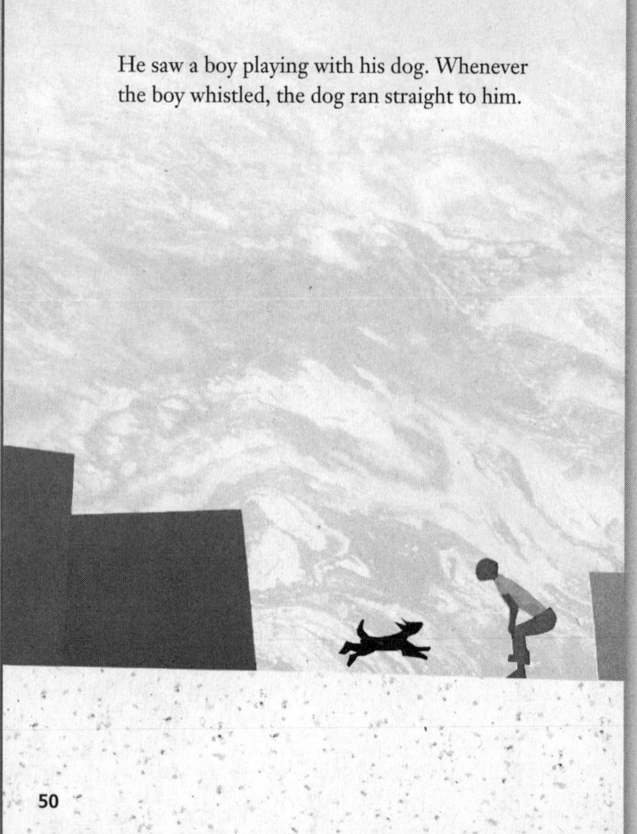
He saw a boy playing with his dog. Whenever the boy whistled, the dog ran straight to him.
50

Pages 52–53

When he stopped
everything turned
down ...
and up ...
52

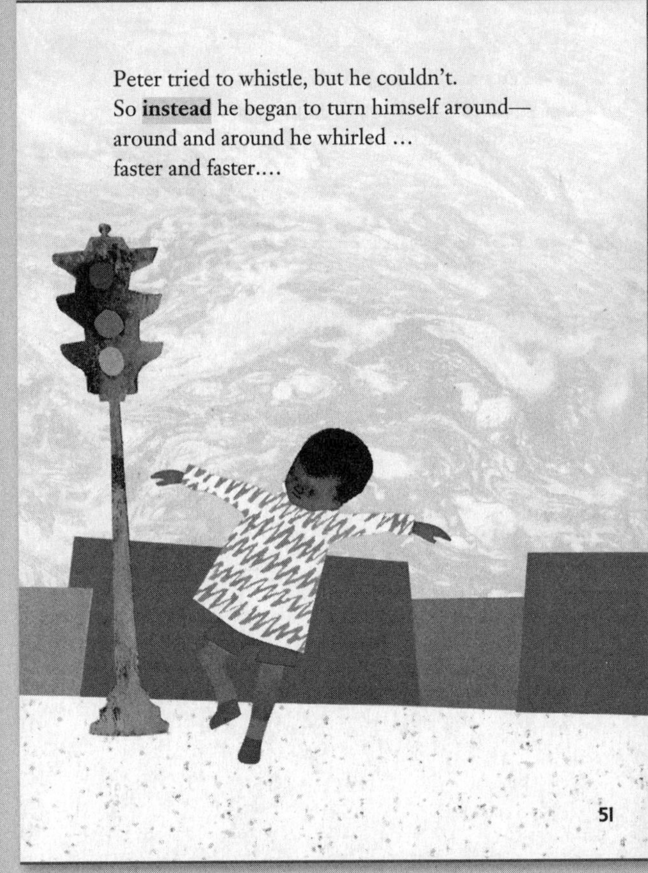
Peter tried to whistle, but he couldn't.
So instead he began to turn himself around—
around and around he whirled ...
faster and faster....
51

and up ...
and down ...
and around
and around.
53

Pages 52–53

Text and Illustrations

- *When Peter stops whirling, everything feels like it's still moving.*
- Look at the pictures of Peter. *Let's stand up and pretend to be Peter. First, let's bend forward like him.* (demonstrate) *Then let's bend backward like him.* (demonstrate) *It's hard to get our balance.*
- *Look at page 52. Pretend you are Peter. The sidewalk seems to be going down.* (Point to Peter, and then move your finger down toward the traffic light.)
- *Now look at the picture on the other page. Point to Peter, and then move your finger up toward the traffic light. Which way does the sidewalk go now?* (up)
- *Now look at the traffic lights. They look like they are bouncing off the pole, like balls.* (Point to them.) *Are they really doing that?* (no) *That's just the way they look to Peter.*

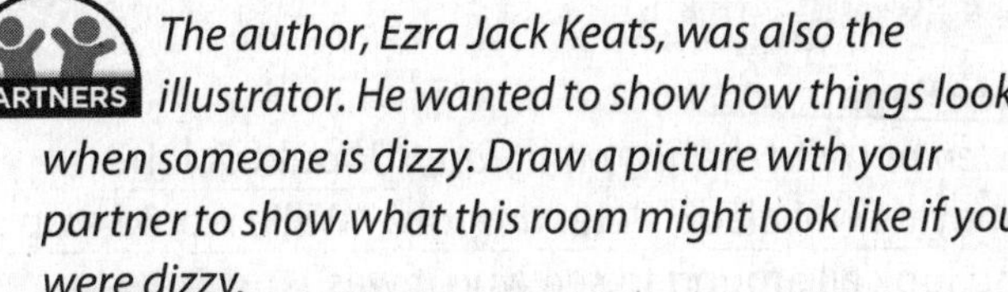
PARTNERS
The author, Ezra Jack Keats, was also the illustrator. He wanted to show how things look when someone is dizzy. Draw a picture with your partner to show what this room might look like if you were dizzy.

- *I am going to say some words. Clap when you hear the word that tells how Peter feels:* sleepy, sad, dizzy. (Children clap after you say *dizzy*.) *Peter feels dizzy from all that whirling!*

Page 54

Whole Page

- *This is a carton.* (Point to the carton.) *Say it with me:* carton. *Another word for* carton *is* box. *The carton is on the sidwalk. Point to the sidewalk.*
- Let's read this page together: Peter saw his dog, Willie, coming. Quick as a wink, he hid in an empty carton lying in the side walk.
- *I am going to wink.* (Demonstrate winking.) *Peter got into the box quick as a wink. Did he get in slowly or suddenly? Why?* (suddenly, because a wink is something that happens very fast)
- *Show me that you understand* quick as a wink. *First, raise your hand slowly. Now, raise your hand quick as a wink.*

Think about times you've hid from others. Why do you think Peter decides to hide from Willie? (to surprise him; to play a game with him)

Page 55

Whole Page

- *Listen as I read the first paragraph:* "Wouldn't it be funny if I whistled?" Peter thought. "Willie would stop and look all around to see who it was."
- *Now let's read the second paragraph together:* Peter tried again to whistle—but still he couldn't. So Willie just walked on. *Did Willie stop and look around?* (no) *He just kept walking.*
- *Now let's role-play what happens. I will call on two children at a time. One child will pretend to be Willie. Willie will start walking around the room. The other child will try to whistle. Willie will just keep walking.*
- *How do you think Peter feels now?* (sadder, discouraged, more determined to learn)

Pages 54–55

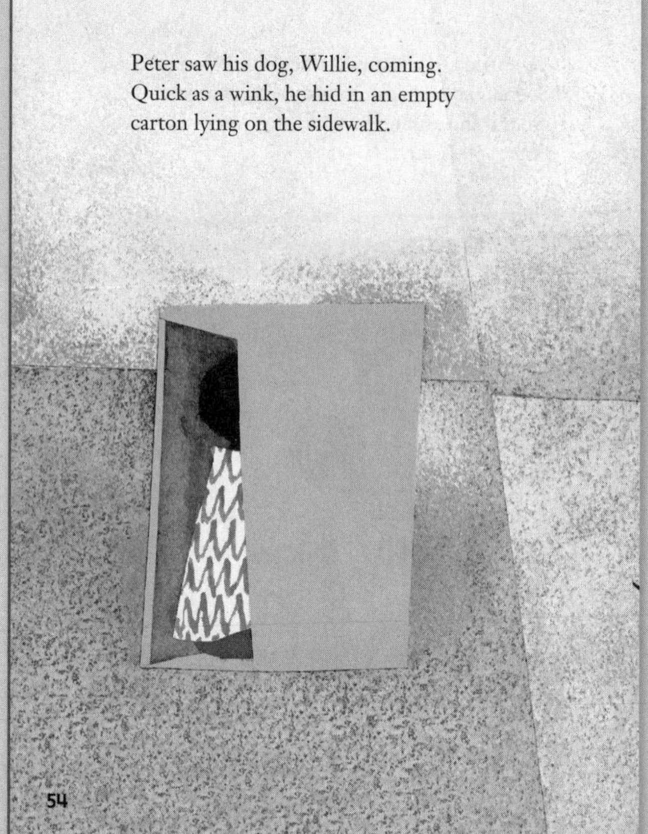

Pages 56–57

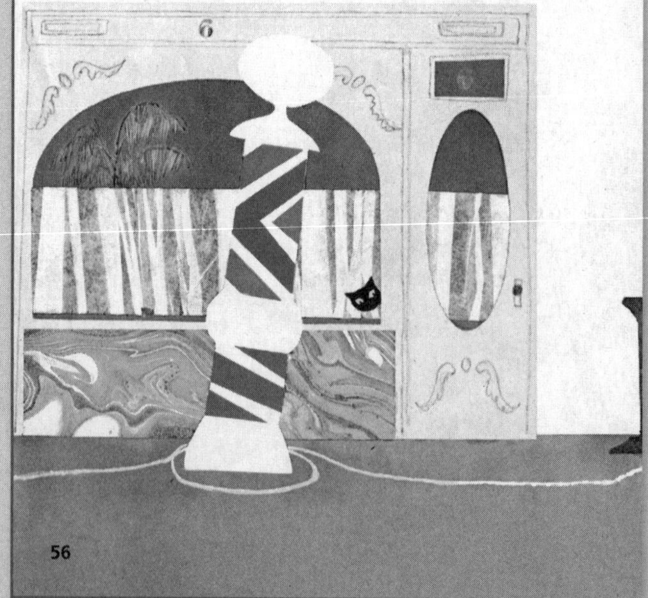

Peter got out of the carton
and started home.
On the way he took some
colored chalks out of his pocket
and drew a long, long line
right up to his door.
6
56

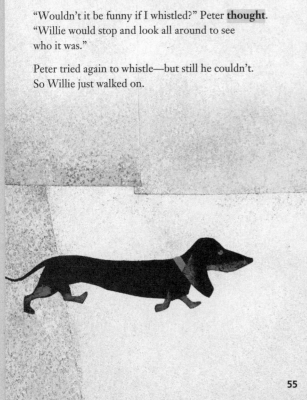

"Wouldn't it be funny if I whistled?" Peter **thought**. "Willie would stop and look all around to see who it was."

Peter tried again to whistle—but still he couldn't. So Willie just walked on.

He stood there and tried to whistle again.
He blew till his cheeks were tired.
But **nothing** happened.

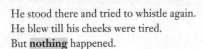

Pages 56–57

Whole Page

- *Peter takes some colored chalks out of his pocket. What does he do with them?* (He draws a line all the way to his door?) *Why do you think he does that?* (because it's fun; because it makes him feel better)

- *Look at the picture on both pages. What colors did Peter use?* (yellow, pink, white) *Use your finger to trace what Peter drew.*

Page 57

Whole Page

- *Peter doesn't give up. He keeps trying to whistle. He tries so long that his cheeks get tired! Let's keep trying to whistle like Peter does. Now let's stop. Are your cheeks' tired like Peter's?* (Answers will vary.)

Why does Peter keep trying to whistle even though he cannot? Talk about your ideas with your partner. (Learning to whistle is important to Peter. He really wants to learn.)

Pages 58–59

Illustration

- *Look at the picture. Point to the pretty wallpaper. Peter is inside the house now. What is he wearing?* (his father's hat) *He is looking at himself in the mirror. Say it with me:* mirror. *Point to the mirror.*

Paragraph, Choral Reading

- *Let's read the paragraph together:* He went into his house and put on his father's hat to make himself feel more grown-up. He looked into the mirror to practice whistling. Still no whistle!

- *The author does not tell us what the hat has to do with whistling. Let's try to figure it out.*

We read that the hat makes Peter feel more _______. (grown-up) *What do we know about grown-ups and whistling?* (Lots of grown-ups can whistle.) *So Peter might think that if he were more grown-up, he could* ______. (whistle)

Pages 58–59

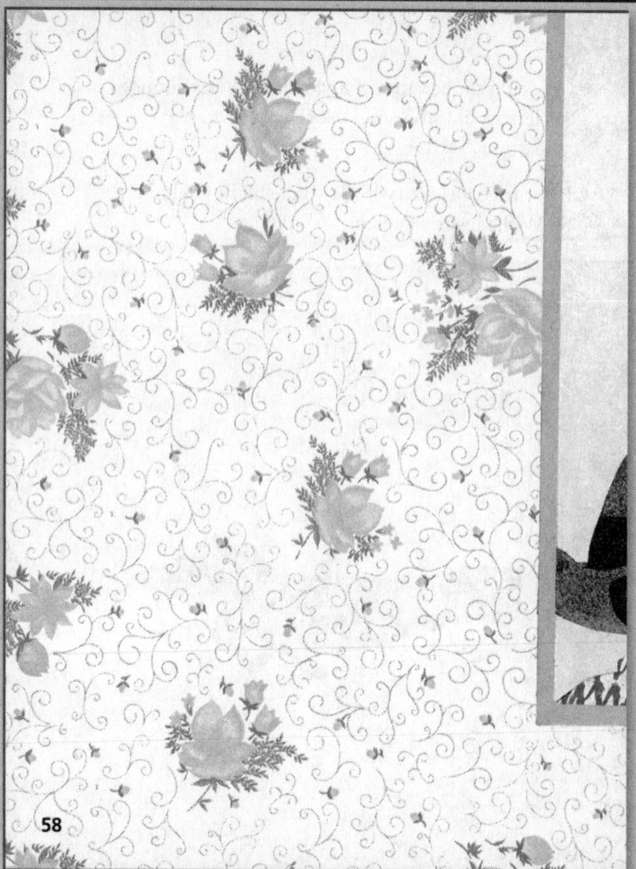

Pages 60–61

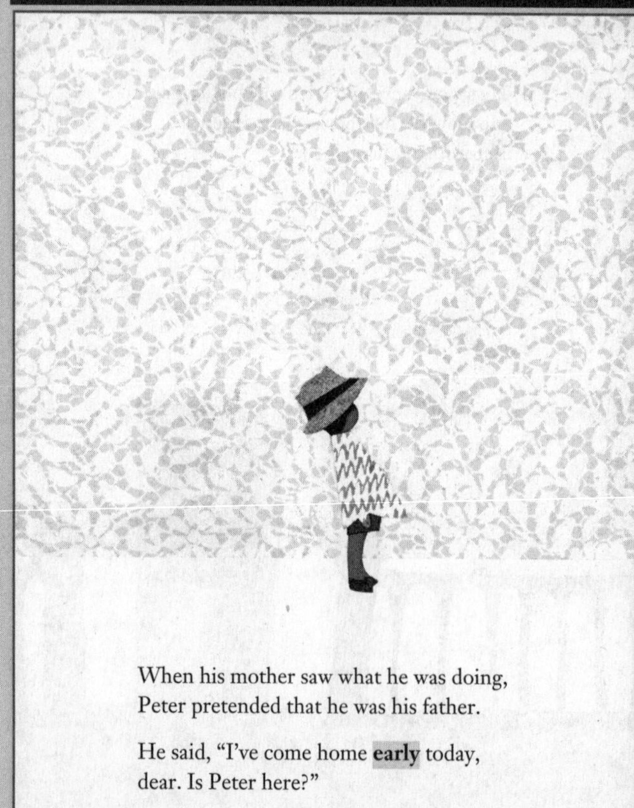

When his mother saw what he was doing, Peter pretended that he was his father.
He said, "I've come home **early** today, dear. Is Peter here?"
60

His mother answered, "Why no, he's outside with Willie."
"Well, I'll go out and look for them," said Peter.
61

Pages 60–61

Whole Page

- *Peter asks his mother:* "Is Peter here?" *Why does he ask her that?* (because he is pretending to be his father)
- *Do you think Peter really fools his mom?* (no) *Do you think she really thinks Peter is his father?* (no) *Putting on a hat would not make a boy look like a grown-up man.*
- *Peter's mother answers as if she were talking to Peter's father. Why do you think she does that?* (She is pretending with Peter.)

Act out this scene with a partner. Take turns being Peter and his mother and saying their lines. When you say Peter's lines, try to use a man's voice.

Request Assistance

Remind children of expressions they can use to request assistance from the teacher or their partners, such as *Can you show me in the picture? Can you explain this part of the story?*

Pages 62–63

Illustrations

- *Peter is outside now, wearing his dad's hat. Let's pretend to do the first thing Peter does. Look at the picture on page 62 to see how Peter puts his feet one in front of the other in a line.*
- *Now, look down at the floor. Pretend you see a crack or line on the floor. Walk along it. Put one foot in front of the other the way Peter does. Is it hard to stay on the line?* (yes)

Text

- *Let's read the paragraph together:* First he walked along a crack in the sidewalk. Then he tried to run away from his shadow.
- *When it's a sunny day, we have a shadow. Look at the blue shape in the picture.* (Point to it.) *This is supposed to be Peter's shadow.*

Pages 62–63

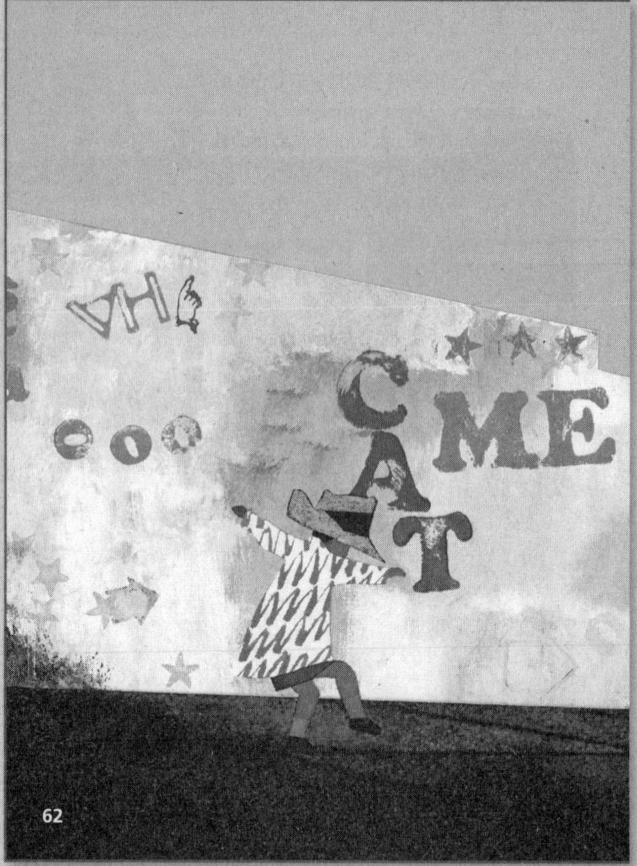

Pages 64–65

He jumped off his shadow,
but when he landed they were
together again.
64

First he walked **along** a crack in the sidewalk. Then he tried to run away from his shadow.

63

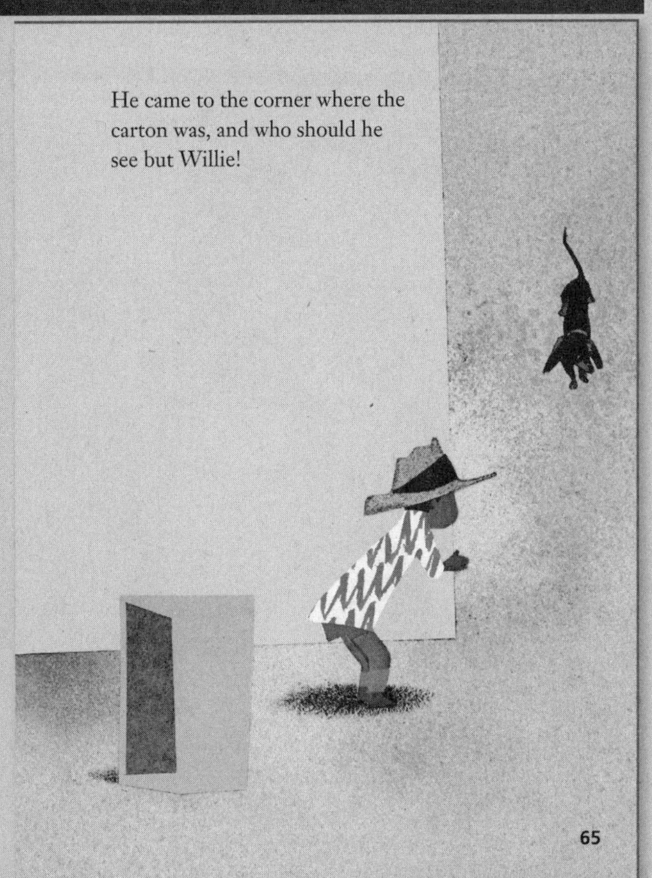
He came to the corner where the carton was, and who should he see but Willie!

65

Page 64

Whole Page

- *Look at the picture. It shows Peter jumping up. He is trying to get off his shadow. Is he able to?* (no) *Then he comes down and lands. That means that he comes back to the land, or ground.*

Think about all the different kinds of things Peter has done in this story. He found lots of ways to have fun by himself. Tell your partner about things you enjoy doing when friends aren't around.

Page 65

Whole Page

- *Let's read the page together:* He came to the corner where the carton was, and who should he see but Willie!
- *Let's point to the corner in the picture.* (Point to it.) *Say it with me:* corner. *Now let's point to a corner of our room.*
- *Peter did not know that Willie would be there. Do you think that Peter is surprised and happy or sad and mad?* (surprised and happy)

Page 66

Whole Page

- *Look at the picture. What do you think Peter is doing?* (hiding from Willie)
- *Listen as I read the first sentence:* Peter scrambled under the carton. *That means that he moved quickly. Why do you think he moved quickly?* (because he wanted to get in before Willie saw him)
- *Let's read the rest of the page together: He blew and blew and blew. Suddenly—out came a real whistle!*

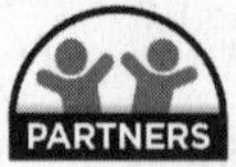
PARTNERS

How do you think Peter feels after he finally whistles? Tell your partner. (happy, surprised, excited, pleased) *Talk with your partner about a time that you were able to do something after trying really hard.*

Page 67

Whole Page

- *Look at the picture. Peter is still under the carton. He has just whistled. What is Willie doing? (*He is looking around to see who whistled.)
- *Let's read the page together:* Willie stopped and looked around to see who it was.
- *Peter was under the carton once before in the story. Was he able to whistle then?* (no) *So Willie didn't stop and look around. He just kept walking.*

Pages 66–67

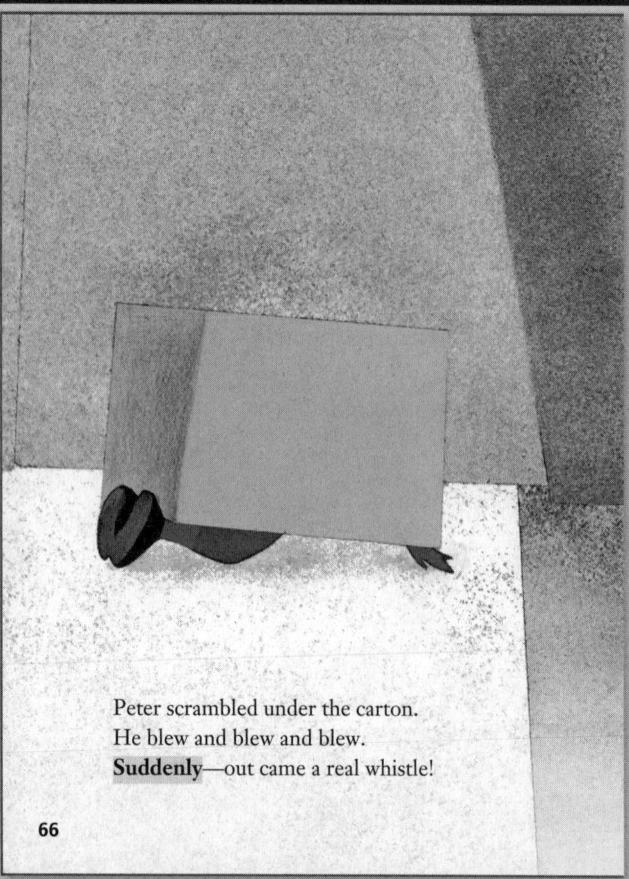
Peter scrambled under the carton.
He blew and blew and blew.
Suddenly—out came a real whistle!
66

Pages 68–69

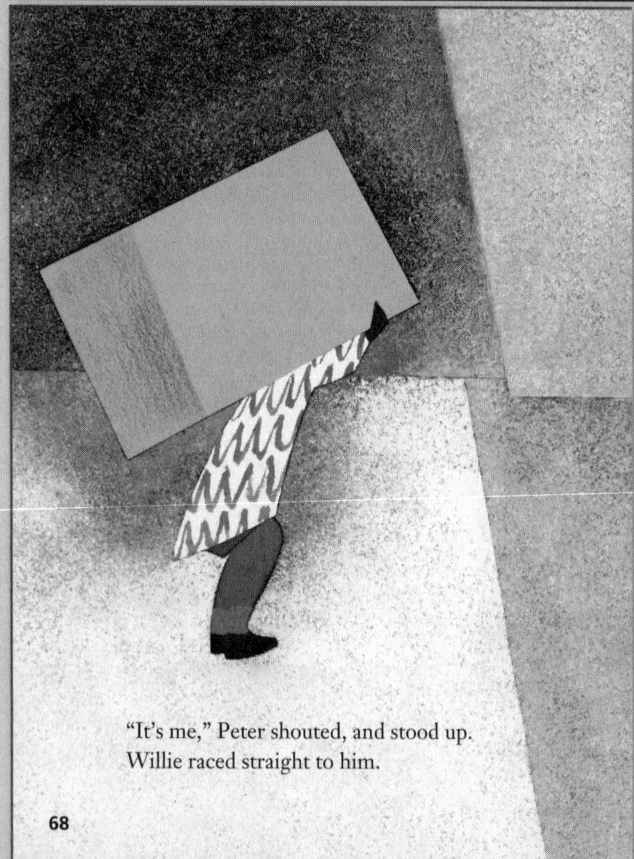
"It's me," Peter shouted, and stood up.
Willie raced straight to him.
68

Willie stopped and looked around to see who it was.
67

69

Pages 68–69

Text and Illustrations

- *Let's read this page together in an excited voice:* "It's me," Peter shouted, and stood up. Willie raced straight to him.
- *Look at Willie. What is he doing?* (running to Peter) *Can Willie see Peter's face?* (Question is open.) Would Willie be able to tell that it is Peter from his voice? (yes)

Pages 70–71

Whole Page

- *Look at the pictures. Why is Peter whistling.* (to show his parents) *His mother is clapping. How do you think she feels?* (proud, happy)
- *How does Peter feel?* (happy, proud) *Why?* (because he learned something that was hard for him to learn)

PARTNERS *You and your partner will take turns being Peter and one of his parents. Peter has just come home to show his parents that he can whistle. What might Peter say when he comes in? What might Peter and his parents say after he whistles?*

Pages 70–71

Pages 72–73

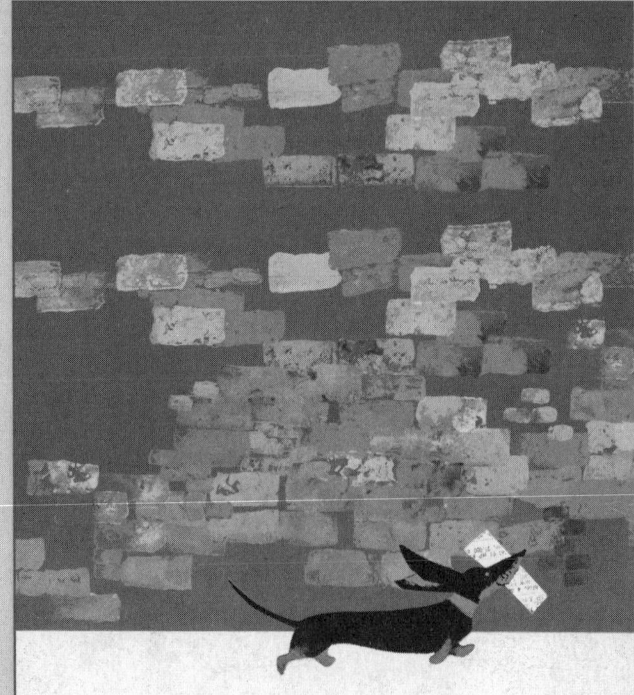

Peter's mother asked him and Willie to go on an **errand** to the grocery store.
72

Peter ran home to show his father and mother what he could do. They loved Peter's whistling. So did Willie.

71

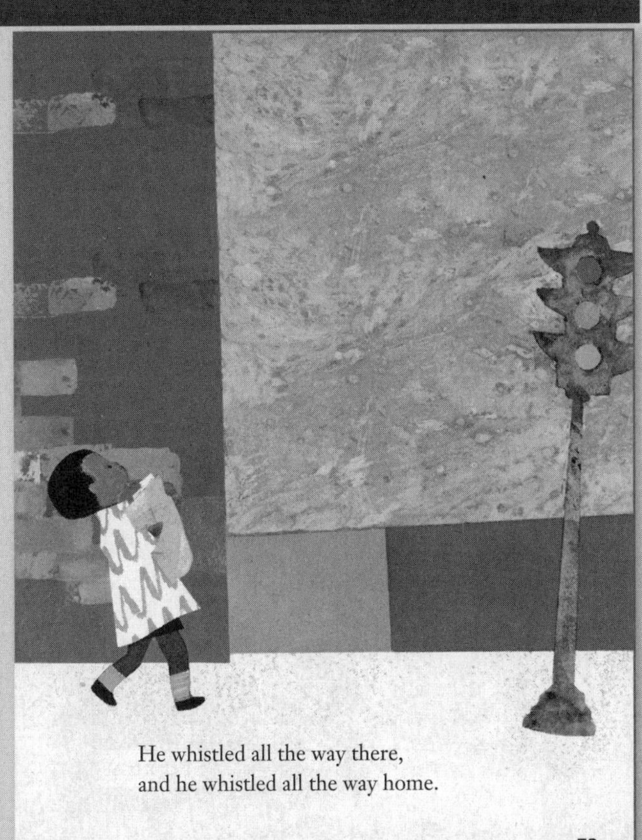

He whistled all the way there, and he whistled all the way home.

73

Pages 72–73

Whole Page

- *An errand is a little job. What kind of errand might Peter's mother ask him to do at the grocery store?* (get milk, buy food)
- *Look at the picture. Willie is carrying the piece of paper we saw on the first page of the story! What is Peter carrying?* (a bag of things from the store)
- *Let's read together the ending of the story:* He whistled all the way there, and he whistled all the way home.

Peter sure is whistling a lot. Why do you think he is whistling so much? (Peter is happy about learning to whistle.)

- *Peter kept trying. If we want to do something badly, we should not give up. We should keep trying.*

Seeing-Eye Dogs

Pages 76–77

Access Core Content

Teacher Note Pose the questions after you read the paragraph or page indicated.

Page 76

Title and Text

- *We just read about a pet dog. What was its name?* (Willie) *Now we're going to learn about dogs that have a special job. The title of this article is* Seeing-Eye Dogs.
- *Listen as I read the paragraph aloud.*
- *Seeing eye-dogs help people. Do they help people who can't see or people who can't hear?* (people who can't see)

Photo

- *Look at the picture of the seeing-eye dog. It is wearing a harness. Say it with me:* harness. *The top part is like a handle.* (Point to it.) *A person who can't see holds onto it. That way, the dog can lead the person.*

Page 77

Paragraph 1 and List

- *Another name for a seeing-eye dog is* guide dog. *A seeing-eye dog guides people, or shows them where to go. Point to the list at the top of the page.*
- *The list tells the traits of a good guide dog, or what a good guide dog should be like. Listen as I read the list aloud.*
- *Number five says that the dog must be in good shape. Would a dog that is in good shape be healthy or sick?* (healthy) *Would it be weak or strong?* (strong)

PARTNERS *Talk with a partner about the list. Why is it important for the dog to like people and be kind? Why is it important for the dog to be smart?* (Questions are open.)

Pages 76–77

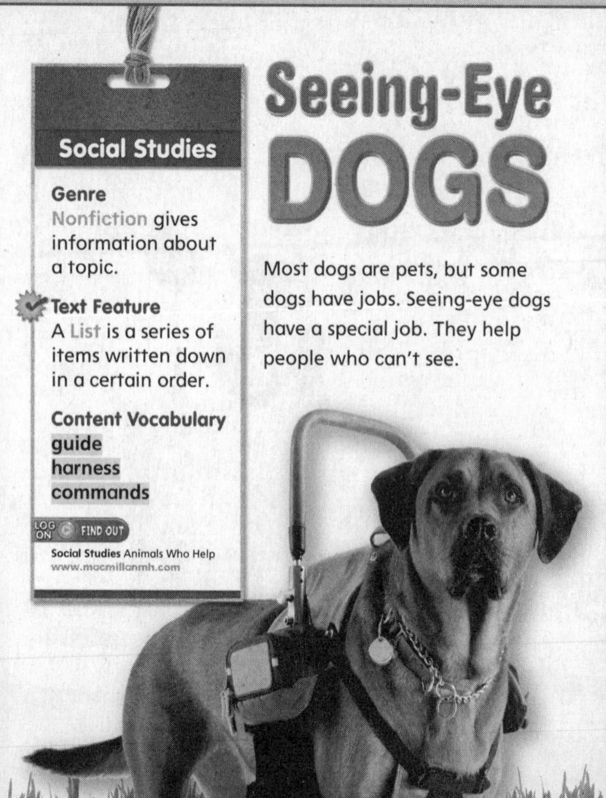

Social Studies

Genre
Nonfiction gives information about a topic.

Text Feature
A List is a series of items written down in a certain order.

Content Vocabulary
guide
harness
commands

LOG ON FIND OUT
Social Studies Animals Who Help
www.macmillanmh.com

Seeing-Eye DOGS

Most dogs are pets, but some dogs have jobs. Seeing-eye dogs have a special job. They help people who can't see.

76

Pages 78–79

If a puppy shows it can learn fast, it will go to a special school. That is when the real training starts!

At school the dogs learn a lot. They get used to wearing a **harness**. They learn how to lead someone on a sidewalk. They learn how to cross a street and ride a bus. When they finish school, they can follow 20 **commands**!

78

Social Studies

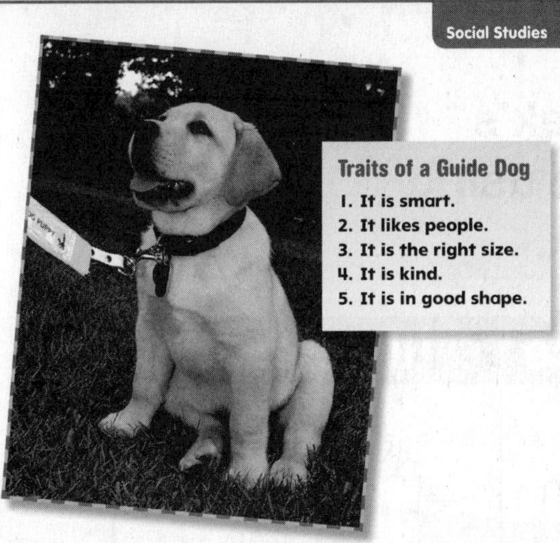

Traits of a Guide Dog
1. It is smart.
2. It likes people.
3. It is the right size.
4. It is kind.
5. It is in good shape.

Seeing-eye dogs are also called **guide** dogs. These dogs guide, or lead, blind people. The dogs can help them get anyplace they want.

How do guide dogs learn this job? Training starts when they are six weeks old. They go to live with a puppy raiser. The puppy raiser takes care of them for a year.

77

Next the dog meets its new owner. They must learn how to work with each other. They train together at the school for four weeks. Then it is time to go home. They are now a team!

Connect and Compare

- What kind of guide dog do you think Willie would make?
- What did you learn from the list?

79

Paragraph 2

- *A puppy raiser teaches puppies to be guide dogs. Say it with me:* puppy raiser. *The puppies live with the puppy raiser for one year. Do the puppies stay with the puppy raiser for many years or for one year?* (for one year)

Page 78

Whole Page

- *The smartest dogs go to a special school for training. Listen as I read the second paragraph aloud.*
- *At school, the dogs get used to wearing a harness. Point to the harness on this page. Now pretend that you are walking with a guide dog. Show me how you would hold on to the harness.*
- *Look at this picture.* (Point to the picture on the left.) *The man is teaching the dog to be a guide dog? Why do you think the man is wearing something over his eyes?* (He is pretending that he can't see. He is teaching the dog how to guide.)

Page 79

Whole Page

- *Listen as I read this page aloud.*
- *The dog gets training, or is taught, at the school. Who else gets training there?* (the owner) *The dog and the owner get trained together. They learn how to be a _______.* (team)
- *Look at the picture on this page. Is the dog working or playing?* (working) *The dog must keep the woman safe.*

Name ____________________

Use the word chart to study this week's vocabulary words. Write a sentence using each word in your writer's notebook.

Word	Context Sentence	Illustration
errand ______	Dad and I went on an errand to the store.	What kinds of errands do you go on?
suddenly ______	A chipmunk suddenly popped out of its hole.	

© Macmillan/McGraw-Hill

Name ______________________________

Book Talk

Read each question and prompt. Discuss the answers with your group. Use your Leveled Reader to find details to support your answers. Then write your answers on another sheet of paper.

1. Describe a child and a teacher in the book you read.

2. What does the child want to learn to do? How does the teacher help?

3. Who else helps? Name other characters who help the child.

4. Talk about how hard the child tries. Does the child succeed?

5. Has someone helped you learn to do something new? Share your experience.

© Macmillan/McGraw-Hill

Cool Jobs

Pages 86–87

Prior to reading the selection with children, they should have listened to the selection on **StudentWorks Plus**, the interactive eBook. In addition, selection vocabulary should have been pretaught using the **Visual Vocabulary Resources**.

Access Core Content

Teacher Note Pose the questions after you read the paragraph or page indicated.

Page 86

Title and First Heading

- *The title of this article is* Cool Jobs. *The word* cool *can have different meanings.* Cool *can be the opposite of* warm. Cool *can also mean "excellent" or "special" This article tells about jobs that are special.*
- *Look at the heading.* (Point to it.) *It names the first cool job the article will tell about:* Zoo Dentist. *Ordinary dentists fix people's teeth. What do you think a zoo dentist fixes?* (animals' teeth)

Text and Photo

- *Let's read the first page together.*
- *Zoo animals take care of the teeth of many different kinds of animals. What animal do you see in the picture?* (a tiger) *What other animals does this article mention?* (alligator, elephant)
- *Zoo dentists are not very different from ordinary dentists. They pull teeth. They might even might pull an elephant's tusk. A tusk is one of the two long teeth you can see when an elephant closes its mouth. Zoo dentists also clean teeth. What do they fill?* (holes)

Page 87

Whole Page

- *Zoo dentists work on wild animals. What do they give the animals so they won't bite—candy or medicine?* (medicine) *What does the medicine do to the animals?* (puts them to sleep)

Pages 86–87

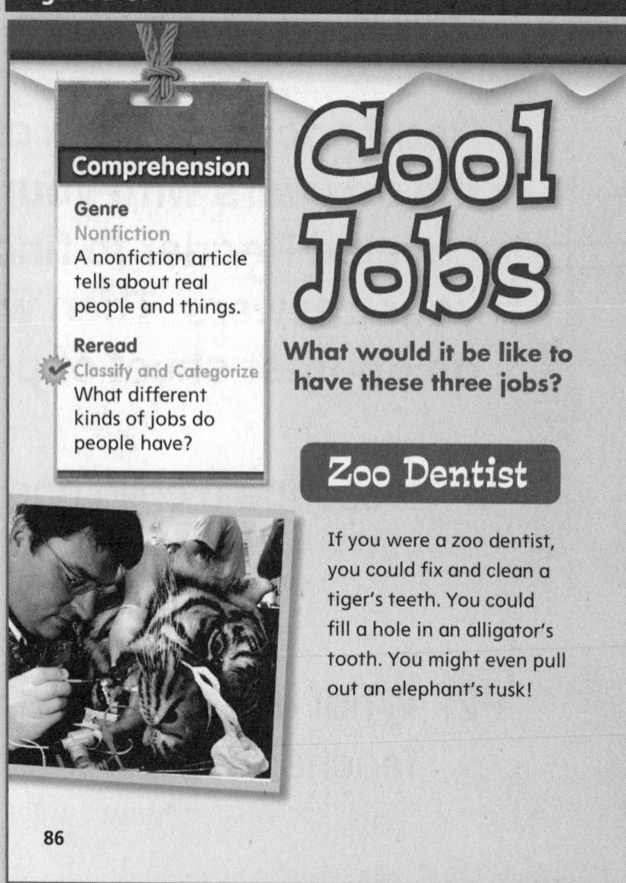

Comprehension
Genre
Nonfiction
A nonfiction article tells about real people and things.
Reread
Classify and Categorize
What different kinds of jobs do people have?
Cool Jobs
What would it be like to have these three jobs?
Zoo Dentist
If you were a zoo dentist, you could fix and clean a tiger's teeth. You could fill a hole in an alligator's tooth. You might even pull out an elephant's tusk!
86

Pages 88–89

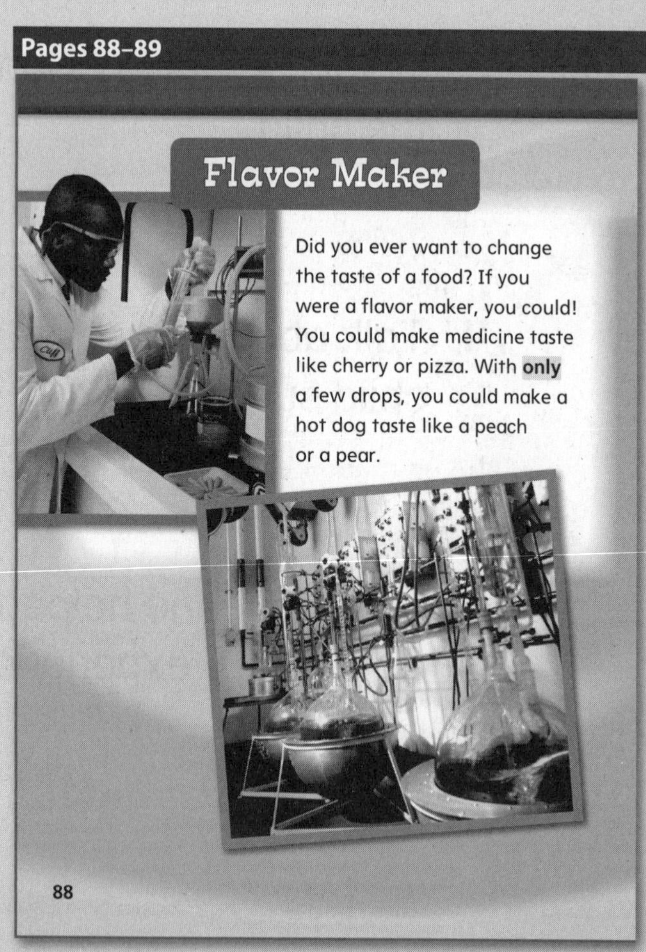

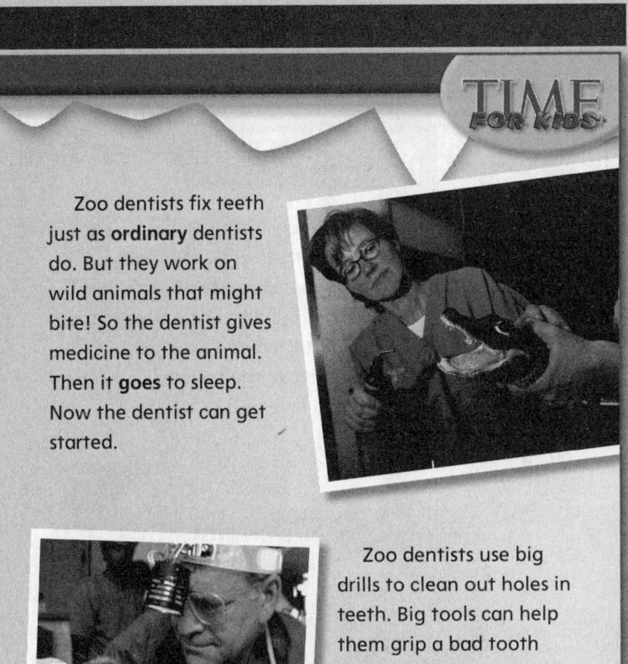

TIME FOR KIDS

Zoo dentists fix teeth just as **ordinary** dentists do. But they work on wild animals that might bite! So the dentist gives medicine to the animal. Then it **goes** to sleep. Now the dentist can get started.

Zoo dentists use big drills to clean out holes in teeth. Big tools can help them grip a bad tooth and pull it out. If it's a lion or bear tooth, that can be a big job!

87

TIME FOR KIDS

Flavor makers work in a lab. They use chemicals to make flavors. Their best tools are their noses and mouths. They do a lot of tasting and smelling!

Flavor makers help make a lot of tasty food! Can you think of a new flavor for a food that you like?

Cheese-flavored crackers

Cherry-flavored medicine

Fruit-flavored cereal

89

- *Look at the woman dentist. She is holding a tool called a drill. Does the drill pull teeth or clean out holes in teeth?* (clean out holes in teeth)

People in other jobs also work with animals? Let's name some of these jobs. (vet, animal trainer, cowboy, circus performer)

Page 88

Heading 2 and Text

- *The heading for this part of the article is* Flavor Maker.
- *Let's read the first two sentences together to find out what a flavor maker does:* Did you ever want to change the taste of a food? If you were a flavor maker, you could! *What can a flavor maker change?* (the taste of a food)
- *Flavor makers can make medicine taste like cherries or pizza? Why might they do that?* (so the medicine will taste good and be easy to take) *Would you want a hot dog to taste like a peach?* (Answers may vary.)

Photo

- *Flavor makers work in a lab.* Lab *is short for* laboratory. *The man in the picture is making a new flavor.*

Page 89

Whole Page

- *Flavor makers must taste the flavors they make. What else must they do?* (smell them) *Their mouths and noses are their best ______.* (tools)
- *Pretend that you are a flavor maker. Pretend that your hand is a bowl with a new flavor you have made. Show how you would try out the flavor.* (Children act out tasting and smelling a pretend food.)
- *Look at the pictures on the page. As I name each item, raise your hand if you have ever tried it:* cheese-flavored crackers, cherry-flavored medicine, fruit-flavored cereal. (Responses will vary.)

Think of a food that you and your partner both like. Pretend that you are both flavor makers. You are having a meeting about this food. Talk about new flavors you could make for the food.

Page 90

Whole Page

- *The heading for this part of the article is* Beekeeper. *Let's read together what a beekeeper does:* Bees make honey. A beekeeper helps the bees do their job.
- *Beekeepers build hives for bees to live in. What do the beekeepers use to build the hives?* (wood) *Point to the wooden hives on this page.*

Bees make something we eat: honey. What other animals make foods that people eat? What do the animals make? (Hens make eggs. Cows make milk.)

Page 91

Paragraph 1

- *Bees can sting people.* (Jab at your hand with a finger to pantomime stinging.) *Ouch!*
- *Beekeepers wear special clothes to keep the bees from stinging them. They wear a hood, which is like a hat. Point to the beekeeper's hood on page 90. What is the beekeeper wearing on his hands?* (gloves) *What do beekeepers wear over their faces?* (nets)

Paragraph 2 and Photos

- *Look at the picture at the top of the page. The beekeeper is putting smoke in the hive. Why does he do this?* (so the bees will leave and he can get the honey)
- *Echo the last two sentences after me:* It can take a lot of work to get honey. But the end is always sweet! *What does the beekeeper get at the end of his job?* (honey) *Is honey sweet or sour?* (sweet) *That's why the end is always sweet!*
- *Look at the picture of the girl. What is she eating?* (bread with honey) *Raise your hand if you have eaten honey on bread. How else have you eaten honey?* (Responses will vary.)

Seek Clarification

Some children may be confused by complex syntax. Encourage children to always seek clarification when they encounter a sentence that does not make sense to them. For example, *I don't understand this sentence.*

Pages 90–91

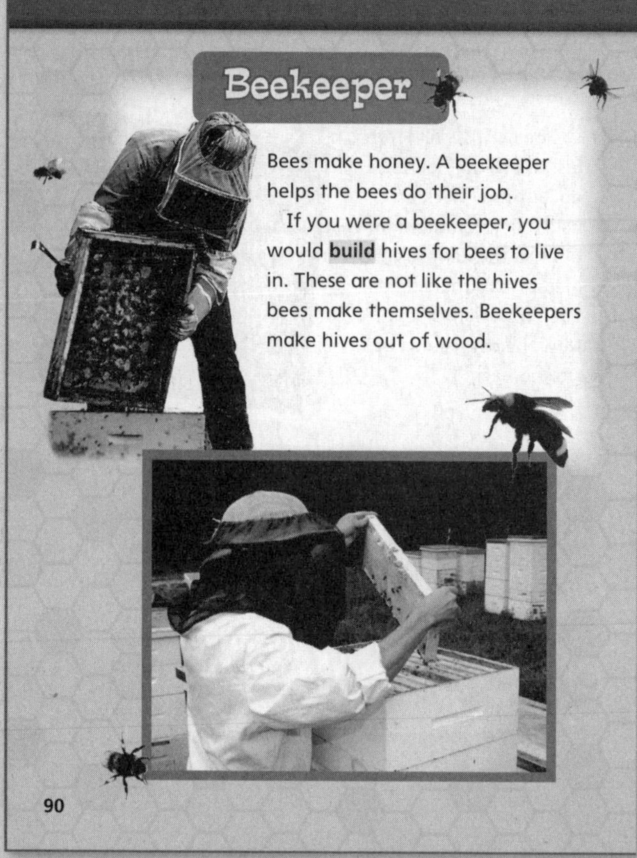

Beekeeper
Bees make honey. A beekeeper helps the bees do their job.
If you were a beekeeper, you would **build** hives for bees to live in. These are not like the hives bees make themselves. Beekeepers make hives out of wood.
90

Pages 92–93

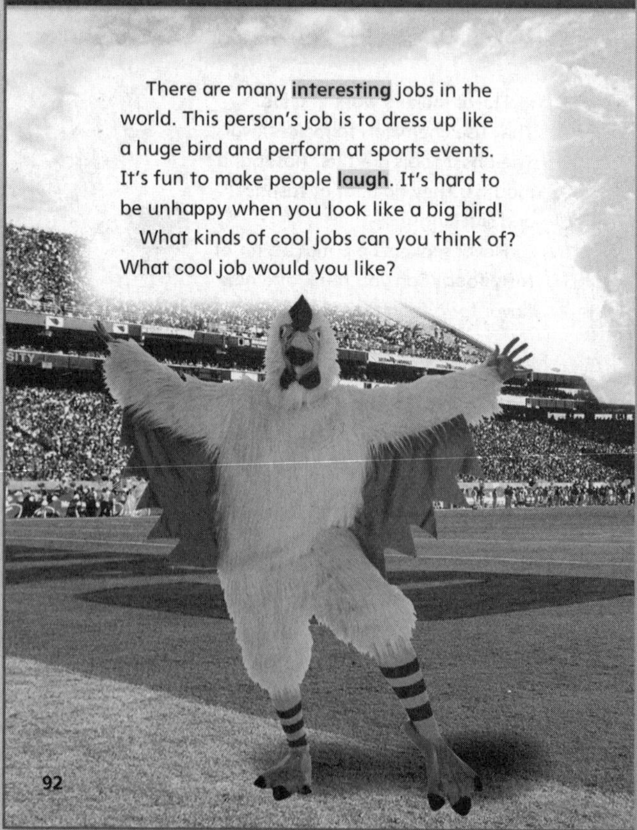

There are many **interesting** jobs in the world. This person's job is to dress up like a huge bird and perform at sports events. It's fun to make people **laugh**. It's hard to be unhappy when you look like a big bird!
What kinds of cool jobs can you think of? What cool job would you like?
92

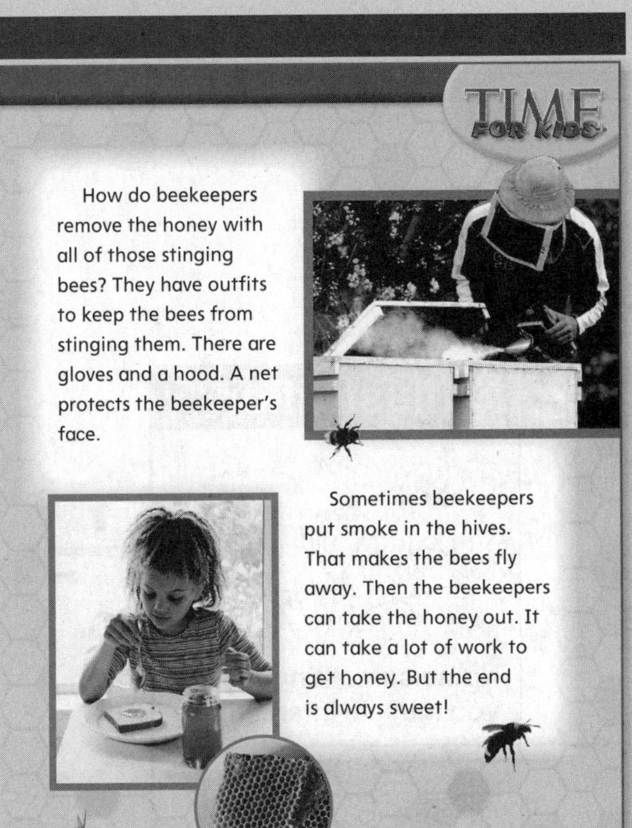

TIME FOR KIDS

How do beekeepers remove the honey with all of those stinging bees? They have outfits to keep the bees from stinging them. There are gloves and a hood. A net protects the beekeeper's face.

Sometimes beekeepers put smoke in the hives. That makes the bees fly away. Then the beekeepers can take the honey out. It can take a lot of work to get honey. But the end is always sweet!

91

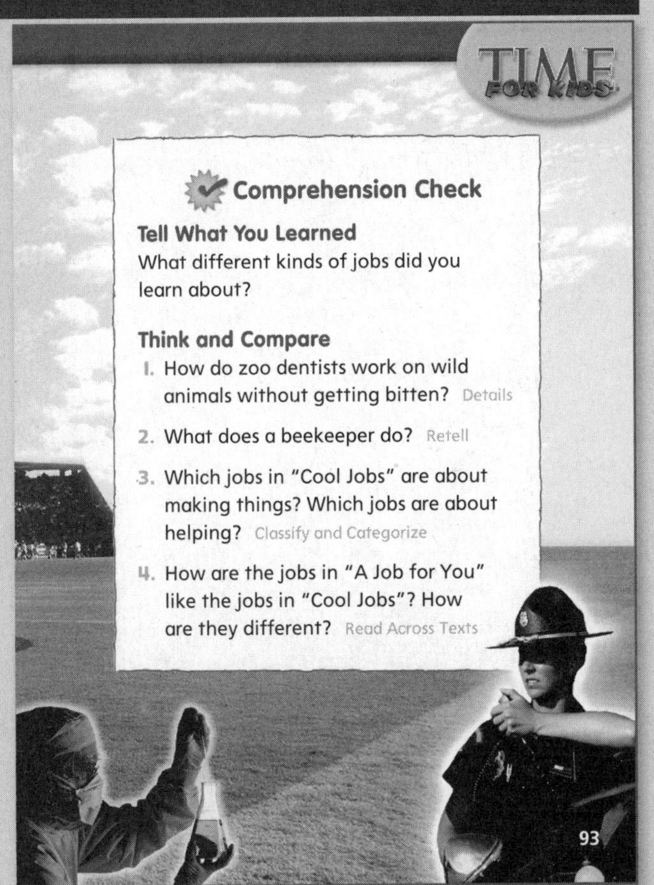

TIME FOR KIDS

Comprehension Check

Tell What You Learned
What different kinds of jobs did you learn about?

Think and Compare

1. How do zoo dentists work on wild animals without getting bitten? Details
2. What does a beekeeper do? Retell
3. Which jobs in "Cool Jobs" are about making things? Which jobs are about helping? Classify and Categorize
4. How are the jobs in "A Job for You" like the jobs in "Cool Jobs"? How are they different? Read Across Texts

93

Page 92

Whole Page

- *Look at the picture. The person is dressed up like a giant bird. This person's job is to make people laugh. What do you think this person might do to make people laugh at a football game or other sports event?* (Responses will vary.)
- *Let's read the last paragraph together:* What kinds of cool jobs can you think of? What cool job would you like to have? *What are some jobs that you think are cool?* (Answers will vary.)

Now think about the kinds of things you like to do. What kind of job might you like to have one day? Talk about it with your partner.

Non-verbal Cues

Remind children that they can use non-verbal cues to share information when they are not able to do so verbally. Encourage children to use pantomime and draw.

Name ____________________

Use the word chart to study this week's vocabulary words. Write a sentence using each word in your writer's notebook.

Word	Context Sentence	Illustration
interesting ____________	This interesting plant eats bugs.	Name something that you think is interesting.
ordinary ____________	Some ordinary flowers grow everywhere.	

© Macmillan/McGraw-Hill

Name ____________________

Book Talk

Read each question and prompt. Discuss the answers with your group. Use your Leveled Reader to find details to support your answers. Then write your answers on another sheet of paper.

1. Describe why it is important to save trees.

2. List five things made of paper.

3. Give examples of ways you can help recycle paper.

4. Share with classmates ways that you and your family help recycle paper.

5. Explain the process for recycling paper.

© Macmillan/McGraw-Hill

Interactive Question - Response Guide

Dot and Jabber and the Big Bug Mystery

Pages 102–103

Prior to reading the selection with children, they should have listened to the selection on **StudentWorks Plus**, the interactive eBook. In addition, selection vocabulary should have been pretaught using the **Visual Vocabulary Resources**.

Access Core Content

Teacher Note Pose the questions after you read the paragraph or page indicated.

Pages 102–103

Title and Illustration

Let's read the title of this book together: Dot and Jabber and the Big Bug Mystery. *Dot and Jabber are the names of the main characters in this story. The main characters are the most important characters.*

- *A mystery is something that happens that we don't understand. Think about the title. What might this mystery be about?* (something that Dot and Jabber don't understand about bugs)
- *Do you think this story will be about things that could really happen or things that could not happen in real life? Why?* (about things that could not happen, because the mice don't look like real mice)

Pages 102–103

Pages 104–105

Dot and Jabber, the mouse detectives, were looking for a mystery to solve. They walked through the meadow and stopped to watch some bugs.
104

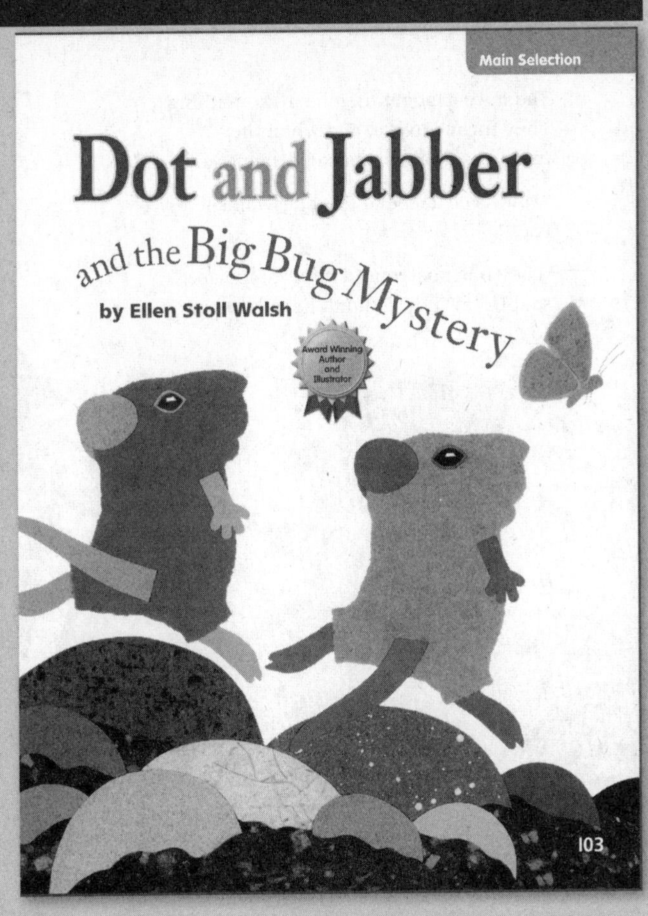

Main Selection
Dot and Jabber
and the Big Bug Mystery
by Ellen Stoll Walsh
103

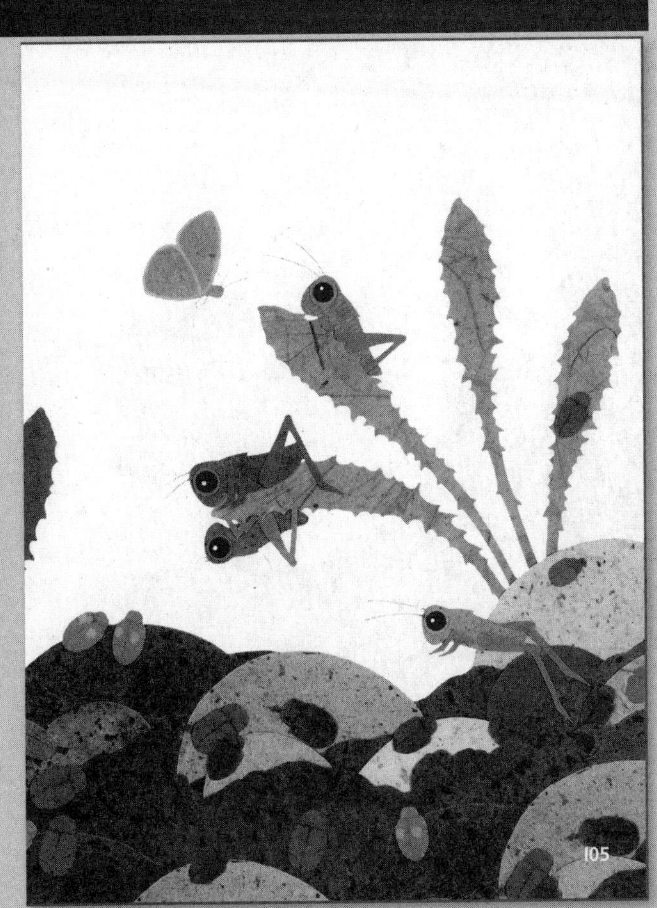

Pages 104–105

Text

- *Dot and Jabber are mouse detectives. Detectives are people who solve mysteries. What are Dot and Jabber doing?* (looking for a mystery to solve)

Share with your partner anything you know about detectives. What do they do? Tell about detectives you have seen in the movies or on television.

Illustration

- *The picture shows a meadow. A meadow is a flat, grassy place. What do you see in this meadow?* (bugs, mice, plants, rocks)

- **Directionality**

  Ask children to place their finger where you start reading (top left). Ask where you finish reading on this page (bottom right).

Interactive Question - Response Guide

Dot and Jabber and the Big Bug Mystery

Page 106

Paragraph 1

- *Listen as I read the first paragraph:* The mice thought they heard something. (Cup your hand around your ear.) They turned to see, (Turn your head.) and when they turned back, (Turn back to your original position.) the bugs had disappeared. (Look surprised.)
- *Now I'll read it again. Let's do the actions together.*

Paragraph 2

- *The bugs vanished. Let's use clues on the page to figure out what* vanished *means. The author uses two other words that mean the same thing. Look at the end of the first paragraph:* the bugs had disappeared.
- *Now look at the last sentence on the page:* "They couldn't have gone away so fast." *What two words on the page have the same meaning as* vanished? (disappeared, gone)

Let's predict what mystery the mice will try to solve. (where the bugs went) *What helped you make that prediction?* (A mystery is something we don't understand. The mice don't understand where the bugs went.)

Pages 106–107

The mice thought they heard something. They turned to see, and when they turned back, the bugs had disappeared.

"Wow," said Jabber. "The bugs vanished. Poof!"

"They must be around here someplace," said Dot. "They couldn't have **gone** away so fast."

106

Pages 108–109

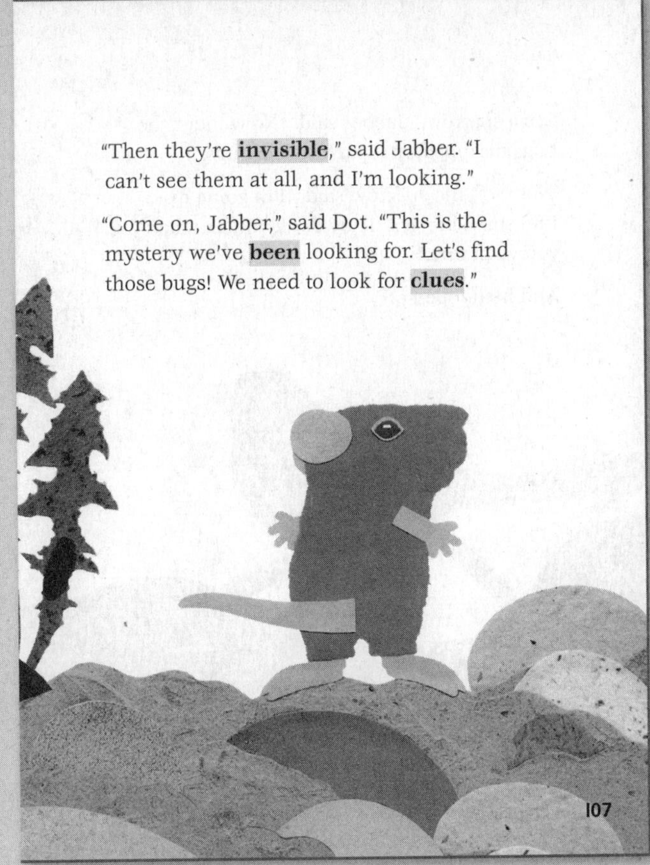
"Then they're **invisible**," said Jabber. "I can't see them at all, and I'm looking."

"Come on, Jabber," said Dot. "This is the mystery we've **been** looking for. Let's find those bugs! We need to look for **clues**."

107

"Dot, listen," Jabber whispered. "I think I hear one."

"One what?" said Dot.

"One clue. *Shhh.* Let's go check."

The mice crept over the hill.

109

Page 107

Paragraphs 1 and 2

- *Jabber can't see the bugs at all. Why does he think he can't see them?* (They're invisible)
- *Dot says this is the mystery they've been looking for. What is she talking about?* (where the bugs went)
- *Let's read the second paragraph together. The mice are excited and curious. We'll use excited, curious voices when we read.* "Come on, Jabber," said Dot. "This is the mystery we've been looking for. Let's find those bugs! We need to look for clues."
- *Let's pretend we are Dot and Jabber. We will pretend that our classroom is a meadow. We will do what detectives do. Let's walk around and look for clues.* (Lead the group in a walk around the classroom. Have them look on, in, under, and behind things.)

Illustration

- *Let's look closely at this picture. Where did the bugs go? I see one clue. There's a bug hiding on a plant. Point to it.*

Pages 108–109

Text

- *Jabber tells Dot to listen. What does Jabber want Dot to hear?* (a clue) *What do you think it is?* (maybe a bug noise)
- *Jabber says* Shhh. (Put one finger to your lips.) *Shhh means "please be quiet." Why does Jabber want Dot to be quiet?* (so she won't scare the clue away; so they can hear the clue)

Dot and Jabber and the Big Bug Mystery

Pages 110–111

Paragraph 1

- *A sparrow is a kind of bird. Point to the picture of the sparrow on page 110.*
- *Jabber thinks the bugs might have disappeared because of the sparrow. Why?* (Maybe the bugs were afraid that the sparrow would eat them.)

Paragraph 2

- *When the sparrow says:* "Not me," *What does he mean?* (that he would not eat the bugs) *What does the sparrow like to eat instead?* (berries)
- *When the sparrow says:* "They don't vanish when you want one." *what does he mean by* they? (the berries)

Illustration

- *Let's look closely at this picture. Where did the bugs go?* (There are bugs hidden among the rocks.) *Point to some of the bugs.*
-

Directionality

Ask children to place their finger where you start reading (top left). Ask where you finish reading on this page (bottom right).

Pages 110–111

Pages 112–113

"Now that the sparrow is gone," said Dot, "why don't the bugs come back?"
112

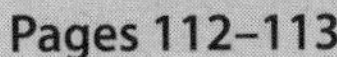

Pages 112–113

Text

- *Dot thinks that the bugs should come back when the sparrow hops away. Why?* (because now they don't have to be afraid that the bird will eat them)

Illustration

Dot asks Jabber why the bugs don't come back. Jabber doesn't answer in words. He uses a gesture. That means he uses his body to show his answer. Look at Jabber on page 113. (Demonstrate shrugging your shoulders.) *Tell your partner what you think Jabber's gesture means.* (It means that he doesn't know.)

Monitor Oral Production

Remember to model self-corrective techniques on a regular basis as you speak to children. Pretend to mispronounce words and self-correct.

Dot and Jabber and the Big Bug Mystery

Page 114

Whole Page

- *Look at the rabbit on this page. Point to it. The rabbit thinks the bugs are hiding from another animal. Whatkind of animal is it?* (a toad) *Why would bugs hide from a toad?* (because toads eat bugs)

Page 115

Paragraphs 1 and 2

- *The first sentence on this page is a question. We make our voices go up at the end of a question. This makes us sound curious. I will read the question with a curious voice. Please repeat after me.* "Where is the toad?" said Dot. (Children echo.)

- *The second sentence answers the question. We will read it in a voice that tells facts. Please repeat after me.* "Hiding from things that eat toads," said the rabbit. (Children echo.)

Paragraph 3

- *Jabber says,* I don't get it. *What do you think he means? What in the story helps you figure out what Jabber means?* (He tells what confuses him so we know there is something he doesn't understand.)

Tell your partner some places you think animals might hide in a meadow. (under rocks, behind leaves, in bushes)

Illustration

- *Let's look closely at this picture. Where are all the bugs hiding? Point to the bugs you see.*

Pages 114–115

"They're hiding from the toad," said a rabbit. "Toads eat bugs, too."

114

Pages 116–117

"Maybe we don't know how to look," said Dot. "Let's keep **searching**. The bugs can't be far away."

"They're watching us," said Jabber. "I can feel it."

"I can, too," said Dot.

116

"Where is the toad?" said Dot.

"Hiding from things that eat toads," said the rabbit.

"I don't get it," said Jabber. "Everybody's hiding, but I don't see anyplace to hide."

"This gives me goose bumps," said Jabber. "They can see us, but we can't see them. I wonder what else is out there watching us?"

Dot caught her breath. "Jabber, quick. Something moved."

"I don't see it," said Jabber.

"Look," said Dot. "It's moving again."

Page 116

Text

- *Dot and Jabber think that the bugs can't be far away. The mice can feel the bugs watching them. How do you think it might feel to have someone watch you? Why?* (creepy, scary; because I wouldn't know why they were watching me)
- *Let's read what Jabber and Dot say. Use the kind of voice the mice might use if they were worried about someone watching:* "They're watching us," said Jabber. "I can feel it." "I can, too," said Dot.

Page 117

Paragraph 1

- *Jabber says he has* goose bumps. *When we say we get goose bumps, we mean we get little bumps on our skin because we feel scared, excited, or cold. Why do you think Jabber has goose bumps?* (He feels funny about the bugs watching him and Dot.)

Tell your partner some things that might give you goose bumps. (Question is open.)

Paragraph 2

- *Let's be sure we know what* caught her breath *means.* (Pretend to catch your breath as if startled.) *Now you show me what* catch your breath *means.* (Children will imitate the action you demonstrated.) *Dot caught her breath because she was startled, or surprised.*
- *Dot is surprised because she sees something move. What do you think it is?* (the toad or a bug)

Illustration

- *Now let's look closely at this picture. What do you see hiding?* (a toad and some bugs)

Dot and Jabber and the Big Bug Mystery

Page 118

Text

- *Let's read the sentence together:* Some butterflies rose from the meadow and flew away. *A rose can be a flower, but rose can also mean "went up." Which meaning fits the way the word rose is used on this page?* (went up)
- *Why didn't Jabber see the butterflies before?* (They were hiding.)

Page 119

Paragraph 1

- *Let's read the first paragraph aloud to find out what Jabber thinks when he suddenly finds the butterflies.* "Wow, butterflies!" said Jabber. "I think the butterflies are a clue. They were hiding in plain sight, and we didn't even see them. Maybe the other bugs are hiding in plain sight, too."
- In plain sight *means that something is right in front of your eyes. Let's find some things in our classroom that are in plain sight but hard to see.* (Give an example such as something on the floor that blends in with the tile or carpet.) *What are some other examples of things that are in plain sight in our classroom but hard to see?* (Question is open)
- *Look at the butterflies in the picture. Why do you think it was so hard to see them in the meadow?* (because they are green, and the grass is green, too)

Pages 118–119

Pages 120–121

"Dot," said Jabber. "Do rocks breathe?"
"Of course not," said Dot.
"Then I've found the toad."
120

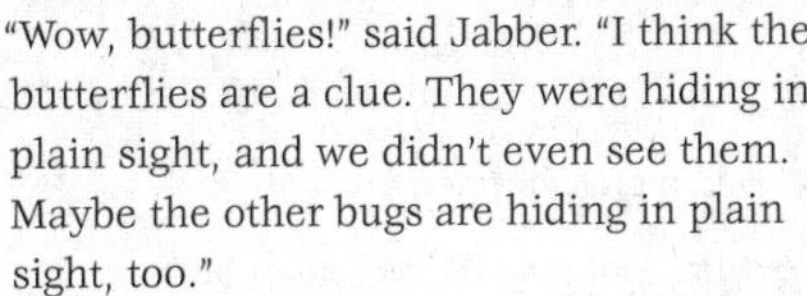
"Wow, butterflies!" said Jabber. "I think the butterflies are a clue. They were hiding in plain sight, and we didn't even see them. Maybe the other bugs are hiding in plain sight, too."

"Oh!" said Dot. "Do you mean they're pretending to look like something else? Let's see if you're right."

Pages 120–121

Text

- *What do you think happens that makes Jabber ask if rocks breathe?* (He sees one of the rocks move.)

How do you think Jabber feels when he thinks he sees a rock move? (surprised) *Show your partner how Jabber's face might look when he thinks he sees a rock move.*

Illustration

- *Jabber doesn't really see a rock move. Look at the picture. What do you think moved?* (a toad)
- *Why does Jabber think what he sees is a rock?* (It looks a lot like a rock. The toad is hiding behind a rock. The toad's color and markings are like the rock's. Jabber can't tell the difference.)

Non-verbal Cues

Remind children that they can use non-verbal cues to share information when they are not able to do so verbally. Encourage children to use pantomime and draw.

Dot and Jabber and the Big Bug Mystery

Pages 122–123

Text

- *Dot tells Jabber that she found the bugs. How do you think she feels?* (happy, excited) *Let's read the first sentence in an excited voice:* "Jabber," said Dot. "I found the bugs!"
- *The grasshopper says* Shhh *to Dot. Why does he want her to be quiet.* (He doesn't want others to know his hiding place.)

Look at the picture on page 123. Two bugs are jumping out of their hiding places. They look as though they are leaving? Why might they be doing that? (They don't feel safe anymore.) *Do you think other bugs will leave? Why or why not?* (Questions are open.)

- *Bugs, toads, and other animals can be hard to see in nature? Their colors and marks can look like trees, dirt, and leaves. What do we have to do to see bugs and animals?* (look carefully; know how to look)

Illustration

PARTNERS *Count how many bugs you see in the picture. If you find more than your partner, show your partner which ones he or she missed. If your partner finds more, ask him or her to show you ones you missed.*

Pages 122–123

"Jabber," said Dot. "I found the bugs!"
"*Shhh*," said a grasshopper.
"You're right, Dot. There are lots of bugs here!" said Jabber. "We just have to know how to look."
122

Pages 124–125

The grasshopper sighed. "Go ahead. Tell the toad where we are. Tell the whole world. What are a few bugs, more or less? I'm out of here."
"Wait for us!" said the other bugs.
124

Pages 124–125

Text

- *Sometimes we say the opposite of what we mean to show that we are upset. What does the grasshopper say that is the opposite of what he really means?* (Tell the toad where we are. Tell the whole world. What are a few bugs more or less?)

- *How does the grasshopper really feel?* (He is upset that Dot and Jabber know his hiding place. He is also upset that they talked about this place out loud. He is afraid that other animals will find the bugs and eat them.)

- *The grasshopper says* I'm out of here. *That's another way of saying I'm leaving. All the other bugs are going with him. Why do all the bugs leave?* (If everyone knows about their hiding places, they aren't safe anymore. Other animals can find them and eat them.)

Dot and Jabber and the Big Bug Mystery

Pages 126–127

Text

- *The mice finally solve their mystery. What was the mystery?* (the mystery of where the bugs were) *How did they solve it?* (They figured out that the bugs were hiding in plain sight.)

Did you predict where the bugs were before Jabber and Dot figured it out? What clues did you use? (yes, because I could see the bugs hiding in the pictures)

Illustration

- *Point to Jabber in the picture. What is he doing?* (trying to hide in plain sight) *Can he do it? Why or why not?* (no; he doesn't have the right color and marks to hide there)

Pages 126–127

"Well," said Dot, "the bugs have really disappeared now. But not **before** the great mouse detectives solved another mystery!" Dot looked around. "Jabber, where are you?"

"Try to find me," said Jabber. "I'm hiding in plain sight!"

126

Go back to the beginning of the story. Take turns with your partner. Try to find all the hidden bugs and animals on each page.

- *How was this story like* Where Has Freddy Gone Now? (Both stories were about missing bugs.) *How was this story different from* Where Has Freddy Gone Now? (In this story, the bugs were in plain sight all the time. In the other story, the missing bug was stuck in a web.)

The World of Insects

Access Core Content

Teacher Note Pose the questions after you read the paragraph or page indicated.

Page 130

Title and Text

- *Listen as I read the title of this selection:* The World of Insects. *What word did Jabber and Dot use for insects?* (bugs)

PARTNERS

Tell your partner some places you have see insects. Describe types of insects you have seen. (Responses will vary.)

- *Listen as I read the first page:* Insects are everywhere. There are more insects than any other kind of animal.

Photos and Illustrations

- *Do the pictures on this page show real or pretend insects?* (both real and pretend) *Point to a real insect. Point to a pretend insect.*

Page 131

Heading and Text

- *Let's read the heading of this page together:* Kinds of Insects. *In this section we will learn about different kinds of insects.*

Photos

- *I will give you some directions about the pictures of real insects on this page. Point to the ant. Put your hand over an insect that can fly.* (Children should put their hands over the bee, dragonfly, or butterfly.) *Tap an insect that lives and works with other insects.* (Children should tap the ant or the bee.)

Page 132

Photos

- *Look at the insect in the middle of the page. How many legs does it have? Count them.* (six) All insects have six legs.

Pages 130–131

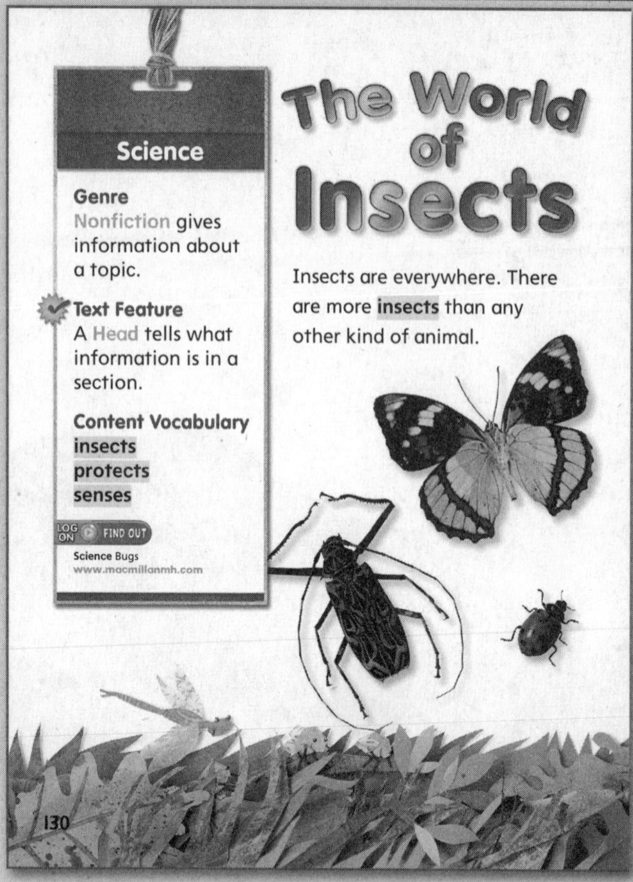
Science
Genre
Nonfiction gives information about a topic.
Text Feature
A Head tells what information is in a section.
Content Vocabulary
insects
protects
senses
LOG ON FIND OUT
Science Bugs
www.macmillanmh.com
The World of Insects
Insects are everywhere. There are more insects than any other kind of animal.
130

Pages 132–133

The Body of an Insect

All insects have six legs. All insects have three body parts. Insect bodies have no bones. The outside of an insect's body is hard. The hard outside protects its insides. Many insects have antennas.

antenna
head
thorax
abdomen
132

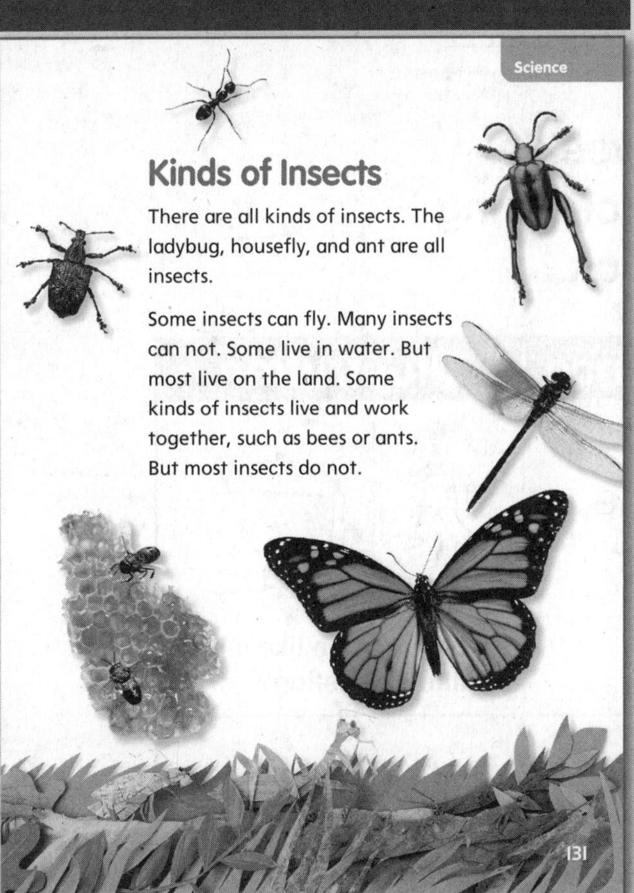

Science

Kinds of Insects

There are all kinds of insects. The ladybug, housefly, and ant are all insects.

Some insects can fly. Many insects can not. Some live in water. But most live on the land. Some kinds of insects live and work together, such as bees or ants. But most insects do not.

131

Insect Senses

Insect **senses** are not like people's senses. Many insects smell with their antennas. Bees taste with their antennas. Flies taste with their feet.

Insects do not see the same as we do. Some insects have more than two eyes. A grasshopper has five eyes. It can see on all sides.

Connect and Compare

- What does the title tell you about this selection? What do the heads tell?
- How are the bugs that Dot and Jabber see like the insects in "The World of Insects"?

133

Text and Diagram

- *The three major body parts of an insect are the head, thorax, and abdomen, or stomach.*
- *Point to the insect's head. Point to your own head. The thorax of an insect is something like our chest. Point to the insect's thorax.*
- *The insect's abdomen is the part that contains its stomach. Point to the insect's abdomen. Point to your abdomen.*
- *A hard outer shell protects insects' insides from getting squished. Do people have a hard outer shell?* (no)
- *Count the antennas on the insect in the middle of the page. How many does it have?* (two)
- *Look at the insect in the middle of the page. Does it look bigger than it is in real life?* (yes) *Why do you think the author wanted the picture to be so big?* (so we could see the parts better)

Page 133

- *This page is about insect senses. People have five senses. What are they?* (Prompt the different senses by pointing to your eyes, nose, mouth, ears, and hands.)(seeing, smelling, tasting, hearing, touching) *Are insect senses the same as people's senses?* (no)
- *Pretend you are an insect. Use your arms as pretend antennas. Where would your antennas be?* (Children put their arms straight up beside their heads.)
- *Now show and tell me how you might use your antenna at lunchtime.* (Children indicate smelling and tasting their lunches.)
- Grasshoppers have five eyes. How might that be helpful? (It could see anything that was coming to eat it and hop way)

Name ____________________

Use the word chart to study this week's vocabulary words. Write a sentence using each word in your writer's notebook.

Word	Context Sentence	Illustration
clues ____________	Lisa followed the clues to find her puppy.	Is a clue more like a hint or like a question?
invisible ____________	We cannot see the air because it is invisible.	

© Macmillan/McGraw-Hill

Name ______________________________

Book Talk

Read each question and prompt. Discuss the answers with your group. Use your Leveled Reader to find details to support your answers. Then write your answers on another sheet of paper.

1. Where do the two friends in the story go? Why?

2. What did you learn about the butterflies that you did not know before?

3. How can you learn even more? Give some ideas.

4. Tell about a surprise in the story. Did you predict this would happen?

5. Which illustration did you like the best? Show the group.

© Macmillan/McGraw-Hill

Super Oscar

Pages 140–141

Prior to reading the selection with children, they should have listened to the selection on **StudentWorks Plus**, the interactive eBook. In addition, selection vocabulary should have been pretaught using the **Visual Vocabulary Resources**.

Access Core Content

Teacher Note Pose the questions after you read the paragraph or page indicated.

Pages 140–141

Title and Illustration

- *Read the title of this story with me:* Super Oscar. *Oscar is the boy in the picture.*
- *Oscar is wearing a tablecloth around his shoulders.* (Point to your shoulders.) *Point to the tablecloth. Oscar is pretending to be a super hero, like Superman. What other super heroes do you know about from television or books?* (Question is open.)

Pages 142–143

Illustration

- *Oscar is standing on the couch. Point to it. He is holding a remote control from a television or a CD player. Now point to the little picture of Oscar. Oscar is holding a microphone.* (Point to it.) *He is dressed in fancy clothes.*
-

Directionality

Ask children to place their finger where you start reading (top left). Ask where you finish reading on this page (bottom right).

Pages 140–141

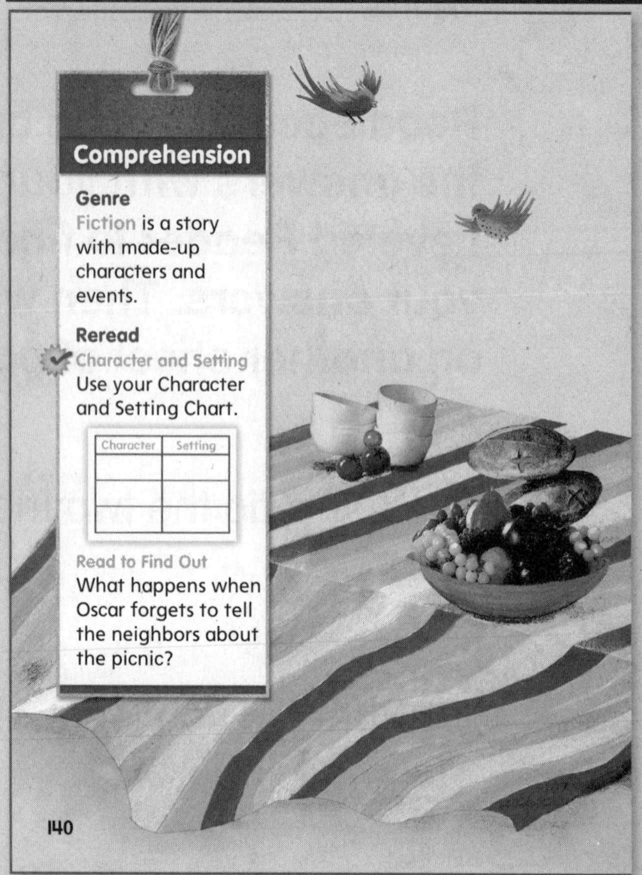

Comprehension
Genre
Fiction is a story with made-up characters and events.
Reread
Character and Setting
Use your Character and Setting Chart.
Character
Setting
Read to Find Out
What happens when Oscar forgets to tell the neighbors about the picnic?
140

Pages 142–143

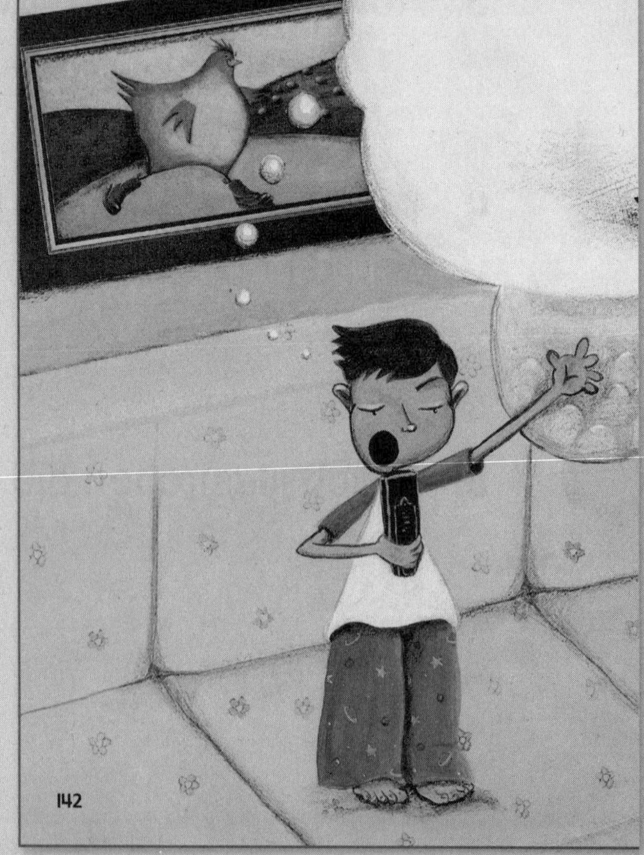

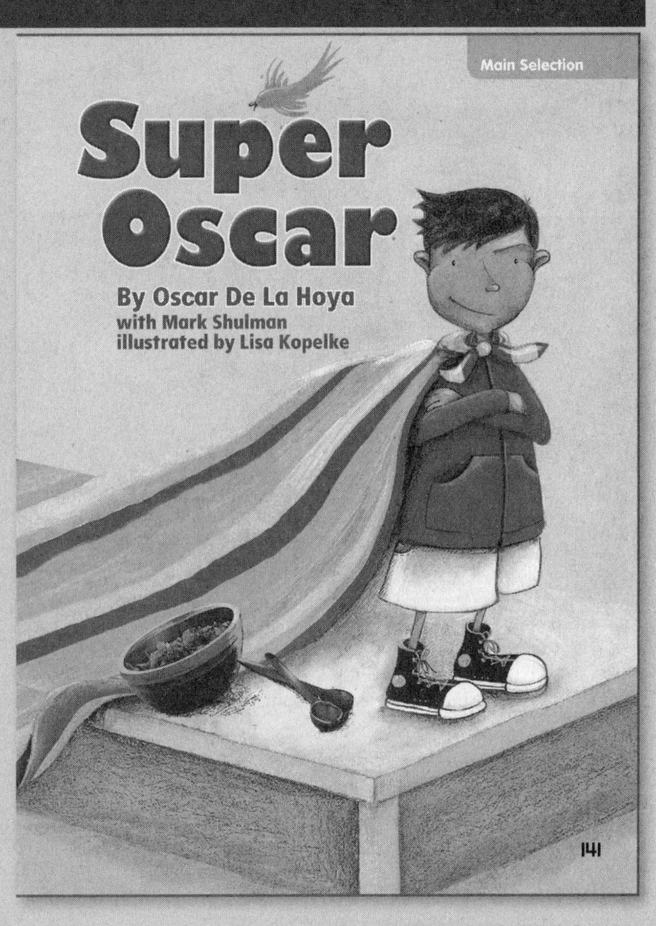

- *Oscar is pretending to be singing on a stage. What is he using to help him pretend?* (the remote control) *How is he using it?* (He is pretending that it is a microphone.)

Talk with your partner about other things kids pretend to be. Talk about any special clothes they wear or objects they use to help them pretend.

Text

- *When people* daydream, *they use their imagination to think about their wishes and hopes. Oscar is a* daydreamer. *He imagines himself doing things he wishes he could do, or going to places he'd like to go.*
- *Let's read this page together:* Oscar was a daydreamer.

The main character, Oscar, is a daydreamer. What are some things that Oscar likes to daydream about? (being a super hero and a singer)

- *Daydreamers are creative and have good ideas. What are some problems daydreamers might have?* (They might not do some things they are supposed to. They might not hear directions their parents or teachers give them.)

Super Oscar

Page 144

Illustration

- *Look at the the dinosaur in the picture. Point to it. What is Oscar daydreaming about on this page?* (about taking a ride on a dinosaur) *What is he really doing?* (riding in a bus)

Text

- *We learn even more about Oscar's daydreaming on this page. Where does he daydream?* (on the bus and at school) *When does he daydream?* (on the way to school, through lunchtime, on the way home)

- *Oscar daydreams most of the time. Do you think that Oscar daydreams more or less than most kids?* (more)

Page 145

Illustration

- *Look at the picture. Point to the pancakes. Point to the spaceship. Are they both round and almost flat?* (yes) *What is Oscar daydreaming now?* (that he is riding in a spaceship) *Maybe he got the idea from the round, flat pancakes!*

Text

- *Oscar daydreams at breakfast and forgets to eat. What happens to his pancakes and juice?* (His pancakes get cold. His juice gets warm.)

- *Oscar's father tells Oscar that sometimes he needs to take his head out of the clouds to get things done. He means that Oscar needs to pay attention to what is happening instead of daydreaming so much. That way he won't forget to eat his breakfast or do other things.*

Pages 144–145

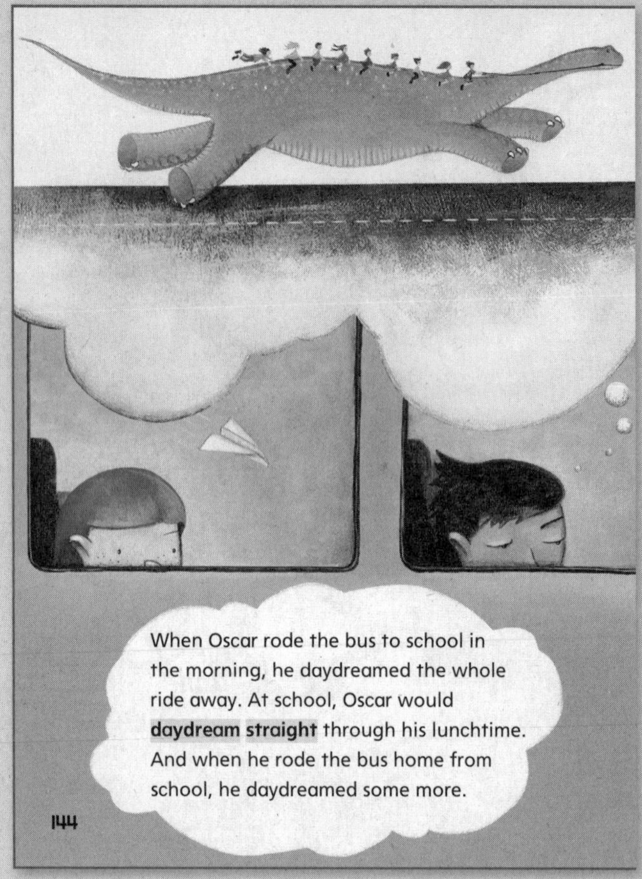

When Oscar rode the bus to school in the morning, he daydreamed the whole ride away. At school, Oscar would **daydream straight** through his lunchtime. And when he rode the bus home from school, he daydreamed some more.
144

Pages 146–147

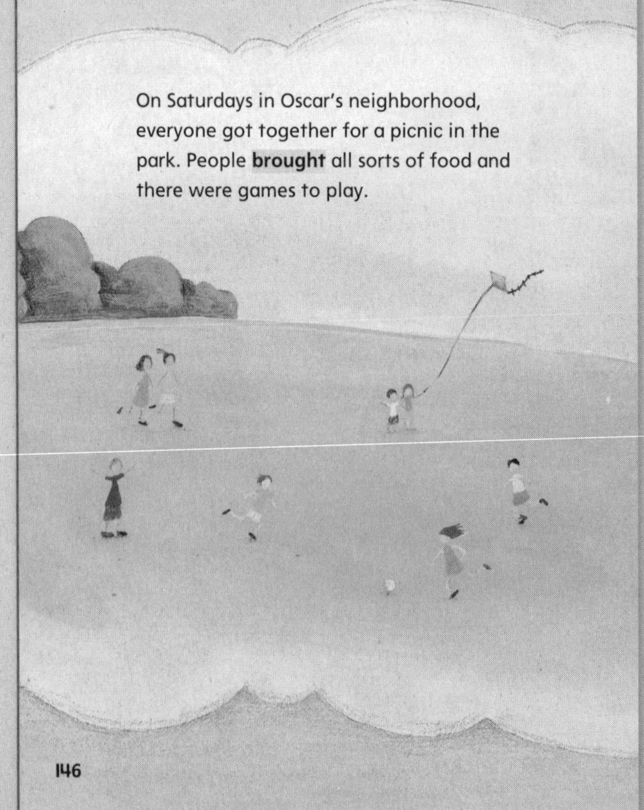

On Saturdays in Oscar's neighborhood, everyone got together for a picnic in the park. People **brought** all sorts of food and there were games to play.
146

At breakfast, Oscar daydreamed as his pancakes got cold and his orange juice got warm.

His father said, "Oscar, it's good to dream. But sometimes you need to take your head out of the clouds to get things done."

"Right," Oscar said.

145

Oscar's mother was in charge of making the lists so that everyone knew what to bring. Oscar would run **around** his neighborhood to give out the lists. One week a **certain** daydreamer forgot to give them out.

147

Pages 146–147

Illustration

- *A picnic is a party or celebration in which people eat their food outside. You can have a picnic at a beach. Where else might you have a picnic?* (Question is open.)
- *Every week, Oscar and his neighbors have a picnic at the park. What are some things that they do? Look at the picture to find out.* (fly kites, play soccer, play catch, run, walk dogs, cook)

The setting of a story is where and when the events happen. Several places are important in this story. Where have we seen Oscar so far? (at home, in the bus) *The park is another important place in the story.*

Text, Choral Reading

- *Oscar's mother is in charge of making lists for the picnic. That means it is her job to make the lists. The lists tell the kind of food each person has to bring. What is Oscar's job.* (to give out the lists)

Pretend that you are Oscar's mother. Make a list of things for the picnic. You and your partner will take turns adding things to the list. (Children will list picnic foods and paper products.)

- *Let's read page 147 together.*
- *Who is the certain daydreamer that forgot to give out the lists?* (Oscar) *Why do you think he forgot?* (He was daydreaming.)

Super Oscar

Pages 148–149

Illustration

- *Look at the picture of the clouds. Oscar is daydreaming about them. How can you tell?* (The clouds are in shapes to show what Oscar is imagining.)
- *Look at the picture of Oscar's mother. What does she have in her hand?* (the lists) *Is she angry or happy?* (angry) *Why does she feel that way?* (because Oscar forgot to give out the lists)
- *Put an angry expression on your face, and stand the way Oscar's mother stands.* (Make an angry expression, and stand with one hand on your hip. Have students imitate you.)
- *Let's read what Oscar's mother says to him:* "OSCAR! You never gave out the lists! We'll have to cancel the picnic. There won't be anything to eat!"

Oscar made a big mistake. What did he forget to do? (Oscar forgot to give out the lists to tell people what to bring to the picnic.) *How would you feel if you made a mistake like that?* (sorry, bad, sad) *What would you want to do?* (fix it)

- *Oscar jumps up, which means that he gets up quickly. He tells his mother that there is still time.*
- *Point to the picture of the boy at the bottom of page 149. Who is the boy?* (Oscar) *Why do you think the illustrator just shows Oscar's feet?* (She is showing that Oscar is moving fast.)

Page 150

Paragraph 1, Echo Reading

- *Oscar leaves* in a flash, *which means that he goes as quickly as a flash of light. What other words in the paragraph show that Oscar is going fast?* (*zipped, rushed, raced*)

Analyze Sayings and Expressions

Help children recognize that *in a flash* is an expression that means very fast. Help them create other examples using this expression.

Pages 148–149

That Saturday, Oscar was lying on the grass, looking at the shapes in the clouds.
His mother called, "OSCAR! You never gave out the lists! We'll have to **cancel** the picnic. There won't be anything to eat!"
148

Pages 150–151

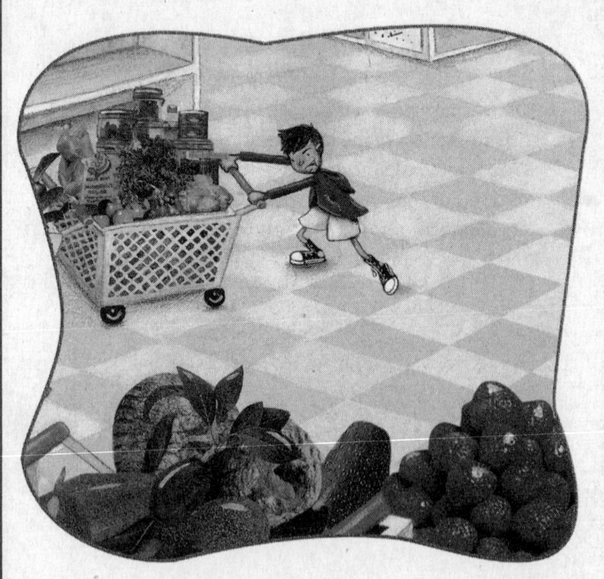

And in a flash, Oscar zipped away. He rushed to the grocery store. He bought everything he needed and raced to the park.

Twenty minutes until the picnic....

150

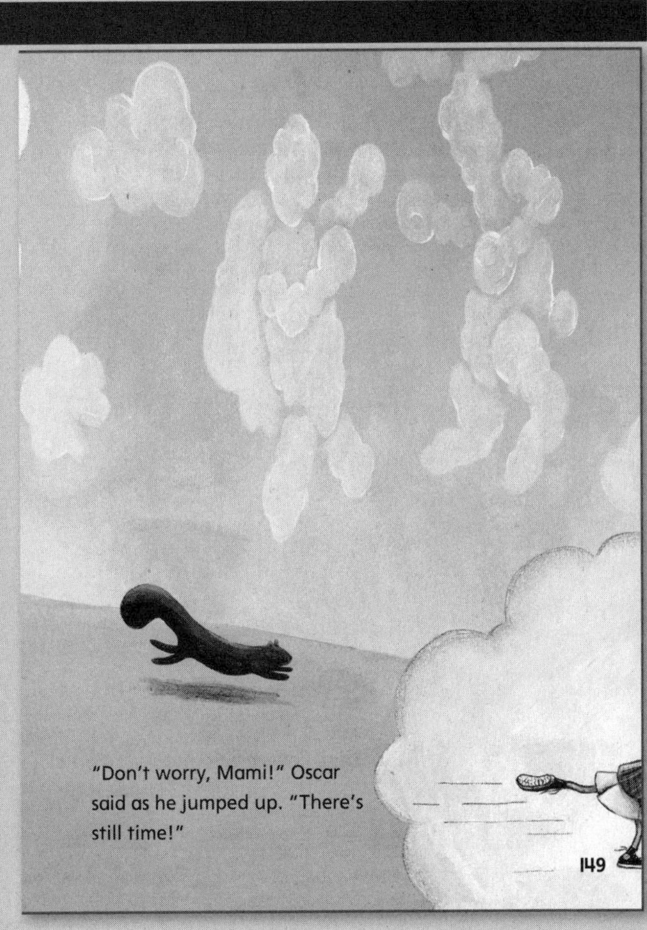

"Don't worry, Mami!" Oscar said as he jumped up. "There's still time!"
149

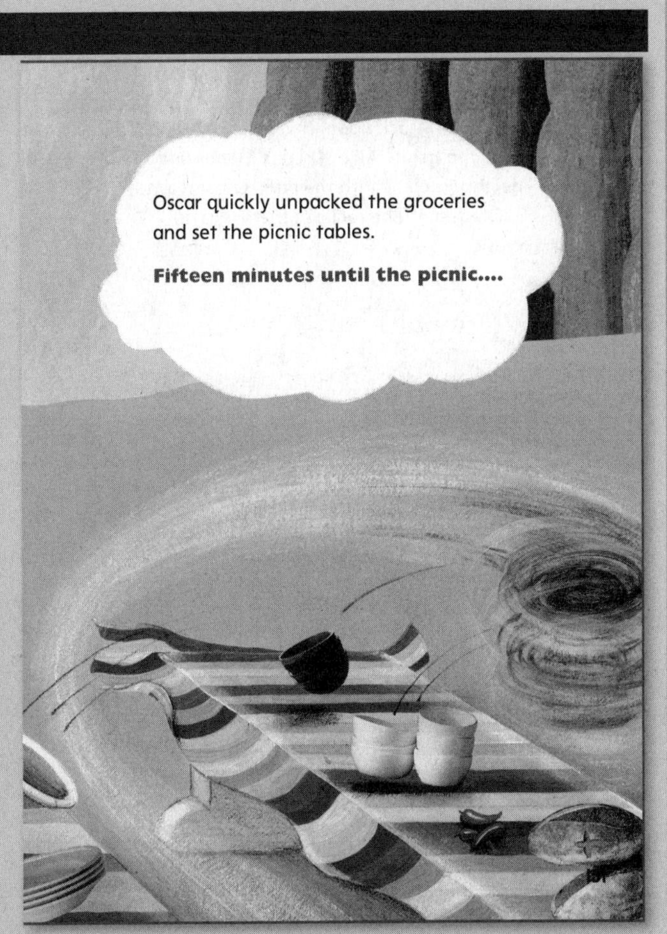

Oscar quickly unpacked the groceries and set the picnic tables.
Fifteen minutes until the picnic....

- *Repeat each sentence after me:* And in a flash, Oscar zipped away. He rushed to the grocery store. (Pause He bought everything he needed and raced to the park. (Pause after each sentence for children to echo.)

In this part of the story, Oscar tries to fix his mistake. What is the first thing he does? (He shops for things for the picnic.)

- *How many minutes are there until the picnic?* (twenty)

Illustration

- *Look at the shopping cart. Are there a lot of things in the shopping cart or just a little?* (a lot) *Oscar has to push very hard to make the cart go. Let's pretend we are pushing heavy shopping carts.* (demonstrate)

Page 151

Whole Page

- *Oscar takes the food, plates, and other groceries out of the bags. What else does he do?* (He sets the tables.)
- *There were twenty minutes left when he got to the park. There are fifteen minutes left now. How many minutes did it take to do everything?* (five) (Do the math problem on the board.)
- *Think about the large number of groceries in that heavy cart. Could Oscar really unpack all of them and set the tables in just five minutes?* (no)
- *Do you think a boy could really do what Oscar did to solve his problem? Why or why not?* (no, because he wouldn't have enough time or money to get a whole picnic ready that fast)

Take turns being Oscar. Pretend that you are . unpacking the bags and setting the tables. Remember to move very fast! .

Interactive Question - Response Guide

Super Oscar

Page 152

Whole Page

- *Guacamole is a smooth green dip made of mashed avocadoes, tomatoes, onion, chilies, lime juice, and spices. Raise your hand if you have eaten guacamole.*
- *A batch of cookies is the amount of cookies you make at one time. Raise your hand if you've helped make a batch of cookies. Now look at the picture. Oscar is making a batch of guacamole.*
- *The author calls it* a humongous batch. *Say it with me:* a humongous batch. *Do you think* humonguous *means "very big" or "very small"?* (very big) *It is so big that Oscar is making it in a swimming pool!*
- *Oscar follows the recipe for guacamole* for the most part. *That means he follows most of the directions, but not all of them. Do you think that the recipe says to mash the avocadoes by stepping on them?* (no)
- *Let's pretend we are mashing avocadoes with our feet.*
- *How many minutes are left now?* (ten)

Page 153

Text, Choral Reading

- *Let's read the first sentence together:* Then Oscar began whipping up the cream for the strawberry shortcake dessert.
- *How many minutes are left now?* (five)

Pages 152–153

Next, Oscar made up a humongous batch of guacamole following Tía Raquel's recipe ... for the most part.

Ten minutes until the picnic....

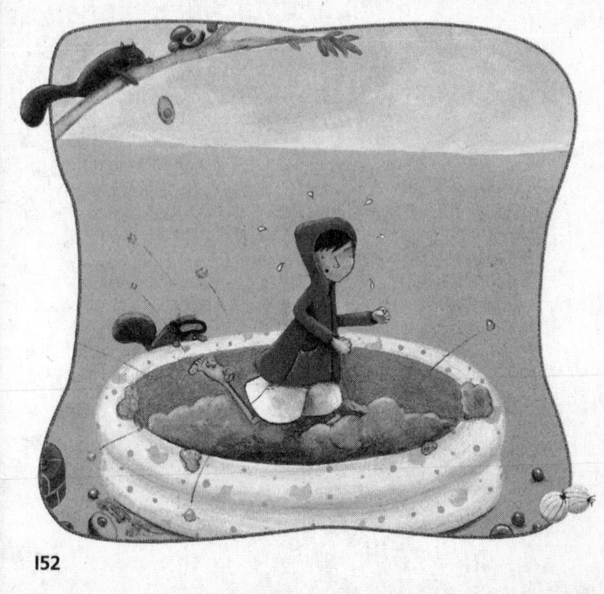

152

Pages 154–155

The clock struck noon. It was time for the picnic to **begin**. All of Oscar's friends and neighbors came into the park. Oscar was excited—until he realized there was no music!

154

Then Oscar began whipping up the cream for the strawberry shortcake dessert.

Five minutes until the picnic....

153

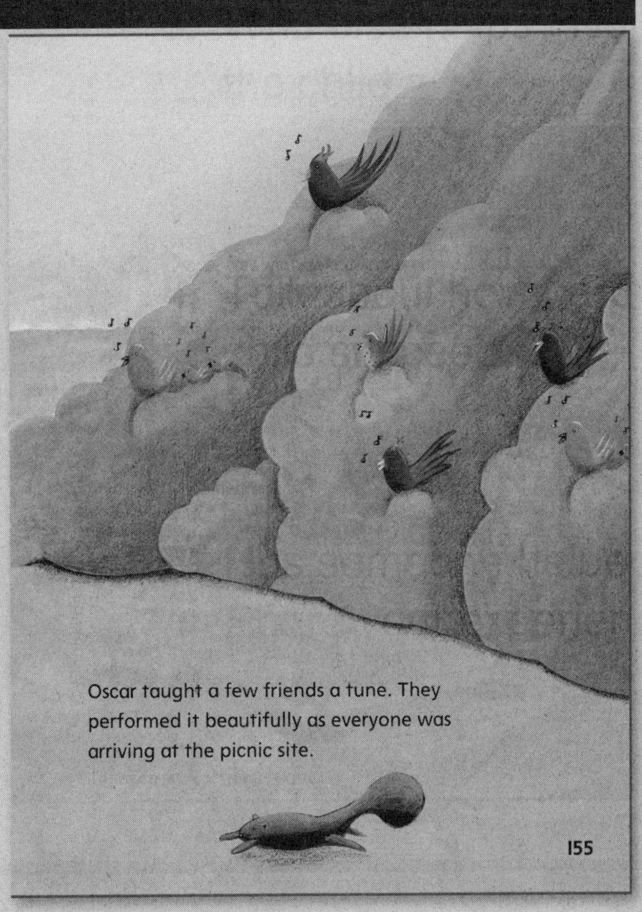

Oscar taught a few friends a tune. They performed it beautifully as everyone was arriving at the picnic site.
155

Illustration

- *There are cartons of cream on the ground. Point to them. Oscar has a jump rope in his hands. Point to it.*
- *What is funny about this picture?* (Oscar is using a jump rope to whip cream in a tub.) *People usually mix cream in a bowl. Do you think all this cream would fit in a bowl?* (no)

Pages 154–155

Whole Page

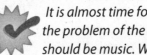

It is almost time for the picnic. Oscar has solved the problem of the food, but now he thinks there should be music. What does he do? (He teaches some of his friends a tune.)

- *Look at the picture. Who might be friends of Oscar?* (the birds)
- *Do the birds perform, or sing well?* (yes) *Look at the squirrels. They are holding acorns. Maybe they will tap them together to the music. Let's pretend to tap acorns together to music.* (demonstrate)

Patterns in Language

Some grammatical structures, such as possessives with *-'s*, pose difficulties to ELLs. Point out that there are several examples of these in this selection, such as *Raquel's* and *Oscar's*. Help children find a pattern.

Page 156

Illustration

- *An empanada* is a pastry with a sweet or spicy filling.
- *Oscar's favorite event, or activity, is an empanada-eating contest. Who do you think wins—the person who eats the most empanadas or the person who eats the fewest?* (the person who eats the most)

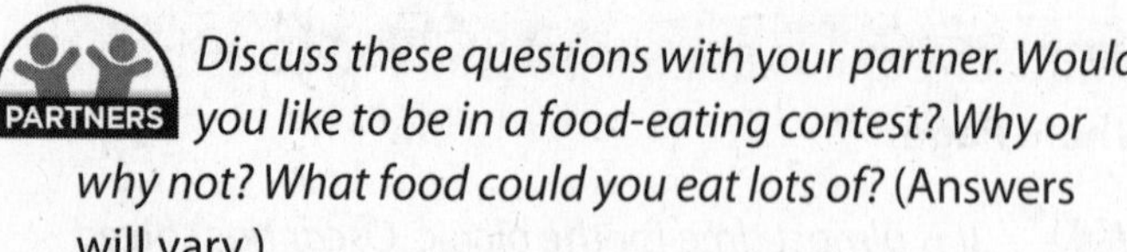

Discuss these questions with your partner. Would you like to be in a food-eating contest? Why or why not? What food could you eat lots of? (Answers will vary.)

Page 157

Whole Page

- *Who is winning the contest?* (Oscar) *How do you know?* (His plate is empty, and the other people still have empanadas on theirs.)
- *Pretend that you are Oscar. Show me how you think he ends up with such a clean plate.* (Children will act out eating empanadas as fast as they can.)
- *Why do you think empanada eating is Oscar's favorite event?* (He is good at it, and it tastes great.)

Pages 156–157

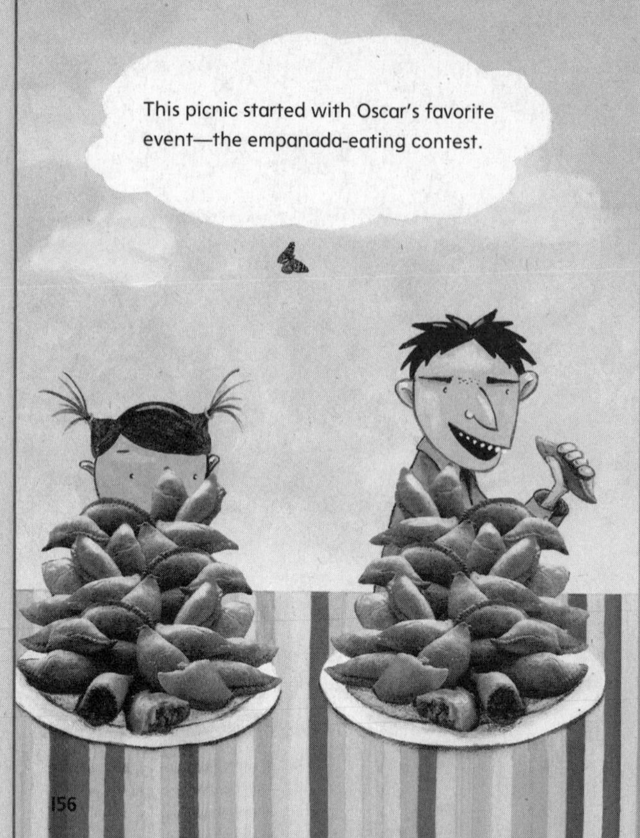

This picnic started with Oscar's favorite event—the empanada-eating contest.
156

Pages 158–159

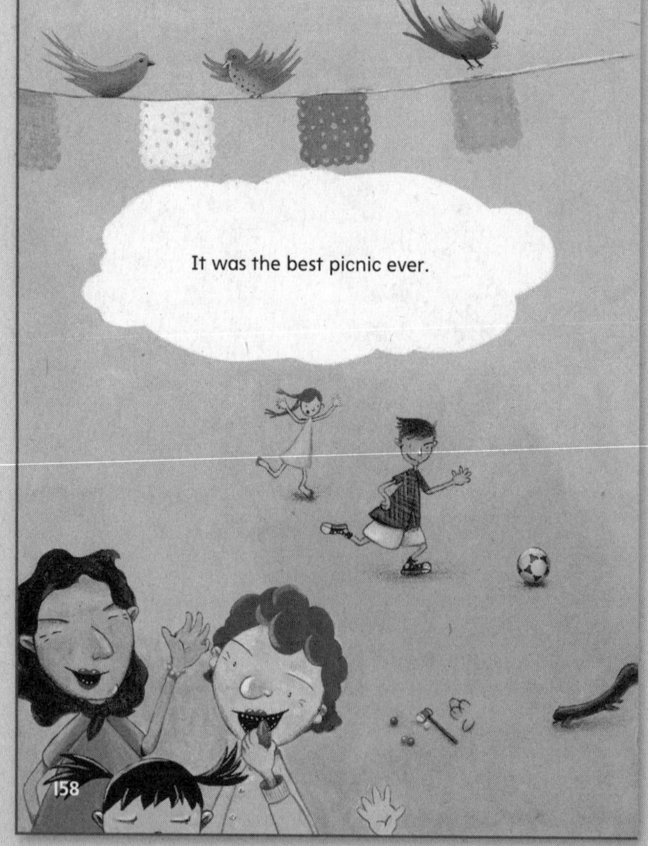

It was the best picnic ever.
158

Pages 158–159

Text

- *Let's read this page together:* It was the best picnic ever.

Illustration

- *How can you tell that people are enjoying themselves?* (They are smiling. They are talking and playing. They look like they are enjoying the food.)
- *Look at the squirrels. Do you think people would really let squirrels eat food at the table?* (no)

 *Tell your partner about a time that you ate outside with other people. What foods did you eat? Were there any special games or music?* (Responses will vary.)

Super Oscar

Page160

Whole Page

- *By the time dessert was served* Oscar was nowhere to be found. *That means that no one could see him.*
- *Why can't anyone see Oscar?* (He is asleep under the table.) *Why is Oscar asleep?* (He is tired because he has worked so hard to make the picnic.)

Page 161

Whole Page

- *Look at the picture. What is* Oscar dreaming? (that he is a super hero)
- *Let's read the sentence together quietly so as not to wake Oscar:* Sweet dreams, Oscar.

Let's think about the end of the story. How did everyone feel about the picnic? (happy) *How did Oscar feel?* (tired but happy)

Pages 160–161

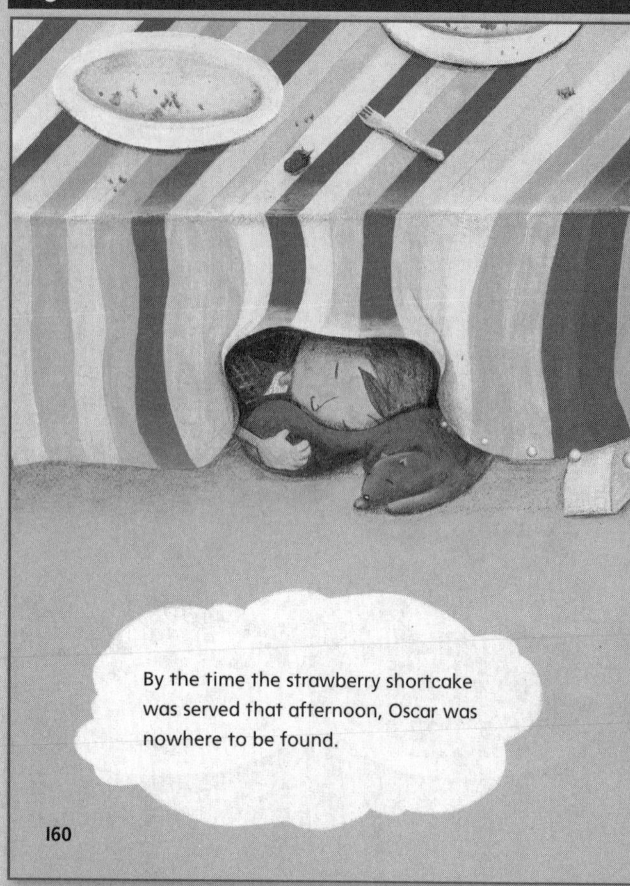

By the time the strawberry shortcake was served that afternoon, Oscar was nowhere to be found.
160

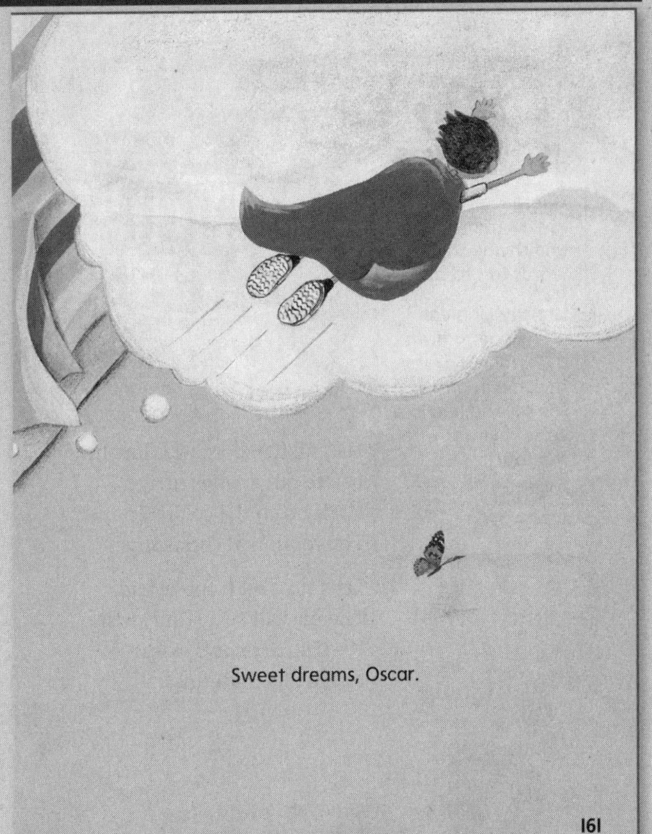

Sweet dreams, Oscar.

161

- *Now let's think about some ways that Oscar's day is like his daydreams. In his daydreams about the dinosaur and the spaceship, Oscar does things that he really can't do in real life.*
- *Let's think about what happens in the story. Could someone really make all that food so fast?* (no)
- *Could someone really get birds to sing a tune?* (no) *Oscar also saves the day, just like a super hero!*

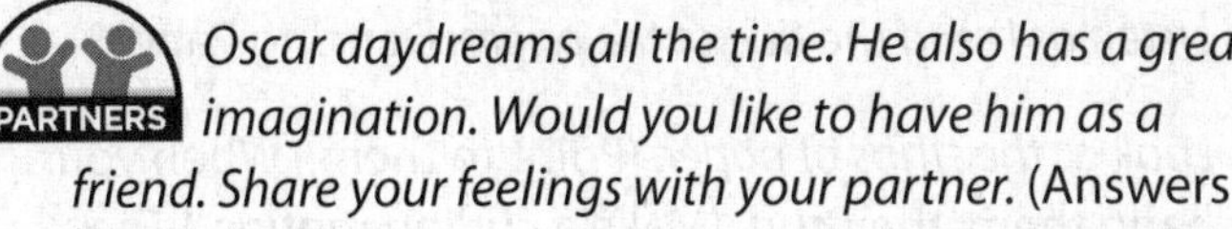

Oscar daydreams all the time. He also has a great imagination. Would you like to have him as a friend. Share your feelings with your partner. (Answers will vary.)

Dancing Paper

Access Core Content

Teacher Note Pose the questions after you read the paragraph or page indicated.

Pages 164–165

Title and Illustration

- *Listen as I read the title of the poem:* Dancing Paper.
- *Look at the strips of paper.* (Point to them.) When you hang them, they curl. (Make a curling motion.) *They also move in the air. Let's pretend our arms are strips of paper and move them in the air.* (demonstrate) *We are dancing paper!*

First Stanza

- *Listen as I read the first stanza aloud. Listen for the two words* arrive *and* alive. *These words rhyme, or sound the same at the end.*
- *Friends are arriving, or coming. The poet wants to make the room come alive. What will make it feel full of life and excitement?* (colored paper)

Second Stanza and Illustration

- *A piñata is a paper shape that is full of treats. Sometimes it looks like an animal. Point to the* piñata *on the second page of the poem. Children hit the piñata to break it. What do you think comes out?* (treats)
- *A papel picado is a kind of banner. It has cut-out designs on it. The designs might be flowers, sun shapes, or even cut-out letters.* (Point to the banners strung across the two pages.)
- *Now listen as I read the second stanza.*
- *The piñata is hung up high. It makes the air seem to sway and swing.* (Demonstrate swaying and swinging.) *Now you sway and swing.*

Pages 164–165

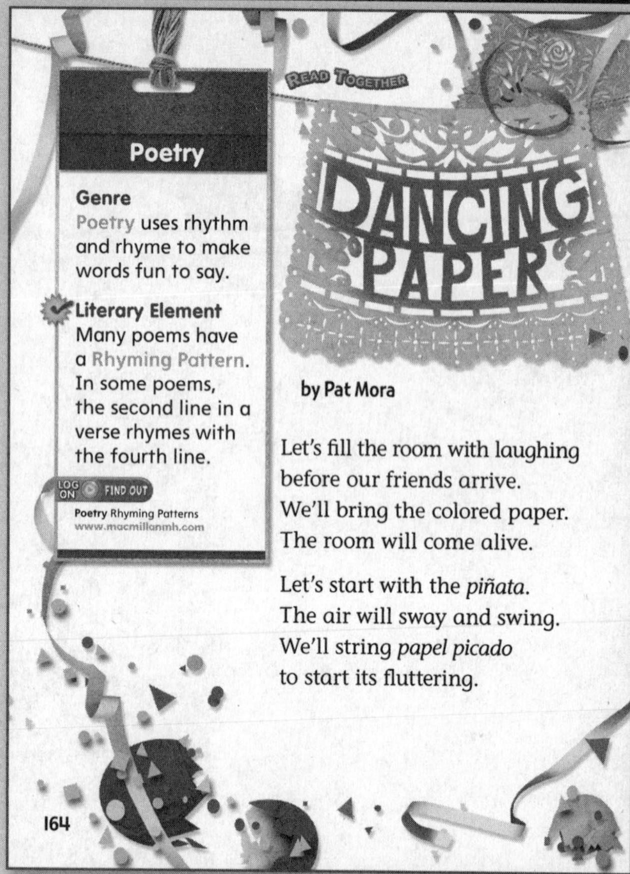

Poetry
Genre
Poetry uses rhythm and rhyme to make words fun to say.
Literary Element
Many poems have a Rhyming Pattern. In some poems, the second line in a verse rhymes with the fourth line.
LOG ON FIND OUT
Poetry Rhyming Patterns
www.macmillanmh.com
READ TOGETHER
DANCING PAPER
by Pat Mora
Let's fill the room with laughing
before our friends arrive.
We'll bring the colored paper.
The room will come alive.
Let's start with the piñata.
The air will sway and swing.
We'll string papel picado
to start its fluttering.
164

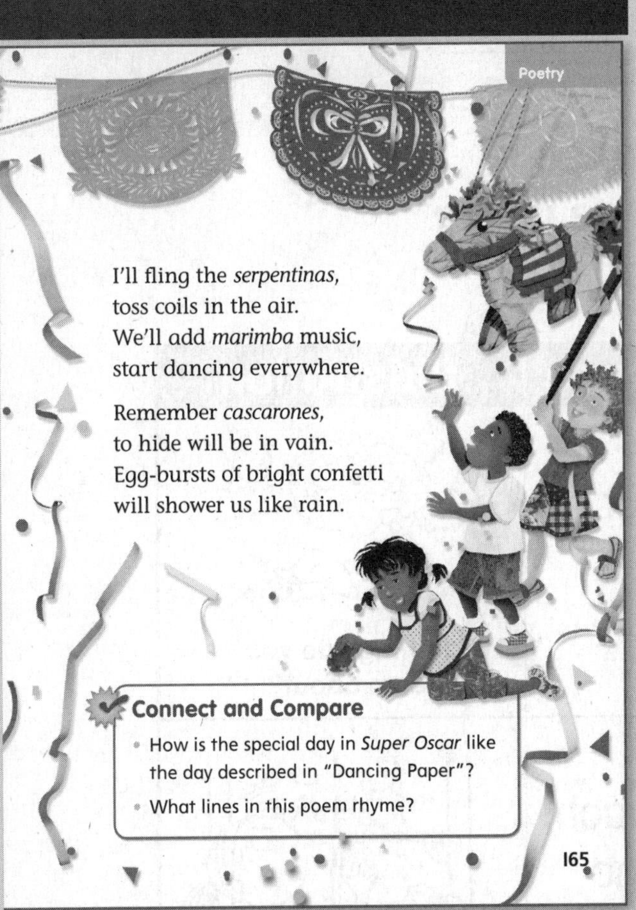

Poetry
I'll fling the *serpentinas*,
toss coils in the air.
We'll add *marimba* music,
start dancing everywhere.
Remember *cascarones*,
to hide will be in vain.
Egg-bursts of bright confetti
will shower us like rain.
Connect and Compare
How is the special day in *Super Oscar* like the day described in "Dancing Paper"?
What lines in this poem rhyme?
165

- *Papel picado banners will be strung across the room. They will make the air seem to flutter, or move back and forth.* (Make a fluttering motion with your hand.)
- *I am going to hold my hand flat in front of me and pretend that it is a papel picado. Watch me make it flutter.* (Make a fluttering motion with your hand.) *Now you do it.*

Page 165

Third Stanza and Illustration

- *Serpentinas are long strips of paper that look like ribbons. Serpentinas come in bright colors. Say it with me:* serpentina. *Point to the serpentinas on this page.*
- *A marimba is a musical instrument. Say it with me:* marimba. *A marimba looks like a table. The top is made of long, flat pieces, or slats of wood.*
- *A marimba player uses sticks with balls on the ends to hit the slats to make different sounds.* (Demonstrate the action of playing a marimba. Say, *bing, bing, bing,* to the tune of a familiar song as you pretend to play.) *Play a pretend marimba with me.*
- *Listen as I read the third stanza.*

Fourth Stanza and Illustration

- *Cascarones are egg-shaped decorations. Say it with me:* cascarones. *Cascarones have confetti, or bits of colored paper, inside. People break the cascarones on each other's heads. What do you think happens?* (Confetti comes out.) *Point to some confetti on this page.*
- *Breaking a cascarone on someone is supposed to bring the person good luck.*
- *Listen as I read the last stanza. Now listen again for the two words that rhyme. What are they?* (*vain* and *rain*)
- *The children in the picture are decorating the room, or making it pretty. What could they be getting ready for?* (a birthday party, a holiday)

Draw a room decorated for a party. Make the papers look like they are dancing! Share and talk about your drawing with your partner.

Name ______________________________

Use the word chart to study this week's vocabulary words. Write a sentence using each word in your writer's notebook.

Word	Context Sentence	Illustration
daydream ____________	Harry likes to daydream about what he wants to be when he grows up.	**What things do you daydream about?**
cancel ____________	It is raining. Coach had to cancel the baseball game.	

© Macmillan/McGraw-Hill

Name ________________________________

Book Talk

Read each question and prompt. Discuss the answers with your group. Use your Leveled Reader to find details to support your answers. Then write your answers on another sheet of paper.

1. Explain why Meena's Mama suggests they make a birdhouse.

2. Who does Meena invite to help her?

3. Describe the problem that makes Meena upset.

4. How does Mama help Meena and her friends solve their problem?

5. Tell your group about a time when you became upset with your friends.

© Macmillan/McGraw-Hill

Oral Language Proficiency Benchmark Assessment

About the Assessment

The Oral Language Proficiency Benchmark Assessment can be given at different points throughout the year to monitor children's oral language proficiency growth. It is suggested that this oral language assessment be administered three times a year. You may wish to administer the test to all of your children, or to those children who have been scored as Beginning, Intermediate, and Advanced in the speaking portion of your state test.

How to Administer the Assessment

Work with children individually. Use the prompts on pages R4-R5. Ask one question at a time, recording the children's answers. Continue asking questions until the children are not able to respond. The guidelines at the bottom of the second page of the Story-Card Prompts/Student Response Sheet will help you to evaluate children's oral language proficiency at this time of year. The first time you administer the assessment, you may wish to model the responses after children give their responses. Model how each question could be answered, using complete sentences, restating, rephrasing, or elaborating on children's responses.

Student Profiles

Use the results of this assessment to monitor children's growth and determine areas in which to focus instruction for each student. Note children's progress on the Oral Language Proficiency Benchmark Record Sheet on page R6 to chart their oral language development throughout the year.

© Macmillan/McGraw-Hill

1

Cat Can Jump

2

Cat Can Jump

© Macmillan/McGraw-Hill

Cat Can Jump

3

Cat Can Jump

4

© Macmillan/McGraw-Hill

GRADE 1

Prompts	Student Responses
Card 1: Let's look at this picture. What do you see?	
Card 1: Where is the cat? What things in the picture tell you where it is? Where is the cat going?	
Card 1: Point to the bird. What is the bird doing? Why do you think the bird has a worm?	
Card 2: What is the cat doing? Why? What do you think the cat wants?	
Card 3: Where is the cat now? How do you think the cat is feeling? Why?	

© Macmillan/McGraw-Hill

Prompts	Student Responses
Card 4: What are the other animals doing? How is the cat feeling now? What clues tell you that the cat is happy? Why is the cat happy?	
All Cards: Let's look at all the cards together. Tell me a story about what is happening in the cards.	

Review children's responses to the prompts. Use the following as a guide to identify children's language proficiency level at this point.

Beginning: Uses few or no words; gestures or points to respond to prompts.

Intermediate: Uses words, short phrases, and sentences to respond to prompts.

Advanced: Uses connected sentences to respond to prompts; responses are more detailed; all prompts are addressed.

© Macmillan/McGraw-Hill

Oral Language Proficiency Benchmark Assessment Record Sheet

Student Name	Beginning of Year	Middle of Year	End of Year

© Macmillan/McGraw-Hill

Acknowledgments

Volume I

The publisher gratefully acknowledges permission to reprint the following copyrighted material:

"Guess What!" by Michael Strickland. Copyright © 2000 by HarperCollins. Reprinted with permission of HarperCollins, NY.

Book Cover, HAVE YOU SEEN MY DUCKLING? by Nancy Tafuri. Copyright © 1996 by Nancy Tafuri. Reprinted by permission of Greenwillow Books.

Book Cover, SPOTS FEATHERS AND CURLY TAILS by Nancy Tafuri. Copyright © 1988 by Nancy Tafuri. Reprinted by permission of Greenwillow Books.

ILLUSTRATIONS
Cover Illustration: Pablo Bernasconi

8-11: Tomislav Zlatic. 12–23: Nancy Tafuri. 26–31: Eileen Hine. 32: Diane Paterson. 36–39: Diane Greenseid. 40–53: Sofia Balzola. 80–83: Steve Haskamp. 84–99: Michael Garland. 108–111: Amanda Haley. 114: Jon Nez. 116: Jon Nez. 118–125: Jon Nez. 128–129: Cheryl Mendenhall. 130: Ken Bowser. 132–133: Benton Mahan. 140, 142-145: Carol Koeller.

PHOTOGRAPHY
All photographs are by Ken Cavanagh or Ken Karp for Macmillan/McGraw Hill (MMH) except as noted below.

iv: Jose Luis Pelaez/Getty Images. v: (tl) Kevin Fitzgerald/Getty Images; (bl) Ken Cavanagh/Macmillan McGraw-Hill. 2-3: Jose Luis Pelaez/Getty Images. 4: Tim Pannell/Corbis. 5: Grant V. Faint/Getty Images. 6–7: Purestock/PunchStock. 24: Courtesy of Nancy Tafuri. 26: Ariel Skelly/Getty Images. 27: Michael Newman/Photo Edit. 28: Airel Skelly/Getty Images. 29: image100/SuperStock. 30: David Young-Wolff/Getty Images. 31: Bluestone Productions/Getty Images. 32: Dynamic Graphics Group/Creatas/Alamy. 33: C Squared Studios/Getty Images. 34–35: Ariel Skelley/Corbis. 52: Courtesy of Ana Costales. 54: Mike Hill/AGE Fotostock. 55: Medford Taylor/National Geographic Image Collection. 56: Tom Brakefield/Corbis. 57: Jeffrey L. Rotman/Corbis. 58: (tc) David Madison/Getty Images; (br) Peter Scoones/Getty Images. 59: Bob Gomel/ Corbis. 60: Comstock. 61: (tr) Ingram Publishing/Alamy; (tcr) C Squared Studios/Getty Images. 62–63: Kevin Fitzgerald/ Getty Images. 64: David Stoecklein/Corbis; (c) Photodisc/ Getty Images. 65: Lawrence Migdale/Photo Researchers. 66: Digital Vision/Punchstock. 67: Photodisc/Punchstock. 68: (t) Blaine Harrington/Corbis; (b) Elyse Lewin/Getty Images. 69: Lawrence Migdale/Photo Researchers. 70: (t) Don Smetzer/ Photo Edit; (b) Cheryl Clegg/Index Stock. 71: (tl) Myrleen Ferguson Cate/Photo Edit; (b) David Muscroft/SuperStock. 72: Digital Vision/Punchstock. 74: Darren Bennett/Animals Animals. 76: Brand X Pictures/Getty Images. 77: (cr) C Squared Studios/Getty Images; (b) Bet Noire/Shutterstock. 78–79: Timothy Shonnard/Getty Images. 98: Courtesy of Michael Garland. 100: Gabe Palmer/Corbis. 101: (l) Richard Hutchings/Photo Edit; (r) Robert Maier/Animals Animals. 102: PhotoStockFile/Alamy. 103: Steve Satushek/Getty Images. 104: Kevin Radford/Masterfile. 105: (t) Bildagentur Franz Waldhaeusl/Alamy; (tr) Yiap/AGE Fotostock. 106–107: Blend Images/Jupiter Images. 112–127: Ken Cavanagh/Macmillan McGraw-Hill. 130: Jose Luis Pelaez/Getty Images. 131: Ken Karp/Macmillan McGraw-Hill. 134–135: G.K. & Vikki Hart/Getty Images. 137: (tr) Tracy Montana/PhotoLink/Getty Images; (br) C Squared Studios/Getty Images. 138: Steve Hamblin/Alamy. 138: Norbert Schaefer/Corbis. 139: Stephen Wisbauer /Jupiter Images. 139: Michael Keller/Corbis. 141: Norbert Schaefer/ Corbis. 141: Steve Hamblin/Alamy. 142: Digital Vision Direct. 143: Stephen Wisbauer/Jupiter Images. 144: Michael Keller/ Corbis. 145: Photodisc Red/Getty Images.

Volume 2

The publisher gratefully acknowledges permission to reprint the following copyrighted material:

"Over in the Meadow: An Old Counting Rhyme" by Olive A. Wadsworth. Copyright © 1991 by Scholastic Inc., 730 Broadway, NY, NY. Reprinted with permission of Scholastic Inc., NY.

Book Cover, TO MARKET, TO MARKET by Anne Miranda, illustrated by Janet Stevens. Text copyright © 1997 by Anne Miranda. Illustrations copyright © 1997 by Janet Stevens. Reprinted by permission of Harcourt Children's Books.

Book Cover, ROADRUNNER'S DANCE by Rudolfo Anaya, illustrated by David Diaz. Text copyright © 2000 by Rudolfo Anaya. Illustrations copyright © 2000 by David Diaz. Reprinted by permission of Hyperion Books for Children.

Book Cover, THE LITTLE SCARECROW BOY by Margaret Wise Brown, illustrated by David Diaz. Text copyright © 2005 by Margaret Wise Brown. Illustrations copyright © 2005 by David Diaz. Reprinted by permission of HarperTrophy.

ILLUSTRATIONS
Cover Illustration: Pablo Bernasconi

28–33: Krystina Stasiak. 38–41: Anna Vojtech. 42–57: David Diaz. 59-62: Tom Leonard. 71: Mircea Catusanu. 73: Mircea Catusanu. 75–76: Mircea Catusanu. 80: Mike Gordon. 84–87: Marisol Sarrazin. 88–105: Pablo Bernasconi. 110: Ken Bowser. 114–117: Laura Ovresat. 118–135: Lynn Cravath. 140–141: Daniel DelValle. 142–143: Stacy Schuett. 150, 152-153 Brian Karas.

PHOTOGRAPHY
All photographs are by Ken Cavanagh or Ken Karp for Macmillan/McGraw Hill (MMH) except as noted below:

iv: (t) Masterfile Royalty-Free; (c) Steve Bloom. v: Image Source/Getty Images. 2–3: Masterfile Royalty-Free. 4: Cathrine Wessel/Corbis. 4–5: D. Berry/PhotoLink/Getty Images. 5: the Granger Collection, New York. 6–7: Steve Bloom Images/ Alamy. 8: Anup Shah/Nature Picture Library. 9: Gabriela Staebler/zefa/Corbis. 10: David A. Northcott/Corbis. 11: Panthera Productions/Getty Images. 12–13: Steve Bloom. 14: Jean Michel Labat/Ardea London Ltd. 15: Art Wolfe/Photo Researchers. 16: Robert Maier/Animals Animals/Earth Scenes. 17: Tom & Pat Leeson/Photo Researchers. 18: Michel & Christine Denis-Huot/Photo Researchers. 19: Peter Lilja/Getty Images. 20: Tim Flach/Getty Images. 20–21: Joe McDonald/Corbis. 22–23: Peter Johnson/Corbis. 23: Inge Yspeert/Corbis. 24: Steve Bloom. 25: JM Labat/Peter Arnold. 26: (t) Courtesy Jose Ramos; (b) Art Wolfe/Photo Researchers. 27: Robert Maier/Animals Animals/ Earth Scenes. 34: Peter Beck/Corbis. 35: Marc Romanelli/Getty Images. 36–37: George Disario/Corbis. 56: Courtesy of David Diaz. 58–59: (t/bkgd) Image 100/Getty Images; (b/bkgd) Digital Vision Direct. 59: (c) AGStock USA/Alamy; (cr) C. Borland/PhotoLink/Getty Images. 60: John Prior Images/ Alamy. 61: (bkgd) Digital Vision Direct; (inset) JW/Masterfile. 62: (t) Larry Lefever/Grant Heilman Photography; (l) Michael Newman/Photo Edit; (cl) Stock Food/SuperStock. 63: Brand X Pictures/Alamy. 64: Tony Anderson/Getty Images. 65: Michael Newman/Photo Edit. 66–67: Image Source/Getty Images. 68: RicPeterson/Alamy. 69: DCA Productions/Getty Images. 70: Tony Freeman/Photo Edit. 72: Swerve / Alamy. 74: Andrea Rugg/Beateworks/Corbis. 76: Bruce Clarke/Index Stock. 78: Jeff Greenberg/Photo Edit. 79: (l) Bill Aron/Photo Edit; (c) Rainer Dittrich/Getty Images; (r) Car Culture/Getty Images. 80: LWA-Sharie Kennedy/Corbis. 81: Bet Noire/Shutterstock . 82–83: Adam Tanner/The Image Works. 104: Courtesy of Natalia Berdini. 106: Mediacolor's/Alamy. 107: Upperhall Ltd./Robert Harding World Imagery/Corbis. 108: Stone/Getty Images. 109: Bryan & Cherry Alexander Photography. 110: Roy Morsch/AGE Fotostock. 111: Design Pics Inc/Alamy. 112–113: ColorBlind Images/Getty Images. 134: Courtesy Anne Miranda. 136: (cr) Canadian Museum of Civilization/Corbis; (bl) David Young-Wolff/Photo Edit; (bc) AllOver Photography/Alamy; (br) Royalty-Free/CORBIS. 137: (c) AP Images/Pat Vasquez-Cunningham; (br) Dynamic Graphics Group/Creatas/Alamy. 138–139: Ken Karp/Macmillan McGraw-Hill. 140: David Schmidt/ Masterfile. 144: Thinkstock/Getty Images. 145: Stockdisc/ PunchStock; (bc) Macmillan/McGraw-Hill. 146: Nic Hamilton/ Alamy. 148: (cr) C Squared Studios/Getty Images; (bl) Jeff Zaruba/Corbis. 149: (t) Robert Maier/Animals Animals; (b) Bananastock/Alamy. 150: Ariel Skelley/Corbis. 151: (t) Robert Maier/Animals Animals; (b) C Squared Studios/Getty Images. 152: Jeff Zaruba/Corbis. 153: Bananastock/Alamy.

Text permissions plus photo and illustration credits for the reduced pages can also be found at the back of the Student Book.

© Macmillan/McGraw-Hill

Acknowledgments

Volume 3

The publisher gratefully acknowledges permission to reprint the following copyrighted material:

"The Sea" by Laura Ranger from poems from *Stone Soup Magazine* May/June 1993 issue. Copyright © 2005 by Stone Soup, Santa Cruz, CA 95063.

"The Sky is Busy" by Ishikawa Megumi © 1993 from *Festival in My Heart: Poems by Japanese Children*, Harry N. Abrams, Incorporated, NY, A Times Mirror Corporations. Reprinted with permission from Harry N. Abrams, Inc., NY.

"Sun Rise" by Camille Pabalan from *KidzPage: Poetry and Verse for Children of All Ages*, November 2000, page 36, Tangled Lives. Copyright © 1998–2000 by Emmi Tarr.

Book Cover, MRS. BROWN WENT TO TOWN by Wong Herbert Yee. Copyright © 2003 by Wong Herbert Yee. Reprinted by permission of Houghton Mifflin.

Book Cover, CIRCUS GIRL by Michael Garland. Copyright © 1993 by Michael Garland. Used by permission of Dutton Children's Books, a division of Penguin Books USA Inc.

Book Cover, FIREMAN SMALL by Wong Herbert Yee. Copyright © 1994 by Wong Herbert Yee. Reprinted by permission of Houghton Mifflin Company.

ILLUSTRATIONS

Cover Illustration: Pablo Bernasconi

8-11: Vincent Nguyen. 12–29: Wong Herbert Yee. 30–33: Mircea Catusanu. 34: Ken Bowser. 35: Diane Paterson. 38–41: Anthony Lewis. 42-59: G. Brian Karas. 76: K. Michael Crawford. 80: Julia Woolf. 84–87: Josée Masse. 88–107: Michael Garland. 108–112: Jessica Wolk Stanley. 114: Daniel DelValle. 142–145: Tomek Bogacki. 146: Ken Bowser. 148–149: Elivia Savadier. 156-157, 159–160: Carol Koeller. 163: Janee Trasler.

PHOTOGRAPHY

All photographs are by Ken Cavanagh or Ken Karp or Natalie Ray for Macmillan/McGraw Hill (MMH) except as noted below.

iv: David R. Stoecklein/drsphoto.net. v: (t) The Art Archive/ Neil Setchfield; (b) Sean Justice/Getty Images. 2-3: David R. Stoecklein/drsphoto.net. 4: Rubberball/PunchStock. 4-5: Farinaz Taghavi/Getty Images. 5: Richard Nowitz/Getty Images. 6-7: Tim Fitzharris/Masterfile. 28: Courtesy of Wong Herbert Yee. 30: (bl) SW Productions/Getty Images; (bcl) Comstock Images/Alamy; (bcr) simplestockshots/PunchStock; (br) Royalty-Free/CORBIS. 31: Richard Hutchings/Photo Edit. 32: (tl) Dave Nagel/Getty Images; (tr) David Frazier/Corbis. 33: (tl) Stockbyte/PunchStock; (cr) Mixa/PunchStock. 34: Bill Frymire/Masterfile. 36–37: Myrleen Ferguson Cate/ PhotoEdit. 58: Courtesy of Aida Marcuse. 60: Ace Stock Limited/Alamy. 60–63: (bkgd) Wetzel and Company. 61: (t) D. Hurst/Alamy; (bcr) PhotoLink/Getty Images; (br) Digital Vision/Getty Images. 62: (t) Blend/PunchStock; (cr) John A. Rizzo/Getty Images; (bl) C Squared Studios/Getty Images. 63: Studio M/Stock Connection/Jupiter Images. 64: Ariel Skelly/Corbis. 65: (tcr) Photodisc/Getty Images; (tr) Hemera Technologies/Alamy. 66–67: The Art Archive/Neil Setchfield. 68: Gail Vachon. 69: Jim Lane/Alamy. 70: (tr) Brooklyn Museum/Corbis; (bl) Scala/Art Resource. 71: Jon Arnold Images/Alamy. 72: Giraudon/Art Resource. 73: Scala/Art Resource. 74: Frans Lanting/Corbis. 75: Brooklyn Museum/ Corbis. 78: Maxppp/Zuma Press/Newscom. 80: Royalty-Free/ Corbis. 81: (br) C Squared Studios/Getty Images; (c) Dian Lofton. 82–83: Anthony Bannister/Corbis. 106: (tr) Courtesy of Mary Anderson; (cl) Courtesy of Michael Garland. 108: Ken Karp/Macmillan McGraw-Hill. 109: Javier Larrea/AGE Fotostock. 110: AP Images/Rich Pedroncelli. 111–112: Richard Hutchings/Photo Edit. 113: Ken Karp/Macmillan McGraw-Hill. 114: LWA-Dann Tardif/Corbis. 115: Natalie Ray for MMH. 116–117: Bryan & Cherry Alexander Photography. 118: Van Hilversum/ Alamy. 119: Paul Chesley/Getty Images. 120: David Morris/ Alamy. 121: Bob Daemmrich/The Image Works. 122: Sean Justice/Getty Images. 124: Robert van der Hilst/Corbis. 125: Karan Kapoor/Getty Images. 126: Digital Vision/Getty Images. 127: Lindsay Hebberd/Corbis. 128: Photodisc/PunchStock . 129: Bob Krist/Corbis. 130: Rebecca Emery/Corbis. 131: Digital Vision/Getty Images. 132: Terje Rakke/Getty Images. 133: Randy Faris/Corbis. 134: Paul Chesley/Getty Images. 135: Alvaro Leiva/AGE Fotostock. 136: Rodolfo Arpia/Alamy. 137: Robert Fried/Alamy. 138: Dennis MacDonald/AGE Fotostock. 139: Avril O'Reilly/Alamy. 140: Courtesy of Minda Novek. 146: Bohemian Nomad Picturemakers/Corbis. 147: Nic Hamilton / Alamy. 150: Enzo & Paolo Ragazzini/Corbis. 151: (br) Sherman/ Getty Images; (bc) David Lassman/Syracuse Newspapers/The Image Works; (tr) C Squared Studios/Getty Images. 152: Ken Cavanagh/Macmillan/McGraw-Hill. 153: Stephen Ogilvy/ Macmillan McGraw-Hill. 154: (cl) Photodisc/Getty Images; (br) Laura Dwight/Corbis. 155: (t) Gary Buss/Getty Images; (b) Getty Images. 156: Bill Hickey/Getty Images. 157: Gary Buss/Getty Images. 158: (t) Getty Images; (b) Tom & Dee Ann McCarthy/ Corbis. 159: Tim Davis/Corbis. 160: Photodisc/Getty Images. 161: Stockbyte/Picture Quest. 162: (t) Joyce Choo/Corbis; (b) Jennie Woodcock/Reflections Photolibrary/Corbis. 163: Joseph Sohm/ ChromoSohm Inc./Corbis.

© Macmillan/McGraw-Hill

Text permissions plus photo and illustration credits for the reduced pages can also be found at the back of the Student Book.

Acknowledgments

Volume 4

The publisher gratefully acknowledges permission to reprint the following copyrighted material:

"The Kite" from *Days with Frog and Toad* by Arnold Lobel. Text and illustrations copyright © 1979 by Arnold Lobel. Reprinted by permission of Harper & Row Publishers, Inc.

"Where?" from *Seasons: A Book of Poems* by Charlotte Zolotow. Text copyright © 2002 by Charlotte Zolotow. Reprinted by permission of HarperCollins.

Book Cover, FROG AND TOAD ARE FRIENDS by Arnold Lobel. Copyright © 1970 by Arnold Lobel. Reprinted by permission of HarperCollins Publishers.

Book Cover, GRANDPA'S FACE by Eloise Greenfield, illustrated by Floyd Cooper. Text copyright © 1996 by Eloise Greenfield. Illustrations copyright © 1996 by Floyd Cooper. Reprinted by permission of Penguin Putnam Books for Young Readers.

Book Cover, OWL AT HOME by Arnold Lobel. Copyright © 1975 by Arnold Lobel. Reprinted by permission of HarperCollins Children's Books, a division of HarperCollins Publishers.

Book Cover, WHEN WILL I READ? by Miriam Cohen, illustrated by Lillian Hoban. Text copyright © 1977 by Miriam Cohen. Illustrations Copyright © 1977 by Lillian Hoban. Reprinted by permission of Greenwillow Books.

ILLUSTRATIONS

Cover Illustration: Pablo Bernasconi

8–9: Sheree Boyd. 10–29: Richard Bernal. 34: Daniel DelValle. 38–39: Patrice Barton. 40–59: Floyd Cooper. 64: Daniel DelValle. 80: Mindy Pierce. 84–85: Jamie Smith. 86–101: Arnold Lobel. 108–109: Ken Bowser. 134–135: Holly Hannon. 138–139: Jannie Ho.

PHOTOGRAPHY

All photographs are by Ken Cavanagh or Ken Karp for Macmillan/McGraw Hill (MMH) except as noted below.

iv: Roy Botterell/Corbis. v: (tl) Larry Bones/AGE Fotostock; (bl) Dana Hursey/Masterfile. 2–3: Roy Botterell/Corbis. 4: Blend/Punchstock. 4–5: imagebroker/Alamy. 5: Mike Powell/ Allsport/Getty Images. 6–7: Jim Cummins/Getty Images. 28: Courtesy of Richard Bernall. 30: Robert C. Hermes/Photo Researchers. 31: (t) Ted Horowitz/Corbis; (cl) Jan Rietz/Getty Images. 32: John B Free/Nature Picture Library. 33: Papilio/ Alamy. 34: Artiga/Masterfile. 35: Eyewire/PunchStock. 36–37: Walter Hodges/Getty Images. 58: (tr) Courtesy of Miriam Cohen; (cl) Courtesy of Floyd Cooper. 60: A.Ramey/Photo Edit. 61: (t) Laura Dwight/Omni-Photo Communications; (b) Brand X Pictures/Picture Quest/Jupiter Images. 62: (t) Lawrence Migdale/Photo Researchers; (cl) Michael Newman/Photo Edit; (cr) Phil Schermeister/Corbis. 63: (t) Ted Streshinsky/Corbis; (cr) Nik Wheeler/Corbis. 64: Juice Images/Alamy. 65: Photodisc/Alamy. 66–67: Larry Bones/AGE fotostock. 68: Mark Thomas/Foodpix/Jupiter Images. 69: Jeff Greenberg/Photo Edit. 70: CSU Archives/Everett Collection. 71: Jupiter Images/Agence Images/Alamy. 72: AP Images. 73: Wisconsin Historical Society/Everett Collection. 74: Jason Laure/The Image Works. 75: AP Photo/Barry Sweet. 76: Arthur Schatz/Time Life Pictures/Getty Images. 78: Jeff Greenburg/The Image Works. 80: Corbis/Punchstock. 81: (b) Bet Noire/Shutterstock; (br & tr) C Squared Studios/Getty Images. 82–83: image100/Alamy. 100: Courtesy of Arnold Lobel. 102–103: Underwood & Underwood/Corbis; (bkgd) Stockbyte/Getty Images. 104: Corbis. 104–105: Stockbyte/Getty Images. 105: National Archives/Handout/Getty Images. 106: Corbis. 106–107: Stockbyte/Getty Images. 107: (tl, tc, tr) Photodisc/Getty Images; (bl, br) Digital Vision/Getty Images; (bc) PhotoLink/Getty Images. 108: Darren Greenwood/ Alamy. 110–111: Tui de Roy/Minden Pictures. 112–113: Fred Bavendam/Minden Pictures. 114–115: Dana Hursey/Masterfile. 116: Photodisc/Punchstock. 117: Georgette Douwma/Photo Researchers. 118–119: Tony Heald/Nature Picture Library. 120–121: Images&Stories/Alamy. 121: Gary Bell/Oceanwideimages. com. 122–123: Karen Tweedy-Holmes/Corbis. 123: Digital Vision/PunchStock. 124: Fred Bavendam/Minden Pictures. 124–125: Stuart Westmorland/Corbis. 126: Arco Images/Alamy. 126–127: Valerie Giles/Photo Researchers. 127: Rick & Nora Bowers/Alamy. 128: Carl Roessler/Animals Animals. 128–129: Fred Bavendam/Minden Pictures. 130–131: Gerard Lacz/Peter Arnold, Inc.. 132: (tr) Courtesy of Julia Smith; (bcl) Rick & Nora Bowers/Alamy. 133: (br) Photodisc/Punchstock; (bl) Karen Tweedy-Holmes/Corbis. 136: Iconica/Getty Images. 137: G.K. & Vicki Hart/Getty Images. 140: Anup Shah/Getty Images. 141: Bigit Koch/Animals Animals. 143: C Squared Studios/Getty Images. 144: (cr) Gary Bell/Zefa/Corbis; (bl) Ken Cavanagh/ Macmillan McGraw-Hill. 145: (b) imageshop/Zefa/Alamy; (t) Stockbyte/Punchstock. 146: (t) BananaStock/Alamy; (b) imageshop/Zefa/Alamy. 147: (t) Stockbyte/Punchstock; (b) William Manning/Corbis. 148: (t) Gary Bell/Zefa/Corbis; (b) Paul Barton/Corbis. 149: Ken Cavanagh/Macmillan McGraw-Hill. 150: (t) David Schmidt/Masterfile; (b) Rommel/Masterfile. 151: (t) Digital Vision/Punchstock; (b) Tetra Images/Punchstock. 152: (t) Paul Freytag/Zefa/Corbis; (b) Masterfile Royalty-Free. 153: (t) Helga Lade/Peter Arnold, Inc.; (b) LHB Photo/Alamy. 154: Dynamic Graphics Group/Creatas/Alamy. 155: Corbis. 156: Banana Stock/AGE Fotostock. 157: (t) Masterfile Royalty-Free; (b) LWA-Sharie Kennedy/Corbis.

© Macmillan/McGraw-Hill

Text permissions plus photo and illustration credits for the reduced pages can also be found at the back of the Student Book.

Acknowledgments

Volume 5

The publisher gratefully acknowledges permission to reprint the following copyrighted material:

"Gray Goose" from *Yellow Elephant: A Bright Bestiary* by Julie Larios, paintings by Julie Paschkis. Text copyright © 2006 by Julie Larios. Illustrations copyright © 2006 by Julie Paschkis. Reprinted by permission of Houghton Mifflin Harcourt Publishing Company.

"Happy Fall" from *Pinwheel Days* by Ellen Tarlow, illustrations by Gretel Parker. Text copyright © 2007 by Ellen Tarlow. Illustrations copyright © 2007 by Gretel Parker. Used by permission of Star Bright Books, Inc.

Kitten's First Full Moon by Kevin Henkes. Copyright © 2004 by Kevin Henkes. Used by permission of Greenwillow Books, an imprint of HarperCollins.

A Tiger Cub Grows Up by Joan Hewett, photographed by Richard Hewett. Text copyright © 2002 by Joan Hewett. Photographs copyright © 2002 by Richard Hewett. Reprinted by permission of Carolrhoda Books, Inc., a division of Lerner Publishing Group.

Book Cover, A HARBOR SEAL PUP GROWS UP by Joan Hewett, photographs by Richard Hewett. Text copyright © 2001 by Joan Hewett. Photographs copyright © 2001 by Richard Hewett. Reprinted by permission of Carolrhoda Books, Inc., a division of Lerner Publishing Group.

Book Cover, A PENGUIN CHICK GROWS UP by Joan Hewett, photographs by Richard Hewett. Text copyright © 2004 by Joan Hewett. Photographs copyright © 2004 by Richard Hewett. Reprinted by permission of Carolrhoda Books, Inc., a division of Lerner Publishing Group.

ILLUSTRATIONS

Cover Illustration: Pablo Bernasconi

8–9: Constanza Basaluzzo. 10–43: Kevin Henkes. 44–49: John Kaufmann. 56–75: John Kanzler. 100–101: Lizzy Rockwell. 102–117: Gretel Parker. 124: Ken Bowser. 129: Tom Leonard. 156–157: Julie Paschkis. 160–161: Melissa Sweet.

PHOTOGRAPHY

All photographs are by Ken Cavanagh or Ken Karp for Macmillan/McGraw Hill (MMH) except as noted below.

iv: Ann Cutting/Jupiter Images. v: (t) Panoramic Images/ Getty Images; (b) Richard Hewett. 2–3: Ann Cutting/Jupiter Images. 4: Scott W. Smith/Animals Animals. 4–5: (bkgd-moss & stream) Digital Archive Japan/Alamy; (ferns) Comstock Images/Alamy. 5: Altrendo Travel/Getty Images. 6–7: Richard Broadwell/Alamy. 44–46: NASA. 47: Dorling Kindersley. 48: NASA. 49: NASA Kennedy Space Center. 50: image 100/ PunchStock. 51: Bill Brooks/Masterfile. 52–53: Jose Luis Pelaez, Inc./Corbis. 54–55: Ken Cavanagh/Macmillan/McGraw-Hill. 74: Courtesy of Phillip Dray. 76: Ken Cavanagh/Macmillan/ McGraw-Hill. 77: (c) Andrew Syred/Science Photo Library/ Photo Researchers; (cr) Davies & Starr/Getty Images. 78: (tl) Steve Gschmeissner/Photo Researchers; (br) Stephen Marks/Getty Images. 79: (tl) Dennis Kunkel/Phototake; (tr) David Sacks/Getty Images. 80: Bananastock/Imagestate. 81: Philadelphia Museum of Art/Corbis. 82–83: Panoramic Images/Getty Images. 84: Derek Davies/Getty Images. 85: (bkgd) C Squared Studios/Getty Images; (t) Wisconsin State Journal/John Maniaci/AP Images. 86: Jim Cummins/Getty Images. 87: Peter N. Fox/AGE Fotostock. 88: John Henshall/ Alamy. 89: (c) Jim Reed/Photo Researchers; (inset) Jim Reed/Photo Researchers. 89: Stockbyte/Punchstock. 90: AP Images. 91: (t) Warren Faidley/Corbis; (cr) Reuters/Jeff Mitchell/Newscom. 92: (tr) Richard Hutchings/Photo Edit; (cl) David Hanover/Getty Images. 92–93: DAJ/Getty Images. 96: Comstock/Jupiter Images. 97: (bc) Bet Noire/Shutterstock; (br) C Squared Studios/Getty Images. 98–99: (bkgd) Bonnie Nance/ Dembinsky Photo Associates. 116: (tr) Ken Cavanagh; (cr) Courtesy of Gretel Parker. 118–119: (bkgd) Ariel Skelley/Getty Images. 119: (b) Jan Halaska/Photo Researchers. 120: (bkgd) Comstock/Punchstock; (b) Jan Halaska/Photo Researchers. 121: (t) Comstock/Punchstock; (b) Jan Halaska/Photo Researchers. 122: (bkgd) Blend Images/Punchstock; (b) Jan Halaska/Photo Researchers. 123: Jan Halaska/Photo Researchers. 124: Dick Luria/Getty Images. 125: D. Hurst/Alamy. 126–127: Tom Murphy/ National Geographic Image Collection. 128: Carl R. Sams II/Peter Arnold, Inc. 131–153: Richard Hewitt. 154: (tl) Joan Hewett. 154–155: Richard Hewitt. 158: Michael Newman/Photo Edit. 15: Arthur Tilley/Getty Images. 162: (cl) Digital Archive Japan/Alamy; (c) Rainman/Zefa/Corbis; (cr) Royalty-Free/ Corbis; (bl) Frank Krahmer/Masterfile; (br) Jim Reed/Corbis. 163: (l to r) Digital Archive Japan/Alamy; Rainman/Zefa/ Corbis; Royalty-Free/Corbis; Frank Krahmer/Masterfile; Jim Reed/Corbis. 165: (tr) Ken Karp/Macmillan McGraw-Hill. 166: (cr) Jeremy Woodhouse/Masterfile; (bl) Denis Scott/Corbis. 167: (t) Royalty-Free/Corbis; (b) Masterfile Royalty Free. 168: Jack Hollingsworth/Getty Images. 169: Jeremy Woodhouse/ Masterfile. 170: (t) Yann Arthus-Bertrand/Corbis; (b) Timothy Shonnard/Getty Images. 171: Joseph Sohm; ChromoSohm Inc./Corbis. 172: Layne Kennedy/Corbis. 173: Royalty-Free/ Corbis. 173: Ryan McVay/Getty Images. 174: Masterfile Royalty Free. 174: Denis Scott/Corbis. 175: David Joel/Getty Images. 176: Rommel/Masterfile. 177: Image Source/Getty Images.

© Macmillan/McGraw-Hill

Text permissions plus photo and illustration credits for the reduced pages can also be found at the back of the Student Book.

Acknowledgments

Volume 6

The publisher gratefully acknowledges permission to reprint the following copyrighted material:

"Dancing Paper" from *Confetti: Poems for Children* by Pat Mora. Text copyright © 1996 by Pat Mora. Reprinted with permission of Lee & Low Books, Inc.

Dot & Jabber and the Big Bug Mystery by Ellen Stoll Walsh. Text and illustrations copyright © 2003 by Ellen Stoll Walsh. Reprinted by permission of Harcourt, Inc.

Olivia by Ian Falconer. Copyright © 2000 by Ian Falconer. Reprinted by permission of Atheneum Books for Young Readers, an imprint of Simon & Schuster Children's Publishing Division.

Super Oscar by Oscar De La Hoya, illustrated by Lisa Kopelke. Text copyright © 2006 by Oscar De La Hoya. Illustrations copyright © 2006 by Lisa Kopelke. Used with permission of Simon & Schuster Books for Young Readers, an imprint of Simon & Schuster Children's Publishing Division.

Whistle for Willie by Ezra Jack Keats. Text and illustrations copyright © 1964 by Ezra Jack Keats. Reprinted by permission of the Penguin Group, a division of Penguin Putnam Books for Young Readers.

Book Cover, HOP JUMP by Ellen Stoll Walsh. Copyright © 1993 by Ellen Stoll Walsh. Reprinted by permission of Harcourt Brace & Company.

Book Cover, GOGGLES! by Ezra Jack Keats. Copyright © 1969 by Ezra Jack Keats. Reprinted by permission of Viking, an imprint of Penguin Putnam Books for Young Readers.

Book Cover, MOUSE PAINT by Ellen Stoll Walsh. Copyright © 1989 by Ellen Stoll Walsh. Reprinted by permission of Harcourt Brace & Company.

Book Cover, OLIVIA AND THE MISSING TOY by Ian Falconer. Copyright © 2003 by Ian Falconer. Reprinted by permission of Atheneum Books for Young Readers, an imprint of Simon & Schuster Children's Publishing Division.

Book Cover, OLIVIA SAVES THE CIRCUS by Ian Falconer. Copyright © 2001 by Ian Falconer. Reprinted by permission of Atheneum Books for Young Readers, an imprint of Simon & Schuster Children's Publishing Division.

ILLUSTRATIONS

Cover Illustration: Pablo Bernasconi

8–9: Tiphanie Beeke. 10–35: Ian Falconer. 40: Ken Bowser. 44–45: Michael-Che Swisher. 46–75: Ezra Jack Keats. 100–101: Will Terry. 102–129: Ellen Stoll Walsh. 130–133: Susan Swan. 134: Rachel Geswaldo. 138–139: Holli Conger. 140–163: Lisa Kopelke. 164–165: Susan Swan. 166: Jenny Vainisi. 168–169: Janee Trasler.

PHOTOGRAPHY

All photographs are by Ken Cavanagh or Ken Karp for Macmillan/McGraw Hill (MMH) except as noted below.

iv: Jason Lindsey/Alamy. v: Photodisc/PunchStock. 2–3: Jason Lindsey/Alamy. 4: Comstock Images. 4–5: Royalty-© The Metropolitan Museum of Art/Art Resource, NY & © 2010 The Pollock-Krasner Foundation/Artists Rights Society (ARS), New York. 34: Courtesy of Roddy McDowell. 36–37: Momatiuk-Eastcott/Corbis. 37: Michael Melford/Getty Images. 38: (cr) Karl Kinne/PhotoLibrary; (t) James Randklev/Corbis. 40: George Shelley/Corbis. 41: Johner/Getty Images. 42–43: Jeff Cadge/Getty Images. 74: Courtesy of Ezra Jack Keats. 76: Digital Vision/Getty Images. 76–77: (b) Westend61/Alamy. 77: Paul Doyle/Alamy. 78: (l) Richard Sobol/Animals Animals; (r) Phanie/Photo Researchers. 78–79: (b) Westend61/Alamy. 79: tbkmedia.de/Alamy. 80: Stephen Simpson/Getty Images. 81: S.Meltzer/PhotoLink/Getty Images. 82–83: Photodisc/PunchStock. 84–85: Zephyr Picture/Index Stock. 85: Jose Luis Pelaez, Inc./Corbis. 86: Tim Wimbourne/Reuters/NewsCom. 87: (tr) Steve Hart. 88: (all) Janet Worne/Lexington Herald-Leader/KRT/NewsCom. 89: (tr) JupiterImages/AbleStock/Alamy; (cr,tl) Burke Triolo Productions/Getty Images; (b) Richard Smith/Masterfile; (cl) Royalty-Free/Corbis. 90: (tc) Stefan Sollfors/Alamy; (tr) Burke/Triolo Productions/Brand X Pictures/Getty Images; (cr) G.K. & Vikki Hart/Getty Images; (tl) Independence Examiner, Margaret Clarkin/AP Images; (tcr) JupiterImages/Creatas/Alamy; (b) JupiterImages/Photos.com/Alamy; (bl) Stefan Sollfors/Alamy. 91: (tr) Rich Pedroncelli/AP Images; (c) Stefan Sollfors/Alamy; (bcl) Julie Toy/Getty Images; (bc) Maximilian Stock-StockFood Munich/Stockfood America; (br) G.K. & Vikki Hart/Getty Images; (bl) Burke/Triolo Productions/Brand X Pictures/Getty Images. 92: Creatas/Jupiter Images. 92–93: Steve Craft/Masterfile. 93: (bl) Photolink/Getty Images; (br) William Fritsch/Brand X Pictures/JupiterImages. 94: Richard Lord/The Image Works. 96: Digital Vision. 97: (bc) Bet Noire/Shutterstock; (c, br) C Squared Studios/Getty Images. 98–99: Patti Murray/Animals Animals. 128: Courtesy of Ellen Stoll Walsh. 130: (c) Burke/Triolo Productions/Brand X Pictures/Getty Images; (br) Photodisc/Getty Images. (cr) Ingram Publishing/Alamy. 131: (t) Charles Krebs/Getty Images; (tr) Ron Wu/Index Stock Imagery; (cl) Burke/Triolo Productions/Brand X Pictures/Getty Images; (cr) Dynamic Graphics Group/Creatas/Alamy; (bl) Brian Hagiwara/Jupiter Images; (br) Bob London/Corbis. 132: (tl) Werner H. Müller/Corbis; (c) Brian Hagiwara/Brand X/Corbis. 133: (tr) Anthony Bannister/Gallo Images/Corbis; (c) IT Stock Free/AGE Fotostock. 134: BananaStock/PunchStock. 135: Digital Archive Japan/PunchStock. 136–137: Masterfile Royalty-Free. 162: J.P. Yim/Zuma/Corbis. 166: Image Source/PunchStock. 167: Creatas/PunchStock. 170: (tl) E. R. Degginger/Photo Researchers; (br) Gail Shumway/Getty Images. 171: (t to b) David M. Dennis/Animals Animals; David Liebman/Pink Guppy; David M. Dennis/Animals Animals; Margarette Mead/Getty Images. 172: (bc) Stephen Ogilvy/Macmillan McGraw-Hill; (br) Royalty Free/Corbis. 173: Nic Hamilton/Alamy. 174: (cr) Burke/Triolo Productions/Brand X Pictures/Getty Images; (l) Dave Reede/Getty Images. 175: (t) Corbis/Superstock; (b) Rommel/Masterfile. 176: Rommel/Masterfile. 177: Photolink/Getty Images. 178: Dave Reede/Getty Images. 179: Ariel Skelley/Corbis. 180: Photographer's Choice/Getty Images. 181: (b) Peter Hince/Getty Images; (b) Burke/Triolo Productions/Brand X Pictures/Getty Images. 182: Royalty-Free/CORBIS. 183: Jim Cummins/Getty Images. 184: Corbis/Superstock.

Text permissions plus photo and illustration credits for the reduced pages can also be found at the back of the Student Book.

© Macmillan/McGraw-Hill